March 16, 2002

W9-CAV-545

Dear Bob -

Have always been partial to movies that take place in New York - think that you will enjoy this book -

Love,

Mom

ALSO BY JAMES SANDERS

New York: An Illustrated History (with Ric Burns and Lisa Ades)

CELLULOID SKYLINE

1. *Five and Ten* (1931).
After a rooftop opening banquet for a new skyscraper, an architect named Bertram "Berry" Rhodes (Leslie Howard) and "five-and-ten" heiress Jennifer Rarick (Marion Davies), convert a party table into a romantic aerie from which to overlook the city below.

NEW YORK AND THE MOVIES

CELLULOID SKYLINE

JAMES SANDERS

ALFRED A. KNOPF | NEW YORK | 2001

THIS IS A BORZOI BOOK
PUBLISHED BY ALFRED A. KNOPF

Copyright © 2001 by James Sanders

All rights reserved under International and Pan-American Copyright Conventions.
Published in the United States by Alfred A. Knopf, a division of Random House, Inc., New York, and simultaneously in Canada by Random House of Canada Limited, Toronto. Distributed by Random House, Inc., New York.

www.aaknopf.com

Knopf, Borzoi Books, and the colophon are registered trademarks of Random House, Inc.

Grateful acknowledgment is made to the following for permission to reprint previously published material:

Random House, Inc.: Excerpt from *The Death and Life of Great American Cities* by Jane Jacobs, copyright © 1961 by Jane Jacobs. Reprinted by permission of Random House, Inc.

Warner Bros. Publications U.S. Inc.: Excerpt from "Going Hollywood" by Arthur Freed and Nacio Herb Brown, copyright © 1933 (copyright renewed) by Metro-Goldwyn-Mayer Inc. All rights assigned to EMI Robbins Catalog Inc.; excerpt from "New York, New York" by Leonard Bernstein, Betty Comden, and Adolph Green, copyright © 1945 (copyright renewed) by Warner Bros. Inc. All rights reserved. Reprinted by permission of Warner Bros. Publications U. S. Inc., Miami, FL 33014.

ISBN: 0-394-57062-6
LCCN: 2001091010

Manufactured in the United States of America

FIRST EDITION

2. **(previous page) Constructing a skyline miniature for *The Hudsucker Proxy* (1994).**

To my father and to the memory of my mother

I am not sure that it is possible for anyone brought up in the East to appreciate entirely what New York—the *idea* of New York, meant to those of us who came from the West and the South. . . . To those of us who came from places where no one had heard of Lester Lanin and Grand Central Station was a Saturday radio program, where Wall Street and Fifth Avenue and Madison Avenue were not places at all but abstractions ("Money," and "High Fashion," and "The Hucksters"), New York was no mere city. It was instead an infinitely romantic notion, the mysterious nexus of all love and money and power, the shining and perishable dream itself.

JOAN DIDION

It is not on any map; true places never are.

HERMAN MELVILLE

CONTENTS

AUTHOR'S NOTE

As *Celluloid Skyline* was on its way to the printers, the events of September 11, 2001, irrevocably altered the skyline of lower Manhattan. The book, of course, had been completed some time earlier, and in the harsh and haunting light of those terrible events, its words and images may in places take on a new and entirely unintended significance. After due consideration, the author and publisher have chosen to proceed with publication on schedule, in the hope that the book may in some way help to further an understanding of why the New York skyline—in both image and reality—has had such profound and personal meaning for people all around the world, and why—more now, perhaps, than ever before—it has been cherished so deeply, by so many.

CELLULOID SKYLINE

MACY'S
MACY'S

INTRODUCTION

Celluloid Skyline is an exploration of two cities, both called "New York."

One is a real city, an urban agglomeration of millions. The other is a mythic city, a dream city, born of that most pervasive of dream media, the movies.

The real place is familiar enough: New York, the largest metropolis in the country, by some measures the largest anywhere; the front door to America, the crossroads between Old World and New, the most important urban center in an increasingly urban world—yet something of a stranger, ironically, to a suburban America.

The dream city may not be quite as familiar, but we know it just as well. For decades we have been visiting it, inhabiting it, thrilling to it—to its cocktail parties and power lunches, its subway chases and opening nights, its playground rumbles and penthouse romances.

We know its people: Jimmy Stewart and Grace Kelly, in a rear apartment in the Village. Fred Astaire and Ginger Rogers, in a glamorous rooftop nightclub. Spike Lee in a Brooklyn pizza shop. Rod Steiger in an East Harlem pawnshop. Woody Allen, just about everywhere.

We know what happens there. An actress twists her ankle, and gives the chorus girl a big break. A boy from one street gang falls in love with a girl from another. Some sailors come to town and spend the day. A big gorilla escapes from a theater, and climbs a tall building.

Above all we remember the moments, the places: the tinkling piano runs and leafy trees outside Holly Golightly's East Side row

3. Reference still of Manhattan, circa 1950. Looking west from the eighty-sixth-floor observation deck of the Empire State Building, this skyline panorama includes the 1910 Pennsylvania Station, designed by McKim, Mead & White (whose distinctive triple-arched roof is visible at center).

house; the midtown sidewalk where Marilyn's white skirt goes flying; the Brooklyn boulevard where John Travolta struts to a disco beat; the ominous peaks and gables of the Dakota, seen from Rosemary's apartment; the Statue of Liberty, half buried in the sand. Or just that familiar New York street—that hydrant-sprayed, fire escape–lined tenement block where a thousand city kids got called home to supper by yelling mothers.

For over a century, movies have been made about New York. Taken as a whole, they offer more than just another genre: they have pieced together, in film after film, the lineaments of a single, coherent place, a place where remarkable people do exciting, amusing, romantic, scary things. It is a "city" so dense in texture, so rich in memory and association and sense of place, that it forms an astonishing urban presence. In its deepest sense, after all, a great city is more than a geographic or economic entity: it is a distinct locus of image and style, memory and dreams. This is precisely what the New York of the movies offers.

Of course, the century of films also provides a fascinating mirror to the real city, to its booms and busts, its crooked mayors and master builders, its waves of immigration, growth, decline, rebirth. We will explore that city as well, and see how the two cities reflected each other, changed each other, taught each other. The real and mythic cities will intertwine, become entangled, just as they so often do in our memory. We will learn from both.

But at the heart of *Celluloid Skyline* remains the proposition that the movie city, the mythic city, is ultimately far more than a mere mirror. It is a place unto itself, an extraordinary cultural construct spanning hundreds of individual films, from works of genius by Wyler, Hitchcock, and Scorsese to the most routine 1930s "Manhattan Melodrama." Perhaps it is precisely because real New York possesses this "other" city as some kind of adjunct or underside or dream version of itself, that it holds a true claim to urban greatness, one shared by only a few places in history: London, Paris, Venice, Rome, Troy, Babylon, Ur. Once they were called the "storied" or "fabled" cities. Today we tell our fables with celluloid.

> It is worth recalling, if only in schematic . . . form, the essential structure of the [movie] industry in its great days: settled financiers on the East Coast were investing in uprooted adventurers on the West Coast because of their supposed expertise on the subject of what the Middle West really wanted. The movies did not describe or explore America, they invented it, dreamed up an America all their own, and persuaded us to share the dream.
>
> MICHAEL WOOD

Nothing about movie New York is more mythic, perhaps, than the story of its origins—a central chapter in the epic twentieth-century story of how two American cities, a continent apart, gave birth to a mass media culture so pow-

4. *On the Town* (1949). At a time when nearly all Hollywood films were made in the studio, co-directors Gene Kelly and Stanley Donen convinced MGM to shoot the opening "New York, New York" number of *On the Town*—the film version of Betty Comden, Adolph Green, and Leonard Bernstein's 1945 Broadway hit—on location in the city. In this view, Jules Munshin, Frank Sinatra, and Gene Kelly—playing three sailors on a whirlwind tour of New York—take in the sights from the Brooklyn Bridge.

erful and seductive that within a few decades it had virtually blanketed the globe. The motion-picture industry was born in New York, of course—one part of the dazzling cultural and technological explosion that, in little more than twenty years, invented or revolutionized modern newspapers, picture magazines, popular songs, musical comedy, phonograph recordings, and network radio. Yet unlike these others, filmmaking thrived in the city only until the time of the First World War, when the early movie moguls shifted the bulk of production (though few other parts of the business) to sprawling new studio lots in and around Los Angeles. For much of the century, an invisible chain linked the industry's financial, administrative, and publicity headquarters in midtown Manhattan to its burgeoning production center in Southern California, which, especially after the coming of sound in the late 1920s, attracted wave after wave of writers, directors, choreographers, musicians, and actors—the basis of an "expatriate" culture that to this day remains a major presence (perhaps *the* major presence) in Hollywood. In recent decades, as Los Angeles has grown into a world-class city and entertainment colossus in its own right, the relationship between the two cities has grown still more complex—not least of all in the film industry, which has doubled back by creating an "independent" satellite in New York, a conscious alternative to Hollywood. From this legendary exchange of money, talent, and ideas, sweeping back and forth across the continent, the two cities gave rise to the popular American culture that now surrounds us everywhere—and, in so doing, linked themselves as perhaps no two other cities in history: physically distant, deeply different in character, yet so intimately conjoined that to those in the entertainment world they often seem a single, strangely distended environment—a city of palm trees and yellow taxis, of cast-iron lofts and blue-tiled swimming pools, a place in which 57th Street and Broadway somehow extends seamlessly into Sunset and La Cienega Boulevards.

5. **Shooting *Do The Right Thing* (1989).** Shot on location over the summer of 1988, Spike Lee's film focuses on a day in the life of a single Brooklyn block (Stuyvesant Avenue in Bedford-Stuyvesant). In this view, a camera crew follows Lee, playing the pizza deliveryman Mookie, making his rounds of the block (note the dolly track beneath the camera, allowing it to glide smoothly along the pavement, matching Lee's pace).

At the heart of this fabled relationship—and, in a sense, a direct product of the historic circumstances that shaped it—lies a remarkable undertaking: the creation of an invented metropolis, movie New York. In the city itself, over a century ago, America's nascent film industry found its first great setting and subject. Yet ironically, it would be the decisive shift of production to Los Angeles that brought the *movie* city into its own, as the studios' unmatched resources were mobilized to reconstruct, at awesome scale and in startling detail, the place that for most members of the film colony (whether ex–New Yorkers or not) remained America's archetypal metropolitan setting. In an astonishing conjunction, the imaginative powers of displaced New Yorkers would be aligned with Los Angeles's unique filmmaking capacities to birth a place of mythic dimension and scope, transmitting it to every corner of the world. In the end, it was this long-standing creative collaboration, between a pair of cities so often considered rivals, that would bring forth and sustain, generation after generation, one of the most familiar and compelling urban visions of modern times: New York of the movies.

> All I need is a brief glimpse, an opening in the midst of an incongruous landscape, a glint of lights in the fog, the dialogue of two passersby meeting in a crowd, and I think that, setting out from there, I will put together, piece by piece, the perfect city, made of fragments mixed with the rest, of instants separated by intervals . . . discontinuous in time and space, now scattered, now more condensed.
>
> ITALO CALVINO

Once we have watched the movie city be dreamed into existence, then seen that dream be physically constructed, only one last daring leap remains: to venture *through* the screen and inhabit—at least briefly—the singular place on the other side. Through a kind of virtual tour or survey, we begin traveling around movie New York—turning a corner, as it were, from one film to another, weaving together their characters, settings, and stories into a continuous urban "fabric." Here, it turns out, a whole city waits to be explored. And what a city! Instantly memorable, visually stunning, it is a place built specifically for action, for drama, for adventure, a city of bright avenues and mysterious side streets, of soaring towers and intimate corners, all designed to heighten and accent the movement of its larger-than-life inhabitants. Employing an entire feature, a single scene, or just a moment (Calvino's "brief glimpse"), we make our way across this magical landscape, guided for the most part not by genre or chronology but by the elements of the city itself. We climb up to its rooftops, step out onto its penthouse terraces, sneak backstage into its theaters, and linger in the spectacular nightclubs that cap its towers. We take in the dazzling lights and signs of Times Square, the leafy backyards of Greenwich

6. Publicity still from *Rear Window* (1954). This composite image shows the photographer L. B. Jefferies (James Stewart) by the rear window of his apartment, surrounded by the activity of the picturesque Greenwich Village courtyard he faces. In reality, the entire film was shot on an immense set at Paramount Studios in Hollywood.

7. **Rooftop nightclub from *Broadway Melody of 1936* (1935).** Designed by Merrill Pye and Edwin Willis of the MGM art department, the huge nightclub appears to float atop the city. In this view, the film's musical climax is led by the brother-and-sister dance team Buddy and Vilma Ebsen.

Village, the gritty stoops and sidewalks of Harlem. We travel to the city's "edge"—its waterfronts filled with gleaming ships and grimy refuse dumps, as well as its train stations and grand hotels—then wander through its office buildings, moving from slender classic towers, symbolic of aspiration and ambition, to the sprawling sea of desks within its modern slabs, the brightly lighted terrain of corporate conflict. Visiting its residential blocks, we glimpse a mighty struggle over the place of the street in city life, then look inside to see personal and societal change reflected powerfully—if not poignantly—in the shape of its mansions, tenements, apartments, and lofts.

Not surprisingly, the past, present, and future all mix together in this imaginary place, mingling indiscriminately: an Art Deco ocean liner departs its Hudson River pier even as an artist's loft is renovated in SoHo, while somewhere in midtown a futuristic aircraft lands atop a skyscraper that never was. In a way, this only reflects our daily experience with cities no less than films: we take in as a single block a group of buildings erected many decades apart, or view in quick succession a 1970s police thriller, a 1930s backstager, and a 1950s Wall Street drama, fusing them effortlessly in our minds as "New York movies."

> [There is a] feeling that you get when you step out of an Italian or Dutch gallery into a city that seems the very reflection of the paintings you have just seen, as if the city had come out of the paintings and not the other way around. An American city seems to have stepped right out of the movies. To grasp its secret, you should not, then, begin with the city and move inward toward the screen; you should begin with the screen and move outward toward the city.
>
> JEAN BAUDRILLARD

In the end, of course, it is not simply a journey but an *exploration* we have embarked upon—an investigation, as it were, into the dream life of a city. Like almost any dream-related inquiry, it centers less on surface appearances than underlying forces—interweaving space and story, urban form and filmic narrative, to learn not only how the city looks, but what it *means*—driven, like Baudrillard, in the belief that movies may hold the key to unlocking the city's "secrets," the hidden meanings beneath its outward form.

In part this is because movie-makers, looking at the real city, so often see more than is there. To the surprise and delight of audiences, Terry Gilliam saw in the heart of Grand Central Terminal not only a great passenger concourse but the world's biggest ballroom, while in the soaring shaft of the Empire State Building, Merian C. Cooper saw not simply a commercial office tower but a prehistoric peak, ready to be surmounted by some timeless figure. In *The Wizard of Oz*, Manhattan's cluster of towers was transmuted—more hauntingly than any literal rendition—into a gleaming apparition, capturing its emotional power as the destination of millions who had come a vast distance to fulfill their hopes and dreams. Especially in those films driven by a sense of the fantastic, from *Ghostbusters* to *Godzilla*, the city is often reshaped bodily to provide a plausible context for the most fanciful scenarios or characters. From such provocative transformations, we gain insight into the city we know.

8. ***The Sweet Smell of Success* (1957).** Though the film's exteriors were shot on location, scenes of columnist J. J. Hunsecker (Burt Lancaster) at his command post at the "21" Club (shown in this view with press agent Sidney Falco, played by Tony Curtis) were filmed on Stage 8 at the Goldwyn Studios in Hollywood, on a set designed by Edward Carrere—and built at a cost of twenty-five thousand dollars—that painstakingly reproduced the famed restaurant's pine paneling, oak bar, and toy models.

But lessons no less significant also emerge from movies rooted in the ordinary sphere of the city, in the everyday places of life, work, and play. In the movies, after all, even the most commonplace settings never exist simply for their own sake; they not only provide the believable background for a film's action but, to a degree rarely appreciated, help to illuminate its characters, propel its narrative, heighten its emotional resonance. "We're talking about *people* when we make movies," the art director Robert Boyle has observed, "we're not talking about sets."

> *We're not talking about brownstone houses; we're talking about people who* live *in brownstone houses. If this girl comes home after a hard day, and she's all alone, and I want to make a statement about how alone she is, I want the room to maybe make a long shot with a certain kind of lens that will say how lonely she is. I don't care about the room. I care about the* woman.

For obvious reasons, this imperative to connect space, story, and character makes the movie city an incomparable resource to explore the complex web of linkages—physical, emotional, imaginative—between urban environments and those who inhabit them. And as we do, the pleasure of simply inhabiting this cinematic metropolis is enriched by a deeper layer of enlightenment. As they move through the streets and buildings of movie New York, its charismatic "citizens"—Cary Grant, Audrey Hepburn, Dustin Hoffman, Marlon Brando, Ginger Rogers, Robert De Niro, Marilyn Monroe, Jimmy Cagney, among scores of others—turn out to provide compelling, almost primerlike lessons, often of quite startling specificity, on how a city and its component pieces function. More than anyone might imagine, feature films, whether made on the studio lot or (as examined in later chapters) shot on the streets of the city itself, offer a superb platform from which to comprehend the urban landscape—at times providing a fresh glimpse of familiar terrain, at other times opening up dramatic new vistas. There are, in the end, simply *so* many films about New York, set in so many different parts of town, that an unusually wide range of ideas and concepts are brought to dramatic life—helping us ultimately not only to understand the city, but to improve it.

9. ***An Unmarried Woman*** **(1978).** Erica Benton (Jill Clayburgh) and the painter Saul Kaplan (Alan Bates) lower a canvas from his loft. Shot on location in SoHo, Paul Mazursky's film captured a crucial moment in the life of the cast-iron district, rapidly transforming from an aging industrial area into an internationally known art community, filled with galleries, shops, and artists' lofts.

> [W]e must remember that drama and theater are not special and separate and private things in our lives. They are the true stuffs of living, the heart and soul of any true city. It follows that we must begin to provide architectural stages upon which our vast populations can act out their lives.
>
> RAY BRADBURY

"Cities, like dreams, are made of desires and fears," Italo Calvino observed in his classic urban meditation, *Invisible Cities*. Constructing a movie city around the needs of story and character, filmmakers have inevitably sought to draw out the human intentionality behind every corner. The result is a place that is, literally, shaped by desire, in which those things that most excite us

about cities—fantasy, mystery, possibility, aspiration, excitement, danger, awe—have become the very blocks from which the place is raised. If the mythic city of the movies has one great lesson, it is to present an urban environment whose form has emerged in the closest possible alignment with human experience. Explore it not only to learn of buildings and streets, but the contours of life itself.

Meanwhile, it is a journey open to anyone. Resting on the stuff of popular dreams, it is intended for all those who, sitting before a cinema or television screen, have found themselves poised between the movie city and the real one. And, as Joan Didion suggests, those who have been lured by the dream can be found not only, or even especially, in New York itself, but wherever those films have been shown—which is to say, everywhere.

10. ***Breakfast at Tiffany's*** **(1961).** Based on Truman Capote's novella, *Breakfast at Tiffany's* follows the intertwining stories of Holly Golightly (Audrey Hepburn) and Paul Varjak (George Peppard), who live in the same converted row house on East 78th Street. In this view, Paul is greeted by the older woman who keeps him (a wealthy interior decorator played by Patricia Neal) as Holly looks on.

PART ONE

MYTHIC CITIES

MYTHIC CITIES

Start not with a myth but a real city. Any city.

It is a worldly place, of course, a focal point of commerce and trade, a propitious meeting of overland routes and waterways that grows over time into an economic engine, a political unit, a sprawling assemblage of places, people, structures. Yet for all its growth, in many ways the city remains exactly what it was at the start, simply a dense human settlement—the most fixed, solid, and earthly of things.

For certain cities, however, something else can happen, something quite magical. From the earthly city there arises an immaterial counterpart, a city of the imagination. This other "place" lives what is an admittedly fictive existence, but one so complete and so compelling that it may come to rival the real city in its breadth and power. When this happens, the city can no longer be defined entirely by its earthly coordinates; it has given rise to a place of mind and spirit—a mythic city.

Few cities ever achieve this status, and those that do generally count among the world's greatest. London. Paris. Rome. But it is not strictly a matter of size. Florence, Jerusalem, and New Orleans have all shared the same magic, yet were far from the largest cities of their times, in either population or extent.

Though it may be rendered in images, in words, in music, a mythic city is no mere copy. It is a world unto itself, its pieces seeming interconnected, self-referential, and full—a vital, living counterpart to the city that spawned it. A mythic city embodies the *idea* of a city, a powerful thing indeed. An idea can travel, after all, as a city cannot—radiating across land and sea into the minds of millions around the world. Those who have never seen or visited the real place can nonetheless imagine it intensely, can picture it. And beyond that, it calls to them, it beckons. They can dream of it.

11. ***Just Imagine* (1930).** This night view of the film's elaborate miniature city—showing New York as it would appear in 1980—includes a series of formal gardens flanking a wide boulevard, inspired by the visionary proposals of 1920s designers such as Harvey Wiley Corbett and Hugh Ferriss.

The first mythic cities were sacred cities, ancient places whose earthly components had been superimposed with a second, spiritual identity. To its earliest inhabitants, Babylon was no mere settlement, but a sanctified space whose outer walls offered a magical zone of defense, dividing the ordered, divine space inside the city from the chaotic, profane wilderness outside. Two Babylons—one of matter, the other of spirit—coexisted in the same urban realm.

Later, the sacred city detached from its worldly counterpart. Jerusalem was such a city: a dream city floating overhead, a vision to sustain the ancient Hebrews during their decades of exile. This mythic Jerusalem was no mere version of the earthly city; if anything, the real city was a version of *it*. After centuries, the solid, real Jerusalem could seem merely a pale copy of the vivid, shining archetype. And why not? The mythic city could travel with them, as the real city could not. In their minds the Jews could aspire to "return" to it—if only, as their prayer proclaimed, in a year still yet to come.

12. **Ambrogio Lorenzetti, *The Effects of Good Government in the City and the Country*, 1338–39.** Though based in many ways on fourteenth-century Siena, this allegorical fresco (located in Siena's Palazzo Pubblico) depicts an imaginary city, the product of virtuous civic leadership. An adjacent companion fresco by Ambrogio, *The Effects of Bad Government*, shows a corrupt and debased city, brought on by municipal corruption and incompetence.

As mythic cities crossed the boundaries of space, so could they travel through time. Transmitted in words or song from generation to generation, these "cities" transcended the rude limitations of stone and brick, the rise and fall of nations, to sing out in clarion tones centuries, even millennia, after any real city had turned to dust. For twenty-five hundred years the world has caught sight of Ilium rising above the Trojan plain, in the "lofty-gated" majesty of its final days. Long ago the city on which it was based disappeared; many wondered if it had ever existed at all. Eventually, traces of a settlement in Asia Minor were unearthed. Through it all, however, the grandeur of the mythic city continued undimmed, fresh and vital in the lines of an epic lyric and the mind of anyone who reads it. Ilium may have long since vanished. But through Homer, Troy lives.

In the Renaissance, mythic cities shed their sacred origins and grew into secular, civic presences. Their "idea" was no longer simple and divine but complex and human; their urban values became specific and individual rather than generic and abstract, in part because we could now *see* them, in elaborate painted images that made them appear so real and compelling it seemed possible—and more than a little tempting—to try to inhabit them. The mythic city created by the artist Ambrogio Lorenzetti in a fresco called *The Effects of Good Government in the City and the Country* has lured generations of visitors with its panoramic urban vision, encompassing the entire spectrum of city life (12). Its people stroll about, sip wine in its cafés, carry goods, dance in its streets. Its interiors include a classroom, a hosiery shop, a tavern with outdoor bar. Its buildings rise proudly, their Gothic and Romanesque windows and tiled rooftops giving way to a distant skyline of towers and crenellated walls. The whole place lives and breathes before our eyes, and is changing even as we watch: workmen on scaffolding are erecting a new structure in the distance. Like generations before us, we feel the urge to enter this city, speak with its people, walk its streets; we can well understand the motivation of a 1930s Italian professor who, working backward from the painting, tried to "build" Ambrogio's city by constructing a wooden model of it. A model, after all, might allow us to peek around the corners, find out what else is happening in this marvelous town. We want to know.

No less than the ancient sacred cities, Ambrogio's city is based on a real one—Siena, of course. Yet like these older mythic cities, it is no mere depiction of actuality, but a true vision: the better, grander Siena that someday might be achieved through virtuous civic effort. Its origins in the particular urbanism of an actual city, however, differentiate it sharply from another concept that emerged in the Renaissance: the ideal city. While the ideal city could be found in books of the time, in Thomas More's *Utopia* and Tommaso Campanella's *City of the Sun*, it resided perhaps most vividly in a painting, *La Città Ideale*, whose authorship has long remained a mystery (13). Its creator's utter mastery of a new technique, linear perspective, makes the image seem like a picture-window view of a real town, encouraging to those who might wish to enter the place. But how different is this *ideal* city from Ambrogio's *mythic* city! Where the mythic city is full of human life, the ideal city is empty. Where the mythic city changes and grows, the ideal city is static, timeless. However much a work of the imagination, the mythic city is clearly based on a real place; it grows from the individual character of a single town. The ideal city is abstract, based not on any particular city but on the generic urbanism of the era. And most important, where Ambrogio's mythic city shows a grander, more shapely vision of real urban life, *La Città Ideale* suggests nothing less than perfection—not just of cities, but of human life itself. Is it empty, we wonder, because people are to be admitted only when they match its level of perfection? Ambrogio's imaginative vision accepts and enhances the messy vitality—both architectural and human—of a specific place. This is indeed the very essence of the mythic city.

13. ***La Città Ideale (The Ideal City)*, late fifteenth century.** Located in the National Gallery of the Marches, Urbino, this painting (attributed to Piero della Francesca and Francesco di Giorgio Martini, among many others) presents a utopian vision of Renaissance urbanism.

The ideal city in contrast banishes both imperfection and specificity; it gives architectural and urban form to the deep utopian impulse to perfect human life and society. Such utopian urbanism would remain a potent but peripheral force until the early twentieth century, when modern architects and planners would bring it to the center stage of city building (127).

Meanwhile, the mythic city would also grow. On the stage of the Teatro Olimpico in Vicenza, the architects Palladio and Scamozzi built a permanent "city" of angled, forced-perspective streetscapes, based on the seven gates of ancient Thebes (14). Converging with drama, the mythic city came to life as a kind of civic arena. Unlike places fixed forever on canvas or between the covers of a book, this theatrical city could enjoy an ongoing existence—one that was always changing, year after year, animated by countless narratives and by generations of actors. Like a real city it could be continually inhabited. Like a real city it was always open to the new—to new characters and situations, conflicts and aspirations.

14. Teatro Olimpico, Vicenza. Designed by the architect Andreas Palladio and completed in 1584, the theater's permanent set (by the scenic designer Vincente Scamozzi) shows a Renaissance-style city that brilliantly employed "forced perspective" to make its streets seem deeper than they actually were—the same technique adopted by Hollywood art directors, three centuries later, to enhance the realism of their miniature cityscapes (44).

In modern times mythic cities have surged in size and complexity, alongside the real cities upon which they are based. The mythic London that swept across late-nineteenth-century English literature, from the epic social novels of Dickens to the popular tales of Conan Doyle's master detective, not only established an indelible urban imagery of foggy nights, cobblestone streets, chimney pots, and hansom cabs; it also suggested that within the borders of a great metropolis could be found not just a city, but all the world itself: infinite human possibility, the extremes of wealth and poverty, misery and comfort, ignorance and knowledge, condensed into a single place. In their breadth these books seem to hold nineteenth-century London within them: from their pages, we feel, one could rebuild the city, brick by brick.

From Paris in the same years rose not one but two mythic cities, intertwined yet distinct. In the mythic Paris of the Impressionist painters—Manet, Renoir, Degas, Monet, Pissarro—we enter a luminous world of stages and rehearsal halls, brasseries and cafés, expositions and racetracks and public gardens, waterside picnics and boating in the parks at the city's edge (15). It is a Paris energized by the new: by the massive mid-nineteenth-century reconstruction of the city under Louis-Napoléon and Baron Haussmann; by the broad, leafy boulevards and squares brought to the heart of the metropolis; by the high, modern railway stations and long iron bridges; by all the strokes of rationalized planning and light and air that sliced through the dark, twisted quarters of the old city. Ironically, it was just this old, vanishing Paris, the working-class districts and narrow streets Haussmann strove hard to eliminate, that animated the *other* mythic Paris, the one brought to life by the writers, by Baudelaire, Balzac, Hugo, Zola. Even when venturing into the new and glittering city, their mythic Paris explores its underside, the demimonde of prostitutes, ragpickers, beggars, and petty criminals who inhabited the arcades and department stores and boulevards alongside the middle class.

Like Paris, New York has given birth to two great mythic cities. The first has arisen in print, in two centuries' worth of stories, novels, plays, essays, poems. It is a dense, sweeping, complex place, full of highs and lows, as damning and celebratory as the real city; it also comprises many of the classics of American literature, works by Whitman, Wharton, and Henry James, by Fitzgerald, Dos Passos, and Thomas Wolfe.

In it we stand at the railing of the Brooklyn ferry and sail up Fifth Avenue in flapper-filled taxicabs; we sit in boxes at the ornate, socially stratified Academy of Music and in the front parlor of a Greek Revival house on Washington Square. We join Holden Caulfield in Central Park, Nathan Detroit and Sky Masterson in Times Square, Stingo in Brooklyn, Gatsby and Daisy at the Plaza. In East Side apartment houses we eavesdrop on John Cheever's bickering young couples and John O'Hara's kept women; on the Upper West Side we hear misery with a different accent in the bleak coffee shops where Saul Bellow and Isaac Bashevis Singer's old survivors drink their sad glasses of tea. We see absurdity and anger mix in the tenement blocks of Langston Hughes's Harlem or in the decaying utopian landscape of James Baldwin's housing projects. We stifle in the hot still air of Harry Hope's bar in Eugene O'Neill's lower West Side and in the midtown hotel room where E. B. White senses a web of historic resonances all around him. With Herman Melville we share the promise of the sea from the Battery; with Frank O'Hara the promise of modernity from the Seagram plaza. Crossing the East River with Walt Whitman, or lingering in the waiting room of Pennsylvania Station with Thomas Wolfe, we listen to the city of the moment, and hear time itself.

15. Edgar Degas, *Aux Ambassadeurs*, 1877. Located in the Musée de Beaux-Arts, Lyon, Degas's painting captures the glitter of a summer evening at the Ambassadeurs, one of the most popular of the outdoor "café-concerts" found throughout late-nineteenth-century Paris.

The source of this fictive city's power is easily located. As the editor Rust Hills once observed, for the storyteller New York is almost irresistible:

> *Because it has more social mobility—both upward and downward—than perhaps any other place in the world, New York City is an appropriate setting for any story of a character's quick rise or fall. Because it has more people of all social classes in close-crowded conjunction, New York City is an appropriate setting for any odd encounter—as between an actress and a bum, between a playboy and a*

secretary—with corresponding opportunities for depicting the injustices of social distinctions and the extremes of poverty and wealth. . . . There are, in fact, so many comings and goings of all sorts in New York that an author can make virtually any plot, no matter how outlandish, or any characterization, no matter how extravagant, seem perfectly convincing.

As the quintessential "big city," New York clearly offers an ideal place to track an individual's arc of social, economic, or personal success—or to expose the hollowness and superficiality of that same success. Good writing always veers toward the specific, the particular; to write about New York is to find a condensed, specific symbol for realities at once larger and more diffuse: modern America, the industrial world, changing times. At the same time the city's character—its distinctive settings, language, moods, and ethnicity—is uniquely flavorful and helps ensure that even the broadest social critique will be grounded in a vivid, precise "world." For almost two hundred years the possibility of joining the specific and the general, of evoking a particular time and place that nonetheless carries resonance everywhere, has propelled writers to remake the city on the page; by now the New York they have built in words stands as one of the greatest of mythic metropolises.

Unlike Paris, New York's other mythic city has not emerged on canvas. Of course the city has been a superb subject for painters, but with rare exceptions, the painted city has not gelled into a place with a coherent life of its own. Painted images of New York have generally remained just that: depictions (however inspired or brilliant) of a real place. Where Impressionist paintings create their own city, New York paintings strive to capture one that exists.

No, New York's other great mythic city arose on film and, despite the enduring power of literary New York, it is *this* city—the New York of the movies—that has become the essential New York of the imagination, the city's true mythic counterpart. Admittedly, it offers few individual artists to rival Henry James or Edith Wharton, few individual works to compete with "Crossing Brooklyn Ferry" or *The Great Gatsby*. Nonetheless it is filmmakers, not writers, who have most fully, precisely, and powerfully developed a mythic vision of New York.

Why? In part, simply because films are so popular. New York has never been an exclusive, aristocratic place but the quintessentially democratic city, open to all. Its true mythic city must match that broad welcome and accessibility. Films do. Across the world—in Europe, Asia, Latin America, and throughout the United States—films about New York have been shown for most of the century. There were few towns and villages so small that their residents could not occasionally see a film, and when they did, it might well portray the movie city of New York, reinforcing its familiarity and asserting its status. For foreigners, this mythical city has taken on special significance because it described a real place, existing in reality at the moment it was being re-created in myth—unlike the Western, for example, which has been widely understood as a world lost in the past. New York, in contrast, has always been really *there*—possible to visit, even as it stands on the screen, scarcely believable, a place at once magical yet real. And unlike novels or stories, which might at best reach a large literate minority, films have been seen by everyone, rich and poor, intellectual and illiterate, forging a common bond of images and ideas that transcends class or nationality. Movie New York turns away no one.

It is also an exact match of medium and subject: New York and the movies seem made for each other. New York is dynamic, restless—ideal for the constantly moving images that make up a film. It is a city of action, a place where things *happen:* perfect for a medium that deals so much better with what is seen than what is thought or imagined. It is a city of powerful imagery, of sharp verticals and rushing horizontals, of bright walls and dark shadows and subtle tonalities in between; in the most elemental sense, it makes a good picture. It is a city of fast-paced living, well suited to the brevity of feature films, which must always tell their stories, even their epics, in little more than a hundred minutes.

16. Establishing shot from *Portrait of Jennie* (1948).

There is also the breadth of material. One of New York's most distinctive qualities is its extraordinary size and complexity. Here films mirror the place through sheer quantity. There are just so many films, so much texture. How many movies have been set in New York, explicitly or implicitly, over the course of the century? Hundreds, certainly. Perhaps thousands. Films began in New York itself; when filmmakers moved to California they made even more movies about New York; now they have returned and make more still. In those endless miles of footage lies a vast, dense texture, a mythic place of astonishing fullness.

This is evident through titles alone. Time and again, the city's place-names have been given over to film titles, and in so doing have transcended themselves, becoming not only geographic designations but resonant gateways, familiar around the world—from those of its boroughs (*Manhattan* and *Manhattan Melodrama, A Tree Grows in Brooklyn* and *It Happened in Brooklyn, Queens Logic* and *Fort Apache, The Bronx*), to its streets (*42nd Street* and *Wall Street* and *Hester Street; Miracle on 34th Street, The House on 92nd Street, Pickup on South Street, Across 110th Street; The Prisoner of Second Avenue, Slaughter on Tenth Avenue, Crossing Delancey*), to its neighborhoods (*Next Stop, Greenwich Village* and *Cotton Comes to Harlem, West Side Story* and *Brighton Beach Memoirs*). New York's shops, clubs, and theaters (*Breakfast at Tiffany's, The Cotton Club, The Night They Raided Minsky's*), its hotels (*Plaza Suite, Week-end at the Waldorf*), even its telephone exchanges and subway lines (*Butterfield 8, The Taking of Pelham One Two Three*) have been transformed into celluloid worlds, making movie New York's geography as familiar to people around the world as the streets and landmarks of their own hometowns. Or more so.

Of course, no other name compares with Broadway, which has constituted a filmic universe in itself, the basis for more titles than any other place on earth. There are, of course, all those *Broadway Melodys* (of 1929, '36, '38, '40). But also *Two Girls on Broadway* and *Two Tickets to Broadway; Angels Over Broadway* and *Bullets Over Broadway. Broadway Rhythm* and *Broadway Serenade* and *Broadway thru a Keyhole; Babes on Broadway* and *Broadway Babies. The Czar of Broadway, King Solomon of Broadway, Dr. Broadway* and *Little Miss Broadway.* There is *Charlie Chan on Broadway, The Barkleys of Broadway,* and *Broadway Danny Rose.* And *Main Street to Broadway, Arizona to Broadway,* and *Broadway to Hollywood*—not to mention the classic *Zombies on Broadway.*

In the end, the linkage is fundamental. Like New York, film is big. Like New York, it is larger than life. And like New York, it embodies—even defines—qualities of romance, glamour, danger, adventure. What New York is, film by its very nature has tended to extend and heighten. If possible, film has transformed New York—a city that looms so large by almost every measure—to an even higher plane. It becomes an elemental force, transcending any earthly place: a super city, a mythic city, a dream city (16).

ONE

SIDEWALK MOMENTS

FILMING THE CITY: 1896–1928

FIRST GLIMPSES

Outwardly, at least, nothing seemed to change. New York looked the same the day before; it would look the same the day after. But on May 11, 1896, something *did* change, something as profound as it was imperceptible. At two o'clock on that Monday afternoon, a man named William Heise initiated a whole new city—through the simple act of recording the existing one.

Heise began by setting up his new device—the latest marvel from America's wizard, Thomas Edison—in a window at the south end of Herald Square. Looking out at the bright spring scene, he could see the energetic heart of a great city, bursting with life. Well-dressed pedestrians mingled with the surging traffic along 34th Street. The elevated train roared periodically along tracks above Sixth Avenue, to the right. Straight ahead, the elegant Herald Building tried its best to inject a note of architectural grace into the square, but could hardly compete with the jumble of signs and marquees in what was still the heart of Manhattan's entertainment district (17).

From the street below, this man in the window could easily have been mistaken for a still photographer, trying to freeze all this lively motion onto a plate of silvered glass. But Heise was not a photographer; he was a *cameraman*—and by the time he was done, just a minute or two later, he had for the first time captured New York, in all its restlessness, onto a flexible strip of celluloid, for a moving picture to be projected the following week under the title *Herald Square.* So on this sunny May afternoon, Heise was also creating a new New York, one that would exist henceforth on film, in the darkened hush of a theater.

This new thing, moving pictures, was just being born—right here, around the corner, down the street. Herald Square itself was the center of a whirlwind of invention that was bringing a whole new medium into the world. Just three weeks before, Americans had seen their first projected motion pictures—their

17. (previous page) Herald Square, circa 1900. Looking north from 33rd Street, this photograph approximates the first projected motion picture ever made of New York City, an Edison actuality called *Herald Square*, shot on May 11, 1896. The elegant, Venetian-style structure at center, designed by McKim, Mead & White, houses the offices of the New York *Herald* itself, from which the square took its name in 1893.

very first "movies"—on the evening of April 23, 1896, in a theater just a few steps from where Heise was now standing, Koster and Bial's Music Hall on 34th Street (the site of today's Macy's). Over the course of the remaining year, vaudeville houses up and down Broadway would present a bewildering variety of competing systems: the Lathams' "Eidoloscope" in May, the Lumière brothers' "Cinématographe" in June, American Mutoscope's "Biograph" in October. The movies were arriving in a wondrous convergence of time and place, across a few short months and a few Manhattan blocks.

Nor was New York just a center of exhibition; the first commercial American films were actually being produced here, in small workshops on these same streets. Edison had taken over the top floor of a walk-up on West 28th Street, while his main rival, American Mutoscope and Biograph, located itself on the sixth floor of 841 Broadway, near 13th Street. In its first decade, most film production in America would concentrate in the heart of Manhattan, within a few blocks of Union and Madison Squares.

It made sense, of course. New York was new to movies but was hardly a stranger to show business. The city had long ago assumed its role as the undisputed center of American theater and in the meantime had become the central hub for the sprawling vaudeville "circuits" crisscrossing the country; it could offer the nascent film industry a huge pool of entertainment talent and a well-developed network for national distribution. No less important was late-nineteenth-century New York's reputation as a tinkerer's town, the kind of place where the complex and innovative hardware of making motion pictures could be developed within the city's industrial loft buildings, amidst a general spirit of ingenuity and invention.

Heise himself worked out of Edison's primitive 28th Street shop, which began to explain why he was filming nearby Herald Square that spring afternoon and why, later that day, he would visit Central Park, just a mile or two away, for some additional footage of Bethesda Fountain. Images of New York were entering the movies at their birth, in no small part, because film was being born in New York.

But there were other reasons, equally basic. Early film stock was so "slow," or insensitive to light (no more than ASA 10 by today's standards), that only by shooting in direct sunlight could a good exposure be assured. And many of the early movie cameras were so bulky and cumbersome—Biograph's weighed a quarter-ton—that filmmakers yearned for subjects that were easy to reach by horse-drawn wagon. New York's sights were thus ideal: close at hand and accessible by paved streets and, in most cases, located outdoors.

Still, the most important reasons were not, in the end, practical ones. It could hardly escape the filmmakers' notice that at their very doorstep was the greatest show on earth. By the turn of the twentieth century New York contained the world's tallest buildings and busiest harbor, the biggest ships and the longest bridges, the densest slums and some of the grandest mansions. It had a statue fifteen stories tall and a park more than 840 acres in size. It had trains that ran a hundred feet above the street and leapt across rivers. And it had people—millions and millions of them, celebrated and obscure, filling every inch of the place.

For a decade, the first cameramen carried their cameras all around this remarkable setting—from street corners to rooftops to boats in the river—making a special kind of documentarylike film that they called "actualities." Usually only a few minutes long, actualities were merely views of actual events, people, or places. They had no plots. They had no stories. They had no characters. Filmmakers still didn't know how to *tell* a story; they hadn't yet discovered editing, the bringing together of two pieces of film to contract time. So these actualities could last only as long as the real event they showed: the cameraman just pointed his camera at something interesting and started cranking. They were simply glimpses, in what today might be called "real time," of the city and its life.

18. ***At the Foot of the Flatiron.*** Photographed on October 26, 1903, by A. E. Weed, for Biograph. In the film, the high winds buffeting the Flatiron Building's prowlike edge seem to confirm the reputed origin of the phrase "Twenty-Three-Skiddoo" as a policeman's warning against lingering near the building's 23rd Street corner, where, since the tower's construction in 1901, men had gathered in the hope of catching a glimpse of ankle beneath the windblown skirts of passing women.

Their deadpan titles suggested just that. *Skating on Lake, Central Park*, or *Excavation for Subway*, these films were called. *East Side Urchins Bathing in a Fountain*, or *Panoramic View of Brooklyn Bridge*, or *New York City in a Blizzard.* One was named *At the Foot of the Flatiron*, and that is exactly what it shows: a stretch of sidewalk in front of the Flatiron Building, on a very windy day (18). During the course of the film, only two minutes and nineteen seconds long, pedestrians—ordinary, turn-of-the-century New Yorkers—simply walk down the street and past the camera, unaware for the most part that they are being photographed. The men grapple with their coats. The women clutch their long skirts. A well-dressed black man stares into the lens with curiosity and suspicion—until his hat flies off. (He disappears offscreen to retrieve it; the camera never moves from its position.) A streetcar can be noticed on the far right, crossing 23rd Street. Then two young women pass by, struggling gleefully against the strong wind. One of them turns and breaks into a wide, joyful smile. The film ends.

It is difficult to overstate the impact of these primitive films. They haunt us with the knowledge that what they show is not a stage but an actual place; that the people in them are not actors, but real New Yorkers; that they offer no invented storyline, but ordinary, everyday life. They are, in the end, not *about* the city: they *are* the city—one or two minutes of it, transposed precisely, second by second, from then to now. Their touching attention to the smallest, most ephemeral details of urban life—a windy day, a passing streetcar, a woman's smile—capture, more than anything, how the city *felt*, what it was actually like to live there. Seeing them, we live there, too.

From Heise's first film to about 1906, Edison and Biograph made hundreds of New York–set actualities, and assembled together they form a stunning urban collage. Cameramen such as Edison's Edwin S. Porter and Biograph's G. W. "Billy" Bitzer were placed in charge of the filmmaking process (another thing that did not yet exist was the notion of a director), and they explored the city encyclopedically. They made films of street kids delivering newspapers, shoppers crowding bargain stores, immigrants first touching American soil at Ellis Island. There were parades of horses, of automobiles, of street sweepers. There were sleek yachts defending the America's Cup off New York Harbor and the squalid "Ghetto" fish markets of the Lower East Side. There was Commander Peary departing for the North Pole and Admiral Dewey arriving from Manila, President Butler being installed at Columbia University and the last rites for Hiram Cronk, oldest veteran of the War of 1812.

The cameramen, in fact, shot just about everything. As fascinated by poverty as by wealth, they traveled as often to the poorest tenement streets as to the grand avenues of the rich. They moved comfortably from the bucolic scenery of the city's parks and rural outskirts to its dense, utterly industrialized core. They were naturally drawn to the bizarre and extraordinary (Edison once made a film at Coney Island called *Electrocuting an Elephant*), but no more so than to the sights of daily life. They were especially absorbed by the city's underlying municipal workings, from the heroic exploits of policemen and fireboat crews to the mundane yet indispensable operations of its health and sanitation departments. One of Porter's films was titled, quite accurately, *Sorting Refuse at Incinerating Plant, New York City*.

19. Fifth Avenue and 42nd Street, circa 1910. In this frame enlargement from an unidentified early actuality film, the majestic facade and famed lions of the New York Public Library are already in place, although the building itself (which opened in 1911) remains under construction.

Of course, the cameramen often left the city to shoot actualities elsewhere, from the battles of the Spanish-American War to the speeches of Teddy Roosevelt. Yet they always returned to New York, filming it again and again to create, in the end, a strikingly complete portrait of the city. This was still due, in part, to sheer convenience. But a more important reason could be found in the audience at the vaudeville halls where these films were shown. New York, on film, proved wildly popular. People all across the country enjoyed seeing both its marvels, suggesting a city of the future, and its scenes of everyday street life, which might seem equally futuristic—or at least alien—to audiences in small towns throughout America. Such continued popularity encouraged companies to keep making New York–set actualities even after the form itself began losing favor in the wake of the first story films.

Together, the actualities were the first group of American films to explore a consistent subject. That subject was New York—not any particular people who lived in New York, nor the stories that could be found there, but simply *New York itself*, its texture and character and urban presence.

With startling clarity, in fact, these films established a number of basic themes, basic ways of looking, that foreshadowed the way films would present New York in the coming century. Lacking stories or characters, for instance, the actualities naturally turned much of their attention to the physical city—but not, interestingly, to its architecture. Which is to say they rarely showed buildings as individual landmarks: they invariably looked instead at the city's *places.* Buildings were a part of these places, of course—but just a part, just one element of the larger urban composition that included streets and sidewalks, traffic, and people. In one early compilation of city scenes, the classical facade of the New York Public Library helps to define the great bowl of space that is Fifth Avenue; but it is the space, not the building, whose activity is the film's focus (19). The film instinctively turned to the library's *urban* role—as a grand street definer—rather than its *architectural* role as freestanding landmark.

20. ***Sky Scrapers of New York City, From the North River.*** Photographed on May 10, 1903, by J. B. Smith, for Edison, this actuality shows the new office towers that had begun springing up at the foot of Manhattan, creating the world's first skyline. The dark spire of Trinity Church, once the highest structure in the city, has already been overshadowed by skyscrapers rising on lower Broadway, including the twin-towered Park Row Building, the tallest structure in the world from the time of its construction in 1899 until the completion of the Singer Tower in 1908.

The same held true of even the city's most daring buildings—its skyscrapers. Actualities almost never isolated a single tower as their subject but looked instead at the city's skyline, at the *grouping* of many towers. These skyline scenes were among the most popular of early films, a truly miraculous sight to audiences living outside New York or Chicago. The turn-of-the-century skyline these films presented is, to the modern eye, exciting and vibrant but curiously unfamiliar, filled not with slender spires but blocky, flat-topped buildings of relatively squat and unromantic proportion (20). The architecture of New York's skyscrapers was still evolving: the graceful towers that would mark the city's maturity had not yet risen, and the eye searches in vain for the cresting peaks of the Singer or Woolworth towers (much less the Chrysler or Empire State) that would give a sense of completion and polish to this spirited, raw upsurge of stone and steel.

Still, this early skyline seemed amazingly alive, especially after it was set into motion by the introduction around 1900 of a new piece of equipment: a swiveling tripod head that allowed the camera to make "panoramic"—or "panning"—motions in films whose titles were quick to advertise their new mobility: *Panorama from the Tower of the Brooklyn Bridge* (1899), *Panorama from Times Building, New York* (1905). Another way to animate the skyline was to view it from a moving platform, such as a boat circling lower Manhattan (*Sky Scrapers of New York City, From the North River*, 1903). Already brought to life by fluttering flags and white plumes of vapor, the skyline was further enlivened by the shifting, waterborne perspective of these views, the towers slowly rotating behind a rapidly shifting foreground of piers and ships. The fixed solidity of the city was being transformed in these films into a dynamic, ever-changing composition, the solid matter of the city giving way to movement and energy.

This transformation of the city—from matter to motion—could be felt throughout this period, perhaps due to the very nature of moving pictures. It was certainly made obvious in the filmmakers' close attention to the multiple forms of transportation the city offered—and often pioneered—around the turn of the century: in films of trolley trips across the Brooklyn Bridge, in a view that followed the precarious curve of elevated tracks from a moving train high above 104th Street, or in one remarkable film in which a camera carried the audience along the entire journey from 14th Street to Grand Central, through the dark tunnels and freshly built stations of the just-completed IRT subway (21). Less obviously, motion could mean change over time as well as space. The early filmmakers were absorbed with the processes of construction: their cameras descended repeatedly into the city's big excavation sites to watch workers cutting down to the bedrock for the footings of a new skyscraper or Pennsylvania Station. They even looked to the underside of progress, in an unusual film that recorded the demolition of the old Star Theatre through an innovative time-lapse process, compressing its weeks-long razing into less than two minutes. The venerable structure's walls and arches seem to disintegrate as if by some strange biological process rather than at the hands of ordinary workmen; by film's end a smooth, empty lot sits where just moments before a big, permanent-looking building stood. A sense of the city's progress through time also informed the many civic ceremonies captured in the actualities, the inaugural moments of bowler-hatted worthies first crossing the Williamsburg Bridge in 1903, or, a year later, descending into the new City Hall Station to dedicate New York's first subway. Even Edwin Porter's strange fondness for dumping wharves and incinerating plants revealed an understanding of the city as a vast

21. ***Interior, N.Y. Subway, 14th St. to 42nd St.*** Photographed on May 21, 1905, by G. W. "Billy" Bitzer, for Biograph. Just eight months after the first subway began operating under the streets of the city, the cameraman Billy Bitzer mounted the Biograph's camera on a utility car and followed one of the new IRT trains on its way uptown to Grand Central. Bitzer solved the challenge of lighting inside the dark tunnel by placing a massive bank of arc lamps on another flat car, which ran on an adjacent track at precisely the same speed.

web of systems and processes, always in motion around us, even when hidden from view.

But the greatest such transformation came near the end of the period, in an Edison film by Porter called *Coney Island at Night* (22). The great amusement resort had been a popular subject from the start, of course, its diverse attractions (diving horses, hippodrome races, elephants "shooting the chutes") portrayed in dozens of actualities that, like nearly all early films, had been shot by daylight. But now the sensitivity of the Eastman Company's film stock had improved and Porter was eager to show off its possibilities. Over a June weekend in 1905, he returned to Coney Island to shoot the dazzling night display that gave the resort its worldwide reputation as the "Electric Eden." He came away with something unlike any New York actuality ever made.

As the film starts, there is nothing, only blackness. Then lights start to emerge—gently at first, soon in a rush—until an entire city of lights arises out of the night air. The name "Dreamland" floats on the dark screen. A sign for Steeplechase tilts crazily from one side to another. Luna Park's arches and domes call to mind an electric Florence, a crashing overflow of light focused on a glowing tower at the center. The magical intent of Coney Island is here perfectly fulfilled: to create an immanent, ethereal world of light and sensation, precursor to Times Square's giant displays. But more so than at Times Square, Coney Island's nighttime landscape complements the plaster architecture of day: not rectangular signboards propped above modest, boxy, commer-

22. *Coney Island at Night*. Photographed on June 3–4, 1905, by Edwin S. Porter, for Edison. Traveling to Coney Island one summer weekend, intent on shooting the famed resort after dark (so as to demonstrate the potential of a new film stock from the Eastman Company), Porter was inevitably drawn to Luna Park, whose fanciful skyline of towers, domes, arches, and minarets was illuminated by an array of 250,000 electric lights.

cial buildings, but a delicate tracery of bulbs, draped like glittering necklaces over the romantic structures of a shimmering fairyland.

Through the same blunt, unmediated technique that had recorded the ordinary life of the city, Porter had created a dreamy urban vision in which matter had been utterly dissolved into energy and movement. He had pushed filmic New York toward a sense of magical possibility, as different as imaginable from the mundane, grounded-in-reality approach with which the actualities began. In the near term, ironically, his vision led nowhere. It would be a quarter-century before its implications could be pursued, in a place thousands of miles away that did not yet even exist. For now, New York films would return to earth—had, indeed, already begun to return to earth, through the simple, human themes of the first story films, using the narrative technique of parallel action invented in 1902 by none other than Edwin S. Porter himself. With the rise of these new story films, the urban prologue of the actualities would soon be over, like the audience's brief view of the scenery before the actors enter at the start of a play. We had seen New York. Now it was time to meet the New Yorkers.

NEW YORK STORIES

From the start, simple films of stage acts and vaudeville routines had complemented the showing of actualities. Searching for a convenient place to make these films, the early companies, located mostly in high-rise loft buildings, looked at first upstairs, to their roofs, where ample sunlight could assure a proper exposure. A primitive, if striking, rooftop stage was erected by Biograph above its 13th Street building; in late 1896, American commercial film production started in this unlikely venue, a rotating platform high above Broadway.

But the obvious limits of space and scenery soon pushed filmmakers to explore other options. One of the first, not surprisingly, was to take a leaf from the actualities and shoot films on the streets themselves. Here they would find the same advantages of convenience and daylight and the rich urban landscape that the actualities had enjoyed, along with a not-undesirable ambiguity about the "reality" of the events they portrayed. An early story film like *What Happened on Twenty-third Street, New York City* (1901) sought deliberately to confuse reality and invention. Its title has the familiar deadpan quality of an actuality, as does its opening view of a man and woman walking down a busy Manhattan sidewalk (23). It is revealed as a staged affair only when the woman lingers atop a sidewalk vent, which—to the delight of her male companion—lifts her skirt and exposes her stockinged legs. Even then, the real city setting continued to offer an invaluable sense of verisimilitude, through the gaping looks of passersby, clearly not actors but ordinary New Yorkers who happened into camera range and were caught staring at this provocative sidewalk moment.

Let loose on the streets, the cameramen discovered possibilities that could

23. ***What Happened on Twenty-third Street, New York City***. Photographed on August 21, 1901, for Edison. One of the earliest efforts at presenting a "story" on-screen, the short film features A. C. Abadie and Florence Georgie, and was shot on 23rd Street, facing Sixth Avenue (whose elevated train station can be glimpsed beyond the lamppost at center). Looking on as a blast of warm air from the sidewalk grating pushes a woman's white skirt around her legs, the film inevitably brings to mind another New York movie moment, enacted half a century later and thirty blocks uptown (215).

never be entertained on a stage set, no matter how big. New York's sprawling urban landscape proved ideal for a new kind of inherently filmic activity—the chase—and soon, story films were being written specifically to initiate sequences that rambled across the city, with cops chasing crooks all over town, for example, in a 1905 film titled *The Life of an American Policeman.* The year before, a Biograph film called *Personal* had been quickly copied in an Edison film whose own title, *How a French Nobleman Got a Wife Through the New York "Herald" Personal Columns*, summarized the plot device that situates the aristocratic Alphonse on the forecourt of Grant's Tomb, only to thrust at him one eligible female, then another, and another, until he is deluged by a horde of single New York women chasing him across the broad, newly planted landscape of Riverside Drive (24).

By the middle of the decade, the story film was clearly the ascendant product of an industry that had firmly established itself as a major new form of urban entertainment. Neither primitive, open-air rooftop stages nor the streets could fulfill the ongoing production needs of these longer, more complex kinds of movies. By 1901, Edison had already created an enclosed, glass-roofed stage on the top floor of 41 East 21st Street. But in 1903 Biograph leaped ahead of its rival by occupying an entire row house at 11 East 14th Street, filling its five stories with the embryonic elements of a full production facility. Banks of long, greenish Cooper-Hewitt lamps lined the walls and ceiling of what was once the house's ballroom and was now the world's first artificially lighted film stage; the basement below and bedrooms above, meanwhile, had been given over to the component parts of the newly emerging industry: wardrobe, editing, set construction, shipping. Here Biograph's filmmakers, including a young director named D. W. Griffith, could expand the length and ambition of the new narrative films.

While spacious compared to before, conditions were still distinctly cramped. In response, Biograph hit upon a formula for making New York story films that would echo down to today, when productions shot in the city still worry about insufficient stage space. Biograph's new generation of New York films would combine the best use of interior stages with outdoor location work. Shot indoors would be scenes that focused on character and advanced the story line; shot outside, on the real streets of the city, would be larger scenes of action and spectacle. With their smaller scale, the staged interiors could explore individual motivation, while the expansive, authentic exteriors could at once suggest larger social forces at work and serve to "open up" the film from its interior limitations. It was an emerging New York style of filmmaking, whose mix of stage and location elegantly combined intimacy and grandeur, the personal and the social. The technique would define New York films for the coming two decades, then vanish, only to reemerge, in the 1960s and 1970s, when filmmaking returned to the city and to the problem of limited stage space that had haunted Biograph.

24. ***Personal.*** Photographed on June 8 and 13, 1904, by the director Wallace McCutcheon and the cameraman G. W. "Billy" Bitzer, for Biograph. Set in front of Grant's Tomb, completed only seven years before and still rising in solitary splendor from the open landscape of Riverside Park, the film presents the startling consequences of a "personals" ad placed by the dapper Alphonse in the New York *Herald:* "Young French gentleman, recently arrived in this country, desires to meet handsome American girl; object, matrimony."

The continued popularity of New York actualities, even as their era was coming to a close, must have suggested to Biograph that story films based on similar city themes would do equally well; these could take plausible advantage of exciting location shots but would now add a dramatic context and identifiable characters. So back the cameras went to the city's construction sites, to the steel framework of an office tower (*The Skyscrapers*, 1906) or the Pennsylvania Railroad tunnel being carved under the Hudson River (*The Tunnel Workers*, 1906), this time to make films enlarged by melodramatic plots about the men who worked in them (25). Back the cameras went to the Lower East Side's streets, to Italian districts (*The Black Hand*, 1906) and Jewish ones (*Romance of a Jewess*, 1908), no longer just glimpsing the inhabitants from afar but now entering into the conflicts of their lives, from the menace of organized crime to the threat of intermarriage. Despite Biograph's best efforts, it would be a long time before the crudely painted interior sets could match the sculptural density and richness of the location backgrounds, and it was indeed the extensive use of locations that gave these films much of their audience appeal. The promotional material for *Romance of a Jewess*, one of Griffith's early films, did not fail to note that "several scenes are decidedly interesting in the fact that they were actually taken in the thickly settled Hebrew quarters of New York City."

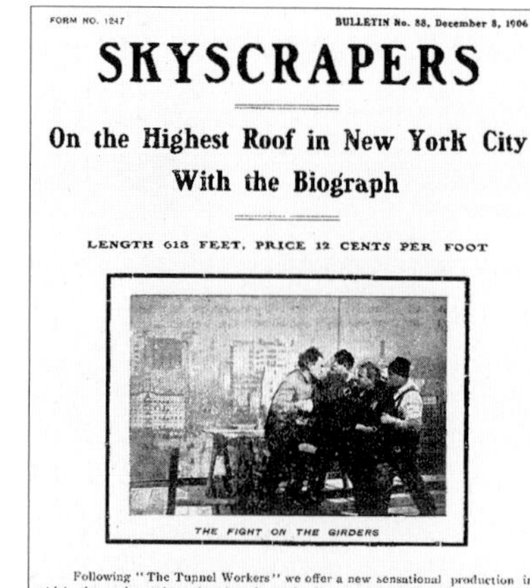

FORM NO. 1247 BULLETIN No. 88, December 8, 1906

SKYSCRAPERS

On the Highest Roof in New York City With the Biograph

LENGTH 618 FEET, PRICE 12 CENTS PER FOOT

THE FIGHT ON THE GIRDERS

Following "The Tunnel Workers" we offer a new sensational production in which the action takes place largely on the dizzy heights of the uppermost girder of a twenty-story skyscraper in the heart of New York. The building is said to be the highest is the city, and overlooks Union Square. In the distance are to be seen the Flatiron Building, the Times Building and other modern marvels.

The opening of the production includes a panoramic view of the skyscraper district and several thrilling "stunts" by iron-workers, such as throwing and catching redhot rivets, riding a girder into its position and adjusting it in place, and a group of workmen hanging to the chains and being lowered by the derrick from the top of the building to the ground.

The action of the story involves the contractor, superintendent and several workmen. "Dago Pete," an iron-worker, is discharged for fomenting trouble, and to get even, steals the contractor's watch and charges the superintendent with the crime. To makes his deed still blacker he conceals the watch in the superintendent's home. The latter is accused of the theft by the owner of the watch, and as a result, the two men engage in a hand-to-hand fight on the very top of the building. The contractor is worsted and narrowly escapes death from a fall. The superintendent is arrested and haled into court, but a little girl who has seen the hiding of the watch denounces the villain. The contractor and superintendent shake hands, while the real thief is hustled off to prison.

No. 3258 CODE WORD—Retusuro.

25. Promotional description of *The Skyscrapers*. Photographed on November 8, 14, and 15, 1906, by F. A. Dobson, for Biograph. Much of the film was shot atop an office building under construction on Broadway and 13th Street. The "skyscrapers" of the title are not the city's tall buildings, but the ironworkers who erected their steel frameworks.

LARGER VISIONS

Although outclassing its rivals, Biograph's house on 14th Street was clearly insufficient for the production needs of films that were growing toward feature length. Filmmaking was beginning to require a lot of room—more room, in fact, than could be had economically in Manhattan. Around 1905, all three film companies turned their attention to the edge of the city, to the open lands of the outer boroughs. Here they could afford to purchase large tracts of land, big enough to hold not one but several buildings, each of specialized purpose. Here, in other words, they could build the first studios.

26. Vitagraph Studios in Brooklyn, circa 1910. Begun in 1903 on East 14th Street in Flatbush, Vitagraph was the first multibuilding complex in the nation devoted to the production of motion pictures—America's first movie studio. Enlarged in the teens, the studio became part of Warner Bros. in 1925, was purchased by NBC in 1952, and remains in use to this day.

Vitagraph opened its studio on Brooklyn's Flatbush Avenue in 1905; Edison moved a year later to the Bronx and was joined there by a new Biograph plant a year after that (26). They could all still take advantage of Manhattan's proximity, just a streetcar ride away; but they had come to the important recognition that studio production is at heart a suburban enterprise. Legitimate theater efficiently combines production and presentation in the same building and thus thrives in the heart of town, where audiences gather. But the functional needs of a movie *studio* and a movie *theater* are completely different, and, because movies are products that can be easily shipped, have no call to take place in the same location. While dozens of smaller film companies still remained in Manhattan, the need for larger settings would push these, too, outward; many soon moved just across the Hudson, making the sleepy town of Fort Lee, New Jersey, into a major production center from about 1910 to 1919.

But if no longer ideal for film production, New York remained a prime subject, and the new, longer movies meant new possibilities for the movie city. Across its full, ten-reel length, a feature like *Traffic in Souls* (1913) could offer a panoramic vision of the city to suggest the extent of a then-current social problem: white slavery. Location shooting would give its sensationalized account a sense of immediacy and veracity; the ability to cross-cut among several stories from different parts of the city would allow it to dramatize the diverse nature of the problem: how both female foreign immigrants (arriving at Battery Park) and domestic country girls (arriving at Pennsylvania Station) were lured to the same evil ends (27). And its feature length would allow a sustained view of the city, far beyond the quick glimpses of earlier films. In it, we see the new Pennsylvania Station, rising in its classicism aloof from the ramshackle district around it, pointing the way to a grander city yet to be achieved. We see the newly built blocks of the Upper West Side, thick with the aesthetic cacophony of hundreds of ornamental schemes, on streets nearly devoid of trees. (If they seem an architectural meal almost too rich to bear, it is in part because these blocks are all so new, their mortar joints almost painfully sharp, their stonework so bright and uniform. While their ornament and composition attempt to recall European cities, in very American fashion they have been put up all at once, with no chance yet for them to mellow or soften into a state of urban grace.) And we see the city's outskirts, scattered tenements and row houses arising with open lots still vacant between them. Ornate street facades stand in striking contrast to the bare side walls that will disappear when the block's missing teeth are filled.

27. ***Traffic in Souls*** **(1913).** Drawn from a congressional investigation three years before, the film sought to expose the "white slave" traffickers who abducted young women into prostitution rings. Shot extensively on location, the film's action swept from the Battery (top), where immigrants arrived after passing through Ellis Island, to Central Park South (center), where a trafficker follows a young American woman just arrived in New York, to the rooftops of Brooklyn, where a policeman closes in on the criminals (bottom) before the raw, unfinished urban landscape beyond.

In the years before America's entry into World War I, vast changes to the industry were under way. Led by Edison, the older film companies banded together to form a restrictive trust, based on their technology patents, that was intent on squeezing out smaller, unaffiliated companies. But the younger independents, it turned out, could not be chased out of the business—only out of New York. With names like Adolph Zukor, William Fox, Samuel Goldwyn, Jesse Lasky, Carl Laemmle, and Louis B. Mayer, this new breed were different from Edison and Porter's generation: mostly Jewish instead of Gentile, mostly showmen and theater owners rather than gadget-oriented inventors. Many had come to moving pictures from New York's garment and fur industries, where predicting next year's trends—and being willing to gamble a big investment to be ready when they arrived—was an essential skill, one that would serve them well in their new line of business. Tired of the legal and sometimes physical harassment of Edison's "patent trust," they boarded trains and headed west, extending their migration well past Fort Lee—all the way, in fact, to the opposite end of the country, to a series of quiet Los Angeles suburbs called Glendale, Edendale, Culver City, and, especially, one called Hollywood.

Here, land to build new studios, and labor to run them, was amazingly cheap; here could be found a wide variety of scenic landscapes, from mountaintop to coastline; here sunlight was endless for shooting outdoors or in glass-roofed stages; and here the Mexican border was close at hand, should the trust ever force them to flee again. The West Coast's film industry grew explosively in the space of a single decade; no more than a tiny rival to New York in 1911, it accounted for four-fifths of all American production by 1920. Yet even before the despised trust was declared illegal in 1915, many of these companies established New York offices, and America's film industry became the two-coast enterprise it would remain for much of the century to come: administrative and financial control remaining firmly in New York while production centered in Southern California.

Meanwhile New York's own film industry enjoyed a wave of growth in the early 1920s, driving a building boom that resulted in four big studios in three years. William Randolph Hearst's Cosmopolitan Studios on East 127th Street and two new Fox studios on Tenth Avenue in the West Fifties brought major production facilities back to Manhattan; even these, though, were dwarfed by the studio that Famous Players-Lasky, later called Paramount, was erecting in Astoria, Queens: a massive facility known as "The Big House." Opened in 1920, it offered what the *New York Times* called "the fittings of a palace." Eventually sprawling over fourteen acres and several blocks, the complex contained laboratory buildings and scene docks, a fifty-seat screening room and a publicity department equipped to turn out ten thousand stills a day. Every star had a personal suite of dressing rooms; long black limousines pulled up under a covered entrance more reminiscent of a grand railway station than a film lot. For a few years, the New York industry seemed poised for a comeback: the arrival of electric arc-lamp shooting suddenly made California's glass-roofed stages obsolete, and enclosed stages like those of New York's "sunless temples" were clearly the wave of the future. But lower land and labor costs and the simplicity of set construction and maintenance afforded under California's benign climate continued to confer a decided advantage. As a Goldwyn executive boasted, "We can build big sets in our big lots and leave them standing as long as we please."

MOMENTS CAPTURED

Perhaps the Goldwyn man was right, but New York's filmmakers did continue to have one set at their disposal bigger than everything else combined: the city itself. The ability to take advantage of spectacular locations remained an important reason why New York's film industry continued to flourish through the 1920s, though on a scale smaller than Hollywood's.

28. **Filming *Play Ball* atop a midtown Manhattan rooftop, 1925.** By the 1920s, the advent of reliable lightweight movie cameras allowed filmmakers to work in nearly every corner of the city. For a Paramount film called *Play Ball*, the actress Allene Ray hangs from a false brick-and-stone parapet that has been built atop an actual rooftop in the West Forties of Manhattan. Minimal protection for the star is provided by a safety mattress placed below the set.

Location shooting itself had grown far easier. Movie cameras had achieved a mature level of reliability with the rugged, lightweight, hand-cranked Bell & Howell models that were now the industry standard. Film stock had improved to the point where only a few reflectors were needed to ensure a clear and consistent outdoor exposure: no lights—and thus no electrical power—were necessary. And sound equipment, of course, did not yet exist. Shooting on the streets of New York in the silent era was simple and light and relatively cheap.

In the teens and twenties, New Yorkers became blasé about seeing films being made around town; in better weather, several location companies from both New York and Hollywood might be working at once. Indeed, in these years the whole city seemed to lay itself bare to feature filmmaking: tales and photographs of early New York location work carry a try-anything flavor which today seems scarcely believable (28). In one case the city was virtually commandeered by a film company with a financial link to a starstruck municipal official—or so the screenwriter Frank Leon Smith recalled of the making of *Into the Net*, a 1924 detective film based on a story written by New York's sitting police commissioner, Richard E. Enright:

> *When I asked [the film's producer] what good the Enright tie-up was to us, with some irritation he said: "Well, what do you want?" In desperation I exclaimed: "The Brooklyn Bridge!" To my amazement he asked, "When, and for how long?"*
>
> *It was as easy as that! The cops roped off the Brooklyn Bridge for us and George Seitz, the director, staged some good fights at mid-day in the middle of the bridge. Chase scenes up and down Manhattan streets became common and ritualized. First Enright's official car and his personal aide ran interference; second, the car with the villains; third, the car with the heroic element; fourth, the camera car, with the director. Traffic cops had no advance notice. When they saw Enright's car, they leapt aside, blew their whistles, and along we sped.*

29. *Speedy* (1928). Though much of Harold Lloyd's film was shot in Los Angeles, the climactic race of Lloyd's horse-drawn streetcar across Manhattan was shot almost entirely on location—from Washington Square (top), still open to vehicular traffic, to Battery Park (center), along whose northern edge can be glimpsed a row of early-nineteenth-century houses, later demolished for the entrance to the Brooklyn-Battery Tunnel. The crash of the streetcar into the column of the "El" (center and bottom) was an actual accident that occurred during shooting, and was then written into the script.

An earlier, no less colorful tale had the director Raoul Walsh making the rounds of New York's dockside saloons and bars to gather gang members and prostitutes to serve as extras for *Regeneration*, his 1915 film set on the tough streets of the Bowery and Lower East Side. Walsh later recalled to the film historian Kevin Brownlow his impressions of the crowd that assembled before the shoot: "Some of the women were obviously hookers, many of the men looked as though they should have been on Death Row for every crime in the book." Brownlow also recounts a charming story associated with the making of *Traffic in Souls*: indignant New Yorkers at the Battery were about to break up the evident abduction of two immigrant girls just off the boat, until someone at the edge of the crowd cried, "Let 'em alone; it's all right!" Another voice chimed in, "Let 'em alone, it's the movies!" The good-natured crowd allowed the scuffle to continue, later watching as the would-be "abductors" and "victims" climbed into a waiting car, and, laughing together in the backseat, were whisked up Broadway.

Despite their new scale and ambition—feature-length, with complex story lines and well-developed characters—the location-shot movies of the 1920s continued to draw much of their appeal from the same source of visual excitement that had propelled the earliest actualities: the sheer spectacle of New York's buildings, streets, and monuments. With a new freedom of movement that allowed the camera to be strapped to the front of cars, hidden in trucks to record the city's street life without being detected, or placed on construction lifts and carried to the tops of skyscrapers, these films seemed to capture every aspect of the city's growth in this busy, frenetic era.

30. ***The Shock Punch* (1925).** The story of an eager Ivy League graduate (Richard Dix) who wants to prove his manhood on the high steel of a New York skyscraper, *The Shock Punch* was filmed in large part on the uncompleted framework of the Barclay-Vesey Building in lower Manhattan, one of the city's first modernistic skyscrapers, designed by the architect Ralph Walker. In the distance rises the neoclassical Municipal Building, completed eleven years before to the designs of William M. Kendall of McKim, Mead & White.

31. Filming *New York* atop a Fifth Avenue roof, 1927. Paramount's *New York*, directed by Luther Reed and starring Ricardo Cortez and Lois Wilson, was celebrated for its unusual New York locations. This still shows a penthouse terrace set that has been constructed atop the roof of a Fifth Avenue apartment house, providing a picturesque view of Central Park South behind the couple.

It was a time when the fast-moving city moved faster than ever before. A new flood of automobiles, trucks, and electric streetcars was rapidly banishing horse-drawn traffic from the streets and with it the last traces of a slower, gentler pace. What better guide to this accelerating moment than Harold Lloyd, the silent film's most agile poet? In *Speedy* (1928), Lloyd plays Harold "Speedy" Swift, whose succession of jobs keeps both him and the film in constant motion (29). As taxi driver for "The Only One Garage," he carries several fast and frenzied fares—including a hilarious race uptown to ensure that his idol, Babe Ruth (playing himself), makes it to Yankee Stadium in time for a game. Speedy can't help but tell the Babe—effusively and at length—just how big a fan he is, constantly turning his head back around to do so. Ruth is polite at first, but soon distracted and then terrified by the view through the windshield, the one that Speedy in his enthusiasm can't be bothered with: his cab wildly careening toward every car and truck it meets on the way uptown. The audience shares the lively action through a point-of-view shot made by a camera mounted to the front of the cab and aimed dead ahead as it whips through New York's traffic-filled streets.

The same technique sets into motion the film's climax, an epic journey that takes Speedy from Times Square to the Battery to preserve New York's last horse-drawn streetcar (whose franchise happens to belong to his girlfriend's grandfather). As we plunge headlong into the traffic, cars just ahead of us flying this way and that, we don't just see a city in motion but actually become *part* of that motion. We are hardly slowed even when the streetcar crashes head-on into a column of the El—an actual accident that occurred during shooting and was then written into the script. (Speedy keeps going by improvising a temporary wheel from a manhole cover.) Although Speedy wins his battle at film's end, and the grandfather receives a handsome settlement from a competing company, the old horse loses the war—it is to be replaced anyway. In the future, the city will only move faster than ever.

Films also caught the moment when the city filled with a different kind of newcomer: not the foreign immigrants of earlier decades, but Americans, come from the nation's heartland to make a name for themselves, crossing the Hudson ferry to take their place among the city's teeming millions. This was the New York of *The Crowd,* King Vidor's 1928 masterpiece; like *Speedy,* it combined scenes shot in Los Angeles with real New York footage, including a rapid montage of city scenes, suggestive of the old actualities but now expressively organized by a master director to capture the excitement and sense of possibility that has drawn Vidor's everyman, Johnny Sims (James Murray), to the city. Seeking to place Sims within the hurly-burly of New York, Vidor hid his camera (and his cameraman, Henry Sharp) in a rubber-tired pushcart stacked high with boxes; the lens, poking through a small hole, was able to photograph Sims walking among the crowds without their knowledge. Though only a few of these shots were used in the final film, they effectively suggest the gradual reduction of Sims's dreams as he confronts the inevitable urban reality of a million other dreams, all vying for greatness. At the same time they catch the special feeling of the city in this era when crowds of domestic newcomers, seeking success at all costs, re-Americanized and reenergized the place.

And last, films caught the exact moment when the city found its own distinctive look, achieved through the maturity of its greatest creation, the skyscraper, and recorded exactly as it happened in *The Shock Punch* (1925). Here the silent camera's freedom of movement was turned vertically to take us right up the side of an office tower under construction. Richard Dix plays Ronny Savage, who, fresh from the Ivy League, wants to prove his manhood by taking a job on the high steel, despite a certain lack of experience. ("What are you?" the hiring boss asks, "riveter—bucker-up—derrick man—or helper?" "Yes," Ronny replies.) Because the lightweight camera could follow the action just about anywhere, much of the film lingered in the airy upper precincts of an actual steel skeleton (30). So this film too recalled its predecessors, from the early construction actualities to 1906's *The Skyscrapers*—but its longer, more sustained look allowed it to reveal something subtle about the new shape of the city.

At the top of the tower *The Shock Punch* revels in the beauty of the steel frame, a spare, three-dimensional matrix of black lines against the sky. Following the course of construction, the film shows us that open frame being wrapped in a masonry skin. But this is not just any skin. For its location, *The Shock Punch* used the 1926 Barclay-Vesey Building, one of the earliest towers in the new "modernistic" style and a landmark in New York's architectural coming-of-age. In earlier films (such as *Little Old New York*, 1923) the skyscraping city had clearly been in search of a style. Towers like the 1914 Municipal Building had brilliantly adapted the classical architecture of low-rise buildings, stretching it over the tall frameworks of modern construction. In the largest sense, then, New York was still borrowing its architectural voice from other places and times. With the Barclay-Vesey Building and its later Art Deco partners, the city finally found its own style, a distinctive look that owed little to any other time or place. Because it was shot on location, a film like *The Shock Punch* could capture the very moment and place of this change—even as it was still happening.

By the late 1920s, New York's movie industry had perfected its own way of filming the city, a highly descriptive approach based on the ability to shoot extensively on location. Roaming the city with impunity, the silent camera offered a direct, documentary-like portrait of New York, closely attentive to its developing character, from the largest shifts in population and geography to finer-grained changes in its physical appearance. However molded to the expressive needs of story and direction, the city shown in the movies remained a representation of New York's reality rather than a transformation of it; there remained a kind of one-to-one equivalence between the real city and its filmic counterpart.

A film like Paramount's *New York* (1927), made near the end of this period and noted for its extensive use of locations, makes it easy to imagine how films might have continued over the coming decades to be shot in New York, faithfully tracking the changing look and feel of its streets, its buildings, and its people—all by virtue of being filmed on those streets, amidst those buildings, and among those people (31). It would be a fascinating portrayal, but it would remain exactly that—a portrayal, a celluloid mirror held up to the real city's growth and change.

Instead, something else was about to happen. Within a few years, the 1920s depiction of New York would be replaced not by another portrayal but by something else entirely: a city of the imagination, an invented city suddenly bursting into life as a consequence of two revolutions in film history, and one in history itself. The first and, for movie New York, most important of these was signaled by nothing more than the scratchy sound of classical music, synchronized to the moving picture of an orchestra playing. Upon that sound, a mythic city waited to be born.

TWO

DREAMING THE CITY

NEW YORKERS IN HOLLYWOOD

GOING HOLLYWOOD

Sound changed everything.

First, it brought on the sudden demise of New York's film industry—an ironic turn of events, given that the whole notion of sound films had begun in New York. In the 1920s, silence was still golden under the California sun, but the industry's East Coast wing, located in the hub of America's music and theater business, anxiously sought a way to synchronize recorded sound to moving pictures. In 1925, Warner's East Coast division bought the old Vitagraph Company and with it their pioneering "vitaphone" system; the following spring they proceeded to film several musical acts to accompany a romantic drama called *Don Juan*. They even used Vitagraph's ancient lot on Flatbush Avenue in Brooklyn. In this oldest of studios the newest filmmaking technique would begin.

It would not stay long. When the rumble from nearby elevated trains seeped through the studio's thin walls, production shifted across the river to the massive Manhattan Opera House on 34th Street. Then blasting started at an adjacent construction site; the sensitive recording stylus jumped the groove with every boom. Sam Warner himself claimed to have suggested the obvious solution—"shoot at night"—by which the film was completed. But it was hardly a permanent answer.

In fact, the arrival of talking pictures—after the tumultuous reception of Warner's third sound film, *The Jazz Singer*, in late 1927—entrenched production in Los Angeles more firmly than ever. Overwhelmed by the need to construct dozens of massive new soundstages, most movie companies could scarcely afford to rebuild their primary West Coast studios, let alone any satellite facilities in the East. Without modern stages, New York's feature film industry soon dwindled; after 1932, Paramount's Astoria studio remained the city's only active major production center and it, too, would essentially shut down within a few years.

32. (previous page) RKO art department sketch of a penthouse set for *The Sky's the Limit* (1943). Under the Hollywood studio system, design sketches such as this were commonly prepared by the art department to establish the look and style of a film's settings before the start of production. Among other considerations, this penthouse terrace set (designed by Carroll Clark and Al D'Agostino) had to be spacious enough to accommodate a romantic dance scene by Fred Astaire and Joan Leslie.

Dimmer still was the prospect for location work in New York. An evocative phrase, "mike stew," described the problems of the earliest microphones, which seemed to pick up everything but the actors' voices—even on hushed soundstages. Making movies on a typical New York street, needless to say, implied a somewhat noisier proposition. The lack of directionality in early microphones ensured that every background sound—car horns, pneumatic drills, tugboat whistles, and always, somewhere, the roar of a distant elevated train—would find its way onto the recording track. From now on, location footage would only be used with postrecorded sound or music; real views of New York would thus be reserved solely for brief sequences, like the introductory shots that established the site of the action to come. The silent camera had roamed the real city fearlessly; the synchronized-sound camera, it turned out, couldn't enter the city at all.

If the cameras could no longer go to New York, the answer was clear: bring New York to the cameras. This is precisely what the studios intended to do. Inside acoustically isolated stages and on outdoor sets—all located within big studio lots and ranches that were themselves placed in the quiet, sparsely developed outskirts of Los Angeles—an artificial New York would arise. It would be a New York where sound could be controlled, a New York distant from any unwanted traffic or background noises. Unable to shoot in the real city, the studios would simply build a city of their own.

But what kind of city would it be? And why would such an effort be made to re-create it in the first place? The arrival of sound merely assured that any New York appearing on screen would be an artificial one. The rise of a genuine, *mythic* New York on film was the unexpected consequence of a second revolution brought on by sound—a consequence, in fact, of the single most crucial fact about talking pictures.

They talked.

Talk meant dialogue, about ninety minutes' worth for every film released. As movie producers realized to their immeasurable dismay, someone had to *write* all that dialogue—and that someone could scarcely be found among the California-bred scenarists on staff, churning out plots and printed titles for silent movies. All their hard-won expertise in sight gags and sentimental titles was of no value now; their early attempts at feature-length dialogue proved stilted and contrived. And audiences, who after all were buying tickets for *talking* pictures, were suddenly demanding sharp, witty dialogue that propelled the story and sketched believable characters.

It was thus in a state of near-desperation that "an SOS was beamed to the East," as the writer Budd Schulberg later recalled, to find novelists, journalists, playwrights—anyone who might be able to write movies. Perhaps the director Josef von Sternberg summed up the predicament most succinctly, noting that the studio bosses "knew what they wanted, but didn't know how to spell it."

CAFÉ SOCIETY

It was to New York that the producers turned, hoping it was where the "real writers" could be found. Their instincts were right. Writers were everywhere in the city, riding a crest of literary industry in the late 1920s that was probably unrivaled anywhere, before or since.

The marketplace boomed. The American publishing industry, long centered in the city, had seen eighteen new houses established in the last decade alone, along with the Book-of-the-Month Club and the Literary Guild. New York's thriving journals, meanwhile, were bolstered by innovative newcomers, such as *The New Yorker* and *Vanity Fair*, that were especially attentive to the city's growing sophistication. On Broadway, seventy-one active theaters showcased over 250 new plays in a single season, 1927. Together with literary agencies and theatrical producers, it all added up to a genuine network, concentrated in midtown Manhattan.

33. Midtown Manhattan, 1930. No part of New York was changing faster or more dramatically in the late 1920s than the area around Grand Central Terminal, which was emerging rapidly as a rival to the traditional downtown business district on Wall Street. Looking north along Fourth Avenue—today's Park Avenue South—toward Grand Central (at far right), this sketch by Vernon Howe Bailey shows several newly erected skyscrapers shooting up behind the traditional low-rise houses and mansions of the Murray Hill district (including the Princeton Club, at center).

Nor was it merely a marketplace. A social and artistic convergence—of friends, places, and informal institutions—helped give definitive shape to the era's culture. These groups consisted not of lonely literary giants but an unusually sociable generation of journalists, critics, novelists, and playwrights who mingled freely, dabbled in each other's crafts, and met each other constantly in bookstores, speakeasies, or their own living rooms. Some gathered at Jack and Charlie's Puncheon Club, later called "21"; others at Horace Liveright's celebrated town-house parties. One especially bright group established a daily luncheon around a table in the Rose Room of the Algonquin Hotel; their repartee soon came to define the era's sophistication and sparkle. "It seemed like we were together constantly," one of them, Marc Connelly, later recalled. Through the newspaper columns, magazine articles, and Broadway shows they wrote, their way of life reverberated throughout the city, becoming an essential part of its identity. To many within and outside its borders, New York literally became a place where people coming in from the rain might conceivably say, "Let's get out of these wet clothes and into a dry martini."

They were in fact a group uniquely of New York, not just the Round Table but the entire constellation of writers who had migrated to the city, hoping to find a generation of like-minded souls who might strip away the sentimentality and narrow-mindedness of mainstream America. Only New York could match their innovations with its own—could, indeed, pace ever faster their lives and writing. For within the space of a few years the city had shed its Edwardian past and burst into a heady and dazzling future. A new generation of young, elite New Yorkers, dubbed "Café Society," had reinvigorated the city's nightlife by patronizing a series of "smart" nightclubs, where debutantes danced with racketeers, and chorus girls with foreign dignitaries, as once-strict demarcations of class and social background broke down. Innovative artists and curators, meanwhile, were busy reshaping modern painting, sculpture, and photography. The city even had a new sound, a fluid, daring kind of popular music called jazz that had been brought up by black performers from the South and was now being honed to lively perfection in the clubs of Harlem and midtown. What just a few decades before had been a bustling but provincial cousin to world capitals like Paris and London and Berlin now sped beyond them into the uncharted territory of the twentieth century, as the harbinger of a new way of life and a new kind of city (33).

Amidst these innovations there was more than a slight edge of lunacy, as the city's sheer intensity overspilled into a kind of absurdity. In part this stemmed from Prohibition, which upended the city's social structure and warped its very fabric. The simple desire to have a drink forced the city's populace underground—literally, into one of the thousands of illegal speakeasies that sat unobtrusively in the half-basements of row houses—while Manhattan's nightclubs became part of a shadowy realm of gangsters and racketeers, strangely ephemeral places that eluded federal agents by constantly changing their identity and location. Only in this context could there emerge improbable characters like "Tex" Guinan, boisterous hostess of bootlegger Larry Fay's establishments (the "El Fey" one week, the "Del Fey" the next), whose siren call to customers about to pay a king's ransom for bathtub gin was, "Hello, Suckers!" (34)

34. ***Tex Guinan's Portable Nightclub*, 1928.** This drawing by Joseph Webster Golinken shows the inimitable nightclub hostess Tex Guinan at center, sitting atop a piano, clutching champagne flutes in both hands, and presiding over the giddy proceedings in her notorious establishment—perhaps loudly proclaiming, as she often did, "Curfew shall not ring tonight!"

The life of the writers in this intense, upside-down city took on an especially wild quality, feeling more than slightly unreal, even as it transpired. It meant slipping in and out of clubs and hotels and restaurants, laughing, punning, playing practical jokes, and sharpening wits. It meant throwing drunken, sexy literary parties that could last all night and into another day with eager replacements. It meant racing through the streets in taxicabs, working in skyscrapers, and frequenting the speakeasies and "portable nightclubs," breaking away from the social life just long enough to make a deadline or rewrite a second act. So much youth, so much speed, so much wit, all packed into a protean city that was charting the course of the new century. In the evening, from their apartment or office windows overlooking Greenwich Village or Times Square, they could sense the pulsing energy of endless possibility beneath them, the dark, glowing city promising still more laughter and more life (35).

GODDAMN LOTUS LAND

This was the city that Hollywood was asking the writers to leave. Unsurprisingly, most of them said no—at least at first. Herman Mankiewicz, one of the few hardy souls who had trekked west in the silent era, couldn't convince more than a handful of New Yorkers to join him, despite efforts like his immortal 1925 telegram to Ben Hecht, which closed, "MILLIONS ARE TO BE GRABBED AROUND HERE AND YOUR ONLY COMPETITION IS IDIOTS STOP DON'T LET THIS GET AROUND." Even with the talkies well under way in 1928 and 1929 and Hollywood producers initiating their habit of offering astronomical salaries and royal treatment, only a trickle of writers made the move. Life in New York was still too sweet, Hollywood still too distant.

35. ***The City from Greenwich Village*, John Sloan, 1922.** In this view, looking south from Bleecker Street, the glowing towers of lower Manhattan rise beyond the densely packed buildings of the Village and the elevated train and bright storefronts of Sixth Avenue, at center.

But that all changed after the fall of 1929, with the coming of the third and final revolution of these short years. The stock market crash and Great Depression promptly shut down the writers' bull market. Nineteen thirty saw fifty fewer plays produced than the year before; by 1932 fully one-half of Broadway's theaters had gone dark. Much of New York still glistened, but the writers could no longer afford it; no one on the East Coast would pay them enough. Suddenly those princely offers from Hollywood looked tempting indeed. In 1931 the trickle became a flood and over the next few years one of the biggest importations of talent in history proceeded west to what was now called "the other end of Broadway." By the mid-1930s the big round table at the Algonquin's Rose Room was empty: Marc Connelly and Robert Benchley and Dorothy Parker and Robert E. Sherwood had all moved to Los Angeles; George S. Kaufman visited frequently. Of the ten original advisory members of *The New Yorker*, six had become Hollywood screenwriters. Throughout the 1930s the flow continued: Maxwell Anderson and Dashiell Hammett and Stephen Vincent Benét went west. So did Gene Fowler and Charles Brackett, Faith Baldwin and Donald Ogden Stewart. Howard Lindsay and Russel Crouse. Daniel Fuchs and Paul Gallico. And Lillian Hellman and Clifford Odets, and John O'Hara and S. J. Perelman, and Damon Runyon and Irwin Shaw and Nathanael West and Preston Sturges. Even F. Scott Fitzgerald himself, who had come out in the mid-1920s but had returned East, now came back again, this time to stay. By 1932, 228 authors were under contract at the major studios; the writers' payroll at MGM alone was fifty-five thousand dollars a week.

It was no small decision, when that telegram from Goldwyn or Mayer or Warner arrived. "Going Hollywood" meant leaving most everything else behind. There was, of course, nothing like today's "red-eye" flight, hopping easily from coast to coast in five or six overnight hours. California was still the full width of a continent away, three thousand miles to be traversed overland, mile by mile, on a railroad journey that required nearly three full days. New York Central's *Twentieth Century Limited* left Grand Central every evening at six p.m., bound for Chicago; once there, the Santa Fe *Chief* (and later the *Super-Chief*) picked up passengers for the extended haul across the plains. If the studio was paying (as it often was) the journey was not long and hard—just long. In a dining car filled with the sweet fragrance of cut flowers, morning-suited maîtres d'hôtel offered diners everything from vintage wines to Malossol caviar. Barbers, bartenders, stewards, valets, and maids stood ready to satisfy any need. But even on these, the fastest and plushest of trains, the hours passed slowly: mile after mile of farmland, mountains, desert, more mountains, more desert. Monday night, and all day Tuesday, then into the night again; another whole day Wednesday and another night until at last, on Thursday morning, the train pulled into the station at Glendale or Pasadena or, a few years later, Union Station downtown. Nearly half a week had passed since the writer had left New York—and his or her other life—behind; it seemed a world away.

36. Los Angeles, 1927. This view looks northeast from Santa Monica Boulevard at Las Palmas Avenue. "It is a kind of boom town," the English author J. B. Priestley wrote a few years later, "that has gone mushrooming itself for scores of miles. . . . [When] you travel along its immense boulevards, you feel you are looking at an immensely swollen small town. There seem to be miles and miles of unimpressive little bungalows and vacant building lots."

Stepping out onto the platform, squinting in the bright sun and already feeling over-dressed in his two-piece wool suit, the writer began to sense the vague unreality of the place. Los Angeles was already a big city—well over a million inhabitants by 1930—but it gave off a very different impression, seeming more like an endless series of small towns spread across four hundred square miles of reclaimed desert (36). The giant freeway system that would knit the region together with its great ribbons of concrete was still decades in the future; movement around town still meant interminable journeys along the wide, barely developed grid of boulevards and avenues, passing low-rise shops and bungalows that multiplied infinitely to the horizon in all directions. Vast in breadth but oddly insubstantial, its human habitation seemed no more than a pale wash across the impressive natural formation of its great basin. "Not a city," one contemporary called it, "but the grandiose sketch of a city."

The landscape was lush, the climate extraordinary. But the newcomers were hardly Iowa farmers come to retire; they were some of the most cosmopolitan souls who ever lived, and they had just left behind the capital of twentieth-century urbanity—which they had helped define. Their new home seemed designed to rob them precisely of the amenities and sophistication they had come to take for granted in New York. Writing home just after he had arrived, Stephen Vincent Benét relayed his discouraged impressions. This was no "city," he reported, but

> *one loud, struggling Main Street, low-roofed, mainly unsky-scrapered town that straggles along for twenty-five miles or so, full of stop & go lights, automobiles, palm-trees, Spanishy—& God knows what all houses—orange-drink stands with real orange juice—studios—movie-theatres—everything but bookstores. I am the only person in the entire 25 miles who walks more than 4 blocks, except along Hollywood Boulevard in the evening. There are some swell hotels—up in the hills or between L.A. and Hollywood—& a few good nightclubs. But in general, everything is dead, deserted at 11:30 p.m.*

"The boys," he added, "go around without hats. They look like prize ears of corn. The girls, ditto."

Nothing embodied the diffuse spirit of the place, the writers soon found, more than the movie business itself. "I don't know why I thought of Hollywood as small and Greenwich Villagey, the studios close together and the picture people a rather compact colony, frequenting the same streets and foregathering in the same clubs and restaurants," a New York observer wrote of her expectations before she arrived. "Instead," she noted, "it wanders over space and has its own vague suburbs . . . Burbank, Culver City, Universal City, Beverly Hills. Hollywood Boulevard is wide and long, more Main Street than Boul' Mich', and about as clubby as the Grand Concourse. To go the rounds of the studios—the five or six big production centres . . . and the half dozen independents still hanging on—is to make a journey of 100 miles."

These studios were in fact veritable kingdoms, a hundred acres big or more, entirely self-sufficient and literally walled off from the outside world, white-painted fortresses that would come to define the writers' professional and social lives. In their physical isolation and rigid hierarchy they could offer little of the freedom available in New York, where multiple activities, woven into the very fabric of the city, created a feeling of possibility and self-determination. Over the length of a single midtown sidestreet an author could easily slip in and out of the Algonquin Hotel, *The New Yorker*'s offices, the Shubert Theatre, a favorite speakeasy. This was more than a matter of superficial urbanity. It symbolized a genuine power: the writer as free agent, able to choose among various venues and platforms through the city's scores of newspapers, magazines, publishing houses, and theatrical producers, always guaranteed at least a measure of editorial deference and authorial control.

But all that was now "back East." In Hollywood, writers soon came to realize that they were professional prisoners behind the studio gate, treated as subservient employees with little say about their product. "You came as a pencil for hire," the writer Ben Hecht observed, "at sums heretofore unheard of for pencils." As long as they stayed within the walls of the lot, the screenwriters remained under the complete rule of the local potentates, the studio chiefs, the "short men chewing on dead cigars," in one writer's words, who ruled the place with absolute authority, and likely shared some of Harry Warner's feelings about authors: "schmucks with Underwoods." Their finished screenplays were commonly handed over to studio hacks to "complete," their names routinely deleted from the screen credits. "In New York what you do is considered distinguished," one writer was reminded by a Los Angeles hostess. "Out here you are on a level with the props." No wonder that the ex–New Yorkers, in the historian Richard Fine's words, were "lonely, out-of-place, frustrated in their work, and depressed generally by their new cultural milieu." "Neither Southern California in general," he adds, "nor the studios in particular struck writers as hospitable."

There was at least no reason to be lonely. The emigré New York writers soon comprised a sizable colony, a mini-Manhattan ensconced in a series of favorite haunts among the palm trees. The expatriates gathered at restaurants like Lucey's, just outside the Paramount gates, or Dave Chasen's, which reminded them just a bit of "21," or at the "bachelor's table" that Herman Mankiewicz presided over at the Montmartre. They lounged at hotels like the Chateau Marmont, tucked quietly off Sunset Boulevard, or at the Garden of Allah, just across the way, whose celebrated bar and pool grew into a West Coast reincarnation of the Algonquin Round Table. Some could be found on a Saturday afternoon huddling in the back room of Stanley Rose's bookshop on Hollywood Boulevard; others on Sunday morning at lavish brunches given by Charlie Brackett in his home in Bel Air. Together they ruefully shared their plush prison sentence, their self-enforced exile in what Mankiewicz called "goddamn lotus land," while pledging themselves to only a "few more years of tripe and then something worthwhile."

THE LOST CITY

> Oh, to be back in Hollywood, wishing I was back in New York.
>
> HERMAN J. MANKIEWICZ

We all know the story, how Hollywood lured the writers away from New York and set them to work writing talkies. For high-minded critics like Edmund Wilson and George Jean Nathan, it was an outrage: an entire American literature going unwritten while some of the country's best authors cavorted amidst the swimming pools and starlets, churning out routine scenarios. For the film critic Pauline Kael, on the other hand, it was a boon, responsible for the special genius of 1930s Hollywood comedies and, indeed, for infusing all of that decade's films with a certain sophistication and spirit—"the twenties moved West in the thirties." But it is possible to suggest another effect of this diaspora: feeding the imaginative wellspring for a mythic, bigger-than-life movie New York.

It was a feeling that started with the most common of emotions, homesickness—for the way of life the writers had left behind, and for the city that had made it possible. It was burnished by the effect that distance so often has on an absent love—as flaws are forgotten and desire enhanced. And it was made pointed by the contrast to their current, straitened circumstance. Hatred of a studio system that systematically robbed writers of their professional dignity quickly grew into an intense aversion for the environment in which that system thrived, and fueled their harsh, perhaps unfair assessment of what they had found—and even more, what they had *not* found—in the nascent and still tentative urbanism of Los Angeles.

37. Garden of Allah hotel, 1936. Along with the Chateau Marmont, located just across Sunset Boulevard, the Garden became the favored stopping place for emigré writers from New York, including Robert Benchley, F. Scott Fitzgerald, Dorothy Parker, Marc Connelly, George S. Kaufman, and John O'Hara. "I used to look around at the dull stucco bungalows of the Garden of Allah," the writer Budd Schulberg later recalled, "and wonder if there had ever been such an assembly of literary lights all on the same hotel register at the same time."

It is not hard to imagine them, sitting poolside at the Garden of Allah (37), amidst the palm trees and flowering bougainvillea, the quiet of the Hollywood foothills interrupted by nothing louder than the clink of ice in a glass of Scotch. In *memory*, at least life in New York seemed sublime—the energizing flow of cars and streetcars and people, the chance sidewalk encounters with friends and acquaintances—especially when compared to the street life of Los Angeles's sunstruck boulevards, where, as one writer put it, it was "as if everyone had gone indoors and pulled down the shades." The writers might fondly recall the rush of 42nd Street's pedestrians, or just ordinary stoop life on a typical sidestreet, in the context of the strange, often isolated existence that now engulfed them, their bedroom windows filled with nothing but empty blue sky and a few palm fronds, their days measured by the dozens of miles between appointments and the familiar face of the gas station attendant. "I'd leave the studio at dusk," one transplant recalled, "and look at the flatlands around me. In the distance stood a solitary oil well . . . [its] lonely silhouette rising out of the ground. It was a strange brand of loneliness, one I hadn't experienced before, relentless and unrelieved."

As the afternoon grew late and dusk approached, thoughts naturally turned to nightlife. In memory, New York nights seemed one long glide into the small hours on a cloud of conversation and music and dancing, among the hundreds of nightclubs, hotels, cabarets, and after-hours boîtes that filled midtown Manhattan (38). Los Angeles's nightlife, on the other hand, was notorious—for barely existing. This was a city, after all, where dancing after midnight was literally forbidden by municipal ordinance (thus forcing revelers to Culver City or the ten-block "strip" of Sunset Boulevard outside the city limits). "You could drop all of Hollywood's people, parties and nightclubs in New York," one contemporary remarked, "and no one would ever notice them." It was a place where most everyone had to be asleep early to make their six a.m. studio calls. That just happened to be about the time the writers, after a long New York night, would have been getting to bed.

In memory, New York seemed nothing less than the ultimate center, the gathering of a whole continent's energies into a single place: an awesome, vertically thrusting core that gave sense to the breadth of the city, to the low-rise outer boroughs and residential districts, the necessarily wide base from which the great central spike rose and drew strength (39). Los Angeles's vastness by the same token seemed dispiriting, precisely because it never came together but remained an endless—and seemingly pointless—repetition of the same low-lying landscape of stucco houses and bungalow courts across mile after mile of the vast plain.

38. RKO art department sketch, late 1930s.

For these cosmopolitan souls, the genuine amenities of Hollywood life—the handsome estates in the hills, the spectacular scenery, the lavish garden parties—could not fully substitute for those well-burnished memories. Something fundamental was missing, perhaps the way New York's excitement built upon itself, its elements reinforcing one another, concentrating their energy until it seemed the most logical thing in the world to shoot a thousand feet into the sky. In contrast, Los Angeles's many attractions remained diffuse, isolated, and private, behind the walls of individual homes or within the gates of studio lots. Its points of excitement, real as they might be, always remained exactly that—individual points, never coming together, never gelling into something larger, grander, more urbane. Yet here the writers remained, in their stucco Elysium, well aware that a return to New York meant the loss of the easy life they had come to rely on, and the easy money that paid for it.

Presently, something else happened: their memories began to have an outlet in the scripts they were asked to write, or were proposing themselves. This was, in effect, what they had been brought out for. Even before the advent of talkies, America's increasingly sophisticated audiences were growing bored with the rustic idylls that dominated Hollywood's first decades. The New Yorkers had been hired specifically to cut through that sentimental haze with rapid-fire dialogue, brisk action, and tales of modern urban characters—newspapermen and lawyers, gangsters and showgirls—placed in contemporary settings. "And the public responded," Pauline Kael later recalled. "Even those of us who were children at the time loved the fast-moving, modern city stories. . . . It's hard to make clear to people who didn't live through the transition how sickly and unpleasant many of those 'artistic' silent pictures were—how you wanted to scrape off all that mist and sentiment."

Except for gangster films that drew specifically upon Chicago's tough reputation, these new urban films were almost always set in New York, which remained *the* city for Hollywood. (A random sample of 115 features made in 1934 found that no fewer than *thirty-seven* of them took place in New York City, making it by far the most popular setting of any kind—urban or rural, foreign or domestic—in American films.) While the actual production of pictures had moved west in the previous decade, New York still exercised a commanding hold upon the industry. Hollywood had been built by New Yorkers, of course, the ex-furriers and glove salesmen turned theater owners who had worked their way up from the Lower East Side, or migrated to New York from Europe and other parts of the country. And it was still directed in large part from New York, from big new office buildings on Times Square, where the "home office" made all the major administrative decisions—what kind and how many films to make each year, where and how to show them, how much to spend on each picture. As Diana Altman describes in her book, *Hollywood East:*

> *Clark Gable may have posed for cameras in Culver City, but his paycheck was signed at 1540 Broadway, across the street from the Camel Cigarette sign blowing smoke rings. When Adolph Zukor, the founder of Paramount Pictures, went to work in the morning, it was to an office in the Paramount building on Broadway. Albert Warner, one of the brothers, ran Warner Bros. headquarters in New York, as David Sarnoff ran RKO's headquarters there. William Fox, who founded the Fox part of 20th Century-Fox, had two offices in New York, one at the Roxy Theater and the other at his newsreel factory on Tenth Avenue and Fifty-fourth Street.*

Even mighty Metro-Goldwyn-Mayer itself was simply the wholly owned production arm of Loew's, Inc., the New York theater chain; its legendary mogul Louis B. Mayer was actually just an employee who answered to the *real* boss back East, Marcus Loew (or his successor, Nicholas Schenck). Long-distance telephone calls crackling across the continent; production logs sent every working day from the West Coast to New York; and the constant two-way traffic of produc-

39. RKO art department sketch, late 1930s.

ers, stars, agents, and publicists on the *Twentieth Century Limited* or *Broadway Limited* (or, by the end of the 1930s, the first primitive cross-country air routes) made New York a constant presence in the minds of everyone in Hollywood. Nowhere could this early bicoastal sensibility be felt more plainly than at RKO, where the very paths and walkways of the Gower Street lot were given the names of Manhattan avenues and Times Square's cross streets: visitors were directed to find the studio commissary on "Broadway," or a rehearsal hall at the corner of "42nd Street" and "Park Avenue" (40). If located physically in the city of Los Angeles, in spirit the RKO lot was clearly a piece of New York that had somehow drifted three thousand miles west.

40. Little Theatre and Rehearsal Hall, RKO Studios, 1941. The sign on the corner of the building (at far right) identifies the names of two of the studio lot's interior streets: Park Avenue and 42nd Street.

The knowing placement of the RKO's music building just off "46th Street" (tallying with the largest cluster of theaters off Times Square) pointed up still another link in the cross-country chain: the dozens of Broadway composers and lyricists, and dance and musical directors, who had been drafted to score, orchestrate, and choreograph the most important new genre of the sound era—musicals. From established Broadway titans like Rodgers and Hart, Cole Porter, Jerome Kern, Irving Berlin, and the Gershwins, to rising newcomers like Roger Edens, Michael Kidd, Harold Arlen, and Betty Comden and Adolph Green, the rehearsal halls and recording studios of Los Angeles were filled from one end to the other with Times Square's creative aristocracy. As with the writers, Hollywood's high salaries and steady work compelled a self-enforced exile from the lights of Broadway; and, as with the writers, many were soon disenchanted. "George was a king in New York," recalled the composer John Green of Gershwin. "In Hollywood, he was invited to homes where there were no pianos or to homes with pianos where people wouldn't ask him to play, or, even if he did play, he was not idolized." It would be easy for the songwriters to look back fondly and transfigure their memory into the unforgettable melodies and rhythms of countless musicals set in the movie city. Just as for the writers and producers, the word "city" for them conjured up New York, and nowhere else—not Chicago, and certainly not Los Angeles.

MEMORY AND IMAGINATION

As they brought New York back to life in the pages of their scripts, the writers could almost feel the warm air and lush landscape outside their windows being replaced by the cool, crisp Manhattan light, the distant bustle of horns and traffic breaking the sunstruck silence of Southern California. To write a picture set in New York was, in a sense, to "live" there for a few hours at a time, inhabiting the world in which their characters would move and speak, love and clash. For a few hours at the typewriter, the palm trees and endless green lawns might slip away and be superseded in the mind's eye by the potent, half-remembered image of their lost city.

Yet the city they were creating was not just the one they were remembering, however romantically. The writers were, after all, professional imaginers, and it was an imaginary city they were bringing into being. It would be animated not only by the memory of what once *had* happened there, but by all the things that *could* have happened, or *should* have happened. To memory was added imagination, and it would be these two potent faculties that would animate the dream city and give it special force and flavor.

The city encouraged such fancy. From a distance of three thousand miles and several years away much of their memories began to look like invention anyway. Could there really have been such characters as Tex Guinan? Had there actually been a round table in a rose-colored room where all those witty things had been said? Memory blurred at the edges, becoming dreamlike itself. Nineteen-twenties New York, after all, was constantly outdoing itself, coming up every year with something bigger, faster, wilder; it was only natural to keep that movement going in the fictive city now taking shape. The city's sense of infinite possibility made it an ideal platform from which to generate new and ever more extraordinary stories, people, and situations.

There was perhaps another motivation. Spending time in an imaginary New York, a place that was everything the real city had been and more, could constitute a kind of secret revenge on their current circumstance. The writers

41. Drawing for a proposed expansion of New York Street, RKO Ranch. Lacking sufficient room in its cramped Gower Street studio in Hollywood for a properly sized back lot, RKO built its permanent New York Street on an outlying "ranch" property in Encino, seven miles to the north, amidst the orange groves and farms of a still-rural San Fernando Valley.

could avoid surrendering their artistic citizenship to the values of Southern California by keeping alive, in their minds and in their scripts, a different and better place, their true cosmopolitan home. At the same time, they could turn around their disdain for their plush prison, Los Angeles, by making every one of its perceived limitations the impetus for an enhanced New York. In this way, L.A. would shape the dream New York as much as the real New York did—only in an entirely contrary fashion.

Los Angeles's horizontal endlessness, for instance, would be avenged by movie New York's overwhelming verticality. If the real New York had many tall buildings, it had plenty of low ones as well, especially in its outer boroughs and residential districts. But the dream city would seem to be *all* vertical, every scene playing in a penthouse, on a terrace, in a rooftop nightclub, every window looking onto a glittering view of rising towers.

Los Angeles's sleepy boulevards, meanwhile, would be retaliated against with an imaginary New York street life that surpassed almost anything the real city could offer (41). The lowliest sidestreet would have scores of pedestrians rushing purposefully across the frame; dozens more sat on stoops and played on the sidewalk. The quiet landscape of Los Angeles's bungalows or the orange groves of the San Fernando Valley would be shattered by the backlot cries of the Italian hurdy-gurdy man, the Irish cop, the Jewish pushcart vendor, as if packing, by scripted instruction, all of New York's human diversity onto a single block. And on these streets, leading men and women would constantly bump into one another, chance encounters that not only served the needs of the plot but worked to demonstrate how a *real* city worked.

42. RKO art department sketch, late 1930s.

With the twilight, imagination took a special leap. The dream city would burn most brightly after dark, would indeed seem to live by night, as if to exorcise Los Angeles's dreary early-to-bed puritanism. The rain-slicked streets, the bright glow of the theaters as audiences spilled out, the warm interiors of the supper clubs, the sequence of overlapping neon signs ("Panorama Club," "Casino Moderne," "Café Intime") that signified a romantic arc from dusk to dawn, all these would feed the projected fantasies of the ex–New Yorkers. The movement, by turns languid and urgent, of the demimondaine through a nocturnal cocoon of dark, slick exteriors and luminous interiors would give movie New York its most dreamlike aspect (32).

The characters moving through these evenings, walking these streets, surveying this skyline from its upper precincts were in some sense the greatest creation of all: idealized "New Yorkers," polished and elegant, or exquisitely rough-hewn, and equipped with all the wit and style that had once graced the

Round Table and its like. In these filmic New Yorkers—Cary Grant and Katharine Hepburn, Fred Astaire and Ginger Rogers, Myrna Loy and William Powell, Jimmy Cagney and Bette Davis—the style of Café Society was wed to the verbal agility of the Algonquin crowd to create an elite worthy of populating the impossibly grand city that the writers were inventing. As Pauline Kael has noted, apropos of one of the greatest of these "New Yorkers":

> *Sitting out in Los Angeles, the expatriate New York writers projected . . . their fantasies of Eastern connoisseurship and suavity. Los Angeles itself has never recovered from the inferiority complex that its movies nourished, and every moviegoing kid in America felt that people in New York were smarter, livelier, and better looking than anyone in his home town. There were no Cary Grants in the sticks. He and his counterparts were to be found only in the imaginary cities of the movies.*

From the moment it was born, this dream city also possessed a dark side. Prohibition's inversion of the social order, by which glamorous supper clubs could be owned by vicious racketeers, informed the mythic city as well; those "smart" clubs or elegant penthouses might well be the turf of rival gangsters whose dramatic shootouts bloodied the shadowy streets, and whose ominous presence could add a layer of threat to the urban night (42). Borrowing headlines from the city's tabloids, the screenwriters revealed the influence of gamblers and racketeers (often played by New York–bred actors like Jimmy Cagney, Humphrey Bogart, and Edward G. Robinson) behind the high-profile worlds of prizefighting, politics, or nightclubs, creating a city of the night whose scary and sometimes shocking character only added to the overall allure of movie New York, enhancing its reputation as a place where life was lived to extremes, with highs *and* lows found nowhere else.

All of this—wealth and poverty, glamour and threat, ordinary daily life and extraordinary nightlife—was part of the scripted urban texture that began to fill the stages and back lots of Hollywood in the 1930s. It soon became the platform for a score of individual fantasies—from *King Kong* to *42nd Street* to *Swing Time*—that pursued particular possibilities within it; at the same time, it became the basis for hundreds of genre pictures whose variations of plot and character were far less important than the sheer atmosphere they created—the "world" of heiresses and shysters, cocktail bars and stage doors.

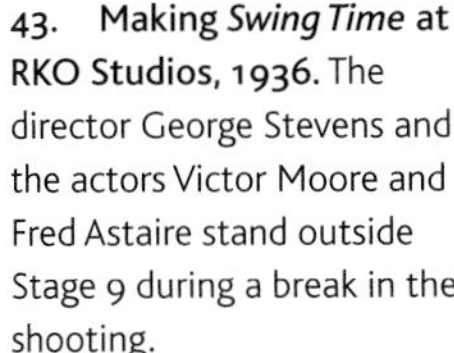

43. Making *Swing Time* at RKO Studios, 1936. The director George Stevens and the actors Victor Moore and Fred Astaire stand outside Stage 9 during a break in the shooting.

Of course, the irony attending the creation of this dream city was inescapable. It was a place sprung from the minds of homesick writers, exiled on the wrong side of a continent, who nonetheless had created something extraordinary, something that would not have arisen had they stayed back East. It was only in "goddamn lotus land" that this New York could be born—and the dream city was, in fact, the unlikely issue of both places, somehow joined together. Years later, a few of the writers came to realize it; as Herman Mankiewicz himself was heard musing over a drink one day in the late 1940s at a midtown bar, "Oh, to be back in Hollywood, wishing I was back in New York." He knew that the real city, for all its excitement, could never compete with the one they had created so convincingly in their minds. No real city could, just as no real lover could ever compete with the perfected image brought on by absence.

In the bright sunlight outside of RKO's Stage 9 stood one of the most elegant of the filmic New Yorkers, Fred Astaire, looking perhaps a touch out of place in his morning suit (43). Here was one of the first citizens of the dream city, ready to inhabit it, ready to bring it to life through dance and song, romance and heartbreak and wit. The lighted darkness inside the boxy stage building behind him stood ready to accommodate. The writers and composers had done their work well, creating the complete and complex blueprint for a mythic New York: the characters, the stories, the situations, the mood and spirit. Astaire, in his dapper perfection, was already living there. He now needed only one thing: a physical city in which to play out the dream.

THREE

BUILDING THE DREAM

THE STUDIO PRODUCTION SYSTEM

THE DREAM FACTORY

> I had the same set in I don't know how many pictures! Ten or fifteen! The opening shot was always an air shot over New York. Then it would bleed into my suite of offices on the fortieth floor of Radio City. Out of the window behind me was always a view of the Empire State Building, in order to identify the setting. I used to say to [cameraman] Joe Walker, "Joe, where was the Empire State Building in the last picture?" . . . He would say, "I had it a little to the left." I'd say, "Well, this time throw it over to the right."
>
> ROSALIND RUSSELL

44. (previous page) Shooting *Romance in Manhattan*, 1934. For this shot of Ginger Rogers and Francis Lederer on Rogers's tenement roof, the RKO art department created not only a rooftop set but a miniature skyline, rendered through five "layers" of buildings, whose dramatically decreasing scale provided an illusion of depth when seen through the camera lens (compare the size of the windows of the foreground tenements with those of the last row of towers).

Even as it was transformed into a physical entity, movie New York remained a profoundly displaced creation. As it rose on the stages and back lots of a dozen Los Angeles studios, teams of designers (including numbers of ex–New Yorkers) would give the movie city a life of its own, fashioning its unforgettable urban presence much as the writers had, by marrying memories of the real place with an intensely felt projection of its possibilities. Born in the early 1930s, just as the Hollywood studio system reached its maturity, the movie city would be shaped for decades by that system's distinctive characteristics—rising as a fabricated construct, created on the studio lot, with a consistent and coherent urban identity that transcended any individual film.

By 1930, Hollywood's moviemaking had been transformed from a semi-improvised, film-by-film proposition to a smoothly rationalized production process. From their big new Los Angeles lots—no longer makeshift ranches but vast modern plants with dozens of buildings, hundreds of acres, and thousands of employees—studios could turn out pictures with amazing regularity (a new feature was completed by MGM, for example, about once every nine days). At any given moment, several dozen films were in some phase of production; all the personnel, materials, and facilities needed to make them were constantly available, and could be smoothly shifted from one film to another. The cost of permanently employing thousands of technicians and maintaining a huge plant was more than offset by the studios' incessant productivity, everyone working eight or more hours a day, five and a half days a week, using resources gathered efficiently in a single, centralized location.

The planning, construction, and operation of these great plants was sustained by a simple economic expedient: the major studios owned most of the biggest theaters where their films would be shown (or more precisely, were themselves owned by large holding companies that owned the theaters as well). Ownership meant exhibitors could be required to accept the studio's lesser products along with its better output. Knowing that everything they produced would find its way to a paying audience, the studios could confidently build their plants and keep them humming.

45. Warner Bros. art department, 1939. Most studio art departments were laid out around a large, well-lighted central drafting room, ringed by the private offices of unit art directors. The zigzag line running near the ceiling is marked out in foot-long increments to help the designers visualize the dimensions of room settings. On the right-hand wall is a background grid, also marked in feet, that allowed the department's draftsmen to accurately draw full-sized architectural details freehand.

What was perhaps the most essential element of the studio system—the physical consolidation of film production onto the studio lot—shaped movie New York profoundly. For one thing, it assured that having left the real city, the movies would not soon return. To studio heads, shooting on location was an anathema, destroying the efficiency and control that made the whole system work. How could a star filming at a distant location do a costume test for her next picture, thus assuring that it got under way quickly? How could the studio moguls review the daily footage (or "rushes") of a picture made in New York, to determine its progress and suggest changes for the next day's shooting, when any film stock shot on the East Coast would take over three days to arrive in Hollywood? Add to this the logistical fears about the disruption of shooting by huge crowds anxious to see and touch their favorite stars, and the old technical problem of recording sound on noisy streets, and it was clear that the real city was not going to make a sustained appearance on screen anytime soon.

At the same time, the concentration of resources onto the studio lot presented a unique opportunity. If shooting the real city was impossible, Hollywood would simply rebuild New York. Building a city would, of course, require an army of craftsmen and a factory of materials and equipment—but that army and that factory already existed, right on the lot, all under the direction of the low-profile but enormously powerful group called the art department.

In a sense, the art department's growing size and significance was a natural consequence of the studio system itself. When nearly every setting had to be artificially created on the lot, the people responsible for building those settings inevitably assumed a huge degree of financial and artistic responsibility within the studio hierarchy (although they remained relatively invisible to the public, certainly when compared to the stars or leading directors). By the 1930s the major studios each employed as many as twenty full-time art directors, supported by another forty or fifty assistants and literally thousands of carpenters, craftsmen, and scenic artists (45). The building of sets paced the studio's entire production schedule; their expense was the highest fixed cost, outside of salaries, in any film's budget. The studio lot was physically dominated by big construction sheds and warehouses, by storage yards and scene docks, and by exterior sets themselves. In fact, one way to conceive of the classic Hollywood studio is as a factory for creating—on a nearly continuous basis—a series of stylized, artificial environments in which to shoot films. It would be this aspect of the studio system, above all, that would give movie New York the sense of being a genuine *place*—a real city that showed up in various films, but somehow enjoyed an independent existence beyond any of them.

With the increased size and responsibility of the art department also came a certain autonomy. With command over so large a portion of the budget and "look" of films in production, the supervisory art director—generally a forceful, strong-willed man who was not only head of the entire art department but, at least nominally, of the construction, props, scenic, and sometimes the "trick" or special-effects departments as well—was given wide berth to build as he saw fit. The elegant, autocratic Cedric Gibbons, to name the classic example, reigned as supervisory art director at MGM from 1924 through the mid-1950s and had the unique contractual right to place his name in the credits of every picture that Metro released during his tenure. During this time, not even the most celebrated MGM directors—Vincente Minnelli, for instance, or George Cukor—could substantially change the stylistic approach of the "medieval fiefdom" (as Minnelli termed it) of the Metro art department. This territoriality was one reason why mythic New York seemed to possess an identity beyond any particular production. With Gibbons in charge, Metro's New York simply *was* the same from film to film, no matter who directed it.

Reinforcing this independence was the studio's distinctively collegial approach to filmmaking, what André Bazin called "the genius of the system." Much less so than today could the director ever be considered the sole creator of a film; the entire style and appearance of a movie were often as much a product of the art director and cinematographer. (Sometimes more so. For budget pictures, the director was often not selected until relatively late in the process, at a point *after* the art director and cinematographer, working with the film's producer, had already laid out the sets and lined up the shots—leaving the director, who appeared on the set a few days before shooting, to work with the actors in a film whose look had already been established.)

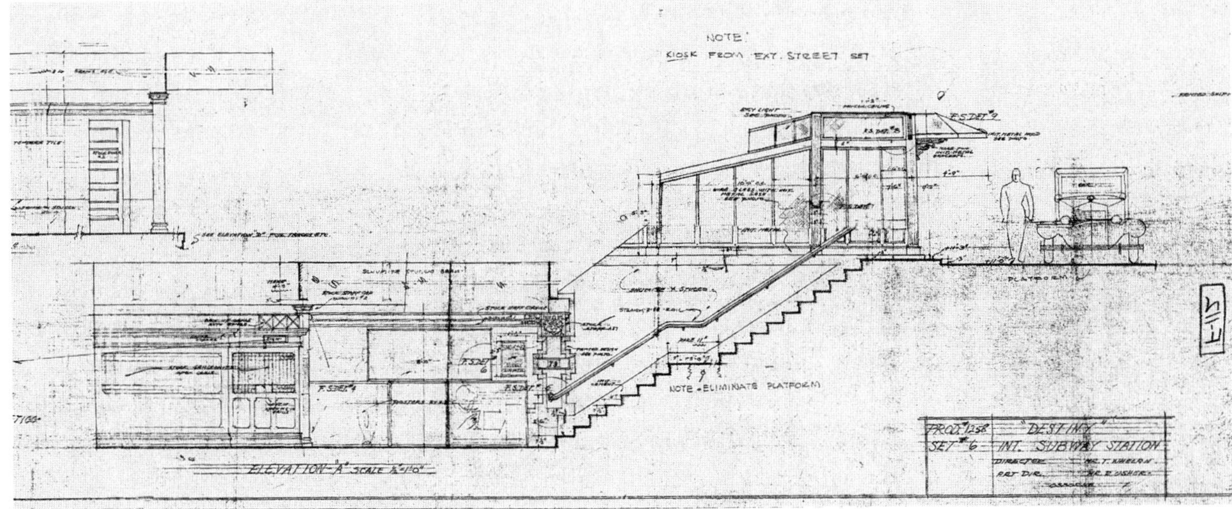

CONSTRUCTING THE DREAM

The making of the mythic city began in the sunny, high-ceilinged office of the supervisory art director, at the "set meeting," the first order of business after a script had been accepted for production. In front of them sat the script, its special blue cover signifying its approved status. At the table was the man charged with giving its imagined world visual reality, the man who would actually design the film: the unit art director. He had been selected by the department supervisor, who rarely picked up a drafting pencil himself but (much like the principal of a large architecture firm) set the tone and style of the whole studio's output by selecting the specific designer for each project, then monitoring and critiquing that designer's work. (For this, the supervisor was generally listed in the credits as "Art Director," while the film's actual art director was given the distinctly subordinate credit of "Assistant.")

The unit art director's initial design concepts were quickly realized through evocative, often masterful drawings prepared by his own hand or by special sketch artists and illustrators (47). Upon approval these were handed to the department's "draftsmen," a team of younger men whose modest title belied their critical role in translating the soft, conceptual sketches into hard-line measured drawings from which the film's sets would actually be constructed (some were licensed architects; nearly all had a few years of architectural training). Working under the constant supervision of the art director, they determined the precise detail, proportion, style, and construction of the film's sets, the rough profiles of the charcoal sketches blossoming into sheet after sheet of precise working drawings (46). They drew plans and elevations not unlike those of real buildings, at the familiar ¼″ and ½″ scales—although

46. (top) Construction drawing of a New York subway station standing set, circa 1940. In the studio era, every Hollywood lot contained a variety of "standing" sets of New York, such as this IRT subway station, which included facing platforms, a ticket booth, a staircase up to street level, and an iron-and-glass entrance kiosk, placed on a raised platform.

47. (above) Sketch of a New York subway kiosk, Anton Grot. Many art directors in the studio era were accomplished illustrators and artists. Anton Grot, a leading art director at Warner Bros. from 1928 to 1948, was especially known for deft, impressionistic sketches—such as this drawing of an IRT subway kiosk—that swiftly evoked the feeling and mood of his proposed settings.

unlike ordinary building plans these drawings might suggest camera angles, or specify "wild" walls capable of sliding easily out of the way to allow camera movement. Their construction details, on the other hand, were quite different from those of most architects: drawn not at intermediate scales but full size, onto enormous sheets of tracing paper that were quickly blueprinted and sent to the construction department to serve as templates for immediate fabrication.

It was here, in the big central drafting room with its ceiling fans whirring to cool the warmish California air, that all the richness of dream New York emerged. Putting in the long years of apprenticeship that would eventually qualify them as full-fledged art directors, the draftsmen spent their days over the boards, painstakingly delineating the Italianate lintels, the Greek Revival pediments, the modernistic cornice lines, the neoclassical fire hydrants, and the thousands of other pieces of a mythic city. Here they assembled, line by line, element by element, the urban particulars that would convince audiences of being the stuff of a genuine metropolis.

To help shape the fine detail of their filmic New York, art directors turned to a wealth of sources on the real city. First stop was the studio reference library, a huge collection that counted among the studio's proudest assets. Tall file cabinets bulged with thousands of special photographs of New York, taken by crews regularly sent back East to shoot parts of the city for a specific film or to supplement the general collection. These crews recorded *everything*, from the broadest skyscraper views to the homeliest details of streets and sidewalks, creating a file-cabinet panorama that comprised one of the most exhaustive urban portraitures ever realized (53).

Many of the collection's images were prosaic, at least when looked at individually. But they gained a kind of cumulative power from the sheer volume with which they were assembled. Nothing was beneath the studio's notice, not even the humblest elements of the civic landscape: the lampposts, fire hydrants, police call-boxes, street signs, and manhole covers that constituted New York's municipal "street furniture," even down to the granite Belgian blocks that gave the street bed its distinctive cobbled texture (48). Other views showed the various building fronts that lined the city's streets: the awnings and show windows of department stores, the classically carved names over the entrances to banks and office buildings, the elegant stenciled lettering on the glazed storefronts of modistes and jewelry shops. The images sought to catalog every element of the urban landscape, both inside and out: the riveted columns and ornate staircases of the El; the benches, water fountains, and statuary of Central and Bryant Parks; the canopies, taxi lights, and uniformed doormen of Park Avenue apartment houses. And onward, through hotel lobbies and elevator cabs, bars and restaurants, tenement hallways and the observation deck of the Empire State Building. Probably never has any living city been documented quite so obsessively, in thousands of sharp, large-format photographs carried across a continent to be assembled, labeled, and filed into an encyclopedic collection, all for the purpose of rebuilding any and every portion of it on a moment's notice. The designers of mythic New York relied carefully on precedent, whether that of the real city or their own versions of it. They always looked before they leaped.

Once approved by the supervisor, the completed drawings were whisked away by the "blueprint boys" starting their apprenticeship in the art department. It was the responsibility of these young men to circulate the drawings among the appropriate construction departments, located across the length of the studio lot. In the massive workshops and storage yards that took up so much of the studio's acreage, the art department's paper vision would become physical reality; here the mythic city would be built.

48. Reference photograph of a lamppost, 1936. In order to accurately re-create physical elements of the city in the studio, still photographers were routinely sent to New York to take reference shots. This view, taken at First Avenue and 53rd Street in Manhattan, was used by the Goldwyn art department in the making of *Dead End*; the measuring rod (lower left) is marked out in foot-long stripes to help studio draftsmen scale the lamppost's size and shape from the photograph.

Its construction would require nothing less than an armada of artisans, probably the greatest collection of diverse skills and crafts ever assembled in a single place. On busy shop floors—each with its own distinctive sights, sounds, and smells—hundreds of superbly talented, mostly anonymous craftsmen would match the dedication that had gone into the mythic city's design with equal care and ingenuity in its fabrication.

Movie New York's underpinnings would be not steel and concrete but, for the most part, wood—thousands of board feet emerging from the huge carpentry department, the "mill," a bright, airy shed redolent of sawdust and varnish. The walls of the movie city would materialize in the plaster or "staff" shop, where a special mixture of plaster of Paris and hemp fiber, called staff, could be cast in panels to simulate just about any surface—from a brownstone wall to carved wood paneling to a limestone facade. Dozens of these panels stood drying outside the shop, awaiting the artful painting that would assure their verisimilitude. The thick plantings of a soundstage Central Park—either real or, more likely, artificial—could be provided by the nursery's greensmen; the enormous plate-glass windows of a mythical Fifth Avenue department store readily supplied by the studio glazier. The Chinese or Yiddish store signage that graced the Lower East Side's streets were no challenge for artisans of the paint-splattered sign shop, while the lacy ironwork of a Gramercy Park balcony was probably not iron at all but inexpensive "pot" metal, cast from a plaster original produced in the high, glassy sculptor's studio. Printed matter from a subway poster to a recent copy of *The New Yorker* was available, or could be created anew, in the paper props department. The hardware for a bank vault, the plumbing for a fire hydrant or steam radiator, the electrical wiring for a street lamp or neon sign:

the construction departments could fabricate literally any piece of the city—or at least a photographically exact facsimile—and with astonishing speed and economy.

There was undoubted spectacle to the building of this mythic city, especially during the war years, when the studios were up and running twenty-four hours a day. A craftsman like Henry Greutert, the head of MGM's sculpture department, might typically start work at 8 a.m. and end at midnight, but his staff would continue around the clock, twenty sculptors in each of four six-hour shifts, shaping architectural details in plaster. "As a young writer," Joe Mankiewicz recalled, "I used to wander around the studio at night. That's when the sets were built. There was all this activity, lights blazing. It was fantastic."

There was also a certain esprit de corps. The art and construction departments embodied a steady, consistent work ethic, far removed from the histrionic excesses of stars, directors, and producers at the front of the lot. Art directors tended to be reticent, quietly capable men, more comfortable with a sketch pencil in hand than expostulating verbally about their work. The scenic artists and carpenters were more taciturn and anonymous still. As screenwriter Gene Fowler noted, watching Fox's art department bring to life the antebellum New York he had imagined on paper for *The Mighty Barnum* (1934):

> *Whenever someone thinks highly of his own ability as a writer or actor, let him visit any of the sets which are built for Hollywood productions. He will come away with a somewhat sad conviction that here, among the designers, the set dressers, and the builders, is exemplified the only honesty Hollywood knows. . . . Their names are not emblazoned on great screens. . . . Yet in the tiddlywinks world of celluloid people . . . these forthright artisans stand as something tangible, real and constructive. . . . The creator of a motion picture set, and the one who "dresses" it, must do his or her work so well that* no one will notice it. *This fact alone conspires to keep the labors of these people anonymous. There must be a fine balance, a superb restraint in the physical creation of a background.*

CITY OF PARTS

49. Set reference still of the Seton mansion interior for *Holiday* (1938). Though considered one of the smaller studios in 1930s Hollywood, Columbia was still capable of building impressive sets, such as the elaborate interior of the Seton mansion—with twenty-four rooms laid out on three levels—designed by Stephen Goosson for the 1938 film *Holiday*.

Once completed, movie New York was located all over the studio lot. Its interiors—the apartments, hallways, shops, and offices of the mythic city—could be found inside soundstages (or "under roof"), usually as temporary sets built for a specific film. These were not complete until the basic structure of walls, doors, and windows had been "dressed" by a team of set decorators. Appropriate furniture, wall coverings, fixtures, and props were selected from vast warehouses that each stored several hundred thousand items. The work of the set dressers might well continue late into the night before filming, but was always ready by morning, when the green dustcovers were pulled off and shooting

began (49). And no sooner was the filming over than these sets were struck and new ones erected in their place, in a constant choreography of construction, use, and dismantling, all directed by the studio's production manager and tracked by the "chart" department.

Impressive as they were, the transient sets of the movie city's interiors were dwarfed in size by the massive outdoor constructions rising from one end of the back lot to the other. These were the permanent (or "standing") sets that represented the movie city's *public* face: its streets and buildings, plazas and parks, theaters and ships, piers and transit systems (50). More than any other single element, the standing set was responsible for establishing the movie city as a real place, with an existence independent of the films in which it appeared. In fact, much of it actually *was* a real and permanent place, standing for years and even decades and reaching a scale that rivaled the big soundstages themselves.

50. Paramount Studios, with New York Street standing set, 1933. Located not in a separate "back lot" outside the studio's walls but next door to the major stages, Paramount's New York Street—its blocks of row-house and mansion fronts—would be reconstructed many times, most recently during a major expansion in 1992, and remains in use in this general location to this day (97).

The use of standing sets reconciled the need for economy with the desire for high production values; it was possible only because of the large tracts of open land that most of the Hollywood studios had acquired in the silent era. An unspoken assumption of American movies was that every filmed environment, large or small, had to be fully and realistically rendered. (Only very rarely has Hollywood flirted with the kind of expressionist approach that allows Broadway's theatrical designers, for example, to "suggest" a setting with a few sticks of furniture.) Yet it quickly became evident that building big new outdoor sets for every film would soon bankrupt the studio. With the ample property now available to most studios, the answer was obvious: build the sets soundly, and *leave them standing*. They would be available for the next film at little or no cost; the price of their construction, however high, could be spread across dozens of films. All that was required from film to film were the minor changes called "redressing" or "revamping": new paint, signs, canopies, or other details to fit the particular needs of a script. Over time, the standing sets would tend to expand, accreting new fixtures, structures or even whole streets for individual films. So while permanent, standing sets were rarely still. Picture to picture, year to year they would change, grow, contract, grow again—just as the city itself might do.

Master drawings at the art department's offices served as the basis for any revamping. These erasable sepia-ink prints, which allowed draftsmen to make only the changes necessary for a specific film and leave the rest untouched, confirmed the wisdom of standing sets. Only a few modifications were usually necessary from film to film, allowing the major investment of the permanent set itself to be quickly recouped. Irish shop names on a tenement street switched to Italian, then Jewish, before reverting back. With a new canvas on its gangway, the French Line pier shifted over to Cunard; a Times Square subway kiosk, with sign panels repainted, suddenly moved to Brooklyn. The sedate, middle-class row of brownstones of one film took a social dive to become a seedy group of boarding houses in another ("Furnished Rooms To Let," read the sign in the window), only to become a chic sidestreet of nightclubs in still another, once a new canopy and neon sign announcing the "Club Continental" had been affixed to the entrance, half a flight down.

The standing set drawings gave off the uncanny sense of being those of a real city—in the way, for example, that they balanced change and continuity. As in any city, each permanent "building" of the standing set had its own number, each street its own name, in order to consistently identify them, even as changes were constantly wrought from film to film. Another example could be found in the countless folders where drawings of individual elements from earlier films were filed. These were usually organized not by those films' titles but by urban category: the canopies of apartment houses from all of the studio's different films were grouped together, as were row-house fronts, theater lobbies, sidewalk clocks, and so on. It made sense: junior members of the art department, assigned to quickly produce a new row-house stoop, could refer to the department's own previous efforts. But it also produced a sense of continuity, of a real city being built and modified, as if the art department considered the films themselves to be merely transient displays of an ongoing urban enterprise. Other sets might be one-of-a-kind constructions with title-related names such as the "Hunchback set" or the "Bounty set." But movie New York was always treated as a continuing design and construction exercise, not tied to any particular film.

51. 20th Century-Fox Studios, with steamship set in distance, late 1930s. One of the most imposing standing sets on the Fox lot was the superstructure of a transatlantic liner, built almost full-scale, that, from a distance, seemed to sail across the lush green landscape of Beverly Hills. The back lots of MGM, Columbia, and Paramount all contained similar landlocked vessels.

The drawing files also revealed the startling variety and number of New York–related standing sets and this, too, made them seem like the elements comprising a genuine city. Paramount's metropolis, for example, included not only New York's street facades, which covered five full blocks and comprised forty-two individual buildings, but also a portion of a full-scale transatlantic liner (51, 183, 184), with dock and pier shed, and the interior of Pennsylvania Station. There was an ornate subway kiosk enclosing a staircase that could actually descend to an IRT station complete with tracks, tilework, and token booth (46). A subway car interior was available on a different set; the interior of the El on still another; on a third was the big, gently curved bow, deck, and wheelhouse of the Staten Island Ferry, as well as the Battery terminal slip at which it docked. One stage held the entire interior of a Broadway theater. There was even an Automat, complete with the little metal cases in which sandwiches and desserts might appear.

Indeed, the standing sets of New York made up a substantial portion of all the permanent sets on the Paramount lot, as they did at every other studio, a revealing testament (especially on smaller lots where space was at a premium) of the primacy of New York in American movies. The sets comprising movie New York were also different in kind from nearly all other standing sets, which were either smaller and sketchier (such as "London Street"), or generic (such as the "Western town," which represented no specific place but an amalgam of idealized images).

52. Installing a scenic backing on the set of *The Fountainhead* (1949). To re-create views of the skyline as seen through the windows of stage sets, scenic departments created immense paintings called "backings." Unlike backdrops used in theaters, scenic backings had no need to be lowered from a fly space above the stage, but were attached to metal frames and simply placed behind the set. In this view, the actor Raymond Massey relaxes between shots as grips behind him remove a scenic backing showing the Plaza, Sherry-Netherland, and Savoy-Plaza hotels.

The extent and complexity of this construct was unique and seemed to fulfill the promise of the reference photographs that had documented the city so completely. And through a kind of financial momentum, the availability of this standing "city" provided a strong stimulus for its continued appearance. Having made the massive investment in movie New York, producers had every interest in encouraging stories and plots to be set there. Hollywood tended toward genre films anyway, in large part to recoup the investment made in their standing sets and costume inventories. New York films had in effect become their own "genre," be they comedies, romances, dramas, or thrillers, made economically within the backlot city that had already been established. So the movie city built upon itself, and reinforced its own continued existence, no less than a real place might.

Of course, parts of the city's landscape defied re-creation on even the biggest and most ambitious standing sets. The Manhattan skyline could obviously not be reproduced full-scale in a Hollywood studio. Nor could the breadth and length of major avenues such as Park or Fifth, or great public spaces such as Times Square. But ever reluctant to return production to the real city, the studios instead developed ingenious techniques that could domesticate even these largest of urban elements and bring them into the controlled confines of the lot.

One technique occupied a building that towered over the rest of the studio. This was the home of the scenic department, which created the giant "backing" paintings that were used to reproduce, on a soundstage, the sweeping views of the skyline and other scenes glimpsed through the windows, doors, and terraces of New York apartments, offices, and other interiors (52). The verisimilitude of these scenic backings was largely a product of their size, which was nothing short of gigantic. At MGM, skyline backings 40 feet high and 120 feet long were not uncommon. The challenges of painting such canvases gave rise to the special features of the scenic loft itself, described quite accurately as "a two-story building ten stories high."

On the upper level, in a skylighted space fully fifty feet tall, reference photographs were scaled up, by stages, into massive painted representations of the buildings, streets, bridges, rivers, and skies of the city—precisely detailed compositions in perfect perspective, with values and colors "forced" to achieve a startling illusion of depth. (For just this reason, photographic blow-ups were rarely used; they might look faded under the bright lights of a film stage.) These compositions were painted on canvases stretched vertically onto giant frames that could be lowered or raised mechanically, like an elevator, through a slot running the length of the floor. The upper portions of these canvases—mostly sky—could thus be painted by men standing comfortably on the loft floor; since the painting moved down to meet *them*, the artists avoided the need for any scaffolding or ladders that might obstruct their view of the work in progress. The lower level, into which the paintings and frames descended, had to be fifty feet high itself in order to accommodate the height of the backings coming down from above. The remainder of this high first-floor space was efficiently used for storage: dozens of older backings were rolled up like so many bolts of cloth and placed on racks over forty feet high.

53. Reference photographs of the Manhattan skyline. Reference shots of the skyline were an invaluable aid in the painting of scenic backings to reproduce views from upper-floor windows. At top is a 1960 view of lower Manhattan, including the slender dark tower of 60 Wall Street (just right of center) and the steel skeleton of the Chase Manhattan Bank headquarters, still under construction (at far left). Below is a 1946 view looking west down 45th Street toward Fifth Avenue, showing the stepped profile of the 1927 Fred F. French Building (at right).

Many of these backings were of New York: by day, by dusk, by night; vistas across the East River of Queens spreading out to the far horizon; dramatic views of lower Manhattan from within its cluster of towers; frontal views of brownstone facades; and vistas of Central Park South through a bosquet of trees. Like the standing sets or the reference photographs, the stored backings constituted a permanent studio asset—a superscaled, two-dimensional New York coiled up in rolls, ready to be unfurled to their full, sweeping extent and astonishing pictorial veracity whenever needed, but existing beyond the confines of any particular film.

The backings showed the city skyline in compositions shaped entirely around their specific purpose: to re-create, on a stage set, a random view of midtown or downtown, as it might actually be seen from an upper-floor office or apartment window. These views thus largely ignored the two most familiar, iconic symbols of the city—the busy streets and soaring skyscraper peaks—to focus on the lesser-known area in between.

54. Scenic backing of midtown Manhattan (top). *The City,* Edward Hopper, 1927 (above). Although their work obviously differed in many ways, both Hollywood scenic painters and fine artists such as Edward Hopper captured distinctive qualities of the city's urbanism, such as the contrast between the ornamental front facades and bare side walls of Manhattan's mid-block towers. Created by MGM's Scenic Department (now J. C. Backings), the painted backing measures fourteen by sixteen feet and shows a portion of the midtown skyline; Hopper's *The City* shows Washington Square North in Greenwich Village (where the artist himself lived for decades).

Into startling focus came the oversized decorative elements that generations of New York architects used to enliven the middle portions of their facades—giant finials, balustrades, cornices, and moldings, designed to be seen from a distance or from the street, but now jumping out in vertiginous proximity (54, top). These carefully composed elements mixed incongruously with the water towers, mechanical penthouses, access bulkheads, and other appurtenances of the city's commercial real-estate traditions. The result was a series of almost surreal juxtapositions of the purposeful and the accidental, of the consciously designed components of New York's traditional high-rise architecture (seen close-up, as never intended) slammed against its casually accreted rooftop structures. Facades that fronted the street, moreover, were highly ornamented, while side and rear walls went largely unadorned; the resulting alternation of decorated and plain surfaces, in frank accordance with the thrifty real-estate dictates of display (in the front) and economy (in the back), offered a distinctly American imagery not unlike the city paintings of Edward Hopper (54, bottom).

It was a further irony that these most contemporary of cityscapes revived one of the oldest traditions in European art. The attempt to render a city faithfully, after all, was hardly a new challenge: it was an essential problem for Renaissance artists, and in its solution lay the visual basis for centuries of art to come. It was precisely to depict his native Florence that the architect Filippo Brunelleschi invented the technique of linear perspective in the early fifteenth century (a pair of images of the city, the octagonal Baptistery across from the cathedral and the towering Palazzo della Signoria a few blocks away, were first used to demonstrate the technique's seemingly miraculous power to render objects receding in the distance). Soon painters like Brunelleschi's friend Masaccio were using the technique to create large frescoes that offered a stunningly accurate depiction of urban space.

Only one limitation remained—but a significant one. Perspective images assumed a vantage point that was firmly fixed: if the viewer stood in exactly the right spot, all the painting's lines converged correctly and a highly realistic image was obtained; if the viewer moved away from that spot, the illusion was more or less ruined. In big, well-filled rooms, such as the public halls in which frescoes were often placed, it was physically impossible for everyone to stand in the same spot. Still, the conventions of linear perspective were so powerful that they held sway over Western painting—not least in the representation of cities—for five hundred years to come (13).

Then, just at the moment it was being firmly discarded by the avant-garde in favor of the "Non-Objective" approach of Modernism, the technique of perspective was reborn, under the distant sun of Southern California, as a skill absolutely necessary to the popular urban mythmaking of the twentieth century. Images of New York's skyline would be painted in precise perspective—at a larger size, and to be seen by a larger public, than any Florentine could have dreamed of. And after five centuries, perspective's greatest drawback would at last be surmounted. Film backings *could* be painted to be seen from one and only one observation point. That point, of course, was the camera lens. Only a few people at a time could stand at the center of a public hall in Florence to see a fresco exactly as it should be seen, but literally millions sitting in theaters could share the single observation point of the camera, viewing the backing from the exactly correct angle—and thus think it not a painting at all, but the city itself. Brunelleschi might have smiled.

55. Constructing a miniature skyline for *Rope* (1948). For Hitchcock's *Rope*, Warner's art department constructed a spectacular miniature skyline, laid out on an eighty-foot semicircle. Its "buildings" were actually shallow cut-outs (far left), rendered on only two sides, which relied on the technique of "forced perspective" to achieve an illusion of depth (compare the relatively large windows on the lower building in the foreground with those of the skyscraper behind it). To provide a convincing transition from day to night, each building was individually wired (at center) with bulbs ranging from twenty-five to a hundred watts, all linked to a "light organ" whose forty-seven switches allowed for the gradual activation of the skyline's eight thousand incandescent lights and two hundred neon signs. At right, Hitchcock "floats" on one of the spun-glass clouds created by technicians. (A Griffith Observatory meteorologist was called in to authenticate their resemblance to New York's actual cumulus clouds.)

56. Miniature skyline in *Rope* (1948). The completed miniature presents a panoramic view looking west from Second Avenue and 54th Street. Among other things, the miniature's construction required a means to slow down the "smoke" that, rising from rooftop chimneys at normal speed, would have instantly given away their reduced size. Dry ice, added to chill the vapor, turned out to do the trick.

The scenic backings lent a presence to the mythic city that was monumental yet motionless, a passive ambience placed behind the penthouse and office sets where endless human dramas might be played out. When the filmmaker desired a city of movement—over time or through space—the art department turned to another technique. Like backings, three-dimensional "miniatures" also reduced the city to soundstage scale, but unlike flat, painted backings they could sustain the motion of a camera passing through and around the skyline, or be wired with tiny electric bulbs to represent the city's passage from day into night, with lights starting to wink from a thousand building windows, accented by commercial signs placed on setbacks or open frameworks, going through their familiar neon dance (55, center).

It might be tempting to call these scaled-down cities "models," but Hollywood usage firmly favored the term "miniatures," and with good reason. Unlike architects' models, studio miniatures were not intended to *represent* a larger reality but to actually *be* that reality—at least when seen through a camera lens. This explained their size, which was larger than any architect's model, a scale considered necessary to sustain a convincing illusion. It explained why their buildings were not rendered on all four sides, but were shaped more like cut-outs with only those two sides visible to the camera depicted in any detail. And it explained their overall layout, which was entirely different from conventional models.

Early experience taught filmmakers that laying out miniature cities to be accurate in plan—like an architect's model—resulted in a phony appearance on screen. The camera lens could not hold the entire depth of this kind of miniature in focus; as a result much of the "city" would be out of focus and thus give away its true size as being a matter of yards, not miles. The solution was to build the city as a series of shallow layers, placed in succession right behind one another. With the entire miniature city only a few feet deep, everything could be kept in sharp focus. The illusion of depth would be provided through the means of "forced perspective": the deliberate manipulation of each layer's scale to suggest that its buildings were set much closer or farther away than they actually were (55, left). The first layer's buildings were big, with large, well-detailed windows and trim; the next layer's buildings might be only half that first layer's scale, with correspondingly smaller windows and trim. The layer behind these would be scaled down half again, and so on, until the distant horizon was reached with tiny buildings in the sixth or seventh layer's skyline. An ingenious refinement added a scrim of fine gauze between each of the last few layers, to replicate the atmospheric distortion that makes buildings in the far distance seem slightly hazy and indistinct. When complete and seen from the correct vantage point, the miniature could offer a remarkable sense of depth. Seen from the side, the illusion was instantly broken (44).

Italian ghosts hovered over the construction of miniatures no less than the painting of backings, but here the activating spirit was not the early Renaissance, with its innocent eagerness to render the city accurately, but the late Renaissance and its sixteenth-century successor, Mannerism, which explored devious ways to fool the eye by manipulating scale and space. In a way, Mannerism's forced perspective turned the earlier, linear perspective on its head: having discovered the rules by which objects could be rendered to seem as if they receded into the distance, forced perspective allowed real objects to seem much deeper or larger than they really were, by falsely manipulating their shape and scale to conform to the pictorial tricks that Brunelleschi had first exploited. Viewers might look down a long Roman arcade toward a giant statue at the far end, only to find once they penetrated the space that the arcade was just a few feet deep and the statue no more than a foot or so high. Assumptions about space and scale, in other words, could be used to deceive as well as depict. Studio art directors and the technicians of the "trick" departments, in charge of designing and constructing miniatures, quickly learned or rediscovered all the sixteenth century's lessons, especially as they proceeded to build a miniature city skyline to be seen beyond a stage-set window or rooftop.

57. **Glass shot from *Broadway Melody of 1936* (1935).** To place live-action sequences within the larger city, technicians often resorted to "glass shots." At top is a view painted on a sheet of glass, with the central area left unpainted. In the middle is a shot of a stage set, built to align precisely with the setting shown in the painting. Cameras filmed the live action on the stage set *through* the glass painting, bringing the two images together in a composite view that completed the illusion (bottom).

However impressive, backings and miniatures showed a city devoid of human life. Adding that life, the movement of people and traffic, required sophisticated techniques that could combine live action on a soundstage with painted or filmed surroundings.

For a "glass shot," a skilled artist would paint an utterly realistic view (of a high building facade, for example) on a piece of clear, optically flat glass. A portion at the center or bottom of the picture would be left unpainted (or be painted and then carefully scraped away) to allow the camera to shoot right through the glass to whatever lay beyond. A stage set was then designed and built to match precisely the perspective and lighting of the painting. A stationary camera, locked down firmly in exactly the right position, would film the painting and through the clear portion would capture the staged action (doormen, partygoers, passing vehicles) occurring on the set beyond, merging the two into one seamless image. It was an ingenious way to provide dramatic composite views of New York—a lively penthouse party, for example, seen among a landscape of roofs—which could not be rendered any other way (57).

Still another technique was employed to bring the activity of the city's busy avenues onto a soundstage. Called "rear projection," this process was straightforward, at least in principle: a movie of the real city's background was projected on a screen behind the actors (58). Although this might seem an obvious expedient for a film studio—in the business, after all, of making movies—it proved a staggering technical challenge.

The process started with a second camera unit, transported to New York, shooting background footage that was carefully planned in advance to coordinate with action to be filmed in the studio. Back in Hollywood, on a special process stage whose interior was painted jet-black to avoid any unwanted reflections, this footage was projected from the rear onto a translucent screen, called a background "plate." In front of the plate, actors played out their New York roles aided by a piece of scenery or two: a couple might flirt in a taxicab whose rear window revealed the moving lights of Times Square, or a divorcée could step from her limousine onto the sidewalk as the traffic and pedestrians of Park Avenue passed behind her.

58. Shooting a rear projection sequence on the Warner process stage, 1944. City scenes that required a moving background were created in the studio using the technique of rear projection. In this view, the Manhattan skyline is projected from the rear onto a screen behind the actors. One rear projector is visible at the top; two others might also be placed at right angles, their beams redirected with prism-like mirrors to converge on the screen, increasing the image's brightness. Stagehands with long sticks rock the taxi body (built in half) to simulate the motion of a moving vehicle.

Simple in theory, the technique proved fiendishly difficult in practice. The bright lights illuminating the actors in the foreground tended to wash out the image on the screen behind them. And the background footage had to be projected in precise synchronization with the camera shooting the actors or a distracting flicker would appear on the screen. These problems were largely solved in 1930 by an ingenious Fox (later Paramount) technician named Farciot Edouart, who used a prismlike mirror to superimpose identical images from three projectors placed at right angles to one another, all precisely synchronized with the camera and held rock-steady.

By the mid-thirties, Edouart's process could almost single-handedly create a filmic New York; in a picture such as *The Gilded Lily* (1935), rear projection could bring Fred MacMurray and Claudette Colbert to the 42nd Street terrace of the New York Public Library (by day and by night), to a speeding tender in the middle of New York Harbor, or onto the hair-raising curves of a Coney Island roller coaster—all without ever leaving the "process stage" on the Paramount lot. Ten years later, Edouart reviewed the technique's rapid improvement:

> *When the process was first used, a scene inside a closed car, with a screen six or eight feet wide was something to be happy about. But demand has forced us to find ways of using screens 12, 15, 18 and 20 feet across. When we succeeded in using a 24-foot screen we already had demand for a 36-foot screen. My most recent scenes have made use of twin screens totaling 48 feet in width—and the end is not yet!*

In Edouart's words we hear more than facts; the prideful tone suggests the mystique of artifice that was unmistakable in the studio era. By the time he was writing, in 1943, the old difficulties of location shooting had begun to disappear. Sound equipment, especially, had improved to the point where synchronized-sound shooting in urban locations was becoming feasible again. But Hollywood studios had grown so comfortable and skilled at making movies their way—doing everything on the lot, using ingenuity and craft to surmount any limitations—that a return to location shooting was still essentially unthinkable. It had become more than a question of technology, or production economy, or even political control. A pride in artifice *for its own sake* had engulfed the studio from the senior producers down to the junior apprentices—a faith in the studio system's ability to build or make anything, a faith that raised the ambition of the constructed city to ever-higher peaks. A single studio, MGM, could, in a single year, 1945, undertake the construction of *two* of New York's greatest landmarks, Pennsylvania Station and the Waldorf-Astoria Hotel, in its Culver City lot. On Stage 27, for *The Clock*, workmen re-created the central section of the vast waiting room of McKim, Mead & White's 1910 station, which rose up at one end in a majestic flight of stairs (complete with a conveyor belt that functioned like the real station's escalator), and opened at the other onto the station's great iron-and-glass concourse (rendered perfectly with a huge painted backing) (59, 192). The re-creation for *Week-end at the Waldorf* was still more complete, including not only the hotel's two main lobbies, but its Park Avenue facade and entrance hall, guest suites and corridors, drive-way, bakery, doctor's office, switchboard, barbershop, elevators, stenographic office, Jade Room, and Star-

59. Set still of the Pennsylvania Station set for *The Clock* (1945). Used in the opening and closing scenes of Vincente Minnelli's first film, this set of the Waiting Room in Pennsylvania Station was erected on MGM's Stage 27 for a cost of $66,450. The only part of the enormous structure that gave the construction department any difficulty was the escalator at center; working parts for a real escalator proved impossible to obtain during World War II, forcing the studio to use a moving belt as a substitute.

light Ballroom. In all, the Waldorf sets occupied 120,000 square feet—half again as large, the art department noted, as the entire first floor of the real hotel. The central lobby set alone, sixty-two by eighty-two feet, boasted walls covered in Oregon maple burl, trimmed with black marble pilasters, and ebony columns with nickel-bronze capitals (194).

To an outside observer, it might have seemed more logical to bring some lights, a few cameras, and a crew into the real Penn Station or Waldorf-Astoria than to literally *rebuild them from scratch* on a Hollywood soundstage. But that wasn't the studio way. And in fact, with the entire system in place, with the cost of the studio's massive investment in buildings, equipment, and personnel spread over the half a hundred films it made each year, a certain economy could be achieved. Not only could Metro's art department turn out its own Pennsylvania Station with ease, it could do so cheaply—the entire set cost less than $67,000.

MGM took special pride in the precise accuracy of its reproductions of landmarks such as the Waldorf or Penn Station. Most of Hollywood's New York, though, was not a precise reproduction. It was instead a subtle reinterpretation of the city, faithful to the spirit of the place, but often quite different in particulars. This held true at many levels. In contrast to today's practice of "product placement," which fills Hollywood movies with recognized brand names, studio attorneys of the time instructed the art department to avoid any legal entanglements by employing invented names whenever possible. So the dream city constituted a self-contained urban universe, not just full of mythical people and stories but of mythical buildings, shops, and establishments as well (as small in-jokes, art directors sometimes slipped their own names into street signage or theater displays). In other cases, a plot turn or musical number might call for the creative manipulation of a city locale, such as the placement of an elegant, if entirely fictive, modernistic band shell within the classical landscape of Bryant Park (60).

60. Set still of the Bryant Park set for *Broadway Melody of 1938* (1937). Rebuilding the city to meet the demands of filmic storytelling, art directors often combined accurate reproductions with fanciful inventions. In the foreground of this MGM set of Bryant Park in Manhattan is a largely faithful re-creation of the actual Lowell Memorial Fountain; the silvery modern band shell in the background, by contrast, is entirely a studio creation, never to be found in the real park.

Indeed, the studios' vast reference sources were often used not for direct copying but as a springboard for the art department's own creations. Knowing the city meant knowing its limitations as well as its strengths, and art directors never hesitated to improve the city for their own purposes, to reshape it to their own ends. For the movie city, the real New York was a starting point, to be closely observed but then transformed, not slavishly imitated. "We didn't want to eliminate reality," noted the art director Eugène Lourié, *we wanted to create the most suitable reality for the film. By omitting certain useless details, by underlining some others, by conveying the mood by lighting, colors, shapes, and linear composition, the designer could make the sets much more expressive than real locations. They could become more real than real. A poetic reality, a reality with a soul. Our town, built on a set, would be a created reality, as when a writer tells a story and creates a projection of real life.*

FULFILLING THE DREAM

61. ***Madam Satan*** **(1930).** The climactic scene of C. B. DeMille's *Madam Satan*—a masquerade ball held in a dirigible cruising over New York—began with this giddy boarding sequence, evidently inspired by the proposal, made a few months earlier, to build a mooring mast for airships atop the Empire State Building.

That movie New York was more than simply a re-creation was apparent almost from the start, as studio art directors sought to make real the supercity lurking in the scripts they had been handed. It would emerge from the same potent mixture of memory and imagination that had inspired the writers—and for good reason. Many prominent Hollywood art directors were themselves former New Yorkers, notably Cedric Gibbons and Van Nest Polglase, respective heads of MGM's and RKO's art departments. Both Brooklyn-born and -bred, they had learned design at the feet of their New York–architect fathers and gone on to enter the city's fledgling film industry in the 1910s (Polglase had actually practiced architecture briefly in New York before working in pictures). By the late 1920s, both had come west and were directing the output of major studios, bringing with them an unmistakable air of New York sophistication—especially Gibbons, arriving for work every morning in a gray homburg and impeccably tailored dark blue suit, speeding through the studio gates in his gleaming white Duesenberg.

For the art directors, the city's possibilities outshone remembrance. Whatever their memories of the real place, it was the new city, still growing in spectacular ways, that ignited their imaginations. Each month, new architecture magazines arrived from the East; each month they held within their pages some stunning new Art Deco skyscraper under construction or just completed in New York. Nineteen thirty brought the Chrysler Building with its gleaming metal spire, an exuberant fantasy over a thousand feet high; with 1931 came the topping off of the Empire State Building, tallest of them all, its spire comparatively sedate—but ready to receive passengers disembarking from dirigibles moored to its 102nd floor, 1,250 feet in the air (61). In 1932, the first structure of an entire skyscraper city, Rockefeller Center, was completed; at *its* top, the

RCA Building offered not another spire but something even more suggestive and inspiring, a great nightclub called the Rainbow Room.

However dazzling these images, the Hollywood art directors were determined to outdo them, making them merely the launching point for an even more extravagant and glittering imagery. Soon they were creating an unforgettable physical counterpart to the superurban vision the writers had initiated. They placed enormous "smart" nightclubs—the Paradise Club, the Silver Sandal, the Moonbeam Room—at the peak of every skyscraper, offering panoramic views of the glowing towers, lighted signs, and starry skies all around. They created sleek lobbies and offices and penthouse apartments of vast dimension and flawlessly smooth finish. They leaped especially at the design possibilities inherent in the silvery, sinuous sleekness of the Art Deco style and remade their city with it.

62. **Art director John Harkrider, with a model of the Silver Sandal nightclub set for *Swing Time* (1936).** Models such as this were used by art directors to study proposed set designs, to coordinate issues of lighting and staging with directors, cinematographers, and choreographers, and, on occasion, to persuade producers to pay for unusual or expensive sets.

Working with unit art directors Hobe Erwin and Frederick Hope, Cedric Gibbons took advantage of technical improvements in film stock and lighting to introduce the "Big White Set" in the New York apartment of Wallace Beery and Jean Harlow in *Dinner at Eight* (1933). The color white had been notably absent from the art director's palette in the 1920s: when photographed under arc lights, white surfaces tended to cause "halation" (a kind of blinding effect) in the old orthochromatic film stock, forcing filmmakers to use light pink or green pastels in their stead. By the 1930s, newly introduced panchromatic film and incandescent lighting permitted all-white sets, which Gibbons proceeded to exploit dramatically. The new film stock would also give these movies their distinctive glossiness.

It was Polglase, though, who carried the Big White Set furthest as the basis for the new city. Polglase ran RKO's art department as a more collegial ship than Gibbons's autocracy at Metro, encouraging younger talents like Carroll Clark, Al Herman, and Perry Ferguson. With Clark, especially, Polglase firmly established the unforgettable style of the mythic New York of Fred Astaire and Ginger Rogers in *Swing Time* (1936) and *Shall We Dance?* (1937). A crucial role in creating this silken, dreamy imagery was played by another ex–New Yorker, John Harkrider, who in his brief stay in Hollywood in the late 1930s propelled the movie city to some of its giddiest and most poetic heights, beyond the wildest imaginings of the real city, even as it was soaring upwards (62).

No less elegant than Gibbons or Polglase, Harkrider arrived in Hollywood

following the well-worn path from Times Square (where he had served as artistic director of Ziegfeld's Broadway extravaganzas). His Silver Sandal nightclub for *Swing Time* adapted Polglase and Clark's Art Deco style into a stratospherically urbane conception of a rooftop pleasure dome that floated high above the skyline, and was itself embraced by a starry firmament (63).

63. Production sketch for the Silver Sandal nightclub set in *Swing Time*, 1936. John Harkrider's initial conception of this rooftop nightclub called for walls and ceiling of transparent glass, bathing the room in starlight; the dance floor would be glazed as well, offering dramatic views of the city below.

In the Silver Sandal, and even greater conceptions to follow (173, 176), could be taken the measure of the art directors' transformation of the writers' imaginative vision into a "poetic reality." By now the distance back to the writers' remembered city of the 1920s seemed long indeed. The famed speakeasies that the ex–New Yorkers had fondly recalled as they wrote the movie city into existence had in truth been small, hastily assembled places, their excitement drawn from an exuberant atmosphere and their wild, anything-goes behavior rather than their physical appearance (34). Even Tex Guinan's famous club had been physically rather modest:

64. Polishing the dance floor of a New York nightclub set, MGM, 1940.

The room is long, but not too long to be homely. No one can be lost in it. The walls are covered with pleated cloth and the roof tented with the same cloth softly toned in old rose, green and sere yellow. There are hanging Chinese lanterns, and on the walls illuminated designs of parrots. There are twenty or thirty tables and a small space in the middle of them for intimate dancing.

In eight short years this homely environment had been transformed into nothing less than Astaire and Rogers's Silver Sandal, with its unforgettable shining surfaces and gleaming black floors. Those floors could be considered a special symbol of the art directors' dream city, of the kind of design magic they brought to their task of fulfilling the writers' conception. Created by placing a layer of Bakelite over wood panels, they were covered with cardboard during rehearsals and polished with Energine between takes to remove any scuffs (64). So Fred and Ginger played out their exquisite choreography of longing and fulfillment on a floor of unearthly polish, a floor, literally, that no one had ever danced on before, or ever would again—a shining, perfect platform sitting atop a city of dreams.

PART TWO

ON THE TOWN

ESTABLISHING SHOT

Welcome to the dream city.

Settle into your seats. Watch the studio trademark go by: the roaring lion, the snow-peaked mountain, the revolving globe, the crossing searchlights. Now sit back as a striking image fills the screen, our first glimpse of this extraordinary place. Filmmakers call it the "establishing shot," the wide view that locates the film or scene to come. But we call it something else.

The skyline.

Over the decades, the New York skyline has opened countless feature films—more films, probably, than any other single place on earth. The specific shot varies all the time, of course: a view of midtown from the East River in one film, downtown Manhattan from Brooklyn in another; a sweeping aerial of the entire island in yet another. We may see the city by day, its towers rising tall and solid, or by night, those same towers dissolved into the tracery of a million points of light (65, 67). Accompanying the view might be that familiar "big city" theme music—its brisk tempo, dissonant brass, and bustling xylophone conjuring up busy streets, taxi horns, and rushing crowds. Or a haunting blue melody, a saxophone and orchestra evoking a kind of sweet urban sadness. Or simply a medley of city sounds—traffic, police sirens, a tolling church bell.

In the end, though, it is not the variety but the *constancy* of the establishing shot that remains with us. The skyline view is a kind of proscenium, after all, a metaphoric arch framing everything to come, offering a reassuring familiarity even as it plunges us into a new and unpredictable experience. How many places are as widely (or instantly) recognizable as New York? Older films sometimes placed a printed title across the view; newer ones rarely do—but in any case the name has always been superfluous. Like Big Ben or the Taj Mahal, the New York skyline is one of the world's unmistakable icons, thanks in large part

65. Establishing shot from *Whispers in the Dark* (1992). Framed by the gently curving spans of the Brooklyn and Manhattan Bridges, this aerial view shows the glittering towers of lower Manhattan rising above the dark plate of the East River.

to films themselves: each new opening shot trades on—and reinforces—the skyline's preexisting fame. Unlike those other icons, though, the skyline carries civic as well as national significance, standing for a city as much as (or more than) a country. And unlike the others it is not just a single structure but an entire place—the very thing, in fact, being symbolized. The Eiffel Tower denotes Paris; the skyline not only denotes but *is* New York.

Of course, the skyline also denotes something else: the "big city," the endless metropolis. This turns out to be less a function of the skyline's vertical thrust, surprisingly, than its horizontal spread: its hundreds upon hundreds of buildings, with their thousands upon thousands of windows—each window providing the symbolic marker of an individual and so, by extension, an individual story. Over the next few hours, the skyline vista suggests, we will follow one such story—but we might well have turned to some other window and there found another, equally interesting story to watch. Next time, perhaps. There are, the skyline proposes, millions of stories to choose from—a whole *city* of stories, all proceeding at once, whether we happen to see them or not.

Some establishing shots try for more, searching the skyline for clues about the story to come. The image that starts *Young Man with a Horn* (1950) gazes high up at the Chrysler Building, soaring into the sky as confidently as the jazz trumpeter on the soundtrack rises into his upper register. But soon the camera begins to tilt down, descending roof by roof to the modest tenement apartment of piano player Hoagy Carmichael, the film's narrator. This turns out to be a sketch of the film itself—a struggle between the transcendent "high note" that cornetist Kirk Douglas dreams of reaching and the worldly complexities of life and love that threaten to wreck his career. An identical shot, opening *Miracle in the Rain* (1956), offers a simpler meaning: New York, as the narrator tells us, is home to not only the high and mighty (the skyscrapers) but to millions of ordinary people—including Jane Wyatt, a tenement dweller who is the film's romantic lead. Barbara Stanwyck's smoky voice-over at the opening of 1949's *East Side, West Side* ("Yes, this is my town . . . the most exciting city in the world, they say, the most glamorous, the most frightening, and above all, the fastest . . .") underpins a glide from the sleek towers of midtown to a modest apartment house on Gramercy Park ("for me, it's home"), again evoking the distinction between the celebrated and the ordinary—and the city's embrace of both.

The same kind of movement is elsewhere turned to very different purpose. Among other things, the New York skyline remains an abiding symbol of American wealth and power; an opening that shifts from the gleaming spires to a slum district effectively reminds the audience that the wretched conditions they will be sharing over the next few hours are to be found not in some obscure locality but in proximity to a national landmark. Over time, the simple tilt or pan from proud skyscrapers in the distance to shabby tenements nearby (in *Street Scene*, 1931, and *The Window*, 1949) has given way to the ambitious, planimetric aerial shots that open *West Side Story* (1961) and *New Jack City* (1991), which, surveying all parts of New York from above—as if through a giant microscope—imply a kind of social-science objectivity, linking the city's richest and poorest districts in a single socioeconomic system (66).

Similar aerial shots begin both *The Broadway Melody* (1929) and *42nd Street* (1933). But unlike *West Side Story*'s, these dramatic views propose no sociological insights; instead, they revel in the skyscrapers' sheer physical excitement and seek to tap it for their own rhythmic ignition. The opening of *42nd Street* relates plausibly to the film's story by flying up Broadway, following the historic northward movement of New York's entertainment district from Herald Square to Times Square; *Broadway Melody*, on the other hand, doesn't even bother with Broadway and instead shows the new skyline of the financial district. But as those amazing towers spike up, straining to reach us, we get a sense of incredible energy before a single toe has started tapping.

For decades, this kind of high, aerial view, shot from the nose of an airplane (or, later, helicopter), represented the closest possible fulfillment of the longstanding cinematic desire to fly *between* New York's towers, right through the narrow canyons that separate them. Once, such daring penetration of the city's airspace was possible only with an artificial skyline, like the one that opens *Reaching for the Moon*, a 1931 Douglas Fairbanks film: we fly headlong down the avenues of a miniature city, turning left and then right as buildings pass by, finally closing in on the tower in which the first scene takes place. More recent films employ a gyro-stabilized camera mount (devised by the cinematographer Nelson Tyler) to dampen aircraft vibration, allowing long tele-

66. Establishing shots of midtown and lower Manhattan. Looking east across midtown Manhattan, the 1975 Paramount aerial view at top includes, from left to right, the Pan Am Building and several other modern towers clustered around Grand Central Terminal, the silvery spire of the Chrysler Building, and, along the East River, the Secretariat building of the United Nations headquarters. The view at bottom, prepared for *Wolfen* (1981), shows a panoramic view of lower Manhattan looking south and east to the Upper New York Bay. The white tower at center is the Irving Trust Building at One Wall Street, designed by the architect Ralph Walker in 1932 and an evident source of inspiration for the towers in *Broadway Melody of 1938* (205).

photo lenses to take us into the very heart of the skyline, while removing any jittering that might reveal the mechanical nature of our platform. Using the Tyler mount and special high-speed film, Ridley Scott's *Someone to Watch Over Me* (1987) opens with an establishing shot that is truly dreamlike: we sail, thrillingly, right *through* the glittering skyline, the Chrysler and Empire State Buildings executing a dazzling dance in the night sky around us. Gone is the distant, flattened, pictorial image of the city's towers; this skyline comprises the most sculptural objects imaginable, popping up in front of us as if in a three-dimensional movie. Avenues become long, glowing wells of light, scooped out of the dark mass of the city and shooting northward like arrows. Continuing our smooth, deliberate glide, we get the sense of actually flying through the night sky, weightlessly, as we might otherwise hope to do only in our dreams. Clearly we have left the real world behind, with its rude constraints (like gravity), and entered a realm where earthly rules simply do not apply.

This last is perhaps the skyline's greatest value, the key to its popularity. As

67. Establishing shot from *The Lost Weekend* (1945). Shot from an apartment terrace in the East Fifties, this view of midtown Manhattan includes (from left to right) the Chrysler and Chanin Buildings, the spire of the Empire State rising beyond the Shelton Hotel (71), the pyramidal roof of the New York Central (now Helmsley) Building, the twin-towered Waldorf-Astoria Hotel, and, at far right, the RCA (now GE) Building.

nothing else, the skyline prepares us—emotionally, viscerally—for the place we are about to enter. It is a cinematic passport, a rite of passage that may last only a few moments but sets us up for the civic hyperreality that lies in store for the next two hours. Forget what you know of real life, it tells an audience, or even the real city you call New York. Grand and strange as that city might be, it still operates by worldly rules. This city is a different kind of place altogether.

It is, in the end, what connects every establishing shot, every skyline. It is there in the river views of lower Manhattan (complete with a sleek liner on its way to France) that opens *How to Marry a Millionaire* (1953)—a place so sophisticated and stylish that Lauren Bacall herself is a mere social climber. It is there in the stately skyscrapers that, rising slender and erect from the mass of lower midtown buildings at the start of *The Hucksters* (1947), recall chess pieces on the biggest gameboard in the world, or perhaps the powerful advertising men—Clark Gable, Adolphe Menjou, Sydney Greenstreet—who move those pieces around the boardrooms of Madison Avenue. It is there in the superheated aer-

ial views of lower Manhattan that start Oliver Stone's *Wall Street* (1987), pushing the audience right up against the sixty-story walls of downtown Manhattan, as if to say, never mind the real Wall Street's kingpins; in *this* Wall Street we will find Gordon Gekko himself. It carries us along, willing or not, in the sweeping opening of *Working Girl* (1988); as we broadly spiral around the head of the Statue of Liberty, then swoop down across the bay and onto a ferry making its way to Manhattan, we know positively that nothing we are about to see could happen anywhere else but movie New York. Sometimes it promises too much: the remarkable establishing shot that opens *Bonfire of the Vanities* (1990), with its time-lapse, dawn-to-dusk vision of the New York universe, suggests a city where the very patterns of sun and clouds and day and night operate by different rules than elsewhere, a city at once frenetically accelerated and oddly eternal, where stainless steel gargoyles, stern and unchanging, look out upon the frenzied traffic and scudding clouds and majestic sunrises and sunsets that come and go in seconds. Sadly we do not get to remain in this amazing, otherworldly city; it is our first and last glimpse of the place.

Is the real New York wild? In *Broadway* (1929) we are introduced to movie New York by a giant Bacchus striding among the towers of Times Square, who then breaks open a jeroboam of champagne and douses the entire district with it, laughing madly. In *Crime Without Passion* (1934), the opening sequence designed by Slavko Vorkapich shows the downtown skyline animated by the Three Furies—complete with flowing gowns, beautiful bodies, and ghastly faces—who fly among its towers, smash its windows, and screech hideously as various inhabitants succumb to acts of passion and murder. Or recall the delicious anticipation of the establishing shot of New York that appears midway through *"Crocodile" Dundee* (1986). The first half of the film has presented Dundee's mastery of the Australian outback, full of terrors at every turn. Yet on seeing the Manhattan skyline, accompanied by distant sirens, we can only smile with delight: now *this*, we say to ourselves, is a *jungle.*

Sooner rather than later, the establishing shot comes to an end; it is time to plunge into the movie city itself. The next image may be the entrance to a mythical structure within that city's borders: "The Dexter Building," "The Ritz-Bilt Hotel," "The Footlights Club," "The Stuyvesant Museum of Natural History." Or it may be an interior, a nightclub where a blowsy singer is finishing a song, a busy skyscraper lobby filled with office workers, a stage whose eager chorus girls are exiting into the wings. These, too, can be called establishing shots in a technical sense: they locate us in space; they set us up for the action to follow. But it is left to that first image—the skyscraper skyline of New York—to perform the truly magical task, not merely placing the audience but transporting it, not just establishing the location of a particular film but asserting once again the compelling reality of an alternative urban realm, a mythic city of reflected light, glowing in the darkness.

FOUR

EMERALD CITIES

SKYLINES OF FANTASY

CITY OF GIANTS

> Oh, we're almost there, at last, at last! It's beautiful, isn't it? Just like I knew it would be.
>
> DOROTHY IN *THE WIZARD OF OZ*

It has been a long and arduous journey, from a tiny village, across miles of rolling countryside, and through the heart of a dense, forbidding forest—all in search of a city of legend. At last they see it, on the distant horizon: a cluster of slender towers rising into an iridescent sky, gleaming and sparkling in the sun. As the music swells in sweeping chords the travelers stand motionless, transfixed by the sight. Then, filled with newfound energy, they break into a giddy dash, heading directly for the glittering apparition (68).

We are clearly in a place nowhere on earth, in a realm of sheer fantasy. Yet the scene is somehow familiar. We *know* that soaring place in the distance—and we know, too, that surge of emotion upon seeing it. Beneath their otherworldly sparkle and hue, the towers of the Emerald City are telling us something important about the skyscraper skyline—and still more about its uncanny power to affect us.

68. (previous page) View of the Emerald City from *The Wizard of Oz* (1939). The famed view of the Emerald City was actually a matte painting, twenty-eight inches by twenty-two inches in size, drawn by the noted MGM matte artist Warren Newcombe with pastel crayons on a piece of black cardboard.

It is a paradox, largely unexplored. Historically, we understand the city's skyscrapers to have arisen from a conjunction of worldly forces: Manhattan's insular topography, nineteenth-century technological innovation, the need for proximity among businessmen and financiers, the speculative impulses of the city's property owners. Yet we also know the skyscrapers to possess an astonishing emotional resonance, a capacity to mesmerize us that plainly transcends their commercial and technological origins—"the most moving buildings of modern times," in the words of the architectural historian Vincent

Scully. Why *are* they so moving? What accounts for their power to affect us so directly? Why should we invest so much of ourselves in these outsized products of cash and steel?

The answer has been elusive, even for those who have deigned to consider the Manhattan skyline an appropriate subject for criticism, and not merely an adventitious collection of overgrown office structures. Scully himself has evoked the towers' striking air of collegiality—"a city of genial giants," he writes, that "stood around and conversed . . . their tripods smoking among the clouds." Thomas van Leeuwen reminds us how much the Manhattan skyline reasserted—at greatly enlarged scale—some of the most venerable Western imagery of cities, from the ancient ziggurats of Babylon, to the many-towered towns of medieval Tuscany, to the church-spired silhouettes of Reformation Europe. Robert A. M. Stern, meanwhile, has called attention to the New York skyscrapers' consciously crowd-pleasing role as "statements" for the major corporations who were their owners or prime tenants.

Yet something still seems missing, something closer to the heart, perhaps, than to the mind. In the end, the Manhattan skyline forms one of the most *expressive* urban groupings ever created. For decades, it has engendered astonishingly personal responses from millions of individuals, who have somehow seen in its towers the embodiment of a remarkable range of human feelings and impulses: of aspiration and struggle, of foreboding and transcendence, of an eerie sense of the future and a haunting sense of the past. If this emotional impact has been relatively underexplored, it is perhaps because it has less to do with the shape of buildings themselves than the imaginative interplay between buildings and people—which is the very stuff of the movie city, of course, even if those buildings and people are sometimes to be found only in a place "over the rainbow."

In fact, the very unearthliness of the Emerald City prompts the notion that the best place to start might be in the most fantastic zones of the filmic city, those places where the skyscraper's worldly origins have been most completely stripped away, where the skyline itself has been transformed most elastically. It may be in just these most unreal and fabular New Yorks—cities of bizarre creatures and superhumans, of projected futures and invented histories—that, ironically, we come closest to the very human impulses to which the skyline gives such striking form.

To begin, we need look no further than the Emerald City itself, as first glimpsed by Dorothy Gale (Judy Garland) and her friends in *The Wizard of Oz* (1939). Much of the scene's power, of course, comes from its place in that film's epic journey—a journey that, though fantastic enough in its details (talking trees, lurking witches, a yellow brick road), nonetheless suggests the very real passage from country to city undertaken by millions over the past century, traveling vast distances of land and water to pursue their hopes and dreams. Seen from a ship's rail or train window, the towers of Manhattan provided an unforgettable confirmation of their decision, the tangible symbol of the goal they had sought for so long.

Perhaps no moment in the filmic city—and certainly no shot of the actual skyline—so effectively reenacts that surge of emotion as this first sight of the Emerald City. Dorothy and her friends indeed stand transfixed—but not by aesthetic pleasure. In that gleaming skyline, they see the fulfillment of their dreams. In that place, perhaps *only* in that place, will each find the special thing he or she is looking for. These towers will somehow change their lives.

That is what makes the view so powerful, so moving. From a distance, the skyline is everything they could have imagined, and more. Soaring, glistening, grand but comprehensible, its upward leap precisely mirrors the feeling in their hearts. Its very improbability—all those slender, dizzying towers, bundled tightly together, cresting at the center—simply adds to its impact. For how could their lives be truly transformed, after all, in a place of ordinary appearance? Magical events call for magical settings.

Through a kind of urban grace, the skyline of New York—in one sense simply the overscaled product of technology and real estate—became the locus of one of the most potent collective emotional experiences in the life of America. Into Manhattan's towers were focused the hopes and dreams of millions, until the very girders and facades were permeated and charged with a sense of human possibility, as the skyline's own skyward aspirations became fused with

69. Preproduction drawing from *King Kong*, 1932. In order to convince skeptical studio heads at RKO of the value of his new concept, Merian C. Cooper had sketches prepared by his production team. This drawing of the film's climactic scene was a group effort by Willis O'Brien (who drew the figure of Kong), Mario Larrinaga (who laid in the skies), and Byron Crabbe (who rendered the skyline). In the film, the pilots who make the fatal aerial attack are actually played by the film's directors, following Cooper's suggestion to his partner that "we kill the sonofabitch ourselves."

70. ***King Kong* (1933).** Kong's rampage through Manhattan was accomplished with a combination of miniatures and stop-action cinematography, under the direction of Willis "Obie" O'Brien. For the scenes of Kong breaking out of the Broadway theater (at left), craftsmen shaped a miniature figure—a posable armature covered in latex and fur—to a scale of one foot to the inch. Kong's height of eighteen feet, impressive enough in the film's Skull Island sequences, suddenly seemed insufficient when he reached Manhattan ("It isn't *big* enough!" director Merian C. Cooper said after seeing the first New York footage). For the city shots, Kong was quietly scaled up to twenty-four feet, with the hope that no one would notice the change halfway through the film. The scene of Kong destroying the Sixth Avenue El (center) had its origins in Cooper's memories of the Third Avenue El, which used to keep his sister awake at nights. "I used to think I'd love to rip the damn thing down," Cooper later recalled, "so when I decided I needed another sequence of Kong in Manhattan, I thought wouldn't that be a helluva scene to tear up one of those things." At right, Kong nears the top of the Empire State Building.

the personal yearnings of millions. The dream city, even in this most unworldly of guises, lets us share that transactive spark.

Of course, much of the scene's seductive power lay in seeing the skyline as a distant prospect. From afar, the composition could be taken in as a whole, its shape seeming clear and purposeful. The broad view offered the skyline without any exposure to its interior reality, in the first—and last—moment when it might seem perfect. From a closer vantage, its perfection could seem less than obvious; upon entry, it might seem hardly perfect at all. Quite the contrary. Those towers, so dramatic and gleaming from a distance, could block the sun and crowd the street with their bulk. Easily comprehended at arm's length, from close up they could be overwhelming or disorienting. From within these dark, dense, hemmed-in streets, the city could seem less an enchanted vision than a mountainous wilderness, teeming with threat.

From this daunting reality, however, one ready escape remains—if only for a few. Even from below we can see that high in the sky, in the city's upper reaches, the world opens up again, the air is clear, the place again seems manageable. Of course, getting there will not be easy. Every force in the world will conspire to stop us from making our way to the top of those tall towers, in an exalted display of individual determination and strength. This, of course, is precisely the premise of the double fantasy known as *King Kong* (1933).

A great ape, called Kong, is king of Skull Island, somewhere in the South Pacific. He makes his throne on a mountaintop, the island's highest point, keeping the other island dwellers at bay. The terrified natives have built a wall to protect themselves; they can do him no harm. Monstrous creatures attack him from time to time, but he beats them off to remain king.

Then one day he is captured by American adventurers armed with gas bombs, and brought against his will to *our* island: the smoky, dark stone and steel jungle that is the New York of the Great Depression. Enslaved for show, he rampages, breaks out of a Broadway theater and makes his way, amid riotous, panicked crowds, down Sixth Avenue, whose elevated train he destroys. His goal is the highest point on *this* island, a manmade mountain called the Empire State Building. By dawn's light he climbs the tower and eventually reaches its pinnacle, high in the air. As they did on Skull Island, threatening forces try to bring him down, but where fearsome dinosaurs failed, a wing of biplanes with .50-calibre machine guns succeeds, riddling him with wave after wave of bullets. Helpless against the aerial attack, he is wounded, swoons, and topples a thousand feet onto the rushing traffic of West 34th Street. His rise to the top was illusory, short-lived. In the end, the city has defeated him (69, 70).

Here is the skyline at its most elemental, as a kind of primeval mountain range. The great tower of the Empire State is shown in near silhouette, its specificity and architectural detail suppressed: it is meant to seem archetypal, almost organic. The city itself is reduced to topographic essentials: streets as canyons, skyscrapers as peaks, the waterfront as island's edge. With its use of the Empire State Building, barely two years old when the film was made and still the marvel of the world, the film held claim to representing the most advanced technology of its time. It is here, the film seemed to say, at the very core of the modern world, that powerful forces and pressures, little changed since prehistoric times, still govern our actions. In this vision, New York has gone further than anyplace else—further, that is, back in the direction of the jungle.

One of the most powerful visions of the movie city ever created, *King Kong* grew largely from the mind of one man: Merian C. Cooper, aviator, adventurer, and filmmaker, best known for his celebrated wildlife movies of large and dangerous animals, shot on location in distant parts of the world. Back in New York in the late 1920s, Cooper wandered the streets, hatching a new idea: a film about a giant gorilla, three or four times the size of any real one, discovered on a remote Pacific island. But he could not imagine a suitably spectacular climax—what he liked to call, in reference to the 1925 epic *Ben-Hur*, a "chariot race." Late one afternoon in February 1930, as he stepped out of his midtown office, Cooper heard the sound of an aircraft engine, and glanced up just as the setting sun glistened off the wings of a plane flying near the New York Life Insurance Building, one of the city's tallest. "Without any conscious effort of thought," he said,

> *I immediately saw in my mind's eye a giant gorilla on top of the building, and I thought to myself, if I can get the gorilla logically on top of the mightiest building in the world and then have him shot down by the most modern of weapons, the airplane, then no matter how great he was in size, that gorilla was doomed by civilization. And I remember saying aloud to myself, "Well, if that isn't a chariot race, I don't know what is."*

As Cooper's fantastic concept moved toward production, the site of the climactic ascent kept changing, keeping pace with the city's dizzying upward growth. In late 1930, the 1,077-foot Chrysler Building became tallest in the world, and thereby replaced the New York Life tower as Kong's destination. But the city kept on building, and by the time the film's actual production began in 1931 the Empire State had topped out at 1,250 feet. The locale of the climax was shifted again, this time for good.

It was Cooper's inspiration to link the two jungle islands so closely and cleverly. Seen from the deck of the ship, Skull Island's blazing bonfires and chanting natives prompt one sailor to remark, "It looks like election night." (Later, a woman in the theater where Kong is to appear wonders what it is they are about to see. "I hear it's a kind of giant gorilla," her companion replies—just as a man rushing to his seat steps rudely on her toe. "Gee," she sighs, "ain't we got enough of them in New York?") Cooper was also careful to establish the motivation for Kong's climb by showing us his elevated lair atop Skull Island. The sweeping view includes the island receding away below, the natives' wall, even the American ship at anchor in the distance. It is indeed a perch fit for a king and prepares us for Kong's later, still more spectacular ascent.

71. View of the Shelton Hotel, 1924. Designed by Arthur Loomis Harmon, later a partner of the architects of the Empire State Building, the Shelton—shown in a rendering by Hugh Ferriss—was among the first buildings to be shaped by the new setback zoning law of 1916. "There is, in the building itself," Ferriss wrote, "something reminiscent of a mountain. Many people choose it as a residence, or frequent its upper terraces, because—known or unknown to them—it evokes that undefinable sense of satisfaction which man ever finds on the slope of the pyramid or the mountainside."

To a large degree, Cooper's provocative parallel could work only because of the specific turn that the design of Manhattan's skyscrapers had taken the decade before. Since the early 1920s, New York's towers had been consciously shaped as stepped, mountain-like masses, with wide, solid bases that narrowed as they rose, soaring high and free until they reached their peaks, which were invariably capped with a spire or pinnacle of some kind. It was a shape generated by the city's 1916 zoning law, as depicted in an evocative series of drawings of skyscrapers real and imagined by Hugh Ferriss (71). The very narrowness of their upper office floors—by law no larger than one-quarter the area of the overall building site—made many of them economically questionable; tall buildings made at least as much sense as gestures of prestige, and even romance, as they did as practical real estate, which is why in part they served so well as a model for the Emerald City.

Their shape was essential to Kong's epic story as well. The canyon-like streets created by their blocky bases established the dense atmosphere of crowds and traffic that seemed to Kong—no less than to us—so jungle-like and oppressive compared to the airy tops above. These towers not only *were* taller but *seemed* taller than earlier skyscrapers—with their sculptural setbacks and soaring shafts they visibly converted their height into movement, appearing to thrust upward with visible force, thinning as they rose, peaking into narrow perches at their tops. "One could well believe," a European observer wrote, "that giants had built this city for giants." In the largest sense, New York's skyscrapers seemed designed not for human beings—the relatively minuscule creatures who filled the buildings' interiors and required mechanical devices to reach their upper floors—but for some sort of new race who might activate the towers' overscaled form in a way that ordinary humans could not. Such was the perfect rightness of Kong. He was the first of a series of fantastic characters, found only in the dream city and possessed of powers beyond those of ordinary men, who could release the latent possibilities of these structures in a way unavailable to the city's everyday inhabitants. In his climb from the dense streets below to the airy sky above, Kong brought to life the aspiration of the building itself—and not just the Empire State, but (as the preproduction shift from one tower to another had demonstrated) an entire city of man-made peaks. Unforgettably, King Kong revealed the essential impulse motivating the skyscraper city: to strive upward and, by dint of superhuman effort, touch the sky. That Kong could succeed for only a moment serves to remind us how fragile—and ultimately tragic—such aspiration can be (72).

72. Cut footage from *King Kong* (1933). This dramatic view of Kong falling down the side of the Empire State Building was not included in the release print of the film, probably because of an evident problem with the matte process: a portion of the sidewalk in the background is plainly visible through Kong's body.

Intuitively, Cooper understood it was the street-level density created by the blocky bases of these buildings—as much as the stepped-back towers themselves—that helped to propel the ascent. He dropped an early notion to have Kong exhibited in Yankee Stadium; though at first glance a promising possibility, Cooper somehow realized it would dilute the sense of tightness and urban compression that sends Kong skyward; he set the scene instead in a crowded theater just off Times Square.

As it happened, the very elements that so perfectly suited Cooper and his giant ape would cause these towers to be rejected by the postwar generation of modern architects. The setback shape and perchlike peaks were deemed romantic, irrational gestures; worse still were the crowded streets created by the wide bases of these prewar buildings. But the answer was at hand. Smoothing their new buildings into sheer, boxy slabs; giving them flat, sheared-off tops instead of spires or pinnacles; and setting them on broad, plazalike open spaces would convert the old, thickly carved city into an airy, enlightened landscape. We need not speculate on how the mighty Kong would have reacted to this rationalized city; we have explicit evidence in the 1976 remake of *King Kong*, produced by Dino De Laurentiis.

From the start, the new *Kong* failed to establish Cooper's imaginative parallel between Manhattan and Skull Island: it begins not on the New York waterfront, but aboard an oil-exploration vessel off Indonesia. And no sooner has the film reached New York than it commits the crucial error that Cooper wisely avoided: it exhibits Kong in a stadium, whose wide open space instantly destroys any sense of crowding or oppression that might motivate a thousand-foot climb. In fact, the entire city that this Kong passes through is virtually deserted, having been conveniently "evacuated." Nothing could be farther from the first film's feeling of intense, panicky compression as Kong moved through the crowded city streets. Palpably devoid of urban excitement, the updated "adventure" comes to its dreary climax when Kong finally reaches the twin towers of the World Trade Center. These buildings had, of course, supplanted the Empire State as tallest in the world (only to be supplanted themselves by Chicago's Sears Tower), and thus formed the likeliest Manhattan site for the new Kong's climactic climb. But what an uninspiring sight greets the big ape upon his arrival! The cold, empty plaza at the base of the towers—thin, desolate, vast—actually dwarfs the creature, intended to seem so ferociously large. Worse still, it offers no motivation at all for his formidable ascent. Where are the madding crowds and canyonlike streets that might propel him to the airier, more kingly precincts above? What lonely grandeur will he achieve up there that he cannot find below?

When Kong actually does start climbing (if only to fulfill expectations established forty-three years before), the sheer, unbroken shape of the World Trade Center's tower makes his effort seem almost absurd. The sight of the original Kong rising up the side of the Empire State, for all its spirit of fantasy, struck a deeply plausible note: the building's stepped-back shape was, at heart, made for ascent—if not by humans, then by something like a three-story ape. But in place of the Empire State's mountainlike, masonry surface, Kong now faces a smooth, metal-sheathed slab, unbroken from top to bottom, endlessly vertical. After watching Kong's attempt to somehow shimmy up this thousand-foot pole, we face a sight no less silly at its top. In the original film, Kong clung precariously to the Empire State's mooring mast, a narrow, vertiginous perch piercing the clouds and sky, where one false step meant doom. The flat tops of the twin towers, by contrast, offer nothing to grab on to—almost nothing to do at all, in fact, except jump from one tower to another, which the great creature inevitably proceeds to do. Atop the second identically large, flat surface, he is forced to stand like a dummy while helicopter gunships open fire. Some effort has to be made, in fact, to ensure that Kong actually falls over the side, rather than simply plops down on this football field of a roof. (In the original film, by contrast, it felt like a sheer act of will, a scary balancing act, for Kong to remain on his narrow roost, reaching out in vain at the circling planes.)

But fall he does, to a final indignity. The huge plaza below swallows up Kong's body and again makes him seem almost puny; the crowd that has gathered for this most remarkable of sights scarcely fills half the space. Kong's body sits like the centerpiece of a party whose guests mill about aimlessly; how different from the original film's rushing crowds and traffic on 34th Street, the dead Kong interrupting the massive urban superflux with his even more massive presence! Even in death, the original implied, Kong belonged up in the sky, not among the thick crowds below from whom he sought so hard to escape. In this last shot of the remake, on the other hand, neither "Beauty" nor aerial gunships seem to have done in the Beast so much as the cool, rational planning of postwar architecture.

Neither the Empire State Building nor the World Trade Center, needless to say, were designed to have a giant ape climb their sides; both were simply large commercial structures, filled with rentable office space. But there is something revealing in the way that the shape of the Empire State lent itself to the film—in fact, in some ineffable way, *became* itself, found its essential identity—through the story of King Kong. The shape of the Trade Center, in contrast, fought the story all the way. The producers of the remake turned inevitably to the World Trade Center as the tallest building in New York, but the Trade Center itself seemed to have forgotten *why* it was tallest. The whole significance of height, its power to impress in more than an abstract, statistical sense—number of stories, distance from sidewalk to roof—had been lost in the interim. The placement of an open plaza at the base of the buildings, meanwhile, removed the extremes of density (at their bottom) and openness (at their top) that gave the old towers their drama, making them, in Vincent Scully's words, "not salubrious but sublime." It was hardly surprising that New York's newer office buildings offered so little to the fantasies of the movie city—or to fantasies of any sort.

The mismatch emerged all over again when another legendary figure made his feature film debut, a year or so later. Like the producers of the second *King Kong*, the makers of *Superman: The Movie* (1978) wanted to set their film in the present and to shoot it on location in the real city. But a problem immediately presented itself: the soaring skyscrapers of Superman's 1930s "Metropolis" had long since been elbowed out by the glass boxes of postwar Manhattan. Their solution was to turn to a surviving icon of Superman's original era—the Daily News Building, a classic 1930 tower by the architects Raymond Hood and John Mead Howells—to provide the headquarters of the *Daily Planet*, employer of Superman's alter ego, reporter Clark Kent. Of course, using the venerable structure in a film set within the contemporary postwar city suggested a certain confusion about what era the movie was meant to be in. In fact, just about the time of the film's production, the first critical reconsideration of New York's Art Deco skyscrapers was getting under way, and the film served as a timely reminder of their values: not only their distinctive look, but their excitement about the possibilities of building tall, a true exhilaration about "skyscraping" that was markedly absent from later, boxier structures. Yet at the same time the film marked its distance from that world: by the late 1970s, the Daily News tower was no longer one of New York's higher buildings, a monolith rising from the rest of the city, but had become something of an exquisite jewel, wedged between taller and blander structures. Whatever else it was, the Daily Planet was never meant to be *quaint*.

In fact, the film transcended anachronism only when its main character arrived to reassert the essential timelessness of the skyline. Like Kong, Superman's special powers allowed him to activate the spatial possibilities of the skyscraper city as mere humans could not. Unlike the giant ape, however, Superman had no need to climb its tall buildings; he could soar among them effortlessly, and it is a sequence in which he does just this, with Lois Lane on his arm, that offers one of the film's few lyrical moments. Lois lives (perhaps somewhat handsomely for a working reporter) in a penthouse apartment with a lushly planted terrace overlooking Manhattan, and it is by way of this terrace that Superman pays her a visit one evening, quietly gliding in over the parapet—a gentleman caller who communes directly with the city's upper strata, without need of crude mechanical aids such as elevators or staircases. Accepting his offer of a "tour," Lois is carried off on a dreamy night ride around the towers of lower Manhattan, sailing across the bay, around the Statue of Liberty, up into the clouds and then back down to the peak of the Empire State Building, before returning to her terrace as gently and effortlessly as she was lifted off. At some fundamental level, romantic instead of tragic, the potential of New York's skyline is perfectly fulfilled by this unlikely citizen. For what is a penthouse

73. ***Batman*** **(1989).** Gotham City's night skyline was actually a scenic painting more than sixty feet wide, enhanced by three-dimensional miniature elements such as a twenty-foot-long bridge (with red and white "tracer" lights simulating two-way traffic) and tugboats crossing a river of black plastic. A veil of smoke blown across the painting completed the effect by simulating a soft, distant focus.

terrace, ultimately, if not a platform from which to be launched on a magical journey above the city? What is the skyline itself, for that matter, if not the ideal setting for a magical figure who can fly in and around its towers? In his very being, Superman embodies the skyward leap that is, in some sense, the essence of the city itself.

When, a decade later, a fellow superhero made *his* first major appearance in a feature, the filmmakers made a crucial decision that allowed them to avoid the temporal confusion that had dogged *Superman*. The city to be defended in *Batman* (1989) completely turned its back on postwar New York; it was a studio fabrication, built not a continent to the west but an ocean to the east of the real place. At Pinewood Studios, on the northern outskirts of London, *Batman*'s Gotham City took shape through an ambitious blending of thirty-four stage sets, extensive matte paintings and miniatures, and a five-block-long exterior street (73). Where *Superman* had mixed sets with location shooting in New York, *Batman* avoided location work entirely to create a unified, otherworldly setting unburdened by the real city's changes over time. "It is neither 1939 nor 1989," Robert S. Sennett has noted, "but just an ordinary day in Gotham City."

74. Filming *Batman* (1989). To create convincing views of Gotham City, *Batman*'s production team (under visual-effects supervisor Derek Meddings) used the process known as "motion control," in which the camera's movement is tracked and controlled by a computer, allowing it to make repeated, identical "passes" through an extended sequence of moves and turns. In the scenes of the Batplane swooping down on the city during the Joker's "parade," the composite metropolis we see is actually a product of motion control, through which the city's skyscrapers and giant balloons (built in miniature), its street-level crowds (filmed full-scale, with real people), and its darkly glowing sky and clouds (a matte painting)—each shot in a separate pass of the camera—could be superimposed onto the same piece of film. In this view, a motion-control camera climbs the side of one of Gotham City's hundred-story buildings, rendered at 1⁄32 scale in a miniature that stood thirty feet high.

As designed by Anton Furst, Gotham's interiors and details suggest a knowing blend of styles and sources, from Art Nouveau Barcelona, to Secessionist Vienna, to contemporary Tokyo. But in its largest gestures Gotham City clearly looks to prewar Manhattan, to the same kind of setting as that of Kong's original rampage: a city of complexly massed skyscrapers, defining relatively narrow streets below, then rising with terraces and setbacks, catwalk bridges, and ornamental ledges into the night sky above (74). As an urban vision it is even darker, literally and figuratively, than Kong's Depression New York: the streets narrower and more threatening, the buildings less elegant and shapely—a thickly layered, ominous landscape, aptly suited for a character far closer to the dark spirit of Kong than the wholesome rectitude of Superman.

This gesture toward the prewar skyscraper city underscored another similarity between Batman and Kong. Unlike Superman, Batman has no transcendent, dreamlike power to float over the skyline; he must physically exert himself in order to move around the city's higher reaches. To be sure, he has a host of extraordinary resources at his disposal, those "marvelous toys" that the evil Joker (Jack Nicholson) so admires, including a set of ingenious grappling hooks and lines, as well as a level of physical strength far beyond that of most men. But the hooks and lines must tie into something, and for all his stamina Batman must be able to find places on which to stand and maneuver. Batman could not function in a city of sheer glass towers, for what would his hooks tie into, and how would he scale their sides? Introduced, like Superman, in the late 1930s, he is even more a product of the prewar city, denizen of its distinctive stepped landscape of setbacks, bridges, ledges, and cornices. The mythic city had again called forth a character of magical powers to activate its architecture, a being whose resources of agility and strength allowed him to take full advantage of its possibilities.

From our first view of the shadowy figure atop a high terrace, observing two criminals below, Batman's command of the city's height is evident. He swoops down on the malefactors, using the skyline's stepped verticality in a way they cannot. Later, we see him travel the other way: trapped in an alley, he shoots a grappling hook to a catwalk overhead, and lifts himself and photographer Vicki Vale (Kim Basinger) to safety. Like Kong's, his ascent to the heights of the city is physical work; like Kong, he looks beyond the dark crowded streets to the city's upper reaches to find his natural home. The film's climax, in fact, hinges on the notion that it is he, not the Joker, who rightfully belongs at the top of the city. At film's end the Joker lies dead on the sidewalk, people and police crowding him as they did Kong; Batman, on the other hand, is making a final, liberating ascent. He has given Gotham City a signal with which to contact him should evil forces reassert themselves: a searchlight that shines the special bat symbol upon the night sky. From below, the city's mayor and citizens—including Vicki—look up through the canyons and see its reassuring glow. Starting from the street, the camera climbs the sides of Gotham's towers. Bridges, terraces, and exposed steel bracing pass by and still we move upward. Finally, we reach the skyline's top: there stands Batman, protector of the city, on his rightful perch high above the fray, transcended only by the evanescent light that plays upon the clouds and sky (75). Humans like ourselves may have built the skyline, but it belongs, finally, to another kind of being, one who can animate it as we cannot—a figure who, like the skyline itself, resides closer to the air above than to the ground from which we come and to which we must return.

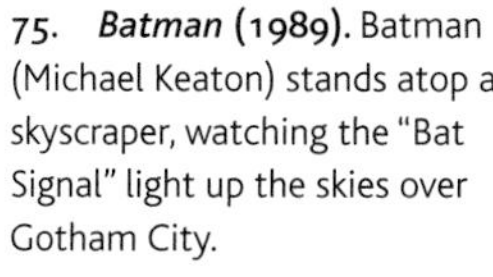

75. ***Batman*** **(1989).** Batman (Michael Keaton) stands atop a skyscraper, watching the "Bat Signal" light up the skies over Gotham City.

A TOWN OF THE FUTURE

> When we were twenty, we heard about the skyscrapers. We discovered them with amazement in the movies. They were the architecture of the future, just as cinema was the art of the future. . . .
>
> JEAN-PAUL SARTRE

The skyline of New York has long offered another powerful sensation: a sense of the future. It has seemed to transport viewers across time, offering a vision of worlds to come.

With good reason. For more than a century, the skyline has in fact been immensely "futuristic," and not only in its technologically advanced construction—the steel framing, high-speed elevators, and complex mechanical systems that were essential to its very existence. The sophisticated organizational skill that brought the skyscrapers into being was itself a potent symbol of the awesome and sometimes frightening scale of the modern world. The intricately choreographed coordination of hundreds of trades, thousands of workers, and millions of structural components that allowed these towers to rise in just months portended more than simply a new type of building; it suggested nothing less than a new shape to society. New York's skyline, many felt, pointed the way toward where all places would eventually go.

76. ***Metropolis*** **(1926).** The film's futuristic high-rise city was inspired by director Fritz Lang's first glimpse of Manhattan, two years before, from a liner moored at a Hudson River pier.

At several junctures, the movie city completed the equation, responding to the skyline's daring architectural vision with a fully rendered new world, filled with people and stories, that might project New York—seemingly so close—completely into the future.

This was precisely the origin of the first and most memorable of futuristic New Yorks, born in October 1924 when the celebrated German director Fritz Lang arrived in the city on the *Deutschland*, en route to California to study Hollywood production techniques. Still cautious about German nationals entering the country, American officials classified Lang as an "enemy alien" and detained him overnight. It was a night that would change the movies, and the city.

From the deck of the ship, moored to Hamburg-Amerika's Hudson River pier, Lang stared for hours at the city he could not enter. Beyond the railing, he saw

> *a street lit as if in full daylight by neon lights and topping them oversized luminous advertisements moving, turning, flashing on and off, spiraling. . . . The buildings seemed to be a vertical veil, shimmering, almost weightless, a luxurious cloth hung from the night sky to dazzle, distract and hypnotize. At night the city did not give an impression of being alive; it lived as illusions lived. [It was] something which was completely new and nearly fairy-tale-like for a European in those days, and this impression gave me the first thought for a town of the future.*

"I looked into the street," he said, "the glaring lights and the tall buildings—and there I conceived *Metropolis.*"

Immediately upon his return, he began work on his new film, directing a large crew at the UFA studio outside Berlin (77). Lang and his team were allowed to develop their setting with a painstaking care almost unknown in Hollywood, spending 310 days and sixty nights building and filming their city of tomorrow. His gifted designers constructed a series of enormous miniatures that brilliantly exploited forced perspective to suggest a convincing urban grandeur, while the special-effects master Eugen Shüfftan pioneered a technique of combining glass paintings and live action that became the industry standard. People seeing the film upon its completion in 1926 could well believe that here indeed was the future, just a step or two ahead of New York.

The idea behind Lang's future city (developed with his wife, the screenwriter Thea von Harbou) was at once provocative and overwrought: a glittering cosmopolis that rested atop a second, subterranean complex, plunged in a grim twilight, where oppressed masses toiled unceasingly to support the cloudlike city above. Lang had recognized something insightful about the skyscrapers of New York: they were the tip of an iceberg, the attractive white-collar pinnacle of an enormous and far less attractive blue-collar pyramid. In real life, the dark, oppressive underworld that supported these towers was to be found not so much in their basements as in grimy industrial towns across the United States, where ten- and twelve-hour days of toil sustained the extravagance of a Chrysler Building or a Rockefeller Center. In the end, the film's absurdly melodramatic story muddled any serious point about class conflict. Yet if it was hard to take seriously the shrieking characters and contrived plot, it was also hard to forget the dazzling "metropolis" Lang and his team brought so convincingly to life.

77. Building the *Metropolis* miniature, 1925. To construct their invented "metropolis," the art directors Erich Kettelhut, Otto Huente, and Karl Vollbrecht created a miniature street more than twenty feet long from wood, plaster, and canvas, in which cars, trains, airplanes, and elevators were set into motion through painstaking stop-motion animation, shot one frame at a time.

Unlike the future city envisioned by virtually all of the modernist architects and planners of the era, Lang's creation was no verdant, low-density setting but an intensely urban place. Though its buildings had a distinctly "modern" look, his city did not suggest that the values of light, air, and greenery would supplant the qualities of energy, movement, and density that were the trademarks of twentieth-century New York. Instead of spreading itself over a field of open space, this city focused its energy along avenues that for all their height were essentially traditional streets—well-defined volumes of space, shaped by buildings on either side. If anything, Lang's "metropolis" extended that energy upward—through sky-high bridges and walkways, through multilevel paths for trains and automobiles, through oversized signs and lights and, finally, through futuristic airplanes that flew between the towers. This was something new: a city whose movement and activity were washed across its entire vertical surface, top to bottom, rather than mostly along its sidewalks and street fronts. Here, for Lang, were the true possibilities for the future city—not less energy and motion but more, and now spread everywhere (76).

This was especially true in the film's nighttime scenes, which gave new form to the "shimmering veil" Lang had first glimpsed in the New York night (78). The bright, busy streets, combined with oversize signs and glittering bridges, create a glow that reverses daylight—rising up from the sidewalk, bathing the buildings' facades from below, and turning the entire street into a pulsing, dazzling river of light.

"Without roofs, crowned by terraces," the French essayist Paul Morand wrote after glimpsing Manhattan in 1925, "it seems to be waiting for airships, helicopters, men of the future with wings." If part invention, Lang's visionary metropolis was also an interpretation of the actual 1920s city. Its main daytime vista, for all the futuristic trappings, looked not unlike Broad Street in lower Manhattan: a curved path extruded twenty stories by solid walls of skyscrapers. Its glowing nighttime boulevard was an evident reworking of a pre-neon Times Square, set aglow by millions of incandescent bulbs. Lang's metropolis reasserted the notion that New York, with a few additional elements, could become the city of the future. It was almost there.

78. Night view from *Metropolis* (1926).

Metropolis also contained a specific lesson for the movie city. Coming in 1926, when American filmmakers were still in the habit of using the real city as a backdrop, the film dramatically demonstrated the potential of a movie city fabricated entirely within the studio. Lang and his team of Germans had showed Americans the filmic possibilities of their own greatest metropolis—possibilities they had never imagined.

The Americans were not slow to respond, especially after *Metropolis* proved a huge success. Film producers at Fox reasoned that a film set in a futuristic city—but without all that ponderous intellectual baggage—might prove an even bigger hit, especially if coupled with a lively musical score by the songwriters DeSylva-Brown-Henderson. The result was *Just Imagine*, a 1930 musical comedy about a contemporary man who is struck by lightning and revives in the New York of the distant future: 1980!

79. *Just Imagine* (1930). Designed by the Fox art director Stephen Goosson and the miniature supervisor Ralph Hammeras, *Just Imagine*'s fantastic vision of New York in 1980 was constructed by 205 craftsmen over a period of five months, at a cost (in 1930 dollars) of $257,000—far more than any Hollywood special effect before it. Measuring an impressive ninety feet by two hundred fifty feet in size, the miniature city—built to a scale of a quarter-inch to the foot—included skyscrapers two hundred stories tall, standing over forty feet high.

In purely cinematic terms, *Just Imagine* is a prime example of what Arlene Croce has called the "period of almost savage incompetence" in movie musicals before *42nd Street*. At interminable length, the revived man (played by an obscure Swedish dialect comic named El Brendel) helps a pilot named "J21" (John Garrick) convince a marriage tribunal to award him the hand of "LN18" (Maureen O'Sullivan) by flying to Mars and back. Frequent references to the Volstead Act and bizarre song-and-dance numbers punctuate the tedious, sometimes incomprehensible plot.

The film's futuristic New York, however, remains a stunning creation (79). Of all the major Hollywood studios, the Fox lot (at the time still personally run by its founder, William Fox) most resembled the relaxed, artistic atmosphere

of a European studio like UFA. The film's producers allowed the art director Stephen Goosson and the miniature supervisor Ralph Hammeras all of the time and money they needed to make a spectacular city of tomorrow, allowing them to set up shop in a vast dirigible hangar on a former army airfield in Arcadia, twenty miles from Hollywood. As a feat of miniature construction, the result outdid even *Metropolis*, but because it was not built with the "forced perspective" technique to create a convincing illusion of depth, *Just Imagine*'s New York looked far less realistic on-screen than the German-designed city. And its use in the completed film was so brief and desultory that it hardly seemed to justify the great effort and expense of construction. It seems to have existed almost for its own sake, a glimpse of a possible future appearing for a few months in a disused airfield near Los Angeles.

80. ***General View of a City Square*, Harvey Wiley Corbett, circa 1927 (top). *City of the Future*, Antonio Sant'Elia, 1914 (above).** *Just Imagine*'s futuristic vision was influenced by the designs of Harvey Wiley Corbett, a New York architect who proposed to separate the city's traffic onto different levels—fast-moving vehicles moving along lowered roadways while pedestrians strolled about on walkways linked by suspension bridges. The influence of Antonio Sant'Elia, a leading member of the Italian Futurist movement, could also be felt in the wide avenues and below-grade railroad tracks, flanked by mid-rise structures and widely separated towers.

But what a vision took shape out in that hangar! Hammeras and Goosson conceived their city as a series of broad avenues, arranged in a rectilinear grid not unlike Manhattan's. But the "blocks" between these avenues are filled with long, stepped buildings from which, at well-spaced intervals, great towers rise, two hundred stories tall. Suspension bridges link the towers, while pedestrian walkways, graced by arcades and lights, run along the setbacks of the lower structures. Some avenues are reserved for traffic—twenty-four lanes of cars flanking a central rail line—while others contain parks and gardens laid out in formal, French-style parterres (11). Like Lang's *Metropolis*, the city includes personal airplanes that fly between the towers—their movement overseen by an aerial traffic cop, shouting commands in a thick Irish brogue.

The designers drew inspiration from a number of sources: from the proposals of the New York architect Harvey Wiley Corbett, from the visionary drawings of the Italian Futurist Antonio Sant'Elia, and especially from the work of the architectural delineator Hugh Ferriss, whose book *Metropolis of Tomorrow*, published the same year as the miniature's design, reiterated the vision of widely spaced towers rising from lower buildings, all linked by multilevel walkways and bridges (80). The interconnected structures, the separation of traffic onto different levels, and the greenery-filled avenues might suggest a kind of modern "superblock" planning, and it is true that the city's traditional grid of streets and blocks has been replaced here by something else. But as in *Metropolis*, the spirit of that substitution is very different from the antiurban superblocks proposed by the 1920s European modernists. *Just Imagine*'s New York is still a place that channels activity into boulevard-like spaces that are defined on either side by buildings. It still uses the street as its generating concept, and achieves not so much a "superblock" as a "superstreet": the linear life of the city laid up in parallel layers and carried up the sides of its buildings—

something entirely different from the diffuse field of space the modernists were proposing.

In fact, the arrangement of these streets and towers draws upon—and calls attention to—one of the most remarkable achievements of New York's twentieth-century urbanism. At their bases, the city's prewar skyscrapers work to shape volumes of urban space, their walls combining sociably with their neighbors to define well-formed streets. As the buildings rise, however, the relationship of mass and space reverses: instead of shaping space, they now pierce the air as sculptural masses. Well-behaved, collegial makers of streets at bottom, these towers become adventurous, solitary explorers of space at top—a superb solution to making a city of towers at once audacious and gregarious.

Goosson and Hammeras achieved something else: managing to imbue their giant construction with a sense of festivity and even delicacy. Their city looks like *fun.* Thousands of small bulbs (a total of fifteen thousand, according to one account) create continuous "necklaces" of light, adding an undeniable sparkle to the structures while also providing a sense of people *living* in this city—each lamp standing for an individual promenading up and down the multilevel paths.

No less than Lang's metropolis, this vision of tomorrow—for all its futuristic flourishes—emerged directly from the real city. Where *Metropolis* seems inspired by lower Manhattan, with its angular streets and closely packed towers, *Just Imagine*'s city suggests midtown, its layout of buildings and avenues more regular and widely spaced. The result is a more relaxed, less disconcerting urbanism; here is a smoothly functioning megalopolis, aggrandized from the existing city, and bathed in a spirit of friendly utopianism.

In his provocative book *Delirious New York,* Rem Koolhaas attempts to trace the origins of New York's skyscrapers in the fanciful towers of turn-of-the-century Coney Island. If the lineage is actually more remote than he suggests, perhaps the New York of *Just Imagine* can be considered a kind of missing link. In it, the festive gaiety of Luna Park and Dreamland has been recast on a truly urban scale, serving all the needs of modern life—an alternative urban vision, still capable of teaching us lessons about the city we know.

Of course, given the age of *Metropolis* and *Just Imagine,* it might be tempting to consider the whole idea of a futuristic New York an historic artifact—a relic of the early decades of the twentieth century, when, as the first and (except for Chicago) *only* skyscraper city on the planet, New York could suggest the future in a way almost unimaginable in today's world. But seventy years after the release of those films—when, for better or worse, the distant future they daringly projected had basically come and gone—a memorable new vision of the city appeared in a film called *The Fifth Element* (1997), a futuristic New York that was as visually stunning and, in its way, as imaginatively provocative as any earlier images.

It is a revealing exercise, indeed, to compare *Fifth Element*'s city with that of

Just Imagine and *Metropolis.* The three have much in common—not surprisingly, perhaps, since the latter-day effort was intended, at least in part, as a tongue-in-cheek homage to its predecessors. Like *Metropolis* it offered a distinctly European vision of New York, a dream of the city's future as imagined from a distance: conceived first by the French director Luc Besson during his teenage days at a boarding school outside of Paris, then refined and developed more than a decade later by an international team of comic artists and illustrators—including Jean "Moebius" Girard and Jean-Claude Mézières—during a year-long series of design meetings in Paris. The result, articulated in eight thousand concept drawings, was a dense, elaborate "backstory" that, although never explicitly described in the film itself, provided a logical—if farfetched—foundation for its creators' vision of the future. By the year 2259, according to Besson's scenario, the vast amount of water needed to "terraform" nearby planets into resorts has caused Earth's sea level to plunge over three hundred feet, transforming New York into a kind of promontory-like settlement, perched above drained riverbeds whose steep banks have been developed with additional tiers of buildings (81). The bottom of the bay, left dry by the receding seas, has been largely filled in with housing and a bustling spaceport, while Manhattan's towers now routinely rise two hundred stories. In the endless search for still more habitable space, municipal builders have tunneled *downward* another four hundred stories, turning New York into a city of no fewer than six hundred levels, in which today's streets and sidewalks have become elevated promenades, high in the air.

This is the city in which a superpowered, skimpily clad young woman named Leeloo (Milla Jovovich)—just minutes after being brought to life in a "nucleolab"—escapes her confinement, racing into a ventilation duct and break-

81. ***The Fifth Element*** (1997). Seen only briefly in the film, this digital matte painting by Kevin Mack and Wayne Hang—based on production art by the French illustrator Jean-Claude Mézières—shows a vista of New York and its surroundings in the year 2259, when, according to the film's "backstory," dropping sea levels have left the city virtually landlocked.

ing through an exterior exhaust grille, only to find herself clinging precariously to a narrow building ledge, several hundred stories high. Alongside her runs an "avenue" that is, in fact, an almost endless canyon: high, deep, and filled with traffic—*aerial* traffic, that is—thousands of fast-moving flying cars, taxis, and buses, whipping up and down the thoroughfare and across side-streets as far above and below as the eye can see. Leeloo is (not surprisingly) dazed and terrified by the spectacle, but the audience is as likely to be amused as dazzled, for anyone can see that, however wild and extravagant this vision of the future, it plainly is New York—indeed, seems somehow *more* New York than the city of today, a place in which the energizing madness and near chaos of Manhattan's surface traffic has been extended in literally every direction. In retrospect, it seems obvious that if New York ever were to be built up in multiple levels (as all three films implied), its traffic would look far more like this than the occasional personal airplane and orderly, well-modulated movement on aerial bridges predicted by *Metropolis* and *Just Imagine* (82).

The amazing spatial dynamics of such a place, of course, cannot possibly be fully experienced from a stationary point of view; we must go with the flow, as it were—which we now proceed to do. With the police closing in, Leeloo avoids capture the only way she can: by leaping off the narrow ledge and plummeting several floors before crashing through the roof of a flying yellow cab driven by Korben Dallas (Bruce Willis), a hard-bitten South Brooklynite who is also, conveniently enough, an ex-fighter ace. Korben's piloting skills quickly come in handy as he attempts to elude the police "flying units" (which, painted the familiar blue-and-white of New York's actual 1990s patrol cars, elicit the same hokey topical pleasure as the floating Irish cop in *Just Imagine*) by careening around the city's giant multidimensional grid. (Korben finally manages

82. ***The Fifth Element*** (1997). Created by the visual-effects group Digital Domain under the supervisor Mark Stetson, the futuristic city shown in *The Fifth Element* relied heavily on the technique of computerized "motion control" to marry views of an elaborate miniature of the city with digitally generated moving objects, such as pedestrians and flying vehicles. Below, a flying yellow cab, piloted by Korben Dallas (Bruce Willis), prepares to descend several hundred levels beneath Times Square—whose distinctive triangular shape can be seen at top.

to elude the cops, in fact, by suddenly plunging hundreds of levels *down*, much against the flow of traffic, to the foggy subterranean depths of the city—which, if not quite the grim workers' quarters of *Metropolis*, are certainly bleak enough.)

The chase is frenetic, exhilarating, and richly suggestive. Since the start of the twentieth century, two distinct kinds of movement—evident in Manhattan as nowhere else—have encouraged observers to see New York as the very embodiment of the modern world. The more obvious of the two was visible on the surface, in the rush of vehicular traffic along the grid of streets and avenues: the endless flow of movement along what a mathematician might call the city's X and Y axes. The second—less obvious as a literal movement than as a direction of thrust—took place in the Z axis, perpendicular to the other two, as year after year, soaring towers were raised straight up into the sky, far higher and more daring than any before. ("Americans have practically added a new dimension to space," a British journalist wrote in 1899, "when they find themselves a little crowded, they simply tilt a street on end, and call it a skyscraper.") For a century or more, the restless horizontal rush of its traffic and the dramatic upward thrust of its skyscrapers have not only combined to give New York its distinctive look and feel, but have become a kind of metaphor for two elemental components of its character: the fast-moving, fast-talking culture of its streets, and the daring, ambitious, aspirational impulse of its towers. While obviously different, they are both linked by a constant, unquenchable sense of *drive* that to many people seems to make visible, more directly than anywhere else, the dynamic, ever-changing quality of contemporary life. In lifting the city's streets into the air with bridges, flying cars, and elevated walkways, *Just Imagine* and *Metropolis* had hinted of a future in which these two kinds of movement, previously linked only in the mind's eye, might be physically joined. But it took the New York of *The Fifth Element* to give the idea full and hilariously literal expression, in which the vertical thrust of the city's skyscrapers is brought to life by delirious vehicular movement, while the surface grid of traffic has itself been replicated up and down in layer after endless layer. The result is a three-dimensional matrix of pure dynamism, a unique combination of movement and mass, order and disorder, sky-high engineering genius and down-to-earth "street smarts" that locates in New York's dedication to movement—to special *kinds* of movement available nowhere else—its continuing power as an icon of the future.

SPOOK CENTRAL

A city is, properly speaking, even more poetic than a countryside, for while Nature is a chaos of unconscious forces, a city is a chaos of conscious ones. The crest of a flower or the pattern of a lichen may or may not be significant symbols. But there is

> no stone in the street and nor brick in the wall that is not actually a deliberate symbol—a message from some man, as much as if it were a telegram or a postcard. The narrowest street possesses, in every crook and twist of its intentions, the soul of the man who built it, perhaps long in his grave. Anything which tends . . . even under fantastic form . . . to assert this romance of detail in civilization, to emphasize this unfathomly human character in flints and tiles, is a good thing.
>
> G. K. CHESTERTON

For over a century, it has been common to denounce tall buildings as "inhuman," and to criticize them for disconnecting people from more traditional ways of life. But it was the special quality of New York, where the tall building first *became* a way of life, to insert a surprisingly resonant sense of history into the fabric of its high-rise buildings. Sometimes scarcely visible from the street, New York's upper reaches offered a whole landscape of ornament, statuary, and structures—temples, obelisks, pyramids—that evoked other times and places, the remnants of earlier cultures. Often enough these elements fulfilled some practical purpose—enclosing a rooftop water tank or equipment bulkhead, for instance, or providing a parapet required by the building code. Yet their cumulative effect outstripped any mere utilitarian value. Together, they provided the city with a kind of narrative richness, transforming its skyline into a "storied" place, permeating the supposedly inhuman urban landscape with a rich layer of human intentionality.

Needless to say, this impulse to veil the most technologically modern of structures in a patina of imagined history was actively despised by postwar architects—who swiftly eliminated the practice. Yet it remained a source of satisfaction to many New Yorkers, who seemed to enjoy the rich contradictions of a skyline that looked forward and back in time, all at once. In 1984, an exuberant fantasy would confirm this sense in the most obvious way: by literally extracting its plot from one of the implicit narrative layers inscribed in the skyline.

From the start, the writers of *Ghostbusters*, Dan Aykroyd and Harold Ramis, were anxious to avoid the conventional "haunted house on the hill" setting of traditional ghost stories. They turned instead to contemporary Manhattan, recognizing that many of the city's buildings (including some of its most familiar) offered half-hidden architectural elements that might plausibly frame a tale of supernatural events. Nowhere were these elements more abundant, it turned out, than atop the city's skyscrapers.

The film does not start high in the sky, just high enough. A few feet above Fifth Avenue, it introduces the theme of hidden meanings through one of New York's best-known landmarks. We see the ornate frieze of the New York Public Library, gleaming in the sun, its allegorical statues—just who are they, anyway?—set between carved inscriptions recounting the institution's origins, half-forgotten history, frozen in stone. Suddenly, a giant animal head fills the screen. It is ominous, even frightening—until we realize that it is just one of the library's celebrated lions, those marble figures by E. C. Potter that are among the most beloved public sculptures in the city. From this slightly elevated vantage point—eye to eye, so to speak—what has always looked familiar and inviting seems strange and scary. If this is what a second glance brings out in one of New York's best-known icons, what might be lurking higher up?

We find out soon enough. A long shot shows us the skyline of Central Park West, rising above the dark mass of greenery. One apartment house, front and center, is quite striking, at once familiar and strange. It rises well above its neighbors, in a ziggurat that seems to carry the avenue's Art Deco traditions to excess, with tier after tier of setbacks and terraces. And it culminates in a windowless, templelike structure, complete with ornamental brazier, that presumably encloses the building's water tank—another instance of grand architecture disguising a utilitarian element (83, 84).

We get an even better look in the next scene, shot from the roof itself. On the street far below, a Checker cab drops off a passenger. But up here the scene

83. Production design drawing from *Ghostbusters* (1984). For the film's major setting, the production designer John De Cuir adapted a real apartment house at 55 Central Park West (designed in 1930 by Schwartz & Gross) by adding several stories and a new roof. This drawing by Michelle Moen was the basis for several matte paintings by Matthew Yuricich seen in the film.

84. **Building the rooftop set for *Ghostbusters* (1984).** For the film's climactic battle atop 55 Central Park West, a set of "Gozer's Temple" was built full-scale at Warner's Burbank studio. The sixty-foot-tall structure was surrounded by a four-hundred-foot-long cyclorama, whose night skyline was brought to life by 7,500 "mushroom" globes of three hundred watts each, used to light the windows of nearby buildings, as well as thousands of tiny Christmas bulbs, by re-creating the lampposts of Central Park.

is dominated by an ominous gargoyle, a perfect example of the overscaled sculptural elements that so often go unnoticed in New York's skyline. Dana Barrett (Sigourney Weaver), the innocent taxi passenger, certainly doesn't notice it, even though her corner apartment happens to sit right beneath the strange rooftop figure. If anything, it is the kind of ornamental flourish she takes for granted as part of her building's historic "charm." This being the film city, however, Dana's life will soon change quite drastically, thanks to these forgotten architectural effigies. Eggs begin to fry themselves on her kitchen counter, while inside her refrigerator a monster is calling out for someone named "Zuul." Who ya gonna call?

Responding from their TriBeCa firehouse, the Ghostbusters (played by Aykroyd and Ramis themselves, along with Bill Murray and Ernie Hudson) are quick to recognize that Dana's apartment house might be the source of trouble. Aykroyd suggests they "check out the structural details. . . . Maybe the building itself has a history of psychic turbulence." Indeed, as supernatural events increase around town, the Ghostbusters come to realize that the strange rooftop on Central Park West is somehow at the center of it all. Its blueprints reveal a framework of "cold-riveted girders, with cores of pure selenium," Ackroyd declares excitedly. "I guess they just don't make 'em like they used to, huh?" wonders Bill Murray, perplexed by this talk of old-time construction standards. "*No,*" Aykroyd explains, "nobody *ever* made them like this." The building, he announces, is actually a "superconductive antenna that was designed and built expressly for the purpose of pulling in and concentrating spiritual turbulence." Dana, he concludes ruefully, "lives in the corner penthouse of Spook Central."

The discussion soon turns to the past, and the forgotten history enshrined in the building's design: a secret society founded in the 1920s by the structure's architect, Ivo Shandor, whose bizarre rooftop rituals were intended to bring about "the end of the world." But the exposition is interrupted by an urgent call from the mayor; it is time to bust some ghosts.

And so they do, in a fight to the finish atop the roof, whose elaborate, temple-like structure turns out to serve not as a water-tank enclosure but, of all things, a temple. Within it, the Ghostbusters find an enormous staircase, the cosmic portal for the evil "Gozer," an ancient Sumerian god whom, with some difficulty, they manage to dispatch back into a hole in the sky. The rooftop is more or less destroyed, but the city is saved (263).

For generations, New York's builders had embellished their towers with richly symbolic elements, aspiring to transcend functional reality with a hint of something grander, more ancient, more poetic. They worked, in effect, in the hope that a water tank enclosed to look like a Greek or Assyrian temple might someday be imagined, however fancifully, as the earthly dwelling of a god or goddess, rather than simply a component of a building's mechanical system. It was an impulse easy to mock or dismiss—as indeed it was by the city's postwar architects, who chose to enclose *their* water tanks with bare brick boxes. But it had the effect of weaving not just a sense of the past, but a whole texture of human intentionality into the stones of the city, all the more evocative for being partly obscure. It was the special gift of *Ghostbusters* to meet those earnest efforts more than halfway: not only noticing those temples and other symbolic structures, but providing a whole story to go with them—right down to the gods and goddesses. As so often happens in the movie city, the imaginative visions of filmmakers served to activate the latent possibilities of the skyline, encouraging us to look twice at that which we usually take for granted.

In the end, it was striking—if not really surprising—how readily the skyline lent itself to these fantastic visions, finding its natural identity in the most supernatural of circumstances. As Nick Carraway mused in F. Scott Fitzgerald's 1925 novel *The Great Gatsby*, his car rolling across the Queensborough Bridge toward the towers of midtown: "Here, I felt, anything could happen. Anything." No one, not even Fitzgerald himself, could have imagined how literally the movie city would fulfill that promise—not least by placing a three-story gorilla atop the tallest of those towers. Thanks to the skyline's stunningly elastic character, the most impossible situations have come to seem not only possible, but downright likely. And so it is that we laugh knowingly at the very last line in *Ghostbusters*—when, upon surveying the nightmarish wreckage of the epic battle high above the city, Ernie Hudson turns to the glowing skyline in the distance, and declares, at the top of his voice: "I *love* this town!"

FIVE

SOMETHING BIG

SKYSCRAPER AND OFFICE BUILDING

SOMETHING BIG

> It's a single master mechanism, set so you can tell the time anywhere on earth: London, Chicago, Honolulu.... It also synchronizes the clocks in this building with those in secondary printing plants in Kansas City and San Francisco and in the forty-three foreign bureaus of the Janoth organization.
>
> TOUR GUIDE IN *THE BIG CLOCK*

85. (previous page) ***The Hudsucker Proxy* (1994).** In this view, set inside the top-floor boardroom of the forty-seven-story headquarters of Hudsucker Industries, executive Sidney Mussburger (Paul Newman) stands silhouetted in a picture window, through which the peaks of nearby downtown towers seem to float mysteriously.

Moving in closer, shifting our focus from the ensemble of the skyline to the individual office towers that comprise it, we soon depart the realms of fantasy to confront a very different reality. For Manhattan's skyscrapers were not only the playground of superheroes, of course, but giant beehives of business: headquarters of global corporations, central offices for far-flung plants and facilities, the focal points of vast commercial energies. Their lines of communication and authority spread to the ends of the planet; with utter confidence, their builders considered them to be the very center of the modern world. No sooner have we entered their doors, in fact, than we are presented with symbolic renditions of the earth itself: an enormous translucent globe in the 1937 lobby of *Top of the Town*'s "Radio Center" (86), for example, or a futuristic, two-story-tall chronometer, ringed by a map of the world and its twenty-four time zones, which sits in the lobby of the Manhattan headquarters of Janoth Publications, a Time-Life-type media empire that is the setting of the 1948 film *The Big Clock.* As a tour guide explains to his group, the clock's complex mechanism does not simply *keep* time but actually regulates activity throughout Janoth's global domain. The symbolism is obvious, of course: the towering device stands for the skyscraper headquarters just as the skyscraper itself stands for New York—the ultimate "big clock," constantly pacing the world and tracking its progress.

These symbolic elements also suggest something else: that the skyscraper holds an entire world within itself—a complex microcosm of society whose trajectory is drawn from the shape of the building. In the movie city, we regularly follow characters on their "way up," locating in the tower's upward thrust a model for other, less visible kinds of movement. Rarely has this parallel been presented more bluntly (or amusingly) than in a racy 1933 film called *Baby Face:* the audience follows the career of an ambitious newcomer named Lily Powers (Barbara Stanwyck) by tracking her physical rise within the offices of the "Gotham Trust." After Lily gets her first job by seducing the manager of the personnel department, the saucy strains of "St. Louis Blues" start to play as the camera pulls out of the forty-seventh-floor window, rises two stories to the filing department, and returns inside. Here Lily meets another supervisor and makes another conquest. "St. Louis Blues" plays again, and again the camera pulls out the window, rising this time to the mortgage department, on fifty-one. And so on, through the accounting and executive offices, until finally Lily has reached the very top of the building—the penthouse of the bank's handsome young chairman, George Brent.

86. Art department sketch from *Top of the Town* (1937). Designed by John Harkrider, *Top of the Town* takes place atop the "Radio Center" in midtown, the world's tallest building. His design for the lobby was evidently inspired by that of Raymond Hood and John Mead Howells's Daily News Building (1930), which features a large globe, from which radiates a star-like pattern of lines showing the direction and distance to cities all around the world.

However unorthodox her technique, Lily at least works her way up one step at a time, her gradual ascent precisely calibrated by the building's tier upon tier of windows. Yet in the classic skyscraper era, lavish architectural efforts were expended precisely to circumvent this sort of plodding, floor-by-floor rise; instead, the exteriors of skyscrapers sought to suggest a single, daring leap, an express track to the sky that would mask the unglamorous stacking of floors within. It is just this disjunction—between interior and exterior, between a hardworking climb and a swift, dizzying leap—that frames Joel and Ethan Coen's parodic exploration of the classic New York skyscraper, *The Hudsucker Proxy* (1994).

It is 1958, and at the center of a mythic Wall Street skyline rises the headquarters of Hudsucker Industries, an imposing Depression-era tower whose exterior design—like those of the actual Manhattan buildings it is based on—seeks to sweep the eye in an unbroken line from bottom to top (2, 87).

And it is precisely at those two extremes that the story begins. At the foot of the building, Norville Barnes (Tim Robbins), a bumbling but ambitious newcomer from Muncie, Indiana, is arriving for his first day on the job, ready and eager to work his way up. At the top, meanwhile, the man who *built* the building—and the immense corporation within it—has chosen that very moment to make a dramatic move in the opposite direction, leaping out of the forty-fifth-floor boardroom window and plunging to his death. Cinematically elongated in

time and space, the fall of corporation chairman Waring Hudsucker (Charles Durning) feels not scary or tragic but oddly exhilarating, as we sail right alongside the plummeting figure, the vertical lines of the building's sleek exterior racing beneath us like railroad track, the camera angled, for much of the distance, *up* the length of the soaring tower—as if to recall, even at this most terrible of moments, its original ascendant promise.

Indeed, within hours, the hapless Norville is making that very ascent—at a rate only slightly less impressive than Hudsucker's fall—when he is elevated from a lowly position in the building's inferno-like mailroom to its airy executive offices, not through any hard work or intelligence on his part, but as the unknowing patsy—or "proxy"—of a boardroom scheme to depress stock values and buy up the company at a bargain. That these executive offices, for all their imposing size and high polish, may have grown a bit *too* detached from the world below is powerfully conveyed by a shot of Hudsucker's successor, Sidney Mussburger (Paul Newman), silhouetted in the high boardroom windows. Not only Mussburger—the cynical, grasping executive who has instigated Norville's rise—but Wall Street's towers themselves are reflected in the mirror-smooth boardroom table so as to appear to float weightlessly, utterly disengaged from everything else (85). But there is far more to the skyscraper than this airy, detached realm at its top, as we discover when Norville pulls an idea out of his pocket—a crude pencil sketch of something that turns out to be the hula hoop—and, indulged by Mussburger, is allowed to carry the idea through to execution. In a succession of rapid shots that, among them, manage to spoof almost every New York office movie ever made (from *The Apartment* to *The Crowd* to *The Big Clock* itself), we tour the divisions that fill the length of the Hudsucker Building: the design department, the advertising department, the accounting department—even a proving lab where Norville's innocent invention is submitted to explosive testing. But all of Norville's good intentions are no match in the end for Mussburger's evil designs, and the film's climax finds the young man in the sad position of Hudsucker himself—standing outside the forty-fifth-floor window, contemplating a fatal plunge. "You had a short climb up, kid," Mussburger gloats, "but it's a long way down." For all its layers of irony, *The Hudsucker Proxy* ultimately takes us on a surprisingly full and complete tour of the New York skyscraper, inside and out, revealing along the way the profound disjunction between the reality of its interior, whose stratified hierarchy of office floors might well take a lifetime to surmount, and

87. Constructing the miniature New York skyline for *The Hudsucker Proxy* (1994). One of the most ambitious New York miniatures ever built, this $250,000 construction contained thirty-three individual structures that were so tall—even at 1/24 scale—that they were constructed sideways to allow cameras to move readily up and down their facades (2). Framed in wood and covered with an easily cut plastic called Sintra, the buildings were detailed with cast ornamental elements and air-brushed stone coursing and "weathered" with a dusting of lacquer and streaks of acetone.

the seductive (if potentially treacherous) promise of its exterior—that the entire length of the building might be negotiated, one way or the other, in a single, breathtaking leap.

If some New York skyscrapers seemed to hold a symbolic world within themselves, others contained the makings of a real city. With working populations in the tens of thousands and activities that ranged from shops and offices to restaurants, broadcasting studios, athletic clubs, and private apartments, these great structures often carried the complexity of a good-sized community. Perhaps no film captured more fully the notion of the skyscraper as a city unto itself, nor more powerfully intertwined personal ambition and high-rise form, than *Skyscraper Souls*, a 1932 film that takes us into just such a city-within-the-city: the Dwight Building, tallest in the world. In this filmic New York, the fevered skyscraper race of the late 1920s, won in reality by the Empire State Building, has produced another, even higher tower, just a few blocks away. Released just a year after the Empire State's completion and scarcely two after the stock market crash, *Skyscraper Souls* captures the era's intense fascination with tall buildings, the combination of awe and apprehension they evoked as symbols of heroic achievement and frenzied speculation.

New York's towers are commonly regarded as supreme *corporate* monuments, the jewels in the crowns of giant national conglomerates. But the more surprising truth, as the historian Carol Willis has pointed out, is that even the most corporate-sounding of skyscrapers—the RCA or Chrysler Buildings, for example—were actually developed as *speculative* ventures, built not by corporations, but by individuals or groups of financiers, as rental propositions.

The Dwight Building is no exception. It may be the world's tallest structure, but it is also a real-estate deal writ in steel and stone, the handiwork of an ambitious, unscrupulous financier named David Dwight. As president of Seacoast National Bank, Dwight has quietly parlayed his depositors' money into his dream tower. With a $30-million loan now coming due, more financial manipulation will be necessary if Dwight is to hold on to what he has made. He can easily obtain the money if he agrees to turn control of the building over to his investors. But Dwight is not interested: "This is a case," he says, "of 'love me, love my building.' " As played by the suave Warren William, David Dwight embodies the complex mix of ego, greed, and idealism that raised the New York skyline.

During the film, we explore the length of Dwight's building via the complexly interwoven stories of the people who inhabit it. This in turn reveals a second surprise, related to the first, and no less rooted in reality: most skyscrapers were filled not by a single large company, but with an intricate cross-section of small- and medium-sized firms. In *Skyscraper Souls*, we meet a young bank teller who works in Seacoast's main branch, off the lobby; a garment manufacturer and his fashion models in a thirty-fourth-floor showroom; a jeweler on a still higher floor; and the employees in the Office of the Building (including Dwight's long-time secretary and devoted mistress Sarah, played by Verree Teasdale, and a young, very innocent assistant, Lynn, played by Maureen O'Sullivan).

Above it all is David Dwight himself. In nearly every way, the hard-driving financier uses the building to extend his reach—for money, power, sex—until the structure becomes indistinguishable from his personality. It is where his bank collects the thousands of deposits to sustain his financial schemes. It is where he maintains his personal apartment (on the top floor, accessible only by private elevator), the site of lavish soirees designed to entertain powerful businessmen, seduce beautiful women, or both. (As the film proceeds he drops Sarah and starts to work on young Lynn.) One financial titan is wooed up and down the building, from a dinner party in the penthouse to a workout in the basement athletic club. Between steambath, swim, and massage, the man is softened up. "Marvelous building you have here, Dave," he says admiringly. "It has everything." "Have you tried the restaurant on the seventy-fifth floor?" Dwight asks solicitously. "No, but I'll work up to it," the other man answers, clearly won over by the fullness of Dwight's realm, and happy to take part in a merger that will save Dwight's financial neck.

Yet soon Dwight is double-crossing this new partner (along with his own investors) through a stock manipulation contrived with an even bigger financier named Hamilton; if successful, it will allow Dwight to take full possession of the building. The demon of rampant speculation is let loose as thousands of ordinary people rush to buy the merged bank's skyrocketing stock on margin (we witness the melee at a broker's office, located, of course, on yet another floor of the Dwight tower), only to be destroyed when its value is intentionally deflected downward. Dwight's investors are utterly ruined. So are the young teller and the garment-maker. The jeweler, a more cautious man, is merely set back a decade.

Though the particular linkage of the skyscraper's financing to a general stock frenzy was a device of this screenplay, it played upon a widely recognized connection. Only a few years before, during the great boom of the late 1920s, a dozen towers in downtown and midtown Manhattan had sprung into the sky within a matter of months, each taller than the one before, as if tracing against the sky itself the market's dizzying rise. Indeed, their rapid rise was subject to the same vicious circle that was pushing stock prices themselves to giddy heights. "[As] land prices rose," Willis has noted, "towers grew steadily taller. Or should the order be: as skyscrapers grew taller, land prices rose?" When it was over, the city skyline had been dramatically transformed by these new structures, shaped by an intense speculative fever that, with the crash in late 1929, broke almost overnight.

Yet the buildings themselves stood—the Empire State and Chrysler Buildings, the needle-like spires of lower Manhattan—permanent additions to the city's topography, already assuming their enduring place as perhaps the most distinctively "New York" buildings ever produced. It is a fascinating paradox.

How and why did these towers, built in a frenzied moment, the very emblems of paper prosperity and the fast dollar, turn out to be some of the city's most stylish and well-made buildings, the very essence of its imaginative spirit?

One answer is that for New York skyscrapers, the term "speculative" carried no implications of the second-rate. "Creating a distinctive image is as important for speculative developers as for corporate owners," Willis has written, "and they use precisely the same strategies to do so, including height, prime locations, and rich materials." It simply made financial sense to build these towers well, with fine detailing and stylish architecture that transcended the frantic upward rush their cresting forms seemed to crystallize.

But another answer is suggested by the film itself, back in the Office of the Building. Dwight's underhanded ploy may have destroyed the lives and fortunes of thousands, but it has allowed him to buy the building outright, and his triumph knows no bounds. He tries to explain it all to Hamilton:

DWIGHT: *They laughed when I said I wanted a hundred-story building. They said it wouldn't hold together. But I had the courage, the vision, and it's* mine, *and I own it! It goes halfway to hell, and right up to heaven, and it's beautiful!*

HAMILTON: *I'll admit it's an achievement . . .*

DWIGHT: *You bet it is. I've achieved something big, something worthwhile. Feel it, under! It's solid! Even the fiercest storm can't budge it. It bends, but it won't break—and it stands here,* defiant! *Hamilton, did you ever stop to think? A million men sweated to build it. Mines, quarries, factories, forests! Men gave their lives to it. . . . I'd hate to tell you how many men dropped off the girders while they were going up. But it was worth it! Nothing's created without pain and suffering—a child that's born, a cause that's won, a building that's built! Say, you don't know what I'm talking about, do you?*

HAMILTON: *Sounds kind of crazy to me.*

Crazy indeed. David Dwight embodies the mix of base and lofty instincts—"halfway to hell, and right up to heaven"—that defines the skyscraper, that monument to greed and power that is also a heady vision of aspiration and achievement. During the course of the film, we see Dwight cheat everyone—partners, employees, lovers—without hesitation. He is utterly and blatantly dishonest, except about one thing: his building. The Dwight tower is not, as one rival claims, a monument to his ego. It *is* his ego.

Final proof, if needed, comes with the film's conclusion. Up in his apartment, Dwight is confronted by his discarded mistress, Sarah, now desperate to save the innocent Lynn from a similar fate. Realizing that nothing can dissuade Dwight from pursuing the younger girl, Sarah pulls out a gun and fires at him at point-blank range. Dwight slumps into his chair, dying. But a mention of the building manages to revive him, and with great effort, he raises himself and shakes his fist in the air. "The building . . . it's a great building," he rambles, just before collapsing one last time. "It's mine . . . I own it . . . a beautiful building." So it wasn't an act; he really did love the Dwight tower—as a part of himself, or something of which he was a part.

Dwight is dead, but the Dwight Building lives, the extension of his will. If she can no longer be his victim, Sarah will become the next best thing—a victim of his building. Utterly distraught, she staggers to the terrace, climbs up to the ledge, and jumps. Pointing straight down, the camera follows her falling body until it seems no bigger, in the classic phrase, than an ant, a potent reminder of the scale of this monument over that of a single, ordinary human being. The instrument of her death is the very height that was Dwight's pride.

The film offers a knowing denouement, sometime later. An elegant middle-aged woman, played by Hedda Hopper, emerges from the ground-floor bank branch, trailed by lawyers. "That's Mrs. Dwight," a guard comments to Lynn. "She's selling the Dwight Building." "Yes," Lynn answers, "it's funny, isn't it?" The great tower, the monument into which an extraordinary man poured his heart and soul, the special product of a special moment in history, is now simply another property to be bought and sold, one piece of the larger skyline, to be viewed by new generations who will never know the confluence of complex, sometimes dark energies that raised it to the sky.

CONFLICT OF FORMS

An ambulance races through the city's streets, rushing the legendary modern architect Henry Cameron (Henry Hull) to the hospital. Inside, the great man is flat on his back, close to death, hardly able to speak—the ideal opportunity, apparently, for him to deliver a lengthy disquisition on the buildings he sees through the ambulance window.

"Skyscrapers," he proclaims, as his protégé Howard Roark (Gary Cooper) draws close, "the greatest structural invention of man! Yet they made them look like Greek temples, Gothic cathedrals, and mongrels of every ancient style they could borrow. I told them that the form of a building was to follow its function! That new materials demand new forms! That one building can't borrow pieces of another's shape, just as one man can't borrow another's soul!"

Catching sight of a modernist apartment house (actually 240 Central Park South), Cameron brightens briefly. "That's one of *my* buildings," he says, before relapsing. If not exactly supernatural, it is indeed a strange world we have entered—the fervid, peculiarly airless precincts of the film called *The Fountainhead.*

Directed by King Vidor and released by Warner's in 1949, *The Fountainhead* closely follows the themes of the best-selling Ayn Rand novel on which it is based—not surprisingly, since Rand herself wrote the screenplay. Most everyone knows the story. Howard Roark, a brilliant modern architect, struggles to build his bold designs in a compromising world. Rival architect Peter Keating (Kent Smith) is a timid, conventional designer who produces neoclassical skyscrapers and at first meets with great success. But when his career stalls, he implores Roark to design a housing project called Cortlandt Homes and let it be submitted under Keating's name. Roark agrees, knowing that no project bearing his own signature would be accepted. When Roark's radical design is grotesquely compromised during construction, he dynamites the structures, reaping widespread public fury. But Roark wins his trial and is vindicated; by film's end he is building the tallest skyscraper in the world.

Intense (and sometimes comically surreal) subplots of passion and ambition embroider the film, but at heart Rand sought to present a parable of ideas, using the battle of architectural modernism against the older eclectic tradition to exemplify her philosophical belief in the value of the individual versus the collective. The year of the film's release, 1949, was propitious: the first modern, glass-walled skyscraper, the United Nations Secretariat building, was just coming out of the ground, soon to be followed by the first steel-and-glass commercial office building, Lever House. New York's skyline was about to receive its first taste of the new International Style.

It was a dramatic change. For generations, New York's skyscraper architects had pursued their own distinctive course as they raised up the world's first and most famous skyline. For them, the skyscraper's internal steel frame was a means rather than an end, something to be freely manipulated wherever necessary to provide a suitable armature for the picturesque exterior effects they sought to achieve. They readily used spires, pinnacles, and complex setbacks to shape their towers into "artistic" compositions, then clad these structures with ornamented masonry facades that first drew from classical and Gothic-inspired styles and then, with the coming of Art Deco in the 1920s, explored their own decorative motifs.

The design of the new postwar skyscrapers, by contrast, proceeded from entirely different principles. For modernist architects, the steel frame beneath the building's skin was not just the enabler of its height but the prime generator of its form. No longer would the steel frame be elaborately shaped to fit the building's exterior; now that exterior would take the form most naturally suggested by the frame itself: simple, repetitive, boxlike. Nor would buildings be clad in masonry, or covered with any kind of applied decoration. Now, sheer flat panels of glass and metal would fill in the frame's openings, allowing the internal grid of columns and beams to become visible on the facade of the building—at least symbolically. (Fire codes generally disallowed the exposed use of actual structural elements.) The building's structure would *become* its decoration.

As Cameron's soliloquy might suggest, *The Fountainhead* took sides without

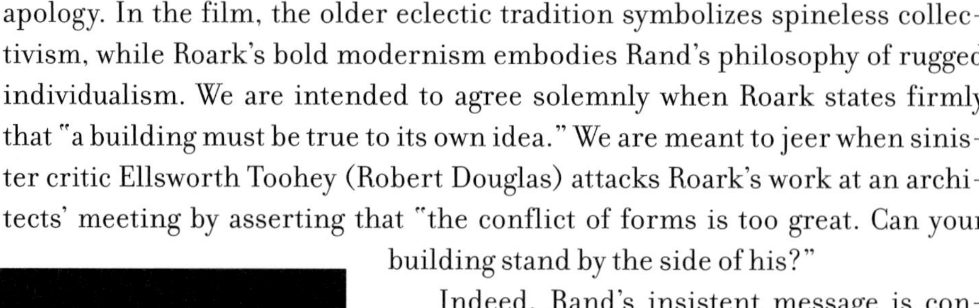

apology. In the film, the older eclectic tradition symbolizes spineless collectivism, while Roark's bold modernism embodies Rand's philosophy of rugged individualism. We are intended to agree solemnly when Roark states firmly that "a building must be true to its own idea." We are meant to jeer when sinister critic Ellsworth Toohey (Robert Douglas) attacks Roark's work at an architects' meeting by asserting that "the conflict of forms is too great. Can your building stand by the side of his?"

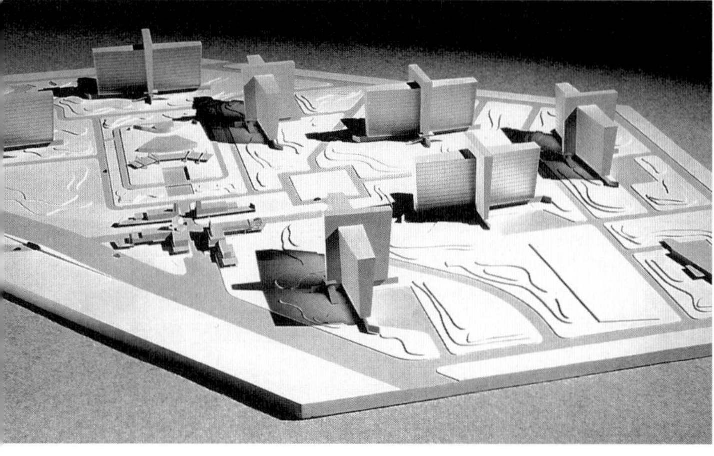

88. Model of Cortlandt Homes from *The Fountainhead* (1949). According to one story, the producers initially asked Frank Lloyd Wright (upon whom the character of the architect Howard Roark had been partly based) to prepare designs for use in the film. When Wright demanded a fee of $250,000 and final approval of the film's sets (and its casting, costumes, and script, as well), Warner's turned back to its own art department, which, under Edward Carrere, designed projects such as Cortlandt Homes, a "tower-in-the-park" housing development that reflected the work of modernists such as Le Corbusier.

Indeed, Rand's insistent message is conveyed not only by the dialogue, but through the film's representations of its competing architects' work. Under the direction of Edward Carrere, the Warner's art department drew up numerous examples of both Roark and Keating's "projects," allowing audiences not only to hear of their relative merits but also actually to see for themselves. We see a model of the modern slab Roark has designed for a New York bank, and stand over the array of widely spaced slabs he has proposed for Cortlandt Homes (88). We also review several renderings of Keating's office buildings, presented by the cynical Ellsworth Toohey (89). The art department did its work well: we instantly grasp the intended distinction between Keating's pallid, overrefined classicism, stretched somewhat absurdly across the face of thirty-story buildings, and the daringly elegant Modernism of Roark's designs. Between these loaded examples and the film's tendentious dialogue (painting everyone except Roark as incompetent, weak, or downright evil) it might be easy to get swept away by Rand's polemic. But in almost every scene, another message keeps intruding, utterly contradicting the rest of the film.

Rand's novel had been set in New York, but in the film the city becomes an active, dominating presence through sweeping skyline views, placed behind almost every one of the movie's interiors. These views are made available to the audience through enormous walls of glass, each one bigger than the last, each allowing in a different part of the skyline—Park Row, Fifth Avenue, or, in one case, a startling composite view that joins midtown *and* downtown Manhattan. The thinnest possible metal mullions, often stretching from floor to ceiling, frame these vivid cityscapes (90).

A moment's reflection reveals something odd about these dramatic window-walls. Nearly all are in buildings that were *not designed by Roark*—buildings that, indeed, predate his rise. Isn't this strange? Shouldn't we have merely glimpsed the skyline through conventional, smallish windows, until we saw it spread out, spectacularly, in the first of Roark's daring modern interiors? Yet every room in the film, the entire "world" in which Roark exists, seems already to have this light and airy architecture in place.

In fact, another priority was at work. The big windows have one overriding purpose: to make the skyline of New York a powerful, near-constant force throughout the film. By allowing the skyline to frame, quite literally, the film's debate about architecture, the filmmakers were likely answering a concern voiced aloud in the movie itself when—in response to the notion that a Roark project might make a good subject for a tabloid exposé—a harried city desk editor wails, "Oh, who cares about a *building*?" Warner's executives may well have had a similar fear, that the popular audience would not easily connect with the film's "highbrow" debate about architectural styles: Hollywood movies, after all, are hardly known for drawing their story lines from obscure aesthetic controversies.

If architecture was an esoteric topic, however, the New York skyline was not. Film audiences everywhere knew it, connected with it—in no small part, of course, thanks to the movies themselves. So the presence of the skyline in almost every frame of *The Fountainhead* was likely prompted by a simple connection. "Pay attention to this debate about architecture," the producers were saying in effect to the audience, "because architecture shapes this skyline that you know so well." The skyline became the popular passport into what might be considered an elitist subject.

But there was a price. The sustained prominence of the skyline, even in the background, worked to subtly subvert the film's intended message. Seen as renderings, one by one, Keating's classical office towers do seem insipid and perhaps ridiculous—the "big marble bromides" that one character calls them.

89. ***The Fountainhead* (1949).** The critic Ellsworth Toohey (Robert Douglas) presents renderings of the architect Peter Keating's skyscrapers to his employer, the press lord Gail Wynand (Raymond Massey)—who brusquely dismisses the neoclassical designs as "great big marble bromides." In the distance, the metal window-wall of Wynand's office frames a panoramic view of lower Manhattan from Park Row, a street near City Hall Park once known as "Newspaper Row" for its concentration of newspaper offices.

But that skyline out there, made up of buildings not at all dissimilar to Keating's, is something else entirely. It is dramatic, exciting, bursting with energy—as no one knew better, obviously, than the filmmakers themselves, who used it shamelessly to capture and hold the public's attention. Roark's modern skyscrapers, meanwhile, undergo a transformation just as profound, but in reverse: while his solitary Manhattan bank tower is convincingly sleek and daring, his plan for the multibuilding Cortlandt Homes appears to be the drab, single-minded work of a dull student. The scheme evinces no notion of a "city" beyond the repetitive placement of identical buildings; it offers no means of varying the mix nor composing the group to achieve any sense of vitality or energy.

We are left with a paradox that has troubled observers of the city for more than half a century—and that still remains largely unanswered. Even the most elegant or dynamic of modern skyscrapers have tended to remain wrapped in a kind of urban solipsism, focused on their own "integrity" at the expense of all else. Obsessed with being "true to their own idea," they speak most signifi-

90 *The Fountainhead* (1949). Ellsworth Toohey (Robert Douglas) and Gail Wynand (Raymond Massey) in Wynand's office, with a spectacular view of downtown Manhattan in the background (including, from left to right, the 1920s towers of Wall Street, the 1915 Equitable Building, and the 1908 Singer Building) provided by a large scenic backing.

cantly to those relatively few observers—critics and historians of architecture, as well as architects themselves—who are inclined to view each skyscraper as an individual work of art, and who, furthermore, consider the skyscraper's status as "the greatest structural invention of man" to be its supremely important *aesthetic* fact, as well. Yet as *The Fountainhead* itself implicitly admits, most everybody else sees things quite differently. The film's high-flown arguments for the skyscraper as a singular work of art, an object whose form is determined first and last by its structure, were entirely undercut by the producers' shrewd and knowing recognition that, in fact, the public was devoted to a skyline built on entirely contrary principles, a skyline in which any single structure was but one piece of something larger, its shape to be freely manipulated to contribute, scenographically, to the overall ensemble. As *The Fountainhead* hinted and we have since come to know too well, now that the boxy progeny of the UN Secretariat and Lever House have spread across New York and every other city in the world, what seemed sleek or dynamic in the individual modern building often became lifeless, anonymous, and dull when repeated even a few times over. By contrast—as *The Fountainhead* made clear almost despite itself—what was perhaps banal or absurd in the single eclectic building could somehow become dramatic and alive when joined with its neighbors. Before our eyes, *The Fountainhead* reasserts the powerful transformation that takes place when the frame of architectural reference shifts from the unit to the group, from the one to the many—a strange and potent alchemy that has proved the puzzlement, and the bane, of the modern city.

ORDINARY POLICY

The widescreen pan that opens *How to Succeed in Business Without Really Trying* (1967) surveys some familiar territory: the prewar skyscrapers of midtown. But it comes to rest not on a slim masonry tower but the wide, modern face of the "Worldwide Widgets Corporation" (actually the Union Carbide Building, designed by Skidmore, Owings & Merrill), whose uniform grid of glass and steel is interrupted only by the maintenance rig of a window washer. More startling still, the camera proceeds to close in *on* that window washer: a minuscule figure, slowly working his way down the building's side, floor by floor.

Things have changed, obviously. Where is Kong now, to make his daring climb? Or Batman, leaping from terrace to terrace? Or even David Dwight, raising his fist to the heavens? This character requires a mechanical device to move across the face of the building, to pursue a goal no more exalted than routine maintenance. He is not even working his way up, but down! Where is the aspiration, the struggle to ascend the lofty spires to the clouds?

All gone, together with the spires themselves. As King Kong discovered when he tried to climb the World Trade Center, the postwar generation of office

91. Reference still from *The Apartment* (1960). By the late 1950s, Manhattan had become the scene of dramatic contrasts between traditional prewar skyscrapers and modern office structures. This shot shows 2 Broadway, a 1959 glass-and-steel office building by the architects Emery Roth & Sons, and its neighbor to the north, the stone-clad headquarters of Standard Oil at 26 Broadway, designed in 1920 by Carrère and Hastings.

buildings—with their boxy shape and flattened tops and abstract, repetitive facades—simply did not lend themselves to any kind of heroic ascent. Surveying the skyline with binoculars from a high office window in *A Thousand Clowns* (1965), Jason Robards confirms as much:

> *Oh, for God's sake, I don't believe it—it's King Kong. He's sitting on top of the Time-Life Building. He seems to be* crying. . . . *Poor gorilla bastard, somebody should have told him they don't make these buildings the way they used to.*

In fact, these newer buildings offered plenty of excitement—just not on the outside. To locate their dramatic center, we must follow that window washer (played by Robert Morse) who, having spotted a conveniently empty office, pulls off his overalls to reveal a business suit underneath, then hops through the window, ready to pursue his corporate destiny within.

We haven't been inside here much. Even though they are the true rationale for any skyscraper, offices were largely ignored in most classic skyline movies. Some films (*King Kong* itself, for instance) never ventured inside at all. Even those that did show a tower's interior usually turned their attention to uncommon spaces, such as the lobby and boardroom in *The Big Clock.* When portrayed at all, ordinary offices were presented in a sketchy, almost notional manner. We might see a few rooms, a secretary typing, someone waiting outside a private office. Solid plaster walls, file cabinets, a desk or two, perhaps a glimpse of a hallway outside. There was rarely anything interesting or memorable about these interiors. Certainly they had little of the style or power of the skyscraper's exterior.

In truth, no great injustice was being done. The classic prewar skyscrapers offered far more excitement outside (and in those special interiors at their tops or bottoms) than in the ordinary offices that filled their core. The slenderness that made these towers so elegant necessitated their smallish office floors, limited in size by the requirement (in those pre–air-conditioning days) to have every desk no more than twenty-eight feet from an operable window, and by zoning laws that restricted the size of the tower's floors to no more than a quarter of the overall building lot. Walls divided the small interiors into even smaller offices, which were then surfaced rather blandly, unlike the exuberant decoration of their exteriors.

But after the war, everything changed. Central air-conditioning, fluorescent lighting, and a new zoning law allowed office floors to become as large as desired—which turned out to be large indeed. Broad interior vistas became common with the advent of "open office" design with its low, flexible partitions. The same wide office floors that caused the building's exterior to balloon from a slender pinnacle to an ungainly box had an additional consequence: creating a vast interior field of space in which to play out a host of stories. The scene suddenly shifted, from the outside in.

It did so without a bump. The philosophy of the postwar International Style encouraged complete consistency between the inside and outside. The modern office building would proudly offer a seamless "package" of style that stretched from the building's exterior, to its lobby and elevators, to the offices above. When we meet Hope Lange at the start of *The Best of Everything* (1959), she is beginning her first day of work for Fabian Publishers. We catch sight of her as she crosses the wide, sunny plaza of nothing less than the Seagram Building, that impeccable exemplar of postwar design, then watch as she glides through the smooth, modern serenity of its lobby. Everything offers a sense of bright, rational possibility, miles removed from the hurrying crowds and Art Deco urgency of earlier skyscrapers.

The same imagery extends all the way upstairs (though we have moved from the real Seagram Building to a studio set at Fox). Lange has arrived a few minutes before nine; the office floor is still empty, offering us an uninterrupted sweep of the place (92). Crisp, rectangular wall panels surround a central open space, filled with desks fronted by still more rectangular panels. Some wall panels are translucent, some transparent, but all offer a kind of glassy lightness utterly different from the solid walls and dark wood partitions of prewar offices. The space plainly shares the same overall imagery that defined the Seagram facade and lobby—a total "look" of tailored rectilinearity that extends from a single cubicle to the entire building. Lange has indeed entered a brave new world.

Every feature of the set is faithful to the International Style as actually built in New York, except one: color. Real postwar offices in Manhattan typically employed a restrained palette of white, beige, and natural wood, set off by the glint of chrome-plated metal. But Hollywood art departments, reveling in the glories of postwar Technicolor and rival film stocks, chose instead to enliven their designs with vivid hues, such as the bright panels of red, blue, and ochre that accent Fabian's offices. In the interiors of *How to Succeed*'s Worldwide Widgets, an even splashier (and less realistic) color scheme prevails. The last word must, however, remain with Kay Thompson, the imperious, Diana Vreeland–like editor in *Funny Face* (1956). As we watch, the modern interiors of "Quality Magazine" are transformed overnight, in strict obedience to her stylistic command: "Think Pink!"

92. ***The Best of Everything* (1959).** Portraying the offices of "Fabian Publishers" in the Seagram Building (to which Caroline Bender, played by Hope Lange, is shown reporting on her first day of work), this Fox stage set by Mark-Lee Kirk and Jack Martin Smith sought to capture the clean lines, simple surfaces, and large expanses of glass that characterized International Style offices in the 1950s.

Of course, the same consistency between interior and exterior, the same complete "look," could easily suggest something more ominous. Even as the voice of C. C. Baxter (Jack Lemmon) blandly narrates an overview of the Consolidated Life Insurance Company at the start of *The Apartment* (1960), the images on screen suggest a darker irony beneath the surface. The home office in Manhattan, he tells us, houses a total of 31,259 employees—more than the population of Natchez, Mississippi. Baxter himself works on the nineteenth floor, in the "Ordinary Policy Department, Premier Accounting Division, Section W, Desk 861." What we *see*, meanwhile, is a high, flat exterior wall with countless windows, a huge modern box that can hold a veritable city—as big as Natchez, surely—within. Every window is identical to all others on its floor, every floor identical to those above and below. We know the nineteenth floor must be in there, somewhere. But where? (91)

The next shot takes us inside the building, to Ordinary Policy—or is it just

93. *The Apartment* (1960). One of the greatest changes to New York's office interiors in the postwar era was the introduction of huge open floor areas. For the work setting of accountant C. C. Baxter (Jack Lemmon), the French art director Alexander Trauner (making one of his few American films) perfectly captured the anonymous character of 1950s offices, with their endless sea of desks framed by an abstract grid of lights and columns.

Section W? As before, the character of the exterior continues seamlessly within. Yet here that character is not stylish but foreboding. The grid of identical desks that fills the sprawling office floor reminds us of nothing so much as the repetitive window grid on the exterior—almost as if the facade had been turned on its side and brought indoors. We can no more locate Baxter's desk amidst this endless sea than we could have found the nineteenth floor amidst the vast matrix of windows outside. Perfection has indeed been achieved, inside and out. Perfect anonymity (93).

The point was hardly new. Thirty-two years before, the director King Vidor had employed the same shot to make the same critique—that giant corporations rob people of their individuality. A dramatic sequence in *The Crowd* (1928) climbs the side of an immense tower and enters one of the windows to find a big room filled with desks within; our hero works somewhere among them. But made in the postwar era, *The Apartment* had a distinct advantage: it had the International Style, whose reliance on abstract, repetitive modules could not help but reinforce the most alienated impression of corporate life. The office in *The Crowd* was simply a large space with lots of desks; the office in *The Apartment*, with its endless grid of ceiling lights and columns, expands the field of desks into an entire universe of repetition. Corporations were already quite big in the 1920s, but the slim massing and rich, individualized ornamentation of their buildings obscured their anonymous nature; the wide, abstract buildings of the postwar International Style, on the other hand, offered a kind of apotheosis of anonymity and alienation—ideal for Billy Wilder's desire to depict a single human soul lost in an ocean of "ordinary policy."

In the coming years, filmmakers would return often to these big modern offices, having noticed something highly attractive about them—at least from a storytelling point of view. Supposedly the last word in abstract, universal space, the modern office floor was actually *filled* with meaning, a kind of full-size map of the organizational hierarchy. An employee's location on the floor conveyed precisely his or her status within the organization; movement around that floor, in turn, made visible the struggle for advancement within an otherwise invisible corporate structure. The modern office floor, it turned out, was a field of play—or of battle.

Seen as terrain, the office floor resembled a series of concentric rings, nestled one into another. The innermost space, the building's core, held only the elevators and mechanical areas and was thus not contested. Surrounding the core was a ring of open floor area—"the bullpen"—given over to junior employees. It is here we would often find our leading characters: ambitious young men and women determined to succeed, sharing the same subordinate status even as their specific tasks and tools changed over time.

In 1960's *The Apartment* the bullpen is home to the dozens of junior accountants like Lemmon's C. C. Baxter, working amidst the roar of mechanical adding machines. In 1959's *The Best of Everything* it is filled with secretaries like Caroline Bender (Hope Lange) clacking away at electric typewriters. In 1988's *Working Girl* it is the domain of "personal assistants" like Tess McGill (Melanie Griffith), the old mechanical sounds replaced now by the pulsing tones and clicks of computer stations. And in 1987's *Wall Street* it is a frenetic trading floor where junior stockbrokers like Bud Fox (Charlie Sheen) make their "cold calls" with one eye cocked to the fast-moving market "zipper" above and another to the Quotron screens below. But in every case it is unmistakably the second tier, the place from which to rise. Open and undivided (except by low partitions), it

94. *Working Girl* (1988). Set in a contemporary skyscraper, *Working Girl* was carefully staged by the director Mike Nichols to reveal the power relationships embedded in the seemingly neutral character of the modern office interior. In this shot, Katherine Parker (Sigourney Weaver) has crossed the aisle that separates her private office (on the building's perimeter) from the desk of her subordinate, Tess McGill (Melanie Griffith), which, located in a central "bullpen," enjoys neither privacy nor genuine views.

is noisy, and lacks privacy. It offers no windows or view, looking out only upon the walls and doors of the floor's third and outermost ring: the private offices reserved for the corporate elite. These offices have actual walls. They are quiet. And occupying the perimeter of each floor, they—and only they—have authentic windows, and real views.

Naturally, everyone wants to achieve this outer ring, to work their way not so much "up" as "out," from center to edge. An arrangement for the illicit use of his apartment wins C. C. Baxter a promotion to a private cubicle, complete with his name on the door, removing him forever from the anonymity of the open desks. Some behind-the-scenes help from financier Gordon Gekko helps Bud Fox move from the trading floor to a private office at its edge. But by far the most emotionally charged—and satisfying—of these floorscape journeys is that of Tess McGill, in *Working Girl.*

Early on, *Working Girl* lingers in the secretaries' bullpen, among the "girls" who share gossip, jokes, and birthday parties and who, on the whole, seem satisfied where they are. Tess is not. She watches admiringly as her new boss, a stylish executive named Katherine Parker (Sigourney Weaver), strides imperiously to and from her private office. Between that office and Tess's desk lies an aisle no more than five feet wide, but to Tess, who dreams of becoming an executive herself, those few feet represent an immeasurable gulf. The offices across that aisle belong to people like Katherine Parker, not to her—at least, not yet (94).

But when a skiing accident keeps Parker away from the office for several weeks, Tess begins to pursue an ingenious business idea she has conceived. One day her partner in the deal, a senior associate from another firm (played by Harrison Ford), pays a surprise visit, propelling Tess, in sudden desperation, to make a quick, unauthorized leap across the aisle, claiming Parker's office as her own. (Another executive, trying to use the office herself, causes a nervous moment when she intrudes on the deception.) In shifting just a few feet, Tess makes the daring decision to inhabit the new identity she has created for herself.

By film's end, Tess—having proved her worth—is starting as an executive trainee at another company. She arrives to find the same layout as always: a woman on the phone in the private office, her own desk just across the aisle. She is setting up at the assistant's desk when the woman emerges from the office and apologizes for using the phone.

WOMAN: *Ms. McGill, that's your desk, in there.*

TESS (confused): *I don't think so.*

WOMAN: *Oh, yes. I sit out here.*

TESS: *I thought the secretary would sit out here.*

WOMAN: *That's right. I'm the secretary.*

Comprehension dawning at last, Tess slowly crosses the aisle—legitimately, this time. In her passage across its narrow width we see her transformed. Our final view of Tess is through her office window—the real window, with its real view, that she risked so much to achieve—allowing us to share the fruits of her victory. The modern office floor, so abstract in appearance, proved anything but, becoming instead the emotionally freighted topography for a series of white-collar struggles—and, occasionally, victories.

HAVE A *POWERFUL* DAY

If the modern office building effectively revealed the *relative* status of its occupants, it failed almost entirely to provide a persuasive image of *absolute* power in the business world. For the most part, films seeking to convey the highest corporate realms turned away from modern offices, instead offering neoclassical interiors that might connect more reliably with the audience's sense of permanence, tradition, and solid extravagance. The International Style, built from the repetition of window and door modules, simply could not awe.

In the mid-1950s, when the modern office building was still new and unfamiliar, it was understandable that a film like *Patterns* (1956) would use the 1915 Equitable Building in downtown Manhattan as the setting for a corporate boardroom struggle. The executive floor's wide, coved-ceilinged hallway could provide the setting for a true battle royal as no modern interior might. The periodic tolling of Trinity Church's bells in the background—evocatively rooting the film in its Wall Street context—sounded fittingly ominous in these baroque quarters; in a modern office their somber tones would seem absurd and out of place.

Yet even by the 1970s, when the postwar office building had become a well-established part of the city, a picture like *Network* (1976) was forced to look elsewhere to convey a sense of *real* power. Most of the film takes place on the floors of a modern network headquarters on Sixth Avenue, and to the concentric hierarchy of the other films it adds an additional twist. Simply having a private office in the outer ring is no longer enough—on which *side* of the building the office is placed, and therefore what it looks out upon, counts heavily in the standings. A young female programming chief (Faye Dunaway), no matter how talented and ambitious, rates only an office on the building's back side, with its motley, midblock view toward Seventh Avenue. She aspires to the office of a corporate executive like Robert Duvall, located in the front and looking out on the great glass slabs along Sixth Avenue that house the rival networks (95).

When the film wants to leap into a celestial realm of corporate power, however, no modern setting will suffice. For a scene in which Ned Beatty, playing the head of the global conglomerate that actually owns the network, darkly warns iconoclastic newsman Peter Finch that he is "tampering with the basic forces of the universe," only the classic trappings of power would serve: an ornately paneled chamber that is actually the boardroom of the New York Public Library. Even as late as 1988's *Working Girl*, the same distinction remains: although a modern corner office signifies Katherine Parker's status as a serious corporate player, the true summit of financial power is represented by the classical marble staircase and dark wood office that, floating a story or two above Wall Street, is the nerve center for the mysterious, all-powerful Trask Enterprises.

But it was just this desire, to project absolute power, that had already begun to change the look of New York's office towers, inside and out. The great room that the persistent trader Bud Fox finally enters in *Wall Street*, the sanctum of Gordon Gekko, is clearly located in a modern office building. Yet it is hardly anonymous: its ceiling has been lifted to double height and its walls layered with marble for an unmistakable impression of wealth and power—even though those marble "walls" (placed within a steel-frame building) can only be a shallow veneer, less than an inch thick.

95. *Network* (1976). Directed by Sidney Lumet from a script by Paddy Chayefsky, *Network* is set within the fictional United Broadcasting Company, whose headquarters (like those of the real CBS, NBC, and ABC) is located in a modern office building on Sixth Avenue. In this scene, a vice-president, Diane Christensen (Faye Dunaway), listens as news director Max Schumacher (William Holden) argues with Frank Hackett (Robert Duvall)—a senior network executive whose office (unlike theirs) looks out onto the imposing glass facades of rival networks across the avenue.

If it was easy to criticize the abstract 1950s office environment as "inhuman," the 1980s office building laid itself open to the opposite charge—of being too nakedly human in its blunt projection of ego and ambition. The old, prosaic rectangular plan disappeared under a wave of willful slashes and diagonals that sought to revive a moribund Modernism through dynamic, angular compositions. The endless grid of windows, so symbolic of the anonymous white-collar masses, was now suppressed into a unified surface of dark glass, projecting a sense of singular executive purpose. The 1950s office buildings so wickedly mocked by Billy Wilder and others came to seem almost innocent in the wake of the ominous dark towers, full of razor-sharp angles, that filled films such as *The Brother from Another Planet* (1984), *The Secret of My Success* (1987), and *The Fisher King* (1991).

So heavy-handed was this attempt to project ego through architecture that it was difficult to take it seriously—at least in the movies. Everyone knew who and what was being satirized in the role of Daniel Clamp (John Glover), builder of the "Clamp Regency Trade Centre and Retail Concourse," in *Gremlins 2: The New Batch* (1990). Every feature of this building, from its pretentious name to its booming public announcements ("Have a *powerful* day," says one; "Mister, welcome to the *Men's* Room," booms another), from its high-tech revolving doors ("The Clamp Entry-Matic") to its atrium lobby of oversized steel trusses and mirrored walls, all suggested the relentless but ultimately unconvincing extension of individual personality in buildings like the Trump Tower. Sheathed in a smooth, featureless skin of black glass (actually 101 Park Avenue, by the architect Elia Attia), the building's diagonal mass draws its shape from Clamp's own office, an acute-angled wedge of space near the top—as if the entire fifty-story structure were simply an extrusion of its owner's triangular executive desk. So great is Clamp's need to express power, in fact, that even an office building has grown insufficient. Now the tower has been fortified by an atrium mall (the "retail concourse") where tourists congregate to buy ice cream or souvenirs, or to join tours of the building that inevitably conclude with the suggested purchase of Clamp's "biography." And so the modern office tower is subsumed as merely one part of a commercial empire that mixes office work with shopping with public relations, generating income and extending ego at every turn.

Needless to say, this smooth, all-encompassing projection of power is undercut throughout *Gremlins 2*, not only by the structure's overblown design, but by the simple fact that many of its most advanced features keep malfunctioning, even before the film's creatures start the mischievous sabotage that leads to the building's ruination. By the end, the mogul Daniel Clamp himself seems philosophical, perhaps even chastened. Walking around the wreckage, he seems ready to consider the notion that the building was not so wonderful after all. "Maybe it wasn't a place for people," he muses. "It was a place for things."

SIX

STREET SCENE

ROW HOUSE, TENEMENT, AND HOUSING PROJECT

NEW YORK STREET

> Think of a city and what comes to mind? Its streets. If a city's streets look interesting, the city looks interesting; if they look dull, the city looks dull.
>
> JANE JACOBS, *THE DEATH AND LIFE OF GREAT AMERICAN CITIES*

With images of the skyline etched in their minds, newcomers to New York are sometimes surprised to find that the city's urban vitality is centered less in its celebrated towers than in the spaces nestled among them—its streets.

Movie New York, in this sense, is no different. Its most common setting turns out to be not the iconic skyscraper but the prototypical city block, a place not of well-known individual buildings but ordinary, generic ones. Indeed, in film after film, decade after decade, from *Street Scene* and *Dead End* and *A Tree Grows in Brooklyn* to literally scores of "Bowery Boys" pictures, the city's streets came to have a mythic status all their own. Thanks in large part to the movies, people just about anywhere can conjure up the classic New York street scene: mothers sitting on stoops, children playing in the spray of a fire hydrant, a cop ambling on his beat, shopkeepers minding their racks of fruits and vegetables, and perhaps an organ grinder, surrounded by small kids, playing "Sidewalks of New York." Films played a crucial role in creating our iconic imagery of New York's street life, so pervasively that it is sometimes hard to say exactly where the real street leaves off and the fictional one begins. And along the way, the place where it all happened took on a life of its own—as the writer Emily Kimbrough discovered on her first visit to Hollywood:

96. (previous page) ***Street Scene*** **(1931).** In directing the movie version of Elmer Rice's Broadway hit, King Vidor closely followed the staging of the original play, which took place on a single exterior tenement set by Jo Mielziner. In the film, Vidor's mobile camera roams across the facade, designed by Richard Day. In this view, Morris (William Collier Jr.) calls up to his girlfriend, Rose (Sylvia Sidney), showing the characteristic connection between the tenement's first-floor stoop and upper-floor windows.

> *I scarcely noticed where we were walking. Then I was aware we were in a strange part of town. There was a drug store on the corner, and a men's clothing store next to it. I could see a display of sporting goods in the window of the store beyond, and the*

unmistakable front of a bar on our side of the street. They seemed down at the heel, and the neighborhood tough, although I could not have said exactly why. I told [our guide] that I thought Paramount Studios owned this whole area. He was talking and answered a little abstractedly that certainly it did. Then he turned back to me with a second thought. "This is a movie set," he said. "Did you think it was real?"

I can only say that, although I was aware that we might conceivably at a motion picture studio see a set for a motion picture, I had no idea that a set could look like that. I have seen them from backstage in the theater—I think I have heard them called "flats"—and that is what I thought I should see—flat pieces representing very accurately the facade of a house or building. But these make-believe buildings had all the dimensions that any buildings require, and they looked, furthermore, as if they had been there a long time, built on good foundations. [Our guide] was comforting. "A visitor on the lot last week," he said, "banged on the counter in that drug store to get some one to sell him cigarettes. He thought the clerk was in the back somewhere."

As visitors to Hollywood soon discover, the phrase "New York Street" is actually a proper name, referring to a kind of permanent outdoor set that is a fixture at almost every major studio. Fully half a dozen can be found around today's Los Angeles; at the height of the studio era, six decades, almost twenty such "streets" stood across Southern California, on lots large and small, celebrated and obscure. Still among the most frequently used of all standing sets, the New York Street—at Warner's, Paramount, Universal, and elsewhere—remains to this day one of the studios' primary assets.

It is also a startling place to visit. Nowhere is the sheer three-dimensional reality of movie New York so plainly in evidence. Seventy feet wide, forty feet high, standing under the bright California sun, it can be walked around and explored as readily as any real city street. Indeed, a stroll down its sidewalk offers a strangely disorienting experience, a sort of eyes-open dream (98). For a moment everything seems familiar, especially if the eyes stay low. Brick facades and brownstone stoops, canvas awnings and fire hydrants and street lamps evoke a New York that is, if anything, a little *too* real, every brick popping out with intense clarity. But soon discrepant details start to creep in, like the strange incongruities of real dreams. There are few people, no traffic, and a very un–New York sense of quiet. Through the upper windows can be glimpsed not bedrooms, but snatches of blue sky. Views of good-sized hills and, yes, snow-peaked mountains appear beyond the building cornices. As in a dream, these peculiar details hint at something about the experience we are having (something, in fact, we already know).

97. **New York Street, Paramount, under construction.** In 1992, at a cost of fifteen million dollars, Paramount completed a new New York Street, whose scale and ambition rivaled anything built in the studio era. Designed by the art director Albert Brenner, the five-acre set drew closely from traditional Manhattan districts such as the Upper West Side, Beekman Place, Washington Square, and Fifth Avenue, as well as from a newer part of town, SoHo—represented by a series of "cast-iron" loft facades. But the biggest innovation lay behind the walls, where the traditional false fronts gave way to fully enclosed steel-framed structures, wired and sprinklered, with operable windows and finished rooms upstairs. Below the street, meanwhile, lay an impressively authentic urban "infrastructure" of pipes and cables, ready to bring power to lampposts and steam to manhole covers all across the set.

But meanwhile the street continues to beckon, encouraging us to stay within its surreal confines. At the end of the block we spot another street, crossing ours. We turn the corner and find ourselves on a new street, somewhat different in style and mood but still plainly part of the same city. Ahead there is another intersection, and another block; by now we realize that the term "New York Street" is something of a misnomer: this is not one street but many, an entire matrix of streets, in fact, meeting at odd angles and T-shaped intersections and spreading over several acres (122).

Eventually, however, we wander a few steps too far, and catch sight of the buildings from the back—only to be instantly confronted by the secret they tried so hard to keep: that they are not buildings at all, but merely false fronts, propped up with bracing (97). Nothing could be farther from the conscious urban clarity of the facades than this behind-the-scenes thicket of raw lumber. The front doors and entries, so prominent from the sidewalk, are from here hardly visible, leading not to actual parlors or lobbies but, we now see, to vestibules just big enough for an actress to kiss the leading man goodnight before scampering down the steps and onto the next scene. Behind the upper-floor windows, meanwhile, are narrow platforms stretched below the sills,

98. New York Street, Warner Bros., 1941. The mythic metropolis through which Bette Davis, Humphrey Bogart, Jimmy Cagney, and others passed on rain-slicked nights was actually located in Burbank, on the north side of the Hollywood Hills, which rise incongruously in the distance. At center can be seen the characteristic "bend" of the New York Street.

99. New York Street, MGM, rigged for a night shoot, 1949. Night scenes on the New York Street were rarely filmed after dark, when expensive overtime provisions would be in effect, but during the day, with sections of street darkened by black tarpaulins stretched from timber frameworks rising above the facades on either side. The result was an almost surreal sight: a cocoon-like enclosure, blocking out the bright sun of a California day to create a sleek, velvety Manhattan night.

allowing grips and stagehands to install curtains or flower pots, or rig lights, or cover the windows with sheets of nonreflective cloth, called duvetyn, to keep the sky from poking through and destroying the illusion. And no matter what elaborate materials are implied up front—granite, limestone, brick—from behind it is plain that these "buildings" are all made of the same stuff: plywood sheets, overlaid with molded veneers of plaster staff or fiberglass. This is a street just inches thick.

It has always been thus, ever since Hollywood first started reconstructing New York on a large scale in the early 1920s. To do so, the city's urban fabric had to be sliced in two—the outer layer of its buildings neatly sheared away from the interiors, which were shot inside enclosed soundstages, some distance away. The reason lay in part with the nature of film stock itself, which responds very differently to natural and artificial light: the higher "color temperature" of the sun's light makes it difficult to blend with that of electric lamps. From this technical constraint arose an entire production strategy, separating the movie city's exterior skins from everything else. Lacking any internal structure, the "buildings" of New York Street formed a membrane-like container, a vessel of space that encompassed only the public, outdoor life of the city—a reality with some provocative implications of its own (99, 123).

Even on their own terms, however, the street facades offered some extraordinary lessons—especially in the big, district-like complexes at the major studios, which included all the various *kinds* of streets one might find in the real city.

As might be expected, many of these were commercial in character, such as the main thoroughfare—called "Fifth Avenue" at MGM, for example—with its shop windows, bank branches, theater marquees, office building entrances; and smaller, specialized offshoots with names like Stage Alley, Warehouse Alley, or Dock Street. As in the city itself, however, most New York Streets were residential, offering a wide variety of character and style, the better to render the city's range of neighborhoods and classes. One end of MGM's Fifth Avenue included the ornate facades of mansions, while around the corner, apartment house entrances could be found on a block called Park Avenue. Warner's included a series of neat little row houses called Brownstone Street, and a dingy, fire escape–lined block known as Tenement Street (the same block, at MGM, was called East Side Street). Paramount, Fox, and Universal offered more or less similar versions of each.

This residential variety was crucial, for there turns out to be a story inscribed in these streets, an epic struggle that has lasted over a century and is still not fully resolved. At its heart has been a fierce debate about the shape of American cities. In what kind of houses should city dwellers live, and on what kind of streets? Still more to the point, *should there be streets at all?* Is the street somehow an enemy to the values of the home—and therefore to be eliminated wherever possible? Or can the street itself be considered a home of sorts, an outdoor parlor that joins the needs of the family with those of the larger community? For generations the debate has raged, the movie city tracking its every turn—and occasionally joining the fray—in a century-long arc that links Henry James with Jimmy Cagney—and both of them, in turn, with Spike Lee. Along the way, we confront some of the most elemental forces that have shaped New York and every American city. For in the end, nothing touches more directly upon the meaning of urban life than the relationship of the two primary places, indoors and out, in which that life proceeds.

100. **Building street sets for *Life With Father*.** In 1946, with great fanfare, Warner Bros. demolished its largest standing set, the Viennese Street, to construct a row of Madison Avenue houses for its new production of *Life With Father*. In this publicity shot, Ellen Day (the playwright's widow), the screenwriters Howard Lindsay and Russel Crouse, and (at far right) the art director Robert Haas "inspect" plans of Day's childhood home on 48th Street and Madison Avenue—a district which, by the time of the production, had been almost completely rebuilt with modern office buildings.

HOUSES OF MEMORY

The origins of the debate lie back in the early nineteenth century, when the streets of the city were first filled with houses—when, indeed, the streets themselves were first laid out. There were no motion pictures back then, of course, but the filmic city nonetheless offers a superb window onto that world—a pair of windows, in fact: two features, both made just after World War II, that looked back with loving care to the New York of an earlier day.

Two films, two families, two houses. Filmed by William Wyler in 1948, *The Heiress* takes us inside 16 Washington Square, an 1830s Greek Revival row house that is the home of Dr. Austin Sloper and his daughter Catherine. *Life With Father* (1947), directed by Michael Curtiz, carries us five decades forward and forty blocks uptown, to the Italianate brownstone of Clarence Day and his family, located at 48th Street and Madison Avenue. Both recall a time when almost every middle-class family in New York inhabited a row house of its own; the difference in style, geography, and period neatly marks the tide of fashion that swept north across the island in these years, as elite families retreated uptown to escape the growing commercial din of lower Manhattan, exchanging their antebellum taste for Greek-inspired brick facades with a post–Civil War preference for somber brownstone fronts.

101. Washington Square North, 1892. This view of the actual row of houses in which *The Heiress* takes place reveals the way the city's row houses have traditionally extended themselves to the street with an array of architectural elements. A pair of Doric columns and a stone entablature surround each doorway, a public gesture that explicitly compares the house to a temple. Wide marble stoops, descending from those doorways, meet the sidewalk alongside gas lamps, thickly planted front yards, and ornate iron fences—creating an intermediate urban zone, shared by both the house and the street.

Both films had literary origins, in books that were themselves a blend of memory and invention. *Life With Father* first appeared as a series of 1930s *New Yorker* stories by Clarence Day Jr. recalling his upbringing in a strict Victorian household a half-century before. Adapted for the stage by Howard Lindsay and Russel Crouse, it became the longest running nonmusical play in Broadway history (100). *The Heiress* also began life on Broadway, as a stage adaptation (by Ruth and Augustus Goetz) of *Washington Square*, the 1881 novel by Henry James that drew on his own childhood memories of New York, thirty years before.

Produced just a few months apart, both films offered a lavish, detailed look at a vanished way of life, lingering on the rituals of nineteenth-century domesticity, and delighting in showing modern audiences how the New York row house functioned in the days when it served a single family (supported, of course, by a clutch of domestic servants). This was especially true of *Life With Father*, whose first ten minutes are wholly given over to a typical "day in the life" of the Day family household on a spring morning in 1883.

Revealingly, our first view is not of the house but the street, an unbroken line of four-story facades stretching into the distance. Even as we draw close to the Day home, it is not the building itself we see, but the stretch of sidewalk in front. Here is a chiseled block of granite near the curb, forthrightly proclaiming the name "Clarence Day" for all to see; here is the high, wide stoop rising from the bluestone sidewalk; here is a housekeeper not sweeping its treads but *hand-scrubbing* them. When a passing policeman declares the steps to be the cleanest on the avenue, the servant's reply is prompt: "That's how Mr. Day wants them kept" (102).

Without meeting him or even entering his house, we have already learned

102. *Life With Father* (1947). The film's opening sequence shows life on Madison Avenue, in front of the home of Clarence Day Jr., on a typical spring morning in 1883. An establishing shot of the long, low-rise thoroughfare—lined as far as the eye can see with four-story row houses—gives way to a close-up of a granite name stone, and, tilting up, to a housekeeper scrubbing Mr. Day's stoop as a passing policeman looks on.

a lot about Mr. Clarence Day, as the filmmakers plainly intended we should. In this middle-class city, the identity of the individual house—and its owner—is allowed to push out into the street, almost to the curb. In a very real sense, the city street is an extension of the house, domesticated through a series of gestures, such as the granite name block and the high stoop, which work to bring the public sidewalk under the home's sphere of influence.

But in approaching the Day home by way of the street, we have learned something else: that this middle-class house draws its identity directly *from* the street, sharing with its neighbors a common language of materials and style, and willingly suppressing its own individuality in order to take its place comfortably within the overall street wall. That wall, in turn, is shown to be one element in the larger "room" that is the street itself, a well-defined outdoor space with a floor of cobblestones, a canopy of trees, and "furniture" ranging from slender gas lamps to the ornate iron railings of the houses themselves. As the house shapes the street, in other words, so the street shapes the house, striking a delicate balance between the demands of the single family and those of the larger community.

Yet the connection between street and house is tighter still, as the opening sequence—which is far from over—proceeds to demonstrate (103).

On the street, a dairy truck pulls up and a servant carries the Days' cannister of milk inside. We watch her descend a few steps into the areaway and slip inside the house's service entrance, tucked beneath the stoop. Lacking an expansive floor area, the New York row house efficiently uses its verticality—a half-flight up to the front entrance, a half-flight down to the service door—to separate its constituent functions and classes. As the camera moves inside the house, we see the same principle extended within. Cutting from one floor to another, the sequence allows us to understand how the various floors of the house are linked (or isolated) as necessary—almost as if we have peeled away the house's walls to reveal a cross-section of the interior (104).

Downstairs, in the half-basement kitchen, the cook prepares breakfast, then places it in a dumbwaiter; upstairs, in a small pantry on the parlor floor, a servant pulls up the breakfast tray, then carries it to the dining room. Meanwhile, Lavinia Day (Irene Dunne), who has already descended from her bedroom above, shouts back up the staircase to her husband, Clarence (William Powell), who, still in *his* bedroom, is seen only as a shadow against the staircase wall as he booms out a string of orders and complaints. Soon the family's four sons have descended, along with father himself. The food has come upstairs,

103. *Life With Father* (1947). This early morning sequence reveals how the vertically organized layout of the nineteenth-century row house functioned on a daily basis. On the sidewalk, a servant takes in fresh milk from a wagon, then steps down to the areaway, on her way to the half-basement kitchen and pantry. In the kitchen, meanwhile, the cook completes breakfast, then carries the tray to the house's dumbwaiter. On the parlor floor above, the servant lifts the breakfast tray up the dumbwaiter and into a small pantry, then carries it into the dining room. In the main hallway, Lavinia Day (Irene Dunne) calls up to the bedroom floor, telling her husband, Clarence (William Powell, seen only in shadow), to come down to eat. Finally, in the parlor-floor dining room, the family gathers at the table as breakfast is served.

the family has come downstairs; everyone gathers around the dining table, and breakfast is served.

It is a revealing sequence, showing precisely how the row house—no more than twenty-five feet wide—sustained the complex social structure of the household. Inside and out, it provided a separate zone for the family's private use, another for their communal use, and still another for the servants' use—each located on its own floor, then linked through parallel pathways (the stoop, the family stairs, the service stairs, the dumbwaiter) to allow movement from floor to floor while still preserving the requisite social distinctions. Using the vertical dimension, the New York row house could thus offer almost a mini-mansion within the confines of its narrow lot.

Finally, with breakfast over, we see Mr. Day himself descending the stoop that has been prepared so carefully for him, on his way to catch a horse-drawn streetcar heading downtown. And we recognize all over again the way the house's entrance and stoop—an elevated perch, fronting the sidewalk—work to establish the clear place of the individual within the community. Part of the common realm, the stoop is also part of the house, and thus slightly more private than the sidewalk, while the home's ornamented entrance, of course, is more private still. It is just this subtle but powerful hierarchy—a hierarchy that continues right into the house itself—that *The Heiress* would use to extend and deepen movie New York's exploration of the row house, and its primal role in shaping the city.

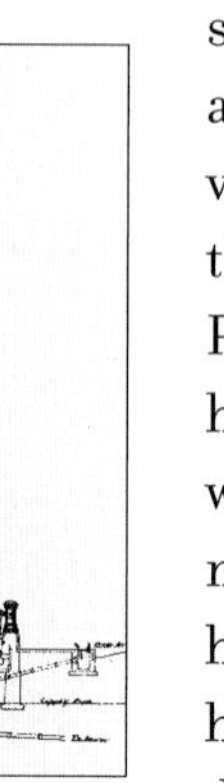

104. Cross-section, New York row house, circa 1880. This cross-section of a late-nineteenth-century row house in Manhattan reveals its characteristic vertical organization: from the sidewalk, the front stoop rises a half level to the high-ceilinged parlor floor, where the home's entertainment and dining rooms are located; a smaller, adjacent set of steps, meanwhile, descends from the street to a half-basement where kitchen and pantry are located. Family bedrooms are located on the second and third floors, with servants' bedrooms placed above them.

105. (opposite) *The Heiress* (1949). Directed by William Wyler from the Broadway play of the same name (itself an adaptation of Henry James's 1881 novel *Washington Square*), *The Heiress* takes place in the Greek Revival row house of Dr. Austin Sloper (Ralph Richardson), who is shown standing by the pocket doors (flanked by columns) that mark a crucial division between the formal front parlor of the house and its more informal back rooms.

Again we start outside, on the street, in a shot that presents the elegant row of houses along the north side of Washington Square (101). Even more than before, we feel the street as an authentic outdoor "room," with every house offering a high level of decoration to the street. That this early-nineteenth-century row of Greek-inspired houses is so different in feeling from *Life With Father*'s later brownstone block suggests how readily this basic "room" could serve as a versatile armature, easily draped with the changing architectural fashions of successive generations, while retaining its essential urban character.

But as in *Life With Father*, the crucial action of *The Heiress* takes place inside the house, in an elaborate interior set whose design would underscore the human conflict at the core of the story. To give it shape, Wyler selected Harry Horner, a gifted Czech-born production designer who had worked with Max Reinhardt in Vienna and with the Metropolitan Opera in New York before migrating to Hollywood. Offered the rare opportunity to research his subject for nearly a year, Horner moved back to New York and spent his Sundays with sketchbook and camera in hand, roaming the quiet streets of lower Manhattan, tracking down the early-nineteenth-century houses still standing among the lofts and factories. He rang doorbells, and, when allowed inside, made extensive notes on the interiors; these were later combined with studio research and period illustrations to create his "bible": a thick notebook documenting every detail about the houses and the people who had once lived in them.

Horner quickly grasped the basics of the early New York row house, especially the layout of its main floor: a front and back parlor, linked by a pair of wide pocket doors which could be closed to conserve the warmth of a fire, or

106. Front parlor of the Old Merchants House (top). Sketch of the front parlor of Sloper house for *The Heiress* (above). In preparing his design for *The Heiress*, the production designer Harry Horner spent a year in New York studying the decoration and architecture of the city's early-nineteenth-century row houses. His primary source was the Seabury Tredwell house (also known as the Old Merchants House) at 29 East 4th Street in Manhattan, a Greek Revival structure built in 1832 for the New York merchant Seabury Tredwell, held in the same family until 1933, and opened to the public three years later.

thrown open to offer a single large space for a party or gathering. Placed alongside was the house's hallway, running front to rear—from the entrance hall, to the staircase, to the back door. In laying out his set, Horner would not hesitate to introduce changes of his own (using angled walls, for example, to allow for deep diagonal sightlines across the length of the house, or placing the dining room and library outside the strict perimeter of the row house's "rectangle"), but he nonetheless remained faithful to its essence. Narrow and long, and butted against neighboring buildings on either side, a row house can only offer two walls with windows. The windows in the front face the sidewalk and street; those in back, the rear yard. This distinction, between front and back, between public street and private yard, would establish the essential dynamic of the film's action. Again the house would be peeled open, this time to reveal not its cross-section, but floor plan (107).

In *The Heiress*, this distinction between front and back would be enriched with a layer of meaning drawn directly from James's novel. Consciously, Horner sought to lace into the house's interior an extended history of the Sloper family—creating the equivalent of what screenwriters like to call a "backstory." "Very often," Horner recognized, "houses that have a memory of one kind or another attached to them are able to dominate the inhabitants and mold them with a definite force of their own."

For Dr. Austin Sloper (Ralph Richardson), 16 Washington Square is certainly a house of memory, a structure he had purchased as a wedding gift for himself and his wife nearly two decades before, built in the fashionable Greek Revival style of the early 1830s. But soon after the birth of their only child, his young wife died, leaving him bereft in a way that neither the rewards of a successful medical practice nor the company of his now-grown daughter, Catherine (Olivia de Havilland), have ever recompensed. His obsessive devotion to his wife's memory is embodied in the formal front parlor, which since her death has been scrupulously maintained in its original Greek style, almost as a shrine (106). The rear parlor, by contrast, has been redecorated in a later, more ornate fashion, and now serves as an informal family room. Behind it are still newer additions, extending the house in back: a library, a winter garden, and a staircase whose distinctive pointed arches reveal it to be a product of the Gothic Revival movement of the mid-1840s (114).

This in itself was no small thing—a house that reveals change over time.

Recognizing that the simple brick box of the row house could be a framework in which time passed and left its mark, Horner managed subtly to intertwine social history (through evolving architectural styles) and individual human stories. Dr. Sloper's residence is "not a house of one period, but of many," Horner remarked. "[I]t must give the feeling of having gone through several styles, thus making that first phase of his life which existed only in his memory stand out and become visible to us."

As the film's story begins, in 1849, the distinction between front and rear is dramatically asserted. Catherine, in her father's eyes a plain and hopelessly dull woman, has found an eager suitor in handsome Morris Townsend (Montgomery Clift). The couple's first romantic encounter carefully lays the groundwork for what is to come. It begins in the classically decorated front parlor, in a polite and cordial tone that matches the formal spirit of the room itself. But soon enough the couple have retreated to the rear parlor, passing through the big pocket doorway that separates front from back. In this informal back room, filled with casual furnishings and facing not the exterior street but the quiet backyard, the couple's connection grows intimate (108). Morris plays the spinet, sings a French song, and, not long after, declares his love for her. A few days later, in this same room, they passionately kiss and decide to marry.

Catherine's father, however, remains deeply skeptical, especially after Morris is revealed to be nearly penniless, and he plainly suspects the young suitor of being more interested in her sizable inheritance than in Catherine herself. And so the two men confront each other, in a sequence that mixes architecture and drama to extraordinary effect (109). First, Dr. Sloper interviews Morris's older sister (Betty Linley) in his library; her answers to his questions about Morris's character (though more than a little ambiguous to our ears) only confirm his worst fears. A while later, the front doorbell is heard; it is Morris himself, come to make his request for Catherine's hand. Catherine excuses herself and retreats upstairs, excited and hopeful, without a clue about what is to come; as the servant moves toward the door, the doctor's sister and a cousin earerly turn to hear his decision about the suitor. Before answering them, he walks over to the pocket doors between the back room and the front and carefully shuts them, then turns back to report that Morris is "worthless," an idler and fortune hunter who on no account will be allowed into the

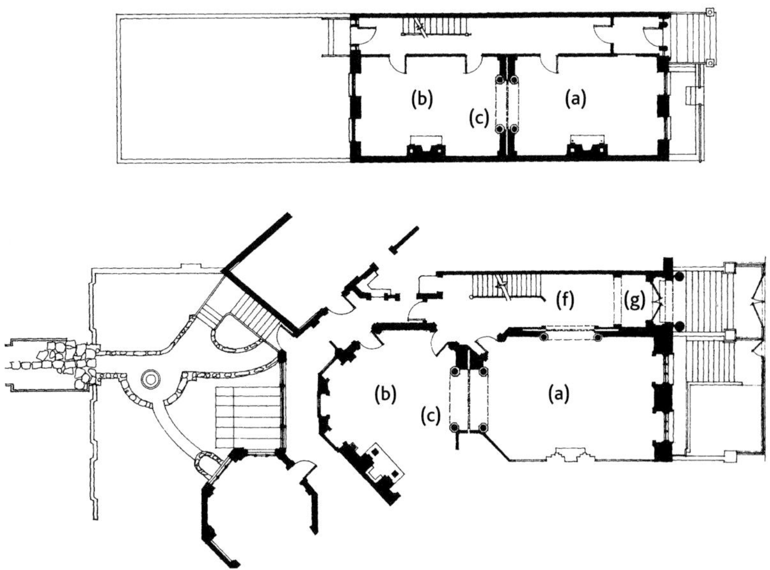

107. Floor plan of Old Merchants House (top) and Sloper house set, *The Heiress* (bottom). Drawn to the same scale, these floor plans show how the production designer Harry Horner freely adapted the layout of a typical New York row house while remaining faithful to its essential features. The plan consists of a front parlor *(a)* and rear parlor *(b)*, connected by a pair of pocket doors *(c)*. Additional doors connect both parlors to a long stair hall *(f)*, running from the front vestibule *(g)* to the back of the house. For ease of staging, Horner located additional rooms on this floor (such as a dining room and a library), technically exceeding the strict rectangular limits of the twenty-five by one-hundred-foot lot on which the city's row houses were almost always constructed.

family. After the crestfallen women depart, Dr. Sloper moves back to the wide pocket doors and opens them to greet Morris, waiting in the front parlor. But in a gesture of crucial significance, he immediately *closes the doors behind him* in a single, smooth motion. The next shot, set in the front room, shows the doctor adopting a pleasant, "social" expression—even as he finishes shutting the doors tightly together, behind his back.

Morris does not know it yet, but the interview is already over. He will get no farther into the Sloper house—or household—than this formal front parlor, where all visitors are received cordially. Those wide pocket doors are more than just a portal from front room to back; they are a threshold between the house's public area, where Morris is more or less welcome, and its private quarters, where he is most definitely not. Indeed, by the conclusion of the interview, Dr. Sloper is brusquely ushering the young man through the parlor's *front* doors, to the entrance vestibule—almost out onto the street. Catherine, waiting on the stair landing, sees the two men arguing and, realizing it has gone badly, races down in desperation. But it is too late. Her heart has been broken. Morris leaves. When he returns, it will not be through the front door.

Rarely in the movie city has so large an insight been compressed into so small a setting; rarer still has it been charged with so much emotional power. For it is crucial to understand that the entire layout of Manhattan's grid of streets and blocks (originally known as the "Commissioners' Plan" of 1811) grew directly from buildings like the Slopers': brick row houses, two rooms deep, with the street in front and a private yard in back. Aligned side by side

108. *The Heiress* (1949). According to the "backstory" that designer Harry Horner prepared while working on *The Heiress* (which takes place in 1849), the rear parlor of the Sloper house, built originally in the Greek Revival style of the early 1830s, had since been redecorated in a more ornate fashion. In this view, a young man named Morris Townsend (Montgomery Clift) courts the daughter of the house, Catherine Sloper (Olivia de Havilland), by playing the spinet.

109. ***The Heiress* (1949).** Among the most dramatic (and significant) scenes in *The Heiress* is Dr. Sloper's interview of Morris Townsend, who wishes to marry his daughter Catherine. Upon hearing the front door bell ring, Dr. Sloper instructs his daughter to wait upstairs during the talk. As the servant, Maria, comes upstairs to open the door, the doctor's family awaits his report of an earlier meeting with Morris's sister. Before answering, Dr. Sloper closes the pocket doors that divide the front and rear parlor, then returns to announce his poor opinion of the young man, even as Maria announces Morris's arrival in the front parlor. Dr. Sloper then opens the doors to greet the waiting guest, but immediately closes them behind him. With the doors fully shut behind him, the doctor assumes a pleasant, "public" face to greet his visitor. Only by the end of the meeting does Catherine, waiting on the landing upstairs, realize that it has gone badly.

and back to back with similar houses and yards, these formed city blocks two hundred feet deep—every block, in effect, a rectangular "ring" of houses surrounding a central core of backyards. Everything built later in New York—tenements, apartment houses, office buildings—would have to contend with this basic template of blocks and streets, born of houses like the Slopers'. New York, it can be said, was designed around the row house.

Not only the layout of the single house, therefore, but that of the entire block (and by extension the whole city) pivoted around the critical distinction between street and yard, front and back, public and private. The street was filled with traffic and strangers; the backyard with only family or friends, and surrounded by neighbors. The house's front rooms, overlooking the street, were inevitably more public in style and feeling than its rear rooms, facing the yard. In practice, as both *The Heiress* and *Life With Father* make clear, the transition from public to private was a gradual one, with many intermediate steps—the street, the sidewalk, the stoop, the entrance hall, the front parlor, and so on—each a notch more private than the one before it.

At some point, however, the transition was complete; the extended "outer" sphere of the street finally gave way to the private inner realm of the home and backyard. In *The Heiress,* that point was precisely and unforgettably located: those pocket doors (105). Here could be imagined a line, drawn through every house and every block in row-house New York, where the street's influence finally waned and was replaced with the intimacy of the block's interior—the great divide, in other words, between the public and private halves of the city in its first, most elemental configuration. It was the triumph of *The Heiress* not only to identify this theoretical line, but to make it wrenchingly meaningful—a threshold not only to the intimate chambers of the city, but also to those of the human heart.

STREET SCENE

As before, we open with a residential street in Manhattan—but hardly the genteel facades of the row-house city. The establishing shot of *Street Scene* (1931) has taken us to a block in the West Forties, the area of Manhattan known as Hell's Kitchen, dominated not by elegant row houses but tall, dark tenements.

Everything has changed.

It is not spring, for a start, but a sweltering day in summer. Children play in the spray of a fire hydrant; ice melts under the blazing sun; a dog lies panting in the gutter; fans blow streams of warm air; a man sleeps on a fire escape. Evening has arrived, but—typical of New York's humid summers—has brought with it little relief from the oppressive heat. As the film's characters gather in front of the tenement we mark still more changes. This is not the home of one family, but of many—poor families, mostly, whose names reveal a mix far removed from the Anglo-Saxon pedigree of brownstone New York. There are the Kaplans, the Olsons, the Fiorentinos, the Maurrants, conducting endless arguments over music, politics—and whether Columbus or Leif Ericsson discovered America.

Directed by King Vidor and based upon the Broadway play by Elmer Rice, *Street Scene* was a groundbreaking work. Structured around a single city block in a single twenty-four-hour period—one of the hottest days of the year—the film introduced a remarkably sturdy premise, one reused six years later in William Wyler's *Dead End*, and still proving serviceable—its ethnic mix updated but in other ways strikingly little changed—in Spike Lee's *Do the Right Thing*, more than a half-century on.

Indeed, more than any other single film, it was *Street Scene* that established the iconic role of the tenement street within New York movies. Films had been located in the city's poorer districts for years (Raoul Walsh's 1915 *Regeneration*, for example, had used exteriors of actual tenements on the Bowery). But Vidor's film offered something new. Following the celebrated staging of the original play (which took place entirely in front of a single exterior set), Vidor never once brought the film's action inside, but instead used a highly mobile camera to roam all across the tenement facade and sidewalk, thus preserving and even enlarging the simple, powerful notion that Rice had inscribed in the play's title—that the street itself could be a scene.

110. ***Street Scene* (1931).** This somewhat staged-looking production image nonetheless captures the classic tradition of stoop- and window-sitting that remained common in New York's tenement districts throughout the twentieth century.

As the setting of both the play (by Jo Mielziner) and the film (by Richard Day) made clear, there was an inherently "theatrical" quality to the tenement front, not unlike that of its patrician predecessor, the row house. Like the row house (from which it had historically evolved), the tenement fronted the street squarely, met its neighbors shoulder-to-shoulder, and provided a continuous street wall, thus shaping the street itself into the same kind of well-defined, outdoor room. Like the row house, the tenement put special emphasis on its street facade, using much the same inventory of architectural devices: decorative treatment around the doors and windows, an ornamental cornice, and a wide stoop, rising a half-flight from the sidewalk to the front door. The detailing was likely to be clumsier and heavier than that of the chaste row house, but the end result was the same: the street became a kind of outdoor auditorium—the decorated facades serving as a backdrop, the stoops as bleachers, and the upper-floor windows, overlooking the entire space, as "boxes." The theatrical parallel was obvious (96).

Yet the row-house street was a stage almost without actors, a place generally empty but for a policeman or a servant or two. By contrast, the front of Vidor's tenement is *filled* with humanity, using it in ways inconceivable to the genteel Sloper or Day families (110). Mr. Kaplan sits in an open window and reads his Yiddish newspaper, holding forth on the failures of capitalism. Mrs. Jones sits on the ledge of the stoop, gossiping with Mrs. Fiorentino, who has made her window a perch upon the world. On the sidewalk, meanwhile, kids race by on roller skates, and yell to upper windows for candy money. Unlike the elegant but silent row-house facade, every inch of the tenement's exterior pulses with life.

The reason for all this activity, of course, was simple: on hot days, no one in his right mind wanted to remain inside the tenement's dark, cramped, fetid rooms. Whatever its external similarities to the row house, the tenement's *interior* was unimaginably different—and unimaginably worse. Yet the decision not to portray the sweltering misery inside the tenement was revealing. Whatever their moral feelings, it is plain that as *dramatists*, Rice and Vidor relished the way in which the tenement's wretchedness caused it to wear its life on its sleeve. As the spacious row house would never do, the cramped, crowded tenement created an outdoor space of remarkable vitality, the staging platform for a universe of interactions, the ultimate "scene."

But if *Street Scene* chose not to enter the tenement, plenty of other films did—not only bringing audiences inside the grim dark buildings but forcing them to remain there, at length. For the tenement was not just a setting but a subject: the greatest scandal, and tragedy, of the modern city.

Although somewhat improved from the worst excesses of a few decades before, New York's tenements in the 1930s remained a vast, horrific agglomeration of substandard housing (111). With their appalling lack of light and air, primitive sanitary facilities, and astonishing population densities, they had been for generations a source of daily misery, a tinderbox for fires, and a breeding ground for disease.

Indeed, their worst horrors were well beyond the capacity of Hollywood to depict, as one anecdote is sufficient to demonstrate. For his 1928 film, *The Crowd*, an unvarnished portrait of working-class life in New York, King Vidor insisted on a blunt, homely setting: a one-room tenement apartment, its shabbiness epitomized by a bathroom toilet bowl visible from almost every corner (112). Upon screening the film, MGM's Louis B. Mayer flew into a rage over Vidor's telling detail. It would have been too costly to reshoot the picture, but a stern decree was issued: *never* again would a toilet be visible in any MGM film. On the real Lower East Side, meanwhile, hundreds of filthy wooden outdoor shacks still stood in garbage-strewn backyards, on blocks where the indoor toilet that scandalized Mayer would have been considered a veritable luxury (113).

111. Aerial view, Lower East Side, 1935. Four hundred thousand New Yorkers lived on the Lower East Side in 1935, in blocks of old-law tenements whose astonishing densities—four hundred people per acre or more—were nonetheless only half what they had been in 1900.

Filmmakers had somewhat better luck depicting the terrible overcrowding of the old tenements, each of which packed a hundred people or more onto a piece of land originally intended for a single-family row house, transforming the once spacious residential grid into a nightmare of tightly packed, tomblike blocks.

An early casualty was the backyard. In *The Heiress*, the backyard had been a lushly planted refuge from the city (114); in *Life With Father*, it was the leafy domain of the family's children, a convenient playground for the youngest boys and the ideal spot for the older son, Clarence Jr. (Jimmy Lydon), to conduct his nascent romance with Mary Skinner (Elizabeth Taylor), out of the family's earshot. But in the effort to cram in as many interior rooms as possible, tenement builders pushed nearly all the way into the rear of the lot, reducing the backyard to a narrow, useless, brick-lined chasm (115).

As for the interior itself, it now contained dozens of tiny, windowless "bedrooms" (actually alcoves, strung along an apartment hallway) with virtually no natural light or ventilation. Legislation in 1879 had required the inclusion of narrow air shafts, but these proved utterly inadequate at providing any real light or air, and, offering direct views into adjacent apartments just a few feet away, only worsened the tenement's lack of privacy. Precisely for this reason, however, air shafts sometimes furnished the movie city with a handy plot device: in *Gold Diggers of 1933*, a trio of hungry chorus girls use pincers to snatch some food from an adjacent apartment, and later, hearing some lively piano music wafting across the shaft, they happily discover their neighbor to be a handsome young songwriter, played by Dick Powell. Over time, many aspects of the old tenement interiors (especially their quirky diagonal walls) became familiar as the settings for countless Depression-era Warner films about working-class New Yorkers.

In the 1930s, conditions in the tenement slums became a rallying point for social reformers, who had succeeded in raising the standards for newer housing, but remained unable to do anything about the tens of thousands of older tenements, still home to nearly a million people. Their greatest challenge was in conveying the misery and dangers of the tenement to a middle-class public who, most likely, had never been inside one; it was thus no surprise that they leapt at the chance to bring audiences into the very heart of the slum, by way of the screen.

Sometimes the journey was enacted literally. Halfway through *Dead End* (1937), a well-to-do woman named Kay (Wendy Barrie) ventures into a nearby tenement to find her struggling lover, Dave (Joel McCrea). The audience measures its own discomfort through Kay's mounting revulsion at the dwelling's garbage-strewn hallways, the sight of a little child playing pathetically in the

112. ***The Crowd* (1928).** King Vidor's portrait of working-class life in New York is set largely in a one-room apartment belonging to Mary (Eleanor Boardman) and John (James Murray). In the interest of authenticity, Vidor insisted that the toilet bowl be visible from almost every corner of the set—a detail that enraged Louis B. Mayer, who, upon screening the film, angrily vowed that no toilet would ever again be visible in an MGM film.

113. **Backyard outhouses on the Lower East Side, 1934.** This view, taken by the New York City Housing Authority on the site of what would become First Houses, shows one of the thirteen hundred backyard outhouses that remained in New York at the time.

gloom of the staircase, a tough-talking prostitute on her way to work, and, finally, the awful detail that sends Kay (and very likely the audience) recoiling in disgust—a trash-can lid literally covered with roaches.

But the most sustained critique of the tenement, without a doubt, was offered by *One Third of a Nation*, a Paramount film adapted in 1939 from a stage play produced by the federally funded Works Progress Administration. Indeed, the picture is actually a seventy-eight-minute polemic for housing reform, disguised—just barely—as a feature film. Anxious to score points any way it can, the film's script moves clumsily back and forth between statistics-laden analysis and high melodrama. The drama builds first, with a terrifying tenement fire: as the dead bodies of victims are laid out on the sidewalk, we see a young boy named Joey (Sidney Lumet, as a child actor) desperately clinging to a fire escape—then watch in horror as it gives way, plunging him to the street, crippling him for life. Can such conditions be legal in the modern city? In an extended courtroom scene, we discover (by way of the cross-examination of a city official) that indeed they are. Joey's building is an "old-law" tenement, built before 1901; there are 67,000 such buildings in New York, each and every one of them a firetrap, with inadequate exits and construction—wood paneling in the public hallways, for example—that allows it to "burn like a matchbox."

114. *The Heiress* (1948). Harry Horner's design for the Sloper house featured an interpretation of the rear yard and mews located behind the houses on Washington Square North. In a subtle touch, Horner's use of pointed arches in the staircase baluster and roof—carried out in the Gothic Revival style that gained favor in New York after 1840—suggest that these elements were later additions, built after the house's original construction.

But fire is the least of it. When young Joey, now on crutches, stands in front of the old tenement, waves his fist in fury, and vows to tear down the "dirty old rat-trap" someday, the building actually responds, its facade surreally transformed into an evil face with a deep, menacing voice: "Lots of people have hated me in my time—with more reason than you. Look what I was like sixty or seventy years ago." A string of historical vignettes then sketches the misery the tenement has caused for generations: a Victorian-era family, dying of cholera in their dark, unventilated rooms; a turn-of-the-century housewife, unwilling to have another child after the others have all died, crying, "It's the houses we always live in. The walls, these lights; no sun, no air. And these stinkin' drains. And you want me to have another kid and have him die before he's a year old. I say no! *NO!*"

The impassioned rhetoric of *One Third of a Nation* sought to make clear not only the misery inflicted on the tenement's own inhabitants, but the enormous costs to the larger city in infant mortality, infectious disease, and fire. Yet in the end, the tenement's greatest liability—at least as far as Hollywood was concerned—was none of these things. It was not even to be found within the tenement's ramshackle walls, in fact, but back outside.

It was the street itself.

CRADLE OF CRIME

It was an extraordinary alignment.

On one side were the reformers—planners, social workers, housing experts—anxious to tackle the old problem of the city's slums, still intact despite decades of limited private initiatives. The only real solution, it seemed clear, was large-scale government intervention. Yet even in the activist mood of the early New Deal, there remained profound reluctance to have public agencies entangled in the quintessentially private enterprise of real estate. By the mid-1930s, reformers needed to build a consensus, to demonstrate to the broadest possible audience how and why the city's slums threatened not only their own inhabitants, but society at large.

On the other side were Hollywood producers, coming off a string of highly successful early 1930s films about big-city gangsters, and looking for ways to spice up a now-familiar formula. One promising possibility lay in reviving an old idea: tracing the gangster's origins, the story of how he came to be. This was

115. *Dead End* (1937). Required by law to preserve only ten feet of rear yard, the builders of New York's nineteenth-century tenements filled their lots with deep, poorly lighted multiple dwellings whose rear rooms faced narrow, chasm-like backyards, as in this view from *Dead End* with Sylvia Sidney.

an established theme in the movie city, dating as far back as 1915 with *Regeneration*, a Raoul Walsh film that followed a gangster from his childhood in a Bowery tenement. More recently, *Sidewalks of New York*, a 1931 film that starred Buster Keaton as a millionaire who falls in love with a tenement girl played by Anita Page, had featured Page's desperate attempt to keep her unruly brother, Clipper (Norman Phillips Jr.), from maturing into a full-fledged gangster.

But in tracking the lives of these notorious figures, the studios now saw the chance to combine social commentary with dramatic action, as the gangster blazed his way from youthful scuffles with the law to an explosive, bullet-ridden demise—just the sort of mixture of high-minded sentiment and crowd-pleasing violence that Hollywood has always found hard to resist. Reformers, meanwhile, recognized that by depicting tenement districts as the "breeding ground" of crime—and thus arousing fear in middle-class audiences—they were far more likely to build support for slum improvement than through any abstract pleas of sympathy for the poor.

In truth, Hollywood's notion of how gangsters came to be was a relatively progressive one: they were made, not born. In an era when many people still believed certain ethnic or racial groups to be somehow predisposed to criminal behavior, Hollywood consistently followed the newer line of thinking: that behavior was profoundly influenced by the "environment"—by nurture, in other words, rather than nature.

116. Studio Tenement Street set, 1930s. In addition to its main commercial street, and a block of row houses called Brownstone Street, permanent New York sets also included a tenement street, complete with pushcarts, grocery shops, and laundry hung to dry from fire escapes.

Yet this only raised another question: What, exactly, was so deleterious about the slum "environment"? By and large, Hollywood chose to ignore the most obvious answer: poverty itself. The existence of a large and near-destitute class of urban Americans was too broad and ultimately frightening a reality for films to tackle—and one, further, whose "solution" implied a more radical agenda than any studio cared to touch. There was also another problem: poverty itself was not particularly photogenic. Hunger, hopelessness, the sheer misery of a life of want—to producers, these were simply depressing subjects, the kind movie audiences were sure to shun.

There was another answer, however, which the producers eagerly leapt upon. For decades, a consensus had been building that much of the slum's problem lay in its physical armature, the street. For reformers, the street's intense activity—its "vitality" for writers such as Elmer Rice—was simply the inevitable result of the tenement itself: with deep, dense, virtually uninhabitable interiors, and the loss of the only other outdoor space available (the backyard), where *else* was life going to concentrate?

Reformers hated everything about the tenement street. Urban planners were appalled by its frightful, almost absurd mix of activities: children playing and adults socializing on the same congested corridor where peddlers sold their wares, cars tried to circulate, and trucks delivered goods to the stores and workshops lining the sidewalk (116). For social workers, the street's greatest sin was its mixture not of different kinds of activities but of different kinds of *people*, including unsavory characters such as prostitutes, gamblers, criminals, and the habitués of saloons and pool halls. Unlike the home, where parents could hope to maintain some level of control, the street promoted unsupervised behavior, a lax social structure that allowed young people to go anywhere and see everything—and surely, to the reformer's mind, be perverted by what they saw.

Here was a promising premise indeed: not the economic problem of poverty, nor the sanitary problem of tenement housing, but the *moral* problem posed by the street, with all its temptations and lack of social controls. In 1930s Hollywood, of course, any talk of sexual temptation was ruled out by the strict Production Code. (A rare exception was *Dead End*, which did make an oblique attempt to suggest a sexual component to the street's iniquities. Returning to his old block, gangster Humphrey Bogart finally locates his childhood sweetheart—only to discover, to his horror, that she has become a common prostitute.) That left only criminal temptation, which was more than acceptable to the producers, since it led straight back to the gangster theme. These films could show how the street turned kids into violent criminals—then offer a taste of that violence for audiences to enjoy. As presented in these films, the process itself was direct, and brutally causal: the street, *Dead End*'s subtitle declared, was "the cradle of crime." Another title, 1938's *Angels With Dirty Faces*, drew only slightly less obviously on the notion that gangsters were simply "good kids gone bad."

It was the group of boys introduced in *Dead End* who became the legendary test subjects of the street's baneful influence. Known as the "East 54th Street Gang," they proved so popular that they were brought back a year later in *Angels*, then continued to appear for over a decade as "the Dead End Kids"—until, pushing middle age, they were renamed the "Bowery Boys." Leo Gorcey, Huntz Hall, Billy Halop, Bobby Jordan, Gabriel Dell: they are all here, right from the start, far tougher and less lovable than in later appearances (151). In *Dead End*, we meet them as they gather in the street on a hot summer morning, the very picture of deprived youth. Their unhealthy environment is sketched in a few strokes: kids swimming in the filthy waters of the East River; one boy nicknamed "T.B." for his chronic affliction; casual tales of family violence and alcoholism. But it is the aimless, unsupervised quality of the street, leaving the kids free to get into all kinds of trouble, that seems most threatening: we watch them hit and abuse each other, extort money from a new kid on the block, gamble at cards, brutally beat up a rich boy and steal his watch. Tommy (Billy Halop) contrasts the white-sock-wearing "sissy" he was when he first came to the block with his current enlightenment: "Yeah, fellas," he says proudly, "it all comes from learnin'."

When we again meet the "kids" in *Angels With Dirty Faces*, a year later, they are slightly less violent but still in fine hooligan form, swaggering down a Lower East Side sidewalk that offers neither adult supervision nor any recreation beyond stealing slot machines and pickpocketing. In fact, one of the pockets they pick belongs to a shady fellow named Rocky Sullivan, a product of the same streets (as we learned in the film's prologue, set fifteen years before). Now a full-fledged gangster, Rocky—played with sly assurance by Jimmy Cagney—follows the boys to their secret clubhouse; he knows its location because it was once *his* clubhouse.

Thus the cycle is completed. Today's street kid is tomorrow's gangster. Today's gangster is yesterday's street kid. In *Dead End*, the end-product of the cycle is personified by "Baby Face" Martin, portrayed by Humphrey Bogart as a notorious "public enemy" who has returned to his childhood block to locate his mother. Running into the youthful Dead End Kids and sizing them up as apt pupils, he teaches them how to make their weapons more deadly and their tactics more violent (117). They are well on their way.

These films were hardly reticent about the determining role of the environment—and especially of the street itself. In *Dead End*, a local architect named Dave (Joel McCrea) defends the kids by arguing, "What chance have they got against all this? They have to fight for a place to play, fight for everything." In *Angels*, Rocky's childhood buddy, Jerry, now the local Catholic priest

117. *Dead End* (1937). Dramatizing the relationship between youthful street gangs and hardened criminals, this scene shows a notorious "public enemy" named Baby Face Martin (Humphrey Bogart, in gray suit at center), who, returning to his old block, passes on his violent lessons to a gang of local boys—the Dead End Kids—gathering around him eagerly.

(Pat O'Brien), vows to bring down his old friend because of "all those other kids, hundreds of them, in the streets and bad environment, who I don't want to see grow up like Rocky."

But what else is there? The middle-class corrective to the streets—a stable home life—seems elusive in the slums. Family and home are embodied by female characters who are, to a woman, almost powerless. Drina (Sylvia Sidney), Billy Halop's hardworking older sister, can't make a dent in her brother's delinquent ways. Nor can Laurie Martin (Ann Sheridan)—a childhood friend of Rocky's who has now become what he calls a "sociable worker"—hope to change him, or the Dead End Kids who idolize him. In one telling scene in *Sidewalks of New York*, Anita Page throws her younger brother a birthday party complete with cake and presents, but he quickly ducks out the bedroom window to rejoin his hoodlum pals downstairs. The home, in tenement districts, is no match for the temptations of the street. Page's romantic admirer, the millionaire played by Buster Keaton, does try to offer an alternative to the street, using his own money to build a gymnasium and community center. Father Jerry, in *Angels*, has a similar answer: a makeshift gym in a local storefront. Both evoke the modest goals of the early slum reformers, as well as the limitations that restrained both private philanthropy and the Church from doing more than merely scratching the surface of the problem.

118. ***A Tree Grows in Brooklyn*** **(1945).** Based on the novel by Betty Smith and set in 1912 Williamsburg, *A Tree Grows in Brooklyn*—the first film directed by Elia Kazan—was shot entirely on the New York Street at 20th Century-Fox. In this scene, a musician named Johnny Nolan (James Dunn) sets off with his daughter Francie (Peggy Ann Garner) on a Sunday promenade around the district.

On the face of it, *Dead End* offers far less hope. The Church is nowhere in sight, and Drina's boyfriend is not a wealthy philanthropist but only Dave, the unemployed architect. But Dave burns with an astonishing vision. He wants to "tear all this down, and all the other places like it," we are told, and "build a decent world where people could live decent and be decent." Unfortunately, no one in the film pays him the slightest attention, and the story concludes with the young Billy Halop being sent off to reform school for attacking the rich boy, which, as Dave bitterly predicts, will only complete his "education." "I've seen you before," he tells Halop. "There are thousands of you on streets like these. Start off with knives and end up with guns." The tenement street remains intact, ready for a new generation.

Yet as it happens, someone *was* listening to Dave: one of the few people, in fact, who could make his dream come true. The guest of honor in the audience at *Dead End*'s premiere in August 1937 was Robert F. Wagner Sr., senior senator from New York, who that very year was sponsoring an epochal piece of legislation, the Wagner-Stegall Housing Act, that finally put the federal government in the business of clearing slums. A few years before, such legislation would have been unthinkable, but now the public mood was changing, thanks in part to films like *Dead End*, which at this crucial moment was helping to convince the American public that the wretched conditions of the slums really *did* affect their own welfare, if for no other reason than fostering a class of gangsters. Wagner had reason indeed to be grateful to *Dead End*'s producer, Samuel Goldwyn; and Goldwyn's publicity department, naturally, was happy to capitalize on the distinguished senator's interest.

119. Red Hook Houses, Brooklyn, 1938. The first housing project in the country built by the U.S. Housing Authority, Red Hook Houses was also the first to be shaped to the revolutionary new template known as "the tower in the park," in which every trace of the traditional urban pattern of streets and blocks was eliminated. Instead, all of the functions that had once come together on the street—transportation, housing, shopping, recreation—were divided into distinct, widely separated zones.

The founding of the U.S. Housing Authority signaled the first federal commitment to slum clearance. Yet with the new agency came a disturbing trend. Earlier model projects in Harlem and in Brooklyn's Williamsburg district had been notable for their humane, low-rise scale and their high level of design. But from the very start, the Housing Authority's efforts lacked even a pretense of architectural quality; designers of the first effort, a huge South Brooklyn project called Red Hook Houses, actually boasted of the economies achieved through the large size and strict uniformity of its high-rise, elevator buildings (119).

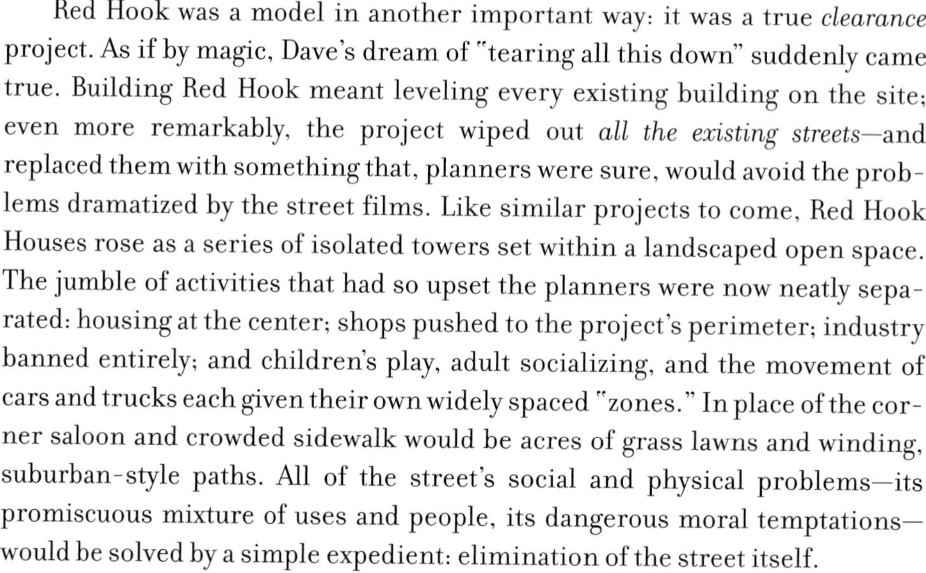

Red Hook was a model in another important way: it was a true *clearance* project. As if by magic, Dave's dream of "tearing all this down" suddenly came true. Building Red Hook meant leveling every existing building on the site; even more remarkably, the project wiped out *all the existing streets*—and replaced them with something that, planners were sure, would avoid the problems dramatized by the street films. Like similar projects to come, Red Hook Houses rose as a series of isolated towers set within a landscaped open space. The jumble of activities that had so upset the planners were now neatly separated: housing at the center; shops pushed to the project's perimeter; industry banned entirely; and children's play, adult socializing, and the movement of cars and trucks each given their own widely spaced "zones." In place of the corner saloon and crowded sidewalk would be acres of grass lawns and winding, suburban-style paths. All of the street's social and physical problems—its promiscuous mixture of uses and people, its dangerous moral temptations—would be solved by a simple expedient: elimination of the street itself.

By now, those problems had been reiterated in a whole series of tenement films—not just *Dead End* and *Angels With Dirty Faces* and *Sidewalks of New York*, but features such as 1939's *One Third of a Nation*, which singled out the street as especially noisome for its unsupervised play, and for the danger of automobile traffic. Unlike earlier tenement films, however, *One Third of a Nation* concludes on a distinctly optimistic note, plainly inspired by the government's recent initiatives: Mary (Sylvia Sidney) explains to her crippled brother that their landlord "is going to give this whole block to the city—and they're going to build new houses, decent houses. And you won't have to play in the streets anymore.

There'll be grass and trees, and regular playgrounds for kids, with swings and a handball court." As the film closes, we see that new housing actually going up, while Sylvia Sidney's brave voice repeats simply, "Grass and trees, parks and playgrounds." The movie city had always *depicted* the shape of the real city, but never before (and never again) did it actively align itself with the effort to transform that shape into something else. At a key historical juncture, the paths of the movie city and the real one had crucially intersected.

Delayed by World War II, the government's slum clearance efforts exploded in the postwar years. Back in 1937, Dave had wanted not only to "tear all this down"—meaning his tenement street—but, far more ambitiously, "all the places like it." That was precisely what the government now set out to do. Across New York (and other big cities), entire districts were soon being reduced to rubble and replaced with the new vision of "tower-in-a-park" projects, housing tens of thousands of people. Without exception, these projects shared the same profound antipathy for the traditional street, an attitude which had attained the status of gospel.

Yet now came a curious turn of events. One might have thought that Hollywood filmmakers, having railed so effectively against the tenement street before the war, would now flock to set their postwar pictures in the new settings that were quickly rising all across New York. Wasn't this precisely the landscape of grass and trees, paths and playgrounds they had been calling for all along?

But they didn't. Not once. Instead, of all things, they kept returning again and again to that old tenement street.

Some went right back to the theme of troubled kids (now called "juvenile delinquents") succumbing to the street's lurid temptations. *City Across the River*, the 1949 film version of *The Amboy Dukes*, Irving Shulman's novel about gang life on Brooklyn's Amboy Street, could be seen as a postwar update of *Dead End:* harsher, more violent, but sharing the same earnest belief that it was the physical failings of the district that caused—or at least reinforced—the violent behavior of its young men. "Sometimes I think the only solution is to clear out all the people and drop an atomic bomb on that whole slum," says one despairing teacher—hinting at the sweeping clearance programs that had already begun to level slum districts with a thoroughness not unlike that of a nuclear weapon, preparing the way for new housing projects.

Other films returned to the street in a different guise. In 1945, Fox released its film of Betty Smith's beloved coming-of-age novel, *A Tree Grows in Brooklyn.* Directed by Elia Kazan and set entirely in 1912 Williamsburg, the film showed the tenement district at a scale larger than ever before—and presented, moreover, a surprisingly complex and shaded appreciation of its street life.

Like the novel, the film is neither sentimental nor moralistic about the realities of tenement life. We see, for example, the dreary stairs that young Francie Nolan (Peggy Ann Garner) must climb every day to her apartment, and can recognize her family's humiliation when a financial crisis forces them to move to a still higher, cheaper unit in the building. Inside the apartment itself, we find a cramped, substandard dwelling, where cooking, dining, and living spaces share a single room. It is obvious why Francie and her brother prefer to spend much of their time on the street outside—even if, in its own way, it is no less crowded and overflowing, an astonishing cacophony of sight and sound.

To offer a complete portrait of Francie's world, Fox redressed much of their studio's New York Street to create a full-blown re-creation of 1910s Williamsburg. In 1945, it might have served as a primer for everything planners despised—and intended to eliminate—about the city's tenement streets. Children play amidst moving wagons, pushcarts, and streetcars (one game calls for flattening pennies under passing trolleys). The housing is intermingled not only with a jumble of commercial shops—butcher, bakery, grocer, saloon, hardware store, cigar shop, laundry—but a host of industrial activities: dressmakers, hatmakers, upholsterers, the Williamsburg Manufacturing Company, and Cheap Charlie's, the junk man who pays the children pennies for rags they collect. The district is an assault on the senses, from the shrill cries of the peddlers, streetcar bells, and organ grinders' music, to the profusion of big, garish signs and advertisements, spread over virtually every inch of wall. In this supposedly "residential" district, there is not a moment's rest, or calm, or peace.

Yet in one memorable scene, we get an entirely different view of the street—through the eyes of Francie's father, Johnny Nolan (James Dunn), a musician, romantic, and dreamer, who takes his beloved daughter in hand for a Sunday "promenade." Suddenly everything appears in a different light (118). Johnny tips his hat to ladies on the stoop and greets the Chinese launderer, Mr. Ching; he seems, in fact, to know everyone on the block. Looking into store windows, he and Francie imagine the pleasure that items on display—a pair of roller skates, for example—might offer. In Johnny's eyes, the street is not a confusion but an abundance of neighbors and attractions, of people to greet and things to admire—a universe of friendship and possibility. Johnny Nolan reminds us that for all its congestion and raucousness, the street could be home.

And what of those original denizens of the street, the Dead End Kids themselves? As popular as ever, they were undergoing a startling transformation. After eight films at Warner's, they moved to Universal for several more features before ending up, by the early 1950s, at Monogram, a small, "poverty row" studio whose only backlot set was a New York Street. They were the Bowery Boys now, their delinquent edge softened and made amiable. They still hung out on the sidewalk, muttered wisecracks, leered at ingénues, and engaged in raucous horseplay; but by film's end, through these and other allegedly comic activities, they would somehow manage to save an orphanage or accomplish some other worthy deed. No longer good kids gone bad, they were in danger of becoming bad kids gone good.

In a sense, a similar destiny overtook the tenement street itself. As popular on the screen as ever, now it was often cast in a different—and far more agreeable—light. By the 1950s, as the social urgency that had driven the old tenement films grew as distant as the New Deal itself, the New York tenement street emerged as a sort of classic American setting, as familiar and identifiable as the New England village, the Midwestern farm, the Western town. To the strains of "Sidewalks of New York," movies returned audiences time and again to the old city block, with all its homely, utilitarian details: the fire hydrants shaped like stubby fluted columns, the ornate "bishop's crook" lampposts, the distinctive street signs with their white serif lettering, the streetbed of granite "Belgian block," the ornate subway kiosks with their studded roofs. To audiences around the world, these films cemented an urban iconography as familiar as the red pillar boxes and double-decker buses of London, or the kiosks, café awnings, and Art Nouveau Métro entrances of Paris. (The unspoken understanding of these films was that New York, like only a handful of cities in the world, had developed a "language" of street elements so distinctive and well-known that they could be identified by audiences everywhere. Ironically, New Yorkers themselves took their city's special style for granted, barely noticing when a new generation of municipal bureaucrats and engineers began in the 1950s to remove these distinctive elements, replacing them with banal new fixtures no different from those anywhere else.)

This inability to leave the old street behind was revealing—and suggestive. Was there actually a *lure* to the tenement street, one that had always been there, perhaps, hidden beneath all the polemics about tearing it down? Filmmakers certainly now had ample opportunity to set movies within the street's enlightened successor, the housing project, with its grassy lawns, trees, and "regular playgrounds"—but they exhibited no interest whatsoever in doing so.

It was easy to understand why. In simplest terms, the housing project didn't "film." As its planners had consciously intended, the project dispersed its population and diffused its functions across the wide expanse of its multiacre site, so that any single view of it, framed in a lens, showed few people and even less activity. In place of the old street's compressed bustle of humanity were—at most—a few isolated pedestrians on the project's winding paths and broad lawns; in place of the well-defined frame of the continuous facades was a loose and amorphous landscape of widely separated towers. Gone was the rich ornament and variety of even the most modest tenement streets; the tall brick slabs of New York's projects were not only individually stripped-down, but nearly identical one to the next. For all its social failings, the tenement street was undeniably picturesque; for all its social superiority, the housing project appeared monotonous, uniform, and dull. It was not a trivial consideration. Before anything else, a filmmaker's priority is to make an interesting picture: to fill the frame with something that holds an audience's attention. (The movies, Alfred Hitchcock once declared, are "first of all . . . a two-dimensional medium. . . . You have a rectangle to fill. Fill it. Compose it.")

This was hard—if not impossible—to do with the housing project. It was terrifically easy with the traditional tenement street.

It was thus hardly surprising that, for more than four decades, the housing project remained absent from the screen. No backlot "housing project" set was ever built in Hollywood; nor were more than a few scenes ever shot in real New York projects. One rare appearance of the projects in a postwar feature was Cortlandt Homes, the development that architect Howard Roark designs, then destroys, in *The Fountainhead.* Significantly, we never get to see Cortlandt as an occupied environment, as any kind of "home" at all. Whether viewed as a pristine tabletop model or a disfigured construction site, the project remained a designer's plaything, a heroic expression of architectural will, wedded to lofty but vague social purpose (88).*

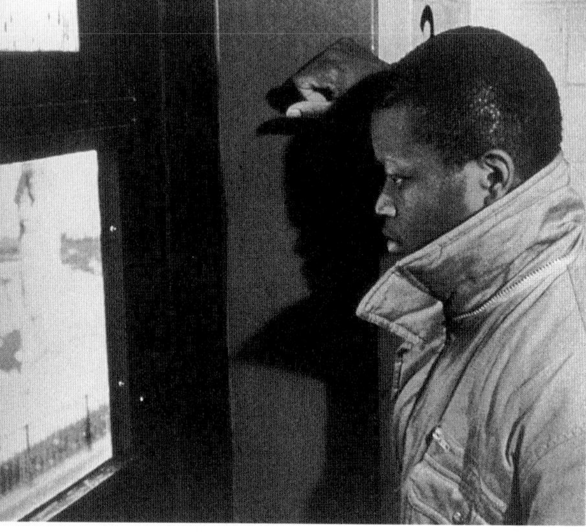

120. *Straight Out of Brooklyn* (1991). Set in Red Hook Houses and made by a first-time director named Matty Rich—who himself had grown up in the very same project—*Straight Out of Brooklyn* told the story of a teenager named Dennis (Lawrence Gilliard Jr.), who dreams of getting out of the project any way he can.

It was not until 1991, in fact, that a feature film took the first truly sustained look at a New York housing project. *Straight Out of Brooklyn* was directed and written by a seventeen-year-old African American filmmaker named Matty Rich, who had been born in the very Brooklyn project he used as the setting for his first film. The project in question, ironically, was none other than Red Hook Houses, the 1938 progenitor of the entire federal housing effort (119).

Straight Out of Brooklyn is very much a first-time work, hampered by shoestring production values. Yet that is part of its impact: an inside look by a young filmmaker at what the housing project had become, more than four decades after its idealistic inception (120).

In the postwar era, New York's public housing had grown into a veritable city within the city—home to well over half a million people, a population larger than most American cities. Its tenantry reflected New York's changing demography, as the city's newer poor—mostly black and Puerto Rican families—came to replace the older project population of white ethnic residents.

As early as the 1950s, it had become obvious that the simple determinism of the early reformers was deeply flawed, especially their belief that the *shape* of the slum was an essential cause of violent antisocial behavior. Given a wholesome environment without tenements or streets, *Dead End* and *One Third of a Nation* had argued, people would surely, in Dave's words, "live decent and be

*Housing projects did make brief, pointedly negative appearances in a handful of later features. In 1971's *The French Connection,* the disheveled project apartment of detective Popeye Doyle (Gene Hackman) plainly implies that the hard-driving cop has no real home life. In *Jacob's Ladder* (1990), Tim Robbins's nightmarish, post-Vietnam existence is set in another bleak Brooklyn project, drawing the sharpest possible contrast to the flashbacks of his happy family life before the war, in a Riverside Drive apartment house replete with canopy, doorman, and other comforting symbols of urban domesticity.

decent." But it wasn't quite so simple. Despite their green lawns and winding paths and widely dispersed buildings, housing projects were proving vulnerable to all the old social ills that had plagued the tenement street, along with a couple of new ones. In particular, as Rich's film demonstrated, the old problem of "good kids gone bad" remained as troublesome into the early 1990s as it had ever been—or perhaps more so.

The film starts inside, in an apartment where a teenager named Dennis Brown, played by Lawrence Gilliard Jr., lives with his family (the scene was shot in the actual Red Hook apartment of the director's grandmother). It is no old-law tenement, to be sure. Gone are the dark, squalid strings of rooms, the rotting plaster walls, the filthy toilets. If spartan and unspacious (Dennis and his teenage sister share a smallish bedroom, for example), the unit is at least clean and well lighted, with a modern kitchen and bathroom. But no less than any tenement apartment we have seen, it is a sinkhole of domestic trouble. Dennis's father (George T. Odom), embittered by societal racism and personal failure, beats his long-suffering wife (Ann D. Sanders) in brutal, drunken rages that the children cannot help but hear through their bedroom door. Dennis's own disputes with his father, meanwhile, grow steadily fiercer.

It is obvious why Dennis retreats outside, to the company of friends Kevin and Larry (played by Mark Malone and by Rich himself) who seem the spiritual heirs of the Dead End Kids—not bad boys, really, but aimless, impressionable teenagers growing up in a harsh, unforgiving place. Beneath the jokes and teasing, we sense the real frustration that is pushing them out into the world. "All we got," Dennis says to his friends, "is the streets."

But there are no streets in Red Hook; the planners have made sure of that. There are only parking lots, and lawns, and playgrounds—and it is in one of these playgrounds that, early on, we see a drug dealer killing someone at point-blank range. As the sound of the gunfire echoes through the project, a wide view of the tall brick faces of the buildings shows how easily the violence is swallowed up by this vast and anonymous landscape. Indeed, as the film continues, it becomes obvious just how little impact the street's elimination has had on the tenacious social problems of the slums. Park-like open spaces cannot prevent the disintegration of Dennis's family, nor keep Dennis himself from succumbing to the classic temptation of easy money and status that comes from criminal activity—in his case the robbery, at gunpoint, of a local drug dealer. Domestic violence, the frustrations of poverty, the lure of crime—all seem to have survived the tenement street, and are thriving perfectly well amidst the lawns and trees.

If anything, the shape of the housing project makes Dennis's descent into crime all the easier. If reformers once attacked the street for its lax, uncontrollable social structure, they could scarcely imagine the effect of the housing project's broad, abstract landscape, in which nearly all connection is severed between the open spaces below and the high-rise apartments above. In one moving scene, the sound of late-night gunfire outside the window awakens Dennis's mother; panicked, she races to Dennis's bedroom and, finding he is not in bed, is sure that her son has been shot. As it happens, Dennis is in no danger at that moment—but we sense her utter helplessness, her inability to exercise any control over the realm outside her apartment door. She has no way of even knowing what is happening out there.

In the wake of Rich's film, housing projects became a more common sight in the movie city, usually as part of the larger landscape of urban poverty. The broken-down Brooklyn project in which the teenage Chantel (Ariyan Johnson) lives, in Leslie Harris's *Just Another Girl on the I.R.T.* (1992), is presented as neither the solution nor the cause of her troubles, but simply another fact of her dismal existence. A similar matter-of-factness informs *Fresh* (1994), Boaz Yakin's compelling story of a clever ten-year-old (Sean Nelson), who lives in the project apartment of his aunt—an apartment he is forced to share with eleven other cousins, three to a bedroom. The film observes but does not comment on this overcrowding (technically illegal but all too common in real projects), which plainly subverts one of the original reasons for building such developments in the first place. Equally unremarked is the apartment's bare, utilitarian interior, which so clearly betrays the project's original unspoken intent to be a kind of filing cabinet for poor people, rather than any kind of real home. One of the film's few explicit acknowledgments of its abject setting comes at the end, when Fresh is offered the chance to live somewhere else. He has only a single request: "I don't wanna live in no more projects."

In 1995, the director Spike Lee offered the closest look yet at the housing project, detailing meticulously what *Straight Out of Brooklyn* had first sketched: the project's role as a modern-day "cradle of crime," a place where decent children grow into destructive adults. Like Rich's film, Lee's *Clockers* made it plain that this troubling social trajectory had survived the key change—eliminating the street—that was intended to defeat it; far more explicitly than the earlier film, it identified precisely how the project's utopian landscape had itself been adapted to illicit purpose—more ominously, perhaps, than the street had ever been.

Based on the novel by Richard Price, *Clockers* was shot in Gowanus Houses, a postwar Brooklyn project here called "Nelson Mandela Houses." For a moment, in the wide opening shot, we see the project as it might have been imagined by its planners, decades ago: a green, landscaped haven from the crowded city, its central bench encircling a tall white flagpole and proud American flag (121, top). The idyllic view is quickly shattered, however, when the bench is taken over by a "crew" of tough-looking teenagers. There is still a faint trace of the Dead End Kids in their lively, raucous debate about gangsta rap, but the chilling new reality is asserted when their leader, Strike (Mekhi Phifer), abruptly cuts off the chatter. "We gots to be about business," he says. For the boys have come into the project not to socialize but to work: to supply drugs to customers—local addicts, young prostitutes, middle-class kids from Connecticut—in good weather and bad, day or night, around the clock. They are "clockers."

But why have they come here? (As the film makes clear, neither Strike nor his boss lives in the project itself, but on its periphery.) With the help of the cinematographer Malik Hassan Sayeed, Lee shows us just how well suited the housing project is for their particular line of business. A telephoto lens picks out a customer, approaching in the leafy distance. One of the young sellers meets up with him, takes his order, then whistles a signal. The camera now whip-pans across to Strike, seated by the flagpole—a central location, we realize, which helps him coordinate the entire operation. Strike taps his chest, and again the camera whips sideways, to a lawn at the project's edge, where a lookout is deployed to watch for police. The lookout signals back that all is clear, information that Strike then relays (by tapping his head) to the actual seller, who remains all the while in relative seclusion. The seller takes the customer's cash and calls into the doorway of a nearby project building; within a few moments a runner emerges and drops a bag into a nearby trash can, followed moments later by the customer himself, who scoops up the bag and is on his way. The sale is complete.

With cruel precision the scene shows us how completely the project's broad green landscape has been turned to unlawful purpose. Offering widely dispersed open areas linked by long, uninterrupted sightlines, the grounds allow the clockers (with their sophisticated division of labor) to be themselves dispersed—not only to guard against the police, but to keep the money and drugs as separate as possible, in case trouble does occur. (Moments after the scene ends, in fact, the police pull up and conduct a search, but find nothing; the main cache of drugs remains safely stored away inside the nearby building.) Shooting the entire scene through a telephoto lens, Lee and Sayeed make the audience complicit in the action: we watch the illicit deal proceed through precisely the same long sightlines that the dealers themselves rely on. The telephoto lens also helps turn the dispersed, isolated landscape of the housing project—once so discouraging to filmmakers—into a series of compressed, incident-filled frames.

Of course, we are not the only ones watching. Occupying the very heart of the project, the clockers are inevitably a focus of attention for younger children—especially one bright, fatherless boy named Tyrone (Pee Wee Love), who idolizes Strike and is now running drug-related errands, his first steps into a life of clocking. Unlike the long-suffering mother in *Straight Out Of Brooklyn*, Tyrone's mother, Iris (Regina Taylor), is young and vigorous, and unwilling to give up her son without a fight; she has even recruited a decent housing patrolman (Keith David) to the cause. But how difficult the project makes her task! Its high-rise buildings, deliberately arranged to avoid enclosing or defining any open space, have severed every shred of domestic life from the public

121. *Clockers* (1995). For the film version of Richard Price's novel, Spike Lee and his crew shot on location for twelve weeks in the summer of 1994 in the Gowanus Houses in Brooklyn's Boerum Hill. As the top view shows, the project's buildings (following the same pattern as the prewar Red Hook Houses) no longer enclosed urban space but instead floated detached in an open landscape, disconnecting the project's private realm from its public space in a way that often proved disastrous for residents. In the bottom view, Iris Jeeter (Regina Taylor) tries to protect her young son Tyrone (Pee Wee Love) from Strike (Mekhi Phifer) and the other drug dealers (or "clockers") who command the project's open space.

realm below. When Iris bravely descends from her home to scold the clockers, to try to restore some sense of community responsibility ("I know you," she says to them, "I know your mothers!") we feel painfully just how little sense of "community" there is, down in this ill-defined, anonymous, deceptively verdant space, where the few symbols of authority—a caring mother, a kind policeman—go unsupported by any larger social fabric, or even a single shopkeeper (121, bottom). By the film's end, Tyrone has been rescued, but another clocker lies dead on the ground, shot in a drug dispute; walking away from the murder scene, a policeman suggests in disgust that "They should blow these projects to Timbuktu."

Once, filmmakers and reformers had agreed, the problem was obvious: the street was the cradle of crime, a hotbed of illicit temptation, the key to the slum's troubles. The answer was no less plain: "clear out the people, and drop an atomic bomb on that whole slum." And that was just what happened, in effect, when the postwar housing project cleared away all the old streets and replaced them with something completely different. Now the circle was complete, and there was still no answer, except explosives.

Perhaps it was time to take a second look at the street.

EYES ON THE STREET

As far back as the late 1950s, a handful of social scientists and design professionals had begun to question the logic that was systematically eliminating city streets in favor of the "superblock" layout of housing projects. In her landmark 1961 book, *The Death and Life of Great American Cities*, the urbanist Jane Jacobs took direct aim at the whole notion of the "cradle of crime"—starting with the "fantasy" that had underpinned *Dead End* and all the films like it:

> *A population of children is condemned to play on the city streets. These pale and rickety children, in their sinister moral environment, are telling each other canards about sex, sniggering evilly and learning new forms of corruption as efficiently as if they were in reform school. If only these deprived children can be gotten off the streets into . . . playgrounds with . . . space in which to run, grass to lift their*

souls! Clean and happy places, filled with the laughter of children responding to a wholesome environment.

Instead, she noted coolly, when the busy street was replaced by the dispersed housing project, "children . . . moved from under the eyes of a high numerical ratio of adults, into a place where the ratio of adults is low or nil." To consider this an improvement in child-rearing, she said, was "pure daydreaming."

But Jacobs's book went much further. It turned the world on its head, challenging the most basic tenet of planners and reformers: their antagonism to the street. Crowded old-law tenements may well have been poor housing, she acknowledged, but that hardly meant that the residential street itself was a bad idea—least of all because it "bred" criminals. "There is no direct, simple relationship between good housing and good behavior," she argued. "Good shelter is a useful good in itself, as shelter. When we try to justify good shelter on the pretentious grounds that it will work social or family miracles we fool ourselves. Reinhold Niebuhr has called this particular self-deception, 'The doctrine of salvation through bricks.' "

Far from breeding criminals, Jacobs insisted, the street was a sort of front line in the fight *against* crime. "Sidewalks, their bordering uses, and their users," she wrote, "are active participants in the drama of civilization versus barbarism in cities. To keep a city safe is a fundamental task of a city's streets and its sidewalks." Her reasoning was simple. Unlike the dispersed residential layout of the housing project, the street *compressed* pedestrian life, while also providing shops, restaurants, and other commercial activities. The result was a continuous stream of "eyes on the street"—residents, shopkeepers, customers, passersby—who, by their very presence, tended to deter criminal or disorderly behavior in a way that the police, in and of themselves, could not.

To be well-used, she said, a street needed to be relatively short, compact, and dense, with plenty of building entrances. But above all, it needed to be *varied*, with shops and services as well as houses; small, older buildings as well as big, newer ones; children and elderly people as well as young adults; single working people as well as large families. As the varied schedules and pathways of different kinds of people and activities overlaid one another, the street would remain busy for much of the day.

The crucial reason to encourage activity, she argued, was to *make the street worth watching.* Few people spend much time looking at an empty street. But "large numbers of people entertain themselves," she said, "off and on, by watching street activity. The sight of people attracts still other people." A well-used street would be a well-watched street, which in turn would help it become even better used.

For the movie city, there was something intuitively plausible in the notion of "watching" as something central to the success of a street. For decades, after all, audiences had been happily "watching" the New York street in literally hundreds of films, and, in the wake of Jacobs's book, it was evident that the filmic New York street offered a virtual checklist of her prescriptions for lively city street life: short blocks framed by dense, low buildings; entrances, stoops, and windows in easy communication with the sidewalk; a combination of houses, shops, and informal play; and a mix of people of different ages and types—children, teenagers, parents, the elderly, shopkeepers and customers, residents and passersby—going about their lives, their paths all intersecting. To be sure, the filmic street was typically busier and more incident-filled than a real one; but as Jacobs herself noted in describing a day in the life of her Hudson Street block, depictions of the street inevitably tend to telescope and compress its activities and rhythms.

Of course, many of these films—*Angels With Dirty Faces*, to give a classic example—had been part of the sustained effort to dismiss the street as a "bad environment." Looking back, it was evident how profoundly ambivalent those films were, how powerfully attracted the filmmakers had been to the street, even as the films themselves—informed by the reformers' morality—were busy proclaiming how pernicious it all was. In the prewar era, they could eat their cake and have it, too, as their cameras lingered lovingly over the street in order to show us why, in principle, it was so bad. But after the war, the game was given away: faced with a choice between the supposedly wicked but undeniably vital street, on the one hand, and the virtuous but lifeless housing project, on the other, moviemakers showed their true colors. The pictorial power of the street, the sheer visual allure of its compressed urbanism and humanity, was simply too appealing to filmmakers.

Yet in their "merely" pictorial orientation, it turns out, filmmakers were on to something that had eluded the reformers and planners. As Jacobs made clear, to be "worth watching" was not marginal but *essential* to the success of a city's public space. The same "visual interest" that intrigued audiences and brought them to the theater would intrigue city dwellers and bring them onto the sidewalk—thus helping, in the process, to make the street not only lively, but comfortable and safe. What made the New York street a good *set* for the movie city, in other words, made it a good *setting* in the real city.

In this light, it was worth taking a last look at the New York Street itself, still standing in the California sun. For clearly it was a place with its own distinctive reality, less a copy of the real city than a vigorous interpretation. This was especially true of its layout, more picturesque than the notoriously rectilinear Manhattan street grid, where except for a few blocks in Greenwich Village and another couple near Wall Street, the streets are arrow-straight, flying off into infinity. The blocks of Hollywood's New York Street, by contrast, had a gentle bend midway in their length, or met each other in T-shaped intersections—very unlike the real city. Though the effect may have been picturesque, the motivation was anything but: bending the street, or having it intersect another,

122. New York Street, MGM, 1951. This aerial view of MGM's famed New York Street—located on Lot 2 of the Culver City studio from 1932 until 1978, when it was demolished to make way for a low-rise condominium development—clearly reveals its character as a vessel of space, defined by building fronts, whose fundamentally urban quality stands in dramatic contrast to the classic suburban pattern, visible at top left, of freestanding houses and bungalows dotting the surrounding landscape.

served to close down the vista and eliminate the need for expensive additional streets trailing into the distance (98).

The curious result, evident in countless films, was to give a distinctly small-town scale to one of the world's largest cities. In doing so, the filmic street illustrated one of the more surprising characteristics of New York: that what outsiders see as endless stretches of avenue actually break down for residents into small overlapping neighborhoods, each just a few blocks in size and encompassing the shops and services of daily life. The New York Street's great conceit, that it could condense the urbanism of the sprawling metropolis into a few blocks, thus made manifest what most New Yorkers know to be the truth, that their "city" *does* in large part consist of the few blocks around them (122).

But the greatest revelation of the New York Street was still more essential and, in its way, poetic. To a far greater degree than a freestanding structure in a rural or suburban setting, a city building can be divided into two conceptual halves, each with its own distinct role. Its interior rooms shelter and enclose the building's inhabitants, while its facade helps frame and define the city's public realm, creating what is, finally, a room of its own—an *outdoor* room with its own distinctive life. Nothing could illuminate this essential difference be-

123. New York Street, Warner Bros., 1947. This view of the Madison Avenue set that was built for *Life With Father* (and probably taken during its production) reveals how the false fronts of Hollywood's New York Street could shape a well-defined arena of civic life within.

tween a city building's *architectural* and *urban* identities more simply—or suggestively—than the backlot New York Street, in which building interiors were simply peeled away, retaining only the facades, sidewalks, and street bed (123). The result—one of the most familiar city settings in the world—was a pure vessel of urban life, demonstrating what Jacobs suggested at the outset of this chapter: that the very essence of a city could be found in its streets.

ONE LITTLE PART OF THE WORLD

Even as Jacobs's principles were revolutionizing modern city planning, a series of trends were gradually undermining her vision of a vital street life. The introduction of residential air-conditioners tended to close up windows, especially in summer; television offered spectacles more distracting than any real sidewalk view; and automobiles, rather than subways, buses, or walking, became an increasingly common means of transport, even in much of New York. Life moved away from the window, away from the stoop, away from the street, as middle-class city dwellers withdrew into secure, climate-controlled interiors.

Amidst all this, only one group remained consistently close to the street: the poor. Despite problems of crime, drugs, and decay, many blocks in the city's poorer districts continued to display a remarkably resilient and vital street life; in 1989, Spike Lee turned to one such block, in the heart of Brooklyn's Bedford-Stuyvesant district, for a film that could almost serve as a Jacobs-like primer on the abiding values of the New York street: *Do the Right Thing.*

Of course, Lee had an agenda of his own in *Do the Right Thing:* to present a passionate and charged exploration of the African American experience in New York in the late 1980s, a world shaped by systemic poverty and its attendant problems. The block that Lee chose to portray, if not at the very bottom of the social ladder, is plainly an economically distressed place, and one, furthermore, racked by racial strife—tensions among blacks, whites, and Asians, as well as routine police brutality—that ultimately explodes in a harrowing riot. Yet unlike his predecessors, Lee was careful to separate the community's larger social problems from its physical context—in other words, from the street itself. Indeed, one of the film's primary goals, Lee wrote, was to show that despite their place in "the bowels of the socio-economic system," poor black New Yorkers could "still live with dignity and humor." Notwithstanding its simmering anger and apocalyptic conclusion, much of *Do the Right Thing* is a series of richly textured, often amusing urban vignettes, revealing a complex and community-sustaining street life (124).

In its setting and structure, Lee's film strongly recalled the classic 1930s New York street movies, especially *Street Scene* and *Dead End:* a single block across a single summer day, caught in a sweltering heat wave that not only brings the block's inhabitants out into the open but escalates tensions toward a violent climax. Unlike those earlier films (and in a victory over the production chiefs at Universal), Lee worked not in the studio but on location, a block of Stuyvesant Avenue between Quincy and Lexington Avenues. Yet ironically, having won his battle for the "authenticity" of a real location, Lee and his production designer, Wynn Thomas, sought to create a setting much like a classic

124. ***Do the Right Thing*** **(1989).** Trying to ease the heat of an unbearably hot day, local residents of a Brooklyn block turn a fire hydrant into a "johnny pump," and frolic in its cooling spray of water.

backlot street—limiting the action to a single block, a precisely bounded bowl of urban space that serves as a microcosm for the larger city. As if to acknowledge this teasing relationship between location authenticity and studio artifice, Lee placed his memorable title sequence—Rosie Perez shadow-boxing to Public Enemy's "Fight the Power"—not on the street itself but in front of a series of theatrical-style backdrops showing the facades of row houses and tenements. The street, in other words, as scene.

125. *Do the Right Thing* (1989). Personifying Jane Jacobs's notion of "eyes on the street," an elderly widow named Mother Sister (Ruby Dee) sits all day in her window, overlooking the Bedford-Stuyvesant block that is the central setting of the film's activity.

As the film begins and the block comes to life in the early morning, a series of carefully composed views emphasize its self-enclosed, almost sheltering character. Our guide is Mookie, played by Lee himself, first seen in an apartment whose dark, stifling atmosphere makes it plain why he would spend most of his time out on the street, even if his pizza delivery job didn't require it anyway. Watching Mookie descend from his stoop and make his way down the sidewalk, we see a man for whom—no less than for Johnny Nolan in *A Tree Grows in Brooklyn*—the street is home (5). If in private life a deeply flawed figure (the irresponsible father of an illegitimate child, among other things), Mookie moves in public as a friend to all, with a greeting for almost everyone he sees. Following his progress past the block's stoops and gardens, children and mailmen, we share in the comfortable domestic rhythm of the sidewalk, in part because the camera itself is dollying right alongside. Borrowing from the photographer Andreas Feininger's classic images of Fifth Avenue, location filmmakers have often pointed a telephoto lens straight down the length of the sidewalk, artificially telescoping the view; by contrast, Lee's sidelong, gliding shot captures a true sense of walking down a block, within an invisible but palpable "bubble" of personal space. Mookie's walk also establishes a central motif: the film itself will spend much of its time simply roaming the block, making discoveries in every corner.

One such discovery is just how many different purposes are served by the street. For the loud but lethargic "corner men" (Paul Benjamin, Frankie Faison, and Robin Harris), planted on chairs beneath a beach umbrella, the sidewalk is a veritable piazza, a spot from which to watch the world go by while debating everything from global warming to Mike Tyson. For young children, the street itself is a canvas for chalk drawings, or a speedway for bicycles. When a fire hydrant is opened and kids splash under its cooling spray, the street becomes an impromptu recreation center—at least until the police shut off the water. The stoop, similarly, is not just a means of access but an entire social center of its own, serving at times as an outdoor extension of the house's rooms, at others like a bleacher facing the action of the street.

Some of the most important street fixtures are not places but people: "regulars," such as those played by the husband-and-wife team of Ossie Davis and Ruby Dee. Dee is Mother Sister, a sharp-tongued widow who sits in her window, dispensing advice to those passing by beneath—the quintessential example of Jacobs's "eyes on the street" (125). "I'll be watching you, son," she tells Mookie. "Mother Sister *always* watches." Davis, meanwhile, is Da Mayor, an elderly rummy with a touch of faded dignity in his scruffy summer suit. Da Mayor does little except sit around the block all day, moving from stoop to stoop, doing odd jobs, enjoying his beer. Yet he, like Mother Sister, embodies what urbanists like William H. Whyte have long noticed—that successful city spaces often have individuals (Whyte actually calls them "mayors") whose familiar presence helps to preserve order and deter crime, or, in one telling vignette drawn from Lee's own childhood, avert catastrophe. A young boy races into the street after an ice-cream truck just as a car comes speeding recklessly down the block; seeing the imminent accident, Da Mayor hurls himself against the child, saving the boy's life.

The film also makes explicit the value of local stores, which on blocks like these take on a role all out of proportion to their commercial utility. Shops are a block's true social centers; like the regulars, they provide a constant familiar presence that helps keep a street safe and well used. The block in *Do the Right Thing* has two corner stores: one a newly opened Korean market; the other an old-time pizzeria, Sal's Famous, the focus of the film's action. As played by Danny Aiello, Sal embodies the complex role that local shops assume in their neighborhoods, well beyond keeping the sidewalks swept or providing jobs for local residents. As Sal asserts with real feeling, the block's youngsters have grown up on his pizza; they are in some sense *his* kids, black or white—a feeling reciprocated, during much of the film, by the kids themselves. Indeed, one of the things that makes the film's escalating racial tensions so painful to watch is their power to undermine, and ultimately overwhelm, this affinity between a shopkeeper and his regular customers. (In many poorer parts of the real city, of course, corner shops like Sal's have long since moved out, and their absence is not only a daily inconvenience to residents but a serious obstacle to rebuilding a sense of community.)

126. ***Crooklyn*** **(1994).** Filmed on Arlington Place, a picturesque block of brownstones in Bedford-Stuyvesant, Spike Lee's filmic evocation of his Brooklyn childhood features a variety of youthful urban pleasures, from elaborate street games to the simple joy of racing down the length of a city sidewalk.

With its tragic, catastrophic climax—in which growing racial hostilities, fueled by a brutal killing by the police, explode in a riot that destroys Sal's Famous—Lee's film offers no pretense that the values of the street, by themselves, can possibly counteract deep-seated social and economic problems. But just as plainly, Lee makes clear that far from being the source of those problems, the traditional street can serve as a kind of harbor against them. If anything, this belief grew stronger in his later films, especially *Crooklyn* (1994), which extended the backlot character of *Do the Right Thing* by literally creating a dead-end block out of a real Brooklyn street, then filling it with a dazzling panorama of street games: handball, hopscotch, double Dutch, dominoes, tops, caps, blowing bubbles, stickball (126). Lee's *Jungle Fever* (1991), meanwhile, enlarged the notion of the street as bulwark against urban decay, using a handsome block of Harlem row houses (Strivers' Row, an 1891 grouping designed by McKim, Mead & White) as the symbol of a struggling, black middle-class order that is threatened both from within—by the marital infidelity of the leading character, an architect played by Wesley Snipes who takes a white lover—and from without, by the continuing nightmare of drug abuse and poverty symbolized by the ragged, graffiti-scarred, prostitute-filled corners where the block meets not just the surrounding avenues but the larger troubles of African American urban life.

Perhaps the most poetic defense of the city street—and especially of the crucial role played by shopkeepers—came from the director Wayne Wang and writer Paul Auster in their 1995 film, *Smoke,* which used a Brooklyn cigar shop as the focal point for the interweaving stories of several local residents. Central among these is the store's manager, Auggie Wren (Harvey Keitel), who for thirteen years, from the same spot across the street, has been photographing the corner in front of his store every morning at eight, just before he opens for business (262). "It's my corner, after all," he explains. "It's just one little part of the world, but things happen there, too, just like everywhere else. It's a record of my little spot." As we view a sampling of his photographs, we hear Auggie's paean to the dailiness of city sidewalk life:

> *They're all the same, but each one's different from every other one. You've got your bright mornings and your dark mornings. You've got your summer light and your autumn light. You've got your weekdays and your weekends. You've got people in overcoats and galoshes, and you've got your people in shorts and T-shirts. Sometimes the same people, sometimes different ones. And sometimes the different ones become the same, and the same ones disappear. The earth revolves around the sun, and every day the light from the sun hits the earth at a different angle.*

The haunting images, coming one after another, day by day, identically framed but subtly different, make visible the powerful bond between the shopkeeper and the street he or she serves. In taking his pictures, which now number over four thousand, Auggie is proud to say he has never missed a day—an apt metaphor indeed for the sense of daily responsibility that a store brings to the street on which it sits. If nothing else, it can always be counted on to be there, open for business, day after day after day. No small thing, it turns out.

Amidst this rediscovery of the street's enduring values, of course, its threats and dangers could not be forgotten entirely. Larry Clark's 1995 film, *Kids*, which followed a roving group of adolescents through the streets of lower Manhattan, reiterated all the classic concerns about the "unsupervised" street. Using a telephoto lens that made cars, buses, and trucks seem to fly out of nowhere, the film offered a heightened sense of the physical danger posed by the street—then reinforced it with some hair-raising videos of kids skateboarding in and around fast-moving city traffic (127). But the focus is on the larger terrors of the street, as its young characters, roaming the city on their own, manage to get into every kind of trouble possible: drug abuse, sexually transmitted diseases, brutal and senseless violence. Perhaps the film overstated its case, but the fact remained that in recent years no urban setting—city street *or* housing project—has been a refuge from trouble, especially for the young. In this context, *I Like It Like That*, a 1994 film by a young Irish–Puerto Rican filmmaker named Darnell Martin, offered a spirited look at the strengths and limitations of both the street *and* the home.

127. ***Kids* (1995).** In this view of a group of New York kids making their way down Houston Street, director Larry Clark's use of a telephoto lens visually compresses the traffic, pedestrians, and landscape—dramatically heightening a sense of urban congestion and threat.

To the infectious rhythm of Tito Puente's title song, we are brought right into the heart of the action. Dusk is falling on East 170th Street, a Hispanic area of the Bronx, and the street is *alive*. More than any film since 1929's *Sunny Side Up*, the film celebrates ordinary street life as a kind of ongoing block party. As the camera swoops across the buildings, we see activity filling almost every window and fire escape, while on the street itself, the "party" is in full swing: a stickball game in progress; the local priest, in shirtsleeves, sweeping in front of his church; kids playing tag; a car pulling up filled with sexy young women who quickly meld into the crowd. There is talk and music everywhere, and the scene is suffused with the balmy, expectant feel of a summer evening. The only ominous note is a sidewalk mural commemorating a heroic Puerto Rican policeman who was killed on that very spot by drug dealers.

Amidst all this, we see Chino and Lisette Linares (Jon Seda and Lauren Vélez) in their apartment, trying to enjoy a session of conjugal sex—even as their kids bang on the bedroom door and the downstairs neighbor hollers out the window that her ceiling is falling down—news which prompts the gang hanging out on the stoop to jeer and mock the married lovers.

In this high-spirited opening lies all of the film's themes. The Linareses' apartment, while not nightmarishly dark or run down, is too cramped to afford a true measure of domestic comfort: the three children are constantly in one another's way, invading virtually every moment of their parents' privacy (at one point, desperate to escape the screeching, Lisette locks herself in the bathroom

128. ***I Like It Like That*** **(1994).** On the sidewalk in front of their South Bronx apartment, Chino and Lisette Linares (Jon Seda and Lauren Vélez) publicly conduct a marital argument, with Lisette's mother (Rita Moreno) and Chino's best friend (Vincent Laresca) taking active part. On the far right, in the distance, stands another source of trouble—a sultry neighbor named Lisa (Magdalena Soto).

and loudly sings along with the radio). We see why and how life moves to the street, in lively stoop and sidewalk conversations with an extended community of friends, family, and rivals. But this means of escape from the claustrophobic apartment is not without its own problems. For reasons of their own, members of the larger group are constantly interfering in the couple's life, spreading rumors of infidelity and fanning discord until Chino and Lisette, after a loud and angry fight—on the sidewalk, and before the entire street crowd—decide to separate (128).

By now, the lines of domesticity and community, of home and street, have grown so confused that Chino and Lisette must spend the rest of the film trying to reestablish their proper boundaries. The final push, unhappy but ultimately necessary, comes from the street itself. Confused and angered by his parents' separation, Chino Jr. (Tomas Melly) suddenly starts sporting expensive clothes, bought with money earned as a lookout for a young drug dealer. When Chino Sr.—whose own brother Hector, it turns out, was the slain policeman memorialized in the sidewalk mural—angrily confronts his son, the dealer (who is all of twelve years old himself) whips out a pistol. However lively, the street offers real dangers and temptations—and their child, Chino and Lisette realize, desperately needs an alternative, a place infused with the moral authority of both father *and* mother. So the separated couple agree to reconstitute their home, in an artificial, divided fashion at first (with Lisette sleeping in the living room) but eventually—as the film closes, in a scene of gentle, late-night intimacy—with genuine feeling.

If the street—as Jacobs, Lee, Wang, Auster, and the others showed so vividly—could be a true extension of the home, then so, too, Darnell Martin reminded us, did the house remain a crucial alternative to the street. It was perhaps not too much to ask, in the end, that a city provide both.

SEVEN

DOMESTIC ELABORATIONS

MANSION, APARTMENT, AND LOFT

SOME SORT OF RESIDENCE

Cary Grant is Johnny Case, a high-spirited young man who has raised himself up from childhood poverty to a banking career on Wall Street. As *Holiday* (1938) opens, Johnny has just returned from a vacation at Lake Placid—in even higher spirits than usual.

At his first stop, we find out why. To his old friends Nick and Susan Potter (Edward Everett Horton and Jean Dixon)—a professor and his wife, who live in a modest apartment near Columbia University—Johnny announces joyously that he's become engaged to a beautiful young woman he met on the trip, one Julia Seton. Now he is off to find her, at some address on Fifth Avenue.

As his taxi rolls up to the house, Johnny is perplexed. The number, 843 Fifth, seems to be correct—but the structure itself, a great stone-fronted mansion that stretches across most of the block, can hardly be his Julia's. Assuming she must be a social secretary of some kind, he ignores the front door, and walks to the service entrance by the side.

His appearance there only enlarges the confusion (130). The butler, relaxing in the kitchen, hastily throws on his coat and snaps to attention while pointing out, as politely as possible, that Miss Julia's callers *usually* enter by the front door. He leads Johnny on a circuitous path across the kitchen and pantry, down a long service corridor and into the main hall. Now Johnny may be properly announced.

129. (previous page) ***Holiday*** **(1938).** Entering the main hall of the Seton residence, newcomer Johnny Case (Cary Grant) crosses paths with the family scion, Ned Seton (Lew Ayres Jr.), on his way to church, hungover from the night before. Directed by George Cukor from a play by Philip Barry, the film takes place almost entirely in the mansion's elaborate interiors, designed by the art director Stephen Goosson.

The reception hall itself brings forth a classic Cary Grant double take. Two stories high, covered in marble and filled with columns, it features an ornate double staircase that sweeps down in two symmetrical arms (49). Their treads, however, go unused; Johnny is brought to the upper landing in a small private elevator. "I could have *walked* that!" he exclaims in disbelief.

Up here, in yet another ornate salon, Johnny at last finds Julia (Doris

Nolan), who explains that this is indeed her home. "But it's enormous!" Johnny cries. "It's the Grand Central Station!" He is inspired to try a yodel—"Bad echo," he notes. In his irreverence he finally grasps that Julia is no social secretary. "Don't tell me you're one of *those* Setons?"

In the years from 1880 to 1914, New York witnessed the construction of a series of houses like no others before or since. So large they could often be shaped as free-standing pavilions, they consciously evoked the grandest castles, mansions, and villas of Europe and symbolized the extraordinary concentration of wealth and power that had made New York the undisputed financial and cultural capital of the United States. Though a few made appearances on Riverside Drive and elsewhere, most were concentrated on a single thoroughfare: Fifth Avenue, whose two miles north of 50th Street became an unbroken line of urban palaces (131).

130. ***Holiday*** **(1938).** Arriving at the Seton mansion by way of the servants' entrance, Johnny Case (Cary Grant) immediately disturbs the social order of the traditional household.

It was hardly surprising that filmmakers—inevitably drawn by the storytelling potential of social extremes—should gravitate to Fifth Avenue's mansions as readily as they did to the Lower East Side's tenements. Mansions provided the kind of mind-boggling luxury that audiences expected from the movie city, an extended look at the rarefied world they might otherwise glimpse only in society columns or the rotogravure sections of the Sunday newspapers.

131. View of Fifth Avenue, 1900. Looking north from 64th Street, this view shows the astonishing row of mansions that stood opposite Central Park at the start of the twentieth century. In the foreground is the home of Mrs. Caroline Schermerhorn Astor, famed arbiter of New York's elite "Four Hundred."

Yet from the start, the filmic representation of the mansion was a complex, contradictory affair. For one thing, in the midst of the heightened class-consciousness of the Great Depression, the mansion's extravagance was more than a little suspect. When millionaire Harmon Van Dine, played by Buster Keaton in 1931's *Sidewalks of New York*, proudly tells tenement girl Anita Page that his grandfather built their enormous house seventy-five years ago, she quickly shoots back, "If it was down in our neighborhood, seventy-five families would live in it."

But it was more than an issue of economic inequality. Art Deco penthouses were certainly homes for the rich, but Hollywood typically admired them as stylish, modern dwellings. By contrast, Fifth Avenue mansions were usually portrayed as dinosaurs from another era, whose heavy architecture and formal way of life grew more anachronistic with every passing year. A stroll down the movies' mythic Fifth Avenue—starting at the Seton house and moving on to the Bullock, Merrick, and Totten mansions, in *My Man Godfrey* (1936), *The Devil and Miss Jones* (1941), and *Ball of Fire* (1941), respectively—thus traces an unmistakable decline; a way of life first threatened, then overrun, by the encroachments of the modern world.

Of course, the film city tried, as usual, to have it both ways. Even as the script challenged the mansion's isolation from an increasingly egalitarian world, the camera luxuriated in its lavish settings and rituals. Thus could *Holiday*'s opening revel in the physical grandeur of the Seton house, even while quietly insinuating the darker social realities upon which it depended.

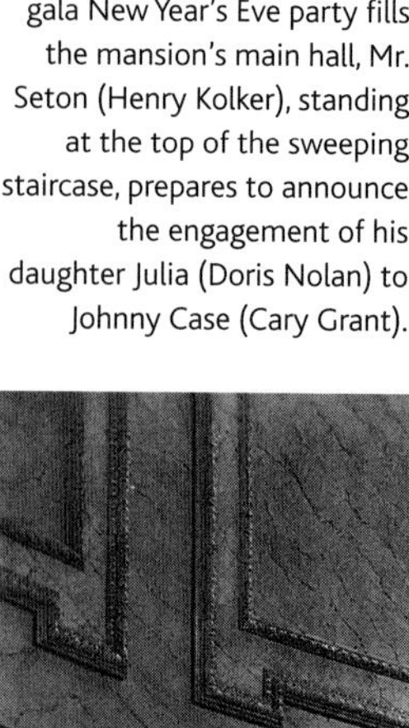

132. ***Holiday* (1938).** As a gala New Year's Eve party fills the mansion's main hall, Mr. Seton (Henry Kolker), standing at the top of the sweeping staircase, prepares to announce the engagement of his daughter Julia (Doris Nolan) to Johnny Case (Cary Grant).

In truth, the two were closely related. Where the old row house had been forced to intertwine its servant and family realms within the narrow confines of a twenty-five-foot-wide lot, the mansion could afford to spread out its various components—entertainment, family, and service rooms—into complete wings, linked by elaborate circulation paths. As the rooms grew more numerous, the spaces connecting them assumed ever-greater importance—especially the stair hall, which became the prime compositional element to unite the sprawling layouts. The staircase itself grew into a major sculptural statement whose complex, elaborate design epitomized the mansion as a whole.

The new scale required equally dramatic changes in social structure. The row house had been predicated on a few domestic servants, but simply maintaining a mansion required a veritable army of butlers, footmen, cooks, maids, and caretakers. With its legions of servants and its acres of rooms and hallways, the Fifth Avenue mansion became a world unto itself, a self-contained and ramified hierarchy of class and position whose physical layout was intended not only to impress outsiders but to keep everyone in his or her proper place.

Until, that is, Johnny Case shows up. Wide-eyed but irreverent, he is the audience's surrogate in this impressive yet alien world. It is hardly an accident that we first meet him not in the mansion but in the Potters' apartment, a benchmark of middle-class life against which he (and the audience) can measure the peculiar extravagance of the Seton mansion. For whether he knows it or not, Johnny, having transcended social class in his own life, represents a threat to the mansion's well-tended world. The amusing confusion of his arrival is actually a carefully calibrated setup: by breaking, however unintentionally, the distinction between the service and family wings of the house, Johnny has begun a breakdown of class structure that, before it is over, will liberate at least one family member from the mansion's powerful constraints.

In the meantime, the film tabulates the cost of those proprieties. Johnny sees Ned Seton (Lew Ayres Jr.), the family scion, on his way to church, plainly hungover from the night before (129). A while later Johnny hears his own reservations about the place echoed by Julia's sister, the family's self-described "black sheep"—Linda Seton, played by Katharine Hepburn. "Don't expect simplicity here," she warns him. "Just think of our Fifth Avenue frontage." Linda is a kindred spirit, no less skeptical of the house and its way of life than Johnny. Yet until now she has been its prisoner, her sole refuge a childhood playroom on the fourth floor, the only space in the house not surfaced in marble, the only one that hints of an ordinary home. Seeing it, Johnny understands immediately. "This is quite different," he says to her, "from the rest of the house, I mean."

In Johnny, Linda sees a ray of hope; eager to celebrate, she decides to throw an engagement party for her sister—a small, intimate affair in the playroom, she insists, not the kind of stuffy, formal reception their father would give.

133. *Holiday* (1938). In a scene that offers an architectural and social cross-section of the Seton mansion, Linda (Katharine Hepburn) begins by comforting her drunken brother Ned in the upstairs playroom that is her private retreat. Descending the main staircase to join the party below, she begins greeting guests, all the while scanning the room for the free-spirited Johnny—who, she is told by a servant, has left the house as he first came in, through the service entrance. Breaking the unspoken rules of the mansion, she traces his steps down the service corridor and into the kitchen, where she heads for the back door and stands in its threshold, eager to follow him but unable—for now—to go any farther.

"Nobody must touch my party but me," she declares to Julia—but as the sisters rise from the foot of the grand staircase where they have been sitting, the wide marble steps seem to exert a pressure of their own. It is hard to imagine *any* sort of informal affair transpiring in this place. And indeed, by the time Johnny has been reluctantly accepted as a son-in-law by their imperious father, Linda's "little party" has been transformed into an immense, formal New Year's Eve reception.

The night of the event, we see the house as it was truly meant to function: hundreds of guests in evening clothes, gliding up and down the grand staircase and assembling in the reception hall (132). The scene is spectacular, at least from a distance; moving in closer, we observe how stiffly the guests move, overhear them bad-mouthing their hosts even as they maintain their frozen, obsequious smiles.

The satire heightens when the Potters make their very *in*formal entrance, Professor Potter handing his humble galoshes to the footman. As with Johnny's first arrival, a great point is made of the staircase's irrelevance. "The *elevator,*" the servants tell the Potters repeatedly, "is to the *rear* and to the *right.*" The point is taken. In ages past, staircases such as these might well have been functional and therefore appropriate things. But in the twentieth century, a time of mechanical conveniences like elevators, the grand staircase is plainly obsolete, an anachronism whose only "function" is social pretension. What is true of the stair must be, by extension, true of the rest of the house, a point the Potters are happy to make as they wander around upstairs like a pair of archaeologists. "It seems to have been some sort of residence at one time," Nick Potter can be heard muttering.

At the party's peak, near midnight, Johnny is to be found not with his fiancée but with her sister. All evening Linda has avoided the crowd downstairs, hiding in her playroom, hosting a casual gathering of the Potters, her brother, and a delighted Johnny; she has managed to give her little party, after all. After the others have left, Johnny and Linda speak at last of their mutual dilemma, of the "vested interests" that have long kept Linda imprisoned in her own house, and which threaten even now to engulf Johnny in a world of deadening responsibility. They stand at an upstairs window, watching the city celebrate the coming of the New Year. The audience does not see the city, but only hears it—a joyful cheer, exuberant and free. Somehow (*we* know) Johnny and Linda belong together, out there. But not yet.

Resisting Johnny for the sake of her sister, Linda sends him down to the party, urging him to stay true to his beliefs, whatever the cost. She will remain up here with Ned, the other outcast, who, drunk as usual, has passed out cold. But a little later, resigned to the situation, she makes her own descent—in a complex passage across the height and length of the house that lays bare the entire relationship of *Holiday*'s story to its setting (133).

She begins by comforting her brother, a tender reminder of all the family feeling that has been lost downstairs. Leaving her refuge, she begins her journey downward, and is still alone as she crosses the third-floor landing, poised and elegant. On the second floor, she catches up with a tearful Julia and is stunned to discover that Johnny has been good to his word; unable to compromise his ideals, he has broken off the engagement, and left the party. Declaring that she will bring him back for her sister's sake, Linda continues down the staircase, gracefully fending off a host of well-wishers while scanning the crowd for Johnny. Like no one else, she seems to activate the staircase, gracefully bringing to life its sinuous, flowing shape; even as she rejects this world, she is revealed as its most authentic citizen. On the main floor she is told by a footman that Johnny has left the way he first came in, through the service entrance. She follows him—breaking, for the first time in her adult life, the rules of social separation upon which the house is built. In a precise reversal of the path Johnny took at the film's opening, she pushes through the door, strides down the long service corridor and into the kitchen itself. The servants point to the back door, telling her Johnny has just left. She opens it, then stands poised in the threshold. As before, the sounds of the city come up, full of promise and possibility. Yet she does not move. Her love for Johnny has brought her this far, allowed her to break through the barriers of class upon which her house and her world are built. But she cannot yet carry her liberation all the way, and leave the house for the larger city and the contemporary world. She is still the mansion's prisoner.

It is not surprising that, when Linda finally makes her break (at the film's end), the setting has changed dramatically. Free of the old house at last, Linda catches up with Johnny on an ocean liner, about to sail for Europe. The location speaks of escape, of course, but also of modernity—the sleek interiors coming as a distinct relief from the heavy classicism of the Seton mansion. The ship's departure horn blows. They have made their escape. They kiss.

A few blocks up the Avenue, meanwhile, the same transition—from aristocratic stricture to modern possibility—was about to be made even more starkly. The mansion at 1011 Fifth Avenue is home to the Bullock family in *My Man Godfrey* and, like the Seton place, it is something of a gilded cage, especially for the Bullocks' daughter, Irene (Carole Lombard). But this particular cage is less that of a prison than of a zoo. A policeman's horse can be found in the library, where Irene has left it after a wild night on the town. And Mischa Auer, playing a "protégé" of Mrs. Bullock with little evident talent for anything except eating free food, does manage (in one memorable sequence) the perfect imitation of a gorilla: roaring incomprehensibly, climbing over furniture, and picking nits off the family poodle. In place of the somber decorum of the Seton mansion we have the screech of a menagerie.

In fact, it requires the services of an unexpected newcomer to restore the mansion's lost dignity. Godfrey (William Powell) is a ragged indigent, a Depression-era "forgotten man" whom Irene has retrieved from a waterfront garbage dump and rashly offered employment as a butler. The scene that takes place the next morning, his first day on the job, inextricably links the elaborate architecture of the mansion to its social workings.

As in *Holiday*, the sequence (brilliantly staged by the director Gregory La Cava) begins in the servants' quarters, a modern, efficient-looking space, an island of relative sanity. Carrying a breakfast tray, Godfrey proceeds into the main hall. Like the Setons', the Bullock mansion offers a majestic staircase as its centerpiece; if possible, this one is even more complex, with runs and landings that seem to go on forever. The camera follows Godfrey up and around the stairs, in a crane shot whose sinuous, effortless movement suggests the ease with which he navigates this intimidating environment. Where Irene, the legitimate heir to the house, is later shown symbolically "imprisoned" by the jail-like balusters of the great staircase, outsider Godfrey proves the complete master of its intricate shapes and turns. The sequence offers the first hint that this bum-turned-butler may not be quite who he seems, and thus that the class distinctions upon which the house is built may be more fluid than ever.

This new servant, in fact, takes it upon himself to restore the household's social order. When Irene breaks into his room to make a breathless declaration of love for him, Godfrey reminds her of "certain proprieties" that should restrain her from entering the servants' quarters. And when the Bullocks face financial ruin, it is Godfrey (now revealed to the audience to be the disowned scion of an old Boston family) who restores their fortune through some clever financial scheming of his own. Yet despite his heroic efforts to shore up the mansion's way of life, Godfrey himself symbolizes the passing of the old order in favor of the new, a world signified by the film's final location: "The Dump." Godfrey has transformed his old abode of shacks and garbage heaps into a stylish Art Deco–style nightclub (designed by John Harkrider) and provided jobs for all the indigents. Now he is busy with plans for winter housing, a new dock, and a seaplane landing, making the place a point of departure in more ways than one—not only onto the water but into the future as well, a future at once technologically advanced and socially humane, in sharp distinction from the stone mausoleums back on Fifth, ever more isolated from the path of social and architectural progress. By film's end, even Irene has dizzily but bravely abandoned the old mansion, ready to join Godfrey in his new world.

Our next glimpse of the Avenue, in *The Devil and Miss Jones*, reveals an accelerating decline. The Merrick mansion is a grim, brooding fortress, darkened within by ornate wood carving and garrisoned by massive iron gates outside. All signs of family life are gone; old John Merrick (Charles Coburn) lives with only his butler and cook for company; forced by doctors to eat pabulum to prolong his life, he rants bitterly at the working people who are on strike against one of his properties, Neeley's Department Store. The house reflects the man and the life: rich, elaborate, yet devoid of any true pleasure or fulfillment.

The frame of reference has changed as well. Most of *The Devil and Miss Jones* takes place not in the Merrick house but in the livelier, if more modest, precincts of the striking employees: apartment houses, Coney Island beaches, and the Neeley store itself. The Merrick mansion, when it does appear, is presented as a world apart, isolated and embittered, the fading remains of an age better forgotten.

By the time of our last stop along Fifth—the Totten mansion in *Ball of Fire*—even the elderly owner has vanished. Daniel S. Totten himself is dead; the house belongs to his foundation, serving as both home and workplace for a group of professors preparing an encyclopedia. The big parlor and library are ideal for their communal research, the structure's isolation from the world perfectly suited to their monastic existence. Only on their daily constitutional in Central Park do the eight scholars, led by a professor of English named Bertram Potts (Gary Cooper), see anything of the larger city.

This comfortable seclusion is challenged when Potts announces he must leave the house's confines. His article on slang is already obsolete, he says, based on dead books rather than the living language. To explore the sources of slang, he must enter the world beyond the mansion's walls: "the streets, the slums, the theatrical professions." The others are shocked; though they live and work in one of the world's raciest cities, the mansion has provided a layer of protection that they are loath to see threatened.

Their fears seem confirmed when, as an unexpected consequence of Potts's expedition, Miss "Sugarpuss O'Shea" comes sauntering into the reception hall late one night. Played to full effect by Barbara Stanwyck, the slinky Sugarpuss is another in the line of outsiders, from Johnny Case to Godfrey, who disrupt the mansion's carefully tended isolation—this time with conga lessons.

Running throughout *Ball of Fire* is a poignant subplot. Early in the film, Mr. Totten's daughter comes by to announce that the foundation has decided to drop the project, sell the property, and demolish the old mansion—to make way for a new apartment house. Through a mixture of charm and eloquence, Gary Cooper persuades her to allow the scholars to remain until the encyclopedia is complete; but it is obvious that he has won only a stay of execution.

The era of the mansion is over. The era of the apartment house has come.

IT'S SO *CONVENIENT*

Two filmic moments construct the New York apartment house.

One takes place at the start of *Mannequin* (1937). We follow hardworking Jessie Cassidy (Joan Crawford) from her garment-factory job to her home on Hester Street, and share her fatigue as she mounts the high stoop of her tenement, only to find the front door propped open, its glass smashed. Once inside, the director Frank Borzage lingers on the long, slow climb to Jessie's third-floor walk-up, allowing us to measure in full the misery that the filthy stair hall engenders. Garbage cans fill the landing. Shoddy wood wainscoting and broken plaster line the stair. Jessie wearily makes her way up the first flight. A baby is wailing in one of the apartments. She climbs another flight, and then still another, every step a struggle, until she reaches her door. Nothing embodies Jessie's hard life more than this lengthy trudge up and down the stairs. We see her do it three times in the picture's first twenty minutes.

By the third time, we can hardly stand it—and neither can she. The piles of garbage are still there; the baby's wails have been replaced by a nasty family argument ("Go on, ya dirty little rat!"). On the last flight, she stops, turns, and runs downstairs, away from everything she knows. "I can't go back up there," she cries.

She doesn't, and soon enough the story finds Jessie in the penthouse apartment of J. L. Hennesy (Spencer Tracy), the owner of New York's biggest tugboat fleet. Like Jessie's tenement, Hennesy's building is also a multiple dwelling, with apartments stacked atop one another, floor after floor. Yet Hennesy's building is a dream for Jessie, whereas her old place was a nightmare. Two things define the difference.

One is that Hennesy's home is a place for the middle class, not the poor. No smelly garbage cans foul its sleek hallways; no crying babies or arguments can be heard behind the solid walls of its large, well-separated apartments. The entrance is not a door propped open to let anyone in, but a doorman-tended lobby offering privacy and personal service.

The other difference is more basic still. Hennesy's apartment, though located much higher than Jessie's third-floor flat, is reached without any hardship at all. A single mechanical device (which we soon see Jessie herself using) has changed everything, making every floor equally accessible: the elevator, of course. Enabling people to ride in comfort rather than climb in misery was the first critical step in transforming the tenement into the apartment house.

134. RKO art department sketch of an apartment house exterior, for *Mr. and Mrs. Smith* (1941).

The element that completed the job, though ordinarily hidden from view, makes a dramatic appearance in a scene in *That Touch of Mink* (1962). Cary Grant, a New York millionaire playboy, has offered to show a new acquaintance, Doris Day, his "apartment." What he shows her is not, in fact, quite his apartment—at least, not yet. It is the steel skeleton of an apartment building still under construction (135). "I'm thinking of putting in some walls," he says wryly, "and perhaps a ceiling—just to give it that traditional touch." As they wander about the open framework, Grant paints a portrait of the home that will someday fill this piece of sky. "The living room will be here, and the bedroom there," he says, pointing at nothing but a grid of steel columns and girders. Standing on the high platform, open to the night air, the pair begin to envision a pleasant domestic life, agreeing that lots of bookcases, fireplaces, good reading lamps, and "plenty of paintings" are important to a home. The whole scene plays off what everyone knows yet takes for granted: that an apartment, with all its familiar domestic proprieties, its ancient associations of hearth and home, rests improbably within the interstices of a huge steel framework, floating high in the air, above the city.

Together, the two scenes suggest the apartment building's decidedly mixed parentage. *Mannequin* hints at the historical evolution by which the New York tenement was transformed in the 1880s into a desirable home for the middle class, when the elevator alleviated the primary physical burden brought on by stacking units vertically. The apartment house thus carried forward a residential tradition that had already passed from row house to tenement. But as *That Touch of Mink* makes clear, the New York apartment house—no less than the skyscraper office tower—was also a modern type of building, made utterly discontinuous from earlier structures by its use of a revolutionary technology: steel framing. While very much a part of the city's residential lineage, the apartment house offered a new, unprecedented scale that boldly challenged tradition.

135. ***That Touch of Mink* (1962).** Millionaire playboy Cary Grant brings Doris Day to inspect his future "apartment" on the upper floors of a Manhattan skyscraper still under construction.

From the outside, this dual identity could be felt strongly. The continuities with the tenement, and the row house before that, were obvious. The facade facing the street, still regarded as more important than the others, was made of better materials and trim, and still shared the three-part, classically inspired composition of base, shaft, and cornice (134). But the differences were equally obvious. The facade could now stretch fifteen stories high, a hundred feet wide, and contain hundreds of windows. For the film city, this explosion of scale called for new techniques. No longer could the entire building's front be created on a back lot, as row houses and tenements had been. Instead, only the lower floors of the apartment-house wall were built full size; the facade above was created with a glass shot of the upper floors, matched carefully to the full-scale set below.

If architecturally evolved from the multifamily tenement, socially the apartment house traced its ancestry all the way back to the row house. Like the old row house, it was expected to provide its middle-class residents with a distinct feeling of propriety, a reassuring sense of the family's place in the bustling city. Except that now, somehow, it was to furnish that feeling of individual propriety in the context of a huge, communal dwelling, home not to one family but to hundreds. Clearly this could not be achieved simply by redeploying the elements of the row house: the stoop, the front yard, and so on. Instead, the apartment house would have to devise new elements, a new "iconography" that residents, visitors, and strangers could understand.

In their hurry to reach the stories proceeding inside the apartment itself, most films quickly passed by this iconography, or took it for granted. But in one film, Alfred Hitchcock's *Mr. and Mrs. Smith* (1941), it was impossible to ignore—because for most of the film, the main character can't get *into* his apartment. His wife won't let him.

Mr. and Mrs. Smith springs from a classic screwball premise: a happily married couple discovering that, owing to an obscure bureaucratic error, they aren't really married at all. The film then follows Mr. Smith (Robert Montgomery) as he attempts to win back his willful, passionate wife (Carole Lombard)—no easy task, as it turns out. With his customary ingenuity, Hitchcock uses urban architecture to play out the couple's changing emotional relationship. A comfortable domestic order is established, then broken, and then, gradually, reestablished—revealing, along the way, the apartment house's subtle interlacing of home and city.

136. **Reference shot of a Park Avenue apartment house entrance, about 1938.** This view shows the traditional means by which the New York apartment house met the street: an architecturally ornamented entrance, flanking beds of shrubbery, street trees planted along the curb, and a dark-green canvas canopy stretching from building to sidewalk—all watched over by a uniformed doorman.

Establishment of the order is accomplished before the first scene even begins, in a sequence of astounding speed and simplicity. Behind the opening credits, Hitchcock flashes five brief establishing shots, taking us from the overall metropolis to a single home. First we see the midtown skyline: the city itself. Second comes the view down Park Avenue: an apartment house district within the larger city. Third, the street sign at 72nd Street and Park Avenue: a single block within that district. Fourth, the apartment canopy of 309 East 72nd Street: a single building within the block. Finally, the name plate on the apartment door itself: a single home within the building.

It is an obvious yet extraordinary sequence, offering a profound lesson about the urbanism of New York in less than a minute. "A city is stones and a city is people," Jacob Bronowski once wrote, "but it is not a heap of stones, and it is not just a jostle of people." Cities are often celebrated for their sheer extent of population. Less noticed is the means they have devised for organizing their residents, so that each person has a clear place among the millions. This is more than a matter of ensuring that everyone can receive his or her mail. It is a question of providing urbanistic subdivisions—neighborhoods, blocks, buildings, and so forth—that give each inhabitant a comprehensible sense of the enlarging environment, intermediate levels of community that mediate between the single home and the immensity of the overall city. At its best, New York not only provided those markers of community, but made them a part of its distinctive urban style, so that a street sign, for example, or an apartment-house canopy, could offer—in addition to its overt information—a larger sense of familiarity and "belonging" by which a city of millions could feel as comfortable as a small town. It has been a conspicuous failure of newer cities and parts of cities (including some in New York itself) to provide exactly the kind of urban iconography that might reduce or even eliminate the feeling of anonymity that sometimes seems an inevitable part of metropolitan life. Though the Smiths live in the middle of one of the world's biggest cities, their individual home is locked into a successive series of layers that radiate outward and merge in clearly defined steps with the public urbanism of New York.

Indeed, once the domestic order has been smashed, those intermediate layers become the film's major terrain; no longer can Mr. Smith pass through them unthinkingly on his way into the cozy confines of his apartment. Now he (along with the audience) must inhabit them from the position of an outsider. He waits on the sidewalk outside the building entrance, hoping to catch Mrs. Smith on her way out; he lingers on a couch in the lobby, near the doorman, seeing her flirt and fend off other suitors. At one point he makes it into the elevator and up to the hallway, only to be foiled at the door of the apartment itself. Not quite a resident of the building, he is not quite a stranger, either, but instead inhabits a realm of communal domesticity that was the apartment house's particular contribution to New York's residential tradition.

137. *Butterfield 8* (1960). In this scene from the film version of John O'Hara's novel, Gloria Wandrous (Elizabeth Taylor) walks down Fifth Avenue, about to return a fur coat she had removed earlier from the home of her married lover, Liggett—until she stops in her tracks, having spotted Liggett's wife (Dina Merrill), just back from the country, entering the apartment house beneath its canvas canopy.

One element above all symbolized this communal realm: the apartment-house canopy (136). By the early twentieth century, the canopy had supplanted the row-house stoop as the common signature of the middle-class New York residence—yet its importance was far more than symbolic. As the apartment house's clearest gesture to the street, it revealed the interlocking of domestic and public realms that made the New York apartment house, for all its layers of remove from the city, a profoundly urban form of housing. The canopy engaged the street—literally—by passing over a portion of the sidewalk and claiming it for the building; yet it simultaneously allowed free passage of the city's street life beneath. In this overlap the film city found enormous dramatic possibility.

In a scene near the middle of *Butterfield 8*, the 1960 film version of John O'Hara's novel, the vivacious young Gloria Wandrous (Elizabeth Taylor) approaches the apartment house of her married lover, Weston Liggett (Laurence Harvey). She carries a fur coat belonging to Liggett's wife, which Gloria angrily removed from his apartment after an earlier liaison and now, in a fit of conscience, intends to return. Walking down the sidewalk, she has almost reached the entrance when Dina Merrill, playing Mrs. Liggett, suddenly pulls up in a car. Gloria freezes in her tracks as the returning Mrs. Liggett is greeted by the doorman who escorts her under the canopy: the very picture of complacent domesticity, the proprieties of home life extended comfortably into the public realm (137). For Emily Liggett, this piece of sidewalk is already "home"—her home, and hers alone, as Gloria is painfully reminded. For a moment, two paths have crossed at right angles: the stream of public life running the length of the sidewalk and the short domestic path set perpendicular to it, from curbstone to doorway. The canopy alone makes possible this crossing, this place where a single plot of ground has two completely distinct meanings, as different as home and city, as wife and mistress, as Dina Merrill and Liz Taylor.

The same crossing shapes the climax of Fred Schepisi's film of John Guare's play *Six Degrees of Separation* (1993), but here the dramatic gesture is precisely reversed. If previously the apartment house had domesticated the public sidewalk, now the sidewalk offers freedom from the social strictures of the apartment house.

Most of *Six Degrees* takes place in the Fifth Avenue apartment of Flan and Ouisa Kittredge (Donald Sutherland and Stockard Channing), an elegant cocoon that floats high above a city whose problems and possibilities are just distant echoes. But the couple's encounter with a remarkable stranger, Paul (Will Smith), a product of the streets below who is at once threatening and inspiring, touches them—or at least, touches Ouisa. It is only in the last scene, during lunch in a Park Avenue apartment house, that she realizes just how much the experience has changed her, and how *little* it has changed her husband, still set in the ways of his class. When she runs from the lunch in tears, the pair argue their way through the building's lobby and out onto the sidewalk, beneath its canopy. Again, two realms meet on the same piece of ground: the comfortable path of the house, and the challenging path of the street. Ouisa makes her choice. She joins the flow of the sidewalk, which instantly sweeps her away from the lobby. Flan remains beneath the canopy, watching her in amazement, then turns around and walks straight back into the building, still locked in the comfortable, narrow path of upper-class domesticity. Ouisa looks around, as if seeing for the first time the city she has always lived in; she smiles and picks up her pace. At that crucial intersection beneath the canopy, she and her husband have—literally—gone their separate ways.

With lobby, elevator, and hallway behind us, we at last open the door and enter the apartment itself—and therein find the single most familiar interior in New York movies. As in the real city, where apartments are by far the most common kind of domestic interior, the movie apartment long ago became the standard setting for middle-class New York life, the background of hundreds upon hundreds of films.

With its relatively simple and standardized layouts, the movie apartment's importance has often been less as a space in itself than as the neutral canvas for a decorating scheme bent on revealing its occupant's personality. A film like *The Best of Everything* (1959) uses apartment interiors almost like Homeric epithets—pithy summaries of their owners' character and place in life, from the chic career-woman's flat of senior editor Joan Crawford, to the art- and book-filled home of theatrical producer Louis Jourdan, to the cramped "starter" unit that the film's struggling young women (Hope Lange, Diane Baker, Suzy

Parker) share in their early days in the big city. Other films savored a different and distinctively New York phenomenon: the startling contrast in decor to be found in the adjacent units of a single building. In *Adam's Rib* (1949), Amanda Bonner (Katharine Hepburn) leaves her classically elegant home to find another world no farther away than across the hall: the exotic, dark-walled apartment—filled with art treasures and show-business mementoes—of her friend and neighbor Kip (David Wayne), a songwriter of ambiguous sexual orientation and extravagantly sophisticated taste. He, in turn, offers her an unusual declaration of affection, explaining how she differs from all the other loves in his life:

> *You're the only one I know* why *I love . . . because you live right across the hall from me. You're mighty attractive in every single way, Mrs. Bonner, but I'd probably love anyone who lived right across the hall from me. It's so* convenient*!*

Over time, the movie city did offer some sense of the apartment's historic evolution. An early film like RKO's *Bachelor Apartment* (1931) suggests in its very name the mid-nineteenth-century origins of the New York apartment house (years before it was adopted by upper-class families) as a transitional home for prosperous, single young men. It is hard to imagine the cosmopolitan main character, Wayne Carlton (Lowell Sherman), living in any other kind of house: neither row house, tenement, nor mansion could serve his suave, unattached lifestyle as well as his elegant apartment at 802 Park Avenue. Nor could Mark Whitney, a similar character played by Clark Gable in MGM's *Possessed* (also 1931), be located anywhere else than *his* apartment, up the street at 1100 Park Avenue. What Whitney's apartment suggests, in fact, is the solidity and comfort of a mansion or country house brought into the twentieth century. With its double-height ceilings, its tall windows trimmed in Gothic stonework, its heavy wooden furnishings and Oriental rugs, Whitney's home feels like an elite men's club lifted into the sky.

138. ***Hannah and Her Sisters* (1986).** During a family Thanksgiving, Lee (Barbara Hershey) stands alone in a doorway of the apartment of her sister Hannah (Mia Farrow), as guests are welcomed in the foyer beyond. Like much of the film, the scene was shot in an eleven-room apartment on Central Park West that, in real life, Farrow shared with her mother, the actress Maureen O'Sullivan.

Significantly, both Sherman's and Gable's homes are located on Park Avenue, the street that became as much identified with the apartment building as Fifth Avenue had been with the mansion. As an apartment-house boulevard, Park Avenue was rivaled only by Central Park West, whose double-towered buildings were the inspiration for countless skyline views, and whose solid, spacious apartments were the very symbol of Manhattan's upper-middle-class life, like the home of Rose and Arnold Morgenstern and their daughter Marjorie

(Natalie Wood) in *Marjorie Morningstar* (1958). A real Central Park West apartment, belonging to actress Mia Farrow and transformed into the fictional home of her character Hannah in *Hannah and Her Sisters* (1986), offers a classic example of the pre–World War II apartment interior, with its generously sized, well-proportioned rooms spun from a central foyer, interconnected to—or isolated from—one another by pocket doors. With the doors open, Woody Allen's camera, gliding from room to room, both imparts and heightens the conviviality of the family's holiday parties; but at crucial moments, when the darker impulses of illicit sexual desire or sibling rivalry divide the happy family into smaller and considerably less happy pairs, the doors are shut and intimate space is achieved amidst the sociable whole (138).

139. ***Adam's Rib*** **(1949).** Directed by George Cukor from a script by Garson Kanin and Ruth Gordon, the film stars Spencer Tracy and Katharine Hepburn as husband-and-wife lawyers named Adam and Amanda Bonner. In this scene, the couple enjoy breakfast in the upstairs bedroom of their duplex apartment near the East River.

Though rich New Yorkers originally shunned the idea of sharing their roof with strangers, eventually even the city's very wealthiest families came to accept apartments as a desirable way of life. Attracted (as always) to the display of wealth, the movie city had more than its share of luxurious apartment sets. Those located near the top of the buildings—penthouses—were so impressive as to constitute a class in themselves, to be explored later. But those placed lower in a building (and thus unable to exploit terraces or skyline views) could still be distinguished from the ordinary run of units by a simple expedient: a second floor. Duplex apartments offered their fortunate residents the best of both worlds: the convenience of an apartment house with the sense of spaciousness and separation offered by the row house's multiple floors. For *Adam's Rib*'s Spencer Tracy and Katharine Hepburn, the duplex suggests the utter stability and comfort of their life in Manhattan. No transitional place, this, but a true home, its upstairs bedrooms as conjugal and its downstairs living rooms as gracious as those of any country estate (139). By contrast, the second floor in Sherman McCoy's Park Avenue apartment in *Bonfire of the Vanities* (1990) seems intended mostly to provide designer Richard Sylbert with the opportunity to create a grandiose, marble-lined stair hall, a return to the sense of ostentatious display that was a hallmark of the movie city's mansions, years before.

In the decades after World War II, as sweeping social changes reshaped American family life, the sprawling formality of New York's older apartments could seem anachronistic, if not downright tyrannical. In 1970's *Diary of a Mad Housewife*, Tina Balser (Carrie Snodgress) is oppressed by many things—from a pair of spoiled and sullen daughters to a demanding, pompous, ferociously social-climbing husband named Jonathan (Richard Benjamin). But as presented by the writer/director team of Eleanor and Frank Perry, among the greatest burdens this "mad" housewife must bear is the house itself: an eight-room Central Park West apartment built before World War I, designed to be maintained by a live-in servant and cook, under the direction of a full-time wife and mother. It is a layout uniquely unsuited for the modern Tina, who, aided by only a part-time helper, struggles with the sheer physical demands of the place. In the very first scene, we see her literally racing back and forth between the oversized kitchen and the formal dining room, trying to serve breakfast to her family; later scenes show her jogging around the apartment's expanses, answering the front door, doing the laundry, preparing dinner, polishing silver, answering the *back* door—fortified by a glass or two of midday Scotch and a chain of cigarettes. Far from being the mistress of her apartment, the long-suffering Tina is its prisoner, a contemporary figure trapped by the expectations embedded in its traditional layout.

140. ***Kramer vs. Kramer*** **(1979).** In his initial conception of *Kramer vs. Kramer*—the story of a young advertising executive (Dustin Hoffman) who must single-handedly raise a son after his wife has left—the director Robert Benton thought to set the film in an old, rambling Upper West Side apartment. But the designer Paul Sylbert disagreed. "I know exactly where Ted Kramer lives," Sylbert insisted, arguing that the setting be moved to a modern building in the East Sixties. "It's got to be a new apartment. It's got to be efficient. It's got to be basically white."

Indeed, as society continued to evolve, and even the wealthiest families began to enjoy a more casual way of life, that layout started to lose some of its very meaning. When the Kittredges review dinner options with their rich South African guest (Ian McKellen) in *Six Degrees of Separation*, the one possibility not even mentioned is eating at home, although their expansive apartment boasts a spacious traditional dining room. Only the surprise arrival of the stranger, Paul, who offers to whip up a meal in their kitchen, convinces them to open up the big darkened room, which has been closed off, a sewing machine on its table. "It's such a treat to eat at home," exclaims Ouisa, delighted at the novelty of using her dining room for, of all things, dining.

Society was changing, and so was the shape of the New York apartment. In the postwar decades, the filmic city tracked the transformation by which the "open plan" of modern architects like Mies van der Rohe was combined with a marked diminution of scale to create the stripped-down, boxy apartments common to the big white-brick buildings along Second and Third Avenues. The Third Avenue apartment of Ted Kramer (Dustin Hoffman) in *Kramer vs. Kramer* (1979) follows the lines of the classic postwar unit, its Mies-inspired layout reduced in size to an L-shaped living room and dining alcove wrapped around a small, galley-style kitchen (140). To be sure, this compressed, informal layout was more practical for modern families such as Kramer's who, like most postwar households, no longer relied on domestic help. But the environmental price of the change was equally obvious, as the film itself could not make clearer. The rooms of Kramer's apartment are so reduced in scale that we sense less their spatial volume than their cheap, percussive surfaces: the parquet-tile floor; the louvered shutters and doors; the white, low, featureless ceiling. And with the reduction of size, the careful zoning and separation achieved by earlier apartment plans have been lost—as evidenced by the embarrassing (if amusing) scene of Kramer's young son, on his way to the bathroom, confronting his father's new lover, who is standing naked in the narrow bedroom hallway. Designer Paul Sylbert carefully shaped the interior around the very *in*stability of Kramer's life:

> *You felt that this guy wanted to be somewhere, he wanted to be bigger than this. The apartment had a lot to do with why you felt comfortable in that movie, why you felt convinced in that movie. You saw his attempt to cook. Can you imagine that scene being anywhere but that confined little efficiency kitchen between the dining room and the hallway? It was made for that.*

Kramer's portrait of the modern apartment, while unflattering, paled next to the frontal attack of *The Prisoner of Second Avenue* (1975), which, as its title hinted, used a modern Upper East Side apartment as the symbol for everything wrong with the postwar city. Though perfectly typical of newer Manhattan units, Jack Lemmon and Anne Bancroft's fourteenth-floor apartment is less a home than a white-walled cell, where the couple live, as Bancroft shouts, "like caged animals in a Second Avenue zoo!" The place is not only drab but cheap, the walls so thin, for example, that Lemmon can easily hear the antics of the young flight attendants who live in the next unit; when he slams his fist against the wall to quiet them down, the plaster cracks open. Far from offering relief from the larger city, the apartment seems to concentrate the city's strains and pressures into a domestic environment.

Across the decades, hundreds of films surveyed the interiors of apart-

141. Establishing shot from *Rosemary's Baby* (1968). This opening shot of the Victorian roofscape of the Dakota apartments establishes a suitably ominous mood for director Roman Polanski's tale of witchcraft in the contemporary city. Designed in 1880 by the architect Henry J. Hardenbergh (who also designed the Plaza Hotel), the Dakota was one of the first apartment houses built in New York.

ments. A few presented the communal space of the building. But it was one film, above all, that conveyed the true complexity of the apartment house, by dramatically linking a single apartment to its neighboring units and to the building as a whole. As if that were not enough, this film also explored the apartment across *time*, understanding a fundamental truth of apartment life—that its occupants are, in the end, a succession of transients who occupy the same space in different eras. Situated precisely in space and time, within a framework of surrounding units and previous tenants, the four-room apartment of Guy and Rosemary Woodhouse, located in a mythical Central Park West apartment house called the Bramford, becomes the animating force of the dark yet often comic story that is *Rosemary's Baby* (1968).

From a vantage point high above West 72nd Street, the director Roman Polanski pans his camera across the line of apartments circling Central Park, before coming to rest on a complex, vaguely ominous roofscape of peaks, towers, and gables. The so-called Bramford is of course the Dakota, a massive ten-story structure built in 1884 as one of the first apartment houses in the city and still standing as an opulent if somewhat grim vestige of late-nineteenth-century Manhattan (141).

We have been brought right to the heart of the apartment-house city, so it comes as no surprise that the first scene shows a primal ritual of that city—the renting of an apartment. Beneath the Bramford's tall arched entrance a rental agent (Elisha Cook Jr.) greets Guy and Rosemary, a young actor and his wife played by John Cassavetes and Mia Farrow, then proceeds to escort them across the building's central courtyard and up one of its slow, manual elevators—prattling nonstop, all the while, about the building's history. His speech comes so rapidly that it plays as comedy, but it actually reveals crucial clues to the story to come.

> *Originally the smallest apartment was a nine; they've been broken up into fours, fives, and sixes. Now, 7E is a four, originally the back part of a ten. It has the original dining room for its living room, another bedroom for the bedroom, two servants' rooms brought together for a dining room or a second bedroom. Do you have children?*

A thick, almost palpable atmosphere envelops us as the Woodhouses step from the elevator into a high-ceilinged corridor lined with dark brick walls and peeling plaster. The twisting hallway carries a claustrophobic, old-world sense of age and history, of mysteries past and present, only accentuated by the faint sound of a piano coming from deep inside one of the other apartments. The sense of the past can be felt no less strongly in the apartment itself, filled with the old-fashioned possessions of its previous tenant, an elderly woman (one of the city's first women lawyers, we are told) who has recently died. But Rosemary is charmed by the apartment's high ceilings and rich woodwork, and after some anxious conversation familiar to all New Yorkers obliged to pay more for an apartment than they had expected, Guy and Rosemary decide to take it.

Soon Rosemary is hard at work redecorating, covering the dark Victorian walls with cheerful wallpaper and coats of white paint, installing crisp new carpets and Scandinavian furniture, appropriating the apartment's ornate interior architecture as the background for a simple, uncluttered, contemporary style of living.

But the history of the place refuses to be papered over quite so easily. The building, it turns out, was once known as "Black Bramford" for its "rather unpleasant reputation" as home to everyone from the Trench Sisters, a pair of nineteenth-century cannibals, to Adrian Marcato, an 1890s tenant suspected of witchcraft. Other aspects of the place are no less disturbing. A heavy wooden secretary has been found wedged—urgently it seems—in front of a closet, which seals off a hallway that once joined the Woodhouses' unit and their neighbors' into a single large apartment. At night, Guy and Rosemary can hear strange, half-garbled sounds coming through the bedroom walls.

142. Rendering of the Castevets' apartment from *Rosemary's Baby* (1968). With its Gothic door frames, ceiling beams, and window surrounds, this atmospheric sketch (by the film's production designer, Richard Sylbert) suggests an apartment interior that has remained unchanged since the building's construction, nearly a century before—thus evoking the larger notion of a dark, ancient way of life persisting into the modern era.

Yet when they finally appear, the neighbors seem amusing enough, an elderly couple named Roman and Minnie Castevet (Sidney Blackmer and Ruth Gordon). In her quintessential New York accent, Minnie invites herself in ("Look how you put the table, isn't that innerestin' "), while Roman regales Guy over dinner with tales of the old New York stage. In contrast to the spare look of the Woodhouse apartment, the Castevets' place is a full-blown Victorian interior, lined with dark, Gothic-style woodwork and filled with heavy, overstuffed furniture (142).

The contrast is crucial as the story heads toward its shocking climax. Rosemary wants a normal life in her bright, modern apartment; when she becomes pregnant, she dreams of a clean, sanitary delivery room. Instead she discovers that she and her unborn baby are being tangled in a web of ancient irrational forces; a witchcraft plot emanates from the Castevets' Gothic apartment, seeping by night through the dark walls in the muffled sounds of strange incantations and music, and manifest by day in the intrusive presence of Roman and Minnie (and their strange friends and neighbors) in Guy and Rosemary's lives. By the film's end, the dark forces have actually entered the apartment itself, as members of the coven pass through the hallway closet that had once blocked off the Castevets' apartment from the Woodhouses'.

As a product of the late 1960s, *Rosemary's Baby* embodies at one level the last vestige of the pervasive anti-Victorianism that animated much of twentieth-century modernism—the sense that the new was not only different but morally *better* than the old. Anything Victorian, the film implies, is unwholesome and possibly evil; anything modern is healthy and good.

At another level, the film carries a dark, antiurban message. Guy and Rosemary typify those driven people who come to New York to find their fame and fortune, in Guy's obvious case as an actor. The apartment house (and by extension the city itself) is presented as a dark, unhealthful, and overpriced place filled with ominous strangers, a place in which success—even if achieved—comes at a price: a real or metaphorical pact with the devil. This particular thread of seeing the apartment house (or the city) as an old, gloomy place with potentially terrifying strangers, where ambitious young people sometimes make the mistake of living, was pursued in *Single White Female* (1992), a less effective but similarly Gothic tale set in another West Side dowager, the Ansonia on upper Broadway—a film to feed the doubts of every parent whose child has moved to New York, inexplicably attracted to its expensive old buildings instead of a cheery, affordable suburb. But unlike *Single White Female*'s heavy-handed atmosphere, the stylishness and wit of *Rosemary's Baby* encourages a look beyond the Gothic darkness of the genre to explore its larger appreciation of the apartment house.

In a most unexpected way, the story serves to remind us of the degree to which New York apartment houses—even big old fortresses like the Dakota—have been transformed over time. Large apartments have been cut into two or more smaller ones, small units have been combined into a single large place, a room from one apartment has been appropriated by another. These physical shifts have reflected changes as small as the arrival of a new baby or as broad as long-term trends in family size, or cycles of national prosperity and depression. It was a frequent habit of modernist architects, proclaiming "flexibility" as a major goal, to invent elaborate, "modular" systems by which, at least in theory, spaces and structures could be easily changed at will. But rarely if ever have these systems worked out in practice as well as the simple taking down and putting up of plaster walls in ordinary New York apartment houses. In *Rosemary's Baby,* this common but often overlooked adaptability becomes the essential premise of the story.

Yet the point is larger than the apartment's *functional* capacity for modification. In allowing change, the apartment house comes to evidence a sense of accrued history, a layering across time, not because its spaces are just as they once were (as in a house museum) but precisely because they are *not:* because the time between then and now has been marked with visible alterations that speak to the distance—in years and social change—that the world has traveled in the meanwhile.

In *Rosemary's Baby,* of course, as so often in the movie city, the theme is raised to full boil: the apartment next door (of which Rosemary and Guy's was once a part) is not just old and eccentric but nothing less than a den of witches.

(It is in a similar spirit, for example, that Jimmy Stewart looks out his "rear window" to view nothing less than a murder.) Yet even without the supernatural overlay, the film's implications are powerful: the apartment house has been here before us, and will be after us, and it reveals what has come before in a series of stratified, often half-erased layers. Story upon story has been embodied in arrangements of plaster and wood, layer upon layer—a process we ourselves will extend and continue for occupants still to come.

ONE BIG FAMILY

Near the start of *The Seven Year Itch* (1955), Richard Sherman (Tom Ewell) has just returned from Penn Station, having sent his wife and child off to Maine for the summer. He's in a good mood, ready to enjoy a few weeks on his own, musing happily about his home. "I like this house," he says:

> *Why does Helen keep talking about moving into those big, enormous buildings that look like "Riot in Cell Block 11"? It's so much nicer here. Just three apartments: ours, the Kaufmans upstairs, and those two guys on the top floor, interior decorators or something.*

The house Richard is describing, a familiar kind of New York residence, is distinguished by the curious fact that it has no name.

To define the building is to tell its history. Originally a row house, built for a single family in the nineteenth or early twentieth century, it has since been converted into apartments, usually one to a floor. Kitchens have been added on the upper stories, and bathrooms, too, to make each floor a self-contained unit. The old house's staircase has become a common area, giving access to each apartment's door. There are thousands of such buildings, all across the city.

Whatever its name, the type was a pure product of the genius loci of the city—a category of housing not created by any architect or planner, but evolved, indigenously, as though shaped by the city itself. A kind of housing meant for one way of life—the large, formal, nineteenth-century family—was altered over time to achieve something of the efficiency and convenience of an apartment house. The result was neither row house nor apartment building, but a different kind of dwelling altogether.

As Richard is about to find out.

Just as he has settled in for the evening, the buzzer rings. Richard opens the front door to find a young woman (in the script called simply "The Girl"), who breathlessly announces that she is subletting the Kaufmans' place upstairs for the summer.

"The Girl," in fact, is Marilyn Monroe. Watching her sashay upstairs,

Richard, grinning stupidly, urges her to call on him if she needs anything (143). "After all," he points out, "we're all one big family here."

The motivation for Richard's remark is all too obvious, but, as he discovers over the next few days, what he's said is more or less true. Although he and his new neighbor live in separate apartments, the connections between them are numerous indeed. Having met her once in the front entry hall, he runs into her again that very evening—when she nearly brains him by dropping a potted plant from an upper terrace onto the backyard garden where he sits, trying to read. This proves the perfect pretext to invite her down for a "neighborly" drink in his apartment, an encounter that sparks his desires but ends with him, guilt-ridden, sending her back upstairs. The next day, trying to forget all about her, he runs into her again as he steps up to the front of the house: she's leaning out the second-floor window, washing her hair. With this excuse for furthering the acquaintance, they have dinner, see a movie, and then—after the legendary skirt-blowing scene (215)—return to his place for a nightcap. Then, just when he thinks she's gone home for good, she appears yet again—having opened up a service stair that once connected the two floors directly until it was boarded up to create separate apartments. "We can do this all summer," she purrs.

143. ***The Seven Year Itch*** **(1955).** In the entry hall of his building, once a private row house but now divided into separate dwellings, Richard Sherman (Tom Ewell) welcomes a newcomer—Marilyn Monroe—who is subletting an apartment upstairs for the summer. The movie's interiors were shot at the Fox studio; its exteriors were filmed on East 61st Street between Third and Lexington Avenues, where, during the shoot, large crowds gathered to catch a glimpse of the famed actress.

Employing nothing more (or less) than Marilyn Monroe in a nightdress, the movie city brought out the unique character of this particular type of urban housing. It is easy to see that this story of cozy summertime desire could have hardly proceeded in a traditional row house or a conventional apartment house. Two adjacent row houses, with one household in each, would never provide so many places for impromptu interaction between strangers. And any story of desire set in an apartment building would have to confront the formality built into its design—especially in the relationship between separate units—specifically to discourage interaction for the sake of privacy. When Richard says "we're one big family here," he touches on the very thing that makes this type of housing special: it *was* once the home of a single family, and still enjoys a kind of domestic ambience, an echo of its former existence, which shapes the spirit of the place in some subtle but perceptible way.

The same echoes of a domestic past could be felt in each of the row house's apartments, from bottom to top. Much of the graciousness of Gene Tierney's apartment in *Laura* (1944) derives from its former identity as the parlor floor of a row house. The wide archways flanked by columns, the sweep of the rooms and bay windows—all imply a kind of residential grandeur (without the daunting upkeep that an actual, multistory row house would entail) that is the perfect setting for this most stylish of New York career women. Laura's apartment, to put it another way, offers the *scale* of a row house without the *size*. Upstairs, meanwhile, entire apartments could be created, sometimes idiosyncratically, from what had once been the row house's high-ceilinged bedrooms. Murray Burns, played by Jason Robards in *A Thousand Clowns* (1965), lives in just such a unit, its high plaster walls ideal for displaying the endless accumulation of what he calls "obsolete structures"—the old radios, metal eagles, bookcases, grandfather clocks, file cabinets, maps, and paintings that are the outward evidence of his eccentric, overflowing personality. Of course, privacy in such a cramped place is hard to come by. Murray must put up a screen around his bed when a young woman (Barbara Harris) comes to spend the night; later, attempting to have an adult conversation, he suggests his young nephew Nick (Barry Gordon) go to his room. "This is a one-room apartment," Nick points out. "Okay," Murray replies, "then go to your alcove."

Small, relatively inexpensive, easy to maintain, the row house apartment found its natural place in the movie city (no less than the real one) as home to young single people starting out in New York. "It's a nice apartment," C. C. Baxter (Jack Lemmon) says of his place in the West Sixties, just off Central Park. "Nothing fancy, but kind of cozy—just right for a bachelor." Yet the portrait drawn early in *The Apartment* (1960) reveals nothing so much as the quiet sadness of single life in the big city. To Adolph Deutsch's poignant music, we follow Baxter's nightly routine: getting the mail, trudging upstairs, pouring himself a martini, and sitting down to a TV dinner heated in his tiny stove, with only the television for company.

Even in this classic portrait of urban loneliness, though, the domesticity of the building reasserts itself. Baxter's apartment serves as a kind of revolving bedroom, the centerpiece of an arrangement with several corporate superiors that allows them use of the place for illicit trysts. The situation's bitter humor is amplified for having a witness—Dr. Dreyfus, Baxter's next-door neighbor, who, watching the liquor bottles pile up and overhearing the sounds of passion every evening, ascribes it all (with some amazement) to the quiet, unassuming Lemmon. Later, when the doctor helps foil the suicide attempt of one of the apartment's female "guests," he proves a good neighbor who tries to dispense some stern fatherly advice—even if it is wasted on the gentle Baxter, the last person responsible for the woman's condition.

This inherently contradictory nature of the building—as a home for solitary young people, yet a domestic environment that encouraged neighborly relations—continued to make it an obvious locale for romance, stories that by their nature tracked the gradual victory of connection over solitude. Without doubt, the most memorable of all such buildings was the one at 167 East 71st Street, home to a writer named Paul Varjak and his downstairs neighbor, Holly Golightly, in the film version of Truman Capote's *Breakfast at Tiffany's* (1961).

The connection among 167's tenants is evident right from the start—if not always romantic in nature. Holly (Audrey Hepburn) has a habit of forgetting her keys, relying on an upstairs neighbor, a Japanese photographer played (in

144. ***Breakfast At Tiffany's* (1961).** Holly Golightly (Audrey Hepburn) waits on the fire escape outside the apartment of her upstairs neighbor Paul (George Peppard), until his "decorator friend" (Patricia Neal) leaves. Holly and Paul's apartments were constructed sets, but the building's facade (with its distinctive blue-and-white striped awnings) was a real Manhattan row house, at 171 East 71st Street, which stands to this day, looking much as it did in the film (10).

the broadest burlesque) by Mickey Rooney, to buzz her in the front door. One day she is called on to do the same for the new tenant, Paul (George Peppard), who greets her in the stair hall; he soon finds himself in her apartment, watching her dress and then depart—but not before stopping briefly in the building's entry hall, which she has converted into an extension of her boudoir, complete with a makeup mirror, lipstick, and perfume tucked in the mailbox.

Despite the differences between the earnest writer on the third floor and the free spirit on the second, they share one important trait: both trade sexual favors—either real or implied—for an artificial bubble of material comfort. Holly picks up fifty-dollar bills for ladies' room tips from her gentlemen "suitors." Paul is being kept by a wealthy interior decorator played by Patricia Neal. Paul has written a collection of short stories called *Nine Lives* but is making little headway on his second work, a novel; Holly has a cat, called "Cat," which someday she'll give a real name. Both live what are—for all their sociable, feline charm—ultimately solitary and expectant lives (10).

The two find a connection that very first night through a special pathway that soon becomes their exclusive preserve. Fending off an overeager suitor, Holly takes refuge in the bathroom, then retreats to the fire escape, located in a side court just outside the bathroom window. Finding it impossible to get through the window in high heels and cocktail dress, she doffs them for a bathrobe and flats, then climbs upstairs and sits outside Paul's apartment (144). After watching Patricia Neal kiss Paul goodnight and depart, Holly simply invites herself in:

> *Look, you can throw me out if you want, but you* did *look so cozy in here and your decorator friend had gone home and it was beginning to get a bit cold out there on the fire escape.*

To which Paul, lying naked under his sheet and looking at Holly in her bathrobe, can only reply: "And I always heard people in New York never get to know their neighbors."

They proceed to share a cigarette and talk about their lives, in a moment of intimacy without sex that is the exact opposite of their other involvements. Holly then suggests that she "just get in with you a minute." After all, she asks, "We are friends, aren't we?"

And so is established a secret route, a private connection between two floors and two souls. The fire escape is theirs; others use the building's staircase (as Paul discovers when, again wearing next to nothing, he leaves Holly's apartment by way of her front door and nearly runs into Patricia Neal in the stair hall, making her way up to *his* apartment).

The film's most tender moment, in fact, comes on the fire escape itself. In the morning quiet after Holly's raucous party, Paul is at last trying to write—in part thanks to her encouragement. The sound of a guitar strumming brings

145. ***Big*** **(1988).** For Josh Baskin (Tom Hanks), a twelve-year-old boy inhabiting the body of a grown man, the value of the loft's large, uninterrupted floor space is obvious. Some moviegoers, easily accepting the notion that a child could be transformed overnight into a full-grown man, nonetheless criticized the film for a lack of realism—arguing that despite his gainful employment at a toy company, Josh could never afford a large loft in SoHo.

him to the window—where he looks down to see Holly, for once clad not in a Givenchy outfit but in simple jeans and pullover, sitting on the fire escape, singing the film's theme song, "Moon River." As she softly intones the lyrics ("We're after the same rainbow's end, waitin' round the bend, my huckleberry friend. . . ."), the film creates for the pair an intimate space that lets them leave behind, for a moment, the stylish yet ultimately lonely worlds they otherwise inhabit.

No one should (or could) confuse this moment with the reality of apartment life in New York—even in a former row house. Indeed, the setting itself is a complete invention: a fire escape lifted off the front of an old-law tenement, then moved around the side to an implausible "air court" placed in what should be the unbroken party wall of a row house.

But however impossibly romantic, the scene still somehow feels *right*, offering, like so many scenes in the movie city, a deeper truth about its setting. The row house turned apartment building, a gathering of separate households amidst the vestiges of an earlier familial wholeness, *did* hold out the possibility of making a connection among its inhabitants, of superimposing a domestic unity atop otherwise solitary paths, of linking the lives, and perhaps even the hearts, of New York's "huckleberry friends."

PEOPLE LIVE HERE?

Near the start of *An Unmarried Woman* (1978), Erica Benton (Jill Clayburgh) rises from bed, alone in her apartment after her husband and daughter have left for the day. Still in her underwear, she begins to dance balletically around the space—leaping and pirouetting from room to room, all the while delivering a breathless, tongue-in-cheek commentary.

Her apartment can barely contain the performance. In fact, it can't. To keep going, Erica must jump over a bed, edge around a potted tree, skirt a coffee table. With its bourgeois clutter of furniture set within a bare, modern container of flat walls, aluminum windows, and a low, percussive ceiling, the apartment seems an inadequate frame for Erica's free spirit—even if it has been a comfortable home for her family for years. Indeed, before the film is half over, Erica (having discovered her husband's infidelity) will jettison her safe middle-class life, and find herself in a completely different kind of environment: the home of a new lover, the painter Saul Kaplan (Alan Bates).

146. ***An Unmarried Woman*** **(1978).** Set in the SoHo loft of the abstract artist Saul Kaplan (Alan Bates), *An Unmarried Woman* actually used the studio (and artwork) of the New York painter Paul Jenkins, who spent a week teaching Bates how to mimic his technique of pouring acrylic paint on canvas.

Saul's place was something new, not only for Erica but for much of the audience. A high-ceilinged, simple volume of space, largely empty of furniture but graced with a row of fluted columns, it was a New York interior unlike any the movie city had yet shown. It was a loft.

By the time of the film's release in the late 1970s, Saul's loft typified a genuine phenomenon: the conversion by artists and others of thousands of industrial spaces in lower Manhattan—especially in the area below Houston Street that had come to be known as SoHo. Like Saul's, most of these were in cast-iron buildings, the products of a pioneering nineteenth-century technology that was the first to introduce metal (in the form of cast-iron pieces, bolted together to make columns and facades) into extensive use in the construction of buildings (9).

Like the row house turned apartment, the loft was not created by any planner but by New Yorkers themselves, determined to transform one kind of space into another. But this change was even more radical—not converting one kind of house into another, but turning an industrial space into a place in which to work *and* live. Watching Saul at work, it is obvious why artists would be drawn to these century-old spaces. Sheer size, for one thing: Saul's canvas is too large to be painted in an ordinary apartment or traditional artist's garret (146). The loft's wide floor spans and high ceilings proved essential to produce artwork that in the postwar era had grown far beyond the dimensions of traditional easel painting. No less important are the enormous banks of windows, which bathe the loft's interior—and the artwork—in a clear, luminous daylight. This is an environment shaped around the needs of a working artist, and it is no surprise to find that it contains only a small, almost monastically simple bedroom area, in the back.

But the attraction of the loft was more than a matter of function. *An Unmarried Woman* instantly grasped—and helped promulgate—the notion of the loft as a world apart, an environment whose simplicity and purity might represent, for Erica, a sort of liberation from the constraints of her bourgeois existence uptown. The final scene, with Erica in a white summer dress sitting next to Saul on the loft's empty floor, suggests an almost Edenic imagery—miles re-

147. ***An Unmarried Woman* (1978).** In this scene at the end of the film, Saul Kaplan and Erica (Jill Clayburgh) sit on the floor of his cast-iron loft, which is almost entirely devoted to work space and storage.

148. ***Mo' Better Blues*** **(1990).** For the home of the jazz musician Bleek Gilliam (Denzel Washington, seen in this view with Cynda Williams), production designer Wynn Thomas used glazed partitions and French doors to subdivide a large Brooklyn loft into a series of deep, layered spaces, evocative of Gilliam's complex personality.

moved from the cluttered, materialist, middle-class setting in which she had begun (147).

There was more than a grain of truth to this. Originally intended for industrial use, the loft was the first type of New York housing to have no connection at all to the city's residential tradition; it stood firmly outside the framework of cues and symbols that clearly designated the level of all other housing—row house, tenement, mansion, apartment house—on the social scale. It was, in short, classless. The loft was thus not only perfectly suited to represent the idealism of artists—from the passionate intensity of actor-teacher Dustin Hoffman in *Tootsie* (1982) to the cranky iconoclasm of painter Max von Sydow in *Hannah and Her Sisters* (1986)—but as a home for anyone outside the conventional structure of society. It was especially rewarding for filmmakers to cast middle-class citizens into a loft setting and show them trying, and often failing, to find their bearings. For the decent, ordinary Manhattan office worker played by Griffin Dunne in *After Hours* (1985), a huge SoHo loft—home to one desirable but obsessed woman, Rosanna Arquette, who eventually commits suicide, and another, Linda Fiorentino, who enjoys bondage and domination games—the loft represents an unfathomable level of psychological and sexual mystery. In *Desperately Seeking Susan* (1985), the meandering loft space of Aidan Quinn, empty but for a giant kung-fu movie billboard, is equally incomprehensible to a New Jersey housewife, Roberta (Rosanna Arquette, yet again), who (through a case of amnesia) has mistakenly taken the identity of a downtown character named Susan (Madonna). "People live here?" she asks in wonderment, as they enter a grim brick alleyway and start up a flight of raw metal stairs to reach the place. Once inside, however, Roberta's domestic sensibilities reassert themselves, even through her amnesiac fog: looking around the big bare room she says, "You could do a lot with this place."

In time, the loft became a kind of shorthand that, contrasted with traditional New York interiors, served quickly to signal a character's distance from the mainstream. The Brooklyn Heights loft of jazz musician Bleek Gilliam (Denzel Washington) in Spike Lee's *Mo' Better Blues* (1990) is rich with revealing character traits—especially in contrast to the high-rise apartment of his rival, Shadow Henderson (Wesley Snipes). To begin with, the loft symbolizes Bleek as the complete artist in an almost Renaissance sense, a man with mastery of both the technical craft and the highest aesthetic challenges of his art. His tool, a trumpet, lays disassembled on a table; we watch him lovingly oil and reassemble its parts, then painstakingly practice the fingering of a new composition; glimpses of the background, meanwhile, filled with the posters and records of Charlie Parker and John Coltrane, reveal his artistic heritage. Bleek's loft, like Saul Kaplan's, is a place of honest work, imbued with the spirit of the countless industrial workers who once labored there, a sense of toil now embodied in one individual: an artist, the ultimate maker of things, a person who manipulates the physical world to the highest ends. As designed by Wynn Thomas, the space is the perfect extension of the man: deep and multilayered, with glazed interior walls that hint of further spaces beyond, not instantly comprehensible, always implying something more. Compare this to the home of Bleek's rival, Shadow: a boxy modern apartment, in which the lack of space and style is disguised with painted wall treatments, faux-marble archways surrounding a trompe l'oeil sky. The contrast is all too obvious: Shadow, the artist as poseur, is revealed by his shallow, flat, socially striving apartment; Bleek, the artist as hero, is just as plainly revealed by his deep, layered, craft-devoted loft (148).

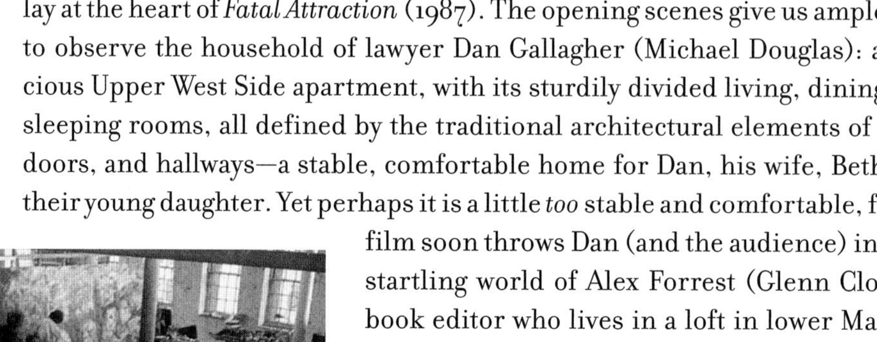

The same contrast—with sympathies now reversed against the "outsider"—lay at the heart of *Fatal Attraction* (1987). The opening scenes give us ample time to observe the household of lawyer Dan Gallagher (Michael Douglas): a spacious Upper West Side apartment, with its sturdily divided living, dining, and sleeping rooms, all defined by the traditional architectural elements of walls, doors, and hallways—a stable, comfortable home for Dan, his wife, Beth, and their young daughter. Yet perhaps it is a little *too* stable and comfortable, for the film soon throws Dan (and the audience) into the startling world of Alex Forrest (Glenn Close), a book editor who lives in a loft in lower Manhattan's meat-packing district near the Hudson River. Here nothing is conventional or stable: a kitchen sink, the very symbol of domestic routine, quickly becomes the platform for Dan and Alex's urgent sexual coupling. No part of Alex's loft, in fact, has any of the clarity of a traditional residential interior. At first, suffused with pure white light, the space suggests for Dan the same kind of liberation that Erica Benton experienced from the gentle suffocation of bourgeois life. But it soon proves more frightening than liberating. Though Alex's loft, like Bleek Gilliam's, offers a complex landscape of screens and layered spaces, it is a complexity that here suggests not depth of character but instability and disorientation; we share with Dan the difficulty of grasping

149. ***Life Lessons, New York Stories*** **(1989).** Lionel Dobie (Nick Nolte) works on a canvas while his assistant Paulette (Rosanna Arquette) looks on. Dobie's paintings were actually those of the painter Chuck Connelly, while his loft, occupying the top floor of the De Vinne Press building on Lafayette Street, was a painstakingly crafted set, designed by Kristi Zea and decorated by Nina Ramsey.

exactly what is happening, or even where we are. Back on the Upper West Side, Dan and his family come and go through a marble-clad, classically decorated lobby and entrance, with their solid symbols of middle-class life; the common spaces in Alex's building, on the other hand, utterly lack the class benchmarks that would fix the loft's place in society and make it knowable and "safe." Instead, the building, an industrial warehouse, offers only a vague sense of menace: the exposed electrical wiring and chipped plaster walls of the dark hallway, or the open-cage elevator—whose metal gate Alex closes with a violent yank and which becomes, in one of the film's most memorable scenes, the setting for another steamy sexual encounter—are exciting precisely for being so frightening. In the end, nothing suggests the bizarreness of Alex's obsessive personality as the fact (of which we are repeatedly reminded) that she makes her home in a *meat-packing district*—all the traditional verities of real estate and rational zoning tossed aside in pursuit of a set of values difficult for many to comprehend.

150. ***Big*** **(1988).** Among the most memorable moments in *Big*, directed by Penny Marshall and designed by Santo Loquasto, was the scene in which the boy-turned-man Josh Baskin (Tom Hanks) convinces his coworker Susan (Elizabeth Perkins) to shed her inhibitions and gleefully jump up and down on the full-sized trampoline he has installed in his SoHo loft.

Over time, the lofts of the movie city diverged sharply from those of the real city. In reality, the skyrocketing cost of real estate in SoHo and other downtown districts put lofts outside the realm of possibility for many artists, even as the spaces became (in no small part thanks to the movies themselves) highly desirable settings for any number of more financially comfortable New Yorkers—lawyers, brokers, account executives—for whom the loft's original rationale as a combined living and working environment gave way to the appeal of its fashionable "look." Yet even as the real city's lofts gradually lost their original purpose and became simply another real-estate option for the upper-middle class, in the film city the loft continued to resonate artistic vigor. The fullest look at the working artist's loft, in fact, did not come until 1989's *Life Lessons*—the segment of *New York Stories* directed by Martin Scorsese and written by Richard Price. Played by Nick Nolte, Lionel Dobie is a celebrated painter—"the Lion"—a middle-aged survivor of an earlier generation of New York artists who saw the downtown loft not as a chic lifestyle choice but as the best possible workshop.

In the center of Dobie's rambling space stands a giant canvas, lightly sketched in; during the course of the film, it will be transformed into a completed work of art. As the dizzying virtuosity of Scorsese's camera follows Dobie in the act of painting—dollying back and forth, craning up and down—we observe the complete synthesis of work and place, seeing how the loft's wide open space is demanded by the scale of the work created within it, how its messy, vital abundance of objects provides the wide array of resources an artist like Dobie needs for his work—from magazine photos to paint-spattered art books, from the portable stereo blaring Procol Harum to the ever-present bottle of cognac at the side of his special "viewing chair" (149).

At one point, frustrated in his painting, Dobie starts playing basketball, making layup shots at a hoop he has installed on one of the walls (a detail borrowed from the real loft of the painter Robert Longo). It is a telling scene, for it reveals the essential relationship between work and play that is near the heart of the loft's appeal and is, indeed, one of the more mysterious aspects of art itself. There might be no better way to characterize the uniqueness of the loft in the city's residential tradition than as the only dwelling in which one could readily play basketball. (Though the rooms might be big enough, one would be unlikely to play ball in the ornate salon or ballroom of a mansion.) If artistic talent, as Charles Baudelaire once observed, is "nothing more or less than childhood rediscovered at will—a childhood now equipped for self-expression," then the loft is the perfect, not-quite-grown-up environment in which artists can pursue their vision, unburdened by the superficial trappings of adult society or the need for middle-class presentability. One of the most memorable lofts in the movie city is that of Rollie (Bryan Brown), the special-effects wizard of *F/X* (1986): it is an adolescent's garden of delights, from the scary animated monster that greets visitors at the door to the prop heads and cast-latex cadavers that fill the shelves and walls, mementoes of past projects like "Vermin from Venus" and "I Dismember Mama." Rollie's creations—amusing, and technically brilliant—bring out even more clearly than high art the complex role of the loft as both playpen and workshop, a place that helps preserve the freshness and creativity so commonly enjoyed by children and so rarely by adults.

It is this duality, finally, that inspires one of the most touching moments in the lofts of the movie city. In *Big* (1988), Tom Hanks plays Josh Baskin, a twelve-year-old boy who has magically inhabited the body of a full-grown man. When it is time for Josh to find a place to live, he is drawn immediately to a loft. The real-estate agent promotes its clean lines, fifteen-foot ceiling, hardwood floors, modern kitchen, and Jacuzzi. For Josh, it is the perfect skateboard slalom (145). He converts the space into a playroom, complete with basketball hoop, pinball and soda machines, and, at the center, a full-size trampoline. Halfway through the film, Josh brings home a coworker named Susan, a brittle, sharp-edged woman played by Elizabeth Perkins. Expecting seduction, she is flustered by his suggestion that she try out the trampoline. In stockinged feet and party dress she makes a few tentative jumps, awkward and unhappy. But as he joins in and encourages her, they jump higher and higher, her hair and skirt flying, her fear turning to glee and pleasure, the superficial sophistication of her adult New York persona peeled away to reveal the simple joy of a child. A final shot from across the street, looking into tall windows framed by the elegant cast-iron facade, shows the two friends mysteriously flying up and down, rediscovering the very essence of space and play that the loft had somehow introduced right into the heart of the old city (150).

EIGHT

WORLDS OF DIFFERENCE

DEAD END AND *REAR WINDOW*

DISTANT NEIGHBORS

Dead End and *Rear Window.*

They are linked first of all by their titles, which, like a handful of others (*The Apartment, On the Waterfront*), achieve their effect not through geographic specificity but the exact opposite: generic, almost abstract place names, with distinctly metaphoric undertones.

They are linked, too, by their status as two of the very greatest products of Hollywood's studio-constructed city, films whose rich physical environments are an essential part of their appeal. In the artistry and sheer scale of their settings, they rise above even the typically ambitious effort, at the height of the studio era, to remake the city from scratch.

Above all, the two films are linked by their lessons. Each, in its fashion, explores one of the most profound challenges to any city, but especially New York: how to accommodate the extraordinary range of human *difference* gathered within its boundaries. Those lessons turn out to be complementary: *Dead End* (1937) looks at the mixing of different *groups* in the city's most familiar outdoor space, the street; *Rear Window* (1954) surveys the mix of different *individuals* within a less familiar (though hardly less common) outdoor space—the backyard at the heart of each city block. Each film sets forth a powerful and troubling critique of the city; each reveals surprising urban values. Both are worth a close look.

151. (previous page) ***Dead End*** **(1937).** On a block by the East River, a group of local boys—including Huntz Hall, Leo Gorcey, Billy Halop, and Gabriel Dell, making their first screen appearance as the "Dead End Kids"—question Kay (Wendy Barrie) about life inside the luxurious River Terrace apartments.

Dead End's setting was explored earlier as a classic tenement street. Yet in fact it is home not only to tenements but, at its very heart, a luxurious apartment house. It thus sustains another layer of meaning altogether, raising issues not only of the poor, but of poor and rich, side by side—issues that cut to the essence of New York's urban character, and, ultimately, to the city's place within the American experiment.

Dead End's intimate conjunction of rich and poor, though dramatic, was hardly fictional. In the early 1920s, a group of elite New Yorkers had begun gravitating to the eastern edge of midtown, renovating old row houses and building new apartment houses along the East River, amid a landscape otherwise dominated by breweries, coal yards, and slaughterhouses. By 1931, their efforts were capped by the completion of River House, a twenty-six-story cooperative apartment building whose water-edge location afforded a private club with dock and floating pier, at which members could moor their yachts (152).

Still present everywhere among the elegant newcomers were the area's old warehouses, factories, and old-law tenements, packed with poor Irish families. With few other outlets for recreation, tenement children turned the commercial piers into swimming holes, diving into the grimy waters of the East River literally steps away from the well-scrubbed docks and gleaming pleasure craft of the richest New Yorkers (153). The striking intersection of society rich and Irish poor soon inspired the use of an old catchphrase for the area's inhabitants: "the Colonel's Lady and Mrs. O'Grady." Then, in 1935, it inspired something else.

152. Private dock, River Club, 1936. Looking south from the tip of East 53rd Street to the base of River House, this view (taken by Goldwyn's art department) shows the landscaped dock and floating pier of the River Club, where members and guests could moor their yachts. Construction of the East River Drive in the late 1930s permanently severed the club from the water's edge.

Though best known as one of America's leading industrial designers, Norman Bel Geddes's first love was theater, and among his close friends was the playwright Sidney Kingsley, with whom he enjoyed regular lunch-hour walks by the river. One day in 1935, the two men came across some neighborhood children swimming at the dead end of East 53rd Street, where the back of River House met a row of dingy tenements, a gravel plant, and a loading pier. Bel Geddes apparently mentioned in passing that the scene could easily frame a modern-day Romeo and Juliet tale, with tenement dwellers and apartment-house elite taking the place of Verona's rival clans. Struck by the notion, Kingsley retreated for several weeks, before emerging with a drama titled *Dead End*, written along those lines. Bel Geddes himself decided to produce the play on Broadway, personally designing the celebrated "dead-end" set on which its action took place. Producer Samuel Goldwyn, always looking for material mixing high entertainment value with "social significance," purchased the movie rights even before opening night.

To create the film version, Goldwyn assembled a stellar team. William Wyler would direct; Gregg Toland would photograph; Richard Day would interpret Bel Geddes's set design for the screen; and Alfred Newman would write the score. To adapt the script, Goldwyn turned to a writer known as much for her crafted dramas as for her radical politics: Lillian Hellman.

Like the play, the whole film would take place on a single dead-end block ("East 54th Place"), constructed inside a Goldwyn soundstage on Santa Monica Boulevard for $90,000, complete with an immense concrete tank, filled with thousands of gallons of water, to reproduce a portion of the East River. Upon seeing Day's finished set, with its roach-infested tenements and refuse-laden river, Goldwyn complained loudly how "filthy" it all looked. When Wyler gently reminded him that the story was supposed to be set in a city slum, the producer countered with a reply that became legendary: "There won't be any dirty slums in a Goldwyn picture!" A strange tug-of-war ensued, with Day and Wyler and property man Irving Sandler daily bringing garbage onto the set, and Goldwyn daily ordering it removed.

153. Swimming pier at the foot of East 48th Street, 1938. Visible in the distance is the setting that inspired *Dead End:* River House, rising at the left, with a motor launch moored at its private dock, right next door to warehouses, a gravel plant, and a grimy industrial pier that (like the one in the foreground) was a favorite recreation spot for poor local children on hot summer days.

Though the action took place entirely on one street, the filmmakers were careful to locate it within the larger city (and society) by way of an ingenious establishing shot that smoothly joined a miniature skyline with the full-scale street (154). As the film opens, we are poised above the city. In the distance we see the towers of Rockefeller Center and the Waldorf-Astoria. At left is the sleek, smooth face of an apartment tower. A prologue appears:

> *Every street in New York ends in a river. For many years the dirty banks of the East River were lined with the tenements of the poor. Then the rich, discovering that the river traffic was picturesque, moved their houses eastward. And now the terraces of these great apartment houses look down onto the windows of the tenement poor.*

And the camera starts to descend.

The distant towers, beacons for the whole city, now give way to the meaner confines of the film's set. The film will close with this same shot in reverse, and the towers will be glimpsed in the background throughout; they are a consistent presence, selected with care. The skyline as a whole tells us New York is a rich city; the sleek, modernistic Radio City in particular tells us New York is also a *progressive* city whose forward-looking structures presage a better world to come.

In this context, the dead-end street offers its own foil. The apartment tower seen at the far left of the opening shot proves to be "River Terrace," a luxurious high-rise jutting into the river, complete with its own yacht mooring—the most striking contrast imaginable to the decaying old-law tenements and grimy warehouses that fill the rest of the block (155).

154. **Establishing shot from *Dead End* (1937).** Combining a painted skyline with three-dimensional miniatures in the foreground, the film's opening shot featured the slab of the RCA Building, the twin-towered Waldorf-Astoria, and, on the left, the facade of the fictional "River Terrace" apartments.

The contrast quickly takes on human dimension. It is morning, and the daily rituals of life among the poor offer sharp contrast to those of the rich. For the tenement dwellers down on the street, filthy garbage cans are dragged out, fly-paper is changed. For apartment dwellers on the terrace above, a birdcage is unveiled and a breakfast table is set alfresco. Below, a poor boy announces his intention to sober up his drunken father; above, a rich boy and his private tutor converse in French. As a white-coated servant polishes the building's brass nameplate, a cop kicks a sleeping bum off a bench.

Thus is the gulf between the classes drawn, in the bluntest possible terms. Yet Wyler's roving camera, moving from vignette to vignette, blurs these stark divisions by way of a familiar urban paradox. As much as the story emphasizes *dis*connection, the camera *connects* everyone living on the block, who, rich or poor, are all greeting the same hot morning. It is an effect reinforced by Day's set, which, by enclosing everything into one easily apprehended space, reminds us that everyone we see on the block is a *neighbor,* however unlikely as such. Social distance and physical closeness; disconnection and connection—it is a tension that will play out across the entire film (151).

It certainly shapes the film's romantic triangle. Dave (Joel McCrea), a local tenement resident who, despite his training as an architect, remains unemployed and desperately poor, has deserted his childhood sweetheart Drina (Sylvia Sidney) for a chic young woman named Kay (Wendy Barrie), who lives in the fancy apartment house. Sexual desire, evidently, can cross the barriers of class. In its way, the street connects, too. Drina, chatting out the window to a neighbor, is distracted by the sight of her stylish rival stepping onto a nearby balcony. In New York, everyone's windows face each other. Still more remarkably, all residential buildings—rich, poor, and middle class—adjoin each other, meeting side by side along a common building wall. For maximum political as well as dramatic effect, *Dead End*'s contrast is unusually sharp, juxtaposing only the very richest and the very poorest; but then as now, it is hardly uncommon for buildings of widely different types and classes—row houses, tenements, apartment houses—to come together on a single New York block, related (for all their differences) by a host of consistent urban gestures and a common urban ancestry. (In this regard, in fact, the design of *Dead End* broke with reality, setting its "River Terrace" apartment house well back from the street. Almost all apartment houses in the real city—including River House itself—were directly aligned with their neighbors, until the 1961 zoning law actually encouraged buildings to break the street wall and be set away from the sidewalk.) (155)

Back down on the street, the social gulf is restated. Amid the general decay, the apartment house's doorman delicately sweeps a cigarette butt off the front step—a scene evoking the sometimes absurd lengths to which the city's rich will go to carve out a zone of well-tended order from the urban chaos around them.

155. *Dead End* (1937). Like the celebrated stage set by Norman Bel Geddes from which it was adapted, the film's dead-end street (by art director Richard Day) offered a striking juxtaposition of buildings: a sleek modern apartment house at left, rundown tenements at center, and a grimy warehouse at right.

The dirty look exchanged by this uniformed guardian and the scruffy Dead End Kids carries in a glance all the bitter enmity that exists between the haves and have-nots of the world.

But again the street connects, or tries to. Seeing the rich boy on the sidewalk, the Dead End Kids entice him into their clubhouse, and he goes in, half wanting to be accepted; once inside, they viciously beat him up and steal his watch. His clothes in shreds, he runs in tears back to the safety of his apartment house. A little later, Kay and Dave meet on the street—their common ground—to discuss the future, looking for a way to make a life together. But again social differences divide them: when Kay tries to visit Dave's home, and glimpses the filthy tenement stair hall—with its ragged children, prostitutes, and roach-infested garbage—she, too, runs back to the comfort of the apartment house. And so it goes, the physical structure of the street throwing the disparate classes together, the economic structure of society separating them. Class differences are brought to life vividly through this constant dynamic of attraction and repulsion, driven by the sheer proximity of rich and poor.

By film's end, difference has won out. Though Dave is no longer poor, having earned some reward money for shooting a gangster, he decides that he and Kay must part: "I don't belong in your world," he tells her, "you don't belong in mine." And though Drina's brother Tommy—wanted for attacking the rich boy—gives himself up to the police, the upper classes, as represented by the rich boy's father, prove stern and unyielding. "For no reason at all, he beat my boy up and stole his watch," the man tells Drina. "There are other boys like mine, and they've got to be protected." Dave will use his reward money to hire a lawyer for Tommy's defense, but the prospects are not auspicious.

The film's conclusion, in fact, is decidedly dark. The authors' message is clear: a vast gulf of economic class divides the world, and must ultimately defeat every effort, social and personal, to bridge it. Perhaps only in the socially conscious mood of the late 1930s could such a pessimistic and politically loaded conclusion have been transmitted by a mainstream Hollywood film. (And ironically, perhaps only Goldwyn, among Hollywood producers, would have allowed such a message to emerge in relatively unadulterated form.)

It is not hard to infer what solution Kingsley and Hellman might favor: social and political revolution, dissolving class differences, and perhaps eliminating classes themselves. The first step, naturally, was to make people aware of the human cost of those economic divisions. In that regard, the value of *Dead End*'s setting was obvious, showing that in New York generally and in this district especially, rich and poor lived so close together, making the tensions between them so obvious and discomforting. From this would come the great response.

In the following decades, a response *did* come, a great one indeed—though hardly the one the filmmakers intended. If proximity between widely different classes made for discomfort, the answer for most Americans was obvious: abolish the proximity.

Clover Leaf
Dairy
Products

Such has been a major thrust of American life, of course, since the time of *Dead End.* The country's great postwar transformation—in which Americans overwhelmingly abandoned public transit for private automobiles, fled city streets for suburban enclaves, and left traditional downtowns for self-enclosed shopping malls and office parks—had its roots, largely, in the broad desire of the rich and the middle class to distance themselves from the poor. The classes of *Dead End* still exist in America, the difference among them no less sharp than at the time of the film's release, but in an automobile-based, suburban-style society, they have far fewer places and opportunities to encounter one another and experience friction. To appreciate the change, we have only to try to imagine a version of *Dead End* set in a typical American suburb, a place zoned specifically to avoid disparities in social class and altogether devoid of sidewalks on which to walk, a place where people enter their private cars to go almost everywhere and remain in them until reaching their destinations—which are themselves usually isolated offices or shopping centers, places where individual behavior is closely monitored, and where those without adequate means are made to feel unwelcome, or are even ejected. In modern America, space has become the great buffer, a means of dampening social tensions by ensuring that, so far as possible, different groups never meet in unregulated settings.

Amidst all this stands New York, where to a surprising degree the premise underlying *Dead End*'s setting—a place in which different classes rub up against one another—still holds. Of course, such heterogeneity is hardly absolute: the rich tend to congregate, as do the middle class, and poor—but to a measure remarkable by the standards of contemporary American life, New York's wide social spectrum of citizens *do* continue to mix within the city's predominantly pedestrian spaces, on streets where buildings of different socioeconomic status are placed closely if not contiguously to one another.

Indeed, this very quality of the city, the historian Thomas Bender suggests, offers a fundamental "myth" for American life, an alternative to both Puritan New England and Jeffersonian Virginia, which for all their distinctions—"one religious, the other secular; one hierarchical, the other egalitarian; one town-oriented, the other rural; one reminiscent of the medieval world-view, the other drawing upon the Enlightenment"—overlap on this critical issue:

> *[B]oth reject the idea of* difference. . . . *You had your place in a Puritan village or town only if your values coincided with your neighbors'. Rather than incorporating difference, Puritan town leaders were quick to offer strangers the "liberty to keep away from us." . . . [T]his theory of America could accommodate inevitable difference, but only in a quite limited way. You cannot stay in our town, but you are free to establish your own town, with your own people and beliefs. So the dream of living surrounded by sameness, with all differences kept at a distance, persists. It is at the heart of much suburban development. . . .*

156. ***Dead End*** **(1937).** Rich and poor, side by side. At left, a young woman (Wendy Barrie) waves from the upper-floor balcony of her elegant Art Deco apartment house, at right, tenement dwellers go about their morning chores.

Perhaps, in this sense, New York fulfills the promise of America itself, extending the notion of *politically* accommodating different groups to the more daring—and potentially dangerous—ideal of *physically* gathering those groups in a single urban place.

Of course, this distinctive way of life has always had its costs, perhaps more so now than at the time of *Dead End*'s release, when the vision of a future without class differences still held sway among many. Today, when those differences seem far more of an enduring fact of life, the city's tradition of public space remains not only prone to the same discomforting and even violent conflicts evident in *Dead End*, but raises what have become essentially unanswerable questions about the inequalities of American life. In a sense, it is no wonder that so many have chosen to avoid the problem altogether, living in environments that are consciously designed to minimize all such tensions, by eliminating any place or circumstance where they might arise. Like the real city, the filmic city gains much of its dramatic impact from the fact that New York, for better or worse, remains a place where such questions must still be asked.

FIFTY WINDOWS

> Ordinarily, we seem to be completely separate from everything and everyone in our surroundings, and our sense of external things (if not of other people) is that they are waiting around until we can find something for them to do. At moments when the boundaries flow together, perhaps even disappear, a different sense emerges.... Our sense of ourselves now has more to do with noticing how we are connected to the people and things around us, part of a family, a crowd, a community.... Through one system of perception we see ourselves as observers of an environment composed of separated objects, but at the same time, through another system of perception, equally active, we look for ways in which we are connected to or are part of our surroundings.
>
> TONY HISS

> Realities keep in the rear.
>
> NATHANIEL HAWTHORNE

With its rich, multifaceted story and its unforgettable Greenwich Village setting, Alfred Hitchcock's *Rear Window*, made in 1954, remains perhaps the most sophisticated and complex exploration of the movie city ever created. Looking at the interaction not of groups but individual city-dwellers, the film gives a subtler, more shaded meaning to the notion of urban "difference" than the blunt class distinctions of *Dead End*. And it reveals not only hidden meanings but a hidden space: the rear yards that combine to create the hollow center of each residential block. Dotting the entire city, these corelike spaces are mostly

157. Publicity still from *Rear Window* (1954). James Stewart, Grace Kelly, and director Alfred Hitchcock pose in the apartment window of L. B. Jefferies (Stewart), overlooking the film's famous courtyard set, which almost entirely filled Stage 18 at Paramount Studios, one of the largest on the lot.

invisible from the street and thus easily overlooked; *Rear Window*'s pleasure, in no small part, grows from its extended view of a part of the city that often goes unseen, at least by outsiders.

Though based on a dark short story by the original "noir" author, Cornell Woolrich, *Rear Window* is leavened by the witty, vignette-filled screenplay of John Michael Hayes; for all the underlying seriousness of its themes, it offers a languorous, urbane tour of the filmic city, the layered density of its setting more than matched by the complexity and delight of its multiple stories, all proceeding at once (157). Its famed courtyard set, a bit picturesque perhaps for an ordinary city backyard (even in Greenwich Village), nonetheless contains the authentic components of the city's residential tradition, mixed in a fashion that is itself not uncommon.

As the opening sequence lets us know in no uncertain terms, the dramatic focus of *Rear Window* is the rear courtyard itself. As the credit titles come up and Franz Waxman's jaunty score begins, three bamboo window shades rise, one by one, to unveil the courtyard view beyond them. It is impossible to miss the theatrical metaphor: a curtain rising to reveal the "stage" behind. Implicit is the notion of a "theater" itself, a fixed place from which to watch the show—what we later discover is the apartment belonging to the character played by James Stewart.

Yet no sooner is this sequence over than the camera moves toward the windows and then *into* the courtyard, executing a broad, sweeping pan of the place it had revealed as framed and distant just a moment before.

The shift between the two shots is profound, and resonates throughout the film. It is not just that a static theatrical view, having been firmly established, now gives way to a dynamic, filmic way of seeing. It is also that the notion of a single, privileged vantage point—Stewart's apartment—has been counterbalanced with that of an omniscient, roving eye that will occasionally go where Stewart himself cannot, passing into the courtyard itself to explore every corner of the place.

As it now proceeds to do, not once but twice.

On the first pass we are alone, except for a cat whose silent footfalls across the courtyard set the tone for our own quiet journey. It is the very early morning and almost no one is about; we see a milkman in the distance, a head or two

158. Courtyard set from *Rear Window* (1954). For reference, Hitchcock sent production manager "Doc" Erickson to New York to photograph three real Greenwich Village courtyards at various times of day. He also ordered ambient sound recorded in the three yards to provide appropriate background effects.

in a window, a flock of pigeons on a roof. Set in the heart of the densely populated city, the landscape is all but devoid of people.

Still, the scene is lively enough (158). Art director Joseph "Mac" Johnson has gathered a realistically rich variety of structures, which we now survey carefully. Over on the right is a glass-walled studio and a couple of brick apartment houses; at center stands a small row house, just two stories tall, sporting a wooden rear porch and open staircase. A small alleyway by the row house's side leads down to the next street, revealing a narrow slice of sidewalk and pavement. To the far left, some diagonally angled brick walls suggest the exposed half of a tenement air shaft.

159. *Rear Window* (1954). "Miss Torso," played by Georgine Darcy (top), and "The Composer," played by Ross Bagdasarian (above).

Though we have yet to meet anyone, we have already learned a great deal about what this place is—and still more about what it is *not.* It is not the street. As that meandering cat first showed us, the courtyard floor is a series of different levels, divided by fences and walls of all kinds, that could not possibly accept any through traffic. Enclosed almost entirely by buildings, the space is connected to nothing else in the city—unlike a street, which is by definition connected to everything else. Though located in the middle of New York, the courtyard is a place apart, a quiet and isolated landscape that is shared only by the people who face it.

The buildings not only reflect but reinforce this feeling. Their walls do not hew to a consistent line but are set forward and back, offering a richly sculptural quality in place of the relatively flat alignment that would be found on the street. They evidence all sorts of accretions and changes over time, having sprouted additions (like the glass-walled studio, or the wooden porch) that sometimes extend a considerable distance into the yard, as they could never do into the sidewalk. They are, in short, the informal *backs* of the city's buildings, as opposed to their formal *fronts.* It is a distinction so crucial that the film's designers—by giving us an explicit comparison—have made certain we won't miss it. In a glimpse of the next street we see a slice of architecture that is unmistakably a building's *front,* a brownstone facade with an elaborate cornice and window enframements. It is a classic example of the carefully composed face that urban buildings put on to meet the outside world; back here, by contrast, where the structures have no need to employ such formality, they can stretch out, improvise, relax.

It is an astonishing shot—but it is not over yet. After bringing us back inside the apartment to glimpse a sleeping Jimmy Stewart and a thermometer pushing ninety-two degrees, the moving camera returns outside, repeating its circuit precisely so that—like a scientifically controlled experiment—we may notice only what has changed.

Which is plenty. For the day is beginning: people are awakening, morning rituals have begun, the block is coming to life. Last time, we now realize, we were shown the courtyard's *form;* now, just as deliberately, we get to see its function. Not just the court, but the people who inhabit it; not just the place, but the way in which it is lived. It is virtually a primer in urbanism.

On the right, the window shades of the studio have been pulled up to reveal its occupant—a musician of some kind, judging by the grand piano in the middle of the room—standing in front of a mirror, in his pajamas, shaving. The Latin rhythm coming from his radio sets a pleasant mood for the entire courtyard, although the music is soon interrupted by an alarm clock ringing on a fire escape that has been transformed by an older couple into an outdoor bedroom, complete with mattress and sheets dragged from inside. Still wearing their bedclothes, they rise and carry their belongings back in through the window. But even this degree of exposure is outdone by that of the resident next door, a young blonde who, just out of the shower, proceeds to put on a pair of skimpy tights and, without donning another stitch, starts to prepare breakfast while practicing leg lifts (159, top).

Having returned inside Stewart's apartment, the camera—still roaming—now efficiently provides the film's backstory: we discover his character's name, L. B. Jefferies, and learn that he is a successful photojournalist, laid up with a broken leg acquired while shooting a race-car accident. Soon enough, we meet Jefferies (or "Jeff") himself, awake now and sitting in a wheelchair at *his* window, sharing in the courtyard's morning rituals: shaving while talking on the phone, explaining to his editor that he still has another week remaining in the cast, after six already passed. As the camera follows his view outside, we continue watching the day begin. The man in the glass-walled studio—he is a composer, it turns out—plays the first tentative notes of a new song. The blonde is still practicing dance moves in her underwear. And another man, a heavyset fellow in hat and coat whom we hadn't seen before, is lugging a big valise into his apartment, pointedly ignoring his nagging wife.

This viewing session, however, is soon interrupted by the arrival of Stella (Thelma Ritter), an insurance company nurse, crisply reciting the provisions of the state penal code regarding Peeping Toms. "We've become a race of Peeping Toms," she declares in disgust. And thus is introduced the overt (and endlessly analyzed) theme of *Rear Window:* voyeurism, the psychological desire or need to observe other people from a distance and inhabit their lives vicariously (6).

But something seems wrong about Stella's pat theory. We have just glimpsed a number of people in the most private of moments—shaving, waking and rising from bed, putting clothes on and taking them off, dressed in pajamas, underwear, tights. We have been able to see all this because it has transpired in front of open windows, or on fire escapes or terraces. No one has bothered to shut themselves off from view by closing blinds, or using interior rooms, or avoiding outdoor areas. And these are clearly *rituals*, performed every day in a casual, unthinking manner, without a trace of self-consciousness. If we really were a "race of Peeping Toms," as Stella claims, would not people regularly try to hide themselves behind solid walls and shuttered windows? Instead, they reveal themselves to an astounding degree. It is no trivial point; in fact, it is the film's first important lesson on how cities work.

Some of their behavior can be traced to the heat; in the days before residential air-conditioning became common, summer life in the city naturally gravitated toward open windows, or to outdoor spaces like fire escapes. But some of their behavior, it is fair to speculate, is encouraged by the space itself. Many of these people might feel far less comfortable performing the same actions on the street side of their buildings, in full view of strangers. Is there something about this courtyard that encourages them to feel comfortable treating it as an extension of their homes?

There is. The courtyard, as Hitchcock shows us, is a place of perceived privacy—a subtle yet enormously valuable quality for an urban space. Real privacy comes from actual isolation, from placing oneself behind closed doors and solid walls. *Perceived* privacy grows from the sense that, while others *might* be looking, it is reasonable to act as if they are not. Perceived privacy allows urban dwellers to go about their lives without the tiresome effort of constantly closing blinds and shades and shutting themselves off from the light, view, and air of windows, doors, terraces, and yards.

Clearly the courtyard's residents share this understanding. They act as if no one is watching—and indeed, no one *would be* watching, were it not for the happenstance of Jefferies's broken leg. Jefferies can see so much only because everyone else shares a sense of perceived privacy; and normally, of course, he would share it too. He obviously never paid much attention to the view before he broke his leg, and will almost certainly become oblivious to it once he has healed and gotten on with his life. (As the film scholar Stefan Sharff has pointed out, "Jefferies . . . is somehow excused for his actions; in a wheelchair, his leg in a cast for nearly six weeks with nothing to do, he looks.")

Valuable as perceived privacy is, it does not occur in equal measure everywhere: in the design of their courtyard, Hitchcock and Mac Johnson brilliantly captured the qualities that best encourage it. Most important, of course, is the fact that the courtyard is a space set apart from the larger city. Because it is not a thoroughfare, there are no passersby and thus no strangers. Anybody in a position to look into one's window must be a neighbor—not necessarily a friend, but a neighbor—into whose *own* windows it is possible to look back, in rough but fair reciprocity. (Shaving right in front of his window, wearing nothing but his bedclothes, Jefferies plainly shares the assumption that no one is bothering to look at *him*.) There is something, too, in the informal character of the place, so lovingly detailed in the opening shot; in the fact that the courtyard's floor is a mixture of different terraces and gardens all set to different levels; in the fact that the building walls that face it are casual, relaxed backs rather than the formal fronts. As the very title of the film makes clear, Hitchcock understood just how important to his story was its setting at a *rear* window. For in this informal, semiprivate courtyard, unlike the formal, public street, people would be more likely to reveal themselves, offering to Jefferies (and the audience) the most entertaining—and potentially dramatic—range of human activity. In its way, it reasserts the profound difference between front and back, public and private, first made evident back in the Sloper's house, in *The Heiress*. Where the row house once stood, new kinds of houses have since been built—but the profound distinction between the outer and inner sides of the New York block remains very much intact.

Under Stella's prodding, Jefferies talks reluctantly about the woman in his life, a stylish, fashion-obsessed beauty named Lisa Fremont (Grace Kelly), whom he cares for but is hesitant to wed. As he speaks of his ambivalence, Jefferies's eye is caught by another window, and its glimpse of a honeymoon couple ceremonially crossing the threshold, then discreetly drawing the shade. The pointed conjunction introduces the notion (suggested by the film scholar Robin Wood and others) that the courtyard's various windows represent alternative scenarios for Jefferies's own life, what one critic calls "a kaleidoscopic prophecy of his future." When Lisa herself arrives that evening, Jefferies points out "Miss Lonelyhearts," an older woman who sets a dinner place for an imaginary beau, pantomiming conversation with him—then descends into lovelorn anguish. This could easily be Jefferies's sad fate, should he continue to spurn the attention of Lisa. "Miss Torso," meanwhile, is the curvaceous dancer, somehow juggling three boyfriends in her tiny apartment, although—as Lisa is quick to point out—she isn't in love with any of them. This could be Lisa's future, surrounded by every man except the one she really wants. And then there is Thorwald, "the Salesman," the heavyset man in the apartment house across the way, constantly fighting with his bedridden wife. For Jefferies, he represents the life sentence of a miserable matrimony. These examples set a dispiriting tone that leads to a fight between Lisa and Jefferies, and a rainy, unsettling night in which Jefferies hears a mysterious scream and the sound of breaking glass, and witnesses the odd comings and goings of the Salesman.

Yet with morning, the courtyard's comforting rituals reassert themselves: the sculptor across the way works on an abstract piece in her backyard; the composer tries to pin down his new tune; Miss Torso practices her steps; the couple on the fire escape unveil an ingenious pulley to lower their dog to the backyard in a basket. This final vignette reminds us again of the special character of the space: the couple would be unlikely, after all, to let their dog wander by itself on the street in front; back here, though, their pet can roam the protected "turf" of the courtyard in safety.

It is in this tranquil context that Jefferies first voices his puzzlement about the Salesman's behavior the night before, and notices the absence of the man's invalid wife. Using binoculars and telephoto lens, Jefferies observes the man cleaning the inside of his sample case, washing knives and saws in the kitchen sink, and staring nervously at the neighbors' dog, who sniffs at a freshly planted flower bed below. It is all decidedly suspicious.

To Lisa, however, Jeff's theory—that the Salesman has murdered his wife and is disposing of her in pieces—is absurd on its face. "You could see all that he did, couldn't you?" she points out. "You could see because the shades were up, and he walked along the corridor, and the street, and the backyard. Oh, Jeff, do you think that a murderer would let you see all that, that he wouldn't pull the shades *down* and hide behind them?" She answers her own question. "A murderer would never parade his crime in front of an open window."

It would sound more reasonable if Jefferies, and the audience, hadn't been seeing, for several days now, just how much people *will* do in front of an open window, in the context of the shared sense of privacy that the courtyard so powerfully engenders. But Doyle (Wendell Corey), a police detective (and acquaintance) who arrives the next day at Jefferies's insistence, remains skeptical. "In full view of fifty windows?" he asks, reiterating Lisa's point.

The courtyard is especially lively this evening, for the weekend has come. (One of the film's many pleasures is the way it is paced to the actual rhythm of a city week, beginning on a Wednesday morning and building toward the weekend's festivities. We emerge with the sense of having really lived with these people for several days.) The composer is throwing a lively party, with the sounds of laughter and boogie-woogie piano spilling out across the courtyard. Yet the host stands alone, looking out the window, as if for something—or someone—he cannot find in the festive whirl behind him (159, bottom). Miss Lonelyhearts, on the other hand, has managed to lure a real beau into her apartment, but the scene turns ugly when the man tries to force himself on her; she throws him out the door, then collapses, sobbing in misery. "That's pretty private stuff going on out there," Jefferies is reminded, while Lisa lowers the blinds, announcing, "Show's over for tonight."

Yet minutes later, attention is wrenched outside again, by a piercing scream. The couple on the fire escape has discovered their dog lying dead in the backyard. Lights are turned on; everyone rushes to the windows; the party-goers step onto the terrace. Even the honeymoon couple raise their shades to see what's going on. "Which one of you did it?" the woman shrieks. "Which one of you killed my dog?" In her anguish, she launches into a tirade against urban life: "You don't know the meaning of the word neighbor! Neighbors like each other. Speak to each other. Care if anybody lives or dies. But none of you do!" It is a harsh indictment, yet there is obvious sympathy in the faces of her own neighbors: Miss Torso, Miss Lonelyhearts, and the sculptor all wear looks of true concern and listen intently to her speech—unlike the party-goers, who *are* strangers, and who return inside abruptly once the excitement is over. Indeed, it is the observation that, alone among the courtyard neighbors, only Thorwald has failed to come to the window (he sits in the dark of his apartment, silently smoking a cigarette), that again convinces Jefferies he *must* be the guilty party, responsible not only for his wife's murder but for the dog's death as well. Intent on convincing us of the high level of alienation in the modern big city, the scene has instead presented a fairly high level of community involvement, and assumed an even higher standard: to ignore a neighbor's plight, it suggests, is an extraordinary act, the sure giveaway of criminal intentions.

The action jumps forward to Saturday evening. Having watched Thorwald all day, Jefferies begins a dangerous game of cat-and-mouse, sending Lisa across the courtyard to obtain some evidence of his presumed crime. Yet as they watch her anxiously (and helplessly) from the window, Jefferies and Stella are distracted by another unfolding disaster: Miss Lonelyhearts, having reached the depths of her despair, is preparing to kill herself with a bottle of potent sleeping pills. Jefferies hurriedly calls the police, though it seems too late.

Unexpectedly, another part of the courtyard comes to the woman's aid. At the studio, a group of musicians have been rehearsing the song the composer has been working on all week. "Okay, boys, let's try it once from the beginning," he says, and as the sound of the ensemble pours across the courtyard, Miss Lonelyhearts—about to swallow the pills—pauses instead to listen. "Look," Stella announces excitedly, "the music stopped her." But there is no time to exult. In the film's climactic sequence, Thorwald realizes he is being watched, identifies Jefferies's apartment, then comes over and attacks him, pushing him out the window. Again, everyone rushes to their window; some quick-moving policemen manage to cushion Jeff's fall, and soon we hear that Thorwald has confessed to the murder.

The denouement, repeating precisely the panorama that opened the film, calls attention yet again to what has changed—and plays out the notion of the windows as alternative futures. Domestic order has been restored; the temperature has dropped at last to a comfortable seventy degrees. In the composer's studio, Miss Lonelyhearts sits listening to the first pressing of his new song, called "Lisa." "I can't tell you what this music has meant to me," she says; for the time being, at least, both seem to have solved their loneliness. In Thorwald's apartment, painters whitewash the walls, preparing for new tenants—a symbolic purification of the evil that occurred there. The couple on the fire escape have replaced their old dog with a new puppy, fawning over it just as before. Miss Torso's steady boyfriend returns from the Army, a short, balding fellow named Stanley who heads straight for the refrigerator. Even the mysterious newlyweds have joined the larger community: their nuptial passion spent, the shades lifted, they sit in the kitchen, bickering. There is Jeff, back in his wheelchair, having broken a *second* leg in his fall—and there, by his side, is Lisa. Her pluck and daring have won his heart; and in bringing the murderer to justice, he has symbolically rid himself of his darker, misogynist side. For Jeff's benefit, Lisa reads a book on Himalayan exploration, but seeing him fall

160. Shooting *Rear Window*. To accommodate the immense set designed by Joseph "Mac" Johnson, the floor of Stage 18 was cut open and the wardrobe rooms beneath removed, adding thirteen feet to the stage's forty-foot clear height. The decision to build downward as well as up not only allowed the set's facades to rise a full five stories, but placed Jefferies's second-story apartment on the stage floor, simplifying access for cast, crew, and equipment. To heighten Jefferies's climactic fall, Johnson ordered the undisturbed dirt beneath the basement excavated; workmen dug so deep—thirty feet below stage level—that they struck water, requiring a pump to be installed during production.

asleep, picks up *Harper's Bazaar* instead. Life in the courtyard, and in the movie city, proceeds. The bamboo curtain comes down, proudly bearing the Paramount trademark.

As well it should. The film was the peak achievement of everything a studio like Paramount had to offer. "*Rear Window,*" noted *American Cinematographer* at the time, "was shot in its entirety on one soundstage and in one set—but a set of which Hollywood has never before seen the like." Combining both the central courtyard and the surrounding apartments in a single, composite construction, *Rear Window*'s set completely filled Stage 18, one of the biggest on the Paramount lot, 98 feet wide by 184 feet long. During the six weeks required for its construction, Hitchcock himself could be seen roving around every corner, delighting in its complexity and verisimilitude, overseeing its smallest details. When completed, the $100,000 set included thirty-one individual apartments, twelve of them fully furnished, and featured a complete drainage system to avoid flooding during the rain scenes (160).

The shooting itself was no less memorable. The apartments all had to be separately wired to allow their lights to be switched on or off individually, as they would be in a real city. A subtle lighting design was required to ensure that the apartment interiors did not appear artificially bright, like shop windows, when seen from outside. And the huge space of the courtyard itself had to be bathed in the glare of a summer day. "Lighting this composite set," cinematographer Robert Burks noted, "was the biggest electrical job ever undertaken on the lot at Paramount—not excepting Cecil B. DeMille's big spectacle sets." Simply controlling the set's three thousand lights required every available switch on the Paramount lot, all connected to a master panel that, Burks boasted, "looked like the console of the biggest organ ever made!" The panel allowed Burks to choreograph the lighting in the courtyard's seventy doors and windows according to a preset chart for mornings, afternoons, and nights. As shooting finally began and the great banks of arc lights were switched on, they generated a heat so intense that the stage's sprinkler system was triggered; it had to be disconnected for filming to proceed. Then Hitchcock, microphone in hand, began calling out directions on a shortwave radio system, allowing actors at the far reaches of the set (wearing flesh-colored headsets) to follow their cues while he stood watching the ensemble.

From the start, critiques of *Rear Window* have admired the film's careful and unusual structuring from Jefferies's point of view. For some, the focus on Jefferies's perspective reflects his character's gradual (and ultimately redemptive) progression from passive, self-involved spectator to active participant in the life of the community. For others, the relationship of Jefferies and his view turns *Rear Window* into a film about film—a meditation on moviegoing itself. Jeff's window becomes a screen, before which he sits as passive and immobile as someone in a movie audience, with the same voyeuristic hope to experience life vicariously. The theorist Jean Douchet takes the cinematic analogy a step further, suggesting that it is the distant windows that are the screens, playing out, collectively, nothing less than the history of movies: Miss Torso's apartment as an early dancing-girl actuality; Miss Lonelyhearts as a weepy 1940s "woman's picture"; the fire-escape couple as a slapstick comedy (at least until their dog is found dead); the composer as a classic Broadway story of the struggling musician who at last makes it big; and the Thorwalds, finally, as a James M. Cain–style *film noir*.

161. *Rear Window* (1954). Alfred Hitchcock, relaxing between scenes on the courtyard set.

Yet a very different approach to the film can be explored, encouraged by production stills that reveal Hitchcock between takes, quietly sitting in different spots around the set, as if to more fully enjoy the "city" he had brought into being (161). It is tempting to do the same, to wander around the courtyard and treat it as an urban construct of fifty windows, of which Jefferies's is just one. We are given some license to do this by the director himself. As critics have pointed out, Hitchcock's camera—though supposedly representing Jefferies's viewpoint—is actually an autonomous agent, seeing things that Jefferies could not (the first tour of the courtyard, for example, shows Jeff himself, asleep). Supported on a long boom into the middle of the space, the camera also offers viewpoints impossible to achieve from the "rear window" itself—dramatically so at the film's end, in a moving shot that follows the police across the courtyard, looking *back* at Jefferies's window, and at Jeff himself, hanging off the sill in terror.

Still more to the point, the film includes a number of interactions around the courtyard that *do not involve Jefferies.* Some are trivial, others not. A woman putting out her parakeet greets the woman sculptor, and is greeted back; the sculptor offers Thorwald some unsolicited advice on his flowers, and is scowled at for her trouble. When the older couple's dog is found dead, Miss Lonelyhearts places it tenderly into the basket, to be raised one final time. And in what emerges as a true subplot, the strains of the composer's song stop Miss Lonelyhearts from killing herself.

These interactions put into perspective the film's urban critique, the troubling accusation voiced by the woman on the fire escape after her dog is found dead: that the courtyard's residents are not "real neighbors," that they don't know or care for each other as neighbors should. The perception of urban alienation implicit in her statement, already on the rise when *Rear Window* was made in the mid-1950s, grew dramatically in the wake of events a decade later, especially the 1964 murder of Kitty Genovese, the young Queens woman whose desperate cries for help went unheeded by nearly forty onlookers. It became common to consider the city an "urban jungle," whose inhabitants sought only to protect their own interests. Social scientists, studying what they called "urban ecology" and turning to animal behavior for clues, emphasized the notion of "territoriality": the way in which individuals define a natural bubble of protective space around them, to be defended at all costs. (The classic illustration was of birds on a telegraph line, all perched at equal distance from one another.) Urban space was seen as the exclusionary province of individual inhabitants, constantly staking out their turf.

Judged by the woman's angry speech, *Rear Window* would seem to share (or even anticipate) this attitude. But the film itself reveals a quite different appreciation. The entire notion of perceived privacy—the attitude that allows Jeff to see so much in the first place—grows from an entirely contrary notion: the idea of *sharing* urban space; of the unspoken rules of behavior by which neighbors agree not to take advantage of one another; of the sense that one's surroundings are not some alien jungle but a relatively benign extension of one's home.

In fact, the interactions among the courtyard's residents are, on the whole, remarkably positive. Despite all of Jeff's self-doubts, his obsession about his neighbor does manage, in the end, to bring a murderer to justice. A domestic homicide could of course happen anywhere; it is urban proximity that allows it to be revealed and punished. Perhaps the murder is too contrived an event, and Jeff's behavior too neurotic, to be regarded entirely positively. But what then of the moment when the sound of the composer's music stays the suicide of Miss Lonelyhearts? Propinquity triumphs over isolation; the sharing of urban space turns out to benefit its inhabitants in ways they could hardly imagine.

The film, in short, presents a very different view of urban life—one with its own analogy in the animal kingdom. Ecologists call it "sympatry," noting that while members of the same species may well fight over turf, those of *different* species more often live comfortably amidst each other, working out mutually beneficial means of coexisting in the same space.

Thus the idea of difference reasserts itself. It is not coincidental that *Rear Window* takes place in Greenwich Village and not, for example, in a suburb or small town. Not the least of the film's pleasures is the sheer variety of lives condensed within the single block it depicts. There are artists, musicians, and performers, older and younger people, singles and families, threadbare households and others that are comfortable. Everyone keeps his own hours, his own habits, his own secrets, without having to worry what others think. It is one of the reasons people come to the Village in the first place—or, as Jane Jacobs points out, to any big city:

> *Privacy is precious in cities. It is indispensable. Perhaps it is precious and indispensable everywhere, but in most places you cannot get it. In small settlements everyone knows your affairs. In the city everyone does not—only those you choose to tell will know much about you. This is one of the attributes that is precious to most city people . . . a gift of great-city life deeply cherished and jealously guarded.*

When the woman on the fire escape denounces the courtyard's missing ideal of intimate neighbors, she is confusing city living with small-town or suburban life. It is precisely the *lack* of involvement in each other's daily affairs that is one of the great attractions of cities, the right to pursue one's life without the petty approbation of one's neighbors. Gathering in a real crisis, on the other hand, marks a robust city district, as the courtyard does on two occasions: when the couple's dog is found dead and again at the film's end, when Jefferies himself is in trouble. In both cases the sense of disconnection among neighbors, so appropriate and useful in keeping people out of one another's hair on a daily basis, is subsumed to an equally appropriate sense of community. Despite the script's overt sentiments, in other words, Hitchcock shows the courtyard to be a superb urban organism, providing both individual freedom and community participation exactly when and where needed.

In the end, Hitchcock's city, revealed through *Rear Window*'s courtyard, is nothing less than a *world* of differences. Its buildings differ from one another—not in the extreme and charged manner of *Dead End*, but in a more subtly (and realistically) graduated mix of tenements, row houses, and apartments, a heterogeneous gathering of housing types on a single block that is the rule, rather than the exception, in the real city. Above all, it is the urban *spaces* of Hitchcock's New York that differ from one another. As the film makes abundantly clear, the courtyards in the middle of each city block are more private, less formal than the streets that surround them. There is, in other words, a clear *hierarchy* to the spaces of this city—which is just another way, of course, of saying difference.

To fully appreciate the power and subtlety of Hitchcock's vision, one need only look at a contemporary project from the world of city planning itself. The year of *Rear Window*'s release, 1954, also marked the construction of a landmark in postwar urban design: the Pruitt-Igoe Houses, an award-winning St. Louis housing project by architect Minoru Yamasaki, a design similar (if architecturally superior) to most postwar housing developments across the country. A series of freestanding slabs poised in open space, it offered no hierarchies at all outside the apartment door. There were no rear windows at Pruitt-Igoe. Or front windows, for that matter. Every window was the same. Everything existed in a field of open space, equal to everything else. As an expression of the professional understanding of cities at the time, it represented what can only be described as a profound impoverishment of urban vision, a broad failure of imagination that transcended this particular project's notorious social failure, which resulted in its state-sponsored destruction by dynamite, two decades later.

What a contrast to the rich vision of city life and form offered by Hitchcock that same year! From its title on down, *Rear Window*'s New York is a world of gradations, hierarchies, and an appreciation of the intertwined nature of human and architectural difference. In our lives there are times when we face the world boldly, publicly; other times when we turn to a smaller, more private group with whom we still balance a degree of sociability; still other times when we are truly alone. Hitchcock's New York mirrors and manifests that richness of possibility, finding in the city a range of states as complex as our own.

NINE

LOFTY PERCHES

PENTHOUSE, TERRACE, ROOFTOP, AND NIGHTCLUB

THE NEAREST THING TO HEAVEN

Deborah Kerr and Cary Grant stand at a ship's rail (in *An Affair to Remember*, 1957), watching the skyline pass by as their ocean liner glides up the Hudson. They have fallen in love on the crossing; now they reluctantly agree to separate for six months to sort out their respective lives and prove their mutual devotion. Only one thing remains: choosing a place to meet, a half-year hence. Gazing at the city, Grant finds the answer right in front of him.

"How about the Empire State Building?" he suggests.

"That's *perfect*," Kerr replies. "It's the nearest thing to heaven we have in New York."

"The hundred and second floor," he confirms. "And don't forget to take the elevator."

For over a century, the insistent verticality of New York has offered more than distinctive profiles on the horizon: it has created the possibility of a remarkable array of elevated *places*, habitable perches high above the ground, settings for everything from flights of romance to the struggles of everyday life. From the soaring upper reaches of skyscrapers to the homely roofs of tenements, the need to make use of every inch of the dense city has encouraged the creation of an entire second plane of urban life, floating above the street—a series of environments that by their very nature looked both up and down, aspiring to the promise of the sky above even as they reflected the world beneath them.

As *An Affair to Remember* reminds us, the most familiar of these were the publicly accessible platforms at the top of New York's tallest structures—especially the Empire State Building, whose two observation decks have long served

162. ***Week-end at the Waldorf*** **(1945).** As the cocktail hour approaches, movie star Irene Malvern (Ginger Rogers) steps onto the terrace of her thirty-ninth-floor suite in the Waldorf Towers, looking south to the Chrysler Building, the Chanin Building, and, in the distance, the skyline of lower Manhattan.

the movie city as places of union and reunion. In *The Thief* (1952), a man and woman (Ray Milland and Rita Gam) meet on the eighty-sixth-floor deck for a secret handoff of information, without exchanging a single word; in *The Moon Is Blue* (1953), a man and woman (William Holden and Maggie McNamara) meet on the same deck and exchange nothing *but* words, the start of an unlikely romance. For the three visiting sailors in *On the Town* (1949), the famous deck—visible from almost everywhere in the city—is a supremely logical place to regroup after a day spent pursuing individual adventures. Yet its functional value as a rendezvous point is quickly transcended when the trio—now doubled in size by the day's romantic efforts—triumphantly come together to celebrate the negotiation of a metropolis they have both symbolically and literally surmounted.

In recent decades, the rise of the preservation movement has given the word "landmark" a precise legal and technical meaning. But in the older, more primal sense, it simply meant a profile on the horizon, a structure of outsized height and repute that offered both practical and emotional orientation for city dwellers. It was the special gift of the movie city to create "landmarks" whose presence could be felt not only across space but also across time. Thus could the deck of the Empire State serve as the locus for a chain of romantic encounters stretching half a century and more.

The rendevous was first set in 1939, with Charles Boyer and Irene Dunne making their shipboard pact in *Love Affair*, written and directed by Leo McCarey. Eighteen years later, remaking his earlier work, McCarey changed the title and the cast but not the meeting place—and it is here, in the darkening gloom of a thunderstorm, that Cary Grant waits, hour after hour, for Deborah Kerr to arrive. She never does; hurrying to the appointment, she is struck by a cab at the tower's base and rushed to the hospital. Unaware, Grant waits until closing time, then descends from the deck in anguish. The emotional power of the moment is lost on no one, least of all Annie and Becky (Meg Ryan and Rosie O'Donnell, in 1993's *Sleepless in Seattle*), as they watch a video of the now-classic film in a Baltimore living room, even as Annie struggles to write a letter intended to win over a Seattle man named Sam Baldwin (Tom Hanks). Suffused with the film's romantic glow, they decide to borrow Grant's shipboard proposal right off the screen, and so it is that Annie finds herself in New York on Valentine's Day, rushing downtown as the theme from *An Affair to Remember* works its way into the score—mingling memories of the filmic city with its own romantic "reality" to reassert the power of a setting that moves so easily from fantasy to reality, and back again. And when at last Annie and Sam do meet up, on the empty deck atop the glittering city, the film simply affirms again the power of this legendary platform—where the plane of city lights joins the firmament of stars to frame a magical realm poised, like love itself, halfway between heaven and earth.

MOONLIGHT AND LOVE

In *The Sky's the Limit* (1943), Robert Benchley solicits some advice from Fred Astaire on how to win over a reluctant Joan Leslie. The setting, Fred suggests, is crucial:

> ASTAIRE: *So, what's your layout?*
>
> BENCHLEY: *Beekman Place. The usual penthouse . . . chromium trimmings, view of the dim-out. Not exactly sordid. I've got a terrace . . .*
>
> ASTAIRE: *Have you ever had her up there?*
>
> BENCHLEY: *Yes, many times.*
>
> ASTAIRE: *Did you dine out on the terrace?*
>
> BENCHLEY: *No, in the dining room, naturally.*
>
> ASTAIRE: *Well, there you are . . .*

It is hardly a surprise when later in the film, Fred puts this same penthouse terrace to the kind of service that he so well understands, and manages to win Joan for himself (32).

"The usual penthouse," Benchley said. It *was* usual in the film city: the quintessential setting, the apotheosis of movie New York. The filmic city abounded in penthouses, to the point where it might seem as though anyone who didn't live in a tenement lived in a glamorous rooftop apartment. At the expressive level (which so often governed the shape of the film city) there was a kind of sense to this: Why have these tall buildings in the first place if some great reward could not be achieved at their tops? In the movie city, the tower's romantic rationale invariably triumphed over its economic one; skyscrapers existed not to maximize the value of expensive city land but to afford the opportunity for new kinds of urban experiences.

At first, real penthouses were simple, single-story affairs placed atop the flat roofs of early apartment houses, taking their name and style from the utilitarian structures that contained the buildings' elevator machinery and other rooftop equipment. But they quickly sprawled and grew elegant as New Yorkers realized the value of their superior views and light, and soon architects were treating penthouses as an integral part of apartment-house design. The city's 1916 zoning law, which mandated that the upper portion of buildings be stepped back in order to provide more light and air for the streets below, turned out to have an important side benefit: the creation of habitable terraces and the encouragement of freer variation in apartment layouts on the upper floors. The tops of New York apartment houses no longer consisted of carved stone cornices and other inanimate architectural devices, but terraces, plantings, windows, doors, and awnings that were clearly signs of life—a whole *way* of life, in fact, that could become the object of fantasy for those below. By the mid-1920s, traditional society-page accounts of Fifth Avenue mansions were being quickly replaced with stories of chic penthouse parties held on expansive terraces high above Park Avenue.

No wonder, then, that the movies, always excited to be revealing secret worlds, were so drawn to the penthouse, seeing it—even more than the mansion—as the essential residence for the city's rich and powerful, one that drew its mystique from the verticality that was New York's special trademark. If the setbacks of the movie city's office buildings became the perches for fantastic superbeings, the upper reaches of apartment houses would become the realm of a group no less magical, though hardly supernatural: the glamorous denizens of movie New York.

As filmmakers soon discovered, the penthouse's attractions went far beyond its spectacular views. Perched, in effect, *on top* of the building's main structure, penthouses could plausibly offer architectural possibilities to sustain the most daring of art directors, such as the huge rooms, high ceilings, and great bank of windows of Greta Garbo's penthouse in *Susan Lenox: Her Fall and Rise* (1931) (163). Then again, the penthouse's floor plan could be looser than the tightly framed apartments below, interlocking with the terraces that surrounded it to create a gracious, almost rambling environment, a kind of private estate in the sky. This was perhaps the penthouse's biggest surprise—that at the peak of the city's tall, steel-framed buildings, the place where they seemed to

163. Set still from *Susan Lenox: Her Fall and Rise* (1931). This spectacular double-height Manhattan penthouse embodies what its designer, MGM's Cedric Gibbons, called the "big white set"—glamorous interiors created for stars such as Greta Garbo, who plays the title character (165).

break most free of the earthly traditions that had ruled house-building for millennia, they should suddenly spring intricate indoor-outdoor relationships reminiscent of traditional country houses, with terraces graced by greenery, outdoor furniture, sunlight, and starlight. At its most unnatural point, the apartment building reverted to naturalism.

It is a love of nature, in fact, that tempts a horticulturist named Brontë Parrish (Andie MacDowell) to do anything to keep the spectacular penthouse apartment of *Green Card* (1990). "What, did you kill someone for this place?" asks friend Bebe Neuwirth upon first seeing the rooftop, and we understand perfectly: a string of lush gardens located in and around an actual greenhouse, it is exactly the kind of layout that could only exist above the rest of the building, its high, wide rooms made bright by skylights and furnished with exotic trees and potted plants. Under Brontë's gifted care, the flowers are soon blooming, the fountain is filled with tropical fish, parakeets are singing in their cages. Water, birds, greenery—so compelling is this miniature paradise, up here where we least expect it, that we easily understand Brontë's frantic efforts to hold on to it, trying to meet the board's strict tenancy requirements through a phony marriage (with an illegal French alien, played by Gérard Depardieu) that has begun to grow disturbingly real (164).

> The sky is decked out. It is a Milky Way come down to earth; you are in it. Each window, each person, is a light in the sky. The stars are part of it also—the real stars—but sparkling quietly in the distance. Feeling comes into play, the action of the heart is released; crescendo, allegro, fortissimo. We are charged with feeling. . . .
>
> LE CORBUSIER

164. ***Green Card*** **(1990).** In Peter Weir's film, a horticulturist named Brontë (Andie MacDowell) enters into a fraudulent marriage with an illegal alien, Georges (Gérard Depardieu), in order to live in a spectacular penthouse. In this view, the couple entertain a friend (Bebe Neuwirth) in the rooftop garden Brontë has lovingly restored.

As much as to the penthouse itself, the movie city was drawn to the outdoor terraces that surrounded it. "What happens after dinner?" the boyish millionaire Douglas Fairbanks asks his butler, Edward Everett Horton, as he awaits a date on his Moorish-style terrace in *Reaching for the Moon* (1931). "Moonlight and love," Horton replies, "one of the advantages of a penthouse, if I may say so." Time and again, the penthouse terrace became a retreat for lovers, a place of intimacy in the crowded city. In *Week-end at the Waldorf* (1945), Army flier Van Johnson and hotel stenographer Lana Turner leave a noisy party to share a moment out on one of the Waldorf's terraces, high above the city. She is a struggling working girl, looking to snag a rich husband; he's just a small-town boy from California. The room inside represents all the societal forces keeping

165. ***Susan Lenox: Her Fall and Rise*** **(1931).** No less impressive than Susan Lenox's thirty-fifth-floor penthouse (163) is the terrace adjoining it, spacious enough to host a formal dinner for twelve. As a maid discreetly sets the table outside, Greta Garbo stands with Hale Hamilton by the penthouse's sleek, minimal window-wall, which seems to dissolve the distinction between indoors and out.

them apart; out here, with only the distant skyline and each other, their desire rises to the surface and overtakes them. James Stewart and Virginia Bruce in *Born to Dance* (1936), Dana Andrews and Susan Hayward in *My Foolish Heart* (1949), Harrison Ford and Annette Bening in *Regarding Henry* (1991)—all would have their turn on the terrace. Nor did the Coen brothers' *Hudsucker Proxy* (1994), a film that sometimes seemed assembled wholesale out of classic New York movie scenes, neglect to put *its* couple, Tim Robbins and Jennifer Jason Leigh, on the same terrace, overlooking the same skyline—and have them fall in love, almost despite themselves.

Underlying the romance of the setting was a powerful urban relationship: the terrace was not only a platform to *view* the skyline, it was among the elements that most *shaped* the skyline. In a very real sense, the distinctive ziggurat top of the traditional New York apartment house was *built* of terraces, of setback after setback carving away the mass of the building in a powerfully sculptural manner. Standing on one of these terraces, the film city's lovers were thus immersed in a subtle but powerful "here-there" relationship, gazing out on a landscape shaped by perches like the one they themselves shared, as if their own intimate sphere had been replicated to make an entire city. Roland

Barthes pondered a similar complementarity in his essay on the Eiffel Tower. "An object while one views it," he wrote, "it becomes in turn a view when one visits it."

> *[it] is an object that sees, or a look that is seen; it is a complete verb, at the same time active and passive . . . [it] transgresses this separation, this common divorce between* seeing *and* being seen; *it accomplishes an unrestrained circulation between the two functions; it is an object that is complete, that enjoys, one might say, the two sexes of "looking."*

Unlike the recent, harder-edged profiles of New York and other cities, the profusion of setback terraces softened the skyline, and textured it, but above all, gave it *life*, making it the public extension of ten thousand private—even intimate—realms. Newer skylines, comprised of smooth, hermetically sealed structures, may be impressive or startling or dramatic, but they don't seem nearly as inhabited, as *alive*, as the classic terraced skyline of New York.

Perhaps the greatest challenge of these high perches was to assure a comfortable relationship between the terrace itself and the great void that lay before it. The movie city offered a compendium of design approaches, from the lacy canopy and awning of Harriman's penthouse in *The Sky's the Limit* (32) to the cypress trees and white metalwork that ringed Lillian Brent's rooftop terrace in *Broadway Melody of 1936* (57). These details ensured that one could lounge, dance, or dine on the terrace without the unsettling feeling of being thrown out into the open space beyond the railing.* They also worked to make the terrace a distinctive place unto itself, a well-appointed roost in the sky. Scenes such as the terrace dinner party in *Susan Lenox*—a white-tie affair transpiring in the soft, silken, breezeless air of movie New York—promoted an urban vision that was as exquisite as it was transparently mythical (165).

166. ***How to Marry a Millionaire* (1953).** Pooling their resources to rent a Sutton Place penthouse, three New York women—Pola Debevoise (Marilyn Monroe), Loco Dempsey (Betty Grable), and Schatze Page (Lauren Bacall)—plot matrimonial strategy over lunch on their penthouse terrace, designed by Leland Fuller.

So intimately did the penthouse and terrace become linked to our notion of urban glamour that by the time of *How to Marry a Millionaire* (1953), it could serve as a veritable plot device. In pursuit of wealthy husbands, fashion models Lauren Bacall,

*From Wini Shaw's nightmarish plunge from a skyscraper nightclub in *Gold Diggers of 1935* to Norman Lloyd's dramatic fall from the Statue of Liberty in Hitchcock's *Saboteur* (1942), the movie city repeatedly exploited the potential danger of New York's tall structures, and the primal fear of falling associated with them.

Marilyn Monroe, and Betty Grable decide to pool their income to rent an expensive penthouse on Sutton Place. As they enjoy their first lunch alfresco on its terrace, Bacall defends the idea. "Where would you be more likely to meet a rich man," she asks, "in a walk-up on Amsterdam Avenue or in a joint like this?" (166)

But the tradition of these wide, setback terraces was about to come to an abrupt end; the city's new 1961 zoning law tossed out the older, stepped design for a new and very different model. Based on the same modernist prototype as the city's boxy new office buildings, apartment houses would now be fashioned as monolithic slabs, rising from sidewalk to roof in a straight line, with little or no variation from top to bottom. Just one element marked them as residential rather than commercial towers: the narrow balconies that were pasted onto the facade at every floor, running up the length of the building. Small and mean, open not to the sky but to the concrete underside of the identical balcony of the floor above, these appendages offered none of the amenities of traditional terraces; indeed, their endless repetition worked to make each apartment (and by extension its occupants) feel like an interchangeable cog in some vast, anonymous machine. If the traditional setback terraces brought profuse signs of human life to the top of each apartment house—while at the same time giving it a distinctively idiosyncratic and highly sculptural shape—the long vertical rows of pasted-on balconies worked only to emphasize (on the very face of the building, for all to see) an interminable, *in*human repetition of units within; an artless, mechanistic stacking of floors; a cookie-cutter mentality that made every new apartment house look just like every other one.

167. ***The Prisoner of Second Avenue*** **(1975).** Mel Edison (Jack Lemmon) rails against the frustrations of city life from the grim brick balcony of his modern apartment house (actually located at 247 East 87th Street, and designed by the architects Paul and Jarmul).

The film city caught it all. In *The Prisoner of Second Avenue* (1975), Anne Bancroft and Jack Lemmon complain of being "overcharged for a growth on the side of a building they call a terrace," a line that suggests one reason for the prevalence of these balconies: the fact that landlords were legally allowed to charge a half-room's rent for them. When Lemmon steps onto his tiny brick-lined opening, it is not to fall in love or view the stars but to smell the garbage rising from the street, to scream angry obscenities into the air, or to rail loudly at his upstairs neighbors—who, screaming back, proceed to douse him with a bucket of water. The image of Lemmon trapped in this narrow brick extrusion, set amidst a banal, oppressive landscape of identical balconies lining not only his building but all the others nearby, proved an irresistible one for filmmakers trying to present the bleakest possible vision of middle-class life in New York (167).

Then, just when it seemed the movie city's terrace would never regain its former glory, there came the moment in *Annie Hall* (1977) when Diane Keaton invites Woody Allen to step onto the terrace outside her East Side apartment. Standing outside, drinks in hand, with a romantic landscape of flowers and chimney pots and the stepped profiles of the city's skyline behind them, the scene reasserted the terrace's value as the ideal platform from which a couple might share a city that was itself comprised of intimate perches (168). As they speak, their new acquaintance gradually blooming into something deeper, the terrace again came to seem the best possible setting, in the high-rise city, for "moonlight and love."

168. ***Annie Hall*** (1977). Annie Hall (Diane Keaton) and Alvy Singer (Woody Allen) talk and flirt over a glass of wine on the terrace of her apartment on East 70th Street.

ROOFTOPS

In *Hands Across the Table* (1935), Carole Lombard plays Regi Allen, a struggling hotel manicurist who, despite living and working in the middle of Manhattan, still manages to spend much of her week under open skies. By day she is often found on the terrace of Suite 1502 at the Savoy-Carleton Hotel, where she manicures—and charms—a wealthy, wheelchair-bound bachelor played by Ralph Bellamy. With all of New York below, she here anticipates the fulfillment of a major career goal: to marry for money, not love. But there is another man in Regi's life, and another outdoor setting. When her fairy-tale day at the hotel is over, she can again be found under the stars—if now only four, rather than fifteen, stories high. Outside the windows of her modest 120th Street apartment is her very own "terrace": the tar-covered roof of an adjoining tenement. This is the space she shares with the charming but penniless Fred MacMurray—all love, and no money (169).

Rooftops have long been the ordinary New Yorker's answer to the penthouse terrace. Like the loft or the row house turned apartment, the inhabited rooftop represents a place discovered rather than designed, an urban improvisation through which countless New Yorkers have taken advantage of the fact that, since the early 1830s (when the smooth, imposing cornices of Greek Revival row houses began replacing the pitched gables of Federal-style houses), most of New York's residential buildings have had flat roofs. The result has been an aerial landscape less picturesque perhaps than the chimney-pots of London or the slate roofs of Paris, but one whose essentially horizontal surfaces can accommodate all kinds of human pursuits and become, in effect, a series of open-air rooms.

The movie city has catalogued a variety of such pursuits, from sunbathing on "tar beach" above Nola Darling's Fulton Street loft in *She's Gotta Have It*

(1986), to outdoor dining such as that enjoyed by Buddy and Vilma Ebsen in *Broadway Melody of 1936* (1935). Breaking into a dance routine after a picnic-style lunch, the Ebsens transform the roof yet again, this time perhaps into its most common filmic incarnation—as an outdoor stage.

Removed from the street, the rooftop provided an invaluable place of refuge in the crowded city. For the anxious store employees in *The Devil and Miss Jones* (1941), a tenement rooftop is the only safe place to hold a union meeting, away from the eyes of the despotic store owner. For the illegal immigrant played by Francis Lederer in *Romance in Manhattan* (1934), the rooftop above Ginger Rogers's tenement offers his first sense of comfort in a disorienting new world; only here, in a place detached from the city's bustle and confusion—yet offering, through its skyline view, a vivid sense of its possibilities—does he realize he has made the right choice. "This is it," he says. "This is what?" she asks. "This is how it was in my dreams" (44).

As an improvised rather than consciously designed space, the humble tenement roof actually offered a narrative advantage over the stylish penthouse

169. ***Hands Across the Table* (1935).** With music from a radio carried outside and bedding provided by some sofa cushions, a modest rooftop becomes the surprisingly romantic setting for a moment under the stars, shared by Regi Allen and Theodore Drew III (Carole Lombard and Fred MacMurray).

terrace. Often as not, tenement roofs carried all sorts of traces of ordinary life, items left by tenants who would gather there by day to wash clothes or do other chores while caring for their children: chairs and tables, toys and baby carriages, washboards and basins, potted plants and flowers, all adding an unexpected domestic touch to an otherwise utilitarian landscape. The ubiquitous clothesline, in particular, with its shirts and underwear hanging out to dry, brought the most personal—even intimate—articles of family life out into the open, transforming the roof into an extension of the apartments below, infusing it with a private scale and character that contrasted dramatically with the vast public spectacle of the skyline beyond (170).

Revealingly, the movies almost never portrayed the daily household activities that created this landscape. Instead, the domesticated rooftop served as a suggestively *symbolic* space, whose elements were the "props" of family life, loaded with meaning. In Preston Sturges's *Christmas in July* (1940), a young couple named Jimmy and Betty (Dick Powell and Ellen Drew), eager to find some privacy in their busy tenement, inevitably turn to the roof. In this surprisingly intimate spot, with a lovely tune playing from the portable radio, they find a landscape that underscores their predicament, the classic dilemma of working-class lovers. Betty wants to get married right away; Jimmy resists, arguing that they are too poor. Debating their future, they amble around a roofscape littered with domestic artifacts: laundry lines, a table set with flowers, potted plants, even a coop filled with rabbits, hinting of fertility. Betty would plainly be happy with the modest life these items imply, a home and children—as long as it included the man she loves. But the rooftop setting also includes something else: the skyline beyond, the siren call for Jimmy's restless ambition—especially the tower of "Maxford House Coffee," whose slogan contest he has entered and whose $25,000 prize he expects (against all odds) to win. For Jimmy, the distant skyline represents everything he wants but cannot have; the rooftop landscape, with its homely reminders of the tattered apartments below, represents everything he has but does not want. The tune on the radio is announced: "Penthouse in Manhattan."

This dual nature of the roof—a place apart from any household, yet an evident extension of the domesticity below—actually triggers the climax of *Hands Across the Table.* Living together for a few weeks in her apartment, Regi (Lombard) and Drew (MacMurray) have quietly grown attracted to each other, even as both remain firmly committed to the notion of marrying for money. On his last night, Drew rises from his customary place on the living room sofa and knocks on Regi's bedroom door. She refuses to open it, though she plainly wants to; he refuses to open it, though *he* plainly wants to. Both continue to respect the proprieties that his presence in the apartment has bent, but not broken.

Alone in the bedroom, she can't sleep; neither can he, alone in the living room. She decides to step out onto the rear part of the roof, just as he steps out onto the front part. A low brick parapet separates front from back. While the threshold between living room and bedroom—interior spaces fraught with meaning and morality—was uncrossable, the division between parts of the neutral roof carries no such freight. Drew crosses the parapet, and their love pours out.

A more recent film, directed by Robert Wise and titled *Rooftops* (1989), demonstrated the surprisingly durable capacity of the tenement roof to create a domestic environment, even when the tenement itself has virtually disintegrated. Set in the worst blocks of the Lower East Side, where abandonment and arson have gutted countless tenement buildings, *Rooftops* proposes a community of young runaways living atop the empty, burned-out shells. On adjoining roofs, T (Jason Gedrick), Amber (Tisha Campbell), and young Squeak (Alexis Cruz) have fashioned strikingly elaborate environments, their "cribs," complete with landscaping, lawn furniture, and artwork. When a friend bluntly points out that her crib is really just a rooftop pigeon coop, Amber counters, "Why not? Great view, low rent, plenty of light. Just what everybody in this city wants. Besides," she says, getting closer to the point, "it's mine, and up here

nobody bugs me." Surviving by stripping fixtures from the abandoned buildings below, these squatters prove fiercely protective of their rooftops, banding together at the climax to thwart the incursions of a local drug dealer.

Though shot on location, an unmistakable quality of fantasy pervades the film's vision of a community of rooftop denizens. T's crib, set within an old wooden water tower like an urban treehouse, looks plausible until one recalls that tenements don't *have* water towers, being only six stories tall; the entire structure was conceived by the film's production designer. Still, *Rooftops*'s adolescent community, ensconced in its aptly named cribs, suggests the roof as an ideal place to play at real life, to experiment with adulthood in a neutral zone, removed from the pressures of the outside world.

Located above and beyond the streets, with the sky and stars for a ceiling, the rooftop, not surprisingly, brought a mysterious and even spiritual aura to the middle of the city. In John Sayles's *The Brother from Another Planet* (1984), the extraterrestrial "brother" (Joe Morton) finds himself sitting with a small child on a Harlem rooftop. "Where are you from?" the boy asks the alien, who hap-

170. Set still from *Big City* (1937). Frank Borzage's *Big City*, produced the same year as *Broadway Melody of 1938*, reused that film's rooftop set, now filled everywhere with signs of daytime life: scrub board, washtub, chairs, baby carriages, plants, laundry, and a hopscotch game.

pens to be a mute. He answers simply by pointing his thumb upward, to the silent dome of stars above their heads. In Jim Jarmusch's 1999 film *Ghost Dog: The Way of the Samurai*, the enigmatic main character—a self-styled modern-day samurai "warrior" played by Forest Whitaker—finds a natural home in this detached, almost unearthly realm. To find him (at the start of the film), we must take to the skies ourselves, sailing in like a bird over Brooklyn's raw industrial landscape to alight on the roof of an old building near the Gowanus Canal. Here, in a dilapidated wooden shack that is half pigeon coop, half apartment, we meet Ghost Dog—a character who, despite his name, seems more closely linked to the flocks of birds that circle endlessly above, only rarely touching down. Like them, Ghost Dog does not really belong on the ground; descending to the streets on occasion to efficiently (if grimly) carry out his duties as a hit man for the Mafia, he moves with a ghostly presence—a self-absorbed, almost spectral figure who walks with silent footfalls and speaks to no one. His true abode is on the roof, where he prays at a Shinto shrine, practices his swordsmanship, and absorbs the seventeenth-century teachings of Hagakure's *Book of the Samurai*. At one point, letting his pigeons out of the coop to make a few circuits, the elusive warrior looks up to the sky as if wishing he could join them—or perhaps, in some way, he *already* has.

Curiously enough, he is not alone. All around him the city's roofs are host to unusual characters and otherworldly pursuits. At one point, Ghost Dog is brought to the top of another building by one of his few acquaintances, a Hai-

171. ***A Tree Grows in Brooklyn* (1945).** Francie Nolan (Peggy Ann Garner), seen in this view with her brother Neeley (Ted Donaldson) on the roof of her Williamsburg tenement. Here she gains perspective on her life, literally and figuratively, by seeing the confined world of her childhood set against the rooftops of Brooklyn and the skyline of Manhattan—a view that holds her past and her future in a single glance.

tian man (Isaach De Bankolé) who speaks not a word of English, to see something "amazing." Looking over the edge, they spy a bizarre sight: a man constructing a full-size wooden fishing trawler atop an adjacent roof. "How the hell is he going to get it down?" Ghost Dog is moved to wonder. "When you're finished," the Haitian man shouts in French to the determined shipwright, "will you sail away into the clouds?"

Perhaps more than anyone else, it was Francie Nolan, climbing to the top of her Williamsburg tenement in *A Tree Grows in Brooklyn* (1945), who cemented the roof's special role as the crucial link between the worldly city below and the celestial realm above (171). Leaving the crowded streets and tenement apartment below, Francie discovers a place where everything opens up—the rooftops of Brooklyn, the distant bridges, the Manhattan skyline, the sky itself—and it is here, in two poignant sequences, that she comes to speak with God: first in confusion and grief after the death of her father; months later, older and wiser, to reflect on her own past and potential future. Just a few floors above the street, and right in the heart of the city, the rooftop nonetheless remains, for many New Yorkers, the "nearest thing we have to heaven."

TOP OF THE TOWN

No other lofty perch matches the allure and sheer drama of the skyscraper nightclub. To be carried upward in an elevator at a thousand feet a minute, to step into a great room at the pinnacle of a tower with nothing but the glittering skyline floating outside the high windows and the starry sky above, is to enjoy a special urban grace in which the complex technology and daring engineering of the skyscraper are put in service of the most romantic of missions: to create a platform in the sky where men and women might converse and play, dance and fall in love.

This vertiginous transition, from the rational and solid to the emotional and ethereal, actually underpins the design of the nightclub featured in *Broadway Melody of 1936.* Here is a place almost transcending physical structure, a place drawn out of light itself (7, 172). Luminescent columns and draped fabric diffuse the glow of the room, while railings of glass block, choreographed in a spirited dance of straight and wavy lines, reflect that glow still further. Holding it all in place is the distant skyline itself, a semicircle of darkened masses and twinkling lights that seems to envelop the nightclub in a glowing embrace.

The effect is festive, lighthearted, sophisticated. With its delicate columns—light poles, really—carrying curtain supports that are more delicate still, we can almost sense the skyscraper beneath being reduced to its frame, a network of members finer than those needed to support the mass of building below. It is the skyscraper in the act of achieving one of its oldest aspirations: shedding its skin, reducing itself to pure structure, and reaching into the sky. And here, using the only thing lighter than structure—light itself—it achieves an even more ethereal countenance, a dream of its own midnight possibilities.

Obviously, the design of such places owed more to fancy than reality. In the real city, perhaps only the Rainbow Room, atop the RCA (now GE) Building in Rockefeller Center, could truly compete with the filmic city's spectacular rooftop nightclubs. A generation before, more than two dozen summer "roof gardens" had dotted Manhattan—including one atop Madison Square Garden, the site of the notorious 1906 murder of the architect Stanford White by the millionaire Harry K. Thaw (an event re-created in *The Girl in the Red Velvet Swing*, 1955, and again in *Ragtime*, 1981). But these resorts had been located mostly on the tops of lower buildings, not true skyscrapers, and their ornate, open-air Edwardian decor was a far cry from the sleek Art Deco look of the movie city's nightclubs. By the 1930s, in any case, they had all but vanished, done in by growing traffic noise from the streets below and the advent of air-conditioned theaters with year-round schedules.

However unrealistic, the movie city's habit of putting its nightclubs atop roofs could be accepted as an act of manifest destiny; this was where nightclubs *ought* to have been in the skyscraper city, even if by chance they were not. And so we could visit the Pinnacle Club (in *Penthouse*, 1933), the Moonbeam Room (in *Top of the Town*, 1937), or the elegant club designed by Kem Weber for *The Big Broadcast* (1932), eventually coming to imagine that every one of New York's great towers had some kind of special club at its top, a sort of elevated city of glamour and light. If fanciful, this vision nonetheless affirmed an essential quality of the prewar New York skyscraper against, say, that of Chicago's proto-modernist version: unlike the overall unity of the single building that was the prime goal of Chicago's towers, New York's classic skyscrapers emphasized the *distinction* between the bottom and the top, between the world of the street and the special realm that existed in the clouds. The kinship of each tower's top, in other words, was not with its own base, but with its fellow tops across the city.

This special realm would provide not just the setting but the underlying theme of what is perhaps the greatest New York film musical of all: *Swing Time* (1936), a film that *lives* in the clouds, leaping from one skyscraper nightclub to another and discovering new planes of romantic possibility as it climbs—scene by scene, dance floor by dance floor—toward its haunting, unforgettable climax.

It begins, to be sure, down on the street. John "Lucky" Garnett (Fred Astaire), professional dancer and amateur gambler, has come to New York penniless, but eager to make a swift $25,000 fortune at the gaming tables in order to win over his hometown sweetheart, Margaret (Betty Furness). On the sidewalk, however, he finds not his thousands but only a "penny," Penny Carrol (Ginger Rogers), whom he quickly (if unintentionally) manages to anger. Hoping to apologize, he follows Penny to her place of employment, the Gordon Dancing Academy, which just happens to be located on the upper floor of an office building—a shiny circular dance floor, ringed by a low railing and framed by big windows through which we see a view of the skyline. Down on the street they could only bicker, but up here, in what proves to be a sort of midlevel platform, a staging area for the further ascent, they are free to discover their common language of music and dance in "Pick Yourself Up," a number so buoyant and spirited that it actually seems to propel the film upward. ("Its compressed energy," writes Arlene Croce, seems "to ignite the air it moves on.") It concludes with the couple leaping into a stroll that somehow whisks them over the low railing, off the dance floor, and toward an elevator that will continue to carry them skyward—at least metaphorically, because the academy's owner, Eric Blore, dazzled by the pair's dancing, has arranged for a tryout at a rooftop nightclub across town.

Much of the rest of the film is played out in a series of nightclubs, each more spectacular than the one before. There is the Club Raymond, sitting atop the thirty-sixth floor of a midtown tower, achieved by a glassy, cylindrical elevator and combining a central dance floor and dining room with a series of gambling tables and a glazed observation area overlooking the city below. Here Lucky and Penny, having already survived another tiff, reunite on the dance

172. **Rooftop nightclub from *Broadway Melody of 1936* (1935).** This shot of Merrill Pye and Edwin Willis's rooftop nightclub set reveals that its columns—which seem to support a roof (7)—were in reality open-topped poles, reaching into the sky like the masts of a ship. The background skyline, meanwhile, was a miniature whose sixty-one structures included a twenty-four-foot-tall Chrysler Building.

173. Silver Sandal rooftop nightclub from *Swing Time* (1936). Designed by John Harkrider (62, 63), the most famous of the movie city's rooftop clubs drew its name from the Silver Slipper on West 48th Street, but its primary inspiration was clearly the Rainbow Room, the spectacular nightspot opened in 1932 atop the RCA Building in Rockefeller Center.

floor to perform the exquisite "Waltz in Swing Time," to the music of bandleader Ricardo Romero (George Metaxa), Lucky's rival for Penny; as always, Fred and Ginger's time on the dance floor reinvigorates and deepens their feelings for each other.

Now the action moves upward again, to the Silver Sandal (which appeared briefly in an earlier scene but which has been, according to the script, "redecorated"). The club's name was plainly derived from the Silver Slipper, located on Manhattan's West 48th Street until 1932, but the setting in the film, designed by John Harkrider, has been lifted into the sky to create what is not only the most glamorous of all the movie city's nightclubs, but one whose design and layout artfully mirrors the emotional narrative of the film itself.

We see it first on its gala opening night (173). The orchestra plays on a platform that seems to float above the skyscrapers of Manhattan. Two broad semicircles of dining tables rise in tiers on either side, forming an elegant sea of silvery tablecloths and glowing Saturn-shaped lamps; a curved pair of black staircases, meanwhile, follows the arc of the tiers as they ascend from the dance floor at the center. A later scene (Astaire's "Bojangles of Harlem" number) reveals a proscenium stage on the far side of the dance floor; the tiers thus serve also as a kind of raked auditorium (62).

But there is an additional agenda to the design, a narrative intent to be fully played out only in the film's climax, but hinted at when Astaire and Rogers's comic sidekicks, Victor Moore and Helen Broderick, begin descending from the central platform above, deep in conversation and oblivious to the fact that each has taken a different wing of the curved staircase. Their discovery comes only halfway down, at the point where the stair's wings are farthest apart; to our amusement, both characters abruptly find themselves standing alone, talking out loud to no one.

It proves an eventful night at the Silver Sandal: Lucky, who had won control of Romero's orchestra through one bet, loses it through another; then his fiancée, Margaret, shows up, sending Penny into Romero's waiting arms. By the evening's end, Penny and Lucky have split up; she is engaged to Romero, he is going back to his hometown girl. "It's all decided now," she insists.

Romero leaves Penny and Lucky alone in the club. A long shot establishes the mood: the deserted room, glittering and elegant as ever but now become the oddly intimate precinct of one couple. If the Club Raymond looked out on the city from a high point, the Silver Sandal seems to exist in an even higher plane—somehow *above* the city, shared only with the stars themselves, a thousand dots of light visible through the transparent walls. It is a zone between the sky above and the city below, between heaven and earth. And it is all theirs.

Penny, looking more desirable than ever, prepares to leave, walking up one wing of the stairs. Lucky sings to her plaintively: if he cannot have her, he is "Never Gonna Dance." She pauses; he grows more passionate, insistent. She turns and comes back down. Though they can never dance again, perhaps they can walk across the dance floor, musing on their fate. Imperceptibly, their walk becomes a dance, an exquisite, elegiac step that is the exact opposite of the buoyant opening number at the dancing academy, when all was new and fresh (174). They have a history now; they have been through everything together; and indeed, the dance proceeds to recapitulate that history: we hear and see snatches of the earlier numbers, from "Pick Yourself Up" to "Waltz in Swing Time" to "Never Gonna Dance" itself—the entire succession

174. *Swing Time* (1936). After a long night at the Silver Sandal, Penny Carroll (Ginger Rogers) and Lucky Garnett (Fred Astaire) share one last dance together, alone in the great room above the city.

that has lifted them both physically and metaphorically to this highest of points. In the diamond-shaped dance floor of the Silver Sandal we can somehow sense the film's other dance floors, the series of ever-higher platforms in the sky that have led us upward—and now, as the number reaches its climax, the ascent takes on its last and most poignant leap. From the dance floor, Penny and Lucky begin to rise, each dancing up a wing of the great staircase, inevitably (as we saw with Moore and Broderick) separating from each other as they climb, only to curve back together as they continue to ascend, at last joining, joyously, at the upper platform—reunited again, yet changed by the separation that has brought them to a higher, more intense plane of emotion. And we realize that the club's design is in fact a metaphor of the entire film's spatial and emotional narrative—a complex three-dimensional path by which the two lovers must separate and then rejoin, rising as they do to an ever higher level of ecstasy. The camera, itself set aloft through a breathtaking crane shot that sweeps across the entire set, closes in on the lovers at the summit, on the upper platform, where their dancing—reaching its own climax in what Croce calls "a spine-chilling series of turns" by Rogers—suddenly ends with her flying out of the scene, and out of Lucky's life. We close with an image of Astaire, arms outstretched, the very picture of romantic longing.

175. Production sketch of the Radio Center lobby, from *Top of the Town* (1937). One of a series of production drawings by John Harkrider, this view shows a bank of glassy cylindrical elevators, whisking patrons to the Moonbeam Room on the building's 114th floor.

The film's denouement takes place the next day, back at the Club Raymond: Margaret has found another man, freeing Lucky to marry Penny; Romero graciously bows out, freeing Penny to marry Lucky. The final shot finds the couple standing by the observation window, high above a snow-covered city, Central Park stretched out like a great white carpet beneath them. As they embrace, even the falling snowflakes are set aglitter by a sudden, unexpected burst of sunlight. Here they will marry and live, floating in their romantic realm above the city, perhaps never to touch the ground again.

No film ever surpassed *Swing Time* in its brilliant linkage of soaring romance and physical ascent. But the following year, the designer of the Silver Sandal made one last attempt to extend his extraordinary vision to its logical conclusion, in a design that carried the celluloid city to an extreme at once breathtaking and slightly ridiculous.

Working for Universal, which hired him away from RKO in 1936, John Harkrider designed a new rooftop nightclub as the centerpiece for the musical *Top of the Town* (1937). As the film's title implies, the club was again to be placed at the highest point of the city, but Harkrider's Moonbeam Room would dwarf even the Silver Sandal in size, scale, and sheer daring.

A series of preproduction sketches capture Harkrider's overall conception:

the "Radio Center" building, tallest in Manhattan; the bank of glassy cylindrical elevators (like that of the Club Raymond, only multiplied a dozen times) ready to shoot patrons upward (175); the observation deck on the 114th floor, offering a vantage so high it reduces the city to geography.

But all this is mere preparation for the club itself, as envisioned in the most spectacular sketch of the series (176). The Moonbeam Room sits atop not one skyscraper but four, bridging the airspace among them with decks of seating and—if the drawing can be believed—a *transparent glass dance floor,* allowing patrons to look straight down a thousand feet or more to the city streets below. All around, meanwhile, the club shoots up in a series of helical, tiered, and crescent-shaped terraces that provide seating areas, an orchestra pit, an observation deck, and, over to one side, a great searchlight rising to the heavens. The design made explicit Harkrider's fantastic goal, first hinted at in the design of the Silver Sandal, with its view down to skyscrapers beneath: to make a place that allowed its swirling, dancing patrons to float—not just seemingly but actually—*above* the city.

176. **Production drawing for the Moonbeam Room, from *Top of the Town* (1937).** The climax of John Harkrider's extraordinary vision of movie New York, the Moonbeam Room—poised over a thousand feet above the city, on four separate towers—offered a glass floor that allowed patrons to literally dance *above* the city.

Harkrider's nightclub appeared in the finished film largely as designed, but stripped of its extraordinary setting. The glass floor revealing the city below was replaced with the shiny but opaque Bakelite surface common to most nightclub sets; the surrounding skyline, shooting up in all directions in Harkrider's drawing, was traded for an abstract field of stars not dissimilar to the Silver Sandal's. It was an impressive set, nonetheless—said to be the largest ever built in Hollywood, covering over an acre and costing more than $100,000. With room for a thousand patrons, it made the Silver Sandal, which seated 360, seem almost *intime.* But it had lost the magic of the original, hallucinatory vision that the Silver Sandal had implied and the Moonbeam sketch confirmed: dancers in evening dress swirling above the glow of a city that lay a thousand feet beneath them—a dream of dancing on air, fulfilled quite literally in a place that linked the aspiration of skyscrapers to the limitless possibilities of the sky itself.

TEN

EDGE OF THE CITY

WATERFRONT,
TRAIN STATION,
AND GRAND HOTEL

ON THE WATERFRONT

> For three hundred years the weeping and the panic and the laughter and the hope and the chancing of sea journeys through the Narrows from the great landlocked harbor of the Upper Bay. . . . The harbor of New York makes the city of New York and the city of New York is the capital of America, no matter what our civics teachers say. Eight billion dollars in world trade makes this the heart-in-commerce of the Western world. Oh, you simple Hendrik Hudson in your simple little ship . . . looking for India along the palisades of Jersey, look at your harbor now!
>
> BUDD SCHULBERG, *ON THE WATERFRONT* (NOVEL)

Before it was anything else, New York was a port, and for centuries the movement of people and goods has been so central to its identity, so tightly knit into its fabric, that its points of connection with the larger world—not just the waterfront itself but inland settings like railway stations and grand hotels—have offered a potent metaphor for the city as a whole. Defined by their essential urban roles—as crossroads, magnets for strangers; places of exchange, mystery, adventure—these settings have lured storytellers of all kinds, filmmakers not least, with their endless narrative possibilities and their richly suggestive atmosphere.

177. (previous page) *On the Waterfront* (1954). Working on location, director Elia Kazan adapted numerous elements of Hoboken's existing waterfront landscape, from giant ocean liners docked at the Holland-America piers (including the flagship *Nieuw Amsterdam*, seen in this view) to a small wooden shack, floating on the water, which became the "office" of the corrupt union boss Johnny Friendly (Lee J. Cobb).

None of these was more alluring than the waterfront itself, the primal source of the city's power and prosperity. Since the days of the nineteenth-century packet ships, when South Street's piers bustled with the strange names and ensigns of foreign vessels, the hubbub of accents and dialects, and the bounty of exotic goods arriving from the most distant places on Earth—Canton, Singapore, Cape Town, Macao—New York's waterfront has been the country's major place of contact with the world beyond its shores, one of just a handful of spots, in the era before commercial aviation, where America came in regular contact with "the other." The original 1933 *King Kong* derives not a little of its eerie, ominous mood from its opening scene on a mist-shrouded Hudson pier, where the S.S. *Venture* readies to sail on what one character calls a "crazy voyage." There is unusual cargo, we hear, an abnormally large crew, a destination unknown even to the skipper, and a hurried departure, one step ahead of the authorities. Only producer Carl Denham (Robert Armstrong) knows the real destination: a small island, "way west of Sumatra," where, he says, "something" is to be found, "something monstrous, all-powerful, still living, and holding the island in a grip of deadly fear." From New York Harbor, America's doorway to the world beyond, Denham will set off to search for this mysterious "something"—and it is to here that he will return, once he finds what he seeks.

As a maritime center, of course, New York for much of its history was in a class by itself—bigger than any other port on the East Coast, and busier than all of them *combined.* For a script he was researching in the early 1950s, the screenwriter Budd Schulberg sought to convey the sheer scale of the Port of New York (which comprised both the New York and New Jersey sides of the bay). It was nothing less, he said, than "a self-contained city-state—750 miles of shoreline, with 1,800 piers, handling ten thousand oceangoing ships a year, carrying over a million passengers a year and over thirty-five million tons of foreign cargo." In the landmark portrait of the harbor that he and the director Elia Kazan created over the next few years, that extraordinary scale—along with some of the striking contradictions that attended it—would be evident from the start. *On the Waterfront* (1954) opens with a shot of the Hoboken piers, across the Hudson River from Manhattan. At center sits one of the world's largest liners, the *Nieuw Amsterdam,* its sleek black hull and gleaming white superstructure stretching the better part of a thousand feet—a majestic, almost otherworldly sight. Yet around the great ship lies a landscape very much of *this* world: a drab, utilitarian setting of piers and cranes, barges and tugs, cargo and debris, a world of hard labor—and endemic corruption (177).

"We got the fattest piers of the fattest harbor in the world!" crows Johnny Friendly (Lee J. Cobb), the crooked boss of a longshoremen's local. "Everything moves in or out, we take our cut." It is easy to see how. Though capable of landing the most modern ships in the world, the piers in *On the Waterfront* still rely on a technique of handling cargo, called "break-bulk," that had remained essentially unchanged since the days of sail. In the deep holds of each vessel stevedores lift goods by hand—one crate at a time—onto slings, which are then craned up and over to the pier. We see what a temptation the labor-intensive technique offers to pilfer valuable cargo—Irish whisky, say—and how terrifying it makes the threat of a slowdown, which, in the case of perishables such as bananas, could quickly ruin millions of dollars' worth of goods.

Though no one could have known it at the time, *On the Waterfront* offered a glimpse of the New York Harbor in its last moments of glory. At the very moment the film was conducting its unsparing examination of the waterfront, a revolution was brewing, one that would transform the port beyond recognition, and cause the great piers lining the Hudson and East River—after more than three centuries of steady growth—to vanish in a twinkling. It was a revolution brought on, in part, by the corrupt practices the film had documented, and it was hatched, remarkably enough, in the very piers where the film was shot. Even as Cobb's Johnny Friendly boasted of his inalienable "cut," a thirty-nine-year-old Southern trucking company executive named Malcolm McLean was expanding his business to the Hoboken docks, where, frustrated by break-bulk's inherent inefficiencies and opportunities for theft, he conceived a radical new way of handling cargo. Called "containerization," it relied on enormous sealed containers that could be lifted by crane from a ship's deck to waiting trucks or railcars (or vice versa) *without ever being opened,* reducing not only the possibilities for theft but the need for longshoremen altogether. Less than two years after the film's premiere, McLean began putting his system into practice, and within a few decades, it had transformed shipping not only in New York but all around the world, eliminating the jobs of thousands of dockworkers. For traditional waterfronts, such as those lining the Hudson River, there was another kind of price. The very size of the containers, and of the massive cranes and other equipment used to move and store them, required hundreds

178. Filming *A Thousand Clowns* (1965). "Opening up" Herb Gardner's Broadway show for the screen, director Fred Coe shot extensively along the water, where Murray Burns (Jason Robards) enjoys the city's primal pleasures and flees its responsibilities. In this view, Murray and his nephew Nick (Barry Gordon) are filmed on an East River pier, near Wall Street.

of acres of "upland" area, open space that was simply unavailable in the dense urban settings of Manhattan, Brooklyn, and Hoboken. One by one, the older piers shut down, or moved operations to sprawling, low-density port areas in Newark and Elizabeth, New Jersey. The harbor itself remained one of the busiest in the world, but by the 1980s the distinctive environment that had defined the edge of the city for centuries—the special combination of grandeur and grittiness so powerfully evoked in that memorable opening shot of *On the Waterfront*—had all but disappeared.

Along with its foreign vessels, the river's edge was long the home to a different kind of waterfront denizen, unusual characters who lived in a world remote from the rest of the city. In the 1989 film version of Hubert Selby Jr.'s *Last Exit to Brooklyn*, the dark, insular Brooklyn waterfront of the 1950s is plainly a world apart, one where the era's outcasts—prostitutes, homosexuals, ex-convicts—are left to fight it out in a sordid, violent place, which, for the rest of the city, is both out of sight and out of mind. In *Times Square* (1980), two teenage runaways, Pamela and Nicky (Trini Alvarado and Robin Johnson), find refuge in a derelict Hudson River pier in the West Twenties, setting up their own "household" among the old steamer trunks. For the middle-class Pamela, the forlorn and forgotten pier at the edge of the city provides needed sanctuary from her over-protective New York family; for Nicky, a tough, wayward spirit, the waterfront environment—with its wide-open vistas, ship horns, and swooping gulls—evokes a larger sense of escape from society itself. In *A Thousand Clowns* (1965), another kind of outsider, Murray Burns, doesn't actually *live* on the water, but seems to spend most of his time there anyway, having left one job in television and appearing to be in no hurry to get another. Instinctively, he gravitates to the city's edge: fishing off the East River Drive, wandering the Wall Street piers, and riding the Statue of Liberty ferry, binoculars in hand, barely listening as his nephew reads employment ads from the classifieds (178). For Murray, the water signifies freedom, a haven from the conformity of white-collar Manhattan, whose workers prefer—for some unimaginable reason—to huddle inland, turning their backs on this elemental wonder. But there is a price to Murray's solitary way of life—and later, when that price becomes too high, a poignant shot finds him alone on a pier, overlooking the glistening waters, as if for the last time.

There was larger truth at work here. For much of its history, the city *did* turn its back on the water, giving its shoreline over to noisome industries (tanneries, gasworks, slaughterhouses) or refuse dumps, near which only the poorest were willing to live. The bleak parallel between the physical and human "refuse" of the waterfront is evident right from the start of *My Man Godfrey* (1936), which brings us City Dump No. 32, at the foot of the Queensborough Bridge. As a crane drops a new load onto the piles of garbage, we discover that people are *living* here, a community of indigents that includes Godfrey himself—until he is whisked off to Fifth Avenue, a boulevard whose desirability lay precisely in its central location on the island, as far as one could get from both of the noxious riverfronts.

Before it is over, *My Man Godfrey* shows us the next step in the waterfront's evolution: its reclamation by the rich. By film's end, the garbage dump has been replaced by a chic nightclub, well located to serve the expensive apartment houses that—as *Dead End* revealed—had begun to rise amidst the gritty blue-collar warrens. After the war, this stretch of the East River all but lost its distinctive mix of industrial squalor and residential luxury when fancy apartment houses edged out almost everything else—in part because the construction of the FDR Drive in 1940 (one of the few highways in the city *not* built by Robert Moses) replaced the grimy coal docks with a series of picturesque water-edge parklets that enhanced the area's scale and idiosyncratic charm. Not surprisingly, these spots became a favored setting in the movie city, especially for romance—whether re-created for a dance scene between Dean Martin and Judy Holliday in *Bells Are Ringing* (1960), or filmed on location by Woody Allen for an intimate conversation at dawn with Diane Keaton in *Manhattan* (1979) (248).

For others, the waterfront has served as a place to look *inward*—a place for contemplation, for meditation. Barbara Hershey is repeatedly drawn to the edge of the Hudson to reflect on the passing seasons in *Hannah and Her Sisters* (1986), as is Michael J. Fox in *Bright Lights, Big City* (1988). It is not hard to see why. Few spots in the world offer such a dramatic shift in scale and mood as the places where New York meets the water—the dense, frenetic, block-by-block rhythm of streets suddenly transposed against a realm of open sky, wide horizons, and the elemental simplicity of the city's edge. New York's waters—its rivers, its great bay, the Atlantic itself—tend to be broad and flat, with distant opposite banks that offer little of the cozy, two-sided texture common to European waterways such as the Thames or the Seine. Instead, they firmly counterpoise the human fabric of the city with the stern infinity of nature, a philosophical quality which New York filmmakers (no less than New York novelists, such as Herman Melville, who opens *Moby-Dick* in just such a setting) have found irresistible.

"The scene is Rockaway," Woody Allen's voice tells us at the start of *Radio Days* (1987). "The time is my childhood." The opening shot establishes the thematic sweep of the film, which alternates between a loving evocation of daily life in the early 1940s and a bittersweet rumination on the fleetingness of human existence. We see a short street that, like many in this Queens beachfront community, ends abruptly with the Atlantic Ocean. Nothing could be more evocative of ordinary life than the stretch of city in the foreground, with its frame houses, small apartment buildings, stores, cars, sidewalks, telephone poles, clotheslines; nothing could be more evocative of a terrifying unknown than the stormy Atlantic beyond it, whose forbidding gray surface offers not a hint of anything beyond, not even a horizon to mark the edge between water and sky (179).

The contrast comes to life in a later scene, which finds the young narrator (Seth Green) with his friends on a local rooftop, training a pair of binoculars—intended to spot enemy planes—on the more riveting sight of a woman undressing in a nearby window. Soon the friends have parted, leaving the boy alone on the beach in a reverie, his mind filled with "funny" thoughts about women, about life, until he is interrupted by the extraordinary sight of a German U-boat, as gray and fierce as the ocean itself, which surfaces and descends "so mysteriously and silently" that the boy realizes he will never be able to tell anyone what he has seen. The grim and infinite ocean has spawned a creature, a mysterious death-machine, to remind the boy of the ominous realm that lies, always, just beyond the snug streets and houses of his childhood landscape (180).

179. *Radio Days* (1987). Woody Allen's film, set in the 1940s, opens with this moody view of Far Rockaway, a long, narrow peninsula fronting the Atlantic Ocean on the far southeastern edge of Brooklyn. Allen had spent part of his childhood in Long Beach, a shore community three miles to the east, but decided it was too far from Manhattan to provide a suitable location for the film.

Despite a spate of recent waterside developments, many city-dwellers continue to turn their attention inland, more or less unaware that New York even *has* a waterfront. Thus the startling impact of the title sequence of Jonathan Demme's *Something Wild* (1986), in which the camera, skimming above the waves as it circles Manhattan, achieves a potent inversion of accustomed perspective simply by looking from the water to the land, rather than the more familiar way around.

The effect is striking. Objects usually seen in the distance—buoys, barges—suddenly zoom by, close up. From here, we can actually see the city's seawall—the literal edge of the city—rising from the waves; we see one stretch of shoreline that is strewn with debris, and another, a grassy escarpment, that seems positively bucolic. Even the bridges look different from here, their spans seeming higher, longer, more daring than usual. Capping it all is David Byrne, singing in tropical rhythm about "an island in the bay," suggesting an unlikely kinship between New York and some verdant spot in the Caribbean. The result is to remind us what we all know but too often forget: that before all else, Manhattan is an *island*.

It is just this overlooked identity that provides the context for the sweet aquatic fantasy called *Splash* (1984), in which a Cape Cod mermaid (Darryl Hannah), seeking her true love Alan (Tom Hanks), decides to *swim* to the city, by following an eighteenth-century mariner's chart, found in the cabin of a sunken sailing ship, that provides still valid directions down the New England coast. Arriving by way of Liberty Island and joining Alan on land, she eventually decides to give up her watery ancestral home in the name of love—but in the end it is Alan who must forsake his world to join hers, jumping into the East River to save her from overzealous scientists. Visual reminders throughout the film allude to the bond between the city and the water: a mermaid fountain, located in one of the parks above the FDR Drive, and views of the moon that hint of the tidal ebb and flow around the island. But it is the film's arrivals and departures—all by way of the water—that remind us that the busy city is not only ringed by the sea, but deeply bound to it.

Arrival by water has indeed long been a crucial part of the city's myth. Across the twentieth century, tens of thousands came in bright white uniforms, ready to spend a brief moment in the world's most exciting port of call before departing again for potentially perilous seas. One fine May morning in 1949, the film city immortalized their ranks, when Gene Kelly, Frank Sinatra, and Jules Munshin flew down a gangway onto a pier of the Brooklyn Navy Yard, startling a sleepy dockworker with their pent-up energy. To him, the city is a place like any other. But to the three newcomers, "New York, New York" is "a wonderful town!"

We've sailed the seas and we've been the world over
From Maine to Mandalay,
We've seen the Sphinx and we've seen the cliffs of Dover
But we can safely say,
The most fabulous sight is New York in the light of the day—
Our only day . . .

The celebrated opening of *On The Town* (1949), which follows the trio around the city via taxicab, ferry, subway, double-decker bus, bicycle, and even horseback, offers a whirlwind tour that—taking in everything from Chinatown and the Brooklyn Bridge to Rockefeller Center and Grant's Tomb—seems less a single morning's actual sightseeing itinerary than the delirious rush of sensations the bountiful city would offer anyone after months of empty sea (4).

The city's greatest water-based welcome, of course, was reserved not for sailors but civilians—millions of them, entering New York as part of the largest migration of people in history, coming first through Castle Garden and then, after 1892, through the federal immigration station on Ellis Island. Though no more than 2 percent entering Ellis Island were ever turned back, the film city, with its inevitable instinct for conflict, directed attention to the problem cases. The Scottish immigrant Janet Gaynor plays in *Delicious* (1931) and the Czech newcomer played by Francis Lederer in *Romance in Manhattan* (1934) have envisaged their arrival in New York so vividly (Gaynor actually imagining a "Mr. Ellis" welcoming her) that it is the cruelest disappointment when, with the Statue of Liberty and lower Manhattan literally in sight, they are told by harsh immigration officials that (for one reason or another) they may not enter the country. Their frustration is so palpable that it becomes perfectly under-

180. Radio Days (1987). In a meditative moment, Woody Allen's youthful persona, Joe (Seth Green), wanders by himself along the Rockaway beach, looking out onto the stormy ocean—just seconds before spotting a German U-boat cruising on the surface, a few hundred yards offshore.

standable when both decide to sneak their way into the city illegally, even though they must spend the rest of their time trying to elude the authorities.

For young Vito Andolini (Oreste Baldini) in *The Godfather Part II* (1974), similar troubles await on Ellis Island—but only after Francis Ford Coppola's moving re-creation of the epic ritual of entrance: the S.S. *Moshulu* sailing through the Upper Bay, laden with its human cargo; the rows of glistening eyes turned to the Statue of Liberty; the daunting passage through the cattlelike pens of the Registry Hall, where the low roar of the crowd is punctuated by the crying of infants and snatches of a dozen foreign languages; the brusque interrogation process itself, during which Vito's last name is changed to that of his hometown, Corleone; and the hurried medical examination that ends with the boy being detained in the quarantine wards on Ellis Island's south side, where again the Statue of Liberty beckons, out the window, just out of reach.

It would be one very late arrival, ironically, who best captured the haunting quality of the place. The alien hero of John Sayles's *The Brother from Another Planet* (1984), crash-landing in New York Bay, proceeds to enter the darkened Registry Hall, empty and decrepit after decades of neglect. Brushing against a column, the Brother (Joe Morton) is startled by a short, sudden cry from nowhere; touching it again, he hears a distant babble of voices, though he is clearly alone in the silent, peeling hall. As he sits on a leftover bench, the roar returns, strange languages and accents, babies crying, all echoing louder and louder off the darkened vaults—until he himself screams, silently, to make it cease. Thanks to his extraterrestrial powers, the Brother can actually hear what the rest of us must perceive in our minds: the resonance of accumulated humanity, embedded in the very fabric of a hallowed place.

181. Hudson River piers, 1965. This aerial view of the "superliner" piers in the West Forties, where the great transatlantic liners all converged from Europe, includes three of the largest passenger ships ever built: the *Queen Mary* (bottom), the *France* (center), and the *United States* (top), each about a thousand feet—five city blocks—in length.

LIBERTÉ

For decades, the row of the world's greatest passenger ships, lined up side by side on the Hudson piers like some Olympian convocation of titans, was a crucial part of New York's identity. No other American city had anything like it—nor, for that matter, did London or Paris, whose interior locations along winding, narrow waterways kept the biggest liners from landing directly. Not surprisingly, this environment—not the ships themselves but the special place where ship met city—was a setting to which Hollywood returned time and again, recognizing the moored liners as an integral part of the city's own urban character. The pier-and-ship set, found in almost every studio, was among the most imposing constructions on the lot (51, 183).

Each set had two parts. On one side was the pier itself: a high, open, steel-frame structure filled with baggage carts and divided into various classes by white picket fences. Enormous overhead doors running along its length were pulled up to reveal the set's other half: the black wall of steel that represented a piece—a *small* piece—of the liner itself (184). The enormous scale of the ship was effectively conveyed by the fact that the portion visible from the pier, though substantial in height and length, showed absolutely no curve, no taper—nothing at all to suggest the familiar shape of a hull. The flat wall of steel implied, instead, something that went on almost forever.

182. Paramount stock footage of Hudson River piers, late 1930s. In the middle decades of the twentieth century, Hollywood filmmakers were drawn time and again to the extraordinary point of linkage between the world's greatest passenger ships and America's largest city. These views, shot by Paramount cameramen for use as background plates in feature films (58), show the French Line's *Ile de France* docked at Pier 88 at 48th Street (top), and passengers boarding the Cunard Line's *Majestic* for a midnight sailing from Pier 92, at 52nd Street (bottom).

Beyond its impressive scale, the drama of the setting lay in its inherent transience, from the fact that the two giants joined to create it, ship and city, were inevitably—indeed, imminently—to be pulled apart (182). A 1931 film called *Transatlantic* opens with an expectant, festive air: taxis and limousines rush up to the pier entrance and crowds pour up the gangway, a two-sided party with some revelers already on deck while others mill about on the pier below. When the stewards ring the chimes requesting that guests go ashore, few take notice. But when the great ship's horn blows with declarative finality, the mood shifts. This is not a party after all, but a leave-taking, inescapably tinged with sadness. It is, despite the high spirits, a farewell.

Even when they finally sailed, the greatest liners—twelve stories high, five city blocks long, carrying several thousand people at a time—seemed to take a piece of the city with them. With their tiers of humanity, their cross-section of society (featuring extremes of wealth and poverty as well as a typically overlooked middle class), their reliance on technology (structural-steel framing, advanced electrical and mechanical systems), the Atlantic liners were potent symbols for the one city on which they all converged (181).

Some films tightened the analogy, linking the great vessels to a single piece of the city, the skyscraper. The pairing made sense. Both ship and tower were singular creations of hand and mind, working on the same astonishing thousand-foot scale. Yet for their awesome size both were slender and graceful, offering the most elegant of profiles. And while both arose from much the same miraculous technology—especially steel framing—their design was a response not to a simple engineering function (like a bridge or dam) but to the more complex need to support and house miniature societies. Both, finally, were structures deeply *of* New York, gathering and compressing its urban energy into a single overriding gesture, a dynamic leap into the elements.

Shall We Dance (1937) joined the two structures by shifting the setting of Fred and Ginger's evolving relationship, at its midpoint, from the length of a liner to the height of a skyscraper hotel. *An Affair to Remember* linked ship and

tower still more explicitly, seeing the Empire State Building as the natural site to culminate a shipboard romance. But one film above all took advantage of the relationship that New York—and New York alone—offered between these two colossal pieces of urban scenography: Billy Wilder's *Sabrina* (1954).

At the tip of lower Manhattan stands the towering "Larrabee Building." Humphrey Bogart plays the elder brother, Linus Larrabee, serious and dutiful, directing company operations from a commanding office on the twenty-second floor; William Holden is the younger brother, David, a thrice-divorced playboy who enjoys seducing women on Long Island's North Shore. Audrey Hepburn is Sabrina, daughter of the Larrabees' chauffeur, who returns from two years of study in Paris chic and ravishing—and utterly tantalizing to David, who can't figure out where he has met this mysterious beauty before, having never really noticed her when she was living above the garage. For Sabrina, it is the fulfillment of a lifelong crush; for Linus, it is a major obstacle to his plan to have David marry a sugar-cane heiress, expediting a merger with her family's company.

183. Steamship set at 20th Century-Fox Studios, circa 1938. Built in 1928 and standing for more than two decades on the eastern edge of the Fox lot in Beverly Hills, this permanent steamship set was a Los Angeles landmark (51), whose upper decks offered sweeping views of Pico Boulevard and the Hillcrest Country Club to the south.

So Linus intercepts Sabrina, sharing with her all the pursuits—sailing, theater-going, dancing—that his strict devotion to business has never allowed. She speaks to him of Paris, of the pleasures of life she learned to enjoy there; he suggests a sadness beneath his tough exterior, and hints that he is ready for a change. A few days later, he brings her to his office, which he calls "my home." From its high windows he points to the French Line piers, uptown, where the liner *Liberté* readies to sail. He will be on it, he says, "breaking out of here."

184. Steamship set at Paramount Studios, 1940. Like most permanent steamship sets, Paramount's included both a stretch of the liner's superstructure and a portion of the adjoining pier, connected by a gangway. The churning waters between vessel and pier were implied by steam from a pipe running along the base of the ship, tucked out of sight.

"Oh, Linus, I'm so happy you're going," Sabrina says. "Or am I?" she adds, realizing that her lifelong attraction to the younger Larrabee is being challenged by feelings for this older sibling.

To his father, Linus admits that his behavior is a ruse. He *has* purchased tickets on the *Liberté* under his and Sabrina's names, but he himself has no intention of sailing. Miles out at sea, he explains, Sabrina will find an empty cabin and fifty thousand dollars. Once she is out of everyone's life, David's marriage/merger to the sugar-cane heiress can proceed.

The night before the sailing, Sabrina

185. ***Sabrina*** **(1954).** The film's climax vividly links the skyscrapers of lower Manhattan with the liners that regularly passed before them. From a boardroom atop the towering Larrabee Building, Linus Larrabee (Humphrey Bogart) watches the *Liberté* sail down the Hudson with Sabrina (Audrey Hepburn) on board, until his brother, David (William Holden), forces him to admit his feelings and sends him on his way—down the tower's express elevator, and onto a waiting tug, to chase the liner across the bay and be united on deck with his love.

admits tearfully to Linus that it is he, not David, whom she really loves. Noticing the tickets on his desk, she is overjoyed. But Linus, moved by her outburst, cannot keep the truth from her: he has manipulated her, and she will be sailing alone. Heartbroken, she accepts the one ticket. "I was happy in Paris," she says, "I think you would be, too." Filled with feeling, Linus looks uptown to the waiting ship, but says nothing.

Early the next morning, a chastened Linus reveals his scheme to David, then announces (to his brother's astonishment) his belated realization that love is more important than business—at least for David. The merger will be canceled; David can sail with Sabrina at noon. Pleased but puzzled, David sets off.

The meeting to close the merger, in Linus's office atop the Larrabee Building, frames the film's dramatic final scene (185). A glance out the window confirms that the *Liberté* has indeed begun making her stately way down the Hudson; and now she sounds her mighty horn, as if speaking directly to Linus. Trying to turn his attention to the matter at hand, Linus prepares to tell the group, including David's fiancée, that neither marriage nor merger will proceed. But the horn blows again, closer. It is the call of love, of freedom, of "liberté"; it is Linus's final chance for happiness, and it is passing him by.

It was Wilder's genius to see in the urban coupling of ship and tower the perfect embodiment for the emotional dynamic underlying this climax—in which Linus, having tried to deceive Sabrina, realizes that he has deceived only himself. As the ship and tower engage in their heartbreaking ritual—the ship sailing closer and closer, calling out to the tower as it passes by—the two structures begin to act out the roles of the romantic leads on the grandest possible scale. For years Linus, high atop his skyscraper, has watched the liners come and go; he *is* the Larrabee Building, a tower of strength, set in his ways, watching the world of love and freedom proceed beneath his window. Now, seeing *liberté*—Sabrina, of course—pass by, he realizes, a moment too late, that he has missed his last chance.

But just as the ship crosses the view, just as Linus has resigned himself to having let his last chance slip away, the office door flies open and in bursts David. Stunned by the fact that Linus is willing to break up a $20-million deal, David has seen what his brother has not—that Linus really *is* in love with Sa-

186. ***A Thousand Clowns* (1965).** Touring the city, Murray Burns (Jason Robards) brings his new friend Sandra Markowitz (Barbara Harris) to the Hudson piers, where they add their shouts and streamers to the crowd wishing the *Queen Mary* bon voyage—though they know no one on board.

187. ***Working Girl*** **(1988).** Tess McGill (Melanie Griffith) crossing New York Bay on the Staten Island Ferry, between two worlds—her work life in lower Manhattan, and her home life on Staten Island.

brina. In a striking reversal of roles, the newly businesslike David briskly outlines the arrangements he has made, then sends the lovestruck Linus on his way, darting down the tower's express elevator to the street, following a police escort to the pier, before boarding a Larrabee tug to speed him to a midharbor rendezvous with the great liner—and Sabrina.

A moment before, ship and tower had seemed so distant. But are they really? Both share the same immense scale, the same modern steel frame beneath, and so much else besides: What is the ship, in fact, but the great tower turned upon its side and set free? By way of an exhilarating pursuit that begins with a fast elevator ride down the tower's height and ends with a boat chase across the liner's length, Linus converts the commanding verticality of the skyscraper into the horizontal freedom of the liner. Beneath the sturdy walls of the Larrabee Building, it turns out, lies the stuff of the dashing *Liberté*—and it always has. It is never too late.

Through its evocative river-edge views, *Sabrina* effectively suggested how the great ships affected the texture of daily life in New York—not only for those fortunate few who traveled on them but for millions who never set foot on board. In *The Flamingo Kid* (1984), standing at the railing of a Rockaway Beach club, circa 1963, Jeffrey (Matt Dillon) points out distant lights on the dark Atlantic. It is a liner, he tells his girlfriend, "boxing the compass," getting its bearings from the Ambrose lightship before setting off across the sea. How does he know all this? From his father, Jeffrey explains, a nautical buff landlocked in the heart of Brooklyn: "You know, he never actually went anywhere, but he *dreams* about this stuff." In *A Thousand Clowns*, Jason Robards brings his new friend Barbara Harris to a sailing of the *Queen Mary*. Who are they saying goodbye to, she wonders? "Nobody," he answers. "I don't get jealous that way. It's a great thing to do when you're about to start something new," he adds, "it gives you the genuine feeling of the beginning of things." And indeed, as the *Mary* sounds her mighty horn while Robards and Harris throw streamers and add their shouts to the dockside crowd, we sense the commencement of more than one kind of voyage (186).

Of course, the sad reality is that, having worked their way into the life of the city, the liners disappeared with dramatic suddenness in the 1960s and 1970s, their sights and sounds fading into memory almost overnight. During one haunting moment in Francis Ford Coppola's *New York Stories* episode, *Life Without Zoë,* a ship horn is heard on a Manhattan sidewalk, evoking a vanished, almost ghostly presence. Though cruise ships still cross the harbor on their way to and from the Caribbean, New York's waters are more likely to be filled today with the prosaic fleet of vessels that travel no farther than the other side of the bay.

Yet in the movie city, no less than the real, even a humble ferryboat could offer a critical passage. From its opening shot, *Working Girl* makes evident the role the Staten Island Ferry plays in the life of the secretary Tess: it is both pathway and barrier between life on Staten Island and her sky-high career ambitions in Manhattan (187). We join Tess on the ferry as it travels back and forth; the director, Mike Nichols, is careful to show the vessel to us from above as well, through the office window of Tess's boss, Katherine, the stylish executive who embodies Tess's aspirations.

As she inches toward her daring (and utterly illicit) takeover of the absent Katherine's position, Tess remains hesitant, her confidence undercut by the limits of her Staten Island existence. But after that life is destroyed one afternoon with the discovery of her fiancé's infidelity, she is primed for change. Now we see her on the ferry again, at the railing, mysteriously enshrouded by night and fog and heading slowly back to Manhattan. Suddenly the camera races toward the skyline, tearing across the water at fantastic speed, and then, as the music rises, floating into the air as it nears the glittery, unreal towers. No ordinary boat ride, this.

The next shot shows the ferry again by day, plying the water at its conventional pace. But the camera pulls back to reveal that we are viewing this ordinary scene from a most extraordinary vantage—Katherine's office, which Tess has quietly taken over as her own. She has done it; she has flown that imaginary ferry right up into the skyline, and will now follow the crossing not from a railing but from a window in the sky. If less glamorous than the sleek and vanished liners, the unassuming, enduring ferryboat still proved—at least in the movie city—every bit as efficient a vessel of human transformation.

THE BIG SEND-OFF

A drab woman, living in a drab place. Her name is Marian (Joan Crawford), the place is Erie, Pennsylvania, and everything about the scene, which opens *Possessed* (1931), is dull, bleak, washed-out. Marian walks home from her job in a paper-box factory down a rutted street, past shacks and mills, all rendered in a dreary wash of gray. At her side, an earnest young man declares his love, but as Marian explains passionately, she wants to get away: from him, from Erie, from everything. She walks off by herself, and suddenly a stroke of black steel cuts through the grayness and fills the screen: a locomotive emblazoned with the letters "N.Y.C.," passing through the heart of town on its way from Chicago to New York.

What occurs next is a haunting sequence (by the director Clarence Brown and the cinematographer Oliver March) that, though perfectly plausible, feels distinctly like a dream. With lilting music playing somewhere, Crawford stands in front of the black wall of the train, looking up at the lighted windows of a private passenger car as it slowly passes. In the first window, she sees a pair of white-coated waiters preparing dinner and cocktails; in the second, another waiter sets the table. The third window reveals a maid ironing a pair of women's lace underwear, while the fourth shows the woman herself: blonde, beautiful, half-dressed. Through a translucent bathroom window we see the silhouette of her husband, shaving. The last three windows all look into a parlor where another couple, tightly clasped and dancing to the music, glide across the room, finally dipping into a passionate kiss.

The train slows to a halt; the last car ends in an open observation platform. Sitting at the railing is a man in evening clothes, slightly tipsy, martini glass in hand. "Looking in?" he asks Marian. She nods yes. "Wrong way," he replies. "Get in and look out."

With its compelling succession of framed vignettes, the sequence unmistakably recalls the way in which the movies themselves offered tempting, silken glimpses of the dream city to rural and small-town audiences. It also suggests

188. Cross-section of Grand Central Terminal, circa 1913. This cutaway view reveals the station's intricate arrangement of concourses, platforms, drives, and ramps. At the center sits the high-ceilinged Main Concourse, with the Suburban Concourse beneath it; trains pull up to both levels from the left, and circle around tracks beneath the complex. Vehicles skirt the terminal along a system of raised drives, while thousands of pedestrians move among the station's levels on gently sloped ramps.

how (like the liners) the trains that traveled in and out of New York seemed to carry a compressed version of the city wherever they went. The white letters on the locomotive stood for the New York Central Railroad, not the city itself, but the happy ambiguity hardly went unnoticed.

Like the liners, the express trains could be considered great urban lances—black steel and rivets on the outside, delicate tracery and finery within—that extended the city's reach along a series of radiating lines of track. Trains, like ships, have always reinforced an urban way of life, a hub-and-spoke pattern that concentrates people and commerce in a few major centers rather than dispersing them (as automobiles and airplanes tend to do) in a broad, evenly developed network across the landscape.

189. *The Fisher King* (1991). Among the most memorable moments in the movie city is the sequence in *The Fisher King*, directed by Terry Gilliam, when the romantic delusions of a lovestruck, mentally disturbed indigent named Parry (Robin Williams) briefly transform the Main Concourse of Grand Central Terminal into the world's largest ballroom.

Other American cities had equal (or greater) right to be considered centers of rail transport—Chicago, most obviously—but it was New York, with its unrivaled ability to mythologize itself, that has most memorably transformed the railroad into an extension of its own urbanism. Nowhere was this more evident than at its gateways, the two great train stations into which the continent-spanning trains arrived, and which in time became—as much as any structures in the city—touchstones of New York's special identity and style.

Of the pair, Grand Central Terminal has been the more enduring. Built in the first decades of the twentieth century, the project was a pioneer of unified planning and design, rising above two levels of underground track in an imposing series of concourses, linked to each other and a host of surrounding buildings (188). The result was something new—not just a railroad station, but a coordinated complex of structures joined above and below street level through an ingenious system of passages, ramps, and drives. Its designers drew its basic architectural motif from the triple arches of ancient Roman gateways, recognizing that in the modern era the primary point of entry to the city had moved from the periphery to the center—and become the railway station. Having proceeded silently beneath the streets, travelers would pop up in the middle of town, first experiencing the city through a structure described by one of Grand Central's architects, Whitney Warren, as the "triumphant portal to New York."

At the terminal's center stood the Main Concourse, the great room at the heart of the complex. "Nice looking city," observes the country bumpkin Pa Kettle (Percy Kilbride) upon entering the space in *Ma and Pa Kettle Go to Town* (1950). "Pa, this is the station," his daughter explains.

An understandable mistake. The Main Concourse *was* something of a city, a kind of vast urban "well" through which midtown's streams of humanity could flow and collect. In the montage that opens *North by Northwest* (1959) we see waves of New Yorkers rushing through the great room—some on their way to trains and subways, others simply passing through, enjoying a covered shortcut from one part of midtown to another. No wonder that later in the film, Cary Grant—an innocent man now become a fugitive—looks to the concourse and its throngs to provide the anonymity he desperately needs. (Navigating the dense crowds in dark glasses, he is detected only when he tries to purchase tickets.) With its constant rush beneath the lofty ceiling, the film suggests Grand Central's multiple role: not only a gateway for continental travelers and regional commuters, but a crucial part of daily life, Manhattan's great town square. This is perhaps the reason why Grand Central has remained such a mythic presence in the movie city, even into the age of air travel. The city's airports are located at its far edges, and few people pass through them who are not somehow involved in an arrival or departure; unlike Grand Central, they have no secondary urban purpose, and are thus delimited in dramatic possibility.

With its high, barrel-vaulted roof and glassy end walls, the Main Concourse could suggest a palatial hall no less than a town square, and in a memorable scene in *The Fisher King*, the fervid imaginings of a lovestruck Robin Williams actually transforms one into the other. As we watch, the random motion of hurrying pedestrians gradually orchestrates itself into something more organized and rhythmic; one person pairs off with another until everyone—sailors, nuns, cops, rabbis, businessmen and -women, literally thousands of people—are *waltzing*, gracefully, splendidly, under the light of a slowly rotating, glittering ball at the room's center (189). Then, just as quickly, the magnificent cohesion is undone and the random, haphazard motion of everyday reality reasserts itself. But for that brief moment, the station seemed in some odd way fulfilled; what proves striking is not how surprising it is to see everyone waltzing in the great room but how *right* it is, how proper. One has only to imagine the same scene in a typical airport concourse to see what Grand Central embodies in its architecture that other transportation facilities simply do not.

190. Standing set of Grand Central Terminal, circa 1940. Constructed at RKO's Gower Street studio, this set reproduced a pair of platform gates with uncanny fidelity, re-creating the limestone walls, marble floors, ornamental metal, and distinctive painted lettering found throughout the station.

Much of Grand Central's mystique can be traced to its seemingly endless network of corridors and passageways, intricately linking the terminal to its surroundings. The brainchild of the station's codesigners, Reed and Stem, these featured a distinctive iconography: black serif letters, painted above gently curved archways, that beckoned the visitor to still lower and more obscure wings of the station, where entire secondary concourses and lobbies lay hidden (190). When crooked Ned Beatty sneaks onto the tracks of Grand Central in *Superman*, we are delighted but only somewhat surprised to find that his destination, the lair of the evil genius Lex Luthor (Gene Hackman), is one such lower-level concourse, now converted into a stylishly decorated command center. Here are those same distinctive segmental arches, those walls of pale polished limestone, those black serif letters announcing "To Baggage Room" and "To Bar and Restaurant." But now the place has been outfitted with maps, screens, a library, and a well-appointed parlor where Lex lives in secret splendor with flunky Beatty and "secretary" Eve Teschmacher, played by Valerie Perrine (who, when reminded by Lex that their home features a "Park Avenue address," quickly shoots back, "Park Avenue address? Two hundred feet below?"). Other amenities include a lower level flooded with water to create a tropical resort complete with swimming pool, beach, palm trees, and Hawaiian music.

In *Beneath the Planet of the Apes* (1970)—in which astronauts from the future discover that the mysterious world on which they have landed actually sits atop a postapocalyptic New York—the ruined Grand Central has become the temple for a future race; a wide, double staircase serves as the altar. Like Luthor's lair, this set is not a reconstruction of the real building, but a rather free interpretation that takes advantage of the enormous familiarity of the station's design, manifested in details as simple as the shape of an arch or a style of lettering. In such details resides Grand Central's power as an almost universally recognizable "place," even as it offers a superb springboard for fantasy. How many other structures could be so universally identified by a few fragments of their graphics?

In the end, however, the terminal's enduring presence depends not on its details but the grand spatial sequence at its heart, whose sweeping procession of interior spaces hauntingly evoked other, more essential kinds of passage: episodes of parting and return, of change and loss. One composite cycle of departure and arrival—offered in a pair of Metro-Goldwyn-Mayer films made two decades apart—suggested the breadth of human experience the terminal could embrace.

The departure is full of high spirits and youthful enthusiasm; for, as the 1933 film's title declares, Broadway star Bill Williams (Bing Crosby) is *Going Hollywood*. "This is the big send-off!" his press agent says, asking the brass band for "a lot of jazz, a lot of pep!" In a long shot of the concourse, with its great shafts of light pouring through the high windows, crowds move in a whirlwind of activity, all set to the music and choreographed by the publicity man. Giant bouquets are heaped throughout the space. Reporters cluster around, anxious for a story. The porters get into the act, dancing down the wide stairs, bags in hand. Everyone is on the lookout for Bing; telephone operators and ticket agents point this way and that. They've found him! No, it's Ned Sparks. "He's only the director," says the press agent in disgust. One porter offers a cue: "Where y'all going?" "Hollywood!" the crowd shouts back, "*Hollywood!*" "All aboard," he yells, "train leaving on Track 27." A baggage cart topped with a bevy of chorus girls pulls away to reveal the familiar Grand Central gates. Into the dark opening the crowd races, hands raised as if in a revival meeting, before rushing down the platform toward the elegant cars of the *Twentieth Century Limited*. Bing slides on board, turns back to the crowd, and, with flashbulbs popping, caps the festivities with lyrics of exultant farewell:

Out where they say, let's be gay,
I'm going Hollywood . . .
I'm on my way, here's my beret,
I'm going Hollywood . . .

And the train begins to glide away, to start its trip up the Hudson and then across the continent, to fame and fortune and stardom.

Coming nearly twenty years later, the arrival is a return of sorts, proceeding through the same sequences of spaces—but in reverse order, and with a profoundly different mood, for the Broadway star who left the station in triumph is now coming back disheartened and forlorn. In *The Band Wagon* (1953) he is called Tony Hunter and played not by Crosby but by Fred Astaire; it is easy, nonetheless, to imagine him as the same character, two decades later, his film career not at its promising start but at a sad and lonely finish. In the parlor car of the *Limited*, coming down the Hudson, he overhears two passengers offer the conventional wisdom—that Hunter, who hasn't made a picture in years, is all washed up, a has-been. As the train pulls into the terminal, Tony's melancholy gets the best of him; he is reluctant, in fact, to leave the car. When he does, a group of reporters waiting on the platform recognizes him and banter briefly, but when their true quarry—Ava Gardner—emerges, they rush off, leaving him more forlorn than ever.

It is in a mood of resignation, then, that he begins to retrace the steps that, in his earlier incarnation, he had trod so ebulliently. Walking down the underground platform, heading toward the Main Concourse, he is no longer "going Hollywood." He will, instead, "go by myself":

I'll go my way by myself,
Like walking under a cloud.
I'll go my way by myself,
All alone in a crowd.

The platform is an unlikely setting for an epiphany—a long, dark, utilitarian space, lined with the *Limited*'s signature red carpet and silvery railroad cars and bustling with the activity of porters, conductors, and maintenance men, all going about their business without paying him the slightest heed. Yet in the few hundred feet from train car to concourse, Tony finds a moment of unexpected grace. Accepting his situation forthrightly, he grows a new resolve to proceed:

I'll face the unknown,
I'll build a world of my own,
No one knows better than I myself,
I'm by myself,
Alone.

By the end of the platform, a remarkable thing has happened: Tony has regained his poise and self-confidence. He is ready for anything—or, more to the point, for nothing—to happen. He pauses—as if to prolong the moment in this oddly comforting, meditative place—before walking into the high, bright, welcoming concourse, where he is surprised to find a reception committee after all: the playwright couple (Oscar Levant and Nanette Fabray) who have lured him back to New York with the idea of restarting his Broadway career. Here the two of them stand, in the middle of the busy concourse floor, blowing noisemakers and holding handmade signs that say "The Tony Hunter Fan Club" and "Welcome to New York." Unlike the "big send-off" years before, when the entire station was mobilized, this raucous reception draws only a few odd stares from passersby. But what of it? The terminal's enlargening sense of ceremonial greeting remains, whether activated by two people or two hundred. Tony has come to realize that his life and career are not over quite yet.

Onto the station's physical layout, the movie city superimposed a design of its own, uncovering a moving emotional narrative in its architectural procession of concourses and platforms. Intended to ennoble a change in place, the station could also mark a change in time; built as the gateway to a continent, it could serve as a gateway across life itself.

Unlike Grand Central Terminal, which still stands in its original form, the architectural identity of its great companion, Pennsylvania Station, was circumscribed by the demolition of its 1910 McKim, Mead & White building in the early 1960s. The structures differed in a number of other ways, as well. While Grand Central was intricately interwoven into the city around it, Penn Station stood apart. The grandeur with which Charles McKim sought to imbue the station (whose waiting room was based on the Roman Baths of Caracalla, scaled up twenty percent) could seem aloof and even haughty when compared to its somewhat ramshackle surroundings, a tension already evident in 1913's *Traffic in Souls.* In Rouben Mamoulian's 1929 film *Applause* (an early talkie featuring extensive New York locations), Joan Peers leaves the Wisconsin convent where she has been raised to reunite in New York with her mother, a burlesque dancer played by Helen Morgan. From the cloistered landscape of the convent—the most peaceful setting imaginable—we cut to a train door flying open to discharge a throng of passengers. As the other travelers rush off the platform, Joan stops and lingers. She looks up, and Mamoulian's camera shows us why. Hundreds of feet above is an astonishing sight, an airy forest of steel columns and arches, all supporting a distant roof of glass. Craning up, the camera shows us the breadth of the soaring glassy enclosure, then pivots back down to the beehive of activity, the crowds quickly making their way upstairs (the camera is slightly undercranked to emphasize their rush). It was no accident that Mamoulian chose Pennsylvania Station and not Grand Central for a scene designed to evoke the impact of New York's scale and speed on an unprepared newcomer. Compared to this place, Grand Central's concourse seems friendly, even relaxed. This is simply overwhelming.

A civic vision grander than most Americans were familiar (or perhaps comfortable) with, the station could easily seem overscaled for the commercial culture in which it sat (191). But that would change with the coming of World War II, as one remarkable film of the time compels us to recognize. Released in 1945 and directed, like *The Band Wagon*, by Vincente Minnelli, *The Clock* captures Pennsylvania Station at the very peak not only of use (109,000,000 passengers that year, more than any before or since) but of emotional resonance as well. During the war years the station gained, at least for a time, a role commensurate with its size—as the entry point for millions of soldiers from across the country, coming to New York to board the vessels in the harbor that would carry them overseas. It was not just the sheer number of travelers, but the palpable undercurrent of emotions—deep feelings of honor, or pride, or anguish—among those headed to and from this greatest of global conflicts, that at last matched the overarching aspirations of McKim's mighty gateway.

191. Paramount stock shots of Pennsylvania Station, 1940s. Taken from footage used for establishing shots or background plates, these frames present three moments in the day-to-day life of the legendary station: the stone-fronted Waiting Room by day (top), and the iron-and-glass Main Concourse by night (middle and bottom).

Of course, the station could still seem overimposing, as we are quickly reminded at the opening of *The Clock*. An establishing shot of the actual facade—two blocks of Doric columns along Seventh Avenue—gives way to a look at the huge interior: the central axis of the Main Waiting Room, re-created by the MGM art department and surveyed by a crane shot that glides above the floor, looking down on the confluence of humanity below. Even more than Grand Central, Penn Station evinces a Roman grandeur—even in its lampposts, which rest on bases as tall as a man, and rise so high that the craning camera, at least thirty feet up, barely seems to clear them (59, 192).

For Joe, an army corporal (played by Robert Walker) who has just arrived in New York on a two-day pass, the station is not just big, but plainly *too* big:

bewildering, dizzying, frightening. "Can you tell me how to get out of this place?" he asks one passing stranger; "Certainly is a big place, isn't it?" he comments to another. But a walk to the building's Seventh Avenue side (with all those massive columns) gives him his first look at the city's vertiginous skyscrapers, quickly sending him back to the Waiting Room in more of a daze than ever.

Then a voice calls out to him, and suddenly within the vast room he makes a human connection. It is the voice of a woman, a woman who says she has lost her heel; it is the voice of Judy Garland. As Joe sits her up on the staircase's wide stone balustrade to examine her shoe, he at last manages—without quite knowing it—to shape a domestic, even personal space within the station's overwhelming grandeur.

Over the next day and a half, Joe and Garland's character, Alice, share experiences and adventures, and, quietly, fall in love—all in the shadow of Joe's imminent departure for war. Accidentally separated in a crowded subway station on their second day, they are brutally reminded of the city's size as each frantically searches Manhattan, not even knowing the other's last name. Giving up at last, Joe returns to Penn Station to board a train back to base; just then he sees Alice and runs to her, and there, in the very spot where they met just a day before, he proposes marriage—re-creating, with infinitely greater emotional force, the private space they first carved from the station's vastness.

The film's end, the next day, brings the pair back to the station one last time. They have wed and consummated their matrimony; now, with Joe's leave over, they must part. At the gate, Minnelli surveys a distinctively New York parade of departing soldiers and their families: a harried couple still discussing car payments; a handsome black officer with his wife and child; a Jew-

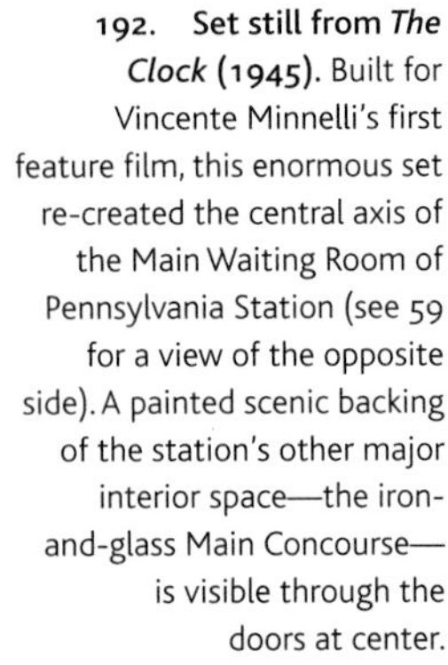

192. Set still from *The Clock* (1945). Built for Vincente Minnelli's first feature film, this enormous set re-created the central axis of the Main Waiting Room of Pennsylvania Station (see 59 for a view of the opposite side). A painted scenic backing of the station's other major interior space—the iron-and-glass Main Concourse—is visible through the doors at center.

ish boy and his doting parents; an older couple sharing a silent moment; and Joe and Alice, saying their final "I love you"s.

Joe passes through the gate; Alice turns and begins to walk away, moving through the crowd, slowly and deliberately. Minnelli's craning camera follows her, and even as it pulls back we keep our eye on her within the vast crowd. When we finally lose sight of her, the huge room seems not the frightening wilderness of the opening shot but a place of great communal purpose, whose scale universalizes the individual story we have just seen: a sense of common mission, at once heroic and tragic, which every audience member of that moment understood and shared—and which we can still recognize today.

As this sense of great collective purpose receded amid the individual pursuits of the postwar era, the station relapsed to its earlier image as something too grand—or grandiose—for the modest civic aspirations of American life. Glimpses in films such as Hitchcock's *Strangers on a Train* (1951) and Kubrick's *Killer's Kiss* (1955) only confirmed that the station—whose high, soot-darkened stone walls seemed almost mausoleum-like to modern eyes—offered little of Grand Central's familiar and comfortable place in the city. Perhaps it was inevitable that by the 1960s the station had been slated for demolition, to be replaced by a facility buried beneath Madison Square Garden, a banal, stripped-down structure that (to put it mildly) has had no memorable place in the filmic city. McKim's vision had aspired to something beyond the reach of everyday society. Perhaps only in that one supreme moment of collective effort, the war, was the scale of the station matched exactly to the society for which it was built—a moment preserved in all its poignancy and grandeur and alive still, like the great station itself, in the dream city of movies.

GRAND HOTELS

It is hardly surprising that the grand hotel should play a vital role in movie New York. As Rem Koolhaas points out, "A Hotel *is* a plot,"

> *a cybernetic universe with its own laws generating random but fortuitous collisions between human beings who would never have met elsewhere. It offers a fertile cross-section through the population, a richly textured interface between social castes, a field for the comedy of clashing manners and a neutral background of routine operations to give every incident dramatic relief.*

Though the movie city abounded in imaginary hotels—the Ritz-Bilt in *Reaching for the Moon* (1930), the Bradbury in *For Love or Money* (1993), Hotel Louis in *Easy Living* (1937)—its greatest hostelries were a pair of quite real establishments, whose names have enjoyed an enduring resonance both on-screen and off. When young Kevin McCallister (Macauley Culkin) first sees the "world-renowned Plaza Hotel" in *Home Alone 2: Lost in New York* (1992), he is still in his bedroom in Chicago, watching television; his confrontation with the real structure in all its Edwardian glory, flags flying and rooftop turrets gleaming in the sun, comes with a sense of recognition, of meeting an old friend. Like Kevin, nearly everyone entering the filmic Plaza, from Maureen Stapleton's suburban matron in *Plaza Suite* (1971) to the rustic hillbilly played by Bette Midler in *Big Business* (1988), knows all about it; or if they don't—like "Crocodile" Dundee (Paul Hogan), a visitor from the Australian outback—that fact becomes in itself a symbol of their profound disconnection from the larger world.

193. Establishing shot of the Plaza Hotel, from *Plaza Suite* (1971). Designed in 1907 by the architect Henry J. Hardenbergh, the Plaza Hotel has long been as prominent a landmark in the movie city as in the real one—in part because its location, facing Central Park and the Grand Army Plaza, allows for wide, unusually photogenic views.

Undoubtedly, much of the Plaza's stature in the movie city—no less than in reality—stems from its singular location, the spot where Central Park South turns to meet Fifth Avenue around the fountains and statuary of the Grand Army Plaza (193, 224). There is also the hotel's urbane layout, which pivots around the central Palm Court to link its east and north entrances in a succession of lobbies and public rooms (including the fabled Oak Bar) that bustle with an intermingled throng of New Yorkers and strangers. If this complex, ultimately unknowable mix of inhabitants—domestic and imported—is what truly defines a grand hotel, the filmic Plaza is without equal, thanks to a roster of guests whose identities are, to say the least, ambiguous.

In *Plaza Suite*, for example, one man (Walter Matthau) turns up as no fewer than three different guests, all occupying Room 719 in quick succession. In *Big Business*, Lily Tomlin and Bette Midler play two different sets of identical twin sisters—West Virginians Rose and Sadie Ratliff and New Yorkers Rose and Sadie Shelton—wandering through lobbies and elevators to the endless confusion of the staff and guests. ("Stand here long enough," says a homeless man who has watched the two pairs pass back and forth through the entrance, "and you'll see yourself come out of that hotel.") Other guests have not too many identities, but too few. "Peter McCallister" is the imaginary father invented by young Kevin, whose improvised presence allows the boy to continue his Christmas jaunt in *Home Alone 2*. And of course there is "George Kaplan," the guest in Room 796, who, despite his daily use of the hotel's valet service, proves (in *North by Northwest*) to be equally imaginary—causing Cary Grant, debonair ad man and Oak Bar mainstay, to be dangerously mistaken for him.

All of these, to be sure, are screenwriters' inventions, deliberately fanciful. Yet they help reveal the authentic essence of the Plaza and places like it. In size

194. ***Week-end at the Waldorf* (1945).** To re-create the hotel's interiors in its Culver City studios, the MGM art department (under art director Daniel Cathcart) constructed sixty-five stage sets and employed a panoply of special effects. In this view, movie star Irene Malvern (Ginger Rogers) and her business manager Henry Burton (Leon Ames) step into the enormous Main Foyer.

and stature a grand hotel might resemble a prominent apartment house, but there is a profound difference: an apartment house, with its established tenantry, would hardly make a plausible setting for such amusing (or scary) misidentifications. But a grand hotel does, precisely because it is, no less than the waterfront or train station, a natural home for strangers, a zone of transience. For all the centrality of its location, a grand hotel is not entirely *of* the city, but a place shared in equal part with the rest of the world.

It is a measure of New York's scale that (as in the case of its train stations) its hotel world offers not one but *two* legendary names. For decades, the Waldorf-Astoria Hotel, located since 1931 in a towering Art Moderne building on Park Avenue, has provided a superb springboard for cinematic fantasy.

Much of that fantasy revolved around sheer luxury. No less than the Plaza (whose ornate, high-ceilinged rooms, entered in countless movie scenes, invariably elicit admiring gasps from on-screen characters as well as the audience itself), the Waldorf symbolized unimaginable levels of luxe, rendered not only in French period decor like the Plaza but along sleek Art Deco lines as well. The duplex favored by film star Alan Swann (Peter O'Toole) in *My Favorite Year* (1982) is remarkable no less for its curved staircase than its expansive bathroom; in *Rich and Famous* (1981), the gigantic suite rented by an author of best-selling romance novels, Merry Noel Blake (Candice Bergen), is contrasted with the modest accommodations of serious writer Liz Hamilton (Jacqueline Bisset) at the Algonquin, a hotel whose own myth is built on its literary reputation, not its physical grandeur. We watch Merry Noel wander through her sprawling suite of reception rooms, planning a party for several hundred guests; Liz, meanwhile, fends off a single upstairs visitor to the Algonquin by noting that "There's only room for me and the ghost of Dorothy Parker." The fact that Jack Lemmon and Sandy Dennis *cannot* get their glamorous, much-anticipated suite at the Waldorf—or find any space at all in the fully booked hotel—seems to predestine, early in *The Out-of-Towners* (1970), everything about the couple's ill-starred trip to New York.

Still, it is more than just luxury. No other hotel lent itself so completely to

195. The Waldorf-Astoria, from Park Avenue, circa 1935. Standing proudly among the towers that rose around Grand Central in the late 1920s, the Waldorf-Astoria (designed by Schultze & Weaver) displays the supremely urban qualities of that era, its lower wings helping to define the city's traditional "street wall" even as its tower, capped by two enormous finials, soars 625 feet into the sky.

the spirit of filmmaking. "With the Waldorf," Koolhaas has written, "the Hotel itself becomes . . . a movie, featuring the guests as stars and the personnel as a discreet coat-tailed chorus of extras." In fact, of all grand hotels, it was the Waldorf-Astoria that was most fully rendered in the movie city, in a splashy 1945 MGM feature called *Week-end at the Waldorf* (194).

Behind *Week-end* lay one of the studio's greatest hits: *Grand Hotel*, the all-star 1932 version of Vicki Baum's 1930 Berlin novel, *Menschen im Hotel*. *Week-end* would consciously mirror the earlier film's structure, with its multiple, intertwining storylines of romance and intrigue played out by guests and staff. But in replacing the earlier film's generic European "Grand Hotel" with a specific establishment in an equally specific city, the later film offered a subtle but important shift of emphasis. The hotel in *Grand Hotel* was presented as essentially a self-contained place, a world unto itself. The Waldorf of *Week-end*, by contrast, is linked inextricably to its larger context; it is a "city within the city." In this interplay between inward and outward focus can be found the special *urban* significance of the grand hotel.

The difference is evident from the first shot, which shows us something we never see in *Grand Hotel:* a view of the building within the city around it (195). Rising on Park Avenue is its seventeen-story base, aligned with the buildings on either side and completing the street wall with impeccable manners. Unlike its neighbors, however, the hotel leaps into the sky for another twenty-five floors, culminating in a twin-peaked rooftop like nothing else around it. This dual identity continues inside: the base contains the hotel's guest rooms; the tower contains residential apartments, the tenants of which enjoy all the services of the hotel while remaining rooted in the life of the city.

One of these residents, in fact, is our guide. "Yes, that's the Waldorf-Astoria," chuckles Robert Benchley. "Big place, isn't it? But it's home to me." Benchley plays Randy Morton, a New York columnist based loosely on the journalist Elsa Maxwell, the self-described "hotel pilgrim" who made the Waldorf her permanent home. A fixture of Manhattan life, yet reliant on the hotel's ever-changing parade, Benchley is the ideal embodiment of a place that joins together the foreign and the familiar, the newcomer and the regular, the world and the city.

A grand hotel must impress us with the variety of its guests, and accordingly, the "weekend" begins with the Friday check-ins of everyone from a celebrated war correspondent, Chip Collyer (Walter Pidgeon), and movie star Irene Malvern (Ginger Rogers), to a wounded pilot played by Van Johnson, and a scheming businessman (portrayed by Eddie Albert). With cosmopolitan ease, the hotel welcomes the most exotic visitors, such as the "Bey of Arijiban," a Middle Eastern potentate whose entourage includes a full-time interpreter and a goat.

But a grand hotel is more than just guests. Early on, we also meet a staff stenographer (Lana Turner), who provides our entry to the world behind the scenes, as complex in its way as that out front. The film revels in the sheer size of that world, from the two dozen switchboard operators (". . . Beverly Hills, calling Miss Malvern"; "Yes, General . . .") to the four employees who do nothing but take room-service orders. Within the hotel, the film delights to show, every whim or need can be satisfied, from a manicure to a physical; every passage of life can be accommodated, from a wedding ceremony to the preparation of a will; and even the most outlandish request can be fulfilled—a pastry miniature of a Midwestern hospital, for example, is added at the last minute to a wedding cake. Glimpses of signboards suggest that for each event we *do* see, several others—perhaps just as interesting—are proceeding unseen: a dinner for the Society of Illustrators, a lunch for the Norwegian navy.

Repeatedly, in fact, the film slips away from its story to provide us with a portrait of the hotel's inner workings. Like contemporary renderings, the film peels back the hotel's facade to show us its daily cycle of activities, from the cleaning of its high windows ("just as they do in Newark or Kansas City, except that the soap has a little farther to fall") to the upkeep of its landmark architecture ("what appears to be a hockey team ready for a scrimmage is merely a crew touching up the mosaic floor, the Waldorf's famous 'Wheel of Life' ").

When, in the end, all the romantic engagements have been settled and all the intrigue resolved, what is left is not the individual stories but a vision of the place that embraces them all. It is a place of temporary visitation and permanent habitation, of ordinary lives and extraordinary ones, of varied spaces for living, working, dining, celebration. In a later era it would be dubbed "mixed-use" and claimed as a new innovation; here it is portrayed as the natural life of a great urban building. Through its first-floor public rooms flows a stream of pedestrians that would do most train stations proud, let alone a hotel; it is hard to believe that the real Waldorf was ever so busy, even in the war years. But MGM clearly saw no risk in contradicting the hotel's reputation for luxury by filling it with a constant flux of moving bodies, perhaps because the actual hotel is laid out around an axis connecting one city avenue to another, just like a typical New York street. Like the Plaza (but unlike so many recent hotels, including the architect-developer John Portman's projects), the Waldorf, for all its grandeur, does not turn its back on its surroundings but extends the city's grid into itself, just as it combines transient lodging for distant travelers with established homes for local residents. Indeed, far from being a fortress against the city, the structure performs its special magic by somehow compressing the whole city's range of possibilities within itself.

Or as Benchley reminds us at the film's close, the chuckle still in his voice: "Anything can happen, in a weekend at the Waldorf."

ELEVEN

DANCING LIGHTS

BROADWAY AND TIMES SQUARE

THE GREAT WHITE WAY

On screen, as in life, one part of the city burned brightest of all. Indeed, Broadway stood in relation to the rest of New York as the city itself stood to other places: the place most charged, most filled with life, most saturated with legend and myth. "More than New York's theater district," Neal Gabler has written, Broadway

> *was as much a mythical city as Hollywood, and made nearly as strong a claim on the imagination. Hollywood was balmy and languorous; Broadway was the place where the pace never slackened, the lights never dimmed, the crowds never thinned, the revelry never stopped—a place where all the hedonistic energy of the age could roar.*

As if to acknowledge this, filmmakers often used a view of Broadway, by day or (more often) by night, as an establishing shot; it was, in this respect, the only part of the city to rival the skyline. But it made sense. Broadway, after all, was the part of New York closest in spirit to the movie city itself, a place physically shaped around the needs of entertainment and spectacle.

Nowhere was that link more obvious than in the heart of the district, Times Square, which offered its own definition of "moving pictures." In its wedge of urban space, an outdoor "theater" darkened each evening by the coming of night itself, shimmering screens of light transformed the solid realities of mass and volume into a realm of liquid energy—overscaled images, flowing overhead, in constant motion (197).

Like the movies themselves, Times Square's signs challenged traditional notions of night and day, darkness and light. As nothing else, they declared

196. (previous page) ***Dr. Broadway*** **(1942).** Directed by Anthony Mann, this film opens and closes atop Times Square, where a Manhattan doctor named Timothy Kane (Macdonald Carey) saves a chorus girl named Connie Madigan (Jean Phillips) from plunging off one of the giant neon signs that lines the space.

Broadway to be a district that came fully alive only after dark, a place whose essential buildings—legitimate theaters—were used for just two or three evening hours of each twenty-four-hour day. By day, the big signs gave away their earthbound reality, the girdered structures that supported them. It was only at night, when those frameworks grew invisible, that the signs presented their intended illusion: floating magically in the air, weightless, alive. Yet the lighted signs were also responsible for the essential paradox of Times Square: that this place, devoted more than anywhere else to the night, should strive like no other to banish it, to replace nocturnal darkness with the glow of an artificial day.

197. Establishing shot of Times Square, 1951. Looking north from the Times Tower, this view shows the distinctive "bow-tie" created by the intersection of Broadway and Seventh Avenue. To the left is the Astor Hotel, built in 1904 and demolished in 1967; to the far right, the enormous Camel sign, famed for emitting actual smoke rings.

In their endless, hypnotic flickering, the signs suggested an illusive, dazzling kind of movement not unlike cinema's own brand of special effects. In a 1949 picture called *Love Happy*, one of the film city's more improbable characters, Harpo Marx, actually links the chimerical movement of Broadway signs to that of the movies. Racing around a Times Square rooftop filled with big neon signs, Harpo first eludes a gang of crooks by magically popping up in widely scattered places with each flicker of light. Still more remarkably, he then "enters" the signs themselves—riding a neon Pegasus across the giant Mobil sign, for example, as if he has himself been somehow transmuted into the evanescent stuff of neon. Knowing Harpo, perhaps he has.

As this scene suggests, Hollywood filmmakers were not content to gaze idly at Broadway's lighted spectacles, but instead put them quickly to work. In pictures stretching from 1929's *Glorifying the American Girl*, to *Broadway Melody of 1938*, to *The Hard Way* in 1991, the district's signs and marquees have done double duty as illuminated title cards, with each movie's cast and credits appearing high over a filmic Times Square. Other moviemakers, meanwhile, used the signs to help tell their stories, recognizing that there could be no quicker or more evocative way to track a show business career, real or imaginary, than by presenting a lighted sign across the face of Times Square. We know instantly that Susan Gallagher (Judy Garland) has achieved a pinnacle of success in *Ziegfeld Girl* (1941) when her name is prominently displayed above the New Amsterdam Theater, just under Ziegfeld's own. The remarkable decades-long string of George M. Cohan's hits is sketched (in *Yankee Doodle Dandy*, 1942) by a slow pan across a landscape of Broadway signs, accompanied by a few bars of each show's best-known song. The fact that the lighted sign for Valerie Stanton (Rosalind Russell) suddenly blinks *out* at the start of *The Velvet Touch* (1948) suggests a different, rather more ominous career turn (200).

Significantly, all of these signs were the kind associated with a theatrical production or personality, not those promoting corporate names or commercial products. For the movie city, the value of Times Square's signs clearly lay in their association with the masses of humanity who regularly gathered in the square itself. In the days when millions of incandescent bulbs fused into the brilliance of the Great White Way, the mapping was straightforward: "a broken heart," the old song lyric claimed, "for every light on Broadway." The conversion to neon, begun in the 1920s, made the analogy less direct, but there remained in the dazzle of Broadway a human presence quite different from the relatively cold-hearted spectacle of Las Vegas, its closest American rival. For the movie city, Times Square's signs served not only as an extension of particular celebrities—especially prominent theatrical figures—but could, on occasion, prompt a meditation on the nature of celebrity itself.

A 1942 backstager called *Footlight Serenade*, for example, includes a romantic scene between Betty Grable and John Payne set on the roof of the Broadway theater in which the pair are rehearsing: she massages his back while a portable radio plays mood music. It is all very intimate and charming—if one can somehow ignore the giant signboard in the background, displaying in huge letters the name of the show that will turn them into stars.

The scene is revealing. Everything about a Times Square sign like this, from its supporting framework to the image it displays, is big—indeed, enormous. But it is not *just* big. Unlike a dam or aircraft hangar or similarly oversized structure, a Broadway sign is not simply large in the abstract: because its subject is almost always a person's face, or figure, or name, it plainly represents an *enlargement*, a scaling-up from ordinary human dimensions to something else, something that is distinct from—yet also related to—the individual on which it is based.

At the start of *The Hard Way* (1991), workmen high above Broadway are installing the sign for "*Smoking Gunn II*," a new film starring a movie actor

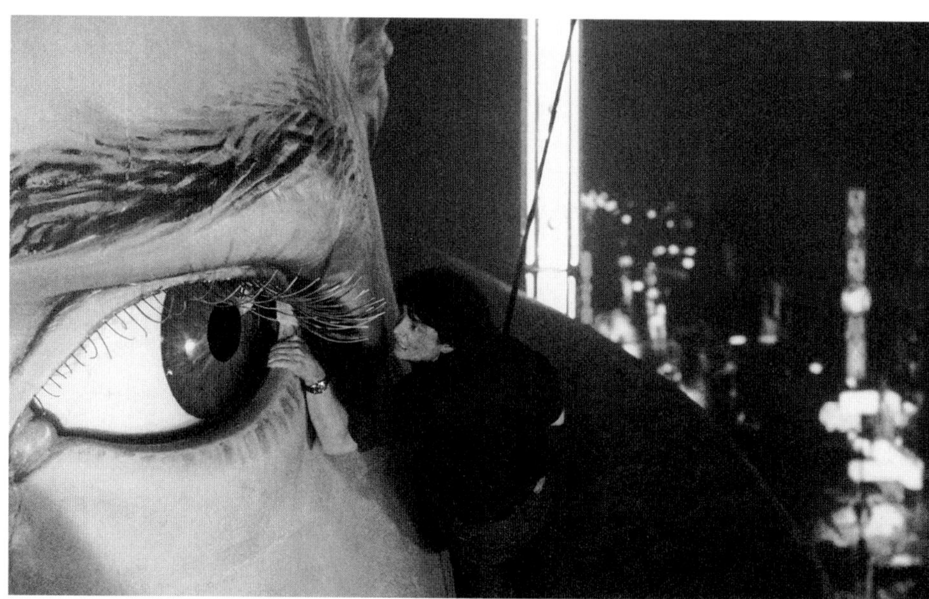

198. *The Hard Way* (1991). In the film's dramatic climax, a terrified Hollywood movie star named Nick Lang (Michael J. Fox) hangs desperately from his own eye—part of a giant Broadway sign advertising Lang's starring role (as the fearless detective Joe Gunn) in *Smoking Gunn II*.

named Nick Lang (Michael J. Fox) as the fearless adventure hero Joe Gunn. In the best Times Square tradition, the sign consists of a huge three-dimensional sculpture of Gunn's head, complete with a cigarette (itself about twenty feet long) that emits real smoke. In contrast to his dashing screen persona, the real Nick Lang turns out to be a shallow, self-involved star, interested only in his career. Perhaps fittingly, the film's climax finds him up on the sign, pursuing a murderer, while at the same time confronting his outsized fictional persona. Flailing around his own giant visage, Lang may be physically tiny—but his selfless gestures (endangering himself in order to save his partner, James Woods and Woods's girlfriend, Annabella Sciorra) are large enough to suggest some kind of reconciliation between an ordinary human being and an overscaled legend (198).

199. ***Radio Days*** **(1987).** At the Kaufman Astoria studios in Queens, production designer Santo Loquasto created a poetic interpretation of 1940s Times Square, as seen from the rooftop of a building on its northern end. In this view, a group of radio stars celebrating New Year's Eve look out onto the lighted signs and great crowds gathered below.

The conclusion of *Radio Days* (1987), Woody Allen's elegy for the lost world of 1940s radio, turns to the lights and signs of Broadway (by way of a superb set designed by Santo Loquasto) for some final reflections on fame itself. It is New Year's Eve, and all the radio stars have come upstairs to the roof of a Times Square nightclub (199). From below we hear the cheers rising from the vast crowd that gathers at the close of every year in this greatest American urban space. On all sides, dramatically visible at eye level, are the glowing neon signs that define Times Square: Camel cigarettes, Pepsi-Cola, even the *New York Times* (for which the square was originally named). But one sign, dead center, especially catches our attention—not least because, seeing it from behind, we have no idea what it is for. It is a giant top hat, outlined in lights and slowly tipping its brim every minute or so. Glamorous, larger than life, ultimately unknowable, it is the symbol not of any particular celebrity but of celebrity itself, a construct of popular culture that grows from and yet transcends individual personality in a way that not even the stars themselves fully understand.

As midnight approaches, the radio personalities mill about the rain-washed roof, sharing a philosophical moment. "The years pass so quickly; where do they all go?" one wonders. "I wonder if future generations will ever even hear about us?" another asks, before ruefully answering his own question: "It's not likely. Everything passes." Then, with a great roar from below, the New Year finally arrives. Afterward, one by one, the famous figures climb back down the stairs—and, as it were, into eternity. Finally, nothing remains except celebrity itself—that mysterious top hat, tipping its brim, yet again, to the unseen crowds below.

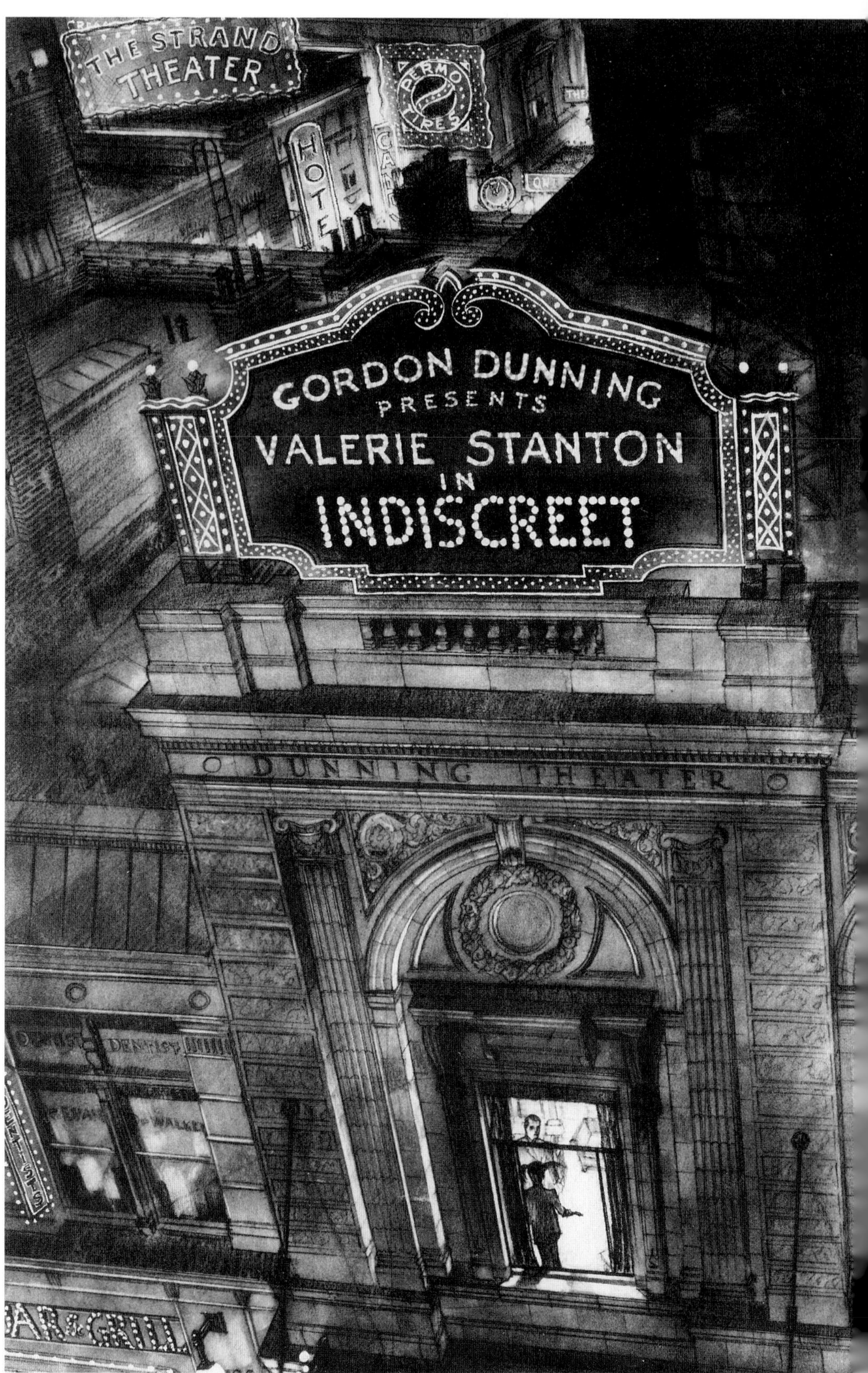

200. Production drawing from *The Velvet Touch* (1948). This view became the basis for the film's opening shot, which tilts down from the dark rooftops and bright sidewalks of Broadway to a lighted window in the Dunning Theater and, coming in closer, to the office where the actress Valerie Stanton (Rosalind Russell) is arguing fiercely with her producer (and lover) Gordon Dunning (Leon Ames).

BROADWAY BABIES

If the lights of Times Square recalled the movies' outward spectacle, a deeper link could be found in the dozens of low-rise buildings, just off the square, that gave the district its essential character. In Broadway's legitimate theaters, the Hollywood studio found its long-lost sibling, and quickly rekindled a relationship that would, in time, change them both forever.

The family connection was obvious: as the two great workshops of American entertainment, the Broadway playhouse and the Hollywood soundstage shared common ancestry and common purpose. Unlike almost any other structure, both were vessels of performance, built to enclose an infinite variety of stories and environments, to hold universes within themselves. It was a parallel filmmakers were not slow to discover or exploit.

The meeting ground was a new genre, made possible only by the advent of synchronized sound in 1927, but quickly becoming a staple of American films: the musical. Indeed, Broadway not only found a place in the movie musical but, virtually from the start, occupied its center. For of all the types of film musicals that have flourished over the decades—period operettas, ballroom duos, even filmed versions of real Broadway productions—which has defined the genre better than those countless films about putting on a Broadway show?

We know the characters by heart: the hard-driving director; the reluctant backer; the tough-talking chorus girls; the glamorous but haughty star; and the young but talented newcomer, with stars in his or (more likely) her eyes. We know the story even better: the endless rehearsals, the last-minute disaster, the unknown snatched from the chorus line and given the lead, the opening night sensation. From its earliest incarnation in MGM's *Broadway Melody* and in Warner's *42nd Street*, *Footlight Parade*, and *Gold Diggers* series, to endless later variations (*Born to Dance*, *Babes on Broadway*, *The Band Wagon*) to more recent appearances in the form of homage or parody (in *Movie Movie*, *The Producers*, *The Muppets Take Manhattan*, *All That Jazz*) the movie musical has been dominated by a tradition summed up by *42nd Street*'s famous line: "You're going out there a youngster, but you've got to come back a star!" "Out there," need it be said, is a fictional Broadway show, set on a fictional Broadway stage (201).

201. ***42nd Street*** **(1933).** In the final number of "Pretty Lady," *42nd Street*'s show within the show, chorus girl Peggy Sawyer (Ruby Keeler) dances atop a taxi as an elaborate street set appears in the background. The film's musical numbers, directed by Busby Berkeley, were filmed at Warner's Sunset Boulevard lot in Hollywood.

Why should this be so? Why should films about the making of an imaginary Broadway show be more central to film musicals than *real* Broadway shows, brought over from New York? One answer lies in a peculiarity of the form itself. Characters in musicals must regularly burst into song and dance, an unlikely occurrence that somehow has to be rationalized if the film is to remain plausible. "The means of moving from one order of reality or style to another," writes Gerald Mast, "became a conceptual problem for every musical film: What conventions would lead from the ordinary prose of conversation to the poeticized expansiveness of song and dance?"

From the moment movies learned to talk, one answer was obvious. "The conceptual problem evaporates," Mast explains,

> *if the musical film's narrative happens to be about a musical performer. . . . Musical performers perform as a matter of course—on a stage, to be sure, but they might even perform in some spontaneous and improvised way within everyday settings, since performers are likely to do just about anything. Performance is a way of life.*

As its title made plain, *The Jazz Singer*, the first movie musical, was just this: the story of a performer (played by the inimitable Al Jolson) struggling to break into show business. But two developments harkened the arrival of the true backstager. The first was the realization that widening the focus from a single performer to an entire company offered far greater potential for narrative interplay and dramatic urgency. The second was that, with the notable exception of Jolson himself, real Broadway stars turned out to have limited appeal to national movie audiences. Performers as celebrated in New York as Fanny Brice and Harry Richman repeatedly failed to carry musical films to success. "The media and audiences were different," the film scholar Richard Barrios has noted, "and idiosyncratic stars that played well across Manhattan footlights wouldn't necessarily go well in Topeka in big unflattering close-ups." For Hollywood, the solution was a familiar one: replace real Broadway performers with invented "Broadway" stars of their own. Out of these building blocks an imaginary theater district would be constructed.

And that was precisely what the first audiences saw: an invented Broadway, encompassing theaters, of course, but extending far beyond the footlights to an entire district of excitement and temptation. With titles like *Broadway Scandals, Broadway Babies, Show Girl, Chasing Rainbows, Puttin' on the Ritz,* and *Glorifying the American Girl,* backstagers were by far the most common kind of early movie musical. Of these, only Rouben Mamoulian's 1929 *Applause*—the story of an aging burlesque queen (Helen Morgan) filmed, significantly, not in Hollywood but at Paramount's Astoria studio—sought to suggest with any realism the sad or sordid aspects of theatrical life; the others were content to revel in a fictive haze of bright lights and show numbers, trading on the district's potent reputation for sex and danger, and intent—as an ad for *Broadway Babies* put it—to "out-Broadway Broadway."

The full implications of this promise became evident in February 1929, with the release of *Broadway*. As a hit stage play in 1927, *Broadway* had told of a struggling dancer in a shabby Times Square nightclub who dreamed of someday playing the Palace. For Universal, the story would be a vehicle to an entirely different urban realm:

> *You'll see things you never saw before in "Broadway." You'll be plunged deep into the blazing heart of New York's mad night life! You'll see people you wouldn't believe existed doing things you wouldn't believe possible!*

In the film, the "shabby nightclub" would be transformed by the art director Charles "Danny" Hall into an Art Deco extravaganza seventy feet high and two hundred feet long. Hall's extraordinary three-level design proved too big to fit into any of Universal's existing stages; unfazed, studio executives ordered the construction of a *new* stage, the largest in Hollywood. The completed set, cinematographer Hal Mohr later recalled, "was like Grand Central Station. It was so big it was almost impossible" (202).

> *This little honky-tonk that [the dancer] was trying to work his way out of turned out to be something like you've never seen in your entire life. . . . Here he wanted to play the Palace—well that nightclub could have taken the Palace, the Winter Garden and the Hippodrome all in one!*

Though it centered on a stage area, the Paradise Club was not a conventional theater; instead, built fully in the round, with tiers of seating on all sides,

202. ***Broadway*** **(1929).** The design of the Paradise Club, by Charles "Danny" Hall, was to be "symbolic not only of one of Broadway's glittering pleasure palaces," the film's press book noted, "but of New York as a whole." At center is the twenty-eight-ton "Broadway" crane, built at a cost of fifty thousand dollars, whose platform could move six hundred feet per minute in any direction.

the set offered unprecedented possibilities for action from top to bottom—possibilities exploited by a remarkable device called the "Broadway crane," the largest camera crane ever built, which featured an arm over forty feet long and which could, in Mohr's words, "do everything but bake beans." With breathtaking mobility, the crane flies all around the vast multilevel interior, swooping down on the show, then rising to the upper balconies before suddenly pivoting back to look down at the stage floor, now forty feet away. As the camera zooms over the balconies—glimpsing wild scenes of revelry among the patrons—the giddy motion and riotous decor combine to make us as lightheaded as if we had joined the party ourselves. The chorus girls on stage are just a small part of the fun; a sense of abandon permeates absolutely every inch of the place. The film fulfills its promise—to present a Broadway that is a seamless web of excitement, a place where the intensity of performance becomes a way of life (203).

203. ***Broadway* (1929).** A dancer named Roy Lane (Glenn Tryon) greets Pearl (Evelyn Brent), a member of a chorus whose vibrant costumes and towering headdresses, designed by Johanna Mathieson, joined on stage to suggest a city skyline.

Yet for all its energy, *Broadway* offered few of the elements now associated with the classic backstager. It was another film, opening two months later, that codified the genre and marked the true inauguration of the movie city's theater district: MGM's *The Broadway Melody.*

We are brought into that district in the very first scene, set in a music publishing house called Gleason's. That this is *not* a theater is much to the point. As in the real city, this theatrical district comprises a large, intricate network of allied operations, radiating from the theaters themselves: rehearsal halls, music publishers, boarding houses, and theatrical agents, all clustered around Times Square, and all places where entertainers might be likely to perform in a casual, spontaneous way.

The film quickly introduces the musical's essential cast of characters: the starstruck neophytes, Hank and Queenie Mahoney (Bessie Love and Anita Page), anxious to make it big on Broadway; the veteran songwriter, Eddie Kerns (Charles King), promising to help them beat the long odds against success; the magisterial producer, Frances Zanfield (his name an obvious play on that of the famed impresario Florenz Ziegfeld), faced with a thousand decisions to be made about sets, costumes, and talent. And the film enshrines, in primitive form, the classic structure of the backstager: an increasingly formal series of performances, from auditions to dress rehearsal to opening night, culminating in the presentation of the show in a Broadway theater.

The heart of that show is a number itself called "Broadway Melody." With its lyrics telling of the promise and heartbreak of the Great White Way and its painted setting of skyscrapers and Times Square, the song introduces another staple of the movies' invented Broadway—its habit of actively mythologizing itself, through performances that, as often as not, were celebrations of the district that made them possible. Significantly, this "Broadway Melody" number remains entirely stagebound: the camera sits rigidly planted in the "audience," viewing a performance staged before a cloth backdrop whose ripples and seams are plainly visible. Except for a few close-ups of a tap dancer's feet, we see exactly what a member of the audience might see, watching from the orchestra seats.

Not least of the film's innovations, the historian Ethan Morrden has noted, was the idea of having its show-within-the-show be a musical revue, in order to answer any concerns about narrative continuity. And indeed, the numbers that make up that show are so varied that it is difficult to grasp the gist of the whole. Still, *Broadway Melody* carried the fiction of the play-within-the-film to a certain extreme, as revealed in publicity stills of the cast assembled proudly beneath a billboard of "credits" not of the actual film but of the invented *show*, also called "The Broadway Melody," featuring everyone from producer Zanfield and songwriter Kerns to costumes by a someone named "Dell Turpe," staging by a man called "Beau Mont," and lyrics by a writer named "Jack Strange."

Jack Strange, indeed. An imaginary lyricist, writing the songs for an imaginary show being mounted in an imaginary theater, which is in turn located in an imaginary theater district. There is a fullness of invention here that begins to hint at why the movies' "Broadway" extended the notion of a mythic city one final, remarkable step. But it would be another film, four years later, that fully revealed the power of this invented district to activate the mythic metropolis all around it.

THE SHOW GOES ON

The dramatic success of *The Broadway Melody* inspired a raft of imitators—almost all of them flops. Indeed, by 1933 the backstager had become so moribund as a genre that Warner's announcement of a new project was considered daring, if not foolhardy. But the quality and impact of the new film, *42nd Street*, would single-handedly reestablish the backstager as the center of the movie musical tradition, this time for good.

42nd Street retained many of the elements pioneered in *The Broadway Melody*, but deployed them to far greater effect, being at once more specific and more fantastic—more precisely reflective of the real theater district, yet more open to the possibilities available only to the filmic version of it. At first, the theater would be evoked with sharp, precise bursts of dialogue and staging; later, that same theater, so carefully delineated, would be exploded into something new and extraordinary. Mixing accurate rendition and imaginative transfiguration to compelling effect, *42nd Street* would suggest the ultimate metaphor for the movie city itself.

The instinct for specificity reveals itself at once, by literally pinpointing our location. After an aerial view flies us north on Broadway, a montage of street signs takes us east to west across 42nd Street, fixing our lines of longitude and latitude, as it were, to the precise place at which they meet: Times Square.

Soon we learn what sort of place this is. News that "Jones and Barry are doing a show" passes as urgent gossip from bedrooms to receptionists to telephone linemen, all sharing a tight circle of interest. From the district's inner sanctum—the office of Jones and Barry themselves—we learn of Broadway as not only a place consumed, but consuming. The brilliant, arrogant Julian Marsh (Warner Baxter) agrees to direct a new show, "*Pretty Lady*," even as he discovers he is dying. "It's my last show and it's got to be the best," he says, looking out the window to the place he has given his life and spirit, the place he calls "that gulch down there."

204. ***42nd Street*** **(1933).** Filmed by Lloyd Bacon in Warner's "Vitaphone Theater"—a standing set located on the studio's Burbank lot—the film's non-musical sequences explored every corner of the theater interior. In this view, the camera looks down from the upper reaches of the fly space to an audition in progress onstage.

Now the focus narrows still further, converging on the structure that *42nd Street* would explore as no film before it. A dramatic shot flies us across the interior of what looks to be a full-sized theater. It is. At Warner's Burbank studio was located the "Vitaphone Theater" set, which, redressed again and again, would serve as the major setting for all of the studio's backstagers. Complete with orchestra seats, balconies and boxes, a full proscenium, and an extensive backstage, the Vitaphone set (here called the "42nd Street Theater") offers us what *Broadway Melody* never did, a clear and comprehensive physical framework for what is to come.

What kind of a place is a theater, anyway? At first, it seems a place of two halves. In front is the auditorium—the "house"—whose elegant ornament, plush red carpet, and velvet-lined seats can accommodate an audience in style and comfort; for now, however, with its seats draped with white cloth, it is a quiet, almost ghostly environment.

At the moment, our attention is turned to the other half. Architecturally, backstage is everything the auditorium isn't: utilitarian instead of plush, a place of work rather than pleasure, not really a "designed" space at all but a functional environment of brick walls and mechanical equipment. Yet with its high fly loft, its dressing rooms tucked around corners (or up a spiral staircase and along a raised catwalk), its thicket of cables and ropes, its stacks of scenic flats—not to mention the broad stage itself, with its battered rehearsal piano, worn wooden floorboards and bare-bulb "equity lights"—backstage turns out to have a distinctive character of its own (204).

It was for its keen rendering of backstage life that *42nd Street* first won acclaim. Compared to *Broadway Melody*'s almost notional presentation of the world behind the curtain, in *42nd Street* we are *there:* from the cattle-call auditions filling the stage with tart-tongued chorines like Una Merkel and Ginger Rogers, to the risqué dressing room encounters between the veteran "juvenile" Billy Lawler (Dick Powell) and newcomer Peggy Sawyer (Ruby Keeler), to the rehearsals in the lobby with star Bebe Daniels and the harassed playwright. The film's sharp wit and rapid-fire pace, celebrated for breathing new life into the backstage genre, are complemented by a precise feeling for the physicality of production as the numbers in *Pretty Lady* begin to take shape. One senses that they are in fact *pieces*, yet to be integrated into a shapely whole—a process relentless and sometimes brutal, as when Marsh throws out a number in disgust: "It smells! What do you think we're putting on here, a revival?" And indeed the piece (which we have just seen) does seem static and lifeless. Allowed to peer over Marsh's shoulder, as it were, we share the process of creation; we can judge for ourselves.

At last the rehearsals are over, and the pieces of scenery arrive; in keeping with the tradition of *Broadway Melody*, these turn out to be elements of New York itself: a subway entrance, a fire hydrant, and a city sidewalk on whose "curb" Marsh now sits, surrounded by the world he has brought into being by sheer force of will. Having come to know the backstage as a field of unremitting drive and superhuman effort, we see a hint of its transformation into something else—a new kind of space that is about to take over both the theater and the film.

But not before the legendary sequence of last-minute tragedy and triumph. When, on the eve of the preview, a drunk and angry Bebe Daniels takes a fall and breaks her ankle, it seems to be the end of the show, and of everyone's hopes and dreams. The next morning, however, an unlikely alternative is proposed: chorus girl Peggy Sawyer. After compressing a month's worth of rehearsals into a few intense hours, Marsh steps outside the dressing room to render his verdict: "All right," he shouts, "the show goes on!"

Then comes the famous speech, delivered moments before Peggy steps in front of the audience. "Now listen to me," Marsh tells her,

> *listen hard. Two hundred people—two hundred jobs—two hundred thousand dollars—five weeks of grind and blood and sweat—depend on you. It's the lives of all these people who've worked with you. You've got to go on—and you've got to give—and give and give—They've GOT to like you—GOT to—you understand—you can't fall down. . . . Now keep your feet on the ground and your head on those shoulders of yours, and go out. And Sawyer—you're going out a youngster, but you've* got to come back a star!

"No one should come to New York to live," E. B. White once wrote, "who is not willing to be lucky." The city had long been regarded, in the Horatio Alger sense, as a place of personal advancement. But this scene recast that vague notion into something more specific, and far more thrilling. That one could be plucked from obscurity and transformed into a star, *overnight*, became a central, animating New York myth. Indeed, it could be argued that the city's theatrical community could not function were it not for the thousands of obsessed young performers who come to New York, willing to work long hours for little pay, in the hopes of achieving a destiny established first and foremost by the mythic city of the movies.

42nd Street is far from over. In a way, in fact, it is just beginning; for having shown us the grueling rehearsals and preparations, it now presents us with their result: *Pretty Lady* itself—or at least several big chunks of it, in three musical numbers. To do so, the film must depart the space that it has delineated so brilliantly—backstage—to activate the theater's two other parts. One is the auditorium, now alive with an appreciative first-night audience. The other is the elusive third space of the theater, its ultimate reason for being. This is, of course, the space of the show itself: a "virtual" space that borrows the backstage's floor area and one of the auditorium's four walls, then superimposes onto them an identity all its own.

That this is indeed a different kind of space is confirmed by a surprising fact of *42nd Street*'s production. While the backstage scenes were shot in the Vitaphone Theater at the Burbank studio, the show numbers of *Pretty Lady* were filmed not only on another lot but in another *city*: at Warner's old studio on Sunset Boulevard, in Hollywood itself. As it happens, they were also directed by a different man: not Lloyd Bacon, who had brought crackling pace and wit to the rehearsal scenes, but someone relatively new to movies, a dance director named Busby Berkeley.

Having made his name in the late 1920s with spectacular dance routines for several Broadway shows, Berkeley had been brought out to Hollywood by Samuel Goldwyn before being lured over to Warner's by producer Darryl F. Zanuck, who hoped Berkeley's innovative approach would bring new life to the stiff, unimaginative staging of filmed show numbers.

It was an approach that at once complemented and contradicted everything that had gone before. If the rest of *42nd Street* had been notable for its careful, realistic rendering of the theater's interior, Berkeley's sequences would explode that space, creating a world with its own rules, transcending anything possible in a real Broadway house.

He introduces it gradually. *Pretty Lady*'s first number, "Shuffle Off to Buffalo," remains utterly stagebound. A passenger train heading for Niagara Falls splits open to reveal the sleeping compartments within—a remarkable set, to be sure, but still plainly a *set*, a distinctly theatrical construction, plausibly fitting into a proscenium stage. At its conclusion, we return to the wings, and watch the cast take their places. We are still very much in a theater.

It is the next number, "Young and Healthy," that crosses the great divide;

here the backstager departs theatrical reality for a realm that can exist only in the movie city. It starts more or less conventionally: Dick Powell singing alone on the stage, then joined by a chorus. But as the floor starts to revolve, we notice something strange. The size of the stage seems to have increased dramatically; it has grown much larger than the one in the Vitaphone Theater, which we have come to know quite well. And there is something even stranger going on: we are suddenly looking straight *down* on the dancers as they form dazzling kaleidoscopic images. This was Berkeley's famous "top shot," and it embodied his fundamental insight—that the movie camera and soundstage allowed for pictorial possibilities far beyond the fixed, frontal viewpoints of real theaters. It was an inspiration that became the stuff of legend. One story has Zanuck coming onto the stage during production and finding the director in the rafters, looking down on the stage floor. "What the hell are you doing up there?" Zanuck shouted. "You can't take an audience up there!" "I know," Berkeley replied, "but I'd like to. It's awful pretty up here."

For all its appeal, the top shot presented a conceptual conundrum. It is, after all, part of a number that is supposed to be occurring in a Broadway theater. If so, *how is the audience viewing it?* Have they suddenly been carried up to special seats in the fly loft, directly above the stage? Apparently not, for the reaction shot immediately following the number shows the audience in their usual orchestra seats, wildly applauding a routine they couldn't possibly have appreciated from where they were sitting. Indeed, these reaction shots would become a standard feature of Berkeley's later films, as if to reassure moviegoers that these astonishing numbers were, somehow or other, transpiring in real Broadway theaters. This quality of exuberant fantasy, presented always within an insistent realism, suggested another intriguing metaphor for the mythic city as a whole.

If the kaleidoscopic patterns of "Young and Healthy" dazzled the eye with spatial possibilities available only to the movie city's theaters, the epic final number would employ that spatial magic as merely one element in a production that sought to capture nothing less than the city itself. It is the theatrical climax of *Pretty Lady* and its name, "42nd Street," again recalls the cyclical spirit of *Broadway Melody* by turning the theme of the show back to the larger urban context. But the crude painted backdrop of the earlier film now gives way to a dazzling three-dimensional rendering of the city, panoramic in scope, filled to the brim with urban vignettes—and *still* supposedly housed within the confines of a Broadway stage.

Standing in front of a vaudeville-style painted backdrop, Keeler first beckons us to "come and see those dancing feet"—but as car horns and street noises blare the camera reveals that Keeler is dancing not on the stage floor but atop a taxicab that has somehow appeared beneath her. As she descends, we pull back to see a deeply receding city scene, its pedestrians—apple sellers, policemen, newsboys—all rushing about in a jaunty, dancelike step (201). Soon the camera carries us to an elegant city district, where a fashionable woman walks her dog, a doorman tips his hat, a nursemaid burps her baby—all in time to the music.

Moving along, the scene turns stranger. Two fruit vendors close up their pushcart and don golf bags and plus-fours, hurrying off to the links. A drunk staggers up the steps of the Hotsy Totsy Club to encounter a wooden cigar-store Indian who, bursting into a little dance, sends the startled inebriate back to the bar. Now we come to a seedy part of town. A man in a doorway tips his hat to a string of women—prostitutes, of course—walking into the "Enterprise Hotel." Through an upper window we see a couple having a brutal fight. The woman escapes through the window and onto a ledge, taking a desperate flying leap into the crowd below—only to be caught, happily, by an Apache dancer on the street. She begins to dance with her savior and all seems resolved when her enraged spouse emerges from the building door and stabs her in the back. She falls in the Apache's arms and a crowd gathers, as the camera climbs the side of the building to find Dick Powell in evening clothes, watching the whole scene from the comfort of his second-floor flat. While a bartender shakes the next martini (still keeping time), Powell toasts the "crazy quilt" of 42nd Street—as if it were a show he has been watching from the balcony.

As the number nears its end, the facades of 42nd Street are rolled away and a group of chorus girls carrying signboards begins dancing up a bleacherlike flight of stairs. They turn around, revealing each signboard to be a building facade, together creating a dancing skyline. A crane shot flies over the painted buildings, recalling the opening shot of the film itself, when we flew up Broadway above the ziggurat tops of midtown. Thus we have been carried full circle: from the city, into Times Square, into the 42nd Street Theater and its musical show and then, within the show, back out to Times Square and finally to the whole city again, now represented in a simple, vivid analogy: each dancer is a building; the chorus is New York.

In one last transformation, the signboards turn into a single enormous building, with Keeler and Powell united at its peak. The camera cranes up again to join them and, as they kiss, an asbestos curtain comes down, at last restoring some sense of theatrical reality to this sprawling, three-dimensional extravaganza. The film itself concludes back at the theater; the audience exits happily while, with infinite poignancy, the dying Julian Marsh sits alone on a fire escape just outside the stage door.

If *Pretty Lady* was for Marsh an ending, it was for Busby Berkeley just a beginning. In three films produced for Warner's over the next eighteen months, he would boldly extend the conceptual conundrum that *42nd Street* had introduced, insisting on the theatrical plausibility of the productions even as their lavishness and complexity reached absurd levels.

The rehearsal scenes in *Gold Diggers of 1933*, for example, work especially hard to convince us of their theatrical reality, with glimpses of the brightly lighted stage as seen from the dark recesses of the wings. But when the show itself (*The Forgotten Melody*) commences, all hints of a traditional proscenium give way to a string of titanic productions ("Pettin' in the Park," "The Shadow Waltz," "Remember My Forgotten Man") that not only could never be staged in any Broadway theater, but challenged the resources of one of Hollywood's biggest studios. No longer content with the crane he had used on *42nd Street*, Berkeley constructed a special "monorail" (which actually ran on two tracks) that could be raised and lowered like an elevator while sliding forward and back like a trolley. Trying to capture ever more dramatic top shots, Berkeley found himself up in the rafters, sixty feet above the stage floor; still not satisfied, he ordered openings cut in the roof, allowing his camera to be placed a few feet higher. (In time, Berkeley cut holes in five or six stage roofs, infuriating the front office. "I've left my mark at Warner Brothers' studios," he later quipped.) For Berkeley's next film, *Footlight Parade* (1933), the maneuvers necessary for an audience to view the musical numbers would have theoretically included not only rising up into the fly loft but somehow descending beneath the stage for the underwater ballet sequences in "By a Waterfall." In *Dames* (1934), the paradox reaches a climax of sorts. Even as the backstage scenes are filled with convincing theatrical detail—the grips, the lighting supervisor with his cue sheet, the frantic jumble of actors and scenery behind the curtain—the show itself (*Sweet and Hot*) transcends theatrical space more completely than ever before. "I Only Have Eyes for You" is set in a city complete with real automobiles, hundreds of pedestrians, full-sized streets and buildings, a subway station, a subway train, and, finally, an entire subway yard with nearly a dozen trains arrayed on their tracks.

Though a few skeptics grumbled that some of Berkeley's musical numbers could hardly have been staged in anything smaller than Yankee Stadium, most audiences seemed willing to suspend their disbelief and accept both parts of the film, the backstage rehearsals and the "shows" themselves, as somehow enclosed within the volume of an ordinary theater—at least the kind found in the movies' mythical Broadway.

From the start, critics were also intrigued by the unusual structure of the films, which essentially abandon conventional storytelling at the halfway point and are given over to full-length performances of the numbers from the show-within-the-show. In the context of a mythic city, this unusual structure prompts a provocative notion. When we watch the performances of *Pretty Lady* or *Forgotten Melody* or *Sweet and Hot*—shows that never appeared in a real Broadway theater, needless to say, but only in the invented Broadway of the movies—it could be argued that we are no longer looking in on the mythic city but have instead *entered it.* During the forty minutes or so that the numbers run, we occupy exactly the same time and space as inhabitants of the mythic New York; it is as if we have walked into a theater in the movie city and are sitting among its audience, watching the same show that they would be watching, judging entirely for ourselves whether we like it or not.

"Houses make a town," Rousseau once wrote, "but citizens make a city." A city is more than a series of physical settings, however complex: it is a vital organism, generating a culture of its own. The mythic city, too, turns out to be more than just a series of places: the backstager reveals it in the process of creating its own culture, and then, most remarkably, allows us to enjoy the fruit of that culture by entering its theaters, taking a seat ourselves, and enjoying the show.

STAGE STRUCK

Responding to the backstager's stunning revival at Warner's, MGM scrambled to recapture the genre they regarded in many ways as their own. Their *Broadway Melody* sequels carried little of Warner's energy and drive but did offer, in classic Metro fashion, a string of dazzling settings, utterly detached from any theatrical reality. In MGM's Broadway, the most humble dressing room or manager's office might resemble one of the more stylish interiors of Rockefeller Center, while the theaters themselves were typically streamlined Art Deco masterpieces. (Occupying two adjacent soundstages, MGM's main theater set boasted a "stage" designed by the architects of Radio City Music Hall, complete with hydraulic lifts and a contour curtain similar to the original in New York.) In one backstager after another, these films told the familiar story of a talented unknown—Eleanor Powell, say, or Judy Garland—achieving sudden stardom, each picture shamelessly recycling not only the plots but often the songs of earlier films (especially "Broadway Rhythm" and "The Broadway Melody" by Arthur Freed and Nacio Herb Brown). And unlike Warner's Broadway, which rarely strayed far from Times Square, MGM's theatrical world stretched over to the blocks near Sutton Place, where sophisticated theatrical couples (like Fred Astaire and Ginger Rogers in *The Barkleys of Broadway*, 1949) maintained elegant apartments with expansive views of the East River.

It was a quality of Metro's backstagers that—unlike many films in the movie city—they were conscious of history, at least in an anecdotal way. In part this was a recognition that the "Broadway" their films were discovering was, in fact, a place whose hold on the American imagination stretched back to the turn of the century, if not before. MGM's embrace of fabled producer Florenz Ziegfeld, for example, in *The Great Ziegfeld* (1936), *Ziegfeld Girl* (1941), and *Ziegfeld Follies* (1944), made clear the studio's presumption of a direct lineage from the past master of American popular spectacle. But the approach was also a response to the sense of time and history that is woven into any stage. In *Babes on Broadway* (1941), Mickey Rooney and Judy Garland explore an old playhouse, long used for storage, in which they plan to mount a new show. The place is musty and creepy, Judy complains. "Every theater is a haunted house," Mickey reminds her. "Think of all the shows that have been in this theater. Flops, suc-

205. ***Broadway Melody of 1938*** **(1937).** Rising tier by tier as Eleanor Powell's number progresses, the glowing, faceted towers (designed by MGM art directors Joseph Wright and Edwin Willis) were evidently inspired by the Art Deco skyscrapers of architect Ralph Walker, especially the Irving Trust Building at One Wall Street.

MARILYN MILLER
Charlie Chaplin
LEW FIELDS
BROADWAY MELODY

cesses, bad shows, great shows. It's all around us right now. Laughter, applause, cheers." Drawing on some old props and costumes and inspired by the faded names on the crates and posters, Mickey and Judy proceed to animate the theater's "ghosts," re-creating the monologues of Richard Mansfield and Sarah Bernhardt and the numbers of Fay Templeton and George M. Cohan.

Broadway Melody of 1938 stretched this sense of continuity to include the future as well as the past. Visiting a theatrical boardinghouse, producer Robert Taylor is impressed by the vibrant memories of its stage veterans; his new show, he decides, will include a performance by the house's proprietor, played by Sophie Tucker. Onstage, Tucker fondly recalls the vanished era of Jolson, Cohan, and Lillian Russell. But even as she sings of the past, a Broadway of the future—a fantastic array of crystalline towers, accented by lights and signs—emerges behind her, rising as we watch, tier by tier, until it is surmounted by a skyline made up solely of lighted profiles, a luminescent urbanism to which the city of the future might aspire (205).

Another historic shift was suggested in *The Band Wagon* (1953), the MGM backstager that mixed past and present (as well as fact and fiction) in the person of Fred Astaire, returning to Broadway after decades in Hollywood. Walking along 42nd Street, he is stunned by the sight of its tawdry, crowded avenues and garish storefronts filled with penny arcades, bars, and movies like *Jungle Tigress*:

> *I just can't get over it. I can't understand it. This used to be the great theater street of the town. The New Amsterdam—I had one of my biggest successes there. Noël and Gertie were over there in* Private Lives *at the Selwyn. Strictly carriage trade, you know what I mean? Why, the first show I ever did was at the Eltinge, and I don't even believe that's here any more.*

In fact, the change Fred decries had been under way at least since the 1930s, when the legitimate theater decamped an increasingly raucous 42nd Street for a cluster of quieter streets to the north. Here, midway between Seventh and Eighth Avenues, could be found block after block lined with theatrical playhouses, the heartland of American drama.

If less prominent than musicals, dramas still had a clear place in the firmament of the movies' mythic Broadway. *All About Eve* (1950), for example, offers us *Aged in Wood*, an imaginary vehicle for the veteran star Margo Channing (Bette Davis), playing at the very real Golden Theater on 45th Street (206). A closer, more intimate look at Broadway's "high" theatrical culture is offered in *A Double Life* (1947)—directed by George Cukor from a script by Ruth Gordon and Garson Kanin—which follows an established Broadway leading man, played by Ronald Colman, through the mounting of a new production of *Othello*. Shot in the venerable (and soon to be demolished) Empire Theater on 39th Street, the film is notable for Colman's stream-of-consciousness narration but even more so for Cukor's remarkably mobile camera, which moves constantly from stage to audience and back, showing us not only the actors as seen by the audience, but the audience as seen by the actors. The result is striking. Even as we gradually inhabit the violent, jealous Shakespearean character, losing ourselves in the "world" of the play, we remain aware that Colman is, in fact, an actor performing a role—that we are not in sixteenth-century Venice but in a playhouse just off Broadway, being watched by hundreds of strangers. We almost viscerally experience, in other words, the strange "double life" that inheres to any theater—and to any actor.

Another institution unique to Broadway provided the subject of *Stage Door* (1938): a boardinghouse for aspiring actresses known as the Rehearsal Club. Renamed the Footlights Club in the film, the establishment sustains a handful of the thousands of struggling young women who come to New York each year to achieve stardom. A hotbed of youth, talent, and ambition, it is the theater district in microcosm, Broadway as seen from up close—perhaps *too* close, as suggested by a giant theatrical sign outside the window, filling the bedroom with its garish blinking light and making it almost impossible to sleep.

206. ***All About Eve* (1950).** Though the exteriors of Joseph Mankiewicz's film were shot outside the Golden Theater on 45th Street, the interiors were actually filmed in the Curran Theater in San Francisco—including this scene of Eve Harrington (Anne Baxter) and Bill Simpson (Gary Merrill) rehearsing on stage as producer Max Fabian (Gregory Ratoff), playwright Lloyd Richards (Hugh Marlowe), and Richards's wife, Karen (Celeste Holm), look on.

Like musical backstagers, films of the New York drama world offered a chance to glimpse the routine, daytime existence of a place meant for nighttime glamour; in *All About Eve* there is an odd, behind-the-scenes pleasure in seeing the theater's interior in the afternoon, its quiet broken only by the sound of cleaning ladies vacuuming the carpet. *A Double Life* also lingers on the theater's quotidian rituals; early on we see Colman walking out of the Empire's stage entrance into the bright afternoon, chatting familiarly with grips hauling signs and scenery. For those who toiled there, of course, Broadway theaters were places of full-time work and life; at least one film, *Stage Struck* (1957), made that "everyday" world its major theme.

Stage Struck was a remake of *Morning Glory* (1933), which a quarter-century earlier had catapulted Katharine Hepburn to fame as Eva Lovelace, an eager young actress just arrived on Broadway, wandering theater lobbies and gazing lovingly upon busts of Cornelia Otis Skinner and Katherine Cornell. The remake, starring Susan Strasberg and filmed by Sidney Lumet in New York's real theater district, updated the familiar fable of overnight stardom with a detailed depiction of the "real" Broadway: not the glitter of Times Square but the blocks just to the west, the authentic home of the business and art of American drama. These blocks offered a panorama of their own—a phalanx of classic Broadway theaters, packed solidly along 45th Street: the Booth, the Plymouth, the Royale—all rendered on a surprisingly intimate scale with their low rooflines, ornate facades, and string of glassy, glittering canopies (a scale and delicacy later compromised drastically by the behemoth constructions of the 1980s). Though not without its legendary qualities—we catch marquee names ranging from John Drew to, again, Cornelia Otis Skinner—we see this as a living *district*, with its local landmarks (Sardi's on 44th Street) and its distinctive rituals (standing outside the *Times*'s truck docks, waiting for the overnight reviews). In one scene, Lovelace's career is changed by a chance sidewalk encounter with a playwright; just being in the district, walking its streets, opens prospects not otherwise available.

When the film leaves the streets and enters the theater for rehearsals, we sense, as hardly ever before, the high, hollow volume of a real Broadway interior, the worn floorboards of its stage. And when it eventually offers up, as it must, the classic scene of Lovelace's sudden star turn, it forces us to wait patiently through the lengthy backstage process of precurtain cueing for lighting and sound effects. More than the most authentic of backstagers, *Stage Struck* reminds us that the much-vaunted "magic" of the theater occurs in the context of everyday routine, spread across three dozen theaters on half a dozen blocks.

It was, finally, this remarkable concentration—not only of the theaters themselves but of the different theatrical "worlds" occurring within them every night, side by side—that made Broadway a place like no other. Most films, portraying a single show in a single theater, did not even try to convey this many-sided phenomenon; one scene in a film called *No Time For Comedy* (1940), however, actually played it for laughs. Jimmy Stewart, a young playwright whose first show is premiering on Broadway, turns to liquor to blunt his opening-night jitters; staggering down the sidewalk, blind drunk and dazed by the whirl of a half-dozen adjacent marquees, he mistakenly passes his own show and walks instead into the theater next door, where a murder mystery is in progress. Standing at the rear of the house, still tipsy, he grows furious with the realization that somehow, behind his back, gunshots and screams have been inserted into his light romantic comedy. Only an angry confrontation with his director, back out on the sidewalk, finally sets him straight. Meanwhile, we have caught a glimpse of what must be one of the world's most extraordinary "cross-sections": the simultaneous series of alternative realities—funny and scary, common and exotic, dramatic and musical—that proceed, every night, in the row of adjacent, brick-and-plaster boxes we call Broadway theaters.

THAT'S SHOW BIZ

The brassy score (by Elmer Bernstein) and the jazzy lights (photographed by James Wong Howe) tell us right off that we have plunged back into the heart of Broadway—not the genteel sidestreets of legitimate theater but the raucous center of mass culture, the populist capital of hoopla and hype that is Times

Square itself. Indeed, as directed by Alexander Mackendrick, *The Sweet Smell of Success* (1957) offers the most charged portrait ever drawn of the people's Broadway that arose parallel to the theater district, a Broadway of nightclubs and tabloids, of hatcheck girls and press agents, and of powerful gossip columnists such as the "Voice of Broadway": J. J. Hunsecker (Burt Lancaster) of the New York *Globe*, a figure based directly on Walter Winchell, the legendary *Daily Mirror* columnist (8).

Viewed from one of the *Globe*'s delivery trucks, making its rounds through the district as the soundtrack's brass reaches its shrieking climax, Times Square's signs appear more frenetic and compelling than ever; it takes a stack of tossed newspapers, hitting the pavement with an audible thunk, to draw our eyes from the distant blaze of light and bring them down, literally, to sidewalk level. Grabbing a copy, press agent Sidney Falco (Tony Curtis) retreats from the busy, brightly illuminated sidewalks of Seventh Avenue to an even busier and brighter all-night lunch counter. The intense white glare and packed midnight crowds suggest Broadway as a dazzling but unnatural environment, a place in which—since night has somehow been turned into day—inversions of all kinds must surely rule (207).

207. Filming *The Sweet Smell of Success* (1957). Taking advantage of Kodak's newly released Double-X film stock—twice as sensitive to light as any commercial stock before it—cinematographer James Wong Howe was able to shoot city exteriors by night; the stock's high-contrast characteristics, moreover, offered a visual harshness that suited the mood of the story.

It is certainly a world with its own geography and schedule, a nocturnal culture that radiates out from Times Square to encompass a circuit of clubs and restaurants (Toots Shor, with its circular bar and plush banquettes; the smooth, even glow of the "Elysian Room"; the baroque, low-ceilinged splendor of "21") where columnists and press agents work their full "day" among the cavorting elite (208). Hunsecker's office at the *Globe*, seen in one of the few daytime scenes, is empty and almost unnecessary; his real work is done in an apartment atop a Broadway tower, where he ends his long night by typing up his daily column. From its terrace, he stares out upon his empire, a slash of light running through the darkened city.

Shot almost entirely on location, *The Sweet Smell of Success* presents a Times Square poised at a point of almost perfect ripeness. Everything about it is full-blown, even overblown, from Ernest Lehman and Clifford Odets's deliciously cynical dialogue (news of a young girl's suicide is greeted with a breezy "That's show biz," while the sight of a bouncer tossing an unruly drunk onto the sidewalk prompts Hunsecker to sigh, "I *love* this dirty town"), to Howe's glossy nighttime shots of the city's lights, endlessly reflected by the rain-slicked streets and gleaming cars. But beneath it all is a sense that this world cannot last, and indeed as portrayed in the film it is already palpably changing. At the old Palace Theater, once the undisputed capital of vaudeville, live comics are now reduced to filling in between film showings; in the theater where Hunsecker hosts his weekly television show, the empty, cavernous old auditorium has been put into the service of the tinny new medium that is robbing the district of its cultural dominance. In the final scene, the dark forces underneath the glitter emerge in a final paroxysm of corruption when, at the very end of a long night, Sidney Falco is brutally beaten by the police on Hunsecker's orders, even as one of the film's only innocents, Hunsecker's younger sister (Susan Harrison), at last escapes his night world, walking into the dawn. It is, we realize, the first sunlight we've seen in the entire movie.

Throughout the decade that followed, films shot on location tracked a Times Square that seemed to grow tawdrier with each passing year. The neon lights still dazzle in *Killer's Kiss* (1955), but there is a new coldness to the streets below. Under Stanley Kubrick's coolly analytic eye, the district's gaudy windows take on an unmistakable freakishness, while the painted signs for an upstairs dance hall ("50 Charming Hostesses") suggest a tired sordidness—a feeling that only enlarges inside the hall itself, where a forlorn taxi dancer played by Irene Kane (the stage name of Chris Chase) wearily fends off groping customers and a leering, aggressive boss. Despite the crowds, the sidewalks have assumed an undefinable air of menace, and the bright lights now mask a sad refuge of the lonely and friendless, the cold heart of a city of strangers. In John Cassavetes's *Shadows*, shot four years later, young Lelia Goldoni walks down 42nd Street, past marquees whose displays of half-naked women are pushing Times Square's erotic energy into an explicit raunchiness. Suddenly a man accosts her, deterred only when another (played by Cassavetes himself) pulls him away. Shaken, Lelia runs off below a marquee that reads "Girls, Inc." In *You're a Big Boy Now*, a coming-of-age film made in 1967 by Francis Ford Coppola, the district's character has almost completely transformed. For twenty-year-old Bernard (Peter Kastner), on his own for the first time and ambling under movie displays for *His Brother's Wife* and *Naked Female*, Times Square is a garden of forbidden fruit, filled with tantalizing glimpses of adult sexuality.

208. ***The Sweet Smell of Success*** **(1957).** Produced in both Hollywood and New York, the film moved between gritty, location-shot exteriors and atmospheric interiors, such as this scene of Sidney Falco and cigarette girl Rita (Barbara Nichols) in the "Elysian Room." To provide the requisite haze of tobacco, Howe brought in a smoke machine, waited patiently until it thickened, then called "action."

By the time of *Midnight Cowboy* (1969), the ripeness of *Sweet Smell of Success* has plainly turned to rot, at least along the stretches of 42nd Street and Seventh Avenue that Joe Buck (Jon Voigt) finds himself wandering. If J. J. Hunsecker and Sidney Falco represented the ultimate Broadway insiders, Joe Buck is the ultimate *out*sider, a young Texan who has come to the city and, not knowing a soul, has gravitated to one of the cheap hotels around Times Square. In sequences set to John Barry's poignant music, Joe—restless, lonely, broke—walks aimlessly around the seedy blocks of the district (209). As before, the bright marquees, turning darkness into light, serve to underline the unnatural status not only of Joe himself (who has come to the city not for stardom but to hustle rich women) but the dozens of other "Texans" he sees on the streets—

male prostitutes on the prowl for customers. What better symbol of a district that deliberately confuses night and day than a group of individuals whose name—"midnight cowboys"—evokes the same internal paradox. This is a place where all sorts of behavior unacceptable in other parts of the city is at least tolerated; a magnet for the neglected and the outcast, for homeless indigents, the mentally disturbed—all hauntingly illuminated (through Adam Holender's superb cinematography) by the bright lights that continue to perform their endless, flickering dance above.

Not surprisingly, by the 1970s, governmental and private interests had begun calling for a safer, less "deviant" Times Square—an effort that, gathering momentum over the next twenty years, would eventually transform the entire district. That effort had scarcely begun in 1980 when a new film—itself called

209. ***Midnight Cowboy*** **(1969).** Wandering the city late at night, lonely and broke, Texan newcomer Joe Buck (Jon Voigt, at left) confronts the tawdry sights of 42nd Street.

Times Square—not only prophesied the change to come, but framed the debate its arrival would spark: between those who wished to restore Times Square as a wholesome zone of popular entertainment, and those who valued the raucous, unsavory character that much of the district possessed in the 1960s and 1970s. Directed by Alan Moyle from a screenplay by Jacob Brackman, *Times Square* opens with a shot of a runaway teenager, Nicky LaMotta (Robin Johnson), dragging her few belongings along 42nd Street between Seventh and Eighth Avenues, past an array of the lurid characters who had come to inhabit that block, night and day. We see men drinking liquor from paper bags and urinating in doorways; we see other runaways, drug addicts, pimps, streetwalkers. But wait! From an office plastered with bright posters saying "Reclaim the heart of the city," two well-dressed assistants carry a model of the area's proposed redevelopment (which includes the towering Marriott Marquis Hotel, by architect John Portman, still unbuilt at the time) into a waiting van. A "Mayor's Commission for Times Square," headed by a young, ambitious, impeccably lib-

201. *Tap* (1989). Playing a tap dancer and professional thief named Max Washington Jr., Gregory Hines (second from right) helps turn a Times Square construction site—actually Universal's New York Street—into the setting for an elaborate musical number.

eral do-gooder named David Pearl (Peter Coffield), intends to "renew New York's finest and most famous landmark . . . to turn the lights back on along the Great White Way." Opposing him is Johnny LaGuardia (Tim Curry), a midnight disc jockey who, from his broadcast booth high atop the Candler Building on 42nd Street, looks down admiringly on the place he compares with "Rio at Carnival time." Calling for "vitality instead of manners," and "slime instead of plastic," Johnny finds unexpected support from David Pearl's own daughter, Pamela (Trini Alvarado), a disaffected teenager who, joining up with Nicky, becomes a symbol of resistance. Known as the "Sleez Sisters" for their outrageous antics, the two girls become performers and then folk heroes, eventually staging an unauthorized free concert atop the theater marquees of 42nd Street itself. Attempting to suggest a kind of "people's reclamation" of Times Square, this climactic scene is less convincing than an earlier, almost throwaway moment, in which the two girls, dancing down the sidewalk as the Talking Heads's "Life During Wartime" plays on the soundtrack, stage a kind of informal parade that (not unlike Rio's Carnival) draws in all kinds of bystanders, and brings alive the quality of street festival that the area always possessed.

Unquestionably idealized—conveniently ignoring the genuinely threatening character these same streets often displayed during that time, especially for women—these scenes also carry a strange, premonitory defensiveness, as if anticipating that, sooner or later, the forces of "improvement" would triumph, and the vitality that Times Square had continued to offer, even at its most disreputable, would someday need to be justified and recalled.

In the movie city, meanwhile, the old Broadway fable about putting on a show continued to demonstrate surprising allure, with filmmakers responding to the challenge of a changing Times Square, and the familiarity of the backstager itself, through a variety of approaches.

One was to adapt the old story to a new medium. The "backstages" seen in *Tootsie* (1982) and *Soapdish* (1991) are those of television soap operas; *Tootsie* in particular captured the nascent character of a new Broadway, visible in the innovative array of small playhouses and broadcasting facilities called "Theater Row," set on the western edge of 42nd Street within an urbane landscape of flower vendors, brick-paved sidewalks, live music, and outdoor cafés—the first tangible evidence of the change that would, in time, extend to the heart of 42nd Street itself.

But at least two backstagers of the era found new possibilities in the classic form. Indeed, one scene in *Tap* (1989) managed—more directly than any earlier film—to connect Broadway's artistry to the urban environment that sustained it.

In the film, Gregory Hines plays Max, the son of the late Sonny Washington, the only old-time tap dancer who, according to fellow veteran Little Mo (Sammy Davis Jr.), did not "borrow" his steps from other dancers. One night, Max lures a dance-club audience out onto the sidewalk to reveal his father's real source of inspiration: the city itself. The thump of tires over a steel plate, a random car horn—all suggest rhythmic motifs to Max, who dashes out his dance steps with a sidewalk as his stage and all of Times Square as his backdrop. Max's provocative thesis—that tap is the outgrowth of the city's restless energies, an art form sprung from the streets themselves—grows more convincing in the number that follows, ingeniously improvised from the elements of a street repair project, in progress nearby. A pile driver sets the basic beat as Max gathers his dancers around; "Don't mind us," he tells the workers, "we're just tap dancing." A bongo player enriches the beat; the club's band add brass, piano, and drums to the pulsing mix. One by one, the prosaic elements of the construction site are transformed: sheets of plywood make a tap floor; big spools of cable become elevated platforms; a window gray with construction dust becomes sheet music when the bandleader traces a staff and notes with his finger. With the work site's generator powering the amplifiers, utility floodlights serving as theater-style spots, and blinking detour lights providing a jazzy strobe, the street becomes the setting for not just a performance but a full-scale production number—an urban fantasia, ingeniously linking Broadway's physical environment and its artistic product (210).

Perhaps the most inventively reimagined backstager of more recent years looked not to the traditional theater but a nearby incubator of talent. Like *Stage Door* years before, *Fame* (1980) borrowed its setting and themes from a real

211. *Fame* (1980). Directed by Alan Parker, the film took advantage of its Times Square locations—especially in this celebrated scene, filmed on West 46th Street, in which students pour out of their high school to dance in the streets, on the sidewalks, and amidst crosstown traffic.

Broadway institution: the High School of the Performing Arts, a public school specializing in music, dance, and drama and located (until 1982) on West 44th Street, just off Times Square.

The unusual setting allowed for a fresh spin on the familiar rituals: the early auditions, filled with disappointment for some, happy surprise for others; the emphasis on sweat and discipline ("This is no Mickey Mouse school," declares one teacher); the quick and ruthless judgment of talent, or the lack of it. The film's documentary flavor allows for frequent shots of the school's gifted, hardworking students—ballerinas, modern dancers, cellists, horn players, pianists—constantly rehearsing in hallways and stair landings and practice rooms, intense vignettes of dedication and concentration. There are also the inevitable love affairs, disenchantments, and other devices that complicate the process of "putting on the show"—the show, in this case, being not so much the formal graduation performance (spirited though it is) as the students' own transformation, over four years, into professionals.

No less than an old Broadway theater, the school (whose interiors were shot at the old Haaren High on 59th Street and Tenth Avenue) is an aging survivor, its peeling walls and worn floors a weary testament to the thousands who have already passed through it; counterpointing this decrepitude, however, is the youthful vitality of the student body, as socially diverse as the modern city itself, but united by ambition and talent.

The film plays knowingly on the school's proximity to Times Square. It is where the students take their lunch or walk to school (sometimes past lurid scenes of drunks and prostitutes); one student lives in an apartment whose garish illumination by a big neon sign just outside the window recalls *Stage Door*'s sense of Time Square's harsh radiance. The school is plainly a staging area for the real Broadway, a block west—and at one point, when the school can no longer contain the youthful energies that have been building up inside, the students create a Broadway all their own. Eager to broadcast his son's musical compositions to the world, a cabdriver rigs loudspeakers to the roof of his taxi, drives up to the school, and blasts a recording of the song "Fame" from the sidewalk. Hearing the music, the students pour outside the school and begin to dance; all the creative energies so long bottled up in the aging structure suddenly explode onto the street, intersecting with the urban flow of midtown Manhattan, literally bringing traffic to a halt. Dancing on cars, lifting their partners, the students stage a dazzling, spontaneous performance that fills 46th Street with color and movement and the sheer exhilaration of musical form; it is also, perhaps, a metaphoric preview of their future, when they will leave school to enter the theatrical world whose center is just beyond their doorstep. The scene resonates in memory—and not only because it provided the model for countless music videos to follow. Exuberantly, buoyantly, the number literally reconstructs Times Square from its constituent elements, identifying it as the precise spot where music and dance intersect with the physical matrix of the city, a uniquely American confluence of performance and urbanism. If there were no Broadway, the scene suggests, it would be necessary to invent it (211).

Yet everything about this vibrant filmic moment—or of entire films such as *The Sweet Smell of Success* or *Midnight Cowboy*—call, finally, for the explicit recognition of what we have really known all along: after abandoning New York decades earlier for the sunny artifice of California, American movies had come back, at long last, to the streets where they were born.

PART THREE

EIGHT MILLION STORIES

UNIVERSAL PICTURES
DASSIN 1551
DANIELS
DAY-EXT.
78 5
7-12-47
SPARKLING WATER

HOT SUMMER PAVEMENTS

Shortly after World War II, Mark Hellinger, the famed New York columnist now producing films for Universal, found himself listening to an unusual script idea from a young screenwriter named Malvin Wald. Wald began by recounting his wartime experience in the Army Air Forces's Motion Picture Unit, turning out training films and learning the power and immediacy of documentary technique. Listening patiently, Hellinger wondered at length what all this had to do with Hollywood. "At last, you've hit on the big question," Wald answered. "Why doesn't Hollywood leave its sheltered studios and go out into the world and capture the excitement of a city like New York in a feature film, instead of using painted backdrops and street sets on back lots?"

It was a daring proposition. Nearly twenty years had passed since the cameras had left New York's streets, after the advent of sound had made shooting in the city all but impossible. In the meantime, New York's once-bustling feature-film industry had more or less evaporated. Other than Paramount, the big studios had ceased making features in the city around 1930; two years later, a nearly bankrupt Paramount turned over its big Astoria studio to its creditor, Western Electric, who rented it out for the occasional feature before selling it in 1939 to the U.S. Signal Corps. Renamed the Army Pictorial Center, the facility had since been used strictly for military training films. Indeed, by the late 1930s, just about the only feature production left in New York was located in Harlem, where, on shoestring budgets, the African American director Oscar Micheaux was producing a series of "race" films with titles like *Swing!* and *Harlem After Midnight*, intended mostly for segregated black audiences in the South.

To be sure, New York's presence in Hollywood films brought a steady

212. **Filming *The Naked City* (1948).** Lee Sievan, the noted New York photographer, took this view of *Naked City*'s film crew (under director Jules Dassin) working on location at 52 West 83rd Street.

stream of production activity into the actual city. Second-unit crews arrived regularly to shoot background plates and establishing shots, studio photographers to take reference photos, art directors to study noted interiors or facades for reproduction back in California. And the studios themselves remained deeply entrenched in New York, which was still home to their financial, distribution, and publicity departments. Fox, Universal, and Paramount produced their weekly newsreels in New York, and MGM maintained a stage on the West Side for screen tests of potential contract players. But by 1946 the human and technical resources for *feature* filmmaking—directors, designers, editors, equipment, facilities—had nearly vanished. New York's cultural dominance in American art, theater, music, dance, and publishing was unquestioned. But the most popular American art form had long ago departed for a place across the continent.

Now this young screenwriter was blithely suggesting something that had never been attempted: a modern Hollywood feature, shot almost entirely on location in the city of New York, on its streets and sidewalks, docks and subways, in its homes and offices. The authenticity of approach, Wald explained, would be integral to the story: a factual, unvarnished account of a murder investigation by the New York Police Department's Homicide Division. While intrigued, Hellinger was frankly nervous about attempting what could easily turn out to be a logistical nightmare. After receiving Wald's script, called "Homicide," he peppered the writer with practical questions, which Wald did his best to answer smoothly:

> *How can you shoot a film on the streets of New York and keep the crowds away? (I explained that the cops would exercise crowd control.) How about the proposed chase on the bridge? Autos used that bridge to get from Brooklyn to Manhattan. (Shut off that section of the bridge and use the lower section; besides, there were three other bridges spanning the East River.)*

When Hellinger remained unconvinced, Wald reminded him that filming in New York *had* been done, on a limited basis, just the previous year. *The House on 92nd Street* (1945) had its roots in one of the few segments of the film industry left in New York—newsreels. Louis de Rochemont, a former producer of *The March of Time* newsreels, working now for 20th Century-Fox, decided to make his first feature—the tale of an actual FBI effort to thwart a Nazi espionage ring in New York—as a "semi-documentary": a scripted story, played by actors, that was nonetheless based in fact and produced, as one reporter described breathlessly, "right out in the open, in the actual localities where the story unfolds, with real honest-to-goodness passersby providing the crowd atmosphere usually supplied by hiring extra players." Years of newsreel experience allowed de Rochement to be comfortable with the complexities of location shooting—changing weather, uncertain light, unwieldy crowds—that had so discouraged

213. **Filming *The Naked City* (1948) at 57th Street and Lexington Avenue.** All through the summer of 1947, the production of *The Naked City*—the first feature shot on location in New York since the late 1920s—attracted huge crowds.

other producers. Directed by Henry Hathaway, *The House on 92nd Street* included scenes shot at the Bowling Green, Columbus Circle, and the Federal Courthouse at Foley Square, as well as the house on 92nd Street itself: the spy ring's headquarters, located on a quiet block off Madison Avenue in the German-American district of Yorkville. (Ironically, the house shot in the film was actually located on *93rd* Street.)

That same year, another Hollywood expedition to the city had drawn even more notice. For his groundbreaking film about alcoholism, *The Lost Weekend* (1945), the director Billy Wilder felt the authenticity of a real location would reinforce a harrowing sequence in which writer Don Birnam (Ray Milland) tries to hock his typewriter for drink money in the pawnshops lining Third Avenue. Taking a cue from *The Crowd* years before, Wilder placed his cinematographer, John F. Seitz, inside a packing crate just large enough to hold a man and a camera; other cameras were hidden in nearby bakery trucks and laundry vans. The trick worked. As the shooting went on, Milland—unshaven, disheveled, genuinely footsore and swayback from carrying the heavy typewriter block after block—portrays true desperation, discovering, to his horror, that all of the pawnshops are closed for Yom Kippur. Darkened by elevated train tracks, hemmed in on either side by tall tenements, the grim, endless avenue perfectly captured Milland's private hell. Critics were outspoken in their admiration for the film's location scenes, whose profound departure from traditional studio ways was wittily summarized by S. J. Perelman. "In transferring *The Lost Weekend* to the screen," he wrote, "the producers sought verisimilitude by bringing Ray Milland to Third Avenue (in the past, Third Avenue had always been brought to Ray Milland)."

At last convinced, Mark Hellinger agreed to produce Wald's script under a title, *The Naked City*, purchased from the photographer Weegee, who had earlier used it for a book of his own. In the summer of 1947, a full Hollywood crew (under the direction of Jules Dassin, another former New Yorker) descended on the city to shoot in 107 different locations around town, including several interiors—a scale of production that dwarfed the relatively brief location sequences in *House on 92nd Street* or *Lost Weekend*. Thousands of curious New Yorkers—as many as two hundred thousand, if Universal's publicity department is to be believed—turned out to watch the camera crews, the first of their kind to be seen in New York in nearly two decades; at one point, the producers turned to a professional juggler to help distract the crowds while the actual shooting was completed. Elsewhere, Dassin reverted to the kind of subterfuge pioneered by Vidor and Wilder, "stealing" his shots by hiding the camera in a telephone booth, a phony ambulance, a moving van. All summer long, local papers entertained their readers with human-interest stories about the production, such as one about the film's star and a dozen extras, who, while shooting a scene in the subway, were accidentally caught by the rush-hour crush and carried off to another station.

In fact, more serious troubles plagued the production, justifying Hellinger's early fears. At several points, the police failed to control the unruly crowds; at other times, city bureaucrats held up the shooting, insisting on payoffs to cut through the red tape. While filming in an empty lot, Dassin cut himself on a rusty nail and had to spend a day in the hospital. In the end, the picture was half a million dollars over budget.

Yet Hellinger himself seemed more than satisfied. Though he died suddenly of a heart attack just after a preview, he had made quite clear his sense of the film's significance in cinema history. The completed picture would open with no titles, no credits, just the drone of an airplane flying over Manhattan and a voice-over introduction, delivered by the once-reluctant convert, now turned proud parent:

> *Ladies and gentlemen, the motion picture you are about to see is called* The Naked City. *My name is Mark Hellinger. I was in charge of its production, and I may as well tell you frankly that it's a bit different from most films you've ever seen. As you*

see, we're flying over an island, a city, a particular city. And this is the story of a number of people, and a story also of the city itself. It was not photographed in the studio. Quite the contrary. The actors played out their roles on the streets, in the apartment houses, in the skyscrapers of New York itself. And along with them, a great many thousand New Yorkers played out their roles also. This is the city as it is: hot summer pavements, the children at play, the buildings in their naked stone, the people without make-up.

But it was another line of the script that would gain immortality, largely through its repetition in the film's later television spin-off: "There are eight million stories in the Naked City," the narrator concludes. "This has been one of them."

It was no empty boast. Unlike any film before, *The Naked City* conveyed the true sense of a city of millions, a feat made possible only by its extensive use of locations. In studio-built New York, to be sure, detectives often walked the streets, searched for clues, and, with any luck, apprehended their suspect. But given the confines of the backlot "city," their enterprise usually had a circumscribed, anecdotal quality, a search not through a whole metropolis but a few streets or, at most, a single district. And the pursuit of the criminal—even if enlivened by a chase—could only turn so many corners before returning to familiar ground. In *The Naked City*, by contrast, a crime investigation became the ideal vehicle to present the genuine scale and complexity of the city—a police effort that "will advance methodically," the narrator tells us, "by trial and error, by leg and brain work, by asking a thousand questions to get one answer." Before it is done, the detectives' search takes us from a cramped Lower East Side tenement to a spacious Park Avenue apartment, from dress shops, beauty salons, and gymnasia to the mortuary at Bellevue (shown to the public, the film's publicity claimed, for the first time ever). Along the way, we meet Jewish shopkeepers, Chinese launderers, an Italian ice man; we hear from wrestlers, fashion models, ironworkers, talent agents, and socialites.

But it is more than just diversity. The sheer size of the city makes the task impossibly daunting. "How many jewelry shops in the City of New York?" the narrator wonders, as a detective trudges from one store to another; every clue requires dozens of such trips. Clearly, this is no filmic sketch of a city, projected from a few particulars as it had been in the studio days, but instead resembles the web of infinities we know the real New York to be. Even as the police begin to close in, the city's sheer immensity continues to frustrate. The detectives have been able to determine that the killer is a male, with a husky build. "Only half a million big men in New York," the narrator observes, his tone combining sarcasm and wonder.

The Naked City opened an entirely new chapter for the movie city—as sudden a shift as the arrival of talkies twenty years before—and within the year, a pair of enthusiasts at MGM were trying to convince their superiors to extend the experiment. Assigned to direct the film version of the hit stage musical *On the Town,* Gene Kelly and Stanley Donen proposed that the entire picture be shot in the city. Shooting a musical on location was, in its way, as ambitious a proposition as *Naked City* itself: synchronizing singing and dancing to a soundtrack, for example, required large playback speakers, placed close enough for the performers to hear, yet out of the camera's sightlines—relatively easy in the studio but next to impossible for the kind of outdoor shots (some on moving vehicles) that Kelly and Donen had in mind. MGM's chiefs fiercely opposed the idea, especially the production manager J. J. Cohn, notoriously cautious about filming anywhere but the Culver City lot. As Kelly later recalled, "The studio executives all said: 'singing and dancing, coming down the streets of New York? You're crazy.' " (According to Donen, it was J. J. Cohn, not the Columbia mogul Harry Cohn, who sent the legendary telegram to a director hoping to work in an exotic location: "A TREE IS A TREE, A ROCK IS A ROCK, SHOOT THE PICTURE IN GRIFFITH PARK.") MGM rejected the idea outright at first, then relented in part by allowing the opening ten-minute "New York, New York," number to be shot on location (4). The rest of the film would be made in the familiar confines of Stage 30 on the Metro lot.

The arrival in New York in May 1949 of the film's first unit, including the stars Ann Miller, Frank Sinatra, and Gene Kelly himself, brought a renewed excitement to the city as well as a new set of production troubles. After days of canceled shooting due to poor weather, Sinatra announced he would remain in his hotel room until the cameras were ready to roll. Later, Sinatra's scheduled appearance for a shoot on a street in Little Italy, supposedly draped in secrecy, was discovered by thousands of delirious, screaming fans. And one notable afternoon, elderly members of the exclusive Metropolitan Club, dozing as usual in the front parlor, were rudely awakened by an orchestral score blaring from playback units placed on the open deck of a Fifth Avenue double-decker bus. The patricians lined the windows to watch Sinatra, Kelly, and crew run the bus back and forth six times before securing a satisfactory take.

Together, *On the Town, Naked City, House on 92nd Street,* and *Lost Weekend* proved location shooting in New York to be not only a practical proposition but an artistically and commercially attractive one as well, a way to bring new excitement to a wide range of different genres. Soon, Hollywood crews were appearing regularly in the city—especially from 20th Century-Fox, which sent Hathaway and others back to New York to shoot sequences for *Kiss of Death* (1947), *Gentlemen's Agreement* (1947), and *Miracle on 34th Street* (1947). Before the war, ironically, Fox had focused on rural and small-town audiences, and of all the major studios had least developed the idea of an invented city; now it offered an entirely different kind of movie New York, built from the crisp, realistic exteriors of location shooting.

There was, in fact, an entirely new look to all these films, which Hollywood technicians—despite their best efforts—could never quite duplicate in the studio. The location camera could shoot wide to encompass actors in a great bowl of urban space that might well include celebrated landmarks or events, such as the Plaza, Rockefeller Center, or Macy's Thanksgiving Day parade. Photographed in the spring or fall, the city proved a cinematographer's delight, with its complex cloud formations, its lucid sea-washed air, and its relatively low sun angles, which softened the daylight and cast long shadows on the buildings' ornamented masonry—offering unbounded visual richness and texture that registered handsomely on black-and-white film.

Technical advances eased the process. Film stock had grown faster and lenses sharper, allowing for simpler, more compact lighting setups. New, portable photoflood lamps, which had let *Naked City*'s cinematographer William Daniels work in spaces as small as a seven-foot-wide bedroom, became a favorite for shooting interiors—especially because they could run off available house current. Outside, powerful new "Brute" and "Titan" lamps introduced by Mole-Richardson allowed lenses to penetrate into the darkest recesses of real streets and doorways, not only those deliberately designed—as the standing "New York Street" sets had been—to minimize shadows. Perhaps most important, microphones had grown more directional, easing the garbled mix of desired and undesired sounds ("mike stew") that had once forced filmmakers from the streets (although most of *Naked City* was re-recorded, or "looped," by the actors back at the studio, a process that soon became common for location-shot films).

Postwar audiences seemed primed for the new look of these films, in part because of the war itself. Before the conflict, wrote cinematographer John Alton, "Hollywood was addicted to the candied . . . type of sweet unreal photography."

> *Then came the war. The enemy was real and could not be present at production meetings. There were no rehearsals on battlefields or during naval or air battles. There were no boosters, no sun reflectors, no butterflies and no diffusers. The pictures were starkly real. Explosions rocked the camera, but they also rocked the world, and with it rocked Hollywood out of its old-fashioned ideas about photography. The year 1947 brought a new photographic technique . . . accepted by the great majority. Let us have more realism.*

As wartime newsreels and documentaries increased moviegoers' familiarity with authentic backgrounds, they revealed by contrast the elaborate artifice of Hollywood's constructed sets and theatrical lighting techniques. Just after the war, moreover, American audiences were being introduced to the work of a new generation of foreign filmmakers, especially those from Italy, who employed extensive location work for their powerful "neorealist" films. Before the war, left-wing directors like Roberto Rossellini had been unwelcome at Cinecittà, the big government-owned movie studio outside of Rome; by 1944, in any case, its stages had been rendered unusable by Allied bombing. Undaunted, Rossellini took his camera into the streets, apartments, and rooftops of Rome itself to tell the story of the city's resistance to its Fascist occupiers. With the sun providing exterior lighting, random citizens serving as extras, and the buildings and rubble of wartime Rome as its "sets," *Open City* (*Roma, città aperta*, 1945) demonstrated an extraordinary new way of filming a city and its people, an experiment extended after the war by Vittorio De Sica's *Sciuscià* (*Shoeshine*, 1946) and *Ladri di biciclette* (*The Bicycle Thief*, 1948), Luchino Visconti's *La terra trema* (1947), and Rossellini's own *Paisà* (1946). (De Sica, ironically, traced his street-based camerawork back to King Vidor's pioneering efforts in *The Crowd*, made twenty years before.)

In Hollywood, meanwhile, troubles from inside and out were threatening the smooth operation of the studios, and especially of the big construction departments that were their special pride. The cost of lumber shot up as a resurgent postwar house-building industry competed for materials. A bitter strike by painters, set decorators, and other technicians in late 1945 shut down production for months and made use of existing locations seem a less risky proposition. More significant still was the landmark 1948 Supreme Court antitrust decision that—in the wake of several earlier consent decrees intended to divide film production from exhibition—forced the major studios to give up their theater chains entirely, thus ending the assured distribution that had been the bedrock of the system. Over the coming decades the studios would be forced to shrink the permanent art and construction departments that had once employed thousands of artisans and craftsmen, creating an endless variety of settings. Just maintaining the vast array of standing sets on each lot would be difficult—and for what should they be maintained? The studios would no longer be turning out dozens of films that needed a back-lot subway station or ocean liner. The change was gradual but the direction unmistakable: in the future, sets would be built for specific films or, better still, films would be shot in a way that minimized the number of sets altogether.

Yet even as it began to transform Hollywood, the new approach reasserted the place of New York in the movies. It was revealing how the makers of *The Naked City* and *On the Town* assumed, almost reflexively, that the city was the first and most interesting place to try the new technique. "Wald's proposal," Carl Richardson has noted, "had only to do with New York."

> *The very idea of location shooting would have been a useless abstraction without this single specification. Not only was the city an object of affection for the filmmakers, but it was a place with a certain mystique that they sought to exploit. An alternative site was never considered.*

Over the next decades, the city would become the essential urban "location" of American films, just as it had been the essential urban set on the studio lot. And with this new kind of movie would come a new kind of movie

New York, combining elements of the studio-made metropolis with pieces of the real city, captured on the spot but, through the power of film, given mythic status of their own.

Since the late 1920s, the movie city had been for New Yorkers a received vision, a version of their home town spun from the dreamings of a magical, somewhat mysterious place, thousands of miles away. Now overlaid on that distant creation were a series of moments snatched from the city's own days, weeks, and months. Legends arose about the production of particular films, linked to the annals of the city in a way that the making of Hollywood's artificial, essentially timeless New York could never be. To see the frigid, fog-bound views of Manhattan from the cliffs of Hoboken, the icy air plainly visible in the mouths of Marlon Brando and Eva Marie Saint ("so cold," Brando later said, "that you couldn't overact") as they cross Stevens Park, is to be instantly returned to the bitter New York winter of 1953–54, as director Elia Kazan and his crew struggled to shoot *On the Waterfront* amidst the tense atmosphere of "observers" sent by the very longshoremen's local whose underworld connections the film sought to expose. (It is a hardness mirrored as well in the faces of the film's extras, many of whom were real dockworkers, collecting a few extra dollars.) The August 1960 shooting of *West Side Story*'s dance sequences, by contrast, proceeded in the steamiest weather imaginable, literally days before the entire area was scheduled to be demolished for the construction of Lincoln Center (the filmmakers bribed the contractor to start work at the other end of the site, to preserve their West 68th Street location for a few additional weeks) (214). By October of that same year, the weather had turned exquisitely mild, just right for the soft morning when *Breakfast at Tiffany's* famous opening scene—with Audrey Hepburn, Danish and coffee in hand, lingering outside Tiffany's show windows—was filmed on the corner of 57th Street and Fifth Avenue. Hoping to avoid crowds, the producers scheduled the shoot for 7:30 a.m. on a Sunday; passersby began to gather anyway, noticing the policemen swarming outside the famed store and assuming that a jewelry heist was in progress.

214. ***West Side Story*** **(1961).** Codirector and choreographer Jerome Robbins demonstrates a dance movement to the actor George Chakiris. The setting of the opening number, much admired for its "realism," was actually a combination of a sidestreet in the West Sixties (about to be demolished for Lincoln Center) and a playground on East 110th Street. "Dancers would jump up on the West Side," Robbins later recalled, "and come down on the East Side."

But the greatest legend of all grew from a single night, Wednesday, September 15, 1954, at the corner of 52nd Street and Lexington Avenue, outside a Trans-Lux movie house and above an IRT subway grating. By 2:00 a.m. that morning, over a thousand New Yorkers had jammed the barricades to watch

Billy Wilder, the director of *The Seven Year Itch*, film a young woman in a white dress enjoying the rush of air from a passing subway train (in fact provided by a fan placed below), as it lifted her skirt above her legs (215). It was a moment that harkened not only back to the 1901 sidewalk filming of *What Happened on Twenty-Third Street* but forward to the production of Nicolas Roeg's 1985 film *Insignificance*, whose dramatic centerpiece was a re-creation of the shooting of *The Seven Year Itch*. On an autumn night in 1984, a feature-film crew could be found on location in New York (not at the Trans-Lux, now long gone, but at the Carnegie Theater on Seventh Avenue), shooting a group of actors who were themselves playing a film crew, working on the streets of New York, precisely thirty years before.

215. Filming *The Seven Year Itch* (1955). The famed location shoot, which drew fifteen hundred onlookers, required fifteen takes and lasted nearly until dawn. Watching the spectacle, Marilyn Monroe's husband, Joe DiMaggio, became enraged by his wife's overt sexual display, and the couple soon separated. Ironically, the location footage was later scrapped, and the scene reshot on a soundstage at Fox.

EASTERNS

By the mid-1950s, as location shooting in New York again became a familiar sight, another group of filmmakers were beginning to be seen around town. They could easily be confused for the location unit of a Hollywood movie, except for one significant fact.

They weren't from Hollywood.

After a lapse of nearly thirty years, New York was again starting its own feature-film industry. A small but dedicated band of moviemakers were determined to restore the city's place as a motion-picture production center, a true alternative to Southern California.

It began gradually. In 1953, director Elia Kazan and writer Budd Schulberg, seeking to escape the influence of Hollywood studios, convinced independent producer Sam Spiegel to finance what they jokingly referred to as an "Eastern": a feature not only filmed but *produced* in the New York area, employing local cast and crew members, and shot on a New York soundstage. Everything about *On the Waterfront* would be different, from its controversial subject and script to the acting style of its stars, trained not by Hollywood drama coaches but in the celebrated "method" of Lee Strasberg's Actors Studio in New York. Even the limitations of New York's primitive facilities were turned to artistic advantage: filming the emotion-laden confrontation of Marlon Brando and Rod Steiger in the backseat of Steiger's car, Kazan had no access to the kind of rear projection plate that, Hollywood-style, would show the city streets through the rear window. Instead, slatted blinds on the car's windows hid the view, except for occasional streaks of light provided by cinematographer Boris Kaufman, passing a flashlight across the vehicle's exterior. Kazan realized later that the apparent drawback had actually helped the scene: realistic streets outside would only have distracted audiences from the dramatic intensity of the action within.

Crucial help for the nascent industry came, ironically, from a rival medium, itself only recently born. With the rise of television in the late 1940s, the networks began presenting most TV programs as they always had their radio shows—from New York. Comedy shows, with relatively modest production needs, could be shot in the networks' existing studios or in rented theaters. But the networks were also presenting what would later be called the "golden age" of television drama: ninety-minute or two-hour teleplays, broadcast live from makeshift or converted studio spaces around town. These programs were the work of a new generation of professionals, bred in New York, with few ties to traditional Hollywood: writers like Paddy Chayefsky, Rod Serling, and Robert Alan Arthur; directors like Sidney Lumet, Arthur Penn, and Delbert Mann. With improvised facilities, primitive equipment, cramped sets, rushed rehearsal schedules, and the obvious limitations posed by putting on live shows for a national audience, they worked in a manner contrary to that of the studio system, learning to value quick and efficient production, realistic dialogue, strong character delineation, and emotional resonance over the showy stars, glossy spectacle, and grandiose settings of Hollywood moviemaking.

When it was decided to produce one of these television dramas—the story of a homely Bronx butcher named Marty—as a feature film, the director Delbert Mann and the writer Paddy Chayefsky chose to remain in the city, hoping to transfer the simplicity and realism of the original story to the screen, with the very unglamorous Ernest Borgnine in the title role. To finance the venture, they turned to United Artists, the traditional maverick among Hollywood studios, now under the reins of an iconoclastic executive named Arthur Krim. Produced for less than $350,000 and lacking any big stars, *Marty* stunned the Hollywood establishment when it received Academy Awards for Best Screenplay, Best Director, Best Actor, and Best Picture in 1955. Coming on the heels of *Waterfront*'s eight Oscars in 1954 (also including Best Picture), this triumph served notice to Hollywood that a genuine rival was emerging in New York—one whose output, though tiny in quantitative terms, could offer an extraordinary level of quality. In the following year two more features were produced in the city, both drawn from live television: *Edge of the City*, directed by Martin Ritt and written by Robert Alan Arthur, and *Patterns*, written by Rod Serling. And a year later, in 1957, a stage play by Reginald Rose called *12 Angry Men*, filmed in New York in an astonishing nineteen days by a former television director, Sidney Lumet, opened to critical and commercial success.

Of course, it was hardly easy to rebuild an entire industry from scratch. In the early 1950s, New York had almost no film stages; the few that did exist were, literally, holdovers from the silent era. Both *On the Waterfront* and *12 Angry Men* had been filmed at the Fox studio on West 54th Street, which dated back to 1920. Yet even this was relatively modern compared to the Gold Medal Studio in the Bronx (where Kazan and Schulberg reunited to make *A Face in the Crowd* in 1957), which was really the "uptown" Biograph studio, opened in 1906. Edison's 1908 studio in the Bronx was also pressed into service for *The Wrong Man* and *The Last Angry Man;* directors like Lumet and Hitchcock found themselves watching dailies in the old screening room, darkened by the original red damask curtains, in which Edison himself had worked. Even the 1905 Vitagraph Studios in Flatbush, the first American studio ever built, was brought back into use. Other spaces were newer but no less improvised, such as Hyman Brown's upper-story studio on West 26th Street, where features like *Stage Struck* were produced next door to television soap operas, or the former bus garage on 127th Street and Second Avenue that became the Filmways Studio (where *Klute, The Godfather, Annie Hall,* and *Manhattan* would all be filmed in later years).

Feature filmmaking required not only specialized space and equipment but skilled labor, and this, too, was difficult to come by at first. There was so little consistent work for grips, for example, that most were actually longshoremen on leave from the Hudson piers. Harder still to find was the cadre of craftsmen essential to feature filmmaking: cinematographers, art directors, costume designers, film and sound editors. Gradually, a small band of talents began to emerge, many deliberately shunning Hollywood predictability in favor of the more idiosyncratic—if also more sporadic—film work available in New York. Working far away from the industry mainstream often necessitated taking any job one could find—in commercials, documentaries, educational and industrial films—just to be available for the occasional feature. Yet these craftsmen persevered, and soon began to develop a distinctive New York style of moviemaking. Boris Kaufman, who photographed *On the Waterfront, Patterns, 12 Angry Men,* and *The Pawnbroker,* became a role model for younger, New York–based cinematographers. The city's only sound editor, Dick Vorisek, brought an authentically rough-hewn flavor to almost every feature made locally, using the city's only sound mixing stage, at Fox's 54th Street studio. The art director Richard Sylbert worked on *Patterns* and designed *A Face in the Crowd* and *How to Murder Your Wife,* becoming celebrated on both coasts for his urbane sense of style. Ralph Rosenblum brought a fresh, unconventional approach to the editing of *The Pawnbroker, A Thousand Clowns* (and, later, *Annie Hall*), while Dede Allen introduced a razor-sharp editing technique of her own, reinforcing the urban edginess of films such as *The Hustler*—and, in time, *Dog Day Afternoon* and *Serpico.*

It was a kind of moviemaking very different from that of Hollywood: drafty rental stages and cramped editing booths instead of big, freestanding buildings on sunny studio lots; a small, collegial band of crew members working from picture to picture instead of the huge rank-and-file of the California guilds; stage-trained New York character actors instead of suntanned movie stars. But for the young filmmakers, it offered real advantages. "Things were much freer in New York," Sidney Lumet later recalled. "There were none of the department heads who had such tremendous power in the studio: the art department, the camera department, the sound department." Even after the advent of nonstop air routes across the country, the process of sending dailies to the West Coast, having them screened by studio chiefs, and getting comments back to New York took at least four days—by which time the filming had moved well along. "It restored power to the director," recalled Lumet.

Not surprisingly, the films themselves turned out to be different: sometimes called "kitchen-sink" dramas, they typically focused on the lives and struggles of working people, emphasized the city's diversity, and sought a darker, more complex ambiguity over the clear-cut optimism of Hollywood. The parallel with postwar Italy was suggestive: a small band of independent-minded filmmakers, breaking away from the traditional commercial studio system, in part by turning to the city itself.

Responding to the same limitations as the silent-era New York filmmakers—inadequate studio space and the difficulty of building large, complex sets—the new generation rediscovered all over again the same "New York style" in which extensive location work provided atmosphere, mood, and context, while interior scenes concentrated on the development of character and plot. As before, they came to recognize that the greatest advantage New York offered filmmakers was the city itself, the world's largest outdoor stage. Far more than their Hollywood counterparts, New Yorkers were willing, even eager, to take their cameras into the city streets.

By now, the value of doing so seemed more obvious than ever, thanks in part to a pioneering generation of avant-garde filmmakers. In the late 1940s and early 1950s, a series of New York still photographers, intent on revealing the everyday street life of the city, had sought to extend the experiment to motion pictures. With the goal, in Phillip Lopate's words, of "catching life at shoe level," the Swiss-born photographer Rudy Burckhardt turned a 16mm camera on Manhattan's shuffling crowds and stony facades for a series of shorts with evocative titles like *The Climate of New York*, *Under Brooklyn Bridge*, and *Millions in Business As Usual*. The photographer Helen Levitt joined forces with the painter Janice Loeb and the critic James Agee, and, borrowing an old Kodak 16mm camera, went up to East Harlem in 1951 to shoot *In the Street*, a twelve-minute film of astonishing emotional immediacy, capturing the daily life of a New York block—children and adults, talking and fighting and playing—as no film before or since.

Another photographer, Morris Engel, shared the same desire to explore New York on film, but made the daring decision to work at feature length and in 35 millimeter, allowing for conventional theatrical distribution. "I had the strange idea," he said, "that a couple of people with the right equipment could compete with Hollywood for next to no money. It was a heretical concept." Aware from his work as a photographer that a tripod and conventional viewfinder tended to attract unwanted attention, Engel decided to shoot the film with a handheld camera and an angled viewfinder—a technique unheard of with bulky, heavy 35mm equipment. He prevailed upon an inventor friend to construct a device to allow the camera operator, Engel himself, to support a custom-built camera on his chest, an early precursor to the handheld "Steadicam" rigs developed years later. The result, a feature called *Little Fugitive* (1953), opened up remarkable new possibilities for filming the city.

The simple storyline offered Engel the loosest imaginable armature to apply his new technique. A seven-year-old Brooklyn boy named Joey (Richie Andrusco), fooled by a practical joke into believing he has killed his older brother, escapes by subway to Coney Island. There he avails himself of every possible offering: the carousel, corn on the cob, bumper cars, cotton candy, and his favorite, the pony ride. When Joey appears at the ride the following morning (after sleeping under the boardwalk), the concessionaire grows suspicious, calls Joey's home and alerts his brother, who eventually retrieves him safely.

216. ***Little Fugitive*** **(1953).** Morris Engel spent the summer of 1952 at Coney Island shooting *Little Fugitive* with a custom handheld 35mm camera rig. In this view, the film's ten-year-old star, Richie Andrusco—searching for bottles beneath the boardwalk—stumbles onto an intimate scene.

The effect of the new technique, which allowed Engel to plunge almost unnoticed into the public space of the city, was extraordinary. In a fashion not seen since the early actualities, the film feels less like a constructed story than a lived experience; watching it, we seem to spend a weekend ourselves in the legendary amusement park, partaking of its garish yet often haunting beauty. We see the sun linger across a long summer afternoon, then watch as the park dazzlingly lights up for the night. When an afternoon downpour forces everyone off the beach, we simply stand for a few minutes under canopies and in doorways, watching the raindrops splash into puddles and waiting for the skies to clear.

Within this apparently casual structure, a powerful theme soon emerges. As he moves across the resort's complex landscape, Joey is constantly watching—and learning. He sees a couple passionately kissing, and a man who has nearly drowned. At one concession stand he has his photograph taken; at another, he studies his body in a funhouse mirror. Surrounded late one afternoon by beach crowds, he wanders the same white sands early the next morning, utterly alone. Running out of pocket money, he discovers to his delight that he can return empty bottles for change, then sets out to amass a small fortune in nickels to buy pony rides, paying his own way for the first time in his life. For Joey, Coney Island's public spaces are a vast outdoor classroom, whose crucial lessons are not about arithmetic or spelling but about love and death, identity and solitude, work and play (216).

Released in 1953, the film proved enormously influential—not least for having been produced and distributed by Engel himself. "Our New Wave would never have come into being," François Truffaut later said, "if it hadn't been for Morris Engel, who showed us the way to independent production with *Little Fugitive.*"

Still another impetus for location shooting came in 1959, when the actor and director John Cassavetes created a film called *Shadows* as sort of an improvisatory dramatic exercise. In an informal, seemingly unstructured fashion, the film follows a struggling black jazz musician (Hugh Hurd) and his younger, lighter-skinned brother and sister (Ben Carruthers and Lelia Goldoni) through a week of New York parties, shows, bar-hopping, and museum-going, all the while exploring issues of personal, professional, and racial identity. Working with available light, a handheld camera, and postrecorded sound, Cassavetes sought to capture the city with the apparent spontaneity that would become his directorial trademark. Moving seamlessly from street and sidewalk into bars and rehearsal halls, he broke down the distinction between interior and exterior that had always shaped studio production, even as he presented the street itself in all its messy fullness: storefronts, trash cans, pigeons, and litter, sidewalks not elegantly slicked with rain but messily splashed with puddles. Upon its release, *Shadows* was hailed for its daring, unconventional technique, its openness to the chaotic texture of daily life. Like Engel, Cassavetes had managed to produce his feature independently, without the aid (or interference) of a traditional studio—a lesson not lost on younger filmmakers, including a student named Martin Scorsese, who later recalled that Cassavetes's film "really made us believe that if he could do it—pick up a camera and go out in the street—so could we. There were no more excuses."

In the meantime, a series of technical improvements had steadily enlarged the range and flexibility of location shooting. In 1954, Eastman Kodak introduced Double-X, a new film stock whose sensitivity to light (at 250 ASA) was literally twice that of its predecessors; the new film made feasible the use of a small, handheld 16mm camera for exteriors, whose images would later be blown up to match 35mm scenes filmed indoors. The new stock also made it possible, at long last, to shoot on location at night, allowing James Wong Howe, for example, to photograph the evening scenes of *The Sweet Smell of Success* on actual city sidewalks. Another leap came in 1961 with the appearance of the first truly portable movie light: a handheld rack of quartz-iodine lamps called the "Sun Gun," originally intended for home-movie buffs but quickly adapted by professionals who could now carry their light anywhere a person could reach. Perhaps the biggest advance came in sound recording, spurred on by a small cadre of young documentary filmmakers—Robert Drew, Richard Leacock, and Donn Pennebaker—who, pursuing a daring new approach called cinema verité, sought to render the world as directly as possible, capturing both images *and* sound with compact, handheld 16mm equipment. Their efforts were reinforced by the introduction of a new generation of synchronized tape recorders, such as the Nagra, built to be used outdoors and small enough to be operated by one person. Camera, lights, sound: each had become compact and reliable. After four decades, filmmakers were again free to roam the city.

By the early 1960s, the desire was greater than ever. A "new wave" had arrived from France, where a group of innovative directors—among them Jean-Luc Godard, François Truffaut, and Claude Chabrol—were turning their cameras onto the sidewalks and rooftops of Paris, using the city's life as both setting and theme for a series of contemporary films. "You have to shoot in the streets, even in apartments," Truffaut insisted.

Impressed with the New Wave's crisp, modern look, American films began including location scenes (in *Mirage, The World of Henry Orient, Love with a Proper Stranger*) to provide a richness of texture unlike anything Hollywood could offer. This was especially true by the 1960s: as the studio system wound down, its stagebound New York took on a bland, tired character that was miles removed from the glossy shimmer and stylish look of earlier decades. "A remorseless stiffening of reflexes had set in," notes Geoffrey O'Brien:

> *The images were born old. Audiences woke as if from a long slumber to find themselves looking at a state-of-the-art wax museum: a Grace Kelly look-alike with dyed hair lip-synched her dialogue against a slightly grainy rear projection representing New York's fashionable East 78th Street, to which the music of Neal Hefti or Frank de Vol tried desperately to lend animation. . . . The latest sophisticated comedy looked like a promotional short for a hotel chain with empty rooms. . . .*

In fact, the rise of location shooting brought about a realignment in the production hierarchy. On the soundstage, the art director worked closely with the cinematographer to establish a film's imagery and style through a combination of set design and photography. On location, where the film's "set"—the city—was already largely built, the art director's role inevitably dwindled. The trick to selecting locations, the cinematographer Carlo di Palma explained to Lumet, was "in picking the right place to begin with and then doing as *little* as possible with it. Given the choice between two equally good exteriors or interiors, pick the one that is already the right color, the one that takes the least alteration by the use of light."

It was indeed the cinematographer—a whole new school of city-based craftspersons such as Owen Roizman, Victor Kemper, Arthur Ornitz, Gordon Willis, and Michael Chapman—who now often "designed" movie New York, by selecting camera angles, lenses, lighting setups, and hour of day to adapt a preexisting urban environment to the film's dramatic needs. On location, the art director's role was often reduced to minor (if crucial) modifications: disguising a lamppost interfering with a shot, adding a mailbox called for in the script, changing a poster in the background. Indeed, as the art of designing the movie city became a matter of selecting the right location, a new member of the crew rose to prominence: the location scout, whose job called for scouring the city before production and bringing potential sites to the attention of the director and producer. No less important, once filming had begun, was the location manager, in charge of all the logistics necessary to prepare a site for production, including city approvals.

This last was no small job. By the mid-1960s, the greatest barrier to working on location in New York was not technological but bureaucratic. Filming in streets and public spaces could involve up to fifty separate permits from a dozen city agencies, who were often perplexed or annoyed by the demanding schedules and unusual—sometimes bizarre—requirements of feature production. (Concerned with public image, agencies were also known to insist on script changes before granting permits.) Once production had begun, corruption was rampant. Producers regularly budgeted as much as $400 a day for police payoffs: $25 per patrolman and $50 for sergeants, to be repeated for all three shifts. The high costs of such "extras" and the lack of help from city agencies dampened the enthusiasm of all but the most devoted directors for working in New York: in 1965, no more than thirteen features were filmed in the city, and only two in their entirety. "Out there," said one New York movie executive, referring to Los Angeles, "motion picture companies get immediate cooperation from the city government. Here they get little or nothing but talk."

217. **Filming *Up the Down Staircase* (1967).** One of the first films to be shot in the city after the founding of the Mayor's Office of Film, Theatre & Broadcasting, the production received a visit from Mayor Lindsay himself, who sat for pictures with members of the young cast.

All that changed in June 1966, when newly elected Mayor John V. Lindsay signed Executive Order Number 10, turning a little-known city agency into the Mayor's Office of Film, Theatre & Broadcasting. The first of its kind (and the model for countless agencies founded later around the country), the office combined forces with a newly formed motion picture and television unit of the police department to transform filmmaking in the city. Obtaining permission for location shooting became a simple, one-stop process; the small, hardworking staff not only issued permits and provided insurance forms for cast, crew, and equipment, but served as intermediary to other city agencies, helping to arrange everything from parking permits to a street repaving to having the Brooklyn Bridge's lights switched on an hour early. Once derided for their lack of cooperation, city agencies became known for bending over backward to accommodate filmmakers. Sanitation workers agreed to *plant* garbage for a scene in *The Out-of-Towners*; a traffic department engineer spent ten days changing lights from red to green for *The French Connection*, and the transit authority provided an entire IRT subway train (at a cost of $275,000) to the producers of *The Taking of Pelham One Two Three.* The somewhat starstruck Mayor Lindsay joined in the act, turning over his own office in City Hall to the director George Seaton for filming a comedy called *What's So Bad About Feeling Good?* and personally calling a former law partner, now a director of the New York Public Library, to allow Francis Ford Coppola access to the library's stacks and reading rooms for *You're a Big Boy Now* (217). Perhaps the most decisive improvement was the special, high-profile police unit, consisting of four sergeants and fifteen patrolmen who, significantly, operated not on traditional police shifts but those of moviemakers, staying with a film from beginning to end. "Right away," Sidney Lumet recalled, "the graft stopped."

The results were extraordinary. In the eight years of the Lindsay administration, 366 films were made; by the second year of Mayor Abraham Beame's term, forty-six features were being filmed in the city. That year, 1975, marked an important turning point. On November 10, a crowd gathered on Stage E of the old Astoria studio to celebrate the commencement of *Thieves*, the first feature to be made in the building in twenty-six years. Since its abandonment by the Army Signal Corps four years before, the great structure had stood virtually empty; now, it was announced, a new foundation would bring the studio into active use. Within two years, the place would be humming with Lumet's *The Wiz*, a project that, budgeted at $25 million, represented the first truly major production in New York since the silent era. Down on the stage floor, twenty sets were under construction; upstairs, Adolph Zukor's old office was turned into a dressing room for Diana Ross. Once a white elephant, the studio had begun its transformation into a major production facility, sizable even by Hollywood standards.

The "big house" had come back to life. New York had reestablished its long-vanished industry. And the dream city of the movies had a new home.

TWELVE

ON LOCATION

FILMING THE CITY AFTER 1945

LEVELS OF MEANING

Though the appeal of location work was based at first on its fresh new look, filming in New York would turn out to carry all sorts of consequences that, in time, came to redefine the entire relationship between the city and the movies. In New York, characters could be placed in the sweep of the city's open spaces—streets, parks, plazas—as never possible on the studio lot. Cameras could survey the entire metropolitan landscape to capture parts of the city never before seen on film, bringing to life the texture and eccentricities of communities in all five boroughs (and beyond) that had been overlooked by Hollywood's geographically circumscribed approach.

Yet at its best, the resulting filmic city would be no less interpretive, or imaginative, than the studio-created version. Movie New York would remain a mythic construct: it would simply be constructed in a new way, with elements of the city's actual landscape recombined and reshaped to emotionally and narratively powerful ends.

No film better revealed this new approach, perhaps, than the very first to be produced in the city itself. *On the Waterfront* (1954) was more than a pioneering effort at local film production and more, even, than a searing portrait of the great but troubled port (218). It presented audiences with a movie city as fully realized as any fashioned in the studio—but one built instead from the elements and layout of a real place. Under the hands of director Elia Kazan, writer Budd Schulberg, cinematographer Boris Kaufman, and art director Richard Day, an entire urban landscape—the city of Hoboken and its waterfront—was reshaped to narrative purpose, creating a self-contained universe that brimmed with meaning.

218. (previous page) ***On the Waterfront* (1954).** Unlike earlier films, shot in New York but otherwise produced in Hollywood, *Waterfront* was the work of a local production crew, assembled by Elia Kazan, that became the nucleus of the city's postwar filmmaking community. In this view, Marlon Brando, as Terry Malloy, waits between takes on the Hoboken docks.

This was possible, in part, because the setting itself was so naturally coherent and contained. Like other communities along the Hudson's western shore, Hoboken sits on an escarpment raised above a thin sliver of land at the river's edge—an area filled almost entirely (at the time) with cargo piers, warehouses, and rail lines. The city above, the waterfront below, the cliff between them making each its own world—it was this essential topography that the filmmakers would fill with narrative and moral significance. It was a topography they would also elaborate, adding two more levels, one above, one below, until they had created a series of *four* tiers, rising like steps from the river to the sky.

Near the bottom is the gritty waterfront itself, a place of hardened workingmen who abide by their own, tightly guarded codes of behavior and spend their lives in tough but honest labor—though hardly as honest as it should be. In fact, the working world of the piers has been corrupted at a level literally below it: the crude wood shack, floating inches above the water, that belongs to a union local chief named Johnny Friendly (Lee J. Cobb). With the help of his "accountant," Charley the Gent (Rod Steiger), Friendly has been extorting everyone in sight—his own struggling membership no less than the big shipping companies—and is willing to use any means, legal or not, to stay in power.

Indeed, to prevent an honest dockworker named Joey Doyle from exposing the local's racket to a newly formed waterfront commission, Friendly enlists Charley's younger brother, an aimless ex-boxer named Terry Malloy (Marlon Brando), to lure Joey to the roof of his tenement, where Joey and Terry have long raised flocks of racing pigeons. Awaiting the would-be informant, however, are not pigeons but a trio of henchmen, who throw Joey over the edge of the roof to his death. The film thus begins with a tragic descent, a fatal fall. "Maybe he could sing," jokes another thug, "but he couldn't fly."

The terrible murder galvanizes the city above, which, long isolated from the docks, has always been able to ignore what goes on below. At the least, it galvanizes two members of that community: Joey's sister Edie (Eva Marie Saint), and Father Barry (Karl Malden), a junior priest at a local church. Descending to the piers, the priest sees firsthand how the corrupt system operates, especially at the morning "shape-up," where Friendly's shifty-eyed hiring boss determines who works that day, and who doesn't. Thwarted by the waterfront's fabled code of silence, the father proposes a meeting at the church, located in the square above the piers and thus, in principle, beyond the boss's influence. But Friendly's evil grasp again reaches up from below; during the meeting, his henchmen surround the church and brutally attack the workers who have dared to come.

In the fight's aftermath we remain with Terry and Edie, following them across the town square as they start to converse. Filled with modest row houses, the church, and a landscaped square, this is a different world from the piers below: it is a civic realm, a place of responsibility and social compact, a world of women and families. It is Edie's world, and Father Barry's—but not Terry's. His connection to Johnny Friendly taints him here as "a bum"—as he is reminded by, of all people, an old rummy in the park. Still, watching him talk gently to Edie while sitting on a playground swing, we sense he might actually like it here.

Where *does* Terry belong? Edie finds out when she comes to the tenement rooftop to search for her dead brother's birds. Terry has made a little world for himself on the roof, a place located as far as possible from the docks below—a realm of sky and clouds, where his only companions are his racing pigeons and a young boy, Tommy (Thomas Handley), who helps train them. Terry's roof is a place of longed-for innocence, of youth, of flight; it is an escape from the worldly responsibility of the city and waterfront that it overlooks—from a distance (219, top).

But down on the docks below, that escape grows harder by the day—especially after Johnny Friendly arranges the "accidental" death of another would-be informant, and Terry, even as he is increasingly drawn to Edie, is served with a subpoena to testify. In anguish and confusion, he comes to the town square to confess his role in Joey's killing to Father Barry; as they stand at the fence above the docks, we can feel Terry's displacement, caught between the corrupt world he has always known, down below, and the honest world he is trying to enter, up here (219, middle). His moral dilemma is resolved only after the famous backseat confrontation with Charley, in which all past hurts are revealed ("I coulda been a contender. I coulda *been* somebody, instead of a bum, which is what I am"). Unable to scare his brother off, Charley is himself killed, and Terry decides to testify—with fierce effectiveness—against Friendly.

Afterwards, Terry tries to retreat to his rooftop refuge. But as the fate of Joey Doyle made clear from the outset, the roof offers only an illusion of escape. To his horror, Terry finds all his pigeons have been killed by the young boy, Tommy, as punishment for breaking the waterfront code of silence. "A pigeon for a pigeon," the boy screams in tearful fury.

Edie suggests escaping, moving inland. But as she speaks, Terry gazes out at a liner sailing down the Hudson, a view that recalls the promise of the film's opening shot (177). He cannot leave this place; he must redeem it. He is done trying to escape. "They always said I was a bum," he says, picking up his longshoreman's hook. "Well, I ain't a bum, Edie. Don't worry, I'm not gonna hurt nobody. I'm just going to go down there, and get my rights."

He leaves the roof—not in a helpless fall like Joey Doyle's, but in a conscious descent to the docks below (219, bottom).

There, pointedly ignored by the shape-up boss, he makes the fateful decision to continue his journey one last step down, to Friendly's shack. A dramatic shot from the level of the shack itself presents the film's entire tiered landscape from the bottom up: the edge of the docks in the foreground, the terrace of city and church above them, the rooftops still higher. Having watched the shack's corrupt tentacles reach up for the docks and the city, we now sense the city and church—embodied by Terry—leading a counterattack. Moving down the ramp, closely watched by the other dockworkers, Terry challenges Friendly and his henchmen—first with words, then fists—until his descent is horribly complete, his bloodied body lying face down on the edge of the shack, half in the dirty water. Yet somehow Terry manages to rise again, staggering back up the ramp, across the dock, and over to the pier door to reenter the world of honest work. Emboldened by Terry's challenge, the rest of the men follow, ignoring Friendly's screaming commands. The pier door closes down; Friendly is closed out.

Produced at the dawn of postwar filmmaking in New York, *On the Waterfront* remains perhaps the most ambitious attempt ever to orchestrate the elements of an urban locale into a unified filmic setting. As distinct from the skills needed to create an effective studio set, built to specification, this effort required a certain improvisational ingenuity, an ability to work with what was available "on site." It was Budd Schulberg's discovery that several Hoboken longshoremen raised racing pigeons, for example, that suggested extending the film's landscape upward to include Terry's rooftop retreat, while the wooden shack in the water—a former boathouse that the film crew happened upon—gave him and Kazan the idea of stretching that landscape *below* the docks. To clarify and sharpen the city's middle "tiers," the filmmakers created a composite town square, mixing waterside views of Stevens Park, directly overlooking the docks, with landside views of Church Square, five blocks inland. They even put the skyline of Manhattan to work, using its presence across from the stepped Hoboken landscape as an "audience," mutely watching the struggle, and as a constant reminder that the stakes counted far beyond this single community.

The result was a narratively charged landscape across which the story could play itself out. Endowing each of the four levels with its own moral status, the filmmakers were able to track Terry's internal changes through his vertical movement from one level to another. In the end, the immorality and corruption of Johnny Friendly's shack—inches above the dirty water—is obviously too low. Yet Terry's rooftop retreat, by the same token, proves too *high*, too detached and irresponsible. The answer is to be found somewhere in between, at the levels of the city and the docks, of life and work—but only after Terry is willing to make his painful descent to the very bottom, in a struggle to save not only himself but his community. From the outlines of a rugged waterfront town, rising from the river, the makers of *On the Waterfront* somehow fashioned a remarkable spiritual landscape, its stepped tiers the stations of an arduous journey from corruption to redemption.

219. ***On the Waterfront*** **(1954).** The filmmakers transformed Hoboken's landscape into a series of tiers, rising from the water, that were each charged with narrative meaning. At the highest level (top) is the tenement rooftop that is Terry's retreat. In the middle is the city (center), where an anguished Terry seeks out Father Barry (Karl Malden). At the lowest level (bottom) is the waterfront—and the floating shack where Terry confronts Johnny Friendly (Lee J. Cobb).

SHOOTING WIDE

If location films immediately looked more authentic than studio-made pictures, it could be traced in large part to a new feeling of space and depth. Long accustomed to seeing actors in front of shallow, projected backgrounds, audiences now reveled at the placement of characters within the fullness of real urban settings. Gregory Peck, for example, is plainly *there*, sitting pleasantly in the Grand Army Plaza in *Gentleman's Agreement* (1947), walking briskly through Rockefeller Center in *The Man in the Gray Flannel Suit* (1956), running frantically through Central Park in *Mirage* (1965). To paraphrase S. J. Perelman, the cameras now came to the city, not the city to the cameras.

But with this new spatial fullness came new challenges, not least among them the need to reconceive—in the most basic visual terms—the relationship of the human being to the city. As the scene grew wider and more spectacular, the figures themselves grew smaller and less significant, dominated by the actual scale of the city's structures. For decades, studio technicians had artfully manipulated the scale and proportion of fabricated urban settings in order to highlight the characters in the foreground. The real city would not be so easily tamed.

At first, in fact, it seemed as if the city's real locations might overwhelm the action altogether. When a Cold War spy played by Ray Milland attempts to elude an FBI agent in *The Thief* (1952), for example, he does so in classic movie-city fashion, by climbing the Empire State Building. But as photographed in the actual structure, the scene bears no resemblance to the fabled ascents of the studio city, where preternaturally powerful figures surmounted the skyscraper's exterior in a few heroic leaps. Milland must do it from inside, floor by floor, using the stairs—the service stairs, to be exact, which carry him, huffing and puffing, from the eighty-sixth-floor deck to the observation platform on the 102nd floor. Still being tailed, he climbs up another flight to the very tip of the structure, allowing us a rare glimpse of its interior construction (among other things, the builders' scrawled markings, dating from 1931, are still visible on the inside of the stainless-steel skin). There is only one place left to go, and we follow with anticipation as Milland opens the upper hatch onto the windy open platform above. With memories of King Kong, we are startled by what Milland discovers up here: nothing, except some broadcast equipment and utility fixtures. We have reached the roof of the city, but the scene is hauntingly empty—no airplanes circling, no ominous music, just the steady roar of the wind and the impossibly distant views of the city beyond. When the FBI man tries to come through the hatch, Milland manages to kick him down the ladder to the floor below, a total of about twelve feet. After that, there is nothing for Milland to do except to climb down the same way he came up. He is just an ordinary human being, after all, atop a very big building. As the film's location work forces us to admit, *this* is the reality of the city's towers. Not King Kong.

220. ***Fourteen Hours*** **(1951).** Filmed by Henry Hathaway on a downtown skyscraper (at the site of today's 140 Broadway), the film follows a young man (Richard Basehart) intent on jumping off the ledge of his hotel room. In the film, Basehart falls but is caught safely by a net; in the actual 1938 incident on which the story was based, the man jumped and was killed.

Yet as filmmakers themselves were quick to appreciate, this disjunction of scale could offer dramatic possibilities all its own. Based on an actual 1938 occurrence, *Fourteen Hours* (1951) follows a disturbed young man (Richard Basehart) onto the fifteenth-floor ledge of a downtown hotel, where he threatens to leap to his death. Even as an earnest traffic cop (Paul Douglas) leans out the window, trying to talk him down, a raucous crowd gathers below, eagerly waiting to see if he jumps. The director, Henry Hathaway, used an actual Manhattan building for its wide shots—and nothing makes us feel the terrifying predicament more than the view of Basehart's tiny figure standing precariously against the high stony facade, as implacable as a mountain face, and equally capable of bringing death with one false step (220). The use of the real location, too, brings out the full comic horror of the incident as a quintessential New York "spectacle": showing the way an individual can command the attention of the crowd (intentionally or not) within the amphitheater of the city's streets and buildings.

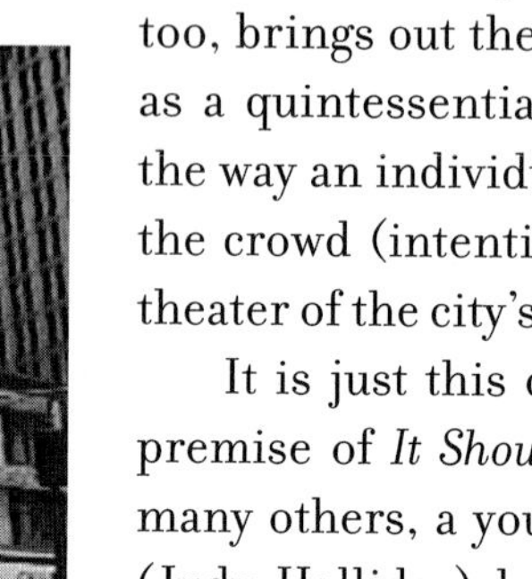

221. ***It Should Happen to You*** **(1954).** From the western edge of Columbus Circle (soon to be demolished for the Coliseum), Gladys Glover, played by Judy Holliday, happily inspects the progress on her giant signboard—until she notices the painters have misspelled her last name.

It is just this capacity that underlies the clever premise of *It Should Happen to You* (1954). Like so many others, a young woman named Gladys Glover (Judy Holliday) has come to New York to make a name for herself. Unable to do so by dint of talent or determination, she hits upon a simpler expedient, using her hard-earned cash to rent a huge billboard overlooking Columbus Circle, with her name painted on it in ten-foot-tall letters. Eerily prophetic in its vision of celebrity as a self-fueling phenomenon—Gladys becomes famous for being famous—the film also offers deep insight into the nature of urban spectacle. New York is a city of crowds, of course, but it is also an instrument by which certain individuals distinguish themselves *from* the crowd, commanding the attention of everyone else. Incapable of activating New York's publicity machine in an institutional way, Gladys taps the city's physical urbanism, which turns out to be shaped along much the same lines: giant signs, placed on buildings facing large public spaces, seek to draw the notice of the thousands of pedestrians below.

Of course, only by showing a real billboard, fronting a real volume of urban space, could the filmmakers offer the authentic interplay of spectacle and crowd, and so transmit fully the strange excitement—and contradictions—of celebrity. At one point, we watch Gladys meandering around Columbus Circle, staring up at her name, deliriously pleased. For the moment, she exists in two places at once—a member of the anonymous sidewalk crowd even as she has literally risen above it (221).

For this relationship to make itself felt, a major public space is not really required: as Sidney Lumet demonstrates convincingly in *Dog Day Afternoon* (1975), an ordinary Brooklyn street will suffice. Lined with small row houses, shops,

and a branch bank, a sleepy Park Slope block is transformed when a robbery of the bank is discovered in progress. The police arrive in force; so do the local residents, eager to see what happens. Lumet lets us watch the transformation: police barricades put into place, street and sidewalk cleared, crowds pushed back to the edges of the block, all creating a well-defined space in which the "event" can occur. The spectacle itself begins unexpectedly when the bank robber Sonny (Al Pacino) steps onto the sidewalk, senses the crowd's rapport, and starts playing to their antipolice sympathies. "Attica! Attica!" he yells, with clenched fist in the air, conscious of the power of his "performance" to fluster the detectives, now reduced to supporting actors by Sonny's star turn. Later he goes further, enlisting the audience into the act by throwing some of the stolen money into the crowd. In principle, the scene could have been shot on a back lot, but Lumet—no less than Hathaway before him—was deeply aware of the value of a real location. Some of the film's most effective shots are those shot from a helicopter, making clear the scene's extraordinary context: from above, we see exactly how the block has been temporarily carved from the matrix of surrounding streets to serve as the improvised set for this bizarre combination of hostage crisis, political rally, and street theater. Even while implying that, under certain circumstances, any random New York street can serve as a performance space, these aerial views also reassert the underlying reality of this otherwise highly theatrical event, reminding us—as only a location shot can—that this volume of space really exists, in all its three-dimensional fullness, in the middle of Brooklyn (222).

222. ***Dog Day Afternoon*** **(1975).** Directed by Sidney Lumet, the film was shot in Park Slope, Brooklyn, just blocks from the actual bank whose 1972 robbery was the basis for its story. In this scene, the bank robber Sonny (Al Pacino), taunting the police, transforms the street into a theater—turning the sidewalk into a stage, the bank into a backdrop, and the surrounding crowds into an audience.

No setting in the city was enhanced more by the advent of location films, fittingly enough, than the greatest open space of all: Central Park. To be sure, the park had made countless appearances in studio films, including several taking place almost entirely in its boundaries: the 1933 Rodgers and Hart musical *Hallelujah, I'm a Bum,* for example, or a 1932 feature itself titled *Central Park.* Indeed, perhaps the most exquisite single moment in the studio-created city is the "Dancing in the Dark" number in *The Band Wagon* (1953), in which Fred Astaire and Cyd Charisse leave behind the pressures of their Broadway rehearsal to enter a dreamy Central Park filled with horse-drawn carriages, evening strollers, and a small band playing the lilting tunes of Dietz and Schwartz. Dressed in white, dancing in a secluded clearing that is framed by greenery and the twinkle of city lights, Astaire and Charisse match the setting's elemental simplicity with a purity of emotion and gesture that seals their love. It is hard to recall a moment when the film city seemed more romantic.

Yet despite this and other evocations, the studio-built city ultimately proved unable to convey the astonishing reality of Central Park: an open rectangle, 843 acres big, carved into the heart of one of the world's densest cities. It was not surprising, therefore, that location shooting transformed the park into one of the city's most popular movie settings. The opening of *It Should Happen to You*, for example, is set in Central Park on a spring weekend. Here Gladys Glover meets Pete Shepperd (Jack Lemmon), a documentary filmmaker who is shooting real-life vignettes of the park and its people. Unlike Gladys, who puts her faith in such artificial social values as fame and celebrity, Pete is a great believer in the natural and the ordinary (224).

This broad, almost philosophical opposition—nature versus society—was implied by the park's very existence, and all but required location shooting to bring out. No stage set could ever capture the true breadth of the park's landscape, nor the dramatic way its miles of greenery interrupted the solid matrix of Manhattan blocks. For it was not just the abstract distinction between the natural and the man-made but their incredible *proximity* that made the park's place in the city so suggestive.

Curiously, Flan and Ouisa Kittredge (Donald Sutherland and Stockard Channing in *Six Degrees of Separation*, 1993) don't seem to notice the park much, although their sweeping view of its sylvan expanses is presumably the reason they live on Fifth Avenue—for just this reason, the most desirable residential street in the city. Only Geoffrey, a South African visitor played by Ian McKellan, seems interested in the dark mass of green outside the windows. Peering through an expensive antique telescope, Geoffrey wonders why there is a statue of a husky in the middle of the park. Neither Flan nor Ouisa seems to know, or care.

224. ***It Should Happen to You* (1954).** Gladys Glover and Pete Shepperd (Jack Lemmon) meet in Central Park, whose picturesque green landscape is dramatically framed by the high white walls of the city's buildings—including the Plaza Hotel, at center.

Yet the mysterious expanse they float above will soon affect their lives directly. A young black man named Paul (Will Smith), a schoolmate of their children, arrives at their apartment bleeding—having been attacked in the park, he says, while examining that same statue of the husky. In fact, Paul is a hustler, living in the park and using his fervid imagination (along with some crucial inside information) to gain entrance to the wealthy households surrounding it. Once his ploy is revealed, the Kittredges quickly push him out of their house, but they cannot push him out of their minds quite so easily: Ouisa, especially, is haunted by Paul's face and voice, floating disembodied over the park's darkened landscape. Nor can Paul quite forget *them:* we later see him down in the park, amidst the rocks and trees, looking up to the white cliffs of apartment houses and imagining his rightful place there as Flan's disowned child. Park and city, city and park; they prove to be not so easily detached after all, once the membrane of class and race has been punctured, or at least stretched. Several times during the film, the director Fred Schepisi flies us over the tops of Fifth Avenue's proud apartment houses, showing exactly how abruptly they rise from the edge of the dark forest at their feet—the very embodiment, in urban terms, of the troubling closeness of "chaos" and "control" that is one of the central themes of John Guare's screenplay (225).

Six Degrees was not alone in offering a mysterious animal (that unexplained husky) to embody the park as a locus for unknowable forces in the heart of the city. The creatures of *Wolfen* (1981) and *Wolf* (1995)—both rather enigmatic specimens, the former being a race of superintelligent animals, the latter a transmuted Jack Nicholson—gravitated inevitably to the nocturnal park as a suitably wild setting for their mayhem. It was not a new idea: RKO's *Cat People* (1943) effectively used a studio-built Central Park as the stalking ground of its supernatural feline. But the power of location filming to "place" the great greensward in the middle of the man-made city allowed these films to convincingly argue for the persistence of a primitive, atavistic spirit in the heart of modern society.

225. ***Six Degrees of Separation*** **(1993).** Several times during the film, the director Fred Schepisi employs an aerial shot, flying high above Fifth Avenue, that shows its apartment houses rising like a mountain range from Central Park's miles of greenery.

This mystical darkness, of course, undoubtedly built upon the common perception of Central Park in recent years as a uniquely dangerous zone, to be avoided at all costs after sundown; park-set scenes such as that in *Marathon Man* (1976), where Dustin Hoffman and Marthe Keller linger romantically into the evening, only to be pulled into the bushes and brutally attacked, became common. The low point of Jack Lemmon and Sandy Dennis's infamously terrible visit to the city in *The Out-of-Towners* (1970) surely comes with the discovery that they are to be dumped in the middle of its forbidding landscape. "The Park?" cries Lemmon. "*Central* Park? At four o'clock in the morning?" Huddled pathetically under a tree, the couple are robbed while they sleep; upon waking, they are set upon by a vicious dog, chased by a mounted policeman, and attacked by two joggers before they can make their way to the street. Nothing could be more innocent than the festive "Junior Science Fair" at the Bethesda Fountain, filled with colorful banners and eager children, to which millionaire parents Tom and Kate Mullen (Mel Gibson and Rene Russo) bring their son in *Ransom* (1996); but while they are looking elsewhere, the boy is kidnaped, and the child's paradise instantly becomes a parent's nightmare.

In sharp contrast to the city's constant, near-compulsive response to new trends and fashions, the park has always moved to its own rhythms, cycling dramatically through the seasons but changing little one year to the next—or, for that matter, one decade to the next. In Woody Allen's *Everyone Says I Love You* (1997), a series of stunning views of the park's foliage across the four seasons helps structure the story as a year-long—yet essentially timeless—romance. Similarly, the producers of *Hair* (1979), having begun production of the celebrated 1960s musical on the eve of the 1980s, made the ingenious decision to set much of the film in the park, softening the anachronisms that might otherwise be inevitable. Inside the park, the film's hippies and war resisters could exist in a world of their own, a place wrenched out of time. Indeed, in using Central Park as an escape from the city's constraints, the filmmakers were interpreting, in their own way, the original intent of its designers, Frederick Law Olmsted and Calvert Vaux, who conceived the park as an escape from the social pressures and divisions of the city. The park we see in *Hair* is an urban arcadia, an artfully improved nature, dedicated to the renewal of the human spirit. The film's characters celebrate the "Age of Aquarius" in a grassy meadow where police horses mirror their dance steps; they ride along the park's bridle paths and take a midnight swim in its pond; they move to Twyla Tharp's choreography on the stagelike steps of Bethesda Fountain and eventually gather at the Sheep Meadow for a peace festival. Reveling in the sheer range of environments contained inside the park's borders, *Hair* presents—as no studio-shot film ever could—the expansiveness and variety of its landscape.

In the end, that landscape even transcended arcadia. By design, Olmsted and Vaux allowed certain parts of the park to retain an untamed appearance, offering a contrast of the well-tended and the wild. In this mix, filmmakers found a metaphor not only for the park, but the city itself.

In *Green Card* (1990), the director Peter Weir sees in New York's diverse moods a mirror for the contrasting personalities of Brontë (Andie MacDowell) and Georges (Gérard Depardieu). As a leader of a volunteer civic group, the "Green Guerillas," Brontë brings order out of chaos, letting gardens bloom on empty slum lots. Georges, a composer of maniacal piano music, connects instead with the pulsing energy that runs everywhere beneath the city, starting with the driving beat of the drummer Larry Wright performing on a subway platform during the film's opening credits. Nervous and pounding and barely skirting chaos, the city also surprises with a gentle spirit of community: it is tame and rough, garden and jungle, all at once. Nowhere is this more apparent, the film suggests, than in Central Park itself. On a spring weekend it is Brontë's park: New York's public garden, with grassy lawns and lush plantings and the supremely civilized landscape of the Bethesda Terrace. But later, as Georges and Brontë race through the park, late for an important meeting with the immigration service, its landscape seems almost African in spirit: a place of high grass, rugged terrain, a forest or savannah to be traversed while drums beat in the distance—Georges's park, a place of dark, mysterious energies. By the end, the couple has rediscovered what Olmsted and Vaux proposed more than a century and a half ago: that the orderly and the wild can indeed coexist—and that life, in its fullness, needs both.

URBAN VILLAGES

FADE IN:

NEW YORK CITY, 187TH STREET. A SUMMER DAY.

Just east of Webster Avenue in the North Bronx, 187th Street is a predominantly Italian community and the commercial avenue of the neighborhood. Fruit and vegetable stands, pizzerias, butcher shops, bakeries, cleaners and dyers and bars flourish. It is Saturday morning around eleven o'clock—a market day.

WOMEN, dark, gesticulative, with bulging cloth shopping bags, baby carriages.

MERCHANTS at their improvised street stands, hawking their wares, disputing with their CUSTOMERS, roaring salutations to PASSERSBY.

In the midst of all this, CAMERA HOMES IN on a typical neighborhood BUTCHER SHOP. . . .

PADDY CHAYEFSKY'S SCREENPLAY FOR *MARTY* (1955)

In Hollywood's vision of New York, neighborhoods could be easily distinguished by style and class but almost never, ironically enough, by geography. Studio-made films offered only the sketchiest idea of where Manhattan's communities actually *were*; produced three thousand miles away and intended for a national audience, they were less interested in physically locating the city's districts than in giving each an easily comprehensible character. Beyond Manhattan, moreover, the movie city all but dropped off the map: Brooklyn was reduced to a handful of picturesque blocks, while the Bronx, Queens, and Staten Island scarcely existed at all. The resulting vision of New York, however cosmopolitan, conveyed neither its true expanse as a sprawling metropolis of more than 327 square miles—its five boroughs each the size of a major city—nor its somewhat contradictory (but no less accurate) identity as what the writer Alistair Cooke once called "the biggest collection of villages in the world."

From the very start—as *Marty*'s opening made clear—New York–based filmmakers would view things differently, not only casting their gaze across the full breadth of the city's landscape, but seeing in it a patchwork of "urban villages"—to use a term introduced by Herbert Gans in his landmark 1962 study of Boston's West End, an Italian American district whose residents, he found, pursued strikingly traditional ways of life within the modern city. Under the guise of conventional storytelling, location-shot features would examine New York's neighborhoods with an almost anthropological precision and care, exploring their local ways of life, observing their streets, shops, homes, and gathering places—and ultimately revealing them to be not merely background settings, but powerful sources of narrative tension and conflict.

Some of these "villages" turned out to be right in Manhattan itself, and for these, one source of conflict was supreme: How could any kind of traditional neighborhood survive so near the heart of the most restlessly changing city in the world, a place whose very layout—its diffuse, open-ended grid of streets—seemed to encourage the fluid movement of boundaries? How could a community ever find anchor on this ever-shifting urban sea?

In *Crossing Delancey* (1988), directed by Joan Micklin Silver, the struggle is largely over. The old Lower East Side is mostly gone, surviving at street level in a few specialty food shops selling lox, kosher wines ("the wines you can almost cut with a knife"), and pickles—like the store on Essex Street, just south of Delancey, that Sam Posner (Peter Riegert) has inherited from his father. The once-vast population of immigrant Jews, now dwindled and aged, lives largely in the union-built housing projects that have replaced many old blocks of tenements, where they mix somewhat incongruously with the younger Asian and Hispanic families who have since filled the area. In one such project apartment, Ida Cantor (Reizl Bozyk) lives with her old furniture and memories, enjoying weekly visits from her granddaughter, Isabelle "Izzy" Grossman (Amy Irving), who comes down by subway from the Upper West Side. Like most young Jewish New Yorkers, Izzy has never lived down here, and has no interest in starting now, even when Ida tries to match her up with the pickle man, Sam. To Izzy, Sam—however charming and sincere—represents the provincialism she has sought to escape in the larger city. At one point, approaching Sam's shop, she glimpses him serving customers by plunging his hands into the pickle barrels lining the sidewalk; we can see how much the scene, so redolent of the district's earthy past, offends her assimilated sensibilities. Having long ago "crossed Delancey," Izzy must struggle to cross back, at least emotionally, to find her heart (226).

226. *Crossing Delancey* (1988). Isabelle "Izzy" Grossman (Amy Irving)—a young Upper West Side woman visiting her grandmother—makes her way down Delancey Street amidst the Yiddish signs and ethnic shops of the old Lower East Side.

A very different, but no less authentic, kind of Manhattan community came into focus in *Metropolitan* (1990), Whit Stillman's affectionate look at what one of his characters terms the "urban haute bourgeoisie": the teenage sons and daughters of the elite Protestant families who occupy the exclusive cooperative apartment houses of the Upper East Side. Over a Christmas week, we witness their holiday rituals and survey the unusual geography of their district, a linear construct that links the two miles of residential Park Avenue with the luxury hotels south of 60th Street—the Plaza, Waldorf, and St. Regis. As the young people stroll between debutante balls and the late-night parties held in spacious Park Avenue apartments, we glimpse a private, privileged world, embodied by the avenue's sparkling Christmas lights and by glowing hotel entrances that promise to soften winter's chill with music and flowers within.

One might think the wealth and comfort of this community offers a sense of security, but no: one of the film's tropes is the elegiac pronouncement of imminent "doom." ("This is the last deb season as we know it," one young man sighs. "I don't want to watch the decline.") As the film itself recognizes, this is fashionable hyperbole: this powerful, moneyed community is in no danger of disintegrating. Still, it is striking how Manhattan, whose extraordinary densities have long forced even the richest New Yorkers to be stacked in high-rise structures, stretched on a long, arrow-straight thoroughfare, offers this social elite little of the physical cohesiveness of a traditional neighborhood. Through the film's location shots, we sense how the larger city, interlacing and intermingling with this oddly elongated "community" at every corner, inevitably challenges the desire for exclusivity that is at its core.

By contrast, the far less privileged citizens of Manhattan's Little Italy—as Martin Scorsese demonstrated in his classic *Mean Streets* (1973)—enjoy a district whose compressed, dense fabric provides a bulwark against the pressures of the larger city. Yet as the film makes clear (and subsequent history has borne out), they too are fighting what is ultimately a losing battle: trying to preserve their enclave against the insistent press of change.

From the start, Scorsese, himself raised on nearby streets, wanted his audience to feel the tribal interiority of Little Italy, evident not only in its inhabitants but its physical character—a district that turns in on itself, away from the outside world. Repeated daytime shots, looking down on narrow intersections from nearby rooftops, offer a sense that the city's streets, like those in old European cities, have been carved out of a dense, solid mass. Even more European are the passageways and internal spaces within each block that Scorsese reveals—especially one high, brick-walled courtyard that evokes the slums of southern Italy and is the setting for an urgent conversation between two illicit lovers. Little Italy, Scorsese suggests, is a place of secrets, of hidden layers, of rooms within rooms.

At night, the district's tribalism comes alive. The camera looks down on the Feast of San Gennaro, with its dazzle of lighted arches and booths, jaunty band music, and the ceremonial procession of its decorated shrine through the narrow streets. This is a world defined by rituals, primarily those of two ancient institutions, the Catholic Church and the Mafia, whose contradictory influences can be felt in the internal struggles of Charlie Cappa Jr., played by Harvey Keitel. Charlie is very much a man of this place, entirely comfortable within its tight confines: a scene at the beach, in fact, finds him restless, ill at ease, declaring his dislike of open water and his preference for mountains. "There aren't any mountains in Manhattan," his girlfriend Teresa (Amy Robinson) points out. "Tall buildings," he replies, "same thing." Yet even as Charlie tries to make his way in this small, ramified world, playing by its elaborate rules and hoping to rise within its hierarchy, he can feel it all slowly slipping away. Like so many other ethnic neighborhoods in Manhattan, Little Italy is being diluted by the forces of assimilation; Teresa, for example, wants nothing more than to leave the old district for a new life uptown. She asks Charlie to join her, but he refuses, clinging to the world he knows: "All I got right now," he says, "is the neighborhood." A different threat to the community is embodied by Johnny Boy (Robert De Niro), an edgy, self-destructive character who—planting a bomb in a mailbox, beating up a stranger, or randomly firing a revolver into the night sky (trying to shoot out the lights of the Empire State Building, he says)—gives uncontrolled expression to the violence that has always lurked just beneath the surface of a district that is, among other things, the historic capital of organized crime in America.

As the film moves toward its explosive conclusion, Scorsese inserts a pair of images that symbolize the challenge facing this community—and all others like it—trying to survive in contemporary Manhattan. The first looks down again on the San Gennaro festival by night, the band still playing its lively tunes, the bulbs now merged into a single slash of light through the mass of darkened buildings—a river of energy held tightly within the community, symbol of its fierce intensity and inward-turning instincts. The next shot is simply a wider, more distant view of the same scene. The glow of San Gennaro has been reduced to a tiny sliver of light at the lower part of the screen, and the band's music now sounds remote and thin; and at the top of the frame, in the distance, rises the Empire State Building, projecting itself over a broad swath of silent, darkened Manhattan—aloof in its vastness and utterly unconcerned, finally, about the life or death of this tiny corner of the city.

Perhaps preserving a sense of community would be easier elsewhere, in the four outer boroughs of New York. With little of Manhattan's cosmopolitan glare or insular concentration, these boroughs have always exerted less pressure on their constituent neighborhoods, allowing a measure of stability and continuity over time. If anything, their problem may be too *much* stability, too little change, especially for the young. Or so suggests a quartet of films, strikingly similar in theme despite being set across four communities, three boroughs, and thirty-five years—from the central Bronx of *Marty* (1955), and Bay Ridge, Brooklyn, in *Saturday Night Fever* (1977), to the northern Bronx of Throgs Neck and Pelham Bay in *True Love* (1989), and the Astoria district of Queens in *Queens Logic* (1990). In each, a young resident struggles against the pull of family and tradition, an interior conflict that is linked to the distinctive, deeply contradictory character of these outerborough communities: small towns in the big city, insular parts of a metropolitan whole, places that by their very nature look both outward and inward.

From the street, this dual identity can be confirmed just by glancing up to the high elevated structures that ride incongruously over the modest houses and shops, as if to frame the community's place within the larger city. The viaduct of the Hell Gate Bridge hovers over Astoria in *Queens Logic*, much as the Verrazano-Narrows Bridge towers over Bay Ridge in *Saturday Night Fever* and the elevated subway runs above the Bronx avenues of *Marty*—all serve to remind us that what might seem like self-contained communities are really the outlying satellites of an immense metropolitan system.

If these giant structures seem like visitors from another planet, it is precisely because everything else is so small. Lined with low-rise houses and stores, these neighborhoods are closer in scale and spirit to a traditional American small town than to the skyscraping city across the river. At the heart of each, appropriately enough, is a Main Street, an urban version of the classic small-town spine. All four films explore this thoroughfare; one transfigures it.

It is just an ordinary chore: a gallon of paint to be carried from one shop to another on Bay Ridge's Fourth Avenue. But as performed by John Travolta at the start of *Saturday Night Fever*, to the infectious beat of the Bee Gees, it became an unforgettable New York movie moment, the click of Travolta's cowboy boots keeping time with the music as he strides down the avenue, a man completely in his element. The task at hand cannot keep Tony Manero from noticing some pretty girls, stopping by an open pizza stand, or window-shopping for a dress shirt. He is plainly a *boulevardier*, Brooklyn-style, for whom Fourth Avenue is not merely a place of work but a way of life (226).

Yet it *is* a place of work, as we are reminded once Tony enters his shop. The music is suddenly cut short; his boss chews him out for taking so long. If main street is a social environment, it is also a collection of businesses, an artery of commerce. Many of these are specialty shops, catering to the community's particular needs, like the Italian grocery where Michael (Ron Eldard) holds down the counter in *True Love*, or the butcher shop, specializing in Italian meats, where Marty spends his days. As much as anything, these ethnic stores define each

226. ***Saturday Night Fever* (1977).** Making his way down Fourth Avenue in Bay Ridge, Brooklyn, on a work-related errand, Tony Manero (John Travolta) nonetheless manages to enjoy the pleasures of the boulevard. The trestle of the elevated subway, on the left, is a reminder that this insular community is, in fact, part of a sprawling metropolis.

district's identity, differentiating it from the larger city. We see something else, too. Along with their order, every customer in these shops brings a question: When is the wedding? they ask Michael; Why aren't you married? they ask Marty. These *are* small towns, to a fault. Everyone knows everyone else's business.

With the workday done, we follow our characters home, literally around the corner. Turning off the commercial avenue, we enter sidestreets that again recall the mixed extraction of these districts. There are row houses, even a small apartment house or two—buildings very much of the city. But there are also plenty of detached frame houses, like those in any small town or suburb, surrounded by yards filled with trees, shrubs, driveways, and garages.

As Tony rounds the corner, the shift is palpable. Back on the boulevard, he was his own man, strutting down the sidewalk, relaxed and poised. Here on the sidestreet, among the yards and houses, things are different: family and tradition rule, and Tony is late for dinner. Marty experiences the same thing. Walking down Webster Avenue with a young woman he has just met, he is ebullient and self-confident; bringing her home to his mother's house—where he still lives—he grows defensive and sullen. As we looked inside the shops, so we go inside the houses, observing family meals that often descend into family fights, as sons and daughters rebel against the pressures of tradition. They have lived all their lives in these dark, thickly decorated interiors; it may well be time for them to go, to shape their own futures.

But not just yet. For now, they continue to play out the rituals of youth, hanging out in local taverns with friends from childhood. Here Marty begins a typically aimless Saturday night with his buddy Angelo. ("So whaddaya feel like doing tonight?" asks Angelo in their classic exchange. "I don't know, Ang', whadda you feel like doing?") Often as not, the night ends at another center of local life, the dance hall. In *Marty* it is called the Stardust Ballroom, with swing music played under a suspended glitter ball. In *Saturday Night Fever,* its name has been updated to 2001 Odyssey and the music to disco, but the role of the place remains much the same: the site of mating rituals, where daily life is left behind for an evening of dancing, socializing, and sexual promise. Among the high-tech flashing lights, there is even that same glitter ball.

In *Queens Logic* and *True Love,* the mating process is much further along; both films take place on the eve of a wedding. Perhaps inevitably, the old friends want to enjoy a last night of raucous bachelor abandon before their world changes forever. Seen as they are ending, these rituals—played out by groups of friends that have stayed close since childhood—not only carry the poignancy of growing up, but reassert the unusual stability of these outerborough districts. Unlike many urban areas (or, for that matter, many suburban ones), people in these communities tend to stay put.

At least till now. For we have come in at a time of change, disorienting to characters who have enjoyed so much continuity in their lives. Not surprisingly, they respond by turning to local landmarks, the touchstones of their youth. What *is* surprising, however, is that these landmarks turn out not to be local in character at all, but the massive artifacts of the metropolitan city, the great public works that have been in the background all along.

Many are the products of New York's legendary master-builder, Robert Moses. Though his hand touched nearly every part of the city, Moses's impact was most obvious in the sweeping outerborough areas that he literally reshaped through his park and highway programs. The studio-created city, with its tight Manhattan focus, tended to understate his presence. But the moment the cameras left Manhattan, they could hardly miss his mighty works, tarnished by neglect and time, perhaps, but still overwhelming in scale and vision. Yet what these films reveal is something else entirely: the way in which these immense structures, built to meet the needs of a whole region, turn out to carry intensely personal meaning to those who live right in their shadow.

In *Saturday Night Fever*, for example, the Verrazano-Narrows Bridge towers over not only Bay Ridge, but also over Tony Manero's life. His teenage gang has long hung out in the park beneath its access ramps and played dangerous games on its upper deck. Tony is now outgrowing these pranks, in part due to a new dancing partner, Stephanie (Karen Lynn Gorney), who urges him to look beyond Bay Ridge to the promise of upward mobility that is Manhattan. Yet he cannot abandon his roots quite so quickly—as is revealed by a quiet rhapsody he shares with her about, of all things, the bridge itself. "That tower goes up 690 feet," he says, surprising her with a string of statistics: forty million cars a year, 127,000 tons of steel, a 4,230-foot central span. "I know everything about that bridge," he admits. The structure's place in Tony's life is sealed in one last scene, when the pranks on the upper deck turn fatal: a troubled member of the gang wanders out too far, loses his footing, and plunges to his death in the dark waters below. Talking soberly to the police afterward, Tony is no longer a boy, but a man; the Narrows crossing has marked one part of his transition, as another—the Brooklyn Bridge, fabled gateway to Manhattan—will mark the rest.

228. ***Queens Logic*** **(1991).** After failing to relive a childhood triumph (climbing the Hell Gate Bridge) and nearly falling to his death in the process, Al (Joe Mantegna) turns to the awe-inspiring view—sunrise over the Manhattan skyline and Triborough Bridge—to celebrate another day of life.

In *Queens Logic*, another Moses project, the big Astoria swimming pool, serves as a key gathering place for a group of old friends. But it is the structure rising just beyond it, the steel arch of the Hell Gate railroad bridge, that proves the crucial landmark in their lives. At the start of the film, a flashback recalls a great childhood moment for Al (Joe Mantegna), who climbed a long dangling rope up to the bridge's deck. Al now cruises the same area in his white convertible, still something of an overgrown adolescent. For his friend Ray (Ken Olin), an artist who likes to paint the city from his apartment roof, the same bridge is a commanding presence on the horizon, and no less significant in his life; he has arranged for his upcoming wedding to take place in the park just beneath it. Yet Ray is also torn between the desire to leave Queens (for Manhattan, Italy, anywhere) and the desire to settle down. The giant bridge embodies it all: the most permanent of objects, fixed in the landscape, it is also a link with other places, a constant reminder of the world beyond.

The climax of the film turns back to Al at a moment of crisis: fearful of growing old, he again tries to climb the bridge, hoping to reenact his childhood triumph. But he fails and, for a terrifying moment or two, nearly loses his grip. Struggling back, he clings to its sturdy riveted steel for dear life—then stands, and with arms raised to the sky, celebrates the simple, adult act of surviving (228). Ray, at last reconciled to his home and borough, decides to proceed with the wedding, and as the end credits roll, we see a white wedding carpet being rolled out across the green lawn, while high above the giant arch prepares for its final role as a great conjugal bower—a surprising marker of roots, in a city whose inhabitants are so often regarded as rootless.

THIRTEEN

NIGHTTOWN

THE DARK SIDE OF THE CITY

HORROR CITY

"When Mayor Lindsay began his efforts to attract the movie production business," Pauline Kael observed in 1971, "it probably didn't occur to him or his associates that they were ushering in the new movie age of nightmare realism."

> *With practically no studios for fakery, the movie companies use what's really here, so the New York–made movies have been set in Horror City . . . a permanent record of the city in breakdown. The city has given movies a new spirit of nervous, anxious hopelessness, which is the true spirit of New York. It is literally true that when you live in New York you no longer believe that the garbage will ever be gone from the streets or that life will ever be sane and orderly.*

229. (previous page) ***Death Wish*** **(1974).** Paul Kersey (Charles Bronson) is confronted by a gang of muggers in Riverside Park. "Sunk in Stygian darkness or illuminated by a sickly orange light," Foster Hirsch has written, "the film's graffiti-coated city is a cauldron of crime."

The screen connection between the city and crime was hardly new, of course. Back in 1912, D. W. Griffith's *The Musketeers of Pig Alley* had not only introduced the first movie gangster (The Snapper Kid, played by Elmer Booth), but directly linked him to New York's dense urban spaces in the cinematically groundbreaking shot of Snapper and his gang walking down a narrow alley, right *toward* the camera, their faces soon filling the screen. *Traffic in Souls*, the exposé of "white slavery" made the following year, introduced another key notion: a pervasive "underworld" operating throughout the city, just beneath its surface. Two decades later, in the late 1930s, the two elements—gangster and underworld—were combined to unforgettable effect at Warner Bros., which followed its early 1930s flirtation with Chicago's Prohibition gangsters (in such films as *Little Caesar* and *The Public Enemy*) by turning to Manhattan's colorful gamblers and racketeers for a series of pictures featuring its distinctive stable of New York–bred stars: James Cagney, Humphrey Bogart, George Raft, Edward G. Robinson, John Garfield. Revealing gangland's sinister presence behind the worlds of prizefighting (*Kid Galahad*, 1937; and *City for Conquest*, 1940), city politics (*Bullets or Ballots*, 1936), and, of course, nightclubs and gambling (*Marked Woman*, 1937; *The Roaring Twenties*, 1939; *East of the River*, 1940), these films offered a heady mix of gunplay and nightlife within a series of highly stylized settings (rain-slicked streets and glowing hotel lobbies, shabby tenements and tough saloons, lavish penthouses and sleek nightclubs) built on the stages and backlots of Warner's Burbank studio. Meanwhile, detectives and sleuths of every stripe could be found roaming the movie city, from insouciant prewar amateurs like William Powell in *The Thin Man* (1934) and Warner Baxter in *Penthouse* (1931), to hard-boiled postwar professionals like Kirk Douglas in *Detective Story* (1951) or Dana Andrews in *Laura* (1947)—quintessential big-city characters, to be sure, but not especially different from their counterparts in Chicago, San Francisco, or Los Angeles.

Kael's "Horror City," on the other hand, was something else, and something new. While plainly the outgrowth of a dramatic increase in crime in the 1960s, it was (as Kael herself recognized) less about crime itself than a crisis in the city's *order*. By the time she was writing, a sharp rise in urban disorder—exacerbated by a slew of larger social troubles, from rising welfare rolls and delinquency rates to growing racial tensions and the accelerating flight of the middle class—was making the city no longer merely a plausible setting for crime stories, but a place the critic Vincent Canby would call a "metaphor for . . . the last days of American civilization."

To calibrate the change, it was necessary only to look back to the original location film, *The Naked City*. Centered around the dreadful story of a young woman's murder, the 1948 film nonetheless asserts the city's fundamentally healthy civic order. "Like the human organism itself," Parker Tyler noted about the film, "Manhattan Island . . . can catch a disease—the criminal." In *The Naked City*, the detective's job is basically immunological: to isolate and remove whatever threatens the city's natural—that is to say, healthy—functioning.

The idea informs the film right from the start, with our introduction to the city's homicide squad, which operates "rather quietly," the narrator tells us, from a modest precinct house in Chelsea. "Don't bite your nails, honey," he later reassures a subway rider, frightened by screaming headlines. "Very few stenographers are murdered." However terrible, the killing is to be understood as a rare event—the stuff of scary tabloid articles, but no real reason for ordinary people to fear. Indeed, the investigation proceeds in an urban context that seems remarkably safe and orderly. Outside the station house, children frolic in the spray of an open hydrant; at one point, detective Barry Fitzgerald actually shuts his window to close out the kids' joyful cries before turning to a disagreeable interrogation. Later, on the Lower East Side, other children at play innocently guide a detective to the suspect's apartment. Even at the climax, as the murderer tries to escape up the walkway of the Williamsburg Bridge, we see him race past happy families enjoying their leisure, then watch him break through a jump rope stretched by two girls across the pathway—literally rupturing the city's peaceful order (230). And in a telling detail near the end, as the chase carries us high into the bridge's towers, we glimpse tennis players on the public courts far below—tiny figures dressed in white, utterly unaware of the life-and-death battle occurring far above their heads. Even in this supremely dramatic moment, in other words, ordinary life in the city proceeds.

Given the film's insistence on realism, it was not surprising that *The Naked City* depicted a community that, while not crime-free, was essentially a place of civic order. This image was nothing less than accurate at a time when, by almost any standard, the city was astonishingly safe; in 1945, with a population of nearly eight million, New York recorded exactly 292 murders.

But by the mid-1950s, a new trend was emerging, first apparent in gang battles that somehow seemed more ominous than earlier crimes: rooted in broad social problems, often senseless, these brutal conflicts posed a threat not only to their individual victims but to entire neighborhoods. On screen, the rising tide of violence was tracked not in traditional police stories, but in a series of socially conscious dramas that recognized it as part of larger urban troubles. In 1955, *Blackboard Jungle* followed an idealistic young teacher (Glenn Ford) inside the grim fortress—part school, part jail—called "North Manual High," where his very life is threatened by a vicious classroom gang. *The Last Angry Man* (1959) charted the growing menace, as youth gangs overran the rough Brooklyn neighborhood where an aging, idealistic doctor (Paul Muni) provides a lonely island of civility. In *West Side Story* (1961), the gangs were poeticized by choreographer Jerome Robbins into a mythic presence, moving down the streets of the West Side with a kind of stylized swagger stretching up and out, as if trying to command the urban space around them (214). Nevertheless,

230. *The Naked City* (1948). Attempting to escape the police, a murder suspect (Ted de Corsia) races up the walkway of the Williamsburg Bridge, past hundreds of families. Covering more than a mile and a half, the climactic chase required three weeks to film; the director Jules Dassin used roller skates to line up the sequence on the bridge.

in its opening shots *West Side Story* crystallized a disturbing new sense of a city that was slipping out of control. Looking down on Manhattan from above, we hear a strange and ominous whistle: a secret signal, like that which some fearsome creatures might use to alert one another as they surround their prey. As the camera descends, we see a school yard, carved from the thick mass of tenements—plainly a clearing of some kind. And now we see the "creatures" themselves, "sharks" and "jets," tangling in a complex choreography of attack, feint, and counterattack: an aggressive battle over turf, imaginary territory in a landscape which neither group actually owns. This is not a city, in other words, but a jungle.

Something else had changed. Shot on location, *West Side Story*'s opening scene made a larger claim—explicit and implicit—to be presenting the reality of the city. Warner's prewar gangster films may have been drawn from headlines (*Marked Woman*, for example, was closely based on Thomas Dewey's prosecution of Lucky Luciano's prostitution rings), but few could genuinely confuse its mythical backlot New York for the actual place. The presence of the real city in the background of postwar films, on the other hand, inevitably lent an air of authenticity to the action—even if (as in any feature) that action was entirely scripted and performed by actors. Born of the close association of location shooting with documentary films, this implied authenticity would have complex and sometimes troubling consequences, as the trajectories of the real city and the film city grew increasingly confused.

For a while, to be sure, the two seemed close enough, as both films and the city (beset by crime, decaying slums, and social unrest) grew steadily more troubled. By 1968, when *The Detective* was released, the traditional order of the city was being questioned even by those sworn to uphold it. The film's first shot shows us the Manhattan skyline *inverted*, a reflection in the car hood of detective Joe Leland, played by Frank Sinatra. The entire city was now turned upside down—a place whose problems reached far beyond any particular crime, such as the death of a businessman that Leland is trying to solve. "Do you know the rising rate of crime in this town?" a local politician asks Sinatra. "Do you know the statistics?" Later, when a group of black demonstrators tries to break into the station house, their angry action is defended by Leland himself, who argues that the poor "do not like living in garbage cans," in "ghetto-type housing," which is, he reminds us, "the most profitable type of housing!" The police, he adds bitterly, do not address the city's real problems, but merely "sit on the lid of those garbage cans" to prevent an explosion. As it happens, the case Leland is working on may save the city after all, since it exposes the corrupt workings of a powerful "borough planning commission," which (by not creating enough housing or hospitals) is evidently responsible for the city's decline. The city of *The Detective* is still potentially salvageable, but the scale of the mandate has grown large indeed—too large for Leland, who resigns the force at the film's end.

By the time of *The French Connection*, in 1971, a corner has been turned:

now, not even the most vigorous police initiative can redeem the city. Crime is worse than ever (in one tragicomic sequence, the sidewalk stakeout of a late-night drug deal is interrupted when another, unrelated gang of car thieves shows up on the scene), while the police have grown almost as dangerous as the criminals themselves. Detective Popeye Doyle (Gene Hackman) is honest and energetic but sadistic and maniacal; in the film's famed chase scene, he nearly kills several pedestrians while tearing up a Brooklyn avenue in pursuit of a killer. In any case, no longer can individual competence make much of a difference: though Doyle and his partner (Roy Scheider) finally manage to recover the heroin and kill several smugglers in the bargain, they are reassigned, their partnership dissolved.

The upside-down city glimpsed at the opening of *The Detective* was now firmly in place. Where the police once helped maintain a healthy civic order, now that very order is seen as diseased: ordinary urban life, according to *The French Connection*, is a nightmare. Its sound is a cacophony of sirens and

231. ***Midnight Cowboy* (1969).** Captured by cinematographer Adam Holender's telephoto lens, a Texan newcomer named Joe Buck (Jon Voigt) is the sole passerby to pause for a man sprawled on the sidewalk in front of Tiffany's.

horns, reinforced by an unrelentingly harsh and jangly musical score; its dirty, decaying, traffic-choked streets are uniformly dingy (having been deliberately bleached of color by the cinematographer Owen Roizman, who underexposed the film stock while shooting, then overdeveloped it in the lab). Is there a solution? Perhaps that offered by a radio commercial heard during the film, promoting Florida real estate: "Join the great escape," it suggests. "Say goodbye to rising taxes, air pollution, commuting, high prices and cold, depressing winters."

By the early 1970s, there seemed to be few other answers. In the real city, soaring crime, social crises, and countless municipal strikes were causing a precipitous decline in the quality of life. The biggest change could be felt at street level, where new trends—including the loosening of vagrancy laws and the deinstitutionalization of the state's mentally disturbed population—now brought a new character to the sidewalks, and the breakdown of traditional middle-class standards for public behavior. It was a change summed up in a single shot from *Midnight Cowboy*, in 1969, showing newcomer John Voigt standing on Fifth Avenue, stunned not only by the sight of a man sprawled face down on the busy sidewalk, but of everyone else ignoring him, literally stepping around the body as they pass (231).

Importantly, the decline in public order was affecting not only the poor (who had always suffered hardship), but middle-class New Yorkers, who found their relatively comfortable way of life threatened by forces that no one seemed able to reverse, or even slow. So universally recognizable was this change, in fact, that no fewer than three times in this period, filmmakers used it as the premise not of crime stories, but of *comedies.*

In a strange way, the trio of films—*The Out-of-Towners* (1970) and *The Prisoner of Second Avenue* (1975), both written by Neil Simon, and *Little Murders* (1971) by Jules Feiffer—only confirmed movie New York's status as a larger-than-life place. For what they showed was no ordinary city confronted with problems, but a place of *titanic* failure, of continuous catastrophe. Yet in their endless, sometimes implausible (and, in *Little Murders*, almost surreal) accumulation of indignities and disasters, the three films revealed the distinctive outlines of middle-class order in New York—even as they sought to obliterate it, piece by piece.

To be sure, that middle-class order is certainly not the standard American model, such as the one that out-of-towners George and Gwen Kellerman (Jack Lemmon and Sandy Dennis) are leaving behind in Twin Oaks, Ohio: a single-family house on its suburban plot, with a station wagon in the driveway. In most of the country, being middle class means owning a tract of land and its necessary corollary, an automobile. Middle-class life in Manhattan, on the other hand, is sustained by other means: with his new high-paying job in town, George explains, they will be living in a rented apartment near the park, and won't *need* a car. Yet as the Kellermans soon find out, to their horror, this life-

232. ***The Out-of-Towners*** **(1970).** Unable to get a hotel room, or a taxi, or even a subway train, George and Gwen Kellerman (Jack Lemmon and Sandy Dennis) are obliged to spend their first night in New York walking down Park Avenue in the pouring rain, past giant piles of uncollected garbage.

support system is on the verge of a complete breakdown, thanks to simultaneous strikes suspending all subway, bus, taxi, and sanitation services; they must walk for blocks in the pouring rain, wading past enormous piles of garbage, only to discover they have been turned out of their hotel room (232). Unable to find a foothold in the city, robbed of all their money, they are reduced to indigents, living not near the park but *in* it, helpless against a barrage of assaults and humiliations. Afterward, Gwen pleads with George to return to the snug certainties of their automobile suburb, hoping George has told his prospective New York employer that "you never want to see a big city again."

> *You don't want to live where people have to live on top of each other, and don't have enough room to walk, or to breathe, or to smile at each other; you don't want to step on garbage in the streets, or be attacked by dogs or have to give away watches in the middle of your sleep. You wish you never came here.*

Unlike the disillusioned out-of-towners, the main characters in *Little Murders* and *The Prisoner of Second Avenue* are native New Yorkers, for whom the street is already something of a lost cause, a place of random murders, muggings, smashed phone booths, fires, sirens, accidents (233). (*Prisoner* is punctuated by radio bulletins of the larger city—heat waves, blackouts, strikes—that carry the flavor of wartime dispatches.) For these characters, the problem is that the *apartment*, the traditional middle-class refuge from the street, is now under siege, no longer capable of protecting its residents from the city's troubles; indeed, it may actually magnify those troubles, turning its tenants into inmates. In *The Prisoner of Second Avenue*, Upper East Siders Mel and Edna Edison (Jack Lemmon and Anne Bancroft) are gradually being driven crazy by their apartment building, as doormen prove surly or incompetent, as the sounds of noisy neighbors penetrate their walls and the smell of garbage rises to their windows, as broken elevators turn the structure into a fourteen-story walk-up—one without running water, because the pipes have failed. Eventually the apartment itself is penetrated by burglars, stripping the couple of their last illusion of protection.

The Upper West Side family in *Little Murders* is under even more direct assault: from the first moments, the home of decorator Patsy Newquist (Marcia Rodd) is being invaded by heavy-breathing phone calls and the sound of a gang fight in the street below. Yet Patsy somehow still believes in the possibility of civic order, even in the face of the blackouts and mysterious explosions that rock the West End Avenue home of her parents (Vince Gardenia and Elizabeth Wilson) or the murder of her brother—a war hero who survived Korea and Vietnam, we are told, only to be shot down on 97th Street and Amsterdam Avenue. Patsy's formidable optimism (when her own place is ransacked, she simply sees a chance to redecorate) and sense of civic commitment is so strong, in fact, it might just bring her zombie-like, "apathist" boyfriend, Alfred (Elliott Gould), back to life. But brutality prevails, as Patsy herself becomes the target of a random sniper. Soon, similar shootings—little murders—have become routine. ("I get shot at every day," Patsy's mother observes as another victim is wheeled through the lobby. "We all do.") Their apartment is no longer protection enough, even with elaborate bolts and alarms installed across the front door. Now, massive steel shutters must be fitted over all the windows ("It has to be put in every room," the mother points out. "It says so in the building code")—and a good thing, too, since the constant ricochet of bullets can be heard outside. Their home has been reclaimed as a refuge, though now more a jail cell than an apartment.

233. ***Little Murders*** (1971). Written by Jules Feiffer, *Little Murders* takes place in an urban environment so broken-down and disorderly that Patsy Newquist (Marcia Rodd) doesn't even notice the smashed glass panel of her telephone booth.

Unlike the Kellermans, the Edisons and Newquists decide to remain in New York, finding an insane joy in surmounting the city's problems. Mel Edison snaps out of his breakdown when he races after a pickpocket (Sylvester Stallone, in a bit part) to retrieve his wallet—only to discover later that he has the *other* man's wallet, that the "pickpocket" was actually the innocent victim of Mel's own maniacal aggression. Happiness is restored at the Newquists' when Alfred buys a rifle and lets everyone take turns shooting pedestrians from the apartment window. No longer automatically granted by middle-class status, urban survival can be assured only by becoming as predatory as the rest of the city's inhabitants.

This same message, unleavened by any trace of humor or surrealism, was delivered by *Death Wish* (1974), a film that fulfilled (and reveled in) the fantasy of middle-class urban revenge that the other films had only hinted at. As a "development engineer," Paul Kersey (Charles Bronson) is an obvious exemplar of traditional civic order. But according to the film, that order has completely vanished, replaced by a "war zone"—as Kersey discovers when a trio of leering thugs break into his Riverside Drive apartment house, viciously rape his daughter, and beat his wife to death. Convalescing in Arizona, Kersey is presented with a different urban model: cities like Tucson are safe, the film claims, because ordinary citizens ("honest men") employ personal firepower at will. Though tempted to leave New York, Kersey decides to remain, redeeming it through his own kind of civic gesture, what critic Carlos Clarens calls "the perfect vigilante fantasy":

> *keeping bachelor hours, most of which are spent not at the local singles bar but cruising parks and streets where men go after each other with sex or murder on their minds. Bronson offers himself as bait, luring those he is about to kill at the first sign of aggression, but, curiously, no one ever makes a pass at him. . . .*

"The camera doesn't turn a corner," Clarens notes, "where a mugger is not caught in the act, and junkies and weirdos run rampant wielding switchblades in front of apathetic subway riders; they are the same faceless fiends who once wore war paint and feathers to furnish a similar provocation." After a few weeks, we are told, Kersey's deadly late-night rambles have driven the entire city's crime rate down (229).

Whatever its claims of social relevance, the film's graphic scenes of violence deeply implicated *Death Wish* in the kinds of behavior it claimed to deplore; the movie was plainly intended first and foremost to satisfy its audience's blood lust (a notion only confirmed by the film's still more violent sequels). But the quality of authenticity associated with postwar films, the sense of realism that came from actual locations, now proved to have far-reaching—and for the city's public image, disastrous—consequences. New York's undeniably high crime rate, combined with its traditionally larger-than-life status and its growing popularity as a production location, now made it by far the most common setting for violent American films. It was no use for officials to point out that New York was far less dangerous, statistically, than many other big American cities—especially Sunbelt cities like Tucson, which (despite *Death Wish*'s claims to the contrary) consistently ranked higher in almost all major crime categories. Nor was it any use for city dwellers themselves to criticize the film's strangely unrealistic portrait of urban crime, with its cartoonish muggers roaming empty parks and alleyways and its stagy late-night clashes. The makers of *Death Wish* were plainly offering up a projection of middle-class fears about crime—and urban life itself—rather than even a vaguely accurate depiction of a real problem or place. Thanks largely to movies, crime and urban violence were now uniquely associated in the public's mind with New York, as glamour and sophistication had once been. Though its crime problems were in fact little different from those of any other American city, New York's very preeminence, the urbanist Marshall Berman observed, enlarged its troubles "into something mythical."

> *In the late 1960s, New York came to symbolize "urban violence." This wouldn't have been so bad if it had enabled Americans to confront the rapidly rising tide of violence throughout American society. But the symbolism took on an insidiously twisted form: poverty, easy access to drugs and guns, desperate rage exploding into mayhem, were considered* our *problems; out-of-towners seeing our town come apart concluded complacently that it could never happen to theirs. . . . Our own media mythicized us into America's Other, which could be blamed for everything that the country didn't want to see in itself.*

Ironically, the problem only grew worse when filmmakers sought a higher degree of authenticity by focusing on certain parts of the city—especially those associated, for better or worse, with lawlessness. Over more than twenty years, in two great waves of "action" films—including *Cotton Comes to Harlem* (1970), *Across 110th Street* (1971), *Shaft* (1972), *New Jack City* (1991), *Juice* (1992), and *Sugar Hill* (1993)—movie cameras descended on Harlem, known decades before as the vibrant center of African American culture but in recent years as a deteriorated area struggling with poverty and crime. Inevitably revolving around illegal drugs and gang warfare, these films were in effect updated versions of the classic 1930s Warner's gangster pictures, with heroin and cocaine replacing bootleg liquor, and black and Puerto Rican drug lords replacing the old Irish and Italian hoodlums. (*New Jack City* actually made the link explicit, modeling its narrative on Raoul Walsh's *The Roaring Twenties* and having its characters consciously recall the likes of George Raft and James Cagney.)

In fact, the African American and Latino directors of these films—Ossie Davis, Gordon Parks, Mario van Peebles, Ernest Dickerson, Leon Ichaso—generally made a conscientious effort to present Harlem as something more than a decaying background for violent confrontations, in the hopes of revealing a community that, however ravaged, still possessed a vital urban heritage. Following John Shaft (Richard Roundtree) as he searches streets of ornate row houses (in *Shaft*), or traveling with detectives "Coffin" Ed Johnson and "Grave Digger" Jones (Raymond St. Jacques and Godfrey Cambridge, in *Cotton Comes to Harlem*) from houseboats on the Harlem River to landmark churches on St.

Nicholas Avenue, audiences glimpsed an area of startling architectural richness, evidence of the strange equation by which economic impoverishment—by discouraging new construction—can often prove a friend to historic preservation. Yet in the end it was obvious that the overall effect of these films—obliged by their genre to be filled with stabbings, shootings, and machine-gun battles—was to reinforce the image of Harlem as a place soaked in blood. Two decades later, *New Jack City*, *Juice*, and *Sugar Hill* were still determined to show the decent side of Harlem life, even as they portrayed ever more graphically the invasion of crack cocaine, for which entire buildings and armies of kids were now being mobilized. These newer films also took cinematic advantage of problems that were more *visible* than ever before: not just the poor housing and high unemployment that had always plagued slum communities, but new patterns of arson and abandonment that were leaving burned-out tenements and empty lots in their wake. Plainly, larger forces were at work in Harlem, but whatever their broader concerns, these films tended to reduce just about everything to the familiar themes of drugs, crime, and violence (234).

If troubling when applied to Harlem, this easy reductiveness had far more dire consequences when films began turning to the South Bronx, a catch-all name for a series of poor and working-class neighborhoods whose rapid social decline in the 1970s had resulted, by decade's end, in a level of physical devastation unlike anything since the wartime destruction of German and Japanese cities: first buildings, then streets, then entire districts burned out through arson, until whole square miles of the borough had become little more than the hollowed-out shells of tenements and apartment houses, or rubble-strewn fields, eerily outlined by sidewalks and streets. Vivid and mesmerizing in ap-

234. ***New Jack City*** **(1991).** After chasing down a vicious drug dealer on a Harlem fire escape (encouraged by a crowd gathering below), a vengeful detective named "Scotty" Appleton (Ice-T) prepares to shoot—even as his partner Nick Peretti (Judd Nelson) attempts to dissuade him.

pearance, the area offered an ideal setting for the ever-more violent films of the period. How better to present an utterly dysfunctional urban context, the true "jungle" in which even the most shocking acts of violence might seem perfectly plausible?

Of course, by now (several years after *Death Wish*), the crucial role played by movies in reinforcing—or creating—public images was becoming all too apparent. Not least of the problems faced by the borough's residents was the fact that the very phrase "the South Bronx" had become a national symbol of urban failure, a term of almost demonizing power. When 20th Century-Fox announced the release in 1981 of a film called *Fort Apache, The Bronx* (using the slang term for the police department's 41st Precinct, located near the heart of the devastated area), a storm of protest arose, with one City Council committee passing a resolution urging New Yorkers to boycott the film. In response, the producers reluctantly agreed to add a disclaimer: "Because the story involves police work," the notice read, "it does not deal with the law abiding members of the community, nor does it attempt to dramatize the efforts of individuals and groups who are struggling to turn the Bronx around."

The conflict haunted the film itself. Concerned with authenticity, the script offered a level of social analysis far beyond Sinatra's "ghetto-type housing" speech in *The Detective*. The precinct, explains the departing police captain to his replacement (played by Ed Asner), covers "a forty-block area with 70,000 people, packed in like sardines . . . the lowest income per capita, the highest rate of unemployment in the city, largest proportion of non-English-speaking population, families that have been on welfare for three generations." Still, it was obvious that for the filmmakers, the area's decline merely provided the license to present scenes of lurid violence, committed by vaguely demonic characters. In the film's opening moments, two patrolmen are shot dead—point-blank and for no apparent reason—by a drug-addicted prostitute (Pam Grier); instantly, zombie-like residents emerge from the wreckage of nearby buildings to strip the men of their wallets. Grier is herself later murdered by a pair of drug dealers, who roll her corpse in a rug and dump it into the rubble of some demolished tenements. Then the drug dealers themselves are killed, and the rug is carted away with the rubble; the patrolmen's deaths are never solved. The point is clear: where the police had once caught criminals to restore civic order, then later settled for catching criminals without restoring order, now there was no real hope of catching criminals—and almost no civic order left to restore.

Near the end of the film, when the cameras turn from battered but still-functioning streets to the hollow heart of the burned-out area, the movie's fundamental disjunction became unavoidable—the unspoken chasm between the kinds of troubles shown on screen, the drugs and street crime familiar to the genre, and the uncanny views of endless ruins and fields of rubble. *Fort Apache* lingers on the terrible sight but does not even try to explain it, certainly never hinting that any larger forces—chronic patterns of disinvestment, bank "red-lining," landlord abandonment, or arson—might be at work. Instead, seeing only the crimes and social failures of the local residents, we are left with the impression that they must have somehow destroyed all their own houses, too, in their spare time.

So otherworldly and eerie were these views of the Bronx's devastation that they soon called forth a fantasy of their own—a film that responded to this strange and terrible landscape by offering up an imaginary horror to inhabit it. If *Fort Apache* could be criticized (by one local paper) for "suggesting that the people of the Bronx are animals to be controlled, rather than human beings to be respected," *Wolfen* (1981) made the comparison literal, extending the demonization of the area one crucial step by making it the home of *actual* demons: supernatural wolves, a race of superior beings who have fled human expansion by moving, we are told, into "the new wilderness, the great slum areas, the graveyard of your species." Feral and nocturnal, the "wolfen" are, in effect, superrats who scuttle through the crevices of the urban landscape; the audience shares their perspective—almost viscerally—through low, fast, color-shifted images intended to reflect the swift creatures' "infrared" and "heat-detecting" vision. From a wrecked church near Charlotte Street (the symbolic center of the Bronx's devastation), the creatures fan out across the city, trying to halt, by way of multiple murders and dismemberments, an urban renewal scheme to rebuild the area as luxury housing. If the precise identity of the creatures remains somewhat unclear—perhaps they are wolves, perhaps they are American Indians, perhaps they are simply local residents (with whom, at several points, they are confused)—the general thrust is clear: they are monstrous creatures, products of a monstrous place. Looking out on the stunning and horrific spectacle of the borough's devastation, and unwilling (or unable) to explore or understand the all-too-human realities underlying it, the film city turned to the inhuman, the supernatural, in the hope of giving it meaning (235).

235. ***Wolfen*** **(1981).** Searching for clues to several mysterious murders, detective Dewey Wilson (Albert Finney) prepares to enter a burned-out church amidst the most devastated blocks of the South Bronx. Designed by Paul Sylbert, the church was the single largest exterior set ever built in New York.

These images of the devastated Bronx—darkly fantastic in spirit, yet evidence of a real (and seemingly unstoppable) decline—allowed filmmakers to imagine a plague of decay engulfing the entire city. A ruined New York—not the Bronx, but Manhattan itself—would provide a potent setting for a dystopian vision of the future, while offering a certain apocalyptic titillation all its own; it would be a place, moreover, whose nonexistent civic order would inevitably allow room for all kinds of violence to satisfy contemporary film audiences, increasingly accepting—if not actually desirous—of on-screen bloodshed and mayhem.

Written and directed by John Carpenter, *Escape from New York* (1981) vividly demonstrated how the dramatic rise in crime and disorder could reinvigorate the most ancient fears and suspicions about the city. For beneath its futuristic trappings, the film embodied a notion dating back to the mid-nineteenth century, when New York City was limited to Manhattan, isolated by wide rivers from mainland United States and even from its sister city, Brooklyn. It was easy for Americans of the time to consider the city as a place apart, a narrow, confined island whose strange and different ways were often unfathomable to the rest of the country. The notion was diluted somewhat in the twentieth century, when Manhattan was laced to the larger world by dozens of rail and road crossings, and the city itself redefined as an enormous, five-borough metropolis—but it has retained a residual power in the American imagination. *Escape from New York* would bring the old vision back to life with a vengeance: Manhattan as nothing less, literally or figuratively, than America's Devil's Island.

The film's prologue describes the city's conversion into the federal government's penal colony in the late 1980s, conveniently eliding all social or economic detail to focus instead on topography: the distinctive shape of Manhattan now outlined by a bright green line indicating a high "containment wall" that, as if quarantining a virus, has finally rid the nation of its offshore anomaly. The great river crossings, the bridges and tunnels that allowed the metropolis to transcend its geography, have literally been subverted—mined with explosives—in order to restore the city to its nineteenth-century boundaries.

The film then surveys the dark jungle that the city has become: its buildings vandalized and burned, its nighttime streets filled with "crazies" who come up from the subway, and its population a throng of criminal gangs, wreaking havoc under the supremely violent Duke of New York (Isaac Hayes). At times, the place portrayed hardly resembles New York at all: the climactic escape takes place on the "69th Street Bridge"; power is provided by pumping crude oil from deposits beneath the island; and the exterior scenes take place on ruined blocks that look nothing like Manhattan—for the good reason that they were shot in downtown St. Louis, in an area that had been recently ravaged by fire. Yet at other times the film plays off the audience's shivery recognition of the city's landmarks: the World Trade Center, now a hulking ruin toward which Snake Plissken (Kurt Russell) glides his sailplane; Central Park, now a jungle clearing where inmates gather for monthly food drop-offs; the Statue of Liberty, now the island's security post. In its way, the film offers a kind of inverted tribute to the sheer iconic status of New York. As Carpenter surely appreciated, a film titled "*Escape from St. Louis*" would hardly draw much of a crowd.

Far from falling into a spiral of decay, of course, the real Manhattan rebounded in a binge of shiny prosperity in the 1980s, even while struggling with civic problems more visible than ever—especially the increasing number of indigents inhabiting its public spaces. Though homelessness, like crime, was hardly a problem unique to New York, the city's version took on the same kind of mythic distinctiveness on film, in part because of the very number of the city's homeless, and in part because of the powerful contrast they offered to the raw display of wealth that marked the decade, and to the public grandeur that had long been the city's hallmark. Indeed, one film devoted to the subject—*The Saint of Fort Washington* (1992)—actually *used* civic architecture to underscore the magnitude of the problem. We watch sympathetically as a mentally troubled man named Matthew (Matt Dillon)—made homeless when his single-room hotel is demolished by a greedy developer—tries to navigate the city housing bureaucracy, then is carted off to one of the city's emergency shelters: the Fort Washington armory, a block-long Romanesque-style fortress in upper Manhattan. Nothing can prepare us, however, for the astonishing sight within: a huge, open space filled with thousands of beds, laid out in endless aisles beneath the high, cavernous ceiling. Thanks to the grandeur of this older civic building, what might otherwise be a statistical abstraction becomes easily comprehensible, visually compelling—and deeply moving.

In *The Fisher King* (1991), Terry Gilliam's darkly baroque vision of New York is essentially defined by the interplay between the homeless and the rich (hardly anyone else seems to live there). It is an interplay, moreover, that the audience witnesses from both sides, through the roller-coaster experience of a radio disc-jockey named Jack Lucas (Jeff Bridges). Wealthy and successful at the start, Jack is sealed behind the dark glass of sky-high apartments and black limousines, attempting to shut out a public realm that has become untenable—a realm in which trash flies everywhere through the air, and half-crazed indigents abound. Later, when he is down on his luck, Jack sees this lower world through the eyes of a troubled homeless man played by Robin Williams. If anything, from street level the contrast seems even greater between the city's looming towers and its ragged population of vagrants, who sleep under plastic bags at the edge of its public spaces. Toward the film's end, Jack, wealthy once more, again sees the homeless only as annoyances who occupy the stretch between limousine door and office lobby. In Gilliam's vision, to be rich is to be socially connected but physically detached from the city; to be poor is to inhabit the city's spaces but be utterly disconnected from its social system. Few other options are evident.

After more than two decades, the portrait of New York as "Horror City" had grown so familiar and conventionalized it could be the stuff of humor: young Tom Hanks, spending his first night alone in a cheap Times Square hotel (in *Big*, 1988), turns off the canned gunfire of *The French Connection* on his television only to hear the real thing just outside his window; newcomer Michael J. Fox, calling his mother in Iowa from a phone booth (in *The Secret of My Success*, 1988), somehow neglects to mention the burglary, gunfight, and arrest that is occurring on the sidewalk right in front of him. Violent urban films tended to be set in New York as a matter of course, even if they had no thematic connection to the city; many were actually shot in Canadian cities, whose lower labor costs and flexible work rules made them popular with the producers of low-budget action films. Sprayed with graffiti and strewn with garbage, streets in

Toronto and Montreal became blandly familiar stand-ins for crime-ridden "New York" neighborhoods. Audiences seeing *Rumble in the Bronx* (1995) were perhaps understandably confused by views of snowcapped mountains in the distance; the film had been shot entirely in Vancouver, its title chosen (by Hong Kong filmmaker Jackie Chan) for its presumed association with violence and "action."

But in the real city, enormous changes were under way. Back in 1983, the social scientists George Kelling and James Q. Wilson had published their "broken window" theory, calling explicit attention to the link between serious crime and broader urban disorder:

> *Crime, as well as fear of crime, is closely associated with disorder. For most people, New York's crime problem comes down to the fear they endure as a consequence of disorder—the well-founded belief that in disorderly places society has ceded control to those . . . who are outside the law, and therefore that anything might happen.*

236. ***The Warriors*** **(1979).** Spray can in hand, a member of the Coney Island gang, the Warriors, leaves his "tag" on the walls of a subway car, as another passenger looks on helplessly.

Even in troubled parts of the city, they pointed out, acts of violence remain relatively rare, so the judgment about the safety of any particular area must be made on secondary evidence—especially signs of physical disorder, such as "graffiti, abandoned cars, broken windows and abandoned buildings." Though often minor in themselves, these breed serious crime, not only by discouraging law-abiding citizens, but by encouraging would-be criminals to feel they can get away with anything. "Yet disorder," Kelling observed, had been "largely ignored by official police doctrine." Concerned mostly with providing a quick response to the short list of "major" crimes, most police officials regarded disorder as a petty annoyance, unrelated to their central mission. "Disorder does not exist on any FBI index;" Kelling noted bluntly, "therefore, it has not been a priority."

In retrospect, it was clear that filmmakers had understood—intuitively—something many police officials had not. For years, films had employed exactly the kinds of physical disorder Kelling identified (vandalism, graffiti, smashed phone booths, trash-filled streets, broken windows) to establish the plausible setting for acts of urban violence, knowing full well that in the minds of their audience—the general public, in other words—disorder was *intimately* connected to serious crime. Indeed, from the start, the Horror City of the 1970s and 1980s had been specifically identified (by Kael and others) with a breakdown in the city's *order*, very different from the ordinary run of crime—and crime movies—that had been a part of the urban landscape since the early years of the century. Even at its most gratuitously or implausibly violent, the filmic

Horror City clearly recognized disorder and crime not as two isolated issues, but deeply interlinked phenomena (236).

By the mid-1990s, after Kelling's theories had been put into widespread practice, New York's crime rate began plummeting to levels not seen in decades. Meanwhile, painted subway graffiti had all but disappeared, and areas such as the South Bronx—in the popular mind still the wasteland of *Fort Apache* and *Wolfen*—had been largely rebuilt. Though New York still sustained enormous human and social problems, it was no longer the ultimate symbol of urban decay: that distinction had passed to another city, which firmly supplanted New York as the quintessential filmic dystopia: Los Angeles.

The shift had begun in 1982 with *Blade Runner*, whose mesmerizing urban vision presented a toxic Southern California of 2012. The gloomy destiny it predicted seemed prophetic when Los Angeles was later beset with a series of human and natural cataclysms: fires, droughts, earthquake, crime waves, economic downturn, and riot. By the time of *Falling Down* (1993), in which newly unemployed defense worker Michael Douglas leaves his traffic-jammed car on the freeway and makes a brutal trek across a racially and economically riven landscape, Los Angeles had replaced New York as the preferred setting for filmic apocalypse, a shift ratified in 1996 by John Carpenter's *Escape from L.A.*, which proposed a ruined, postearthquake Los Angeles as an armed camp for the deranged. By the time of that film's release, New York—whose extraordinary crime drop had made it by far the safest big city in the United States—no longer seemed like much of a candidate for urban dystopia, even as fantasy.

Crime films would continue to be made in New York, of course. But Horror City—the nightmarish vision that for decades had shaped both the real and filmic city—had vanished with startling rapidity. Even as it receded, however, its lasting mark on the fabric of the city grew clearer than ever. In a 1996 film called *Ed's Next Move*, a young newcomer from rural Wisconsin, Ed Brodsky (Matt Ross), never witnesses a single serious crime. But the city he comes to has been completely transformed, nonetheless, by decades of *responding* to crime. "I put bars on the window and they cost," one potential roommate tells him; "I put in a Fichet lock so it's ultrasafe here," boasts another. Trying to enter an apartment building to meet a veteran New Yorker named Ray (Kevin Carroll), he is brusquely turned away at the locked front door by another tenant, who plainly looks at any stranger—even the innocent, fresh-faced Ed—as a dangerous threat. The place Ed does finally share with Ray sports security grates on every window, converting a decent living space into a jail-like environment, not all that different from the steel-shuttered nightmare in *Little Murders*. Ray's car is no less well-protected, with not just an alarm but also a heavy chain and a Club device locking down the steering wheel. "Did you think New York would be like Wisconsin with more people and a subway?" Ed's girlfriend (Callie Thorne) wonders in amazement. "You have to deal with New York on its own terms."

If New York's epidemic of disorder had abated with surprising speed, its legacy—a city physically reshaped around security, safety, and the *fear* of crime—would clearly take far longer to change. Such would remain, for the foreseeable future, New York's "own terms."

ALL THAT FRANTIC MOTION

For most of its length, *The Naked City*—shot on location more extensively than any film before it—is given over to a systematic homicide investigation, carried on patiently across the breadth of the city. At its climax, however, the picture explodes into something very different—and no less innovative. As the police close in, we see the murderer, Ted de Corsia, fly out of his tenement, sprint across a series of backyards, then over to the Williamsburg Bridge. Suddenly, the use of locations pays a new dividend, as the deliberate investigation becomes a dramatic chase, racing across a landscape of startling complexity (one of the backyards, for example, turns out to be a mortuary yard, filled with headstones). It is only as the camera reaches the bridge itself, however, that the true impact of the new technique becomes evident. The giant river-crossing offers an arresting setting for the pursuit, as we follow the police and the suspect scrambling across an immense steel framework of girders and beams. Even more than its sheer scale, the great structure's intertwining of so many different kinds of movement—cars on its roadways, subways on its tracks, pedestrians on its intricate walkways and staircases—makes it exquisitely apt as a setting for the breathless chase. Built specifically to enable movement, the

237. ***Shaft's Big Score!*** **(1972).** In the film's spectacular climax, the detective John Shaft (Richard Roundtree) attempts to elude a pursuing helicopter in a speedboat—barreling down the East River (with the Williamsburg Bridge in the background)—and on foot, amidst the gantries of the old Navy Yard in Brooklyn.

bridge is readily supercharged by the police pursuit—which becomes, in a sense, simply another stream of motion weaving through its daily flux.

For filmmakers no less than audiences, *Naked City*'s stunning climax offered a revelation—that New York, the city devoted to movement as no other, provided the greatest context imaginable for that most primal of cinematic devices, the chase. The real city offered a resource simply unreproducible in the studio: a nineteenth-century street grid superimposed with a series of twentieth-century marvels—massive engineering projects, crossing and re-crossing the city, above and below the ground. In the years to come, directors would flock to set crime films in New York not only for sociological reasons, but to make the kind of action films in which, as Carlos Clarens later observed, "cutting and the logistics of stunt work collaborate to cancel any but the most visceral commitment; [and] moral issues are left suspended by all that frantic motion" (237).

Along the way, these films would offer audiences a remarkable look at the city's unique infrastructure. Could there be any closer examination of the subway, for example, than *The Taking of Pelham One Two Three* (1974), a film whose incredible premise—the hijacking of an IRT train—was balanced by its superbly credible locations? In the film, the audience not only learns more about the subway than they ever dreamed (that each IRT car is seventy-two feet long, costs $150,000, and weighs seventy-five thousand pounds, for example) but gets a full cross-section of the system itself—from the transit authority's drab command center in downtown Brooklyn to an underground control "tower" at Grand Central, whose primitive display boards and telephones seem hardly newer than the IRT itself, originally constructed in 1904.

238. ***The French Connection* (1971).** Determined to chase down a killer in the elevated subway above him, detective Popeye Doyle (Gene Hackman) commandeers a car and races down Brooklyn's 86th Street—nearly hitting several pedestrians (including the woman and baby in this view) along the way.

The climax, shot from a camera mounted on a runaway train, barrels us headlong through the tunnels and stations of the Lexington Avenue line—a scene that, whatever its contemporary overlay of suspense, essentially offers the same primal thrill as the old Edison actuality (which, as it happens, ran precisely through the same stretch of tunnel) (21). But the film also offers a *second* chase, in which police cars tear up the avenues, trying to keep up with the train that is racing along, somewhere, beneath their feet. In the most exciting terms possible, the action thus traces for us the parallel paths of movement—running visibly on the street, and invisibly, below it—that define modern Manhattan.

It was another, still more famous chase scene, however, that dramatized most vividly the way the city, with its constant premium on space, learned to overlay its streets with a parallel system of transport—in this case not below but *above* the ground, along an elevated train track. Halfway through *The French*

Connection, a gunman jumps onto an IND train after trying to kill Popeye Doyle (Gene Hackman). Commandeering a car, Doyle roars up Brooklyn's 86th Street trying to overtake the train, which is being forcibly run through the stations without stop. Foot to the pedal, frantically honking the horn, Doyle tears up the length of the avenue, one eye on the speeding train above and another on the street-level havoc he himself is creating, as he runs every light, slams into cross traffic, and terrifies pedestrians. The director William Friedkin's camera flies right alongside the two-level chase, looking across to the madly racing train above and even more madly racing car below—an amazing spectacle that not only takes advantage of but also fulfills, in the strange but satisfying manner of the movie city, the extraordinary possibilities of this double pathway, built to multiply the capacity of the crowded city's corridors (238).

Perhaps the most surprisingly poetic vision of the subway appeared in a film called *The Warriors* (1979), a darkly stylized adventure of a Coney Island gang trying to make their way back home through the endless city night. Like no other film, *The Warriors* managed to convey the extraordinary breadth of the city's transit system, the hundreds upon hundreds of track miles that make it one of the largest such underground networks in the world. Indeed, the film managed to imbue the New York subway, for all its besmirched reputation, with a distinctly epic quality—not surprisingly, in a sense, for the film's original story was drawn directly (by the writer Sol Hurick) from the *Anabasis* of Xenophon, whose ancient themes of distant journey and embattled return were transposed neatly from first-century Persia to twentieth-century New York, a sprawling urban archipelago linked from one end to the other by a continuous ribbon of steel.

The story opens with the outbound voyage, traced for us on a subway map by a young gang member: across the width of Brooklyn, up the length of Manhattan, and on to the far northern border of the Bronx, where an extraordinary conclave of all the city's violent gangs—the Riffs, the Saracens, the Moon Runners, and dozens more—has been arranged by a supreme leader named Cyrus. But Cyrus is soon assassinated by someone in the crowd, and in the ensuing melee, the Warriors are falsely accused of the murder. Now they must somehow make their way home to Coney Island, even as all of the other gangs unite to stop them.

The return trip passes through a landscape at once gritty and fantastical—a shabby and alienating universe of empty stations, gloomy tunnels, and spray-painted graffiti. Yet it is a magical pathway all the same, whose vibrant strokes of lurid, electric color—signals and lights suddenly looming in the darkness—provide the haunting setting for a night voyage of the imagination. Along the way, one gang member is caught by the police, another dies on the tracks—but slowly, tunnel by tunnel, station by station, the surviving Warriors make their way south until they return exhausted to their Coney Island home station, with its suggestive name, Stillwell. The sun is rising, the Atlantic beckons; the northern Bronx seems distant indeed, and some strikingly ancient echoes resound.

Inspired by films such as these, location scouts continued to comb the city's inventory of transportation systems for new possibilities. Only a few years after planners introduced an innovative aerial tramway system to Roosevelt Island, for example, it was called into service as the site of a deadly hostage crisis in *Nighthawks* (1981), its car brought to a terrifying dangling halt, midway across the East River, by a group of terrorists. Yet even this scene was outdone by an earlier sequence, which was shot on location in the IND subway and reached its climax with a pursuit through a section of tunnel still under construction, deep beneath 63rd Street—a huge underground concrete chamber, lighted by the dazzling blaze of arc welding.

As it happens, the 63rd Street line was one of the transit system's last efforts at large-scale construction. In fact, very few public works of any kind have been built in New York in recent decades, forcing moviemakers—always looking out for new scenarios—to propose ever more extravagant scenes within existing assets. *The Cowboy Way* (1994) found Oklahoma rodeo champion Woody Harrelson leaping from a galloping police horse to a subway speeding across the Manhattan Bridge, a stunt at once impressive and absurd. *Money Train*, a 1995 feature about the special subway car that collects token revenues, reached new heights of fantasy, especially in its vision of the "money train" itself, not the grimy yellow utility car actually in service but a gleaming, silvery high-tech transport—a mobile Fort Knox, by way of NASA.

As if to seal the bond between action films and the city's heroic engineering heritage, *Die Hard with a Vengeance* (1994) turned to New York's last great public works project of the twentieth century, Water Tunnel Number 3, a vast network of steel and concrete, five hundred feet below the street, as ambitious as it is little known. It is precisely this obscurity that makes the tunnel ideal for its role in *Die Hard*, as the less-than-obvious escape route for master-criminal Simon Peter Gruber (Jeremy Irons) and his truck armada, laden with Federal Reserve bullion. Following their tracks, policeman John McClane (Bruce Willis) is as surprised as we are to discover how remarkable a construction lies buried beneath his feet: an immense steel cylinder, at least fifty feet across—a water pipe big enough to fill not one but ten million faucets, and thus a sort of metaphor for the metropolis it serves. When, at last, a giant wall of water comes slamming down toward McClane, we can perhaps spare a moment from the exhilarating terror to recognize, as in so many action scenes, an inverted honor to the remarkable feats of construction the great metropolis calls forth, simply to exist.

By the same logic, there could be only one greater—and more paradoxical—tribute to the vast city: its destruction, through some natural or man-made disaster. Such a disaster could arouse the same apocalyptic thrill engendered by *Escape from New York*, but without any implications of urban or social failure.

Some terrible catastrophe has occurred worldwide; New York is simply the most effective place to show it.

Thus the astronaut George Taylor (Charlton Heston in *Planet of the Apes*, 1968) walks the beach of a strange and distant planet that is dominated, nightmarishly, by apes. For the moment he has eluded them, but now something catches his eye, something terrible, something that brings him to his knees in horror. We see him from a high vantage; in the foreground are some oddly familiar, spikelike forms. Then comes the famous shot, summing up the shocking truth: it is the Statue of Liberty, half-buried in the sand. The planet of the apes is Earth, destroyed by man.

Scenes like this one traded yet again on the iconic power of New York. How better to convey the end of the world than to show the destruction of its best-known place—a place, further, that was construed in postwar decades as the closest thing to its capital? In the nuclear era, the greatest symbol of civil society was inevitably the greatest possible target, whose annihilation would pro-

239. ***Beneath the Planet of the Apes* (1970).** Accompanied by a native called Nova (Linda Harrison), astronaut John Brent (James Franciscus) descends beneath the surface of the planet on which he is stranded to discover the ruins of New York—including the marble facade of the Stock Exchange.

240. ***Independence Day* (1996).** This startling view of the Statue of Liberty face-down in New York Harbor was in reality a composite image, combining a five-foot-tall foam replica of the statue, a forced perspective miniature of lower Manhattan, and thirty other layers of film—including fire and smoke elements, the background sky, the alien spacecraft, and subtle touches such as the moving reflections in the water's surface.

vide the most wrenching symbol of atomic nightmare. Of course, actually *showing* the destruction of something as big as New York was a cinematic challenge of the first order. Stock footage of the London blitz, standing in for the atomic bombing of New York in *Invasion, U.S.A.* (1952), was somewhat less than convincing, though perhaps acceptable once it was discovered that the "invasion" was actually the product of mass hypnosis, performed on the patrons of a midtown bar by a Cold War zealot. An indirect yet effective approach was taken by Sidney Lumet in *Fail-Safe* (1965), to portray the bombing of New York by an American war plane, the price of avoiding a general holocaust after Moscow is destroyed in error. A series of quick-cut location shots shows the final few seconds of the city's life, ending in blackness and the high-pitched squeal of a melting phone.

"What a ruin it will make!," H. G. Wells is reported to have said upon first seeing the skyline of Manhattan. Nuclear war provided the plausible springboard for fantasies of New York bombed back into a jungle (in *Captive Women*, 1952), or buried underground (in *Beneath the Planet of the Apes*, 1970). In the latter, astronaut John Brent (James Franciscus) drops through a deep cave to discover that the place the apes reverently call "the forbidden zone" is, in fact, Queens. With further exploration he locates the Stock Exchange, the New York Public Library, Radio City, and St. Patrick's Cathedral, all deep beneath the surface. We see no part of the city, in fact, that does not carry the power to shock us through recognition of its name or architecture. In this ruined city, there are only landmarks (239).

Of course, the filmic scenarios of the city's destruction were not limited to nuclear war. In *Deluge* (1933), made years before the atomic bomb had been invented, New York was destroyed by a giant tidal wave—a fate it would suffer once more in *When Worlds Collide* (1953), and yet again in *Deep Impact* (1998) (240). Given the city's traditional link to the sea, there was a certain aptness to these watery catastrophes; a special shock was provided in the 1953 film by the view of ocean liners floating *between* the city's buildings. The sight of titanic walls of water pouring into the city, moreover, played upon not only the canyonlike character of Manhattan's streets but also of their widely apprehended sense of scale. This latter factor was especially crucial for special effects created in miniature, which succeeded only if audiences believed that waves a couple of yards high, for example, were really hundreds of feet tall. The widespread familiarity of moviegoers with the approximate shape and size of New York's buildings and streets, in fact, made the city the indispensable target for cinematic disasters of all description, from the prehistoric "rhedosaurus" in *The Beast from 20,000 Fathoms* (1953) and the giant mutant lizard in *Godzilla* (1998), both rising from the East River to "hide" among Manhattan's canyons, to the speeding cosmic fragments of *Meteor* (1979) and *Armageddon* (1998), which manage to hit such photogenic targets as the Chrysler Building, Central Park, and Grand Central Terminal. It is perfectly plausible that the invading aliens in *Independence Day* (1996) would seek out New York as one of their first targets, but it is their arrival over Manhattan, in fact, that first gives audiences a sense of how large their ships are meant to be. (Neither Washington nor Los Angeles does the trick as well.) *Independence Day* also reaffirmed the city's continuing iconic power: when the aliens attack Los Angeles's highest structure

241. ***The World, the Flesh, and the Devil* (1959).** A coal miner named Ralph Burton (Harry Belafonte), spared the "atomic poisoning" that has killed off the world's population, searches an empty Fifth Avenue for other survivors. In a logistical triumph, the production team—obliged to shoot between 5:30 and 6 a.m. each morning—arranged with city officials and scores of private companies to halt all traffic and shut off every light and sign in view.

(the First Interstate Bank, designed by I. M. Pei), it is just another tall building being hit; when they do the same thing in New York, it is the Empire State Building being blown up—an image of the city's destruction rivaled in shock value only by a later one of the Statue of Liberty, facedown in the water of New York Harbor.

Yet of all the filmic catastrophes to beset New York, perhaps none was so haunting in the end as a Cold War fantasy that did not destroy the city but, far more strangely, emptied it of people. In *The World, the Flesh, and the Devil* (1959), worldwide "atomic poisoning" spares only Harry Belafonte, caught in a Pennsylvania coal mine during the attack. He makes his way to New York, motorboats across the empty bay, and sets foot on a Manhattan Island, which, he soon realizes, he has all to himself. Searching for other survivors, he wanders around a deserted Wall Street and Times Square and rings the bells of Trinity Church, listening to them echo off the silent streets. Eventually the plot turns up a woman (Inger Stevens) and another man (Mel Ferrer), and ends with the two male rivals, rifles in hand, hunting each other through the city's canyons. But it is those early shots that remain in the mind, the views of Belafonte pulling his wagon of supplies up the middle of an empty Fifth Avenue, the realization of a strange and, in some ways, not unappealing dream of solitude, within the least solitary place on earth (241).

THAT DANGEROUS CITY OF THE IMAGINATION

In his classic 1948 essay, "The Gangster as Tragic Hero," Robert Warshow was among the first critics to observe that urban crime films were not necessarily—at least in any obvious way—about the actual city at all:

> *The importance of the gangster film . . . cannot be measured in terms of the place of the gangster himself or the importance of the problem of crime in American life. Those European movie-goers who think there is a gangster on every corner in New York are certainly deceived, but defenders of the "positive" side of American culture are equally deceived if they think it relevant to point out that most Americans have never seen a gangster. What matters is that the experience of the gangster* as an experience of art *is universal to Americans. . . . For the gangster there is only the city . . . not the real city, but that dangerous and sad city of the imagination which is so much more important, which is the modern world.*

"The real city," Warshow added, "produces only criminals; the imaginary city produces the gangster: he is what we want to be and what we are afraid we may become." Since Warshow's essay, a new kind of "nighttown" has emerged, an unforgettable vision of urban alienation and decay that is not intended, in some sense, as a literal rendering of the city at all. It is a dark city of the mind, a place where outward troubles symbolize inward needs, where social breakdown reveals psychological distress—a filmic vision that *uses* the city, in effect, to make tangible the profound interior conflicts of its characters.

The origins of this shadowy place can be traced to a celebrated group of low-budget, black-and-white films that, even as Warshow was writing, were extending his "dangerous city of the imagination" beyond the singular character of the gangster himself. These pictures—dubbed *film noir* by a group of postwar French critics—centered on ordinary city-dwellers trapped in a grim web of passion, betrayal, and murder. Their distinctly urban flavor was evident in names such as *Where the Sidewalk Ends* (1950), *Cry of the City* (1948), *Scarlet Street* (1945), *The Dark Corner* (1946)—or, in one writer's words, "any movie with *City*, *Night* or *Street* in its title"—and the city in which they took place (if named at all) was more than likely to be New York.

Some *noir* films were shot on location. But it was those pictures shot in the studio that created what the writers Charles Higham and Joel Greenberg call "the specific ambience of *film noir*"—a dismal yet somehow alluring imagery of neon signs and rain-swept streets that has turned out to be one of the most enduring cinematic visions of the city:

> *A dark street in the early morning hours, splashed with a sudden downpour. Lamps form haloes in the murk. In a walk-up, filled with the intermittent flashing of a neon sign from across the street, a man is waiting to murder or be murdered. . . . here is a world where it is always night, always foggy or wet, filled with gunshots and sobs, where men wear turned down brims on their hats and women loom in fur coats, guns thrust deep into pockets.*

Produced for the most part on minuscule budgets, *noir* films (like the gangster films before them) relied heavily on the studio's inventory of standing sets, but they jettisoned the upscale nightclubs and hotels of gangster films to focus almost exclusively on the seedier side of city life: cheap rooming houses, drab lunch counters, and anonymous sidestreets, now given a strange and alienating character through slanted camera angles, unbalanced compositions, and shadowy lighting—the stylistic hallmarks of the genre. "The set itself," in Michael Wood's words, "fell under suspicion."

The effect is startling. The same familiar backlot blocks that had once suggested a compact and comprehensible city neighborhood now came to feel, in Foster Hirsch's words, "airless and claustrophobic . . . a dark, urban world of neurotic entrapment," the ideal setting for "stories of obsession and confinement in which the world begins small and then progressively closes down." Revealingly, this sense of menacing enclosure had nothing to do with the kinds of social concerns about density and congestion evidenced in 1930s tenement films; *noir* films were not set in slums but ordinary, lower-middle-class streets, and offered no images of overcrowding. If anything, *noir* streets tended to be strangely empty of people: it was the implicit *feeling* of confinement in their built-up walls and closed-down vistas that seemed so suffocating.

In the context of American cities that were still, in the late 1940s, overwhelmingly prosperous and secure, *noir*'s "nightmarish world," as the writer and film scholar Paul Schrader observed in his 1972 essay "Notes on *Film Noir*," could seem "far more of a creation than a reflection." In retrospect, it is obvious that *noir* films were capturing not so much the existing urban reality of the early postwar era as an emerging attitude about the city—an incipient claustrophobia felt by many city dwellers as the suburbs began to beckon. Beneath it, too, was a new fear of urban density itself, understandable enough in the aftermath of the strategic bombing campaigns intended to devastate the urban industrial centers of Europe and Japan, culminating in the atomic destruction of Hiroshima and Nagasaki. Planning was already under way for a network of federal "defense highways" (later known as the Interstate Highway System) that would help quickly disperse the nation's population to low-density areas, thus offering a less inviting target to potential aggressors. Public agencies and private lenders, meanwhile, were busy skewing their mortgage and housing policies away from anything resembling traditional urban settings in favor of suburban-style communities that not only offered a high degree of social homogeneity but, to put it bluntly, simply didn't have all those dark old buildings and streets.

As New York was overwhelmed with an array of social problems in the decades following the 1950s, the old *noir* city was left far behind—but only for something more ominous still. In the years to come a new city of the imagination would emerge, all the more powerful for being filmed not in the studio but on real locations: not the confined, claustrophobic city of the back lot, but a dark and alienated vision of the real city, permeated by decay, corruption, and, above all, disconnection.

This sense of disengagement could be felt almost viscerally in Sidney Lumet's *The Pawnbroker* (1965), the story of a concentration-camp survivor who has utterly detached himself from the mainstream of urban life. Having lost his wife, children, and almost everything else to the Nazis, Sol Nazerman (Rod Steiger) lives out his days in a shabby pawnshop in Harlem, an area itself isolated from the city by a long history of prejudice and poverty. Here he watches the world pass him by, quite literally: every few minutes, a train speeds over the elevated tracks of the New York Central Railroad just across the street, carrying its prosperous passengers into and out of town. Self-exiled to this backwater, Nazerman will allow nothing to touch him emotionally—neither the sad, desperate customers who parade through his shop, nor the brutality he sees on the decrepit, trash-strewn streets outside. Yet as the film proceeds, the horrors and misery of the contemporary city increasingly overlay themselves onto the atrocities that haunt his memory—triggering him, much against his will, to remember.

By 1969's *Midnight Cowboy*, the feeling of disconnection has spread over the whole city. Even bustling Fifth Avenue offers no place for a Texan newcomer, Joe Buck (Jon Voigt). Using the photographer Andreas Feininger's classic technique—a telephoto lens pointed straight down the length of the avenue, visually compressing its pedestrians atop one another—the director John Schlesinger makes the elegant boulevard seem alienating and anonymous, with Joe barely visible, lost in its restless crowds.

On the sidewalk, the story is much the same: Joe dreams of making an easy fortune as a hustler, but cannot manage to connect with the flow of the city. On Manhattan's sidewalks there are wealthy, desirable women all around, but somehow they walk too quickly, too determinedly; Joe cannot quite pick up their pace. There are other fortunes at hand, too—jewels in Tiffany's windows, the great open vault door of Manufacturers Hanover Trust—all in plain sight, but utterly beyond reach. Then there is that man sprawled on the sidewalk, of whom no one except Joe takes more than a passing notice. It is the ultimate symbol of the alienated city: New Yorkers cannot connect to each other; and Joe can't connect to anyone at all (231). Eventually he is reduced to wandering the streets, until his money runs out, and he has nowhere to live.

242. *Midnight Cowboy* (1969). Through a freezing winter, "Ratso" Rizzo (Dustin Hoffman) and Joe Buck (Jon Voigt) struggle to survive in Ratso's unheated tenement apartment.

Finally Joe does manage to make a connection, with Enrico "Ratso" Rizzo (Dustin Hoffman), a fast-talking character whose very name suggests a night crawler, scuttling through the cracks of the city—an identity that proves to be literally true, we discover, when Ratso offers to share his "home" with Joe. The place turns out to be the very embodiment of disconnection: a condemned tenement apartment with broken windows, peeling paint, raw mattresses, its power and heat long ago switched off—not just poor but drained of all warmth and all life, a place that is the cold blue of death itself. It is one of the saddest, most miserable dwellings ever portrayed in the movie city, the symbol of those who live within the city's borders yet can find no way of attaching themselves to its currents. Here Joe and Ratso struggle to survive as winter sets in, as the demolition workers draw nearer, as the apartment grows so frigid they must dance around to avoid freezing (242). Relief comes only when the city is left behind. As they near Miami, a feeling of normalcy blows through the film like a warm breeze: Joe sheds his cowboy attire along with his sordid dreams. Ratso never survives the cold city he has left behind.

Another kind of urban disconnection, more common still, was hauntingly explored in *Klute*, a 1971 thriller directed by Alan J. Pakula. The theme is set early on, as we follow Bree Daniels (Jane Fonda)—an aspiring actress and hard-working call-girl—back to her Manhattan apartment. In an all-too-familiar ritual of modern life, we watch her unlock her door, enter the apartment, and instantly lock up again. Bristling with dead bolts, security bars, and chains, the door is the crucial barrier that separates Bree (like almost every city dweller) from the rest of the world—protecting her, to be sure, but enforcing a certain isolation, too, as we realize watching her inside the apartment, smoking and drinking alone, even singing a hymn to herself.

But this fragile isolation is now threatened, first by a string of anonymous phone calls (reinforcing her suspicion that she is somehow being "watched"), and then by a strange man at the door the next day. She looks through the peephole, then cracks open the door, careful to leave the security chain in place (243). The man is John Klute (Donald Sutherland), a small-town detective from Pennsylvania, come to New York to track down a missing friend who is feared dead. They converse through the narrow gap, Bree mocking Klute's accent and asking for identification; just as it seems she is going to let him in, she slams the door shut, locks it, then double locks it, shutting him out completely.

The locked door is a metaphor for her whole existence—and for the modern city itself, where anonymity and fear have brought on an obsession with security and isolation. The very appeal of being a call-girl, Bree explains to her therapist, is that, "You don't have to feel anything; you don't have to care about anything; you don't have to like anybody." Beneath her shallow bravado, of

243. *Klute* (1971). Bree Daniels (Jane Fonda), a call girl living in the West Forties, cautiously keeps her apartment door chained as she speaks with a stranger—a private detective from Pennsylvania named John Klute (Donald Sutherland).

course, we sense a deep unhappiness: prostitution, she admits, "made me feel like I wasn't alone"—and it is only after working closely with Klute that Bree realizes he is a different kind of person, someone willing to risk a real connection. But the alienated city keeps getting in the way, upsetting the balance between interaction and privacy, discouraging supportive relationships even as it encourages twisted ones—especially that mysterious voyeur, who continues to spy on Bree, his ominous presence reinforcing all of her instincts for isolation and disengagement. Still, her relationship with Klute gradually deepens, until the day when Klute finally lets *himself* into the apartment, having been given his own set of keys. She has begun to *feel,* Bree tells her therapist, and soon we see Bree and Klute spending time together, very much the loving couple—until one day they return home to find the door broken open, the apartment ransacked and ruined. The threat of violation has been made real by the voyeur, who is also, not coincidentally, the murderer Klute has been looking for. Bree and Klute have managed to establish an intimate bond, but it is obvious that New York cannot sustain them; by film's end they are moving to Pennsylvania, leaving the city—and its world of locked doors—behind.

From the first shot of *Taxi Driver* (1976)—a yellow cab looming from the blackness of the urban night, gliding through an infernal shroud—we know we have entered the ultimate city of alienation and disconnection, the definitive nighttown. It is hard to imagine a more faithful or powerful rendition of Warshow's notion of a "dangerous and sad city of the imagination" than *Taxi Driver*'s New York—a place that, however much a dark reflection of the real city, is even more the external projection of one man's interior struggles.

Like Joe Buck, Travis Bickle (Robert De Niro) is a lonely newcomer to New York, perhaps even less capable than Joe of finding a healthy connection to the city. As the film's writer, Paul Schrader, has pointed out, any taxi driver is a symbol of urban disengagement, a man "who moves, works, walks and talks and yet somehow is invisible to the eyes of his fellow men. He is acknowledged briefly when the passenger enters the cab and then consigned to limbo, to nonexistence." Yet Travis's disconnection from the city is deeper and far more threatening. Driving his cab each night from dusk to dawn, he moves through the sordid nighttime streets but does not really enter them, remaining isolated behind the glass of his windshield, whose rain-sprayed surface often transforms the urban surroundings into an abstract haze of colors. Clamping his camera to the cruising Checker taxi, the film's director, Martin Scorsese, viscerally evokes Travis's extreme isolation: we see startling views of the cab's fenders, windows, and hood medallion, all held rock steady and in sharp focus, even as the background—the city itself—becomes nothing more than a blur of lights.

If anything, this sense of isolation only increases when Travis returns "home" to his shabby one-room apartment, with its peeling walls, hot plate, bare bulb, army cot, and clothes hanging from a rope strung up in a corner—a

244. ***Taxi Driver*** **(1976).** In this view—as throughout the film—the director Martin Scorsese (working with cameraman Michael Chapman) employs telephoto lenses and carefully staged camera set-ups to visually isolate Travis Bickle (Robert De Niro) from the life of the city around him.

space, the film scholar Patricia Kruth has observed, that is not only detached but literally barred from the rest of the city by security grates across the windows. Even on the few occasions when Travis leaves his cab to walk the streets with everyone else, Scorsese invariably employs long, telephoto lenses, or carefully composed camera setups, or, in one case, slow motion, to separate him from the city all around (244).

Which is not to say the trouble is all in his mind. Indeed, it is the teasing interplay between reality and projection—combined in some mysterious, indeterminable ratio—that gives the New York of *Taxi Driver* its enduring, mythic power. Though hardly intended as a literal representation of the city, or even the seedier parts of it, the place to which Travis is obsessively drawn does have some kind of objective reality—it is a world, in the words of the critic Joy Boyum, of "darkness, filth, and violence."

> *[Travis] prefers to drive at night and he chooses to cruise the most foul of New York's streets: 42nd Street, with its garishly lit porno theaters and its sidewalks littered with prostitutes and drifters; the East Village with its overstrewn garbage pails, its broken bottles and pasty-faced teenage addicts; the dark and threatening streets of Harlem where even small children pick up a contagious anger, flinging trash at Travis' taxi.*

Filmed, Scorsese later recalled, over "forty days and forty nights" during the unbearably hot summer of 1975, the film was a product of what was surely the nadir of the modern city—a moment when, after mounting for years, New York's enormous, seemingly insoluble problems of crime and social unrest were coming to a terrible crescendo in the fiscal crisis that erupted that same fall, bringing its government to the very edge of bankruptcy. In this context, the squalid, filthy city that Travis confronts at every turn—filled with muggers, pimps, underage prostitutes, and crazed street people—seemed to many at the time a reasonably accurate portrayal of the contemporary urban environment. Rarely, however, has any film offered so intense or disturbing a vision of a city literally steeped in random violence and madness: a gang of street kids smashing bottles against Travis's cab for no reason; a store owner viciously beating the body of a mugger who has already been shot dead; a deranged homeless man racing down the sidewalk, screaming to himself, "*I'm going to kill her! I'm going to kill her!*" It is all too easy to see why Travis describes the place as an "open sewer," and calls for a "great rain" to redeem it.

Still, the film is no documentary. A distinct sense of unreality permeates *Taxi Driver* from start to finish—in part because of its almost exclusively dark focus (Travis almost never picks up a fare, for example, who is not sex-crazed or homicidal), but even more because "almost every shot," in the critic Amy Taubin's words, "is calculated in terms of filmic expression and razzle-dazzle." Nowhere is this more evident than in the movie's famous opening image—evoking a "thin cement lid," Vincent Canby wrote, "over the entrance to hell"—which is in fact built from nothing more frightening than a cab driving through some excess water vapor, a byproduct of the belowground steam network that efficiently heats and powers Manhattan's biggest buildings. Brilliantly framed and backlighted, those harmless clouds—mistakenly referred to by some critics as "sewer vapors"—are just one of the countless elements Scorsese employs within the film to transform the everyday streets into a hellish but haunting setting.

Indeed, as framed by the windows of Travis's cab, the city created by Scorsese (with the help of cameraman Michael Chapman) often seems less an actual environment than a kind of movie—and not just any movie, but a classic *film noir* (not surprisingly, given the close involvement of Schrader, whose celebrated "notes" on *noir* had been published just a few years before). Corrupt and venal, *Taxi Driver*'s New York is also an almost voluptuously lurid place, filled with old-fashioned neon signs (THE BELLMORE CAFETERIA, THE TERMINAL CAFÉ) straight out of a 1940s movie—especially as reflected in the glistening, rain-washed streets visible throughout the story (the original *noir* films, Schrader observed, had "an almost Freudian attachment to water"). The garish green and red light those neon signs emit, in turn, seems to bathe the entire city in a thick expressionistic gloom, completing its transformation into a fully rendered nightworld—a place at once "seductive and terrible," Janet Maslin has noted, that is "a physical manifestation of the forces tearing Travis apart."

As in *The Pawnbroker*, *Midnight Cowboy*, and *Klute*, those "forces" are revealed precisely as the main character tries to find some kind of connection with the city—this time with consequences no more successful, though far more violent. With increasing desperation, Travis attempts to break through the shell that isolates him, linking himself first with an attractive political campaign worker played by Cybill Shepherd (who soon rejects him), and eventually with an underage prostitute named Iris (Jodie Foster), who is confused but somehow touched by his attention. But as before, New York seems to discourage healthy relationships even as it encourages depraved ones, and as the film approaches its climax the only "connection" Travis can conceive is a direct attack on the corruption he sees all around him: by arming himself to the teeth, rehearsing fantasies of violent encounters with strangers ("You talking to *me*?"), attempting a political assassination, and, when that fails, deciding to "free" Iris by entering her East Village tenement and shooting everyone he finds there—a gruesome, horrific seven-minute expedition that leaves the hallway literally sprayed with blood. He himself has brought on the "great rain" he called for, and by the time it is over, several men are dead, Iris has been returned to her grateful parents in Pennsylvania, and Travis has become a hero of sorts. But by the film's end he is back where he started, in his cab, the city of the night again sliding by his windows like a dream. The final shot, as the first, shows New York again transfigured into a place of mythic darkness: a pair of ominous figures, silhouetted against a field of headlights, within a city of undefinable—but unmistakable—menace.

FOURTEEN

CHANGING CITY

RENEWAL AND PRESERVATION

A TINY BIT OF CONSTRUCTION

"Cities reveal as much about time as about place," observed the architect Nathan Silver in his haunting inventory of vanished landmarks, *Lost New York*. Ever since the early actuality films eagerly recorded the construction of new buildings and the demolition of old ones, New York's restless drive to remake itself has drawn special cinematic notice. Change was the city's trademark, after all, the distinguishing feature of what O. Henry once famously said would be "a great place if they ever finish it." What could better reveal this constant change than a medium with the word "motion" in its very name?

In the studio era, New York's constant rebuilding was seen as an essential part of its fabric, as necessary to reproduce as any other. One of the biggest standing sets on the Fox lot in Beverly Hills was an East River vehicular tunnel under construction, an interior tube of raw, exposed steel plating. Built for a 1933 picture called *Under Pressure*, the set remained on the lot for decades, forever "unfinished," a testament to the city as an ongoing work in progress. Other films, meanwhile, used New York's dizzying rate of change to calibrate the arc of human experience. Carlotta Vance, the former Broadway star played by Marie Dressler in *Dinner at Eight* (1933), has returned to the city after several decades in Europe. But she isn't staying. "I've been in New York four days," she says, "and I'm lost already."

245. (previous page) Illustration from *Life* magazine, 1959. Featured in an article on the changing city landscape, this lone row house standing in a razed block at 69th Street and Second Avenue was seized upon by the director Vincente Minnelli as a model for the offices of "Susanswerphone" in *Bells Are Ringing* (1960).

> *Everything's changed. I couldn't stand it here. I'd die. I belong to the Delmonico period. Ah, a table at the window, looking out on Fifth Avenue. Boxes with flowers, pink lampshades, string orchestras, and, yes, willow plumes. Inverness capes, dry champagne, and snow on the ground. Say, they don't even have snow anymore!*

After World War II, however, something else happened, as the nature of change itself was transformed. Before, New York's physical evolution—however furious and constant—had been relatively organic, the result of advancing construction technology and the understandable economic desire to replace smaller, older buildings with larger, newer ones. But now the city's change took on a systemic, even ideological cast. The advent of urban renewal in the postwar years not only made the city's reconstruction far more sweeping—not just buildings but entire *districts* leveled, to be rebuilt as institutional or housing complexes—but assigned it a different mission: no longer merely to make bigger and more profitable buildings, but a better world. By the same token, old buildings were now seen, as never before, as a genuine source of embarrassment, to be wiped away as quickly as possible.

In 1950, Universal released *The Sleeping City,* a thriller shot on location in New York's venerable municipal hospital, Bellevue. Along the way, the film offered audiences an extensive tour of the hospital's aging plant, a turn-of-the-century congeries of structures by McKim, Mead & White that provided a superbly atmospheric setting for the film's tale of a narcotics ring operating within the hospital's walls. Yet when the picture was complete, a disclaimer was added at the insistence of Mayor William O'Dwyer, evidently shamed by the institution's appearance. The star, Richard Conte, comes on-screen at the start of the film to earnestly promise the audience that "on this same site will rise . . . the new buildings of Bellevue, already planned and begun, and they will form the world's most complete research and teaching hospital." However photogenic, the city's older buildings (we could rest assured) would soon be making way for shiny new ones.

Another city property, Calvin Coolidge High School (in *Up the Down Staircase,* 1967), is not much newer than Bellevue and only marginally less grim—a great brooding pile rising from a depressed East Harlem landscape of empty lots and decaying tenements, with dingy but richly decorated Gothic Revival interiors (actually those of Haaren High School on Tenth Avenue, the same building used in *Fame*). Though Calvin Coolidge (a "so-called problem-area school," according to its principal) suffers from a wide variety of ills, the condition of the old building itself tops the list—and its planned replacement is the cherished dream that keeps its teachers going. The blueprints for a new building are complete, but the $7.5 million needed to construct it remain elusive. "It's been six years," one teacher complains wearily, "and we're losing heart." The film never questions whether the school's profound social problems might transcend its architecture. The new building equals salvation itself.

If Coolidge's new building stood as a distant dream, in the real city the process of renewal was in full swing, as tenements, apartments, and offices gave way by the thousands to modern structures (247). The most dramatic physical transformation in the city's history, it could hardly be ignored, even in films not concerned at all with social issues. The title sequence of *Bells Are Ringing* (1960), a musical comedy about a telephone answering service, offers a striking pictorial essay on these changes at their very zenith. In midtown, glass facades are popping up everywhere, while seemingly solid masonry buildings are quickly being reduced to smoky piles of rubble. In their bright-red primer paint, new steel skeletons stand out like colorful Erector sets, or are reflected in the glassy walls of other new structures. Finally we see an excavation site: the newest of the new, just beginning.

This theme—the old making way for the new—goes on to define the film's main set, the house in which "Susanswerphone" operates. Once part of a row of similar neighbors, it now stands alone in a field of rubble, the last holdout on the site of a new apartment house (245, 246). On either side, what were once the interior walls of adjoining row houses are exposed to the world; a sliver of the neighboring building's stoop and railing remain, the sole trace of its former existence; and Susanswerphone's backyard, once framed by neighboring yards, now stands oddly open amidst the surrounding rubble. The house looks sad and forlorn; it is the end of the cycle begun with the solitary houses and tenements in 1913's *Traffic in Souls* (27, bottom). Those buildings were awaiting some neighbors. This building has outlived them.

Bells Are Ringing does not show us what is to replace Susanswerphone's house, but plenty of other films did, mermerized by the contrast of old and new.

246. Set still from *Bells Are Ringing* (1960). On a Culver City stage, MGM's art department (under Preston Ames) re-created the *Life* magazine illustration (245) with startling accuracy, from the air conditioner in the bay window to the sliver of stoop and railing left over from the previously demolished house on the right.

"This is Mr. Ford's town," announces the impeccably elegant Terry-Thomas in *How to Murder Your Wife* (1965), as an aerial view of Manhattan floats by. "And this is Mr. Ford's town*house.*" In his role as manservant to a successful magazine illustrator named Stanley Ford (Jack Lemmon), Terry-Thomas conducts a tour of the gracious West 54th Street home, guiding us through French doors onto a terrace adorned with canvas awnings, wicker furniture, trellises, and flowers. But the urbane charm is undercut by the sound of jackhammers, forcing Terry-Thomas to admit that "like everyone else in New York, Mr. Ford has a *tiny* bit of construction going on next door." A dramatic zoom out offers the truth: right next to Ford's little house, a gigantic skyscraper is going up. In fact, office buildings are rising on every side—"a world gone mad, *mad!*" cries Terry-Thomas, in anguish. In their size, scale, and style, these modern structures have no use for the traditional urbanity of buildings such as Ford's. It is probably only a matter of time before this little row house disappears, like the rest.

The opening of *West Side Story* (1961) offers an even better sense of what is coming. Though its aerial survey covers both new and old parts of the city, it is the newer landscapes—the arterial highways and bridges, the United Nations, Stuyvesant Town—that seem to jump off the screen, their precise edges, crisp green lawns, and box-like buildings promising a new world of order and simplicity. If these projects look especially seductive from here, it is hardly surprising, for this is precisely how their architects and planners envisioned them, in sweeping aerial views from which their dramatic scale and simple plans might be best appreciated (66). By contrast, the city's older districts, from this viewpoint, appear a jumble of crowded buildings and narrow streets, hopelessly deficient and impossible to save—except by the cleansing hand of urban renewal, ready to wipe it all away and start over. And this is just what we see happening in later shots that show unfinished housing projects rising from the rubble of demolished tenements. In *West Side Story*, the only problem with urban renewal remains that, despite the city's best efforts, there is still not enough of it to go around: the Jets and the Sharks continue to battle over a turf of narrow sidewalks and playgrounds among the thick tenements, with the occasional warehouse or gas tank adding to the general unwholesomeness. The old must still make way for the new, without question.

It was only with the making of *A Thousand Clowns*, in 1965, that the movie city began to hint at another point of view. Murray Burns (Jason Robards) lives on an Upper West Side block of aging row houses, long ago divided into small apartments. In this old and unconventional place, Murray enjoys his offbeat way of life, shouting into an airshaft to berate his neighbors about the quality of their garbage ("I want to see more empty champagne bottles and caviar tins!") and exploring the faded glitter of an abandoned Chinese restaurant on the building's first floor. But a host of dark portents suggest that the building—and indeed the entire row in which it sits—may not be long for this world. The block across the street has already been leveled, and as Murray crosses its field of

247. Filming *The Naked City* (1948). Carrying his cameras and crew high up into the scaffolding, director Jules Dassin shoots a scene in which two homicide detectives, tracking a lead, ride an exterior elevator to the top of an office building under construction at 57th Street and Park Avenue (the new headquarters, not coincidentally, of Universal Pictures, the studio behind *Naked City*). One of the first modern structures put up in New York after World War II, the Universal building stood out dramatically from the older urban landscape around it—and signaled a sweeping change that would soon transform this once-residential stretch of Park Avenue into a boulevard of glass-and-steel commercial towers.

rubble (or passes other parts of the city, like Lincoln Center, rising in its fresh marble blandness) it is hard to avoid the feeling that his old block may be the next to go. *A Thousand Clowns*, however, has taken us inside, showing us that the house is as charming in its own peculiar way as Murray himself; it has, in short, assigned a positive value to the old. Not that it matters, really. Murray's block will likely come down anyway; the new and modern must still march inevitably over the old and idiosyncratic. Yet for the first time, the city's single-minded drive for progress had been seriously questioned. Something had happened.

VITAL STRUCTURES

Something *had* happened.

In 1963 the demolition of Pennsylvania Station began, a monumental act of civic destruction that was accepted with hardly a murmur. (A small band of architects and historians, protesting the decision in front of the station in August 1962, were regarded mostly with amusement by the public and press.) Only by 1966, when the last of the great Doric columns had been carted off to the Secaucus Meadows, did the magnitude of the loss become evident. For the first time, the automatic assumption that change was good—or that the new was inherently better than the old—came into question.

For most, this growing awareness still took the form of a vague unease rather than a specific program or agenda. It could be sensed best in an oblique, unexpected manner—as it was in a pair of disturbing psychological thrillers that both drew on an ominous feeling, just beneath the surface, about the seamless modern future into which the city seemed so intent on heading.

Mirage (1965) opens with a dusky view of the lower Manhattan skyline, glittering as ever—until the lights in one modern tower suddenly blink *out*, rendering it a tomblike slab. Inside, we meet businessman David Stillwell (Gregory Peck), trying to make his way downstairs in the dark. With his gray suit, narrow tie, and attaché case, Stillwell seems at first to be just another of the thousands of midlevel executives who fill these buildings. But over the next few hours, a series of unaccountable experiences—lapses in memory, confusing responses from acquaintances, bizarre approaches by a vicious gunman and a beautiful stranger—bring Stillwell to the stunning realization that he has no idea who he is, or where he comes from. To discover his own identity, he must set out across the city, picking up clues here and there—from the police, a psychiatrist, a private detective—while trying to elude a group of professional killers who are out to get him for reasons he himself doesn't understand. His search ranges all over Manhattan, from the Central Park Zoo to Battery Park—but as it does, a subtext begins to emerge, a contrast between the humane scale of the old city and the inhuman anonymity of the new, especially the glass-and-steel office buildings of which the clean-cut Stillwell seems so much a part. New York's traditional urbanism is represented by the teeming ethnic district where a gentle building attendant named "Turtle" lives—until he is brutally killed by the mysterious thugs—and by a gaggle of schoolboys on a Central Park field trip, with whom Stillwell surrounds himself when another gunman threatens him. The newer city is symbolized by automatic elevators, instant coffee, and latchkey children, but most of all by a modern office building owned by the mysterious "Unidyne Corporation" (with its motto, "The Future is Here"), which is somehow at the center of the forces trying to destroy him. Piece by piece, Stillwell rebuilds his true identity—and with it, the traumatic memory of the evil he found in a darkened office high in the Unidyne building. Stillwell manages to break through, but the message is clear: the new city, the modern city, is stripping us of a humanity the old city had somehow sustained.

An even more frightening fate awaits Joe Turner (Robert Redford), an iconoclastic researcher who is employed by a cover agency of the CIA in *Three Days of the Condor* (1975). Turner works in a handsome old East Side town house, and likes to use an obscure rear exit in the basement that, through a circuitous series of yards and service alleys, offers a rainy-day shortcut to a lunch counter on the next block. One morning the unorthodox pathway saves his life, when a team of assassins enters the building's front door and efficiently murders everyone inside. Alone, terrified, unsure who has committed the horrific crime, Turner proceeds to play cat-and-mouse all over New York with the CIA and whomever else may be out there. Having seen how one urban eccentricity allowed him to live, now we see how other qualities of the older city—its small scale and dense humanity—help him survive. At one point, the landlady of his row house pleasantly mentions two "friends" waiting for him; at another, he uses a crowd of strangers, just as Stillwell does, to create a human shield against a sniper. Turner kidnaps a young woman (Faye Dunaway) and briefly finds a haven in her home, which is also in a row house. In fact, he and Dunaway turn out to have a lot in common: both are sensitive young people living solitary lives in the city, trying to find a human connection.

Meanwhile, the other half of the chase proceeds, directed from that most overbearing symbol of the new city: the twin towers of the World Trade Center, home in this context to the CIA's "New York Center." This is the rationalized future, with hermetically sealed offices detached from the rest of the city, limousines and underground garages tied by helicopter to the even more anonymous CIA headquarters off a highway in suburban Virginia. "Do you think he's still in New York City?" someone asks the agency's deputy director. "I wouldn't be," comes the answer. But Turner *is* still in New York, which is somehow protecting and nurturing him, until he is ready to strike back at the soulless world the Trade Center symbolizes. Like Stillwell, Turner finally breaks through his mystery, but the disturbing question remains: Why are we so anxious to replace the old city with a new one—and what might we be losing as we do?

As the 1970s proceeded, the awareness of the city's history was inflected by larger events. One was the Bicentennial, which focused the entire nation's attention, at least briefly, on its historic heritage. Another was the fiscal crisis that brought New York to the brink of bankruptcy and necessitated a humiliating request for federal loan guarantees; the financial emergency crystallized not only the enormous social problems that had engulfed the city over the previous decades, but the distance that had grown between New York and the rest of the nation. Most of America now devoted itself to highways, automobiles, suburban tract homes, and office parks; New York, once an exemplar of the future, now seemed a surprisingly old-fashioned place, filled with historic buildings and a traditional street life. To many both outside the city and within, New York's aging physical plant seemed one more problem, a potent symbol of decline.

Soon after the crisis, however, a new film arrived that suggested a different way of looking at New York's past. In both its timing and theme, Woody Allen's *Annie Hall* (1977) reflected the defensive mood of a city just back from the brink of financial catastrophe. In the film, Alvy Singer, played by Allen himself, repeatedly defends the city in almost quixotic terms, resisting the entreaties of a fellow comedian (Tony Roberts) to leave for Southern California. It may be Alvy's personality, which, he's told, is "like New York . . . an island." Or it may simply be his neuroses: as Alvy himself admits, the country makes him nervous. No matter what the reason, he is stubbornly devoted to the city, whatever its troubles.

With the appearance of Annie Hall (Diane Keaton), Alvy's feelings for New York expand into something larger. As in countless earlier films, Annie and Alvy's romantic relationship evolves against a backdrop of the larger city. That backdrop, however, is not the familiar place of postwar romantic comedies, the sleek Madison Avenue of Doris Day and Rock Hudson's "pillow-talk" films or the sparkling Park Avenue offices surrounding Audrey Hepburn and George Peppard in *Breakfast at Tiffany's.* Very deliberately, Allen turned not to the newest but some of the oldest parts of the city to frame his "nervous romance." Following Annie and Alvy to an East River pier at dusk, or past the exquisite facades of Washington Square, the film seemed to discover—almost to its own surprise—that for all its immediate troubles, the city remained a resonant, visually compelling environment. Seen today, *Annie Hall* captures a moment of dawning awareness when, having averted disaster and taking stock of their town's strengths, New Yorkers began to realize that the city's older urban inventory was not a liability at all, but a unique asset. In an increasingly tinny, suburbanized world (symbolized in the film by Los Angeles's architectural motley of mirror-glass facades and roadside stands), New York's landscape was suddenly valued because it was *not* built yesterday.

Still, nagging doubts persist: "New York," Annie Hall herself declares, "is a dying city." By the time of Allen's next film, a year later, with the financial crisis receding and an upbeat set of leaders at the city's helm, his declaration of faith in New York grew firm, even exultant—and reliant more than ever on the conviction that the city's physical heritage was something to be celebrated. For *Manhattan,* he created an unforgettable, nine-minute introductory montage that shifted the city from the background to a place unmistakably front and center.

"He adored Manhattan. He idolized it all out of proportion," begins the narration in Allen's distinctive voice and accent. "No matter what the season was, this was still a town that existed in black and white, and pulsated to the great tunes of George Gershwin." And this indeed is just what we get: a series of moody black-and-white views of the midtown skyline, set to the anthemic urban strains of "Rhapsody in Blue"—a combination of music and imagery that inevitably recalls not only the real city but the movie city itself, the dream New York that, Allen suggests, might well still exist. The voice, we now realize, is that of a writer, trying out different "takes" on the city, proposing it as a symbol for society's decline, a place of noise and garbage, then stressing the street-smart qualities necessary to survive its tough environment. And still the images keep coming, alluring, ugly, striking: an arriving ferry, a tenement facade, a basketball court, heaps of garbage, Park Avenue in a blizzard, a parade, Washington Square, 57th Street, Macy's, the Guggenheim, the Plaza. In the end, Allen's abiding love of the place wins out: "New York was his town," he concludes, "and it always would be." As the music reaches a crescendo and the sun begins to set, the images grow unabashedly starry: dusky views of Central Park West; a couple kissing on a twilight terrace; the glitter of Broadway, Lincoln Center, Radio City—all racing faster and faster until a single, breathtaking long shot slows the pace and makes the audience gasp in amazement—the vast bowl of Yankee Stadium, filled to capacity, lighting up the sky, erupting in a great cheer even as a glowing subway train glides into the station in the foreground. The next shot can top it only by literally exploding: a climactic fireworks display over Central Park, whose dazzling burst of shells seems to synchronize with the last thunderous chords of Gershwin's music.

In the broadest terms, the sequence was a timely reminder—for New Yorkers no less than those who lived elsewhere—that for all its troubles the city still possessed an urban character of unmatched power, well worth fighting for. But the film also left no doubt that the most precious parts of that urbanism—at least in Woody Allen's eyes—were those of the past. *Manhattan*'s best-known shot shows the filigreed span of the 1909 Queensborough Bridge rising out of a misty dawn, moving Allen to reassert that "This is really a great city. I don't care what anybody says. It's a knockout" (248). Still more to the point is a later scene on Park Avenue, in which Allen and Diane Keaton bemoan the loss of an older building, whose masonry facade is being ripped down as they watch. "Can't they have those things declared landmarks?" Keaton wonders.

They could. And they did. If not that particular building, perhaps, then hundreds of others—and entire blocks in what were called "historic districts"—that had come under the jurisdiction of the Landmarks Preservation Commission, a city agency founded in the wake of Penn Station's destruction. Although

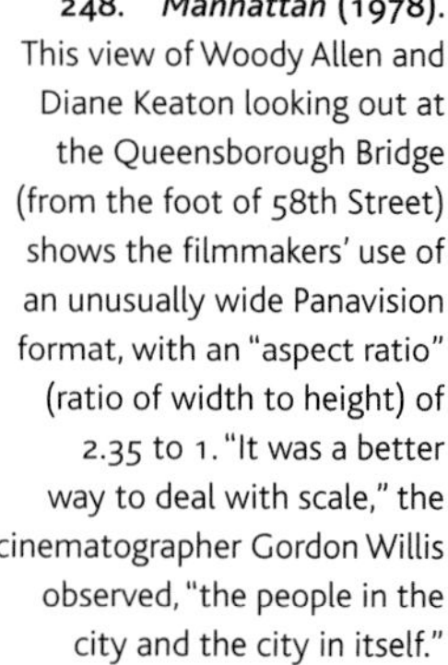

248. *Manhattan* (1978). This view of Woody Allen and Diane Keaton looking out at the Queensborough Bridge (from the foot of 58th Street) shows the filmmakers' use of an unusually wide Panavision format, with an "aspect ratio" (ratio of width to height) of 2.35 to 1. "It was a better way to deal with scale," the cinematographer Gordon Willis observed, "the people in the city and the city in itself."

the commission had been designating buildings since 1965, it was only as the 1970s ended that it firmly entered the public's awareness. By the 1980s, New Yorkers had become highly conscious—if not, indeed, self-conscious—about their historic architectural heritage.

Again, Woody Allen embodied the mood perfectly. Released in 1986, *Hannah and Her Sisters* was quickly recognized as a successor to his earlier pair of "classic" New York comedies. The new film again featured the older city, but with a revealing difference. At a party, a charming, handsome architect named David Tolchin (Sam Waterston) asks a pair of single women, April (Carrie Fisher) and Holly (Dianne Wiest), if they would care to see a building of his design; both of them, not surprisingly, jump at the chance. Encouraged by April's eager effort to articulate her admiration for his work, David remarks that "People pass by vital structures in this city all the time and never take the time to appreciate them." This, in turn, leads to a tour of some of David's favorites—the Ansonia and Alwyn Court apartment houses, the Graybar and Chrysler Buildings, the New York Yacht Club and the Jefferson County Courthouse—before concluding at a neoclassical town house. "It's romantic," he declares, "and it's got a handsome partner sitting right beside it. And your eye goes along, lulled into complacency, and then . . ." As if following his directions, the camera pans across two classical facades and comes to a stop on a blunt modern building. "That's disgusting," April responds. "Really sad," adds Holly. "A monstrosity," says April, unwilling to be topped. It was a long way from *The Sleeping City*, which had all but apologized for the continuing existence of the city's older buildings. Now it was almost taken for granted that a historic structure was preferable to anything new.

Something else was different. *Annie Hall* had quietly rediscovered the value of New York's landmarks and *Manhattan* had celebrated them with thrilling freshness; this "tour," by contrast, presented them explicitly and self-consciously, mirroring the change that had overtaken New Yorkers—once famed for destroying old buildings frantically, but now busy revering them, no less frantically, through walking tours, exhibitions, and guidebooks. (The release of *Hannah* itself, in fact, was accompanied by a spate of articles pinpointing the landmark structures shown in the film.) It was undoubtedly progress of sorts, but there was also perhaps a loss involved: the new attitude—venerating individual buildings as precious gems—replaced an earlier, more robust sense, evident in *Manhattan*, of New York's buildings as supporting members of a larger urban ensemble, the city itself.

YOU CALL THIS AN APARTMENT?

For Woody Allen, the value of the old was primarily aesthetic: historic buildings were simply nicer to look at than new ones. But to the writer and director Paul

249. ***Next Stop, Greenwich Village*** **(1976).** Set in the 1950s, Paul Mazursky's film was shot in period locations throughout the Village—including the Caffé Reggio on MacDougal Street, the oldest coffee house in the city, where a circle of bohemian friends, played by (clockwise from the front) Ellen Greene, Lenny Baker, Lois Smith, Christopher Walken, Dori Brenner, and Antonio Fargas, gather regularly.

Mazursky—who, like Allen, made an important pair of films during New York's "comeback" period in the late 1970s—older buildings had an even more essential (if less visible) significance.

In *Next Stop, Greenwich Village* (1976), Mazursky's look back at his days as a struggling young actor in the early 1950s, the neighborhood of the title is not yet the official historic district it would become later. But the film shows us an area whose fundamental character had changed little since the days when it first became a magnet for American bohemia: a place of old, small buildings set on winding streets and irregular blocks, of cramped walk-up apartments and crowded cafés where intense conversations could be pursued late into the night; a place where the strictures of conventional propriety might be loosened, and all kinds of conformity challenged.

The Village's iconoclasm had once been mostly political: the pre–World War I enclave portrayed in Warren Beatty's *Reds* (1981) is the natural home to young radicals like John Reed (Beatty) and Louise Brooks (Diane Keaton). By Mazursky's time, however, the area had become known as a refuge for those whose nonconformity was artistic or sexual in nature. For Mazursky's alter-ego, Larry Lapinsky (Lenny Baker), recently arrived from deepest Brooklyn, the Village is the only place to pursue his goal of becoming a serious actor; here he befriends a circle of young people, each somehow an outsider to the mainstream culture of the 1950s. There is Bernstein Chandler (Antonio Fargas), a gay black man whose name derives, he says, from that of the Jewish family whose house his mother once cleaned; Robert (Christopher Walken), a handsome poet and womanizer; the depressive Anita (Lois Smith), a costume designer who is chronically unlucky in love; and the friendly, supportive Connie (Dori Brenner), whose basement apartment across from the Caffé Reggio serves as a convenient way station for the group. Through race, sexuality, and choice of career (or lack of it), they are all misfits in a conformist society, and each nurses a private sadness. Yet in the Village they have managed to find one another, and together enjoy a series of rituals: long coffees at the Reggio talking art and politics; lively rent parties where wayward debutantes mix with sullen painters; and regular excursions over to Anita's apartment—everyone dancing in a sidewalk conga line—to thwart one of her repeated suicide attempts. Rejected everywhere else, they have briefly discovered community, however fragile and imperfect, in this one place (249).

It was not a coincidence. In ways both symbolic and real, Greenwich Village provided an ideal urban context in which to express (or create) an unconventional personality. After all, how could this district—with its eccentric street plan, jumble of structures, web of crooked streets—ever impose a code of conformity? In the Village, any single block was likely to contain a bewildering variety of buildings—row houses, warehouses, tenements, garages—of widely different ages and styles (250). What better metaphor could there be for the ragtag group of young people inhabiting them?

250. ***Next Stop, Greenwich Village* (1976).** In a pouring rain on a winding Village street, Larry Lapinsky (Lenny Baker) walks with his girlfriend Sarah (Ellen Greene) to his nearby apartment.

But as Mazursky makes clear, the neighborhood's value was more than metaphoric. Filled with old, decrepit buildings, it offered relatively cheap rents, making it affordable to young people pursuing careers of uncertain financial reward. The film brilliantly portrays Larry's $25-a-month apartment—a fifth-floor walkup in the back of an old tenement—by showing it both through his own eyes and those of his mother, a Brooklyn housewife played by Shelley Winters. Even before her first visit, Larry can predict his mother's response: "You call this an apartment? You call this furniture?" Through her, we see the apartment's miserable reality: dark, dingy, with peeling paint and ancient appliances, a tiny kitchenette and a single small room for living and sleeping. But we also see it as Larry does, as a place with everything he really needs: a phonograph, some books, a picture or two, and a couch-turned-bed he can share with his girlfriend. It is affordable, and it is his own; little else matters.

"Cities need old buildings," wrote Jane Jacobs. "Not museum-piece old buildings . . . but a good lot of plain, ordinary, low-value old buildings, including some rundown old buildings." With construction costs long ago amortized and mortgages paid off, only older buildings could offer rents cheap enough to sustain the economically marginal activities that make a city interesting. "Chain stores, chain restaurants and banks go into new construction," she noted.

> *But neighborhood bars, foreign restaurants and pawnshops go into older buildings. Supermarkets and shoe stores often go into new buildings; good bookstores and antique dealers seldom do. Well-subsidized opera and art museums often go into new buildings. But the unformalized feeders of the arts—studios, galleries, stores for musical instruments and art supplies, backrooms where the low earning power of a seat and a table can absorb uneconomic discussions—these go into old buildings.*

Next Stop, Greenwich Village not only understood all this—showing us the coffee houses, acting studios, and other "marginal" elements essential to an urban bohemia—but extended Jacobs's premise to reveal the special relationship between old buildings and young people that makes preserving historic parts of the city more than a matter of aesthetics.

The point is still valid—even if the Village itself, with its rising rents, is no longer the primary site of that relationship. In *Married to the Mob* (1988), director Jonathan Demme updated the connection between old structures and new lives, shifting the location a mile or two eastward.

Angela de Marco (Michelle Pfeiffer) is the wife of a successful Mafia hit man (Alec Baldwin) and lives accordingly, in a big suburban house filled with new appliances (some still stacked in their boxes) and garish furniture. But Angela is discontent, tired of a life in which, as she says, "Everything we own fell off a truck." When her husband is mysteriously killed, she chooses to break free, donating the house to charity and moving with her young son Joey back to the city, to a tenement on Rivington Street in the Lower East Side. No one—not the FBI agents who are following her, nor the Mafia family who refuse to leave her alone—have any idea what she is doing. "It's a real hell of a place," one of the Mafia men reports. "I wouldn't have a dog live there." On first sight, the apartment truly is depressing: the bathtub sitting in the middle of the kitchen, the peeling paint and grimy walls, the rotten wood and cracked tiles that were already the shame of New York in 1939's *One Third of a Nation,* now a half-century older. But as Angela explains to her son, "This is all we can afford right now, Joey. We're gonna lead a good life, a life we can be proud of, and that's what really matters now." "Okay," he agrees gamely, "but this place really sucks."

As she starts a new life—even while dogged by her sordid past—Angela discovers in this place of poverty and privation a kind of freedom, a liberating spirit that grows from the very diversity at the low end of the economic spectrum. The Lower East Side, while not the old bohemian Village, is perhaps its closest modern equivalent, where relatively cheap rents have brought together a multicultural mix that is miles removed from the insularity of Angela's earlier suburban existence. "Hello, Gorgeous!" is the name of a funky haircutting salon, run by Rita Harcourt ("Sister" Carol East), an easygoing West Indian woman whose window display asks, "Are you ready for a brand new you?" Angela, in fact, is more than ready, and inside the vibrantly painted interior, filled with Bob Marley posters and Jamaican flags, she is transformed with a new haircut, a new job, and the beginnings of a new existence—materially modest, perhaps, but unquestionably authentic, and emotionally rich.

WE'RE NEIGHBORS

Angela was not alone. All across town, young people were discovering historic parts of the city and moving in. Not content with a tiny apartment like hers, however, many newcomers were renovating entire buildings—nineteenth-century row houses, once the homes of single families but now, often as not, divided into cheap rental units. Known as "brownstoning," the arrival of middle-class newcomers into older, poorer districts (mostly in Brooklyn) came also to be known by a more critical term, "gentrification." To many it was a promising sign of reinvestment in the city by young families; to others it represented the displacement of the poor and working classes by those with more security and wealth. What could be a liberating gesture at the scale of an individual such as Angela, might, when carried out on a wider basis, carry social costs for those already living in the older districts.

251. ***The Landlord* (1970).** Arriving for the first time, houseplant in hand, at an aging Brooklyn brownstone he has just purchased, the ingenuous Elgar (Beau Bridges) is mocked by the building's longtime residents. Directed by Hal Ashby, the film was shot in large part on location in Park Slope.

Released in 1970, when the trend was still new, *The Landlord* follows the experience—by turns comic and tragic—of a rich young white man who has purchased a run-down house in Park Slope, a district of Brooklyn filled at the time with poor black families. Starting as satire, the film becomes a sober look at the clash that can occur when the older city, suddenly "rediscovered," turns out to have preexisting human and social complexities.

"It's an old goddamned house, y'know, lots of molding," is the way Elgar Enders (Beau Bridges) describes his new purchase to a squash partner. Elgar's plan is simple: rid the place of its tenants, gut the interior, and create for himself a single giant space from basement to skylight, complete with a hanging psychedelic sculpture. "Restored landmarks will be the latest urban trend," says the real-estate agent who shows him the exquisitely renovated row house of another "pioneer" down the street. "This neighborhood is going to be very chic, very chic," the proud owner agrees, before opening a package and announcing, "the sconces came!" Suddenly, a projectile flies through the open window—"eviction powder," the agent unhappily explains, intended to put a voodoo spell on the newcomers. Perhaps it will not be so simple.

In fact, from the moment Elgar arrives at the building, he realizes his presence will be met with more than a little resistance. At first, the situation is played for laughs. Elgar is instantly harassed by local residents; within an hour, his life has been threatened not once but twice—with a shotgun and, of all things, bow and arrow. If Elgar is a satire of white naïveté and ingenuousness, the black tenants seem painted in equally broad comic strokes of paranoia and distrust (251).

But the film's tone changes when Elgar actually moves into the building and, unable to act on his plans until he receives buildings department approval, becomes intimately involved in the life of the place. He is fed and mothered by Marge (Pearl Bailey), and befriended by a young boy (Douglas Grant) who, like everyone else, simply calls him "Landlord." Later, he spends a long evening with the boy's mother, Fanny (Diana Sand), and she, unhappy with her absent husband, ends up in bed with him. Meanwhile, Elgar falls in love with another woman, Lanie (Marki Bey), who herself confounds racial certainties through her half-black, half-Irish ancestry. Gradually, he comes to

252. Production still from *The Pick-up Artist* (1987). Jack Jericho (Robert Downey Jr.) makes his way down Columbus Avenue, moving from one young woman to another (until, in a later scene, he meets his match in Randy Jensen, played by Molly Ringwald). A Steadicam operator and sound man capture the scene, which, like much of the film, was shot on location on the Upper West Side.

realize that the building is something more than a plaything, and toward the end he has all but given up his boyish plans, not even trying to collect the rent.

Fanny's discovery that she is pregnant by Elgar sets off a climactic chain of events. Hearing the news, her deranged husband tries to murder Elgar—a serious attempt, this time—but instead suffers an emotional collapse and is taken away; chastened, Elgar decides to take responsibility for the baby himself. By film's end, he has decided to turn over the building to Fanny; he himself will start a new life in Brooklyn Heights with Lanie and his own racially mixed child. The old house remains much as it was before; it is Elgar who has changed.

If Elgar chose to leave, however, tens of thousands of actual New Yorkers did not, and by the 1980s, district after district of Brooklyn (not least Park Slope, much of which did become as chic as the man predicted) had been transformed into middle-class areas. Even the impoverished Bedford-Stuyvesant block that is the setting for *Do the Right Thing* (1989) includes at least one restored brownstone, belonging to a prosperous white newcomer, played by John Savage. "Go back to Massachusetts!" the local kids taunt him. "I was born in Brooklyn," he replies. Their reaction can be imagined.

Though premised on preserving rather than destroying the past, gentrified districts nonetheless had a look and feel all their own. In areas like Columbus Avenue on the Upper West Side, an upscale veneer was superimposed on the aging urban fabric—especially at street level, where clusters of outdoor cafés, designer clothing shops, and gourmet ice-cream parlors replaced the homely bodegas, tailors, and hardware stores that had clung on for decades. With the new retail uses came a new sidewalk life, an open-air playground for the growing population of young professionals, students, and artists who filled the renovated apartments—and the setting for the extended sidewalk excursion known as *The Pick-up Artist* (1987).

We meet our guide (Robert Downey Jr.) in his bathroom, rehearsing before a mirror. "Hi, I'm Jack Jericho," he says to himself with a winning smile. "Has anyone ever told you you have the face of a Manet and the body of a Botticelli?" With such lines will Jack seek to find romance, or some vague approximation, on the streets below. Soon he is bounding down the steps of his row house—located on a sidestreet, just off the avenue—and with a boyish spring in his step, heads into action (252).

There is no lack of opportunity. Along the pedestrian paradise that is Columbus Avenue, he sees possibilities everywhere: beautiful girls on skates, beautiful girls jogging, even a pair of beautiful girls carrying a ladder, surely to work on their renovated apartment. The camera follows Jack's progress down the sidewalk as he sidles up to one woman after another. Sometimes his lines work, sometimes not. No matter—as soon as he has finished with one, or sooner, he spies the next and is off in a new direction. On the avenue, hope springs eternal.

Throughout these scenes, there is something striking about Jack's bouncy walk: it seems to transform the hard concrete sidewalk into a sprung surface, almost like the wooden floorboards of a stage. Suddenly we get it, the underlying perception about Columbus Avenue that the film has been suggesting all along. For Jack, the whole district is a kind of stage, filled with actresses opposite whom he can play leading man. His bathroom is the "green room" where he rehearses his lines and prepares to go on, while the quiet sidestreets down which he bounces are the "wings" feeding onto the wide, busy stage—the avenue itself—where his "performance" proceeds.

There was a real insight here (by the writer and director James Toback) about the essential theatricality of these gentrified streets—not the one-time spectacle of a *Dog Day Afternoon*, but a regular performance put on every weekend by the crowds browsing the shops or meeting each other at outdoor cafés. The sidewalk tables and chairs—itself a new tradition for New York—became ringside seats for an almost Mediterranean display of urbanity, far removed from the purposeful Nordic rush of the 1950s city. But there was also a new self-consciousness, a sense of "seeing and being seen" that resembled nothing so much as the mutual pact between actor and audience. Once simply a place to live and work, the city had become something of an open-air carnival or fairground.

Such perceptions might prompt cynics to question whether historic preservation had, in the end, become simply a means of enhancing the already attractive lifestyle of young professionals. But the film city could also movingly evoke the original impetus of the preservation movement, by looking not at a chic and successful urban district, but at the most ordinary of city dwellings, fighting for its life.

Preservationists are not especially interested in saving 817 East 8th Street at the start of **batteries not included* (1987). In fact, just about no one is. A typical Lower East Side tenement, it is the last building standing on a block that has been otherwise leveled, thanks to an ambitious urban renewal scheme that now threatens 817 as well. Hoping to have the building designated a landmark, one tenant has called in a city official, but to no avail: "We do have a minimum standard," she notes coolly. In truth there is not much to recommend the building: the depredations of time and vandalism have taken their toll on whatever architectural merit it ever had. But as we soon learn, the building *does* have real value—a whole range of values, in fact, as various as the people who inhabit it.

To Frank Riley (Hume Cronyn), 817 is the repository for a lifetime of memories—the place he has shared for decades with his wife, Faye (Jessica Tandy), the place whose first-floor lunch counter, Riley's Café, has always supported them. The title sequence charmingly sketches Frank and Faye's past through old black-and-white photographs, showing the life they once obtained on East 8th Street, until a haunting shot dissolves the block's solid, vibrant past into its empty, rubble-strewn present, with the solitary tenement its only survivor.

To the painter played by Dennis Boutsikaris, the structure's appeal lies in

253. ***batteries not included* (1987).** Unable to find a suitable freestanding tenement on the Lower East Side, the designer Ted Haworth and his crew spent ten weeks constructing this four-story exterior set, built on three sides and open in the back, whose facade of brick-patterned fiberglass was "aged" by burning, chipping, and staining. The result looked so authentic that passersby inquired about available apartments and the sanitation department emptied prop garbage cans in front of the building.

its authenticity. His departing girlfriend cannot understand his fascination with the "old depressing building." It's real, he says, to which she replies, "This is the eighties; nobody likes reality." For the pregnant Hispanic woman next door (Elizabeth Peña), the building's value is more basic still: affordable shelter for herself, and for a baby on the way. But it is Harry (Frank McRae), a mute ex-boxer working as the building's superintendent, whose connection to the structure is most touching and profound. He simply loves the building itself, and spends his days vainly trying to repair it, resetting the ornamental hallway floor, tile by tile. His struggle is, in a sense, the largest one—not against the specific threat of redevelopment but the gradual, inevitable decay that plagues every old building and neighborhood.

Ironically, it is their very diversity that makes 817's tenants so ineffectual against the forces that are seeking to push them out. A local tough, Carlos (Michael Carmine), has been hired by the developer to offer relocation bribes to the tenants; when that fails, his gang vandalizes the hallways and destroys the café. With so little in common, the tenants remain isolated, cowering in their apartments. Yet their mutual devotion to this battered old house—however unlikely an object of affection—is so real, so heartfelt, it would be obvious to any outside observer. A Martian would see it in a minute.

As it happens, a Martian does. Or at least someone from the same general

vicinity. In this particular world (the film was coproduced by Steven Spielberg), help arrives from an unusual source: a pair of alien flying saucers who are also living creatures—and small enough to grasp in one hand.

It is not only their diminutive size that is surprising. In contrast to the countless malevolent aliens who come to New York to rampage and destroy, these little creatures enjoy rebuilding and restoring. "They're the fixers," explains Faye, who is the first to befriend them, "they like to fix things. They have that knack."

But why have they come? The answer lies on the roof, where the miniature aliens have created a kind of nest. The mother craft is apparently trying to give birth, but needs more electrical power. Working together, the tenants string an extension cord from below; encouraging the apprehensive "father" saucer to accept the wire, Frank says, "Take it, we're neighbors." As the tenants watch in amazement, two "baby" craft emerge; the third, sadly, seems stillborn. But Harry, showing the same devotion he has displayed toward the building, somehow nurses the little creature back to life. By their joint efforts, the tenants—who have in fact become neighbors to one another no less than to the aliens—reiterate that 817, despite its troubles, is indeed a home, a nest, a place for life and growth.

Now the clever little saucers repay the favor. After Faye shows them old photos of the lunch counter in its heyday, they miraculously restore the place overnight, and with a bump to the jukebox, Riley's Café is back in business, fresh and humming to the sound of swing music. The effort breeds its own success, as the café starts drawing customers from all around—including the demolition workers, who are now beginning to regret they have to tear the place down.

Watching the unlikely turn of events, Carlos may not grasp the cause, but he can judge its effects clearly enough. "They're getting organized," he says, "somebody's bringing them together." With permits soon to expire, the developers turn to a drastic measure—the same terrible technique, in fact, responsible for untold tragedy in New York's poor neighborhoods in the 1970s. With chilling precision, a professional arsonist puts in place the accelerant fuel that will not only send the building up in flames, but make it all look like an accident. He ignites the fuel and, like thousands of other tenements in Brooklyn and the Bronx, 817 East 8th Street is quickly blazing against the night sky (254). How fragile a thing, we realize, is any home! How easily and quickly destroyed, by anyone sufficiently motivated.

The next day there is nothing left but the stoop and a few charred walls; demolition crews are ready to bulldoze away. But they can't, because Harry, sitting on the stoop and nestling the little saucer he helped to save, won't move. His fierce devotion to the building seems to have crossed a line into irrationality. But in this extraterrestrial fantasy, his faith is rewarded when the saucer family returns for their baby, having brought a few friends along—a few *thou-*

254. ***batteries not included* (1987).** In a shot that chillingly recalls the destruction of many of the city's poorer districts in the early 1970s, an arsonist's blaze rips through a tenement at 817 East 8th Street on the Lower East Side.

sand friends, that is, filling the night sky from end to end, a veritable army of fixers who have come to help.

The next morning, the building stands again, restored to pristine perfection. A crowd has gathered to witness the miraculous sight, in a festival of renewal. Even the snooty preservationist is bowled over: "I love it," she says, "the whole thing, especially the sconces and the corbelling, the molding!" It is a sharp-edged point: now that the structure is alive again, it has "architectural" values that were somehow invisible before. The tenants, amazed as anyone, scamper up the steps and into the hall, where the restored tilework quietly announces the building street number, "817." How strange to think that the structure's appeal has been there all along, could we have seen it through the surface of grime and decay (253).

In the end, **batteries not included* is a paean to the act of preservation, all the more effective because its subject is not a celebrated architectural jewel but the most common and disregarded of buildings. As the film reminds us, even the humblest urban structure can be a vessel of meaning and value—a touchstone of the past, a source of affordable shelter, an object of affection, of authenticity, of care. A home, finally.

In its way, the film anticipated the trend by which thousands of houses in the city (many no more distinguished than 817 East 8th) have been resuscitated by the more earthly—but no less heroic—efforts of dedicated civic groups and city agencies. Along the way, the value of preservation has been recognized to extend far beyond traditional "historic" houses and districts to include all manner of urban neighborhoods.

While the final credits roll, the story is amusingly completed. Just as 817's old neighbors faded away at the start of the film, so its new neighbors now fade in: giant black towers rising on all sides, a huge development with the tiny tenement at its center, still surviving in a landscape that is, in its own way, quite alien. In its final moments, the film thus offers both of the visions that have defined the city in the postwar era: urban renewal and historic preservation.

One sought to eradicate the past, and looked to the future for answers. The other argued that the past was precisely where those answers might be found. But both turned time itself, and change, into a shaping force in the landscape of the present.

FIFTEEN

A HEIGHTENED REALITY

STREET MEETS STAGE

THE WORLD'S BIGGEST BACK LOT

> People like to do films in New York because there is an energy that is conducive to good filmmaking, that gets into the crew and cast and elevates it, lifts everybody up, brings everybody to another level. It's a vortex of energy and it gets into people and makes them vibrate. That's the magic of New York. And things happen—serendipitous, spontaneous events that you're just not going to get anywhere else. That's why people want to film here.
>
> FRANK PELLEGRINO

By the 1980s, filmmaking in New York had blossomed into a major industry. Not only were more features being shot on location in the city than ever before—seventy-six films in 1981—but the scale and ambition of location work had expanded dramatically. Prompted by the need to shoot longer and more complex scenes in the streets, a series of technical advances emerged to provide filmmakers on location with the control and flexibility that they had long enjoyed inside the studio. In the early 1970s, a new generation of 35mm sound-synch cameras were introduced, including the Panaflex and Arriflex BL—the first to be battery powered, and thus genuinely portable. With power packs strapped to their waists and the new lightweight cameras balanced on their shoulders, operators could plunge fully into sidewalk crowds, without any trailing cables—a freedom expanded a few years later when the cinematographer Garret Brown introduced the Steadicam, an ingenious gimbal-mounted support that almost magically smoothed out the jerky, distracting motion of a handheld camera (252). In 1979 came the French-built Louma camera crane, a kind of portable, remote-controlled "sky-hook," to give directors on location the ability to employ the high, swooping shots that had once been limited to a

255. **(previous page) Shooting *Born to Win* (1971).** Working on location on Duffy Square at the northern end of Times Square, a film crew directed by Ivan Passer shoots a conversation with George Segal and Hector Elizondo.

soundstage. Location lighting, meanwhile, had been transformed in the mid-1970s by the advent of efficient metal-halide arc lamps, which required smaller generators than the old quartz lights; those generators, in turn, were now part of a specially outfitted truck called the "cinemobile" that was, in effect, a movie studio on wheels.

As the streets of New York increasingly became (in the oft-heard phrase) "the world's biggest back lot," the nature of the movie city was changing. If the studio-built city had whisked audiences away to a dreamy, almost otherworldly urban realm, the location-shot city stayed close to the ground, drawing on the spontaneity of daily street life, entertaining audiences with flavorful vignettes that might well be glimpsed in the real city, it was implied, on any given day.

256. (top) ***Midnight Cowboy* (1969).** Walking with his new friend Joe Buck (Jon Voigt), Ratso Rizzo (Dustin Hoffman) angrily confronts a driver on West 58th Street.

257. (above) ***Manhattan* (1978).** An idyllic moment with Mary Wilke (Diane Keaton) on Central Park Lake is marred when Isaac Davis (Woody Allen) makes the mistake of running his hand through the water.

Thus the knowing smile that John Schlesinger's *Midnight Cowboy* induced with its scene of Sylvia Miles at the curb of her East Side apartment house, urging her reluctant French poodle to "Do it for Mommy." Or, later in the same film, the shot of Ratso Rizzo (Dustin Hoffman) blithely stepping onto West 58th Street against traffic—then yelling at a cab that has stopped short: "Hey, we're *walkin'* here!" Much of the spirit of Woody Allen's classic 1970s comedies, *Annie Hall* and *Manhattan*, likewise relied on distinctive New York "moments." Seeing a group of African diplomats stepping out of Zabar's delicatessen, or watching Allen mock passersby at the Central Park Zoo ("Here's the winner of the Truman Capote look-alike contest"), or solicit romantic advice from random New Yorkers on the street (one attractive couple, asked the secret of their success, simply explain they're "very shallow and empty and have no ideas and nothing interesting to say"), or dip his arm in Central Park Lake only to come up with a handful of sludge, audiences everywhere experienced a nudge of recognition, a sense that these moments somehow embodied—in heightened form, perhaps—the texture of the city's daily life (256, 257).

A new sense of New York was emerging in these films: America's urban menagerie, where a remarkable collection of idiosyncratic and sometimes bizarre individuals were not only assembled but on *public display*, at all hours, in its streets and outdoor spaces. Inevitably, filmmakers shooting on location drew increasingly *from* that display, allowing their films to be shaped, or at least influenced, by the sights and sounds around them. Indeed, for some, such was the very appeal of filming on location. "The great thing about shooting in New

York," the director Andrew Bergman observed, "is that you don't work under laboratory conditions."

> *You have to* deal *with the city every second that you are shooting; the place doesn't stop. The chaos, of people and traffic, is simply the chaos of life itself. And the movie, if you allow it, feeds off that life. If I see an interesting soul walking down the street—say a ragged man carrying a large, ornate floor lamp, or a well-dressed woman pulling a shopping cart—I'll ask if he or she would like to be an extra, just for that moment, for that hour. And if God and union regulations permit, that person's in.*

For another group, capturing the vitality and texture of the real city would be nothing less than the essence of moviemaking. New York's independent film movement could trace its distant roots back to the avant-garde filmmakers of the 1950s, but its true incubator was the film program at New York University, which by the mid-1960s had become home to a new American film sensibility that prized authenticity, expressiveness, and immediacy above all. "At NYU," Martin Scorsese has recalled of that time, "the French New Wave, the Italian New Wave, some new British films, and the New York underground of Shirley Clarke, John Cassavetes and Jonas Mekas were all combined to give us a new sense of freedom and enthusiasm." No one embodied the new spirit more than Scorsese himself, who first as a student, then as an instructor, produced a series of low-budget films drawn from the landscape he knew best: the sidewalks, social clubs, apartments, hallways, and rooftops of nearby Little Italy. They were "real films," he said, "based on real incidents, the daily life of the neighborhood." For the last film of the series, the feature-length *Mean Streets*, Scorsese was obligated to work in Los Angeles, but, insisting that he needed the look of New York for certain settings (authentic tenement hallways, he noted, were impossible to find in California), managed to obtain funds for an intense, six-day shoot in Manhattan, using a crew composed largely of students, and working around town under the guise of making a "thesis" film.

The impact of *Mean Streets* and Scorsese's subsequent films (especially among young filmmakers) transformed NYU into a true rival of the older, established film departments at USC and UCLA. Oriented to the needs of the Hollywood studios, the West Coast programs had always emphasized high production values and technical polish; NYU, by contrast, was notorious for the simple, basic equipment it offered its students. But unlike California, where only a few, relatively expensive projects were produced each year, almost every student in New York was expected to make a short film, and, armed with the school's battered but rugged 16mm cameras, fanned out onto the streets—using the rich landscape of the city to sustain what was becoming known as "guerrilla-style" filmmaking.

As they moved on to direct their first features, NYU graduates such as Susan

Seidelman, Spike Lee, Jim Jarmusch, and others were determined to extend the same approach, shunning traditional studio projects to develop personal films that could be produced in the city on minuscule budgets. Inspired by Scorsese's example, they used ingenuity and willpower to work in New York for almost no money—asking actors and crew to defer their salaries, for example, or borrowing the necessary equipment and supplies in order to get something, *anything*, on film. Unable to afford elaborate sets, they inevitably set their movies in existing locations (not only streets and sidewalks, but interiors, as well) that could be "dressed" at minimal cost. "See what's there and make a film about what's there," Seidelman advised, "rather than trying to re-create a script that calls for specific locations. Go out and see what's available." Pioneering the kind of creative dealmaking that would become common with later independents, Seidelman gained use of East Village clubs by offering to bring in a crowd of extras who would pay for their drinks, then managed to convince the DuArt film lab to put up half her processing costs in return for a portion of the profits.

For these young directors, using locations was far more than a matter of production economy. In shaping their films around the existing landscapes of the city, they were mapping out an alternative approach to the making of American features, laying the groundwork for the emergence of a new, homegrown industry that would look to New York not only as a base of production, but as a major source of inspiration. As nothing else, they demonstrated the possibili-

258. *Smithereens* (1982). Susan Seidelman's first feature, produced independently and shot on location throughout the East Village, tracks the downward spiral of Wren (Susan Berman), who—having been evicted from her apartment—stands by helplessly as her clothes are thrown onto the sidewalk.

ties of making small, expressive features by taking a crew and cast into the streets, relying on the city to provide endless opportunities for story, incident, and character.

Seidelman's first film, *Smithereens* (1982), for example, grew directly out of its East Village setting (258). Its main character, Wren (Susan Berman), is one of the thousands of aimless young people who have gravitated to downtown Manhattan—hardly able to survive its harsh, unwelcoming environment, yet unwilling to leave. Callous and disaffected from the start, Wren grows increasingly lost—morally as well as physically—as the film proceeds. Evicted from her apartment, she stands by helplessly on the sidewalk as her clothes are tossed from the window (a little boy, watching from the side, makes off with her panties). She briefly takes advantage of another free-floating soul, a Montana boy named Paul who lives in a van parked in a vacant lot; but when he proposes leaving the city for a more rooted way of life, she pushes him away. Now truly homeless, she is reduced to dragging her bags around the streets, trying in vain to sleep on the subway. At one point, in the rubble of an empty lot, Wren spray-paints a circle on the ground around her feet, as if trying somehow to create a fixed place to inhabit in this shifting, rootless landscape. But the film ends with her more adrift than ever, wandering along the West Side Highway.

Spike Lee's first effort, *She's Gotta Have It* (1986), emerged no less directly from another part of town—a cluster of Brooklyn neighborhoods encompassing the downtown shopping streets, the old waterfront, and several residential districts. But where Seidelman used her settings to emphasize a kind of rootlessness, Lee brought out a strong sense of place—deftly using his locations, in fact, to sketch out his major characters, Nola Darling (Tracy Camila Jones) and her unlikely trio of suitors. Nola meets Jamie Overstreet (Tommy Redmond Hicks) one Saturday at the Fulton Street Mall; later we see him on a bench in Fort Greene Park in the heart of brownstone Brooklyn. Jamie represents Brooklyn's black middle class—solid, dependable, if perhaps a trifle earnest and bland. We first glimpse Mars Blackmon (played by Lee himself) on his ten-speed bike, screaming wildly down "Dead Man's Hill" in the warehouse district near the waterfront. An unemployed messenger, he is working-class Brooklyn, raw and crude, yet funny and vital. Nola's third suitor, Greer Childs (John Canada Terrell), is a male model, stylish and handsome but striving and self-involved; revealingly, he has abandoned Brooklyn altogether for upscale Manhattan, where he entreats Nola to join him. Nola herself—free-spirited, independent—lives in a former warehouse space near Fulton Ferry, the closest thing Brooklyn had, at the time, to a bohemian loft district.

Ironically, even as independent filmmakers were demonstrating the value of minimal, guerrilla-style location work, studio films were busy expanding *their* location shoots into full-fledged production venues. By the late 1980s, the single cinemobile truck had been superseded by a formidable armada of vehicles: two or three big location trucks for camera and lighting equipment, along with a generator truck, a makeup truck, a wardrobe truck, several campers with dressing rooms, the craft-services truck (operated by a catering firm, and known affectionately as the "roach coach"), and last but not least, the so-called "honey wagon" with its toilet facilities. With its fleet of hired vans to transport the stars and crew, chartered buses to carry extras, and the various "picture cars" appearing in the film itself, a location shoot could easily require forty vehicles or more, and take up entire blocks and avenues of the crowded city.

By 1989, when 143 features were shot in New York—double that of just a decade before—the constant presence of these large film crews was beginning to wear a little thin for some residents, for whom closed-off streets and rerouted traffic was tarnishing the excitement of living in the world's biggest back lot. In July 1990, the production of *Hudson Hawk* closed the Brooklyn Bridge's eastbound lanes for six consecutive nights and the Brooklyn-Battery Tunnel for another three. The mayor's film office sought to deflect the criticism by noting the half-million dollars *a day* the production was pumping into the local economy. But the grumbling continued, especially from those who lived on the picturesque blocks of Greenwich Village, SoHo, and the Upper East Side that were the favorites of location scouts. "Having a film crew in your neighborhood," one Village resident complained bitterly, "is like being occupied by a foreign army."

At that very moment, however, a still greater problem was looming for the industry—an authentic disaster, in fact. In 1990, the major studios decided to force the East Coast craft unions—the camera operators, set dressers, property and wardrobe masters, grips, electricians, and members of a dozen other trades—to agree to the same contract terms recently accepted by the Los Angeles unions. Hollywood producers had long complained about the high cost of shooting in New York, especially the strict overtime rules that substantially raised the cost of working at night and on weekends, as was so often necessary on busy Manhattan locations. When the unions refused to give up their cherished overtime provisions, the studios took the extraordinary step of boycotting *all* production in New York. Films slated for shooting in the city were suddenly shifted to Chicago, or Atlanta, or Toronto—anywhere but New York.

The result was devastating. More than a hundred million dollars in business was lost; by some estimates, the overall size of the industry contracted by half as production personnel, desperate for work, relocated elsewhere. Eight months into the boycott, the local unions agreed to accept the new rules, softened by some enhanced health and pension benefits.

Ironically, the bitter episode proved a kind of catharsis, ushering in a new era of cooperation. During the boycott, with all studio work at a halt, the unions came up with an innovative program called the East Coast Council, an alliance of craft locals intended to *assist* the producers of independent low-budget films, by allowing them to negotiate a coordinated package of wage deferments, to be repaid only if the film recouped its cost. Meanwhile, the city government—realizing how close it had come to losing a major industry—was jolted into action, elevating the head of the mayor's film office to commissioner status, sponsoring a package of local tax incentives, and aggressively wooing the studios to work in New York. Somewhat belatedly, the city had come to appreciate not only the size of the film industry but the economic reality that, because it comprised a large number of small companies, its dollars tended to change hands frequently, creating a still greater stimulus to the economy—"real money, true billions," observed the former New York City film commissioner Richard Brick, "leveraged by a much smaller amount." In a city whose manufacturing base had been shrinking for decades, motion-picture production, which soon represented fifty thousand jobs and $850 million a year in direct spending, offered a rare opportunity for industrial growth.

259. TriBeCa coffee shop set from *It Could Happen to You* (1994). Located on North Moore Street and West Broadway—half a block from the Ghostbusters' firehouse, visible on the left—Bill Groom's elaborate set included a four-story warehouse building, a two-and a-half-story Federal-style row house, and a fully furnished coffee shop interior.

Indeed, as the boycott receded into memory, New York's motion picture industry embarked on a wave of growth like nothing before it. Location shooting soared: 175 films in 1995; 201 in 1996; 223 in 1998. The craft unions began displaying a striking collegiality, attributed by some observers to a shift within the locals themselves: "The fathers' attitude was, How much can we beat you out of," one industry veteran noted. "Today's attitude is, What can we do to help you?" At the same time, production in the city was evolving beyond its gypsylike origins with the construction of substantial facilities. Transformed into a profit-making venture by the developer George Kaufman, the old Astoria Studio was overhauled and expanded at a cost of $50 million into a six-stage, fifteen-acre lot, complete with Hollywood-style scenic shops, wardrobe department, and dining commissary. A few years later, to meet the burgeoning demand for stage space, a former bakery in Long Island City was converted to Silvercup Studios, offering twenty-four stages and an even wider array of services. Still more space would be added with the opening of the Chelsea Piers Studios in Manhattan and other stages around town, but demand continued to outpace supply, and as developers floated increasingly ambitious proposals for new studios around the city—in the Brooklyn Navy Yard, atop a truck terminal in downtown Manhattan—producers were busy putting city armories and warehouses into near-constant service as "temporary" stages.

Still, New York's greatest advantage remained the city itself, and as the scale of production increased, an ironic new trend emerged: large, studio-style sets erected on the streets themselves—transforming the real city, as it were, into a back lot. For Spike Lee's *Crooklyn* (1994), the designer Wynn Thomas stretched a series of five-story brownstone fronts across the middle of Arlington Place in Brooklyn, transforming a typical city street into something resembling the classically enclosed New York Street as constructed back in California. Residents of TriBeCa, meanwhile, were startled when a pair of new buildings suddenly appeared on an empty site on West Broadway, including a fully furnished diner at street level. A few eager passersby came inside and asked for the lunch menu. But the entire construction was in fact a set for Andrew Bergman's *It Could Happen to You* (1994), designed by Bill Groom (259).

By now, it was evident that New York had become home to *two* film industries, flourishing side by side. Each year, several big-budget studio features were shot in New York, which remained, as always, one of the principal settings of Hollywood films. Often these drew on some quintessential corner of the city: Ron Howard's *The Paper* (1994), for instance, revolved around the newsroom of a New York tabloid, reveling in its distinctive rituals (the telltale vibration that runs through the building each evening, for example, as the big presses in the basement start up) as well as its fierce parochialism (five wall clocks, typically showing the time in cities around the world, here display the names of the five boroughs, and all show local time). Barry Sonnenberg's *For Love or Money* (1994) anatomized a New York grand hotel, mixing the exteriors of the Pierre with an elaborate interior stage set, built to reveal the complex (and surprisingly intimate) intertwining of the hotel's glossy public rooms and raw, brick-lined service spaces. Nora Ephron's *You've Got Mail* (1998)offered audiences the startling sight of a newly gentrified Upper West Side—the drug-ridden, nightmarish setting of 1971's *Panic in Needle Park* now transformed into a gleaming demi-paradise of refurbished brownstones, Starbucks coffee shops, farmer's markets, and street fairs, whose greatest urban challenge rested in the protection of its local independent bookstores from predatory chains.

Other films, tied less to a specific site, grew instead from the sensibility of filmmakers who—whether living on one coast or another—maintained strong emotional and professional links to the city, including Mike Nichols, Jonathan Demme, Andrew Bergman, Garry Marshall, Paul Mazursky, Barbra Streisand, Sidney Pollack, and Nora Ephron herself. Occupying a special place within this group, of course, were the four directors most closely identified with New York—Martin Scorsese, Woody Allen, Spike Lee, and pioneer Sidney Lumet—a quartet whose ethnic and artistic diversity itself provided a rough gauge of the city's social complexity.

But it was the stunning rise of the city's *independent* industry—growing in a decade from a distinctly marginal alternative to a major presence in American film—that signaled an extraordinary new chapter in the relationship between New York and the movies. Even as studio-financed films began flocking back to the city following the end of the boycott, the East Coast Council had remained active, assisting the production of dozens of smaller-budget features and encouraging a whole generation of producers and directors to work outside the traditional Hollywood system. At the same time, an entire apparatus for independent financing and distribution emerged within the city, in the form of companies such as Miramax, Gramercy, and Fine Line, that were attuned to the needs and potential of small, unusual films (and proved so successful commercially that they were, in most cases, acquired by major studios). Unlike their larger California equivalents, these companies did not maintain sprawling production facilities or studio lots, but instead clustered in modest offices, many in or around a former coffee warehouse on Greenwich Street that the actor Robert De Niro had transformed in 1989 into the TriBeCa Film Center, a state-of-the-art complex of production offices, screening rooms, and editing booths that soon became a hub for the city's independent film community.

Not all independent films were set in New York, of course. But to a remarkable degree the city now became associated with a kind of readily identifiable American film: small in scale, idiosyncratic in theme and mood, the product not of studio story conferences but of the personal—or downright quirky—vision of its writer and director (who often enough were one and the same). Like independent films before them, these films used the city both as an expedient background and a narrative resource. But now there were literally dozens of them, produced year after year, deliberately seeking out the subtler, inconspicuous precincts of the contemporary city.

260. ***The Brothers McMullen* (1995).** With twenty-five thousand dollars raised from friends and family, the screenwriter Ed Burns shot his first feature almost entirely on location. This view, filmed in Washington Square Park, depicts the three McMullen brothers—Jack (Jack Mulcahy), Barry (Burns), and Patrick (Mike McGlone)—as well as the striking young woman, Audrey (Maxine Bahns), who has caught Barry's eye.

Some explored the ethnic neighborhoods that continue to coexist, if often uneasily, on the city's periphery. Three closely observed portraits of New York's Italian American community—Nancy Savoca's *Household Saints* (1994) and *True Love* (1990), and Martha Coolidge's *Angie* (1994)—tracked the characteristic passage of the city's ethnic groups from its center to its edge, from the flavorful, congested streets of Little Italy to the leafy, semi-suburban environs of the Bronx and Brooklyn. A similar trajectory of Irish New Yorkers informed Edward Burns's *The Brothers McMullen* (1995) and *She's the One* (1996). Although both the McMullen and Fitzpatrick families have settled in low-rise neighborhoods in Brooklyn and Nassau County—solid, stable communities where the old verities of family and religion rule—their sons (played in both films by Burns and Michael McGlone) remain drawn to the dense and fluid environment of Manhattan, filled with all manner of desire, temptation, and possibility. Indeed, it is the back-and-forth movement of characters and cameras—between the lively, serendipity-filled streets of Manhattan and the quieter, tradition-bound communities on the outskirts of the city—that helps to give each film its narrative rhythm (260).

Even films that focused exclusively on Manhattan often bypassed its famed icons to explore lesser-known subcultures and communities beneath its surface. Tom De Cillo's *Living in Oblivion* (1995) offered an amusingly self-referential look at the world of independent filmmaking, proceeding fitfully in the improvised, low-rent conditions of a West Side warehouse. In *The Real Blonde* (1997), De Cillo widened his scope to encompass a rondelet of friends and lovers who are all (in one way or another) sustained by Manhattan's interlocking networks of art and popular culture: the overlapping worlds of museum exhibitions, daytime television shows, music videos, and fashion photography. In *The Last Days of Disco* (1998), Whit Stillman tracked another Manhattan subgroup, the insular young elite who arrive in the city out of Ivy League colleges, filling the lowest rungs of the publishing industry as they try to make their own way in cheap, dormlike rental units on the East Side.

Perhaps inevitably, independent filmmakers were especially drawn to the new communities emerging downtown. Scorsese himself explored SoHo in *After Hours*, a film produced in 1985 but intended to portray the district as it had been a decade earlier: an urban netherworld, isolated from the rest of Manhattan, whose dark, deserted streets offer few outward signs of life—yet a real community all the same, whose seemingly isolated pockets of activity (a bar, a diner, a loft, a nightclub) turn out to be complexly interconnected, as an uptown visitor played by Griffin Dunne discovers to his nightmarish surprise. Eleven years later, in 1996, *Basquiat* (directed by Julian Schnabel from a script written with John Bowe) again looked back—this time to the SoHo of the mid-1980s—to plumb the strange contradictions of a place that had become a kind of global village unto itself. Tracking the artistic career of the painter Jean-Michel Basquiat (Jeffrey Wright), the film revealed SoHo's surprisingly small-town character—its intimate scale, casual sidewalk encounters, and distinctive community rituals (gallery openings that typically spill onto the pavement, for instance, taking on an almost block-party atmosphere). Yet the film also shows a place that had quickly become the undisputed center of the art world, filled with the heady, disconcerting atmosphere of influential gallery owners, rich collectors, and famous artists. Racking between one reality and the other, trying somehow to reconcile the two, we share Basquiat's profound disorientation (261). Daisy von Scherler Mayer's *Party Girl* (1995) shifts the focus a few blocks east and a few years forward, to the still-evolving downtown world—a wildly flamboyant subculture of transvestite dancers, nightclub owners (and bounc-

261. ***Basquiat* (1996).** Making his first foray into motion pictures, the painter Julian Schnabel filmed his biographical portrait of the artist Jean-Michel Basquiat in the galleries, restaurants, and sidewalks of SoHo and the East Village. In this scene, the newly successful Basquiat (Jeffrey Wright) returns from a shopping spree with Andy Warhol, played by David Bowie.

ers), and disaffected "party girls" such as Mary (Parker Posey), superimposed incongruously on a daytime community of hardworking, newly arrived immigrants. For Mary, switching back and forth between her job at the local public library and her evening vocation as a party habitué, attracted both to the earnest attention of a young Lebanese pushcart vendor (Omar Townsend) and to the noisy blandishments of drag queens such as "the Lady Bunny," the neighborhood's contradictions become the markers for her own confused search for identity.

This effort to grasp the elusive (and often paradoxical) identity of the city was central to many independent films—especially a pair of features that the director Wayne Wang and the writer Paul Auster produced in the summer of 1995: *Smoke* and *Blue in the Face.* Though the two films (shot in succession on the same set, with much of the same cast and crew) apparently share the same tight focus—a single cigar store in Park Slope—their field of view is in fact much wider, encompassing an entire borough (262). *Smoke*'s seemingly random web of stories turns out to evoke two very different Brooklyns—scarcely a mile apart, but each, according to one character, its own "galaxy." There is the Brooklyn of Park Slope itself, the neighborly community enjoyed by the novelist Paul Benjamin (William Hurt) and the shopkeeper Auggie Wren (Harvey Keitel), its urbane streets filled with families, cafés, and friendly local stores. But there is also the harsh, dangerous Brooklyn of Clinton Hill, whose grim housing projects are home to two black teenagers, Thomas (Harold Perrineau Jr.) and Roger (Walter T. Mead). In one plot turn, Thomas shares Paul's

262. ***Smoke* (1995).** As he has done every morning for thirteen years—at precisely eight a.m.—Auggie Wren (Harvey Keitel) crosses the street from his cigar store on 13th Street and Seventh Avenue in Brooklyn's Park Slope to take a photograph of his "little corner of the world." (Elsewhere in the film we see a sample of the photographs themselves, which were actually shot by K. C. Bailey.)

life; in another, Auggie briefly shares Roger's. The unlikely train of events that brings the four characters and two worlds together only reinforces our sense of their separateness, as does the film's coda, which relocates us from the cozy sidewalk life of the Slope to the forbidding landscape of Clinton Hill, seen in grainy black and white. If both of these places are Brooklyn, the film asks implicitly, then what exactly *is* Brooklyn?

Blue in the Face poses the same question, this time explicitly. By way of Harvey Wang's cinema verité interviews with various residents, and the recitation of startling statistics about the borough by an astonishingly diverse assortment of inhabitants—Indian, Arab, Chinese, Jewish, African American, Hispanic—the film questions whether Brooklyn possesses an identity at all, anything that might unify its sprawling communities and fragmented population. The one indisputable source of borough-wide identity that once existed, the Brooklyn Dodgers baseball team, is long gone, together with Ebbets Field (whose demolition is recalled through newsreel footage), and nothing has replaced it—certainly not the little cigar store, a single thread in the borough's fraying social fabric, which is itself, in any case, scheduled to be closed. It requires nothing less than a visit from the ghost of Jackie Robinson himself to convince the owner (a former Brooklynite, now relocated to Long Island) to keep the shop open; the spectral Dodger succeeds by recalling for him the meaning that Brooklyn once had—and, all things considered, might still have.

By the late 1990s, when it seemed as if every corner of New York was appearing in a low-budget feature, a new development brought filming in the city full circle: the "no-budget" feature, made for a hundred thousand dollars or less by young, aspiring filmmakers. In 1996, the director John Walsh and his producer Sally Roy made *Ed's Next Move* for $93,000; the following year, Greg Mottola shot *The Daytrippers* for $60,000; other efforts included Matthew Harrison's *The Rhythm Thief* (1995)—made in eleven days, for $11,000. Like all location films, these took advantage of advances in technology—not elaborate cranes and Steadicams, but basic camera and sound equipment that had grown lighter and more flexible than ever, as well as sharper film stock that allowed the use of Super 16mm rather than expensive 35mm equipment. Perhaps more than any films before them, these features relied completely on the city. Their stories—as often as not a series of New York vignettes, strung together—were told through the simplest (and cheapest) of production techniques: handheld cameras tracking the characters' conversation around the city's streets, lofts, coffee shops, apartments. Indeed, in a manner not unlike the very first movies ever made in New York—the actuality and early story films, a century before—these features returned filmmaking in the city to its essentials. They were shot in New York because New York was the most convenient place to bring a camera, cast, and crew; because the city itself could provide the basis for endless stories; and because—even with the absolute minimum of means—the city could be transmuted into so powerful and compelling a celluloid presence.

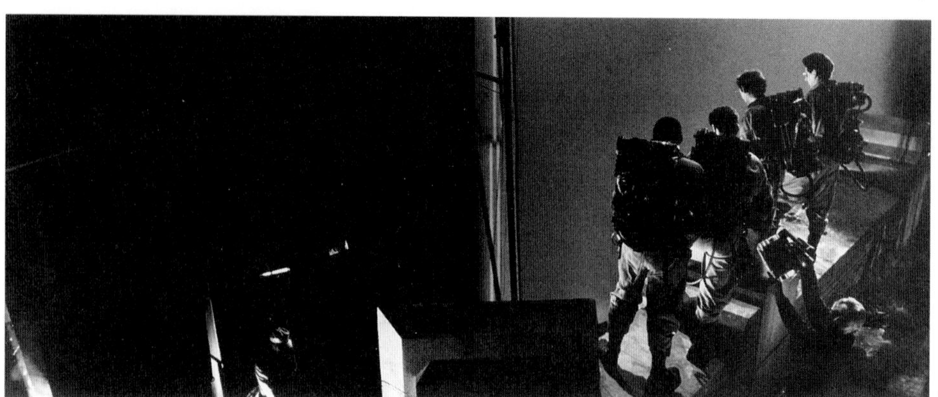

263. ***Ghostbusters*** **(1984).** To create this image of the Ghostbusters confronting the Stay-Puft man (bottom), the film's visual-effects team (under supervisor Richard Edlund) optically combined a shot of the principal actors, standing on a fragment of the building cornice (top); footage of an operator inside a Stay-Puft costume, standing on an elaborate miniature of Central Park West and the park itself (second down); and a matte painting by Matthew Yuricich of background building facades and rooftops (third down).

THE MAGIC CLUB

By the 1980s, location filming had come to overwhelmingly dominate the relationship of New York and the movies. Not only were the exteriors of most New York features shot in the city itself (interiors continued to be filmed largely on Hollywood sets), but the spirit of location-shot New York—gritty, authentic, realistic—had essentially superseded the old, stylized city of the studio era. For audiences now deeply familiar with the sights, sounds, and rhythms of the real city's streets, the notion of an artificial, studio-built city seemed a thing of the past—as dated, in its way, as silent pictures themselves.

Yet just as it was pronounced dead, the stylized, invented city of the movies came suddenly back to life and was soon coexisting quite comfortably with the location-shot city that was supposed to have replaced it forever.

It was, in part, the price of success. With New York locations now appearing endlessly in feature films—and even more endlessly on television programs such as *McCloud*, *Kojak*, and *The Enforcer*—it was hard for audiences to find urban location work as automatically fresh as they had decades before. It was the idea of a *constructed* city that came to seem uncommon and novel, not only for audiences, but filmmakers as well.

In the late 1970s, in fact, the desire to create an imaginary New York had propelled two of the directors most closely associated with location filmmaking—Martin Scorsese and Sidney Lumet—to attempt to create studio-constructed cities for *New York, New York* (1977) and *The Wiz* (1978). The former, filmed at Goldwyn Studios in Los Angeles on elaborate sets by Boris Leven, was a full-blown homage to 1940s Hollywood's New York, right down to the artificially high street curbs that Scorsese recalled from his earliest days of moviegoing. The latter, produced at the newly reopened Astoria studio to the designs of Tony Walton, combined fantastic images of the real city with soundstage constructions of the Emerald City. Despite sincere intentions, neither vision proved especially convincing: Scorsese's studio-built New York seemed plagued by self-consciousness, an act of embalming rather than reanimating, while Lumet and Walton's fantasy creation was diffuse and confusing, without the clarity of the simple country-to-city journey that made the original *Oz*, for all its air of fantasy, feel so credible. It would be a few years before the third leading proponent of location New York—Woody Allen—at last rekindled the magic of the stylized city of the studio. Indeed, the very premise of *The Purple Rose of Cairo* (1985) arose from the notion that an invented city could offer as sturdy and compelling a presence as any real place, or more so. Physically, Cecilia (Mia Farrow) inhabits a drab New Jersey town, wracked by the Great Depression; imaginatively, she lives in the dream city of the movies, manifested (this week) by an RKO feature called "The Purple Rose of Cairo." She sits through every showing, every day, absorbed less by the film's routine plot than its glamorous characters and setting—a carefree penthouse world of "cocktail parties and opening nights," where a "madcap Manhattan weekend" is under way. Just when this imaginary city feels so real she can almost touch it, it turns around and touches *her:* a character named Tom Baxter (Jeff Daniels) notices Cecilia in the audience and steps out of the screen to join her in the real world. Back *in* the screen, meanwhile, life in the movie city proceeds—after a fashion. Unable to continue the film's original story without Tom, the remaining characters (including the maid) settle down for a game of cards in the penthouse's living room; later, other characters drop by, having tired of waiting at the "Copacabana" for Tom's party to arrive. What simpler or more effective argument could there be that a whole city really does lie beyond that penthouse's walls, where all sorts of people interact in all sorts of places, as they would in any city! What is *not* behind those walls, by the same token, is any trace of an RKO stage on Gower Street in Hollywood.

Ultimate proof of the solidity of this "city," if needed, comes when Cecilia fulfills her wish and steps through the screen herself, right into movie New York. She joins the party in progress at the Copa: aside from champagne that tastes like ginger ale, the filmic metropolis more than lives up to her expectations, as Tom whisks her from one nightclub to another, before returning her to the penthouse and romantically "offering" her the skyline. Tempted to stay, she has come to realize her place is on the other side of the screen. "I'll never forget our night on the town," she says, by way of farewell.

At one level a loving tribute (by the production designer Stuart Wurtzel) to the sleek Art Deco settings of Van Nest Polglase and the RKO art department—right down to the white telephone and baby grand piano that were the touchstones of the Big White Set—the film also spoke to a broader desire to inhabit again a movie city not wholly tethered to reality. And that was precisely what began to appear on screen in the mid-1980s, as the city once again became fertile ground for filmic reinvention and reimagining of every kind.

There was, of course, the fantastic vision of New York that began with *Ghostbusters* and its 1989 sequel, continued through *Batman* and its later sequels, and reappeared in *The Hudsucker Proxy* (1994), *The Shadow* (1995), and *The Fifth Element* (1996). As much as the movie New York of decades earlier, this imaginary new city owed its very existence to a blend of art direction and special effects: gigantic stage sets and elaborate miniatures, mixed with state-of-the-art optical and digital techniques (2, 73, 74, 81, 82, 84, 87). As before, too, a strong sense of continuity could be felt from film to film, and for the same good reason: portions of the enormous (and enormously expensive) miniature Manhattan built for *Hudsucker Proxy*, for example, were bought and reused by Universal for *The Shadow*, then adapted once more by Warner's for *Batman Returns.* Once again the movie city seemed to exist outside any particular film.

With a knowing wink, the makers of these films also reintroduced the kind of larger-than-life figures that have always been among the most distinctive citizens of movie New York. *Ghostbusters* brought on the fiendishly grinning, hundred-foot-tall Stay-Puft Marshmallow Man, making his thunderous way down Central Park West—a classic oversized New Yorker in the tradition of King Kong, Macy's Thanksgiving parade balloons, and that original urban giant, the Statue of Liberty (263). In *Ghostbusters II*, the Statue herself (sprayed inside with a "psychoactive substance") dramatically comes to life, wading across the bay and up Fifth Avenue to save the city, while in *Godzilla* (1998), the

264. ***Men in Black*** **(1997).** Shot on location, this view shows an alien character scaling the exterior of Frank Lloyd Wright's Guggenheim Museum on Fifth Avenue. A complex winch and cabling system, controlled by high-speed governors, allowed the figure to leap up the side of the building.

legendary giant lizard races with surprising stealthiness around the corners of a distinctly *noir*-like Manhattan. Yet perhaps the ultimate outsized New Yorker appeared in a film by Woody Allen himself: Mrs. Millstein, the giant Jewish mother (played by Mae Questel) who appears hovering over the city in *Oedipus Wrecks*, part of the *New York Stories* trilogy (1989). Comparing baby pictures and chatting volubly with sidewalk crowds below, the enormous floating lady is soon accepted by New Yorkers as "another part of life in the city" (Mayor Koch, on television, loudly defends her civil right to remain over the city as long as she likes), but her presence is an unimaginable nightmare for her assimilated son, Sheldon Mills—especially when she begins complaining about Sheldon's Gentile girlfriend, and his desire to downplay his Jewish identity. In the movie city's instinct for oversized spectacle, Allen found the ideal external context to play out a host of deeply *internal* conflicts—between child and parent, between public and private personas, between the appeal and abhorrence of an ethnic heritage. In the unforgettable figure of Mrs. Millstein, in turn, Allen gave movie New York—famously the home not only of giant buildings but giant characters—a worthy successor to King Kong (255).

Importantly, this new fantasy city did not preclude the use of locations. The New York that Mrs. Millstein floated over was authentic—the city's real streets and skyline, shot on location, above which her head was "placed" through the optical ingenuity of R/Greenberg Associates. "New York City is always New York City; it can't be used for anything else," Pauline Kael had insisted in 1971. But it turned out that the real city, shot on location, could provide a superb platform for a fantastic *version* of itself. Among the major pleasures of a film like *Men in Black* (1997) was its clever use of postwar New York landmarks, from Frank Lloyd Wright's 1959 Guggenheim Museum to Philip Johnson and Richard Foster's New York State Pavilion at the 1964 World's Fair, to suggest an other-

265. *Desperately Seeking Susan* (1985). To create this exterior of the film's fictional Magic Club, the production designer Santo Loquasto dressed the existing facade of the aging Audubon Ballroom on Broadway in upper Manhattan.

worldly dimension woven right into the city's fabric (264). In lower Manhattan, a strangely featureless building serves in the film as the secret entrance to the headquarters of a shadowy agency located deep below the surface. In fact, this monolithic structure (a ventilator tower of the Brooklyn-Battery Tunnel) really *is* a telltale sign of a pervasive yet hidden bureaucracy: the Triborough Authority, one of the powerful semiautonomous agencies formed by Robert Moses to determine the destiny of the city and the region.

The film's knowing use of locations proves even more appropriate when the true identity of this underground facility is revealed: an interplanetary Ellis Island, where refugees from across the galaxy are processed and admitted to Earth. "There are fifteen hundred aliens on the planet," agent Tommy Lee Jones tells the newly recruited Will Smith, "most of them right here in Manhattan." He provides this information, appropriately enough, at the Battery, the exact spot where the original "aliens"—immigrants—first set foot in the city. New York's historic cosmopolitanism has apparently extended not only across time (as we are reminded by shots of the city's newest arrivals driving cabs, working newsstands, and running restaurants), but across space as well. "It makes total sense," says Linda Fiorentino upon learning the truth. "How else do you explain New York?" It is precisely the film's ability to move between location (the city we know) and fantasy (the city we don't) that gives *Men in Black* its evocative power. Breaking down the old distinctions between the real and the imaginary city, it sits comfortably poised between them.

Indeed, after nearly a century, the two venerable traditions—studio fabrication and location realism—were at last beginning to merge. Inserting imaginatively created settings into the matrix of the location-shot city, filmmakers created what the director Susan Seidelman called "a heightened realism," through which the gritty, authentic city was "made to seem magical." Nothing embodied this, in the end, better than Seidelman's own *Desperately Seeking Susan* (1985), in which the real city was transmuted (by the cinematographer Ed Lachman and the designer Santo Loquasto) into a stylized, slightly fantastic urban world. In it, the George Washington Bridge is not just a river crossing but a mystical gateway, through which a bored housewife named Roberta (Rosanna Arquette) is able to leave behind a confining suburban existence in Fort Lee, New Jersey, to follow—and gradually emulate—a brash downtown character named Susan (Madonna). Battery Park's promenade, meanwhile, becomes a cauldron of ambiguity and confusion, in which Roberta is mistaken for Susan and then, through an ill-timed bump on the head, comes to believe she *is* Susan. Even the ordinary streets and interiors of this city—rendered in electric colors, or bathed in deep chiaroscuro—seem eerily unfamiliar and mysterious, though they have been filmed on real locations and plainly reflect the layered grittiness of contemporary Manhattan. Sailing through the heart of Times Square on the back of a motor scooter, the dazed Roberta takes it all in as if she's never seen it before—as does the audience, who are seeing the city turned into a strange and dreamlike place before their very eyes. Inhabiting her new name and identity—which includes a new boyfriend (Aidan Quinn) and a new job (as a magician's assistant)—"Susan" eventually finds her way to the heart of this strange, swirling urban vortex: an establishment called the Magic Club, located in a shabby but once-grand Broadway storefront (265). As designed by Loquasto, the Magic Club is like nothing else and everything else in the city, from its fading exterior signs (complete with a neon rabbit jumping out of a neon hat) to its vaguely Oriental interior, filled with an aging band, young cigarette girls, hackneyed magic acts, and more than a hint of New Wave style. Here, at the film's climax, all the characters converge, the two Susans meet, and Roberta (confronting her suburban husband) comes to realize that although she may not be Susan, she is not the old Roberta, either. Rendered through a richly stylized mix of real locations and invented settings, the city has itself been transformed, even as it continues to perform its best and longest-running "trick"—transforming those who have come to it, allowing them to realize unimagined possibilities within themselves. The magic club, indeed.

STAND BY . . .

The "No Parking Tuesday" signs have been up since yesterday morning. Late last night, production assistants started placing the orange cones in the street, reserving parking spaces for the trucks and campers that rolled in this morning and are now lined up, end to end, over the length of the block (the big generator trucks have been placed at the far end, to keep their noise as far as possible from the action). The rigging crew, meanwhile, has been hard at work for days, mounting an impressive array of lights on nearby roofs. The city's own lampposts have been switched off; in place of their harsh sodium glare, a softer, more artful urban light is being sculpted from a hundred sources, near and far. Above the central action is the key light, a "brute," held in place by a twelve-foot crane. Tucked into corners are smaller incandescent lights, "inkys," angled precisely to light the starring actors as they stand at their marks. Halfway down the block, a massive crane supports the pair of twenty-kilowatt "Titans" that will provide the scene's basic ambient light, while atop several buildings across the street are the biggest of all, the "dinos"—giant arrays of fifty lamps or more, providing the "scratch" light that will keep the distant recesses of the block from fading into blackness. The gaffer announces he is ready; the generators are switched on; the motors turn over; and the scene blazes into brilliance (266).

The effect is uncanny. An intense pool of light bathes the scene, bringing out the ornamental richness of the cast-iron facades, while throwing unintended but eerily beautiful shadows outside the camera's field of view. "There's a wonderful intensity about night shooting," Sidney Lumet has noted. "Here, in the midst of blackness, a group of people are painting with light." The lights also create an unmistakable beacon, visible for blocks, and soon the location is surrounded by a crowd of onlookers: neighborhood residents, couples on their way to dinner, a tourist or two. Some just glance at the shoot and walk away, grumbling about "another damn film crew in the neighborhood." Others will spend the entire evening watching the free entertainment—"a cocktail party without alcohol," one crew member calls it. The onlookers strike up conversations with one another and with newcomers, who, arriving on the scene, ask excitedly what is being shot. It's a feature, someone says, coming out next year; no one in the crowd seems quite sure of its title.

Within the company, tension is running high, because—as the production manager needs not remind anyone—this is the last night of location work. Tomorrow the crew and cast will pack up for California, to start shooting the day after that. In Los Angeles, where it is still late afternoon, the rigging grips, scenic artists, and set dressers are just ending their day, putting the finishing touches on the loft interior inside a giant soundstage. An enormous "duratrans" photomural transparency, representing the cast-iron facade across the street in New York, has been hoisted into place, and lit up from behind. Now the men step out from the relative darkness of the stage onto the lot, surprisingly quiet in the late afternoon; in the distance, the lowering sun bathes the Hollywood hills in a soft, golden light.

Back in New York, the preparations are complete, and shooting is about to begin. Until now, the stars have remained in their trailers, receiving last-minute touches to their wardrobe and makeup, deliberately kept off the set by the director until the last moment. Now they emerge, and the impromptu audience is instantly abuzz. The actress is much prettier in person than on television, the onlookers agree, while others call out to the leading man, "Hey, Jack!" as they might to a familiar neighbor. He, in turn, makes a few jokes with the crowd, and casually wonders about the score of a playoff game; the answer is shouted down from a window.

The small army of technicians wheel into action. The camera operator and assistant can be seen up on the crane platform, next to the

266. Night shoot in Greenwich Village, 1997.

big Panavision camera, practicing the focus changes for this dramatic, swooping shot, while the cinematographer, director, and producer cluster around the "video-assist" to watch the shot through several large monitors while sitting on canvas-backed chairs stenciled with their names in script. No one sits in the proper chair.

The director points out a distracting street sign in the frame. Grips cover it over with sheets of nonreflective duvetyn. He decides he wants more traffic in the background. A dozen "show cars," including a couple of gleaming yellow taxis, are wheeled around the corner, where they have been waiting for hours. Now it is time for the final touch, the "wet down," the light wash of rain that will heighten the classic city look of the scene. A "rain tower," with four long arms radiating from the top of a hundred-foot-tall crane, is positioned above the action. Fed by hose from a tank truck, halfway down the block, the sprinkler heads, "rain birds," start spinning and a wide spray begins to fall, washing the sidewalk—"like diamonds," a crew member observes. But the director is still not quite satisfied.

"Move the rain," he says.

"Rain moving," the operator responds.

Walkie-talkies crackle with obscure commands to production assistants (PAs) at the edges of the shoot, blocks away, as sightlines and coverage, focus and exposure are checked one last time. "Sweep 'em out," yells a producer, anxious to clear the area of bystanders. The haughty, self-important young PAs strive to catch passersby from intruding into the shot; one woman, kept for a few minutes from entering her loft, is furious: "I couldn't get into my office today because of Woody Allen—and now this!" Still, sometime next year, sitting in an audience, she will nudge her neighbor as her building—the home of the leading man, and focus of the action—appears on the screen.

Everyone waits, as more time elapses, for reasons unclear. Finally, the assistant producer relays his instructions to the crowd: please be quiet while the shot is in progress; *please* do not use a flash camera. "Stand by," the assistant director says into the mike.

The air is hushed with anticipation: shooting is about to begin. The city's intensity, energy, and concentration are all superheated tonight, to be captured forever on celluloid. Even at a distance, one can see that something big is happening, yet again: a more dramatic, a more frightening, a more beautiful New York is in the making.

"Stand by." "Background action?" The background players are set at their marks. "Stand by." An intent silence comes over the area.

"Camera?" "Speed."

"We're rolling."

"And . . . action!"

AFTERWORD AND ACKNOWLEDGMENTS

When *Celluloid Skyline* first began to take shape, nearly fifteen years ago, I realized it would call for an unusual (and relatively extensive) research effort. Surveying the resources publicly available at the time, I found very little—in words or images—along the lines I needed. For the most part, the role of the city in film, when considered at all, was treated in the traditional literary sense of a "setting," to be understood essentially in symbolic terms, as one would the setting of a story, novel, or play. Occasionally a critic might go so far as to claim that in a certain film, the city had been elevated to being "almost a character."

I had something different in mind. Perhaps because of my background as an architect, I was determined to look at New York in the movies, first and foremost, as a *city*—to be explored and apprehended as one would any city: by wandering through it, coming to know the character and mood and rhythm of its spaces, large and small, public and private, indoors and out. Unlike stories, novels, and plays, films occur in fully rendered environments, robustly three-dimensional landscapes through which their characters move and interact, and it was this *spatial* character that, in the end, I most wanted to understand fully. To do so, I realized that I would have to "cross the screen," so to speak, to enter the world of film production—not only to bring the movie city to life in words, but also to locate the kind of illustrative materials that would visually re-create that city on the printed page.

I thus embarked on a decade-long odyssey, traveling to specialized archives and collections in New York, Washington, London, and Los Angeles, haunting studio lots and location shoots, getting to know the remarkable men and women who design, direct, and produce feature films. It was difficult—especially at first—to breach the barriers that the film industry has always erected against civilians, and I will always be grateful to two of my early guides into this unknown territory. In New York, Donald Albrecht, whose landmark book *Designing Dreams: Modern Architecture in the Movies* had just been published, furnished me (in a gesture of true scholarly generosity) with every art department contact he could think of. In Los Angeles, with amazing luck, I happened on Joan Cohen, film researcher extraordinaire, who seemed to know everyone—and who proceeded to open up one door after another.

What I was looking for, to begin with, was a certain kind of film image—not the familiar "headshots" or "two-shots" of the stars, but views that depicted a film's characters within its larger environment: wider views, for the most part, that carried a feeling of urban space and life, without looking particularly staged or artificial. I was searching, too, for images that revealed how filmic settings were created—allowing the book's illustrations to reach behind the scenes as well as in front of them.

267. (previous page) Publicity still from *Rope* (1948).

For films produced in the studio era, such images turned out indeed to exist, in a quantity and quality that astounded me. Every studio in Hollywood, I discovered, had once maintained an entire stills department—a dozen or more photographers, all working on the lot, each assigned to a picture in production. Unlike their equivalents today (who typically work in 35mm), these professionals used large-format bellows-type view cameras to take big, superbly detailed 4 × 5 negatives documenting every aspect of a film's production. Upon release, large prints of these images were gathered into what were known as key books (for the metal pin-and-key device that bound the stills together) and distributed to the film's producers. I spent endless days and hours in Los Angeles studying folder after folder of these exquisitely lighted, elegantly composed views, as well-crafted in their way as the films themselves.

There was more. For continuity purposes, studios routinely produced a second series of images, called "set reference" stills. Photographed after the final take of each scene, these images recorded in precise detail every aspect of the setting: not only the larger "architectural" elements but—in a strange, almost *Marie Celeste*–like fashion—every chair, lamp, rug, potted plant, table setting, piece of luggage, and so forth, as it had been left moments before by the film's actors (who were themselves nowhere to be seen). No studio produced these stills as comprehensively as MGM, which, ever since the days of Irving Thalberg (whose famed perfectionism led the Culver City studio to be known as "Retake Valley") had been notorious for revising whole scenes or even entire endings in response to audience previews. Created to help the art department accurately re-create film settings long after the original sets had been dismantled, these reference stills provided a remarkably rich view of studio-created New York.

The search for usable stills took me to more than a dozen archives on both coasts and in Europe. In New York, I enjoyed the help of Mary Corliss and Terry Geesken of the Museum of Modern Art Film Stills Archive, Jeremy McGraw at the Billy Rose Collection of the New York Public Library, Shawn Miller at the Museum of the Moving Image, Eve Povzea and Ron Harvey at the Everett Collection, and Allen Reuben at Culver Pictures. With the aid of the diligent staff at their agency, Photofest, Ron and Howard Mandelbaum—twin brothers with an encyclopedic knowledge of American film—were able to locate a large number of striking images for me. In London, the staff of the Kobal Collection and Bridget Kinally at the British Film Institute were unusually helpful.

Traveling to Los Angeles, I had the opportunity to explore some of the world's greatest film still archives, and I wish to extend a special thanks to Ann Schlosser, Leith Adams, Ned Comstock, and Carlos Noriega at USC's Special Collections, and to Brigitte Keuppers and Julie Graham at UCLA's Theater Arts Library. It was a treat to meet Marc Wanamaker, who, after a childhood spent wandering the MGM back lots, became one of the leading experts on the history of Hollywood. After a remarkable initial conversation in which he walked me, studio by studio, through the geography of early filmmaking in New York and Los Angeles, Marc generously made available the resources of Bison Archives, his superb picture collection of studio lots, standing sets, and historic Los Angeles. Another giant of early film scholarship, Kevin Brownlow, graciously loaned me his frame enlargements from *Traffic in Souls*.

It was my privilege, finally, to work in the Margaret Herrick Library, the archive of the Academy of Motion Picture Arts and Sciences, and a film resource like no other. In the course of the project I returned to the library again and again, reviewing thousands of images in its core and special collections with the help of staff members Janet Lorenz, Kristine Krueger, Alison Pinsler, and Richard Stermer; archivist Sam Gill; and its supremely knowledgeable curator, Robert Cushman. I never watch the Academy Awards ceremony without the warm knowledge that a substantial fraction of its revenue helps to sustain this worthiest of scholarly enterprises.

Given the abundance of studio-era stills, it was surprising (not to mention dismaying) to find that equivalent images from *recent* films were, ironically, far harder to come by. Perhaps because movies are no longer advertised through lobby cards, publicity kits for new releases typically contain only a handful of photographs—many of them the conventional head-shots and two-shots that were of little use to me. Talented photographers continue to document films exhaustively during production, but because of the costs involved, studio publicity departments are generally reluctant to release a broad selection of images. To find the kind of unusual shots I needed, I would have to work directly with filmmakers, photographers, and the studios themselves.

I was able to do so, in the end—thanks to the exceptional help I received from a wide variety of individuals. At Fox, I had the good fortune to meet a trio of women who shared the same encouraging spirit as well as the same first name. Melissa Duke in the publicity department pointed me toward Melissa Totten, the supremely capable director of the Fox Studio Archives, who in turn had her assistant, Melissa McCollum, pull dozens of folders of recent Fox releases. At Warner Bros., the soft-spoken Steve Rogers, Leith Adams (whom I had first come to know at USC, years before), Marlene Eastman, and Judy Singer, vice president of film clips and stills licensing, were immensely helpful, as was Ugene Park at MGM/UA. At Universal, executive director Cindy Chang and publishing coordinator Tom Meissnest went out of their way to assist my research, making special arrangements with archivist Marla Ryan to have me spend a day up at the studio's warehouse in the remotest recesses of the San Fernando Valley. There, among other discoveries, I found stills from several Spike Lee films, which Mr. Lee graciously consented to allow me to include in the book. The photographer Brian Hamill took it upon himself to arrange for me to view the archive of his stills from Woody Allen's films—a selection of which Mr. Allen generously allowed me publish. Many, many thanks to them all.

Even this great bounty of images turned out to be only one part of the rich array of visual materials associated with film production. I was deeply impressed by the superb quality of the New York sketches and renderings produced by Hollywood art directors—and even more so by the generosity of the industry professionals who readily made those drawings available to me. John Mansbridge, who began working at the RKO art department in the 1930s, and later saved the department's sketch archive after the studio closed in 1957, eagerly gave me permission to publish half a dozen images from what is now known as the Mansbridge Collection at UCLA. The noted visual-effects supervisor Richard Edlund agreed to lend me rare original materials from his work on *Ghostbusters*, while special-effects supervisor Micheal McAllister offered dozens of photos he took during the construction of the *Hudsucker Proxy* miniature. R/Greenberg Associates courteously provided their composite from *Oedipus Wrecks*. Several hard-to-locate images from *Batman* were provided by the photographer Stefan Lang and by the wonderfully helpful Don Shay, editor of *Cinefex*. The production designer Richard Sylbert graciously allowed permission to publish his rendering from *Rosemary's Baby*, while Wynn Thomas enthusiastically approved my using his sketch layout from *Do the Right Thing* (which, due to the vicissitudes of publication, does not appear in the final book—but for which I remain grateful nonetheless). Michelle Davidson generously gave me complete access to the Paramount stock library, where, among other treasures, I found Billy Wilder's original footage from the establishing shot of *The Lost Weekend* and the climax of *Sabrina*. At the Lillian Michelson Reference Library, one of the last of its kind in Hollywood, I found tall file-drawers crammed with clippings and reference shots of New York—a stunning archival resource all but unknown in the city itself. I want to thank Lillian and her husband, the noted art director Harold Michelson, not only for the images they lent me from the collection, but also for all the support and affection they have extended to me over the years.

As an architect, there was another set of documents I was especially anxious to examine: the art department's construction drawings, the blueprints from which studio sets were actually built. I was horrified to discover that in many cases these have been lost forever—decades of work chucked into the trash when studios shut down or moved. But at least two great collections survive. Warner Bros. donated its drawings to USC, where, thanks to Noelle Carter—and to Judy Noack at Warner Bros. itself—I was able to examine them in detail. Paramount has maintained their old art department files right on the lot, and thanks to Mike Daly, Roberto Ruiz, and Jim Arnold, I was able to descend to a deep basement to get a good look at dozens of folders. Few experiences were as thrilling as that of holding in my hands not prints but the *original drawings*—sheet after sheet of tracing paper, thick with easily smudged charcoal or graphite—used to build *Rear Window*'s courtyard, or *42nd Street*'s backdrops, and Holly Golightly's town-house apartment. At one level, it allowed me to enter the minds of men and women who created these environments, to study their choices, to glimpse them at work, as it were. But there was something else about these exquisite drawings, each dated a few weeks before the start of shooting, and signed-off by the art department head—a haunting feeling that one had entered the time and space in which those classic films *were still yet to be made*, when no one could know that the places they had just drawn up in detail would turn out to live forever in the imagination. I will always be grateful to those who helped me examine firsthand these marvelous documents.

Not surprisingly, it was immensely useful (not to mention thrilling) to spend time exploring the studio lots, something possible only through the assistance of several colleagues. With the help of Sheila Slate, I got a look at *Batman*'s impressive Gotham City street at Pinewood Studios. At Paramount, Earl Lutz, Ellen Hamilton, and the studio's planning team—including Christine Essel, Ann Gray, and my old friend Natalie Shivers—encouraged me to follow the progress of their ambitious New York Street expansion from design to reality. (Later, Jonathan Dolgen, chairman of Paramount Pictures, graciously gave me permission to have my photograph taken on the same landmark street set.) At the former MGM studios, now Sony/Columbia, Daren Janes gave me access to a trove of art department stills and plans of Metro's standing sets, located in a room adjoining the old office of Cedric Gibbons himself (whom I half expected to see striding in at any moment, double-breasted suit and all). Elsewhere on the historic lot, I had the pleasure of riding the charmingly tiny elevator (once the private lift to Louis B. Mayer's office) to what was once the MGM scenic department and is now J. C. Backings—where, to my astonishment, Jim Spadoni and Lynne Coakley obligingly unrolled their huge backings of Penn Station (from *The Clock*) and the United Nations (from *North by Northwest*), and later allowed me to reproduce similar images in my book. My deepest appreciation to them and to everyone who, over the years, helped me breach the fabled studio gates.

One of my first and most unexpected discoveries was the Paper Print Collection at the Library of Congress, where dozens of early actuality films shot in New York from 1896 to 1906 are lovingly preserved. The collection's very existence is something of an epic story itself, starting in the earliest days of the movies, when film companies—unsure of the copyright status of celluloid images—sent motion pictures to the Library in the form of long strips of opaque photographic *paper* onto which frames were printed. After celluloid images were deemed copyrightable in 1912, companies began the practice of sending actual nitrate negatives (which, considered a fire hazard, were often destroyed soon after being registered). For decades, meanwhile, hundreds of the old deteriorating paper strips remained in storage, impossible for anyone to view—until, in the late 1940s, a heroic effort by Kemp Niver painstakingly *re-photographed* them, frame by frame, onto modern safety stock. Today these films can be viewed not only at the Library's Motion Pictures Division (where, thanks to librarian Madeline Matz, I was first able to see them), but also on the World Wide Web, where fifty-four New York actualities have been gathered under the title *Scenes in the Life of a City* (//memory.loc.gov/ammem/papr/nychome.html).

During the course of the project, I had the rare pleasure of interviewing several major filmmakers associated with New York. The directors Sidney Lumet, Susan Seidelman, and Paul Mazursky all generously took time from their busy schedules to meet with me, and I was able to speak by phone with two key figures in the history of New York independent film, Morris Engel and Helen Levitt. The cinematographer John Bailey graciously invited me onto the location shoot of *As Good As It Gets*, then patiently answered my endless questions between takes. I also had the stimulating experience of speaking at length with a number of legendary studio art directors, including Robert Boyle, designer of *North by Northwest* and *Saboteur*; Henry Bumstead—"Bummy"—who sketched for me the ingenious section he developed with Mac Johnson for the *Rear Window* set; Gene Allen (formerly president of the Society of Motion Picture and Television Art Directors), who explained in detail how the studio art direction system worked; Al Brenner, who walked me through his plan for the expansion of Paramount's New York Street; and the late Harry Horner, with whom I spent a delightful afternoon discussing his Oscar-winning design for *The Heiress*. I also enjoyed conversations with younger professionals such as William McAllister, Nina Ramsey, John Muto, and the inimitable Syd Mead, "visual futurist" for *Blade Runner*. I am profoundly grateful to all of them.

Other valuable interviews included Peter K. Schnitzler and Scott Fleischer of Panavision New York, the Hon. Patricia Reed Scott, New York City Commissioner of Film, Theatre & Broadcasting; and her predecessor at the Mayor's Office, Richard Brick. At several junctures, I turned for help to my friend and colleague Phillip Lopate, who directed me to film experts David Sterrit and Kent Jones. Stanford Anderson, Keller Easterling, Karrie Jacobs, Christopher Gray, and Andrew Dolkcart provided help with urban and architectural questions. I thank them all.

My research and publication of this book would not have been possible without the generous financial assistance of several foundations and public agencies, and it is an honor to publicly acknowledge the support of Furthermore, the publication program of the J. M. Kaplan Fund, and its director, Ann Birckmayer, and president, Joan K. Davidson; the Graham Foundation for Advanced Studies in the Fine Arts, and its director emeritus, Carter Manny; the Design Arts Program of the National Endowment for the Arts, and its former director, Adele Chatfield-Taylor; and the Architecture, Planning and Design Program of the New York State Council on the Arts, and its director, Anne Van Ingen. In addition, Mary Holloway, executive director of the Association for a Better New York; Steve Zeitlin, executive director of City Lore; Rochelle Slovin, director of the American Museum of the Moving Image; and Rosalie Genevro and Anne Rieselbach, executive director and program director, respectively, of the Architectural League of New York were all instrumental in obtaining support, and I wish to express my gratitude to them all.

Over the years, a series of gifted young men and women in and out of my office helped to research this book and its illustrations, and it is a great pleasure to at last acknowledge in print the diligent efforts of José Gatti, Catherine Taylor, Dottie Northup, Gina Pollara, Caroline Abitbol, Darcy Cosper, Norman Cohen, Laurie Ouliette, Rebecca Moyle, Kelly A. Feeney, Sari Siegel, and Katie Pearl. In the end, it was the marvelous Heather MacDonald who carried out the truly herculean task of securing camera-ready art and permissions for the book's three hundred–odd images.

Throughout the writing process, a number of friends and family members provided crucial help and moral support, including Deborah Bergman (who first encouraged me to begin the project); Ingrid Bernstein; Marisa Bowe; Ric Burns; Richard Kaplan; Maria Reidelbach; P. B. Turgeon (whose venerable friendship was supplemented by a formidable computer expertise that on more than one occasion salvaged precious files I had managed to "corrupt"); my sister, Avis Sanders; my step-brother, John Wellington; and my father, Albert Sanders, whose intense, lifelong fascination with cities—coupled with his strange habit of taking his young children to 1930s movies at revival houses—was, in some sense, a root cause of this book. My mother, Edith Sanders, did not live to see the book beyond its earliest phases, but her unique spirit and energy, I believe, permeate its pages throughout.

The long gestation of this work has inevitably challenged everyone involved in its creation, and I wish to reserve a special thanks for those publishing colleagues who have helped the book see the light of day. In the course of the project I have worked with three extraordinary literary agents—Geri Thoma of the Elaine Markson Agency, Joy Harris of the Joy Harris Literary Agency, and Lydia Wills of the Artists Agency—and I wish to thank them all for their superb efforts on my behalf. Likewise, I have worked with three remarkable editors: the late Lee Goerner, who first acquired the book and helped me to understand its meaning; Elisabeth Sifton, who with characteristic energy and enthusiasm picked up the baton and carried it forward; and the amazing George Andreou, who, in the end, carried out the heavy lifting of editing the book with the lightest, most exquisitely calibrated touch imaginable.

Given this lengthy list of distinguished names, it may seem all the more surprising that I have had only one publisher throughout. There are, in the end, no words to properly thank Alfred A. Knopf and its president, Sonny Mehta, for their unwavering belief in this book and their astonishing patience during the years necessary to bring it forth—except to say that, if possible, I am even prouder today to be a Knopf author than I was the day I first learned of my proposal's acceptance. As the book has moved into production, I have had the wonderful opportunity to work again with my colleagues there, including the always inspiring managing editor, Katherine Hourigan, and a wonderful production team under Andy Hughes and Roméo Enriquez, as well as Knopf's superb publicity department, including Paul Bogaards, William Loverd, and Sheila O'Shea. I cannot express my gratitude sufficiently to Ralph L. Fowler of the Knopf art department, whose extraordinarily elegant design for the book is everything I dared hoped for and more, and to Chip Kidd, who with infinite enthusiasm and professionalism—not to mention incomparable talent—has created its hauntingly beautiful jacket.

When all is said and done, three individuals deserve special acknowledgment for their efforts on behalf of this book and its author. From start to finish, my friend Eliot R. Brown has not only seemed to have an answer for every technical question I could conjure up, but also—as he has always done—offered his help in every way he could. Margot Wellington, my stepmother, has been a colleague as well as a source of inspiration who, for almost as long as I can remember, has helped me think more sharply about my home town, and muse more richly about hers. And Geri Thoma made this book possible in ways I shall never forget—and for which I will always remain profoundly grateful.

My deepest, deepest thanks to them, and to all those who have helped me realize what has been, in the end, a dream as much as a book.

NOTES

viii *"I am not sure that it is possible":* Joan Didion, "Goodbye to All That," *Slouching Toward Bethlehem* (New York: Farrar, Straus & Giroux, 1968), 229.

"It is not on any map . . .": Herman Melville, *Moby-Dick* (Harmondsworth: Penguin, 1977), 150.

PART I: MYTHIC CITIES

16 *a vision to sustain the ancient Hebrews during their decades of exile:* Much of that exile, ironically, took place in Babylon—for the Jews not a sacred city, of course, but the very emblem of earthly corruption.

17 *the better, grander Siena that someday might be achieved through virtuous civic effort:* A nearby companion painting, also by Ambrogio, shows the debased city that Siena might become without conscientious improvement.

19 *"Because it has more social mobility":* Rust Hills, ed., *New York, New York: The City as Seen by Masters of Art and Literature* (New York: Shorecrest, 1965), 17.

CHAPTER 1: SIDEWALK MOMENTS

24 *he had for the first time captured New York:* This represented the first use of a new "taking" camera that had been designed by Edison specifically for shooting outdoor scenes. Though earlier cameramen may have shot scenes of New York for Kinetoscope strips (see below), Heise's May 11 film, taken just three weeks after the night of the Koster and Bial's premiere, was almost certainly the first footage of the city intended to be projected on a screen—in other words, the first *movie* of New York.

25 *The movies were arriving in a wondrous convergence:* Koster and Bial's premiere is generally regarded as the first showing of projected films in the United States (the Lumière Brothers had debuted their Cinématographe in Paris in December 1895; some scholars have claimed projected films were shown in New York by the Lathams as early as May 1895). All early projection systems (including that of the Lumières) had a common heritage in Edison's original Kinetoscope strips—looped motion pictures, viewed through the eyepiece of a wooden cabinet—which had been introduced on August 14, 1894, in an entertainment parlor at 1155 Broadway (corner of 27th Street) in Manhattan.

34 *The promotional material for* Romance of a Jewess*:* *Biograph Bulletin,* No. 181, October 28, 1908.

268. (previous page) ***Taxi Driver*** **(1976).** Robert De Niro speaks with the director Martin Scorsese between shots.

36 *"the fittings of a palace"*: "Sunless Temples of New York's Movies," *New York Times*, November 7, 1920, 6.

"We can build big sets in our big lots": Ibid.

37 *or so the screenwriter Frank Leon Smith recalled:* Kevin Brownlow, *Beyond the Mask of Innocence* (New York: Alfred A. Knopf, 1992), 165.

38 *Walsh later recalled to the film historian Kevin Brownlow:* Ibid.

Brownlow also recounts a charming story: Motion Picture Story Magazine, December 1914: 89.

CHAPTER 2: DREAMING THE CITY

45 *"an SOS was beamed to the East"*: Budd Schulberg, "The Writer in Hollywood," *Harper's*, October 1959, 133.

the studio bosses "knew what they wanted": Josef von Sternberg, quoted in Alice Goldfarb Marquis, *Hope and Ashes: The Birth of Modern Times* (New York: The Free Press, 1986), 54.

46 *"real writers"*: Budd Schulberg, "The Writer in Hollywood," 133.

"It seemed like we were together constantly": Marc Connelly, quoted in Richard Fine, *Hollywood and the Profession of Authorship* (Ann Arbor, MI: UMI Research Press, 1985), 37.

48 *"MILLIONS ARE TO BE GRABBED AROUND HERE"*: Ibid., 64.

50 *"It is a kind of boom town"*: J. B. Priestley, *Midnight on the Desert* (New York: Harper Brothers, 1937).

"Not a city," one contemporary called it: Anne O'Hare McCormick, "The Great Empire of Celluloid," *New York Times*, November 29, 1931, Section V: 1.

51 *This was no "city," he reported:* Stephen Vincent Benét, *Selected Letters of Stephen Vincent Benét*, Charles A. Fenton, ed. (New Haven, CT: Yale University Press, 1960), 194.

"I don't know why I thought of Hollywood as small": McCormick, "The Great Empire of Celluloid," 1.

"You came as a pencil for hire": Ben Hecht, "Let's Make the Hero a MacArthur," in *The Grove Book of Hollywood*, Christopher Silvester, ed. (New York: Grove Press, 1998), 193.

52 *"short men chewing on dead cigars"*: Fred Lawrence Guiles, *Hanging on in Paradise* (New York: McGraw-Hill, 1975), 35.

one writer was reminded: Quoted in Sheilah Graham, *The Garden of Allah* (New York: Crown, 1970), 74.

"Neither Southern California in general": Fine, *Hollywood and the Profession of Authorship*, 129.

"goddamn lotus land": Herman Mankiewicz, quoted in Richard Meryman, *Mank: The Wit, World and Life of Herman Mankiewicz* (New York: Morrow, 1978), 131.

"Oh, to be back in Hollywood": Ibid., 289.

"the twenties moved West in the thirties": Pauline Kael, "Raising Kane," *The Citizen Kane Book* (Boston: Little, Brown, 1971), 17.

53 *"as if everyone had gone indoors"*: Joseph Hansen, "A Country of the Mind," *L.A. Style*, Vol. 2, No. 1, June 1986: 70.

"I'd leave the studio at dusk": Vincente Minnelli, *I Remember It Well* (Garden City: Doubleday, 1974), 118.

"I used to look around at the dull stucco bungalows": Budd Schulberg, "The Writer in Hollywood," *Harper's*, 134.

53–54 *"You could drop all of Hollywood's people"*: Leo Rosten, *Hollywood: The Movie Colony and the Movie Makers* (New York: Harcourt, Brace & Co., 1941), 191.

54 *"Even those of us who were children at the time"*: Kael, "Raising Kane," *The Citizen Kane Book*, 13.

55 *"Clark Gable may have posed"*: Diana Altman, *Hollywood East: Louis B. Mayer and the Origins of the Studio System* (New York: Birch Lane/Carol, 1992), xii.

56 *"George was a king in New York"*: Aljean Harmetz, *The Making of the Wizard of Oz* (New York: Alfred A. Knopf, 1977), 65.

59 *"Sitting out in Los Angeles"*: Pauline Kael, "The Man from Dream City," *When the Lights Go Down* (New York: Holt Rinehart Winston, 1975), 5.

CHAPTER 3: BUILDING THE DREAM

62 *"I had the same set in I don't know how many pictures!"*: Rosalind Russell, quoted in Howard Mandelbaum and Eric Myers, *Forties Screen Style* (New York: St. Martin's Press, 1989), 42.

64 *"the genius of the system"*: André Bazin, 1957, quoted in Thomas Schatz, *The Genius of the System* (New York: Pantheon, 1988), 1.

the director was often not selected until relatively late: A list of forthcoming productions in the March 29, 1937, issue of *Variety* (kindly provided by Sidney Lumet) shows directors still unassigned for three of the seventeen films ready to roll that same week. Of the thirty-four pictures scheduled to begin within the month, twelve remain unassigned—including prestigious projects such as *Goldwyn Follies* and *Dead End.*

65 *At the table was the man:* There were no women art directors or illustrators in Hollywood in the 1930s. In general, the only creative positions in the studio open to women at the time—other than acting—were found in the wardrobe and editing departments.

68 *A craftsman like Henry Greutert:* Harmetz, *The Making of the Wizard of Oz*, 233.

"As a young writer": Joe Mankiewicz, quoted in Stephen Farber and Marc Green, *Hollywood Dynasties* (New York: Delilah, 1984), 236.

"Whenever someone thinks highly of his own ability": Gene Fowler and Bess Merdyth, *The Mighty Barnum: A Screenplay* (New York: Covici-Frede, 1934), xiii.

73 *"a two-story building ten stories high"*: Dore Schary, *Case History of a Movie* (New York: Random House), 147.

78 *"When the process was first used"*: Farciot Edouart, "The Evolution of Transparency Process Photography," *American Cinematographer*, October 1943, in *The ASC Treasury of Visual Effects*, Linwood G. Dunn and George E. Turner, eds. (Hollywood, CA: American Society of Cinematographers, 1983), 107.

80 *"We didn't want to eliminate reality"*: Eugène Lourié, *My Work in Films*, quoted in Howard Mandelbaum and Eric Myers, *Screen Style* (New York: St. Martin's Press, 1989), 42.

84 *"The room is long"*: Stephen Graham, quoted in Howard Mandelbaum and Eric Myers, *Screen Deco* (New York: St. Martin's Press, 1985), 102.

PART II: ON THE TOWN

CHAPTER 4: EMERALD CITIES

94 *"the most moving buildings of modern times"*: Vincent Scully, "American Architecture: The Real and the Ideal," *American Architecture: Innovation and Tradition*, David G. De Long, Helen Searing, Robert A.M. Stern, eds. (New York: Rizzoli, 1986), 20.

95 *"a city of genial giants"*: Vincent Scully, *American Architecture and Urbanism* (New York: Praeger, 1969), 146.

97 *"It isn't big enough!"*: Orville Goldner and George E. Turner, *The Making of King Kong* (South Brunswick, NJ: A. S. Barnes and Company), 159.

98 *"Without any conscious effort of thought"*: Merian C. Cooper, quoted in Ronald Haver, *David O. Selznick's Hollywood* (New York: Alfred A. Knopf, 1980), 77.

99 *"There is, in the building itself"*: Hugh Ferriss, quoted in Jean Ferriss Leich, *Architectural Visions: The Drawings of Hugh Ferriss* (New York: Watson Guptill, 1980), 85.

102 *"not salubrious but sublime"*: Scully, *American Architecture and Urbanism*, 144.

104 *"It is neither 1939 nor 1989"*: Robert S. Sennett, *Setting the Scene* (New York: Abrams, 1994), 65. A thousand feet long and five stories high, the Gotham City exterior street set served as base for the thousand-foot towers above. It required five months and, at its peak, 250 men to build—the largest exterior set built in Europe since *Cleopatra*.

105 *"When we were twenty, we heard about the skyscrapers"*: Jean-Paul Sartre, 1946, quoted in Caroline Mierop, *Skyscrapers: Higher and Higher* (Paris: Norma, 1995), 37.

106 *"a street lit as if in full daylight"*: Fritz Lang, quoted in Frederick Ott, *The Films of Fritz Lang* (Secaucus, NJ: Citadel Press, 1979), 27.

"I looked into the street": Fritz Lang, quoted in Peter Bogdanovich, *Fritz Lang in America* (London: Studio Vista, 1967), 15. Recent scholarship has suggested that initial work on *Metropolis* had already begun by the time of Lang's trip to New York, and that Lang later exaggerated the impact of his visit on the film.

108 *"Without roofs, crowned by terraces"*: Paul Morand, 1929, quoted in Mierop, *Skyscrapers: Higher and Higher*, 25.

"period of almost savage incompetence": Arlene Croce, *The Fred Astaire and Ginger Rogers Book* (New York: Dutton, 1972), 14.

114 *"Americans have practically added a new dimension"*: William Archer, quoted in Bayrd Still, *Mirror for Gotham* (New York: Fordham University Press, 1994), 206.

CHAPTER 5: SOMETHING BIG

124 *"As land prices rose"*: Carol Willis, *Form Follows Finance: Skyscrapers and Skylines in New York and Chicago* (New York: Princeton Architectural Press, 1995), 88.

125 *"Creating a distinctive image"*: Ibid., 149.

CHAPTER 6: STREET SCENE

142 *"Think of a city and what comes to mind?"*: Jane Jacobs, *The Death and Life of Great American Cities* (New York: Random House, 1961), 29.

"I scarcely noticed where we were walking": Emily Kimbrough, *We Followed Our Hearts to Hollywood* (New York: Dodd, Mead, 1943), 47.

152 *"Very often," Horner recognized, "houses that have a memory"*: Harry Horner, "Designing the Heiress," *Hollywood Quarterly*, Vol. 5, No. 1 (Fall 1950): 2.

153 *is "not a house of one period, but of many"*: Ibid., 4.

174 *"A population of children is condemned to play on the city streets"*: Jacobs, *The Death and Life of Great American Cities*, 74.

175 *"There is no direct, simple relationship"*: Ibid., 113.

"Sidewalks, their bordering uses, and their users": Ibid., 30.

But "large numbers of people entertain themselves": Ibid., 35.

CHAPTER 7: DOMESTIC ELABORATIONS

197 *"A city is stones and a city is people"*: J. Bronowski, *The Ascent of Man* (Boston: Little, Brown, 1973), 96.

202 *"I know exactly where Ted Kramer lives"*: Vincent LoBrutto, *By Design: Interviews with Film Production Designers* (Westport, CT: Praeger, 1992), 81.

203 *"You felt that this guy"*: Paul Sylbert, quoted in Vincent LoBrutto, *By Design: Interviews with Film Production Designers* (Westport, CT: Praeger, 1992), 80.

CHAPTER 8: WORLDS OF DIFFERENCE

227 *"[B]oth reject the idea of* difference": Thomas Bender, "New York as a Center of 'Difference,'" *Dissent*, Fall 1987: 429.

228 *"Ordinarily, we seem to be completely separate"*: Tony Hiss, *The Experience of Place* (New York: Alfred A. Knopf, 1990), 21.

"Realities keep in the rear": Nathaniel Hawthorne, *The Blithedale Romance*, 1852; reprint (New York: Meridian Classic edition, 1981), 119.

233 *"Jefferies . . . is somehow excused for his actions"*: Stefan Sharff, *The Art of Looking in Hitchcock's* Rear Window (New York: Limelight Editions, 1997), 6. The film scholar Patricia Ferrara makes an even stronger argument against *Rear Window*'s "voyeurism," reminding us that Jefferies's "passivity is forced upon him by his broken leg, and he is impatient to go out on a new assignment and bored with inactivity. . . . His handicap is physical, and temporary, and does not indicate a corresponding mental vice." ("Through Hitchcock's *Rear Window* Again," *New Orleans Review*, Fall 1985, 21.)

234 *"a kaleidoscopic prophecy of his future"*: Thomas M. Leitch, "Self and World at Paramount," in *Hitchcock's Rereleased Films*, Walter Raubicheck and Walter Srebnick, eds. (Detroit: Wayne State University Press, 1991), 39.

237 "Rear Window," *noted* American Cinematographer: Arthur E. Gavin, "237 Window," *American Cinematographer*, Vol. 35, No. 2 (February 1954): 97.

"Lighting this composite set": Robert Burks, quoted in Gavin, "237 Window," 97.

"looked like the console of the biggest organ ever made!": Ibid.

240 *"Privacy is precious in cities"*: Jacobs, *The Death and Life of Great American Cities*, 58.

CHAPTER 9: LOFTY PERCHES

247 *"The sky is decked out"*: Le Corbusier, *When the Cathedrals Were White* (New York: Reynal and Hitchcock, 1947), 90.

249 *"An object while one views it"*: Roland Barthes, "The Tour Eiffel," in *Structures Implicit and Explicit*, Vol. 2, James Bryan and Rolf Sauer, eds. (Philadelphia: Graduate School of Fine Arts, University of Pennsylvania, 1973), 164.

259 *"Its compressed energy,"* Arlene Croce, *The Fred Astaire and Ginger Rogers Book* (New York: Dutton, 1972), 104.

262 *"a spine-chilling series of turns"*: Ibid., 113.

CHAPTER 10: EDGE OF THE CITY

267 *"a self-contained city-state"*: Budd Schulberg, *On The Waterfront: The Final Shooting Script* (Hollywood, CA: Samuel French, 1980), 142.

272 *"New York, New York" is "a wonderful town!"*: Comden and Green's original Broadway lyric—"New York, New York is a *helluva* town"—was forbidden by the Hays censorship office.

273 *Francis Ford Coppola's moving re-creation of the epic ritual of entrance:* Though *The Godfather Part II* is noted for the accuracy of its historical re-creations, this sequence contains several errors. The shot of the *Moshulu* arriving past the Statue of Liberty shows it clearly pointed *away* from the city, heading out to sea. And contrary to legend, no Ellis Island official ever changed an immigrant's name; the officers wrote no names down, but simply confirmed the names written in the ship's manifest (which may have been changed at the port of departure by the steamship company itself).

286 *Here the two of them stand:* The scene is based on a real incident. Returning from Hollywood at a low point in his career, a despondent Adolph Green was met at Grand Central by Betty Comden, carrying a sign that read, "Adolph Green Fan Club."

289 *"A Hotel is a plot, a cybernetic universe"*: Rem Koolhaas, *Delirious New York* (New York: Oxford University Press, 1978), 124.

293 *"With the Waldorf . . . the Hotel itself becomes"*: Ibid.

CHAPTER 11: DANCING LIGHTS

296 *"More than New York's theater district"*: Neal Gabler, *Winchell: Gossip, Power and the Culture of Celebrity* (New York: Alfred A. Knopf, 1994), 88.

302 *"The means of moving from one order of reality or style"*: Gerald Mast, *Can't Help Singin': The American Musical on Stage and Screen* (New York: The Overlook Press, 1987), 88.

"The conceptual problem evaporates": Ibid.

"The media and audiences were different": Richard Barrios, *A Song in the Dark: The Birth of the Musical Film* (New York: Oxford University Press, 1995), 57.

"out-Broadway Broadway": Miles Kreuger, *The Movie Musical: From Vitaphone to 42nd Street* (New York: Dover, 1975), 64.

303 *"You'll see things you never saw before in 'Broadway' "*: Ibid., 51.

studio executives ordered the construction of a new stage: Nestled into the foot of the Hollywood Hills, Universal's Stage 12 (now called Stage 20) was known for years after as "the *Broadway* stage."

"was like Grand Central Station": Hal Mohr, quoted in Leonard Maltin, *Behind the Camera* (New York: Signet, 1971), 117.

307 *"No one should come to New York"*: E. B. White, *Here Is New York* (New York: Harper and Brothers, 1949), 10.

309 *One story has Zanuck coming onto the stage*: Bob Pike and Dave Martin, *The Genius of Busby Berkeley* (California: CFS Books, 1973), 33. Berkeley was no stranger to revolving stages, which had been a feature of Ziegfeld's Broadway shows since 1906, but had been unable to use them in films until *42nd Street*.

314 *"I just can't get over it"*: Vincente Minnelli, Betty Comden, and Adolph Green, *The Band Wagon* (London: Lorrimer, 1986), 26.

323 *whose interiors were shot at the old Haaren High*: Discomfited by the script, the city's Board of Education refused permission for the film to be shot in the real High School of Performing Arts; a number of the school's actual teachers, however, did appear in the movie, more or less playing themselves.

PART III: EIGHT MILLION STORIES

327 *"At last, you've hit on the big question"*: Malvin Wald and Albert Maltz, *The Naked City* (Carbondale, IL: Southern Illinois University Press, 1979), 137.

328 *"How can you shoot a film on the streets of New York"*: Ibid., 43.

"right out in the open": Thomas M. Pryor, "Blazing a Trail: Feature Film on FBI Will Be a Blend of Factual and Entertainment Techniques," *New York Times*, April 1, 1945, Sect. 2: 3.

330 *"In transferring* The Lost Weekend *to the screen"*: S. J. Perelman, *Keep It Crisp* (New York: Random House, 1943), 5.

333 *"Hollywood was addicted to the candied . . . type of sweet unreal photography"*: John Alton, *Painting With Light* (New York: Macmillan, 1949), 134–5.

334 *"Wald's proposal . . . had only to do with New York"*: Carl Richardson, *Homicide: The Story of* The Naked City (unpublished manuscript), 9.

335 *"Dancers would jump up on the West Side"*: Jerome Robbins, quoted in *Film Review*, June 1994, 28.

338 *Both* On the Waterfront *and* 12 Angry Men *had been filmed at the Fox studio:* Later, it would house *Fail-Safe, The Pawnbroker,* and, when renamed Cameramart, everything from *The Producers* to *The French Connection.*

339 *"Things were much freer in New York":* Sidney Lumet, interview with author, April 26, 1996.

"There were none": Ibid.

"It restored power": Ibid.

"catching life at shoe level": Filmed interview with Phillip Lopate, in *Framed,* a documentary by Simon Fields and Keith Griffiths, 1987.

339–340 *"I had the strange idea":* Morris Engel, interview with author, December 24, 1996.

341 *Cassavetes's film "really made us believe that if he could do it":* Les Keyser, *Martin Scorsese* (New York: Twayne, 1995), 14.

342 *"You have to shoot in the streets, even in apartments":* François Truffaut, "Seule la crise sauvera le cinéma français," *Arts* (8–14 January 1958): 1.

"A remorseless stiffening of reflexes had set in": Geoffrey O'Brien, *The Phantom Empire* (New York: W. W. Norton, 1993), 151.

The trick to selecting locations: On more than one occasion, locations helped to shape the stories themselves. When Woody Allen accompanied the art director Mel Bourne to Coney Island during the making of *Annie Hall,* the discovery of an old wooden house sitting directly beneath the roller coaster inspired Allen to add childhood scenes for the character of Alvy Singer.

343 *"Out there," said one New York movie executive:* Max E. Youngstein, in *New York: True North,* Gilbert Millstein, ed. (Garden City, NY: Doubleday, 1964), 130.

344 *"Right away . . . the graft stopped":* Sidney Lumet, quoted in Peter Biskind, "The Crucible," *Premiere Special Issue: New York and the Movies* (1994): 105.

CHAPTER 12: ON LOCATION

357 *"FADE IN: NEW YORK CITY, 187TH STREET":* Paddy Chayefsky, *The Collected Works of Paddy Chayefsky: The Screenplays,* Vol. I (New York: Applause Books, 1994), 3.

"the biggest collection of villages in the world": Alistair Cooke, quoted in *Quotable New York: A Literary Companion,* William Cole, ed. (New York: Penguin Books, 1992), 31.

CHAPTER 13: NIGHTTOWN

366 *"Sunk in Stygian darkness":* Foster Hirsch, *Detours and Lost Highways: A Map of Neo-Noir* (New York: Limelight Editions, 1999), 235.

"When Mayor Lindsay began his efforts to attract the movie production business": Pauline Kael, *For Keeps: 30 Years at the Movies* (New York: Dutton, 1994), 389.

367 *"Like the human organism itself":* Parker Tyler, "Documentary Technique in Film Fiction," *American Quarterly,* Summer 1949, reprinted in Lewis Jacobs, ed., *Documentary Traditions* (New York: W. W. Norton, 1979), 251.

368 *we glimpse tennis players on the public courts far below:* When *The Naked City*'s screenwriter, Malvin Wald, remarked to the director Jules Dassin how lucky it was that the courts happened to be in use during the filming, the director commented, "Lucky? I planted those tennis players there—they're extras!" (Quoted in Malvin Wald and Albert Maltz, *The Naked City,* 145.)

374 *"the perfect vigilante fantasy":* Carlos Clarens, *Crime Movies* (New York: W. W. Norton, 1979), 321.

"keeping bachelor hours": Ibid., 322.

"The camera doesn't turn a corner": Ibid., 321.

375 *"In the late 1960s, New York came to symbolize 'urban violence'"*: Marshall Berman, *Dissent*, Fall 1987: 424.

378 *"suggesting that the people of the Bronx are animals to be controlled"*: quoted in Richard Goldstein, "Fort Apache: The Bronx," *The Village Voice*, February 18–24, 1981: 46.

381 *"Crime, as well as fear of crime, is closely associated with disorder"*: George Kelling, "Measuring What Matters," *The City Journal*, Spring 1992: 21.

384 *"cutting and the logistics of stunt work"*: Clarens, *Crime Movies*, 312.

that each IRT car is seventy-two feet long: This particular piece of information is, in fact, incorrect. IRT cars are actually fifty-one feet long.

390 *"The importance of the gangster film . . . cannot be measured"*: Robert Warshow, "The Gangster as Tragic Hero," *Partisan Review*, February 1948: 242.

391 *"any movie with* City, Night *or* Street *in its title"*: Eddie Muller, *Dark City: The Lost World of Film Noir* (London: Titan Books, 1998), 10.

"airless and claustrophobic": Foster Hirsch, *The Dark Side of the Screen: Film Noir* (San Diego: A. S. Barnes, 1981), 4.

"a dark urban world of neurotic entrapment": Ibid., 10.

"stories of obsession and confinement": Ibid., 15.

392 noir's *"nightmarish world"*: Paul Schrader, "Notes on Film Noir," *Film Comment*, 8:1, Spring 1972: 13.

396 *"[Travis] prefers to drive at night and he chooses to cruise the most foul of New York's streets"*: Joy Gould Boyum, "On Film" [Review of *Taxi Driver*], *Wall Street Journal*, February 9, 1976: 11.

CHAPTER 14: CHANGING CITY

400 *"Cities reveal as much about time as about place"*: Nathan Silver, *Lost New York* (Boston: Houghton Mifflin, 1967), 1.

411 *"Cities need old buildings"*: Jacobs, *The Death and Life of Great American Cities*, 187.

CHAPTER 15: A HEIGHTENED REALITY

422 *"People like to do films in New York"*: Frank Pellegrino, filmed interview, April 1997.

423–424 *"The great thing about shooting in New York"*: Andrew Bergman, "'Action!' Central," *Premiere Special Issue: New York and the Movies* (1994): 36.

425 *"See what's there and make a film about what's there"*: Interview with Susan Seidelman, *American Cinematographer*, Vol. 64, No. 5, May 1983: 68.

427 *"Having a film crew in your neighborhood"*: S. W. Stout, "Street Gangs from Hollywood," *New York Times*, September 30, 1991: 34.

428 *"real money, true billions"*: Richard Brick, interview with author, November 11, 1993.

"The fathers' attitude was, How much can we beat you out of": Peter Schnitzler, interview with author, January 15, 1997.

438 *"New York City is always New York City; it can't be used for anything else"*: Kael, *For Keeps: 30 Years at the Movies* (New York: Penguin, 1994), 389.

439 *"a heightened realism"*: Susan Seidelman, interview with author, November 11, 1993.

440–441 *"There's a wonderful intensity about night shooting"*: Sidney Lumet, *Making Movies* (New York: Alfred A. Knopf, 1995), 135.

BIBLIOGRAPHY

269. (previous page) Filming *Annie Hall* (1977). Woody Allen and crew on location at Coney Island, with the Parachute Jump in the distance.

GENERAL FILM HISTORY

Balio, Tino. *The American Film Industry*, rev. ed. Madison: University of Wisconsin Press, 1985.

Baxter, John. *Hollywood in the Thirties.* New York: Warner, 1970.

Berg, A. Scott. *Goldwyn: A Biography.* New York: Alfred A. Knopf, 1989.

Biskind, Peter. *Easy Riders, Raging Bulls: How the Sex-Drugs-and-Rock'n'Roll Generation Saved Hollywood.* New York: Simon & Schuster, 1998.

Charyn, Jerome. *Movieland: Hollywood and the Great American Dream Culture.* New York: New York University Press, 1989.

Day, Beth. *This Was Hollywood.* London: Sidgwick and Jackson, 1960.

Gabler, Neal. *An Empire of Their Own: How the Jews Invented Hollywood.* New York: Crown, 1988.

Haver, Ronald. *David O. Selznick's Hollywood.* New York: Bonanza, 1980.

Higham, Charles, and Joel Greenburg. *Hollywood in the Forties.* New York: A.S. Barnes, 1968.

Kael, Pauline. *For Keeps.* New York: Penguin, 1994.

——. *When the Lights Go Down.* New York: Holt, Rinehart & Winston, 1980.

Kazan, Elia. *A Life.* New York: Anchor Books/Doubleday, 1989.

Mordden, Ethan. *The Hollywood Studios: House Style in the Golden Age of the Movies.* New York: Alfred A. Knopf, 1988.

O'Brien, Geoffrey. *The Phantom Empire: Movies in the Mind of the 20th Century.* New York: W. W. Norton, 1993.

Ott, Frederick W. *The Films of Fritz Lang.* Secaucus, NJ: Citadel Press, 1979.

Rosten, Leo. *Hollywood: The Movie Colony and the Movie Makers.* New York: Harcourt, Brace, 1941.

Schary, Dore. *Case History of a Movie.* New York: Random House, 1950.

Schatz, Thomas. *The Genius of the System: Hollywood Filmmaking in the Studio Era.* New York: Pantheon, 1988.

Sklar, Robert. *City Boys.* Princeton, NJ: Princeton University Press, 1992.

Thomson, David. *America in the Dark: The Impact of Hollywood Films on American Culture.* New York: Morrow, 1977.

Truffaut, François. *Hitchcock/Truffaut*, rev. ed. New York: Simon & Schuster, 1983.

Walker, Alexander. *The Shattered Silents: How the Talkies Came to Stay.* New York: Morrow, 1979.

Webb, Michael, ed. *Hollywood: Legend and Reality.* Boston: Little, Brown, 1986.

INDIVIDUAL FILMS AND GENRES

Altman, Rick. *The American Film Musical.* Bloomington: Indiana University Press, 1987.

Atkinson, David. "Hitchcock's Techniques Tell Rear Window Story." *American Cinematographer,* Vol. 71, No. 1, January 1980: 34.

Auster, Paul. Smoke *and* Blue in the Face. New York: Hyperion, 1995.

Balio, Tino, ed. *42nd Street.* Madison: University of Wisconsin Press, 1980.

Barrios, Richard. *A Song in the Dark: The Birth of the Musical Film.* New York: Oxford University Press, 1995.

Belton, John. "The Backstage Musical," *Movie* 24 (Spring 1977): 22.

Bergman, Andrew. *We're in the Money: Depression America and Its Films.* New York: New York University Press, 1971.

Clarens, Carlos. *Crime Movies: An Illustrated History.* New York: W. W. Norton, 1980.

Coen, Joel, Ethan Coen, and Sam Raimi. *The Hudsucker Proxy.* London: Faber and Faber, 1994.

Comer, Brooke. "Byzantine Business Plot Begets *The Hudsucker Proxy.*" *American Cinematographer,* Vol. 75, No. 4, April 1994: 36.

Cowie, Peter. *Annie Hall.* London: BFI Publishing, 1996.

Croce, Arlene. *The Fred Astaire and Ginger Rogers Book.* New York: Galahad Books, 1972.

Feuer, Jane. *The Hollywood Musical.* Bloomington: Indiana University Press, 1982.

Forden, Hugh. *The Movies' Greatest Musicals.* New York: Ungar, 1984.

Gambill, Norman. "Harry Horner's Design Program for *The Heiress.*" *Art Journal,* Fall 1983: 223.

Gavin, Arthur E. "Rear Window." *American Cinematographer,* February 1954: 76.

Goldner, Orville, and George E. Turner. *The Making of King Kong.* South Brunswick, NJ: A. S. Barnes, 1975.

Harvey, James. *Romantic Comedy.* New York: Alfred A. Knopf, 1987.

Hirsch, Foster. *The Dark Side of the Screen.* New York: Da Capo, 1983.

——. *Detours and Lost Highways: A Map of Neo-Noir.* New York: Limelight, 1999.

Hoberman, J. *42nd Street.* London: BFI Publishing, 1993.

Horner, Harry. "Designing *The Heiress.*" *Hollywood Quarterly,* Vol. 5, No. 1, Fall 1950: 1.

Kendall, Elizabeth. *The Runaway Bride: Hollywood Romantic Comedy of the 1930s.* New York: Alfred A. Knopf, 1990.

Krohn, Bill. *Hitchcock at Work.* London: Phaidon, 2000.

Lang, Fritz. *Metropolis.* London: Faber and Faber, 1973.

Lee, Spike, and Lisa Jones. *Do the Right Thing: A Spike Lee Joint.* New York: Simon & Schuster, 1989.

Levy, Emanuel. *Cinema of Outsiders: The Rise of American Independent Film.* New York: New York University Press, 1999.

Maltz, Albert, and Malvin Wald. *The Naked City.* Carbondale: Southern Illinois University Press, 1948.

Minnelli, Vincente, Betty Comden, and Adolph Green. *The Band Wagon.* London: Lorrimer, 1986.

Mordden, Ethan. *The Hollywood Musical.* New York: St. Martin's Press, 1981.

Muller, Eddie. *Dark City: The Lost World of Film Noir.* London: Titan Books, 1998.

Odien, W. C. "The Rise and Fall of Norville Barnes." *Cinefex* 58, June 1994: 66.

Ottoson, Robert. *The American Film Noir.* Metuchen, NJ: Scarecrow Press, 1981.

Pike, Bob, and Dave Martin. *The Genius of Busby Berkeley.* California: Creative Film Society, 1973.

Rubin, Bruce Joel. *Jacob's Ladder.* New York: Applause Books, 1990.

Salamon, Julie. *The Devil's Candy: The Bonfire of the Vanities Goes to Hollywood.* New York: Houghton Mifflin, 1992.

Schrader, Paul. *Taxi Driver.* London: Faber and Faber, 1990.

Schulberg, Budd. *On the Waterfront: The Final Shooting Script.* Hollywood, CA: Samuel French, 1980.

Seldes, Gilbert, "Man with Camera." *The New Yorker,* May 30, 1931: 21.

Shay, Don. "Willis O'Brien, Creator of the Impossible." *Cinefex* 7, January 1982: 4–70.

Shay, Don, ed. *Making Ghostbusters.* New York: Zoetrope, 1985.

Silverman, Stephen M. *Dancing on the Ceiling: Stanley Donen and His Movies.* New York: Alfred A. Knopf, 1996.

Spoto, Donald. *The Art of Alfred Hitchcock,* 2nd ed. New York: Doubleday, 1992.

Taubin, Amy. *Taxi Driver.* London: British Film Institute, 2000.

Thomas, Tony, and Jim Terry (with Busby Berkeley). *The Busby Berkeley Book.* Greenwich, CT: New York Graphic Society, 1973.

Turner, George E. "*Rope*—Something Different." *American Cinematographer,* Vol. 66, No. 2, February 1985: 35–40.

Wood, Robin. *Hitchcock's Films.* New York: Castle Books, 1969.

PRODUCTION DESIGN, CINEMATOGRAPHY, AND SPECIAL EFFECTS

Affron, Charles, and Mirella Jona Affron. *Sets in Motion: Art Direction and Film Narrative.* New Brunswick, NJ: Rutgers University Press, 1995.

Albrecht, Donald. *Designing Dreams.* New York: Museum of Modern Art/Harper & Row, 1986.

Barsacq, Leon. *Caligari's Cabinet and Other Grand Illusions.* Elliott Stein, ed. New York: New American Library, 1978.

Brosnan, John. *Movie Magic.* New York: New American Library, 1976.

Deschner, Donald. "Anton Grot, Warner's Art Director," *Velvet Light Trap,* No. 15, Fall 1975.

Dunn, Linwood G., and George E. Turner. *The ASC Treasury of Visual Effects.* Hollywood, CA: American Society of Cinematographers, 1983.

LoBrutto, Vincent. *By Design: Interviews with Film Production Designers.* Westport, CT: Praeger, 1992.

Maltin, Leonard. *Behind the Camera.* New York: New American Library, 1971.

Mandelbaum, Howard, and Eric Myers. *Screen Deco.* New York: St. Martin's Press, 1986.

——. *Forties Screen Style.* New York: St. Martin's Press, 1989.

Neumann, Dietrich, ed. *Film Architecture.* Munich: Prestel, 1996.

Polglase, Van Nest. "The Studio Art Director." in Joe Bonica, comp., *How Talkies Are Made.* Hollywood, CA: J. Bonica and Co., 1930.

Preston, Ward. *What an Art Director Does.* Hollywood, CA: Silman-James, 1994.

Rainsberger, Todd. *James Wong Howe: Cinematographer.* San Diego: A. S. Barnes, 1981.

Schaefer, Dennis, and Larry Salvato. *Masters of Light: Conversations with Contemporary Photographers.* Berkeley: University of California Press, 1984.

Sennett, Robert S. *Setting the Scene: The Great Hollywood Art Directors.* New York: Abrams, 1994.

Spiegel, Ellen. "Fred and Ginger Meet Van Nest Polglase," *Velvet Light Trap* 10, Fall 1973: 17–22.

MOTION PICTURE PRODUCTION IN NEW YORK

Alleman, Richard. *The Movie Lover's Guide to New York.* New York: Harper & Row, 1988.

Altman, Diana. *Hollywood East: Louis B. Mayer and the Origins of the Studio System.* New York: Birch Lane/Carol, 1992.

Ampil, Cristina C. *Film and Television Production in New York City/Behind the Glitz: Lights, Camera, Jobs.* New York City Economic Policy and Marketing Group/Office of the Deputy Mayor for Finance and Economic Development, 1993.

Brownlow, Kevin. *Hollywood: The Pioneers.* New York: Alfred A. Knopf, 1979.

——. *Behind the Mask of Innocence.* New York: Alfred A. Knopf, 1990.

Bowser, Eileen. *The Transformation of Cinema, 1907–1915.* New York: Scribner, 1990.

Boyer, Jay. *Sidney Lumet.* New York: Twayne Publishers, 1993.

Carney, Ray. *The Films of John Cassavetes.* Cambridge, UK: Cambridge University Press, 1994.

Everson, William. *American Silent Film.* New York: Oxford University Press, 1978.

Kelly, Mary Pat. *Martin Scorsese: A Journey.* New York: Thunder's Mouth Press, 1991.

Keyser, Les. *Martin Scorsese.* New York: Twayne Publishers, 1995.

Koszarski, Richard. *An Evening's Entertainment: The Age of the Silent Picture, 1915–1928.* New York: Scribner, 1990.

——. *The Astoria Studio and Its Fabulous Films.* New York: Dover, 1983.

Lee, Spike. *Five for Five: The Films of Spike Lee.* New York: Workman, 1991.

Leyda, Jay, and Charles Musser, eds. *Before Hollywood: Turn of the Century Films from American Archives.* New York: American Federation of Arts, 1986.

Lippy, Tod, ed. *Projections 11: New York Film-makers on New York Film-making.* London: Faber and Faber, 2000.
Lumet, Sidney. *Making Movies.* New York: Alfred A. Knopf, 1995.
Musser, Charles. *Before the Nickelodeon: Edwin S. Porter and the Edison Manufacturing Company.* Berkeley: University of California Press, 1991.
——. *The Emergence of Cinema: The American Screen to 1907.* New York: Scribner, 1990.
"New York and the Movies," *Premiere* special issue, 1994.
North, Joseph H. *The Early Development of the Motion Picture (1887–1909).* New York: Arno Press, 1973.
"Our Love Affair With the Movies," *New York* Magazine special year-end movie issue, Vol. 9, No. 1, December 29, 1975.
Thompson, David, and Ian Christie, eds. *Scorsese on Scorsese.* London: Faber and Faber, 1989.

NEW YORK WRITERS IN HOLLYWOOD

Aylesworth, Thomas G. and Virginia L. Aylesworth. *New York: The Glamour Years (1919–1945).* New York: Gallery Books, 1987.
Corliss, Richard. *The Hollywood Screenwriters.* New York: Avon, 1972.
——. *Talking Pictures: Screenwriters in the American Cinema.* New York: Overlook Press, 1985.
Fine, Richard. *Hollywood and the Profession of Authorship.* Ann Arbor, MI: UMI Research Press, 1985.
Freeman, Everett. "Hollywood and the New Yorker." *The Screenwriter,* June–July 1948: 30–33.
Fuchs, Daniel. "Days in the Gardens of Hollywood." *New York Times Book Review,* 28 July 1971: 3.
Graham, Sheilah. *The Garden of Allah.* New York: Crown, 1970.
Guiles, Fred Lawrence. *Hanging on in Paradise.* New York: McGraw-Hill, 1975.
Kael, Pauline, Herman J. Mankiewicz, and Orson Welles. *The Citizen Kane Book.* Boston: Little, Brown, 1971.
Marquis, Alice Goldfarb. *Hope and Ashes: The Birth of Modern Times.* New York: Free Press, 1986.
Meryman, Richard. *Mank: The Wit, World and Life of Herman Mankiewicz.* New York: Morrow, 1978.
Podeschi, John. "The Writer in Hollywood," Dissertation, University of Illinois at Champaign-Urbana, 1971.
Powdermaker, Hortense. *Hollywood: The Dream Factory.* Boston: Little, Brown and Co., 1950.
Schulberg, Budd. "The Writer in Hollywood," *Harper's,* October 1959.
Schultheiss, John. "A Study of the 'Eastern' Writer in Hollywood in the 1930s." Dissertation, University of Southern California, 1973.
Torrence, Bruce T. *Hollywood: The First Hundred Years.* New York: New York Zoetrope, 1982.

ARCHITECTURE, URBANISM, AND URBAN HISTORY

Anderson, Stanford, ed. *On Streets.* Cambridge, MA: MIT Press, 1986.
Bender, Thomas. "New York as a Center of 'Difference,'" *Dissent,* Fall 1987: 429.
Berman, Marshall. "Ruins and Reforms," *Dissent,* Fall 1987: 421.
Dickstein, Morris. "Neighborhoods," *Dissent,* Fall 1987: 602.
Gans, Herbert J. *The Urban Villagers.* New York: Free Press, 1962.
Herbert, Robert L. *Impressionism: Art, Leisure and Parisian Society.* New Haven, CT: Yale University Press, 1988.
Le Corbusier. *The City of To-morrow and Its Planning.* New York: Dover Press, 1987.
Links, J. G. *Townscape Painting and Drawing.* New York: Harper & Row, 1972.
Jacobs, Jane. *The Death and Life of Great American Cities.* New York: Random House, 1961.
Scully, Stephen. *Homer and the Sacred City.* Ithaca: Cornell University Press, 1990.
Scully, Vincent. *American Architecture and Urbanism,* rev. ed. New York: Henry Holt, 1988.
Sharpe, William, and Leonard Woolcock, eds. *Visions of the Modern City: Essays in History, Art, and Literature.* Baltimore: The Johns Hopkins University Press, 1987.
van Leeuwen, Thomas A. P. *The Skyward Trend of Thought: The Metaphysics of the American Skyscraper.* Cambridge, MA: MIT Press, 1988.

White, John. *The Birth and Rebirth of Pictorial Space.* Cambridge, MA: Harvard University Press, 1987.
Willis, Carol. *Form Follows Finance: Skyscrapers and Skylines in New York and Chicago.* New York: Princeton Architectural Press, 1995.

CITIES AND FILM

Christopher, Nicholas. *Somewhere in the Night: Film Noir and the American City.* New York: Free Press, 1997.
Cites-Cines. Paris: Éditions Ramsay et la Grande Halle/La Villette, 1987.
Clarke, David B., ed. *The Cinematic City.* London: Routledge, 1997.
Doucher, Jean, and Gilles Nadeau. *Paris Cinema: Une Ville Vue par le Cinéma, de 1895 à Nos Jours.* Paris: Editions Du May, 1987.
Fear, Bob, ed. "Architecture + Film II." *Architectural Design,* Vol. 70, No. 1, January 2000.
Lamster, Mark, ed. *Architecture and Film.* New York: Princeton Architectural Press, 2000.
Penz, François, and Maureen Thomas, eds. *Cinema & Architecture: Méliès, Mallet-Stevens, Multimedia.* London: British Film Institute, 1997.
Sorensen, Colin. *London on Film: 100 Years of Filmmaking in London.* London: Museum of London, 1996.

SELECTED FILMOGRAPHY

FEATURE FILMS

In addition to title, release date, and original releasing studio, the following information is provided:

- *d:* director
- *w:* screenwriter (and author of original source material, in cases of adaptation)
- *ad:* art director
- *pd:* production designer
- *c:* cinematographer

Across 110th Street (1972), United Artists: *d* Barry Shear, *w* Luther Davis (from a novel by Wally Ferris), *ad* Perry Watkins

Adam's Rib (1949), MGM: *d* George Cukor; *w* Ruth Gordon, Garson Kanin; *ad* William Ferrari, Cedric Gibbons

An Affair to Remember (1957), 20th Century-Fox: *d* Leo McCarey; *w* Delmer Daves, Leo McCarey; *ad* Jack Martin Smith, Lyle R. Wheeler

After Hours (1985), Warner Bros.: *d* Martin Scorsese, *w* Joseph Minion, *pd* Jeffrey Townsend

All About Eve (1950), 20th Century-Fox: *d* Joseph L. Mankiewicz; *w* Joseph L. Mankiewicz (from a story by Mary Orr); *ad* George W. Davis, Lyle R. Wheeler

Angels With Dirty Faces (1938), Warner Bros.: *d* Michael Curtiz; *w* John Wexley, Warren Duff; *ad* Robert M. Haas

Angie (1994), Buena Vista: *d* Martha Coolidge; *w* Todd Graff (from a novel by Avra Wing); *pd* Mel Bourne

Annie Hall (1977), United Artists: *d* Woody Allen; *w* Woody Allen, Marshall Brickman; *ad* Mel Bourne

The Apartment (1960), United Artists: *d* Billy Wilder; *w* Billy Wilder, I.A.L. Diamond; *ad* Alexander Trauner

Applause (1929), Paramount: *d* Rouben Mamoulian, *w* Garrett Fort (from a novel by Beth Brown)

Armageddon (1998), Buena Vista: *d* Michael Bay; *w* Jonathan Hensleigh, J. J. Abrams, Robert Roy Pool, Tony Gilroy, Shane Salerno; *pd* Michael White

Baby Face (1933), Warner Bros.: *d* Alfred E. Green; *w* Gene Markey, Kathryn Scola; *ad* Anton Grot

Bachelor Apartment (1931), RKO: *d* Lowell Sherman; *w* J. Walker Ruben, John Howard Lawson; *ad* Max Rée

Ball of Fire (1941), RKO: *d* Howard Hawks; *w* Charles Brackett, Billy Wilder (from a story by Thomas Monroe and Billy Wilder); *ad* Perry Ferguson

The Band Wagon (1953), MGM: *d* Vincente Minnelli; *w* Betty Comden, Adolph Green; *ad* Preston Ames, Cedric Gibbons

The Barkleys of Broadway (1949), MGM: *d* Charles Walters; *w* Betty Comden, Adolph Green; *ad* Edward C. Carfagno, Cedric Gibbons

270. (previous page) Filming *The World, the Flesh, and the Devil* (1959). Harry Belafonte, as the last man in New York, being photographed on Maiden Lane in lower Manhattan, in front of the Federal Reserve Bank. The camera's upward angle insures that no background activity will be visible.

Basquiat (1996), Miramax: *d* Julian Schnabel; *w* John Bowe, Julian Schnabel, Lech Majewski; *pd* Dan Leigh

Batman (1989), Warner Bros.: *d* Tim Burton; *w* Sam Hamm, Warren Skaaren (based on the comic book by Bob Kane); *pd* Anton Furst

Batman Returns (1992), Warner Bros.: *d* Tim Burton; *w* Daniel Waters, Sam Hamm (based on the comic book by Bob Kane); *pd* Bo Welch

**batteries not included* (1987), Universal: *d* Matthew Robbins; *w* Matthew Robbins, Brad Bird, Brent Maddock, S. S. Wilson; *pd* Ted Haworth

The Beast from 20,000 Fathoms (1953), Warner Bros.: *d* Eugène Lourié; *w* Lou Morheim, Fred Freiberger (from a story by Ray Bradbury); *pd* Eugène Lourié

Bells Are Ringing (1960), MGM: *d* Vincente Minnelli; *w* Betty Comden, Adolph Green (from a musical play by Betty Comden and Adolph Green); *ad* E. Preston Ames, George W. Davis

Beneath the Planet of the Apes (1970), 20th Century-Fox: *d* Ted Post; *w* Paul Dehn, Mort Abrahams; *ad* William J. Creber, Jack Martin Smith

The Best of Everything (1959), 20th Century-Fox: *d* Jean Negulesco; *w* Edith Sommer, Mann Rubin (from a novel by Rona Jaffe); *ad* Mark-Lee Kirk, Jack Martin Smith, Lyle R. Wheeler

The Bicycle Thief (*Ladri di biciclette*) (1949, USA), Mayer-Burstyn: *d* Vittorio de Sica, *w* Cesare Zavattini (from a novel by Luigi Bartolini)

Big (1988), 20th Century-Fox: *d* Penny Marshall; *w* Gary Ross, Anne Spielberg; *pd* Santo Loquasto

The Big Broadcast (1932), Paramount: *d* Frank Tuttle; *w* George Marion Jr. (from a play by William Ford Manley)

Big Business (1988), Buena Vista: *d* Jim Abrahams; *w* Dori Pierson, Marc Rubel; *pd* William Sandell

The Big Clock (1948), Paramount: *d* John Farrow; *w* Jonathan Latimer (from a novel by Kenneth Fearing); *ad* Roland Anderson, Albert Nozaki, Hans Dreier

The Blackboard Jungle (1955), MGM: *d* Richard Brooks; *w* Richard Brooks (from a novel by Evan Hunter); *ad* Randall Duell, Cedric Gibbons

Blade Runner (1982), Warner Bros.: *d* Ridley Scott; *w* Hampton Fancher, David Peoples (from a novel by Philip K. Dick); *pd* Lawrence G. Paull, Peter J. Hampton

Blue in the Face (1995), Miramax: *d* Paul Auster, Wayne Wang; *w* Paul Auster, Wayne Wang; *pd* Kalina Ivanov

The Bonfire of the Vanities (1990), Warner Bros.: *d* Brian de Palma, *w* Michael Cristofer (from a novel by Tom Wolfe), *pd* Richard Sylbert

Born to Dance (1936), MGM: *d* Roy Del Ruth; *w* Jack McGowan, Sid Silvers, B. G. DeSylva; *ad* Joseph Wright, Edwin Willis, Cedric Gibbons

Breakfast at Tiffany's (1961), Paramount: *d* Blake Edwards; *w* George Axelrod (from a novella by Truman Capote); *ad* Roland Anderson, Hal Pereira

Bright Lights, Big City (1988), Universal: *d* James Bridges, *w* Jay McInerney (from a novel by Jay McInerney), *pd* Santo Loquasto

Brighton Beach Memoirs (1986), Universal: *d* Gene Saks; *w* Neil Simon (from a play by Neil Simon); *pd* Paul Eads, Stuart Wurtzel

Broadway (1929), Universal: *d* Pál Fejos; *w* Charles Furthman, Edward T. Lowe Jr., Tom Reed (from a play by Philip Dunning)

Broadway Babies (1929), First National: *d* Mervyn LeRoy; *w* Monte M. Katterjohn, Humphrey Pearson, Paul Perez; *ad* Jack Okey

Broadway Danny Rose (1984), Orion: *d* Woody Allen; *w* Woody Allen; *pd* Mel Bourne

The Broadway Melody (1929), MGM: *d* Harry Beaumont; *w* Norman Houston, James Gleason, Sarah Y. Mason; *ad* Cedric Gibbons

Broadway Melody of 1936 (1935), MGM: *d* Roy Del Ruth; *w* Jack McGowan, Sid Silvers, Harry Conn; *ad* Merrill Pye, Edwin Willis, Cedric Gibbons

Broadway Melody of 1938 (1937), MGM: *d* Roy Del Ruth; *w* Jack McGowan, Sid Silvers, Harry Conn; *ad* Cedric Gibbons, Joseph Wright, Edwin Willis

Broadway Melody of 1940 (1940), MGM: *d* Norman Taurog; *w* Leon Gordon, George Oppenheimer

Broadway Serenade (1939), MGM: *d* Robert Z. Leonard; *w* Charles Lederer, Lew Lipton, John T. Foote, Hans Kraly; *ad* Cedric Gibbons, Joseph Wright

Broadway Thru a Keyhole (1933), United Artists: *d* Lowell Sherman; *w* Gene Towne, Graham Baker (from a story by Walter Winchell); *ad* Richard Day, Joseph Wright

The Brother from Another Planet (1984), A-Train Films: *d* John Sayles, *w* John Sayles, *pd* Nora Chavooshian

The Brothers McMullen (1995), Fox Searchlight: *d* Edward Burns, *w* Edward Burns

Bullets or Ballots (1936), Warner Bros.: *d* William Keighley; *w* Seton I. Miller, Martin Mooney; *ad* Carl Jules Weyl

Butterfield 8 (1960), MGM: *d* Daniel Mann; *w* Charles Schnee, John Michael Hayes (from a novel by John O'Hara); *ad* George W. Davis, Urie McCleary

Captive Women (1952), RKO: *d* Stuart Gilmore; *w* Jack Pollexfen, Aubrey Wisberg; *pd* Theobold Holsopple

Cat People (1942), RKO: *d* Jacques Tourneur; *w* De Witt Bodeen; *ad* Albert S. D'Agostino, Walter E. Keller

Central Park (1932), Warner Bros.: *d* John Adolfi; *w* Ward Morehouse, Earl Baldwin; *ad* Arthur Gruenberger

Christmas in July (1940), Paramount: *d* Preston Sturges; *w* Preston Sturges; *ad* Hans Dreier, A. Earl Hedrick

City Across the River (1949), Universal: *d* Maxwell Shane; *w* Maxwell Shane, Dennis Cooper (from a novel by Irving Shulman); *pd* Bernard Herzbrun

City for Conquest (1940), Warner Bros.: *d* Anatole Litvak, Jean Negulesco; *w* John Wexley (from a novel by Aben Kandel); *ad* Robert M. Haas

City Hall (1996), Columbia: *d* Harold Becker; *w* Ken Lipper, Paul Schrader, Nicholas Pileggi, Bo Goldman; *pd* Jane Musky

The Clock (1945), MGM: *d* Vincente Minnelli; *w* Robert Nathan, Joseph Schrank (from a story by Paul and Pauline Gallico); *ad* William Ferrari, Cedric Gibbons

Clockers (1995), Universal: *d* Spike Lee; *w* Richard Price, Spike Lee (from a novel by Richard Price); *pd* Andrew McAlpine

The Cotton Club (1984), Zoetrope: *d* Francis Coppola; *w* William Kennedy, Francis Coppola; *pd* Richard Sylbert

Cotton Comes to Harlem (1970), United Artists: *d* Ossie Davis; *w* Arnold Perl, Ossie Davis (from a novel by Chester Himes); *ad* Manny Gerard

The Cowboy Way (1994), Universal: *d* Gregg Champion; *w* Robert C. Thompson, William D. Wittliff, Joe Gayton; *pd* John Jay Moore

Crime Without Passion (1934), Paramount: *d* Ben Hecht, Charles MacArthur; *w* Ben Hecht, Charles MacArthur

Crime School (1938), Warner Bros.: *d* Lewis Seiler; *w* Crane Wilbur, Vincent Sherman; *ad* Charles Novi

"Crocodile" Dundee (1986), Paramount: *d* Peter Faiman; *w* Paul Hogan, Ken Shadie, John Cornell; *pd* Graham "Grace" Walker

Crooklyn (1994), Universal: *d* Spike Lee; *w* Cinqué Lee, Joie Lee, Spike Lee; *pd* Wynn Thomas

Crossing Delancey (1988), Warner Bros.: *d* Joan Micklin Silver, *w* Susan Sandler, *pd* Dan Leigh

The Crowd (1928), MGM: *d* King Vidor; *w* King Vidor, John V.A. Weaver, Harry Behn, Joseph Farnham; *ad* Arnold Gillespie, Cedric Gibbons

Dames (1934), Warner Bros.: *d* Ray Enright; *w* Delmer Daves, Robert Lord; *ad* Robert M. Haas, Willy Pogany

The Dark Corner (1946), 20th Century-Fox: *d* Henry Hathaway; *w* Jay Dratler, Bernard Schoenfeld (from a story by Leo Rosten); *ad* James Basevi, Leland Fuller

The Daytrippers (1996), Metrodome/Fiasco/Trick Films: *d* Greg Mottola, *w* Greg Mottola, *pd* Bonnie J. Brinkley

Dead End (1937), United Artists: *d* William Wyler, *w* Lillian Hellman (from a play by Sidney Kingsley), *ad* Richard Day

Death Wish (1974), Paramount: *d* Michael Winner, *w* Wendell Mayes (from a novel by Brian Garfield)

Deep Impact (1998), Paramount: *d* Mimi Leder; *w* Bruce Joel Rubin, Michael Tolkin; *pd* Leslie Dilley

Delicious (1931), Fox: *d* David Butler; *w* Guy Bolton, Sonya Levien; *ad* Joseph Wright

Deluge (1933), RKO: *d* Felix E. Feist; *w* Warren Duff, John F. Goodrich (from a novel by S. Fowler Wright); *ad* Ralph M. De Lacy

Desperately Seeking Susan (1985), Orion: *d* Susan Seidelman, *w* Leona Barish, *pd* Santo Loquasto

The Detective (1968), 20th Century-Fox: *d* Gordon Douglas; *w* Abby Mann (from a novel by Roderick Thorp); *ad* Jack Martin Smith, William Creber

Detective Story (1951), Paramount: *d* William Wyler; *w* Philip Yordan, Robert Wyler (from a play by Sidney Kingsley); *ad* A. Earl Hedrick, Hal Pereira

The Devil and Miss Jones (1941), RKO: *d* Sam Wood, *w* Norman Krasna, *pd* William Cameron Menzies

Diary of a Mad Housewife (1970), Universal: *d* Frank Perry, *w* Eleanor Perry (from a novel by Sue Kaufman), *pd* Peter Dohanos

Die Hard with a Vengeance (1995), 20th Century-Fox: *d* John McTiernan, *w* Jonathan Hensleigh, *pd* Jackson DeGovia

Dinner at Eight (1933), MGM: *d* George Cukor; *w* Frances Marion, Herman J. Mankiewicz, Donald Ogden Stewart (from a play by George S. Kaufman, Edna Ferber); *ad* Hobe Erwin, Fredric Hope

Do the Right Thing (1989), Universal: *d* Spike Lee, *w* Spike Lee, *pd* Wynn Thomas

Dr. Broadway (1942) Paramount: *d* Anthony Mann; *w* Art Arthur (from a novel by Borden Chase); *ad* Hans Dreier, A. Earl Hedrick

Dog Day Afternoon (1975), Warner Bros.: *d* Sidney Lumet, *w* Frank Pierson (from a novel by Patrick Mann), *pd* Charles Bailey

A Double Life (1947), Universal: *d* George Cukor; *w* Ruth Gordon, Garson Kanin; *pd* Harry Horner

East of the River (1940), Warner Bros.: *d* Alfred E. Green, *w* Fred Niblo Jr. (from a story by John Fante and Ross B. Wills), *ad* Hugh Reticker

East Side, West Side (1949), MGM: *d* Mervyn LeRoy; *w* Isobel Lennart (from a novel by Marcia Davenport); *ad* Randall Duell, Cedric Gibbons

Ed's Next Move (1996), Orion: *d* John Walsh, *w* John Walsh, *pd* Kristin Vallow

Edge of the City (1957), MGM: *d* Martin Ritt, *w* Robert Alan Aurthur (from a play by Robert Alan Aurthur), *ad* Richard Sylbert

Escape from L.A. (1996), Paramount: *d* John Carpenter; *w* John Carpenter, Debra Hill, Kurt Russell; *pd* Lawrence G. Paull

Escape from New York (1981), Avco Embassy: *d* John Carpenter; *w* John Carpenter, Nick Castle; *pd* Joe Alves

Everyone Says I Love You (1996), Miramax: *d* Woody Allen, *w* Woody Allen, *pd* Santo Loquasto

A Face in the Crowd (1957), Warner Bros.: *d* Elia Kazan; *w* Budd Schulberg; *ad* Paul Sylbert, Richard Sylbert

Fail-Safe (1964), Columbia: *d* Sidney Lumet, *w* Walter Bernstein (from a novel by Eugene Burdick and Harvey Wheeler), *pd* Albert Brenner

Falling Down (1993), Warner Bros.: *d* Joel Schumacher, *w* Ebbe Roe Smith, *pd* Barbara Ling

Fame (1980), MGM: *d* Alan Parker; *w* Christopher Gore; *pd* Geoffrey Kirkland, Ed Wittstein

Fatal Attraction (1987), Paramount: *d* Adrian Lyne; *w* James Dearden, Nicholas Meyer; *pd* Mel Bourne

The Fifth Element (1997), Columbia: *d* Luc Besson; *w* Luc Besson, Robert Mark Kamen; *pd* Dan Weil

The Fisher King (1991), TriStar: *d* Terry Gilliam, *w* Richard LaGravenese, *pd* Mel Bourne

The Flamingo Kid (1984), 20th Century-Fox: *d* Garry Marshall; *w* Neal Marshall, Garry Marshall; *pd* Lawrence Miller

Footlight Parade (1933), Warner Bros.: *d* Lloyd Bacon; *w* Manuel Seff, James Seymour (from a story by Robert Lord and Peter Milne); *ad* Anton Grot, Jack Okey

Footlight Serenade (1942), 20th Century-Fox: *d* Gregory Ratoff; *w* Robert Ellis, Helen Logan, Lynn Starling (from a story by Kenneth Earl and Fidel LaBarba); *ad* Richard Day, Albert Hogsett

For Love or Money (1993), Universal: *d* Barry Sonnenfeld; *w* Lawrence Konner, Mark Rosenthal; *pd* Peter S. Larkin

Fort Apache, The Bronx (1981), Time Life: *d* Daniel Petrie, *w* Heywood Gould, *pd* Ben Edwards

42nd Street (1933), Warner Bros.: *d* Lloyd Bacon; *w* Rian James, James Seymour, Whitney Bolton (from a novel by Bradford Ropes); *ad* Jack Okey

The Fountainhead (1949), Warner Bros.: *d* King Vidor, *w* Ayn Rand (from a novel by Ayn Rand), *ad* Edward Carrere

Fourteen Hours (1951), 20th Century-Fox: *d* Henry Hathaway; *w* John Paxton (from an article by Joel Sayre); *ad* Lyle Wheeler, Leland Fuller

The French Connection (1971), 20th Century-Fox: *d* William Friedkin, *w* Ernest Tidyman (from a novel by Robin Moore), *ad* Ben Kazaskow

Fresh (1994), Miramax: *d* Boaz Yakin, *w* Boaz Yakin, *pd* Dan Leigh
Funny Face (1957), Paramount: *d* Stanley Donen; *w* Leonard Gershe; *ad* George W. Davis, Hal Pereira
F/X (1986), Orion: *d* Robert Mandel; *w* Robert T. Megginson, Gregory Fleeman; *pd* Mel Bourne
Gentleman's Agreement (1947), 20th Century-Fox: *d* Elia Kazan; *w* Moss Hart (from a novel by Laura Z. Hobson); *ad* Lyle Wheeler, Mark Lee Kirk
Ghostbusters (1984), Columbia: *d* Ivan Reitman; *w* Dan Aykroyd, Harold Ramis; *pd* John DeCuir
Ghostbusters II (1989), Columbia: *d* Ivan Reitman; *w* Harold Ramis, Dan Aykroyd; *pd* Bo Welch
The Gilded Lily (1935), Paramount: *d* Wesley Ruggles, *w* Claude Binyon
The Girl in the Red Velvet Swing (1955), 20th Century-Fox: *d* Richard Fleischer; *w* Walter Reisch, Charles Brackett; *ad* Maurice Ransford, Lyle R. Wheeler
Glorifying the American Girl (1929), Paramount: *d* Millard Webb; *w* J.P. McEvoy, Millard Webb
The Godfather (1972), Paramount: *d* Francis Ford Coppola; *w* Francis Ford Coppola, Mario Puzo (from a novel by Mario Puzo); *pd* Dean Tavoularis
The Godfather, Part II (1974), Paramount: *d* Francis Ford Coppola; *w* Francis Ford Coppola, Mario Puzo; *pd* Dean Tavoularis
Godzilla (1998), Columbia TriStar: *d* Roland Emmerich; *w* Dean Devlin, Roland Emmerich, Ted Elliott, Terry Rossio; *pd* Oliver Scholl
Going Hollywood (1933), MGM: *d* Raoul Walsh; *w* Donald Ogden Stewart, Frances Marion; *ad* Merril Pye
Gold Diggers of 1933 (1933), Warner Bros.: *d* Mervyn LeRoy; *w* Erwin Gelsey, James Seymour, David Boehm, Ben Markson (from a play by Avery Hopwood); *ad* Anton Grot
The Goodbye Girl (1977), Warner Bros.: *d* Herbert Ross, *w* Neil Simon, *pd* Albert Brenner
Grand Hotel (1932), MGM: *d* Edmund Goulding, *w* William A. Drake (from a novel by Vicki Baum), *ad* Cedric Gibbons
The Great Ziegfeld (1936), MGM: *d* Robert Z. Leonard; *w* William Anthony McGuire; *ad* Cedric Gibbons, Eddie Imazu, Edwin B. Willis
Green Card (1990), Touchstone: *d* Peter Weir, *w* Peter Weir, *pd* Wendy Stites
Gremlins 2: The New Batch (1990), Warner Bros.: *d* Joe Dante, *w* Charlie Haas, *pd* James Spencer
Hair (1979), United Artists: *d* Milos Forman; *w* Michael Weller (from a musical play by Galt MacDermot, Gerome Ragni, James Rado); *pd* Stuart Wurtzel
Hallelujah, I'm a Bum (1933), United Artists: *d* Lewis Milestone, Chester Erskin; *w* S. N. Behrman, Ben Hecht; *ad* Richard Day
Hands Across the Table (1935), Paramount: *d* Mitchell Leisen; *w* Norman Krasna, Vincent Lawrence, Herbert Fields (from a story by Viña Delmar); *ad* Hans Dreier, Roland Anderson
Hannah and Her Sisters (1986), Orion: *d* Woody Allen, *w* Woody Allen, *pd* Stuart Wurtzel
The Hard Way (1991), Universal: *d* John Badham; *w* Daniel Pyne, Lem Dobbs; *pd* Philip Harrison
The Heiress (1949), Paramount: *d* William Wyler; *w* Ruth and Augustus Goetz (from a play by Ruth and Augustus Goetz, based on a novel by Henry James); *pd* Harry Horner, John Meehan
Hester Street (1974), Midwest Films: *d* Joan Micklin Silver, *w* Joan Micklin Silver (from a story by Abraham Cahan), *pd* Stuart Wurtzel
Holiday (1938), Columbia: *d* George Cukor; *w* Donald Ogden Stewart (from a play by Philip Barry); *ad* Steven Goosson, Sidney Buchman
Home Alone 2: Lost in New York (1992), 20th Century-Fox: *d* Chris Columbus, *w* John Hughes, *pd* Sandy Veneziano
The House on 92nd Street (1945), 20th Century-Fox: *d* Henry Hathaway; *w* Barré Lyndon, Charles G. Booth, John Monks Jr., Charles Booth; *ad* Lewis H. Creber, Lyle R. Wheeler
Household Saints (1993), Fine Line: *d* Nancy Savoca; *w* Richard Guay, Francine Prose, Nancy Savoca (from a novel by Francine Prose); *pd* Kalina Ivanov
How to Marry a Millionaire (1953), 20th Century-Fox: *d* Jean Negulesco; *w* Nunnally Johnson; *ad* Leland Fuller, Lyle Wheeler
How to Murder Your Wife (1965), United Artists: *d* Richard Quine, *w* George Axelrod, *pd* Richard Sylbert
How to Succeed in Business Without Really Trying (1967), United Artists: *d* David Swift; *w* David Swift (from a musical play by Abe Burrows, Jack Weinstock, Willie Gilbert, based on a novel by Shepherd Mead); *ad* Robert F. Boyle, Mary Blair

The Hucksters (1947), MGM: *d* Jack Conway; *w* Luther Davis, Edward Chodorov, George Wells (from a novel by Frederic Wakeman); *ad* Cedric Gibbons, Urie McCleary

Hudson Hawk (1991), Columbia TriStar: *d* Michael Lehmann; *w* Steven E. de Souza, Daniel Waters; *pd* Jackson DeGovia

The Hudsucker Proxy (1994), Warner Bros.: *d* Joel Coen, *w* Ethan Coen, Joel Coen, Sam Raimi; *pd* Dennis Gassner

I Like It Like That (1994), Columbia TriStar: *d* Darnell Martin, *w* Darnell Martin, *pd* Scott Chambliss

Independence Day (1996), 20th Century-Fox: *d* Roland Emmerich; *w* Dean Devlin, Roland Emmerich; *pd* Oliver Scholl, Patrick Tatopolous

Insignificance (1985), Island Alive: *d* Nicolas Roeg, *w* Terry Johnson (from a play by Terry Johnson), *pd* David Brockhurst

Into the Net (1924), Pathé: *d* George B. Seitz; *w* Richard E. Enright, Frank Leon Smith

Invasion, U.S.A. (1952), Columbia: *d* Alfred E. Green; *w* Franz Schulz, Robert Smith; *pd* James W. Sullivan

It Could Happen to You (1994), Columbia Tristar: *d* Andrew Bergman, *w* Jane Anderson, *pd* Bill Groom

It Happened in Brooklyn (1947), MGM: *d* Richard Whorf; *w* Isobel Lennart; *ad* Leonard Vasian, Cedric Gibbons

It Should Happen To You (1954), Columbia: *d* George Cukor; *w* Ruth Gordon, Garson Kanin; *ad* John Meehan

Jacob's Ladder (1990), TriStar: *d* Adrian Lyne, *w* Bruce Joel Rubin, *pd* Brian Morris

The Jazz Singer (1927), Warner Bros.: *d* Alan Crosland; *w* Alfred A. Cohn, Jack Jarmuth (from a play by Samson Raphaelson)

Juice (1992), Paramount: *d* Ernest R. Dickerson; *w* Gerard Brown III, Ernest R. Dickerson

Jungle Fever (1991), Universal: *d* Spike Lee, *w* Spike Lee, *pd* Wynn Thomas

Just Another Girl on the I.R.T. (1992), Miramax: *d* Leslie Harris, *w* Leslie Harris, *pd* Michael O'Dell Green

Just Imagine (1930), Fox: *d* David Butler; *w* Buddy G. DeSylva, Lew Brown, Ray Henderson; *ad* Stephen Goosson, Ralph Hammeras

Kid Galahad (1937), Warner Bros.: *d* Michael Curtiz, *w* Seton I. Miller (from a novel by Francis Wallace), *ad* Carl Jules Weyl

Kids (1995), Miramax: *d* Larry Clark; *w* Larry Clark, Leo Fitzpatrick, Jim Lewis, Harmony Korine; *pd* Kevin Thompson

Killer's Kiss (1955), United Artists: *d* Stanley Kubrick; *w* Stanley Kubrick, Howard Sackler

King Kong (1933), RKO: *d* Merian C. Cooper, Ernest Schoedsack; *w* James Creelman, Ruth Rose (from a story by Edgar Wallace and Merian C. Cooper); *ad* Carroll Clark, Alfred Herman

King Kong (1976), Paramount: *d* John Guillermin; *w* Lorenzo Semple Jr.; *pd* Mario Chiari, Dale Hennesy

Kiss Me, Guido (1997), Paramount: *d* Tony Vitale, *w* Tony Vitale, *pd* Jeffrey Rathaus

Kiss of Death (1947), 20th Century-Fox: *d* Henry Hathaway; *w* Ben Hecht, Charles Lederer; *ad* Leland Fuller, Lyle Wheeler

Klute (1971), Warner Bros.: *d* Alan J. Pakula; *w* Andy K. Lewis, Dave Lewis; *ad* George Jenkins

Kramer vs. Kramer (1979), Columbia: *d* Robert Benton, *w* Robert Benton (from a novel by Avery Corman), *pd* Paul Sylbert

La terra trema (1948), ENIC Universalia Produzione: *d* Luchino Visconti, *w* Luchino Visconti, *pd* Renato Silvestri

The Landlord (1970), United Artists: *d* Hal Ashby, *w* Bill Gunn (from a novel by Kristin Hunter), *pd* Robert Boyle

The Last Angry Man (1959), Columbia: *d* Daniel Mann; *w* Gerald Green, Richard Murphy (from a novel by Gerald Green); *ad* Carl Anderson

The Last Days of Disco (1998), Warner Bros.: *d* Whit Stillman, *w* Whit Stillman, *pd* Ginger Tougas

Last Exit to Brooklyn (1989), Cinecom: *d* Uli Edel, *w* Desmond Nakano (from a novel by Hubert Selby Jr.), *pd* David Chapman

Laura (1944), 20th Century-Fox: *d* Otto Preminger; *w* Jay Dratler, Samuel Hoffenstein, Betty Reinhardt (from a novel by Vera Caspary); *ad* Leland Fuller, Lyle Wheeler

Life With Father (1947), Warner Bros.: *d* Michael Curtiz, *w* Donald Ogden Stewart (from the play by Howard Lindsay and Russel Crouse, based on a book by Clarence Day, Jr.); *ad* Robert M. Haas

Little Fugitive (1953), Joseph Burstyn: *d* Ray Ashley, Morris Engel, Ruth Orkin; *w* Ray Ashley, Morris Engel, Ruth Orkin

Little Murders (1971), 20th Century-Fox: *d* Alan Arkin, *w* Jules Feiffer (from a play by Jules Feiffer), *pd* Gene Rudolf

Living in Oblivion (1995), Sony Pictures Classics: *d* Tom DiCillo; *w* Tom DiCillo; *pd* Stephanie Carroll, Thérèse DePrez

The Lost Weekend (1945), Paramount: *d* Billy Wilder; *w* Charles Brackett, Billy Wilder (from a novel by Charles Jackson); *ad* Hans Dreier

Love Affair (1939), RKO: *d* Leo McCarey; *w* Mildred Crain, Leo McCarey, Delmer Daves, Donald Ogden Stewart; *ad* Van Nest Polglase, Al Herman

Love Happy (1949), United Artists: *d* David Miller; *w* Ben Hecht, Frank Tashlin, Mac Benoff; *pd* Gabriel Scognamillo

Love with the Proper Stranger (1964), Paramount: *d* Robert Mulligan; *w* Arnold Schulman; *ad* Roland Anderson, Hal Pereira

Ma and Pa Kettle Go to Town (1950), Universal: *d* Charles Lamont; *w* Martin Ragaway, Leonard B. Stern; *ad* Bernard Herzbrun, Van Enger

Madam Satan (1930), MGM: *d* Cecil B. DeMille; *w* Jeanie Macpherson, Elsie Janis, Gladys Unger; *ad* Cedric Gibbons, Mitchell Leisen

The Man in the Gray Flannel Suit (1956), 20th Century-Fox: *d* Nunnally Johnson; *w* Nunnally Johnson (from a novel by Sloan Wilson); *ad* Jack Martin Smith, Lyle Wheeler

Manhattan (1979), United Artists: *d* Woody Allen; *w* Woody Allen, Marshall Brickman; *pd* Mel Bourne

Manhattan Melodrama (1934), MGM: *d* W. S. Van Dyke II; *w* Oliver H. P. Garrett, Joseph L. Mankiewicz; *ad* Cedric Gibbons, Edwin B. Willis, Joseph C. Wright

Mannequin (1938), MGM: *d* Frank Borzage; *w* Lawrence Hazard, Frank Borzage (from a story by Katherine Brush); *ad* Cedric Gibbons, Paul Groesse, Edwin B. Willis

Marathon Man (1976), Paramount: *d* John Schlesinger, *w* William Goldman (from a novel by William Goldman), *pd* Richard MacDonald

Marjorie Morningstar (1958), Warner Bros.: *d* Irving Rapper, *w* Everett Freeman (from a novel by Herman Wouk), *ad* Malcolm C. Bert

Marked Woman (1937), Warner Bros.: *d* Lloyd Bacon; *w* Robert Rossen, Abem Finkel; *ad* Max Parker

Married to the Mob (1988), Orion: *d* Jonathan Demme; *w* Barry Strugatz, Mark R. Burns; *pd* Kristi Zea

Marty (1955), United Artists: *d* Delbert Mann; *w* Paddy Chayefsky (from a teleplay by Paddy Chayefsky); *ad* Edward Haworth, Walter Simonds

Mean Streets (1973), Warner Bros.: *d* Martin Scorsese; *w* Martin Scorsese, Mardik Martin

Men in Black (1997), Columbia: *d* Barry Sonnenfeld, *w* Ed Solomon (based on a comic book by Lowell Cunningham), *pd* Bo Welch

Meteor (1979), American International Pictures: *d* Ronald Neame; *w* Stanley Mann, Edmund H. North; *pd* Edward C. Carfagno

Metropolis (1926), Paramount: *d* Fritz Lang; *w* Thea von Harbou, Fritz Lang (from a novel by Thea Von Harbou); *ad* Otto Hunte, Erich Kettelhut, Karl Volbrecht

Metropolitan (1990), New Line: *d* Whit Stillman, *w* Whit Stillman

Midnight Cowboy (1969), United Artists: *d* John Schlesinger, *w* Waldo Salt (from a novel by James Leo Herlihy), *pd* John Robert Lloyd

Miracle in the Rain (1956), Warner Bros.: *d* Rudolph Maté, *w* Ben Hecht (from a novel by Ben Hecht), *ad* Leo K. Kuter

Miracle on 34th Street (1947), 20th Century-Fox: *d* George Seaton; *w* George Seaton (from a story by Valentine Davies); *ad* Richard Day, Richard Irvine

Mirage (1965), Universal: *d* Edward Dmytryk; *w* Peter Stone (from a novel by Walter Ericson); *ad* Frank Arrigo, Alexander Golitzen

Mr. and Mrs. Smith (1941), RKO: *d* Alfred Hitchcock; *w* Norman Krasna; *ad* Albert S. D'Agostino, Van Nest Polglase

Mo' Better Blues (1990), Universal: *d* Spike Lee, *w* Spike Lee, *pd* Wynn Thomas

Money Train (1995), Columbia TriStar: *d* Joseph Ruben; *w* Doug Richardson, David Loughery, Richard Price; *pd* Bill Groom

The Moon Is Blue (1953), United Artists: *d* Otto Preminger, *w* F. Hugh Herbert (from a play by F. Hugh Herbert), *pd* Nicolai Remisoff

Morning Glory (1933), RKO: *d* Lowell Sherman; *w* Howard J. Green (from a play by Zoë Akins); *pd* Chick Kirk, Van Nest Polglase

Movie Movie (1978), Warner Bros.: *d* Stanley Donen; *w* Larry Gelbart, Sheldon Keller; *ad* Jack Fisk

The Muppets Take Manhattan (1984), TriStar: *d* Frank Oz; *w* Frank Oz, Tom Patchett, Jay Tarses; *pd* Paul Eads, Stephen Hendrickson

The Musketeers of Pig Alley (1912), Biograph: *d* D. W. Griffith; *w* D. W. Griffith, Anita Loos

My Favorite Year (1982), MGM/United Artists: *d* Richard Benjamin; *w* Norman Steinberg, Dennis Palumbo; *pd* Charles Rosen

My Foolish Heart (1949), Samuel Goldwyn: *d* Mark Robson; *w* Julius J. Epstein, Philip G. Epstein (from a story by J. D. Salinger); *ad* Richard Day

My Man Godfrey (1936), Universal: *d* Gregory La Cava; *w* Morrie Ryskind, Eric Hatch (from a novel by Eric Hatch); *ad* Charles D. Hall

The Naked City (1948), Universal: *d* Jules Dassin; *w* Malvin Wald, Albert Maltz; *ad* Jon DeCuir

Network (1976), MGM: *d* Sidney Lumet, *w* Paddy Chayefsky, *pd* Philip Rosenberg

New Jack City (1991), Warner Bros.: *d* Mario Van Peebles; *w* Thomas Lee Wright, Barry Michael Cooper; *pd* Charles C. Bennett

New York (1927), Paramount: *d* Luther Reed; *w* Barbara Chambers, Becky Gardiner, Forrest Halsey

New York, New York (1977), United Artists: *d* Martin Scorsese; *w* Earl Mac Rauch, Mardik Martin; *pd* Boris Leven

New York Stories/Life Lessons (1989), Touchstone: *d* Martin Scorsese, *w* Richard Price, *pd* Kristi Zea

New York Stories/Life without Zoë (1989), Touchstone: *d* Francis Ford Coppola; *w* Francis Ford Coppola, Sofia Coppola; *pd* Dean Tavoularis

New York Stories/Oedipus Wrecks (1989), Touchstone: *d* Woody Allen, *w* Woody Allen, *pd* Santo Loquasto

Next Stop, Greenwich Village (1976), 20th Century-Fox: *d* Paul Mazursky, *w* Paul Mazursky, *pd* Philip Rosenberg

The Night They Raided Minsky's (1968), United Artists: *d* William Friedkin; *w* Arnold Schulman, Sidney Michaels, Norman Lear (from a novel by Rowland Barber); *pd* Jean Eckart, William Eckart

Nighthawks (1978), Four Corner: *d* Ron Peck; *w* Ron Peck, Paul Hallam

No Time for Comedy (1940), Warner Bros.: *d* William Keighley; *w* Julius J. Epstein, Philip G. Epstein (from a play by S. N. Behrman); *ad* John Hughes

North by Northwest (1959), MGM: *d* Alfred Hitchcock; *w* Ernest Lehman; *ad* William A. Horning, Robert Boyle, Merrill Pye

On the Town (1949), MGM: *d* Gene Kelly, Stanley Donen; *w* Betty Comden, Adolph Green (from a musical play by Betty Comden and Adolph Green); *pd* Cedric Gibbons, Jack Martin Smith

On the Waterfront (1954), Columbia: *d* Elia Kazan, *w* Budd Schulberg, *ad* Richard Day

One-Third of a Nation (1939), Paramount: *d* Dudley Murphy; *w* Dudley Murphy, Oliver H. P. Garrett (from a play by Arthur Arent); *ad* Walter Keller

Open City (Roma, città aperta) (1946), Mayer-Burstyn: *d* Roberto Rossellini; *w* Sergio Amidei, Roberto Rossellini, Federico Fellini; *pd* Rosario Megna

The Out-of-Towners (1970), Paramount: *d* Arthur Hiller; *w* Neil Simon; *ad* Charles Bailey, Walter H. Tyler

Paisà (1948), Mayer-Burstyn: *d* Roberto Rossellini; *w* Sergio Amidei, Federico Fellini, Roberto Rossellini

Panic in Needle Park (1971), Gadd Productions: *d* Jerry Schatzberg; *w* Joan Didion, John Gregory Dunne (from a novel by James Mills)

The Paper (1994), Universal: *d* Ron Howard; *w* David Koepp, Stephen Koepp; *pd* Todd Hallowell

Party Girl (1995), First Look: *d* Daisy von Scherler Mayer; *w* Harry Birckmayer, Sheila Gaffney, Daisy von Scherler Mayer; *pd* Kevin Thompson

Patterns (1956), United Artists: *d* Fielder Cook, *w* Rod Serling (from a teleplay by Rod Serling), *ad* Richard Sylbert

The Pawnbroker (1965), Landau Company: *d* Sidney Lumet; *w* David Friedkin, Morton Fine (from a novel by Edward Lewis Wallant); *pd* Richard Sylbert

Penthouse (1933), MGM: *d* W. S. Van Dyke; *w* Frances Goodrich, Albert Hackett (from a novel by Arthur Somers Roche); *ad* Alexander Toluboff

The Pick-Up Artist (1987), 20th Century-Fox: *d* James Toback, *w* James Toback, *pd* Paul Sylbert

Pickup on South Street (1953), 20th Century-Fox: *d* Samuel Fuller; *w* Samuel Fuller (from a story by Dwight Taylor); *ad* George Patrick, Lyle Wheeler

Planet of the Apes (1968), 20th Century-Fox: *d* Franklin J. Schaffner; *w* Michael Wilson, Rod Serling (from a novel by Pierre Boulle); *ad* William Creber, Jack Martin Smith

Play Ball (1925), Pathé: *d* Spencer Gordon Bennett, *w* Frank Leon Smith

Plaza Suite (1971), Paramount: *d* Arthur Hiller, *w* Neil Simon (from a play by Neil Simon)

Possessed (1931), MGM: *d* Clarence Brown, *w* Lenore Coffee (from a play by Edgar Selwyn), *ad* Cedric Gibbons

The Prisoner of Second Avenue (1975), Warner Bros.: *d* Melvin Frank, *w* Neil Simon (from a play by Neil Simon), *ad* Preston Ames

The Producers (1967), Embassy: *d* Mel Brooks, *w* Mel Brooks, *ad* Charles Rosen

The Purple Rose of Cairo (1984), Orion: *d* Woody Allen, *w* Woody Allen, *pd* Stuart Wurtzel

Puttin' on the Ritz (1930), United Artists: *d* Edward Sloman; *w* John W. Considine Jr., William K. Wells; *ad* William Cameron Menzies

Queens Logic (1991), Seven Arts: *d* Steve Rash, *w* Tony Spiridakis, *pd* Edward Pisoni

Radio Days (1987), Orion: *d* Woody Allen, *w* Woody Allen, *pd* Santo Loquasto

Ragtime (1981), Paramount: *d* Milos Forman; *w* Michael Weller (from a novel by E.L. Doctorow); *pd* George DeTitta Sr., John Graysmark, Peter Howitt, Anthony Reading, Patrizia von Brandenstein

Ransom (1996), Buena Vista: *d* Ron Howard; *w* Cyril Hume, Richard Maibaum, Alexander Ignon, Richard Price; *pd* Michael Corenblith

Reaching for the Moon (1931), United Artists: *d* Edmund Goulding; *w* Edmund Goulding, Elsie Janis (from a story by Irving Berlin)

The Real Blonde (1997), Paramount: *d* Tom DiCillo, *w* Tom DiCillo, *pd* Christopher Nowak

Rear Window (1954), Paramount: *d* Alfred Hitchcock; *w* John Michael Hayes (from a novella by Cornell Woolrich); *ad* Joseph McMillan Johnson, Hal Pereira

Reds (1981), Paramount: *d* Warren Beatty; *w* Warren Beatty, Trevor Griffiths; *pd* Richard Sylbert

Regarding Henry (1991), Paramount: *d* Mike Nichols, *w* Jeffrey Abrams, *pd* Tony Walton

Regeneration (1915), Fox: *d* Raoul Walsh; *w* Raoul Walsh, Carl Harbaugh (from a book by Owen Kildare)

Rhythm Thief (1994), Strand Releasing: *d* Matthew Harrison; *w* Christopher Grimm, Matthew Harrison; *ad* Daniel Fisher

Rich and Famous (1981), MGM: *d* George Cukor, *w* Gerald Ayres (from a play by John Van Druten), *pd* Jan Scott

The Roaring Twenties (1939), Warner Bros.: *d* Raoul Walsh; *w* Jerry Wald, Richard Macaulay, Robert Rossen (from a story by Mark Hellinger); *ad* Max Parker

Romance in Manhattan (1935), RKO: *d* Stephen Roberts; *w* Jane Murfin, Edward Kaufman; *ad* Charles Kirk, Van Nest Polglase

Romance of a Jewess (1908), Biograph: *d* D. W. Griffith, *w* D. W. Griffith

Rooftops (1989), 20th Century-Fox: *d* Robert Wise, *w* Terence Brennan, *pd* Jeannine Claudia Oppewall

Rope (1948), Transatlantic: *d* Alfred Hitchcock, *w* Arthur Laurents (from a play by Patrick Hamilton), *ad* Perry Ferguson

Rosemary's Baby (1968), Paramount: *d* Roman Polanski, *w* Roman Polanski (from a novel by Ira Levin), *pd* Richard Sylbert

Rumble in the Bronx (1995), Golden Harvest: *d* Stanley Tong, *w* Edward Tang, *pd* Oliver Wong

Saboteur (1942), Universal: *d* Alfred Hitchcock; *w* Peter Viertel, Joan Harrison, Dorothy Parker; *ad* Jack Otterson

Sabrina (1954), Paramount: *d* Billy Wilder; *w* Billy Wilder, Samuel Taylor, Ernest Lehman (from a play by Samuel Taylor); *ad* Hal Pereira, Walter Tyler

The Saint of Fort Washington (1993), Warner Bros.: *d* Tim Hunter, *w* Lyle Kessler, *pd* Stuart Wurtzel

Saturday Night Fever (1977), Paramount: *d* John Badham, *w* Norman Wexler (based on an article by Nik Cohn), *pd* Charles Bailey

Scarlet Street (1945), Universal: *d* Fritz Lang, *w* Dudley Nichols (from a play by George de la Fouchardière), *ad* Alexander Golitzen

The Secret of My Success (1987), Universal: *d* Herbert Ross; *w* Jim Cash, Jack Epps Jr., A. J. Carothers; *pd* Peter Larkin, Edward Pisoni

Serpico (1973), Paramount: *d* Sidney Lumet; *w* Waldo Salt, Norman Wexler (from a novel by Peter Maas); *pd* Charles Bailey

The Seven Year Itch (1955), 20th Century-Fox: *d* Billy Wilder; *w* Billy Wilder, George Axelrod (from a play by George Axelrod); *ad* George W. Davis, Lyle Wheeler

The Shadow (1994), Universal: *d* Russell Mulcahy; *w* Walter B. Gibson, David Koepp; *pd* Joseph C. Nemec III

Shadows (1959), Lion International: *d* John Cassavetes; *w* John Cassavetes; *pd* Randy Liles, Bob Reeh

Shaft (1971), MGM: *d* Gordon Parks; *w* Ernest Tidyman, John D. F. Black (from a novel by Ernest Tidyman); *ad* Emanuel Gerard

Shaft's Big Score! (1972), MGM: *d* Gordon Parks, *w* Ernest Tidyman, *ad* Emanuel Gerard

Shall We Dance? (1937), RKO: *d* Mark Sandrich; *w* Allan Scott, Ernest Pagano, P. J. Wolfson; *ad* Van Nest Polglase

She's Gotta Have It (1986), Island: *d* Spike Lee, *w* Spike Lee, *pd* Wynn Thomas

She's the One (1996), 20th Century-Fox: *d* Edward Burns, *w* Edward Burns, *pd* William Barclay

The Shock Punch (1925), Paramount: *d* Paul Sloane; *w* Luther Reed, John Monk Saunders (from a play by John Monk Saunders); *ad* Ernst Fegté

Shoeshine (Sciuscià)(1946), Lopert Pictures: *d* Vittorio de Sica; *w* Cesare Zavattini, Sergio Amidei, Adolfo Franci, C.G. Viola; *pd* Ivo Battelli

Sidewalks of New York (1931), MGM: *d* Jules White, Zion Myers; *w* George Landy, Paul Gerard Smith, Eric Hatch, Robert E. Hopkins

Single White Female (1992), Columbia TriStar: *d* Barbet Schroeder, *w* Don Roos (from a novel by John Lutz), *pd* Milena Canonero

Six Degrees of Separation (1993), MGM: *d* Fred Schepisi, *w* John Guare (from a play by John Guare), *pd* Patrizia von Brandenstein

The Sky's the Limit (1943), RKO: *d* Edward H. Griffith; *w* Frank Fenton, S. K. Lauren, Lynn Root; *ad* Carroll Clark, Albert S. D'Agostino

Skyscraper Souls (1932), MGM: *d* Edgar Selwyn; *w* C. G. Sullivan, Elmer Harris (from a novel by Faith Baldwin); *ad* Cedric Gibbons

The Sleeping City (1950), Universal: *d* George Sherman; *w* Jo Eisinger; *ad* Bernard Herzbrun, Emrich Nicholson

Sleepless in Seattle (1993), TriStar Pictures: *d* Nora Ephron; *w* Nora Ephron, David S. Ward, Jeff Arch; *pd* Jeffrey Townsend

Smithereens (1982), New Line: *d* Susan Seidelman; *w* Susan Seidelman, Ron Nyswaner, Peter Askin; *pd* Franz Harland

Smoke (1995), Miramax: *d* Wayne Wang, *w* Paul Auster, *pd* Kalina Ivanov

Soapdish (1991), Universal: *d* Michael Hoffman; *w* Robert Harling, Andrew Bergman; *pd* Eugenio Zanetti

Someone to Watch Over Me (1987), Columbia: *d* Ridley Scott; *w* Howard Franklin, Danilo Bach, David Seltzer; *pd* James D. Bissell

Something Wild (1986), Orion: *d* Jonathan Demme, *w* E. Max Frye, *pd* Norma Moriceau

Speedy (1928), Harold Lloyd: *d* Ted Wilde; *w* John Grey, Lex Neal, Howard Emmett Rogers, Jay Howe

Splash (1984), Touchstone: *d* Ron Howard; *w* Lowell Ganz, Babaloo Mandel, Bruce Jay Friedman, Brian Grazer; *pd* Jack T. Collis

Stage Door (1937), RKO: *d* Gregory La Cava; *w* Morrie Ryskind, Anthony Veiller (from a play by Edna Ferber and George S. Kaufman); *ad* Carroll Clark, Van Nest Polglase

Stage Struck (1936), Warner Bros.: *d* Busby Berkeley; *w* Tom Buckinham, Pat C. Flick, Robert Lord; *ad* Robert Haas

Straight Out of Brooklyn (1991), Samuel Goldwyn: *d* Matty Rich, *w* Matty Rich, *ad* Walter Meade

Strangers on a Train (1951), Warner Bros.: *d* Alfred Hitchcock; *w* Raymond Chandler, Czenzi Ormonde, Whitfield Cook (from a novel by Patricia Highsmith); *ad* Ted Haworth

Street Scene (1931), Samuel Goldwyn: *d* King Vidor, *w* Elmer Rice (from a play by Elmer Rice), *ad* Richard Day

Sugar Hill (1994), 20th Century-Fox: *d* Leon Ichaso, *w* Barry Michael Cooper, *pd* Michael Helmy

Sunny Side Up (1929), Fox: *d* David Butler; *w* B. G. de Sylva, Lew Brown, Ray Henderson; *ad* Harry Oliver

Superman (1978), Warner Bros.: *d* Richard Donner; *w* Mario Puzo, David Newman, Robert Benton, Leslie Newman; *pd* John Barry

Susan Lenox: Her Fall and Rise (1931), MGM: *d* Robert Z. Leonard; *w* Wanda Tuchock, Leon Gordon, Zelda Sears (from a novel by David Graham Phillips); *ad* Cedric Gibbons

The Sweet Smell of Success (1957), United Artists: *d* Alexander Mackendrick; *w* Clifford Odets, Ernest Lehman; *ad* Edward Carrere

Swing! (1938), Micheaux Film Corporation: *d* Oscar Micheaux, *w* Oscar Micheaux

Swing Time (1936), RKO: *d* George Stevens; *w* Howard Lindsay, Allan Scott (from a story by Erwin Gelsey); *ad* Van Nest Polglase

The Taking of Pelham One Two Three (1974), United Artists: *d* Joseph Sargent, *w* Peter Stone (from a novel by John Godey), *ad* Gene Rudolf

Tap (1989), Tristar: *d* Nick Castle, *w* Nick Castle, *pd* Patricia Norris

Taxi Driver (1976), Columbia: *d* Martin Scorsese, *w* Paul Schrader, *ad* Charles Rosen

That Touch of Mink (1962), Universal: *d* Delbert Mann; *w* Stanley Shapiro, Nate Monaster; *ad* Robert Clatworthy, Alexander Golitzen

The Thief (1952), United Artists: *d* Russel Rouse; *w* Clarence Greene, Russel Rouse; *pd* Joseph St. Amand

Thieves (1977), Paramount: *d* John Berry, Al Viola; *w* Herb Gardner (based on a play by Herb Gardner); *ad* Robert Gundlach

The Thin Man (1934), MGM: *d* W. S. Van Dyke; *w* Frances Goodrich, Albert Hackett (from a novel by Dashiell Hammett); *ad* Cedric Gibbons, David Townsend, Edwin Willis

A Thousand Clowns (1965), United Artists: *d* Fred Coe, *w* Herb Gardner (from a play by Herb Gardner), *ad* Burr Smidt

Three Days of the Condor (1975), Paramount: *d* Sydney Pollack; *w* Lorenzo Semple Jr., David Rayfiel (from a novel by James Grady); *pd* Stephen Grimes

Tootsie (1982), Columbia: *d* Sydney Pollack; *w* Larry Gelbart, Murray Shisgal, Elaine May; *pd* Peter S. Larkin

Top of the Town (1937), Universal: *d* Ralph Murphy; *w* Brown Holmes, Charles Grayson; *pd* John Harkrider

Traffic in Souls (1913), Universal: *d* George Loane Tucker; *w* Walter MacNamara, George Loane Tucker

Transatlantic (1931), Fox: *d* William K. Howard; *w* Guy Bolton, Lynn Starling; *ad* Gordon Wiles

A Tree Grows in Brooklyn (1945), 20th Century-Fox: *d* Elia Kazan; *w* Tess Slesinger, Frank Davis (from a novel by Betty Smith); *ad* Lyle Wheeler

True Love (1989), Oasis: *d* Nancy Savoca; *w* Nancy Savoca, Richard Guay; *pd* Lester W. Cohen

12 Angry Men (1957), United Artists: *d* Sidney Lumet, *w* Reginald Rose (from a play by Reginald Rose), *ad* Robert Markell

Two Girls on Broadway (1940), MGM: *d* S. Sylvan Simon; *w* Joseph Fields, Jerome Chodorov; *ad* Cedric Gibbons, Stan Rogers

Two Tickets to Broadway (1951), RKO: *d* James V. Kern; *w* Sid Silvers, Hal Kanter; *ad* Carroll Clark, Albert S. D'Agostino

An Unmarried Woman (1978), 20th Century-Fox: *d* Paul Mazursky, *w* Paul Mazursky, *pd* Pato Guzman

Up the Down Staircase (1967), Warner Bros.: *d* Robert Mulligan, *w* Tad Mosel (from a novel by Bel Kaufman), *ad* George Jenkins

The Velvet Touch (1948), RKO: *d* John Gage; *w* Leo Rosten, Walter Reilly (from a story by William Mercer, Annabel Ross); *pd* William Flannery

Wall Street (1987), 20th Century-Fox: *d* Oliver Stone; *w* Stanley Weiser, Oliver Stone; *pd* Stephen Hendrickson

The Warriors (1979), Paramount: *d* Walter Hill; *w* David Shaber, Walter Hill (from a novel by Sol Yurick); *ad* Don Swanagan, Bob Wightman

Week-end at the Waldorf (1945), MGM: *d* Robert Z. Leonard; *w* Sam Spewack, Bella Spewack, Guy Bolton (based on a play by Vicki Baum); *pd* Daniel B. Cathcart, Cedric Gibbons

West Side Story (1961), United Artists: *d* Robert Wise, Jerome Robbins; *w* Ernest Lehman (from a play by Arthur Laurents); *pd* Boris Leven

When Worlds Collide (1951), Paramount: *d* Rudolph Maté; *w* Sidney Boehm (from a novel by Philip Wylie and Edwin Balmer); *ad* Hal Pereira, Al Nozaki

The Window (1949), RKO: *d* Ted Tetzlaff; *w* Mel Dinelli (from a novella by Cornell Woolrich); *ad* Sam Corso, Walter E. Keller

The Wiz (1978), Universal: *d* Sidney Lumet; *w* Joel Schumacher (from a musical play by Charlie Smalls and William Brown, based on a novel by L. Frank Baum); *pd* Tony Walton, Philip Rosenberg

The Wizard of Oz (1939), MGM: *d* Victor Fleming; *w* Noel Langley, Florence Ryerson, Edgar Allan Woolf (based on a novel by L. Frank Baum); *ad* Cedric Gibbons, William A. Horning

Wolf (1994), Columbia: *d* Mike Nichols; *w* Jim Harrison, Elaine May, Wesley Strick; *pd* Bo Welch

Wolfen (1981), Warner Bros.: *d* Michael Wadleigh; *w* David Eyre, Michael Wadleigh, Eric Roth (from a novel by Whitley Strieber); *pd* Paul Sylbert

Working Girl (1988), 20th Century-Fox: *d* Mike Nichols, *w* Kevin Wade, *pd* Patrizia von Brandenstein

The World of Henry Orient (1964), United Artists: *d* George Roy Hill; *w* Nora Johnson, Nunnally Johnson (from a novel by Nora Johnson); *pd* James W. Sullivan

The World, the Flesh, and the Devil (1959), MGM: *d* Ranald MacDougall; *w* Ranald MacDougall (from a novel by M.P. Shiel); *ad* Paul Groesse, William A. Horning

The Wrong Man (1957), Warner Bros.: *d* Alfred Hitchcock; *w* Maxwell Anderson, Angus MacPhail (from a novel by Maxwell Anderson); *ad* Paul Sylbert

Yankee Doodle Dandy (1942), Warner Bros.: *d* Michael Curtiz; *w* Robert Buckner, Edmund Joseph; *ad* Carl Jules Weyl

Young Man with a Horn (1950), Warner Bros.: *d* Michael Curtiz; *w* Carl Foreman, Edmund H. North (from a novel by Dorothy Baker); *ad* Edward Carrere

You're a Big Boy Now (1966), Seven Arts Pictures: *d* Francis Ford Coppola, *w* Francis Ford Coppola (from a novel by David Benedictus), *ad* Vassele Fotopoulos

You've Got Mail (1998), Warner Bros.: *d* Nora Ephron; *w* Nora Ephron, Delia Ephron (from a play by Miklós László); *pd* Dan Davis

Ziegfeld Follies (1946), MGM: *d* Vincente Minnelli, Lemuel Ayers, Roy Del Ruth, Robert Lewis, George Sidney, Norman Taurog; *w* Roger Edens, David Freedman, Kay Thompson, Peter Barr, Harry Tugend; *pd* Lemuel Ayers, Edward C. Carfagno, Tony Duquette, Irene, Harry McAfee, Merrill Pye, Jack Martin Smith

Ziegfeld Girl (1941), MGM: *d* Robert Z. Leonard; *w* Marguerite Roberts, Sonya Levien; *ad* Cedric Gibbons, Daniel Cathcart

Zombies on Broadway (1945), RKO: *d* Gordon Douglas; *w* Lawrence Kimble; *ad* Albert S. D'Agostino, Walter E. Keller

EARLY FILMS AND ACTUALITIES

At the Foot of the Flatiron, Biograph, 1903, *c* A. E. Weed

The Black Hand, Biograph, 1906, *d* Wallace McCutcheon, *c* G. W. Bitzer

Coney Island at Night, Edison, 1905, *c* Edwin S. Porter

East Side Urchins Bathing in a Fountain, Edison, 1903, *c* Edwin S. Porter

Electrocuting an Elephant, Edison, 1903

Excavation for Subway, Biograph, 1902, *c* Robert K. Bonine

Herald Square, Edison, 1896, *c* William Heise

How a French Nobleman Got a Wife Through the New York "Herald" Personal Columns, Edison, 1904, *d* Edwin S. Porter

The Life of the American Policeman, Edison, 1905, *d* Edwin S. Porter, *c* Edwin S. Porter

New York City in a Blizzard, Edison, 1902

Panorama from the Times Building, New York, Biograph, 1905, *c* Wallace McCutcheon

Panorama from the Tower of the Brooklyn Bridge, Biograph, 1903, *c* G. W. "Billy" Bitzer

Personal, Biograph, 1904, *d* Wallace McCutcheon, *c* G. W. Bitzer

Skating on Lake, Central Park, New York, NY, American Stereoscopic Company, 1902

The Skyscrapers, Biograph, 1906, *c* Fred Dobson

Sky Scrapers of New York City, From the North River, Edison, 1903, *c* James Blair Smith

Sorting Refuse at Incinerating Plant, New York City, Edison, 1903, *c* Edwin S. Porter
The Tunnel Workers, Biograph, 1906, *c* F. A. Dobson
What Happened on Twenty-third Street, New York City, Edison, 1901

DOCUMENTARY FILMS

The Climate of New York, Rudy Burckhardt
Millions in Business as Usual, Rudy Burckhardt
Under the Brooklyn Bridge, Rudy Burckhardt
In the Street (1948), Helen Levitt, James Agee, and Janice Loeb

INDEX

ILLUSTRATION CREDITS

FRONT MATTER

iii: Photofest. iv–v: Photograph by Special Effects Supervisor Micheal McAllister. Courtesy of Micheal McAllister. 2: Photofest.

INTRODUCTION

5: Culver Pictures. 6: Photograph by David Lee. Courtesy of American Museum of the Moving Image. © 40 Acres and a Mule Filmworks. 7: Photofest. 8: Courtesy of Academy of Motion Picture Arts and Sciences. © 1936 Turner Entertainment Co. A Time Warner Company. All Rights Reserved. 9: Photofest. 11: © 1978 Twentieth Century-Fox Film Corporation. Courtesy of Twentieth Century-Fox. All Rights Reserved.12: Photofest.

PART ONE

14: © 1930 Twentieth Century-Fox Film Corporation. Courtesy of Twentieth Century-Fox. All Rights Reserved. 16: Scala/Art Resource, NY; Lorenzetti, Ambroglio, *Effects of Good Government in the City*, Palazzo Pubblico, Siena, Italy. 17: Alinari/Art Resource, NY; Piero della Francesca and Luciano Laurana, *View of an Ideal City*, Galleria Nazionale delle Marche, Palazzo Ducale, Urbino, Italy. 18: Teatro Olympico, Vicenza. 19: Edgar Degas, *Le Café-Concert des Ambassadeurs*, Musée des Beaux Arts de Lyon. © Studio Bassett. 21: Photofest.

CHAPTER ONE

23: Broadway and Herald Square, ca. 1900. Negative #43231. © Collection of The New York Historical Society 26: Library of Congress, courtesy of Steeplechase Films. 27, 28, 29, 30, 32, 33: Library of Congress. 34: (top) Library of Congress; (bottom) Bison Archives. 35: Courtesy of Kevin Brownlow. 37: Bison Archives. 39, 40: Courtesy of American Museum of the Moving Image.

CHAPTER TWO

43: John Mansbridge Collection, UCLA Arts Library Special Collections. 46: Vernon Howe Bailey, *Magical City*, 1935. 47: Joseph Webster Golinken, 1928. 48: John Sloan, *The City from Greenwich Village*, gift of Helen Farr Sloan. Photograph © 2001 Board of Trustees, National Gallery of Art, Washington. 50, 53: Bison Archives. 54, 55: John Mansbridge Collection, UCLA Arts Library Special Collections. 56: Courtesy of Academy of Motion Picture Arts and Sciences. 57, 58: John Mansbridge Collection, UCLA Arts Library Special Collections. 59, 61: Courtesy of Academy of Motion Picture Arts and Sciences.

CHAPTER THREE

63: Bison Archives. 65: (bottom) Anton Grot Collection, Department of Special Collections, Research Library, UCLA; (top) Private collection. 67: Courtesy of Lillian Michelson Research Library. 69: Courtesy of Academy of Motion Picture Arts and Sciences. 70, 71: Culver Pictures. 72: Courtesy of University of Southern California

Warner Bros. Collection. © 1949 Turner Entertainment Co. A Time Warner Company. All Rights Reserved. 73: Courtesy of Lillian Michelson Research Library. 74: (top) Courtesy of J. C. Backings; (bottom) Edward Hopper (American, 1882–1967), *The City*, 1927. Oil on canvas, Collection of the University of Arizona Museum of Art, Tucson, Gift of C. Leonard Pfeiffer, Acc. No. 45.9.23. 75: (top left, bottom) Courtesy of Academy of Motion Picture Arts and Sciences. © 2001 Universal City Studios. Courtesy of Universal Studios Publishing Rights. All Rights Reserved; (top middle, top right) Courtesy of University of Southern California. © 2001 Universal City Studios. Courtesy of Universal Studios Publishing Rights. All Rights Reserved. 77: Courtesy of University of Southern California Warner Bros. Collection. © 1936 Turner Entertainment Co. A Time Warner Company. All Rights Reserved. 78: Ralph Crane/TimePix, contributed by Black Star. 79: Courtesy of Academy of Motion Picture Arts and Sciences. © 1945 Turner Entertainment Co. A Time Warner Company. All Rights Reserved. 80: Courtesy of Academy of Motion Picture Arts and Sciences. © 1937 Turner Entertainment Co. A Time Warner Company. All Rights Reserved. 81: Courtesy of Academy of Motion Picture Arts and Sciences. © 1939 Turner Entertainment Co. A Time Warner Company. All Rights Reserved. 82, 83: John Harkrider Collection. Courtesy of Academy of Motion Picture Arts and Sciences. 84: Culver Pictures.

PART TWO

86: Courtesy of Paramount Pictures Stock Footage Library. © Paramount Pictures. All Rights Reserved. 89: (top) Courtesy of Paramount Pictures Stock Footage Library. © Paramount Pictures. All Rights Reserved; (bottom) American Museum of the Moving Image. 90–91: Courtesy of Paramount Pictures Stock Footage Library. © Paramount Pictures. All Rights Reserved.

CHAPTER FOUR

93: Courtesy of University of Southern California Warner Bros. Collection. © 1939 Turner Entertainment Co. A Time Warner Company. All Rights Reserved. 96: Concept sketch by Mario Larringa, Willis O'Brien, and Byron Crabbe. 97: Photofest. 99: Hugh Ferriss, *The Metropolis of Tomorrow*, 1929, Courtesy of Avery Architectural & Fine Arts Library, Columbia University, NY. 100: Courtesy of George E. Turner. 103: Photograph by Stefan Lange. © 1989 Warner Bros. Inc. All Rights Reserved. 104: Photograph by Stefan Lange. Courtesy of Don Shay. © 1989 Warner Bros. Inc. All Rights Reserved. 105: © 1989 Warner Bros. Inc. All Rights Reserved. 106: Courtesy of Academy of Motion Picture Arts and Sciences. 107: Courtesy of George E. Turner. 108: Courtesy of Cinematèque Français. 109: Courtesy of New York Museum of Modern Art Film Stills Archive. © 1930 Twentieth Century-Fox Film Corporation. All Rights Reserved. 110: (top) Avery Architectural & Fine Arts Library, Columbia University, NY; (bottom) Antonio Sant' Elia, 1914. 112: Photofest. 113: © 1997 Gaumont. Courtesy of Columbia Pictures. All Rights Reserved. 116, 117: Photograph by Virgil Mirano, production design by John DeCuir. Courtesy of Richard Edlund.

CHAPTER FIVE

119: Photograph by Jim Bridges. © 1994 Warner Bros., a division of Time Warner Entertainment Co. All Rights Reserved. 121: John Harkrider Collection, courtesy of Academy of Motion Picture Arts and Sciences. 122: Photograph by Special Effects Supervisor Micheal McAllister. Courtesy of Micheal McAllister. 128: Courtesy of University of Southern California Warner Bros. Collection. © 1949 Turner Entertainment Co. A Time Warner Company. All Rights Reserved. 129, 130: Photofest. 132: Courtesy of Lillian Michelson Research Library. 134: © 1959 Twentieth Century-Fox Film Corporation. All Rights Reserved. 135: Photofest. 136: Photograph by Andy Schwartz. © 1988 Twentieth Century-Fox Film Corporation. Courtesy of Twentieth Century-Fox. All Rights Reserved. 139: Photograph by Michael Ginsberg, Photofest.

CHAPTER SIX

141: Courtesy of Academy of Motion Picture Arts and Sciences. 143: Photograph by James Sanders. 144: Bison Archives. 145, 146: Courtesy of Academy of Motion Picture Arts and Sciences. 147: *Washington Square*, 1894 (from Mary Black book), negative # 20157. © Collection of the New York Historical Society. 151: Culver Pictures. 152: (top) Gottscho-Schleisner Collection, Library of Congress; (bottom) Harry Horner, Krannert Art Museum, Champaign, IL, gift of Mrs. Joan Horner. 153: Drawings by James Sanders (top) and Harry Horner (bottom). 154: Courtesy of New York Museum of Modern Art Film Stills Archive. © 2001 Universal City Studios. Courtesy of Universal Studios Publishing Rights. All Rights Reserved. 155: © 2001 Universal City Studios. Courtesy of Universal Studios Publishing Rights. All Rights Reserved. 157: Courtesy of Academy of Motion Picture Arts and Sciences. 158: New York City Housing Authority. 159: (top) Photofest; (bottom) New York City Housing Authority Collection, La Guardia and Wagner Archives, La Guardia Communitiy College/City University of NY. 160: Courtesy of Academy of Motion Picture Arts and Sciences. © 2001 Universal City Studios. Courtesy of Universal Studios Publishing Rights. All Rights Reserved. 161: Photofest. 162: Bison Archives. 164: Photofest. 165: © 1945 Twentieth Century-Fox Film Corporation. All Rights Reserved. 166: New York City Housing Authority. 170: Photograph by Sherman Bryce and Rodney Wright, Photofest. 174: Photographs by David Lee, courtesy of Universal City Studios Publishing Rights. © 40 Acres and a Mule Filmworks. 177, 178: Bison Archives. 179, 180, 181: Photograph by David Lee, courtesy of Universal City Studios Publishing Rights. © 40 Acres and a Mule Filmworks. 183: Photofest. 184: © 1994 Columbia Pictures Industries, courtesy of Columbia Pictures. All Rights Reserved.

CHAPTER SEVEN

185: Photofest. 187: (top) Photofest; (bottom) Fifth Avenue No. of 65th St. showing John Jacob Astor's House, 1898, Museum of the City of New York, The Byron Collection. 188: Photofest. 190: © Columbia Pictures Industries. All Rights Reserved. 195: John Mansbridge Collection, UCLA Arts Library Special Collections. 196: Courtesy of Estate of Cary Grant. 197: Courtesy of Lillian Michelson Research Library. 198: Photofest. 200: Photograph by Brian Hamill. Courtesy of Woody Allen. © 1986 Orion Pictures Corporation. Courtesy of MGM Clip + Still. All Rights Reserved. 201: Photofest. 202: © 1979 Columbia Pictures Industries. All Rights Reserved. Courtesy of Columbia Pictures. 203: Courtesy of Paramount Pictures Stock Footage Library. © 1968 Paramount Pictures. All Rights Reserved. 205: Production Design by Richard Sylbert, courtesy of Richard Sylbert. 208, 210: Photofest. 212: Photograph by Brian Hamill. © 1988 Twentieth Century-Fox Film Corporation. Courtesy of Twentieth Century-Fox. All Rights Reserved. 213: © 1978 Twentieth Century-Fox Film Corporation. Courtesy of Twentieth Century-Fox. All Rights Reserved. 214: © 1978 Twentieth Century-Fox Film Corporation. Courtesy of Twentieth Century-Fox. All Rights Reserved. 215: Photograph by David Lee, Photofest. 216: Photograph by Brian Hamill. © Touchstone Pictures. All Rights Reserved. 217: © 1988 Twentieth Century-Fox Film Corporation. Courtesy of Twentieth Century-Fox. All Rights Reserved.

CHAPTER EIGHT

219: Photofest. 221: Courtesy of Lillian Michelson Research Library. 222: The Municipal Archives Department of Records and Information Services, City of New York. 223: Courtesy of Academy of Motion Picture Arts and Sciences and Metro-Goldwyn-Mayer Inc. All Rights Reserved. 224: Photofest. 226: Courtesy of Academy of Motion Picture Arts and Sciences and Metro-Goldwyn-Mayer Inc. All Rights Reserved. 229, 230: Courtesy of New York Museum of Modern Art Film Stills Archive. © 2001 Universal City Studios. Courtesy of Universal Studios Publishing Rights. All Rights Reserved. 231: (top) Courtesy of Billy Rose Collection, New York Performing Arts Library. © 2001 Universal City Studios. Courtesy of Universal Studios Publishing Rights. All Rights Reserved; (bottom) Courtesy of New York Museum of Modern Art Film Stills Archive. © 2001 Universal City Studios. Courtesy of Universal Studios Publishing Rights. All Rights Reserved. 237: © 2001 Universal City Studios. Courtesy of Universal Studios Publishing Rights. All Rights Reserved. 238: Courtesy of BFI Films. © 2001 Universal City Studios. All Rights Reserved. 242: Photofest.

CHAPTER NINE

246: Courtesy of Academy of Motion Picture Arts and Sciences. © 1931 Turner Entertainment Co. A Time Warner Company. All Rights Reserved. 247: Photograph by François Duhamel, Photofest. 248, 249, 250: Photofest. 251: Photograph by Brian Hamill, courtesy of Woody Allen. © 1977 United Artists Corporation. Courtesy of MGM Clip + Still. All Rights Reserved. 252: Courtesy of UCLA Arts Library Special Collections. © 2001 Universal City Studios. All Rights Reserved. 254–5: Courtesy of Academy of Motion Picture Arts and Sciences. © 1937 Turner Entertainment Co. A Time Warner Company. All Rights Reserved. 256: Photofest. 259: Courtesy of Academy of Motion Picture Arts and Sciences. © 1936 Turner Entertainment Co. A Time Warner Company. All Rights Reserved. 260: Courtesy of Academy of Motion Picture Arts and Sciences. 261: Photofest. 262, 263: John Harkrider Collection, courtesy of Academy of Motion Picture Arts and Sciences.

CHAPTER TEN

265: Photofest. 268: Courtesy of New York Museum of Modern Art Film Stills Archive. © 1965 Mrs. Joyce Coe. Courtesy of MGM Clip + Still. All Rights Reserved. 271, 273: Photograph by Brian Hamill, courtesy of Woody Allen. © 1987 Orion Pictures Corporation. Courtesy of MGM Clip + Still. All Rights Reserved. 274: Port Authority of New York and New Jersey. 275: Courtesy of Paramount Pictures Stock Footage Library. © Paramount Pictures. All Rights Reserved. 276: (top) Courtesy of Academy of Motion Picture Arts and Sciences; (bottom) Private collection. 277: © 1954 Paramount Pictures. By permission of Estate of Humphrey Bogart, TM & © Bogart Inc. Licensed by Global Icons, Los Angeles, CA, www.globalicons.com. All Rights Reserved. 278: Photofest. 279: Photograph by Andy Schwartz. © 1988 Twentieth Century-Fox Film Corporation. Courtesy of Twentieth Century-Fox. All Rights Reserved. 281: *Scientific American*, Dec. 7, 1912. 282: Photograph by John Clifford. © 1991 Tristar Pictures. Courtesy of Columbia Pictures. All Rights Reserved. 283: John Mansbridge Collection, UCLA Arts Library Special Collections. 287: Courtesy of Paramount Pictures Stock Footage Library. © Paramount Pictures. All Rights Reserved. 288: Courtesy of Academy of Motion Picture Arts and Sciences. © 1945 Turner Entertainment Co. A Time Warner Company. All Rights Reserved. 290: Courtesy of Paramount Pictures Stock Footage Library. © 1971 Paramount Pictures. All Rights Reserved. 291: Photofest. 292: Museum of the City of New York, The Wurts Collection.

CHAPTER ELEVEN

295: Everett Collection. 297: Courtesy of Paramount Pictures Stock Footage Library. © Paramount Pictures. All Rights Reserved. 298: Photofest. 299: Photograph by Brian Hamill. Courtesy of Woody Allen. © 1987 Orion Pictures Corporation. Courtesy of MGM Clip + Still. All Rights Reserved. 300: John Mansbridge Collection, UCLA Arts Library Special Collections. 301: Photofest. 303: Courtesy of Academy of Motion Picture Arts and Sciences.

304: Photofest. 306: Culver Pictures. 313, 315: Photofest. 317: Courtesy of Academy of Motion Picture Arts and Sciences. 318: Courtesy of Academy of Motion Picture Arts and Sciences. © 1957 Metro-Goldwyn-Mayer. Courtesy of MGM Clip + Still. All Rights Reserved. 319, 320, 322: Photofest.

PART THREE

326: Photograph by Lee Sievan, New York Museum of Modern Art Film Stills Archive. 329: Bison Archives. 335: Photofest. 336: Elliot Erwitt, Magnum Photos. 340: Everett Collection. 343: Photofest.

CHAPTER TWELVE

345, 348, 350: Photofest. 352: © 1954 Columbia Pictures Industries. Courtesy of Columbia Pictures. All Rights Reserved. 353: (top) Photofest; (bottom) Everett Collection. 354: Photofest. 355: © 1993 Metro-Goldwyn-Mayer, Inc. Courtesy of MGM Clip + Still. All Rights Reserved. 358: Photograph by Ken Howard, Photofest. 361: Everett Collection. 363: © New Visions Pictures.

CHAPTER THIRTEEN

365: Photofest. 368: Everett Collection. 370: Courtesy of New York Museum of Modern Art Film Stills Archive. © 1969 Jerome Hellman Productions, Inc. Courtesy of MGM Clip + Still. All Rights Reserved. 372: Photofest. 373: © 1971 Twentieth Century-Fox Film Corporation. Courtesy of Twentieth Century-Fox. All Rights Reserved. 376: Photofest. 378: Photograph by Michael Ginsberg, Everett Collection. 381: Photograph by Michael Ginsberg, Photofest. 383: Everett Collection. 384: © 1971 Twentieth Century-Fox Film Corporation. Courtesy of Twentieth Century-Fox. All Rights Reserved. 387: Photofest. 388: Courtesy of Don Shay. © 1996 Twentieth Century-Fox Film Corporation. All Rights Reserved. 389, 393, 394: Photofest. 396: Photograph by Josh Weiner, Photofest.

CHAPTER FOURTEEN

399: Dmitri Kessel/TimePix, contributed by Dmitri Kessel. 402: Courtesy of Academy of Motion Picture Arts and Sciences. © 1960 Turner Entertainment Co. A Time Warner Company. All Rights Reserved. 404: Courtesy of the Billy Rose Collection, New York Performing Arts Library. © 2001 Universal City Studios. Courtesy of Universal Studios Publishing Rights. All Rights Reserved. 408: Courtesy of Woody Allen. © 1979 Metro-Goldwyn-Mayer, Inc. Courtesy of MGM Clip + Still. All Rights Reserved. 410, 411: © 1976 Twenteth Century-Fox Film Corporation. Courtesy of Twentieth Century-Fox. All Rights Reserved. 413: Photofest. 414: © 1987 Twentieth Century-Fox Film Corporation. Courtesy of Twentieth Century-Fox. All Rights Reserved. 417, 418: Photograph by Ron Batzdorff. © 2001 Universal City Studios. Courtesy of Universal Studios Publishing Rights. All Rights Reserved.

CHAPTER FIFTEEN

421: Courtesy of American Museum of the Moving Image. 423: (top) Photofest; (bottom) Photograph by Brian Hamill, Everett Collection. 425: Photofest. 428: Photograph by James Sanders. 430: Everett Collection. 431: Photograph by Prashant Gupta, Photofest. 432: Photograph by K. C. Bailey, Everett Collection. 434: Courtesy of Visual Effects Supervisor Richard Edlund. © 1984 Columbia Pictures Industries. All Rights Reserved. 437: Photograph by Andy Schwartz. © 1997 Columbia Pictures Industries. Courtesy of Columbia Pictures. All Rights Reserved. 438: Photograph by Andy Schwartz. © 1985 Orion Pictures Corporation. Courtesy of MGM Clip + Still. All Rights Reserved. 441: Photograph by James Sanders.

BACK MATTER

443: Culver Pictures. 449: Photograph by Josh Weiner, Photofest. 459: Photograph by Brian Hamill. Courtesy of Woody Allen. 465, 497: Photofest

271.
Bells Are Ringing
(1959).

A NOTE ABOUT THE AUTHOR

James Sanders, an architect, is the cowriter with Ric Burns of the seven-part, fourteen-and-a-half hour PBS series *New York: A Documentary Film*—which received an Emmy Award and an Alfred I. duPont–Columbia University Silver Baton Award—and coauthor with Burns and Lisa Ades of its companion volume, *New York: An Illustrated History.* He has written for the *New York Times*, the *Los Angeles Times*, *Vanity Fair*, *Architectural Record*, and *Interiors*, and has produced exhibitions on New York housing and the urban heritage of 42nd Street. Mr. Sanders, who maintains a design practice in Manhattan, has completed projects for the Port Authority of New York and New Jersey, the Parks Council, the Landmarks Preservation Commission, and other civic groups and commercial clients in New York and California.

A NOTE ON THE TYPE

The text of this book was set in Filosofia, a typeface designed by Zuzana Licko in 1996 as a revival of the typefaces of Giambattista Bodoni (1740–1813). Basing her design on the letterpress practice of altering the cut of the letters to match the size for which they were to be used, Licko designed Filosofia Regular as a rugged face, with reduced contrast, to withstand the reduction to text sizes, and Filosofia Grand as a more delicate and refined version for use in larger display sizes.

Licko, born in Bratislava, Czechoslovakia, in 1961, is the cofounder of Emigre, a digital type foundry and publisher of *Emigre* magazine, based in Northern California. Founded in 1984, coinciding with the birth of the Macintosh, Emigre was one of the first independent type foundries to establish itself centered around personal computer technology.

Composed by North Market Street Graphics, Lancaster, Pennsylvania, and Ralph L. Fowler

Printed and bound by R. R. Donnelley & Sons, Willard, Ohio

Designed by Ralph L. Fowler